COLOSSIANS & PHILEMON

COLOSSIANS & PHILEMON

ZONDERVAN
Exegetical
Commentary
ON THE
New Testament

DAVID W. PAO

CLINTON E. ARNOLD
General Editor

 ZONDERVAN®

To Chrystal

ZONDERVAN

Colossians and Philemon
Copyright © 2012 by David W. Pao

Requests for information should be addressed to:

Zondervan, 3900 *Sparks Dr. SE, Grand Rapids, Michigan 49546*

Library of Congress Cataloging-in-Publication Data

Pao, David W.
    Colossians and Philemon : Zondervan exegetical commentary series on the New Testament /
David W. Pao.
        pages cm. (Zondervan exegetical commentary on the New Testament; v. 12)
    Includes bibliographical references and indexes.
    ISBN: 978-0-310-24395-3 (hardcover)
    1. Bible N.T. Colossians — Commentaries. 2. Bible N.T. Philemon — Commentaries. I. Title.
BS2715.53.P36   2012
227'.707 — dc23   2012005346

Cover design: Tammy Johnson
Interior design: Beth Shagene

Printed in the United States of America

16 17 18 19 20 21 22 23 24 /DCI/ 25 24 23 22 21 20 19 18 17 16 15 14 13 12 11 10 9 8 7 6 5 4 3

Contents

Series Introduction. 7

Author's Preface 11

Abbreviations 13

Introduction to Colossians 19

Select Bibliography on Colossians 35

Commentary on Colossians 43

The Theology of Colossians 328

Introduction to Philemon 341

Select Bibliography on Philemon 355

Commentary on Philemon 359

The Theology of Philemon 427

Scripture and Apocrypha Index 436

Subject Index. 451

Author Index. 458

Series Introduction

This generation has been blessed with an abundance of excellent commentaries. Some are technical and do a good job of addressing issues that the critics have raised; other commentaries are long and provide extensive information about word usage and catalogue nearly every opinion expressed on the various interpretive issues; still other commentaries focus on providing cultural and historical background information; and then there are those commentaries that endeavor to draw out many applicational insights.

The key question to ask is: What are you looking for in a commentary? This commentary series might be for you if

- you have taken Greek and would like a commentary that helps you apply what you have learned without assuming you are a well-trained scholar.
- you would find it useful to see a concise, one- or two-sentence statement of what the commentator thinks the main point of each passage is.
- you would like help interpreting the words of Scripture without getting bogged down in scholarly issues that seem irrelevant to the life of the church.
- you would like to see a visual representation (a graphical display) of the flow of thought in each passage.
- you would like expert guidance from solid evangelical scholars who set out to explain the meaning of the original text in the clearest way possible and to help you navigate through the main interpretive issues.
- you want to benefit from the results of the latest and best scholarly studies and historical information that help to illuminate the meaning of the text.
- you would find it useful to see a brief summary of the key theological insights that can be gleaned from each passage and some discussion of the relevance of these for Christians today.

These are just some of the features that characterize the new Zondervan Exegetical Commentary on the New Testament series. The idea for this series was refined over time by an editorial board who listened to pastors and teachers express what they wanted to see in a commentary series based on the Greek text. That board consisted of myself, George H. Guthrie, William D. Mounce, Thomas R. Schreiner, and Mark L. Strauss along with Zondervan senior editor at large Verlyn Verbrugge, and former Zondervan senior acquisitions editor Jack Kuhatschek. We also enlisted a board of consulting editors who are active pastors, ministry leaders, and seminary professors to help in the process of designing a commentary series that will be useful to the church. Zondervan senior acquisitions editor Katya Covrett has now been shepherding the process to completion.

We arrived at a design that includes seven components for the treatment of each biblical passage. What follows is a brief orientation to these primary components of the commentary.

Literary Context

In this section, you will find a concise discussion of how the passage functions in the broader literary context of the book. The commentator highlights connections with the preceding and following material in the book and makes observations on the key literary features of this text.

Main Idea

Many readers will find this to be an enormously helpful feature of this series. For each passage, the commentator carefully crafts a one- or two-sentence statement of the big idea or central thrust of the passage.

Translation and Graphical Layout

Another unique feature of this series is the presentation of each commentator's translation of the Greek text in a graphical layout. The purpose of this diagram is to help the reader visualize, and thus better understand, the flow of thought within the text. The translation itself reflects the interpretive decisions made by each commentator in the "Explanation" section of the commentary. Here are a few insights that will help you to understand the way these are put together:

1. On the far left side next to the verse numbers is a series of interpretive labels that indicate the function of each clause or phrase of the biblical text. The corresponding portion of the text is on the same line to the right of the label. We have not used technical linguistic jargon for these, so they should be easily understood.

2. In general, we place every clause (a group of words containing a subject and a predicate) on a separate line and identify how it is supporting the principal assertion of the text (namely, is it saying when the action occurred, how it took place, or why it took place?). We sometimes place longer phrases or a series of items on separate lines as well.

3. Subordinate (or dependent) clauses and phrases are indented and placed directly under the words that they modify. This helps the reader to more easily see the nature of the relationship of clauses and phrases in the flow of the text.
4. Every main clause has been placed in bold print and pushed to the left margin for clear identification.
5. Sometimes when the level of subordination moves too far to the right — as often happens with some of Paul's long, involved sentences! — we reposition the flow to the left of the diagram, but use an arrow to indicate that this has happened.
6. The overall process we have followed has been deeply informed by principles of discourse analysis and narrative criticism (for the Gospels and Acts).

Structure

Immediately following the translation, the commentator describes the flow of thought in the passage and explains how certain interpretive decisions regarding the relationship of the clauses were made in the passage.

Exegetical Outline

The overall structure of the passage is described in a detailed exegetical outline. This will be particularly helpful for those who are looking for a way to concisely explain the flow of thought in the passage in a teaching or preaching setting.

Explanation of the Text

As an exegetical commentary, this work makes use of the Greek language to interpret the meaning of the text. If your Greek is rather rusty (or even somewhat limited), don't be too concerned. All of the Greek words are cited in parentheses following an English translation. We have made every effort to make this commentary as readable and useful as possible even for the nonspecialist.

Those who will benefit the most from this commentary will have had the equivalent of two years of Greek in college or seminary. This would include a semester or two of working through an intermediate grammar (such as Wallace, Porter, Brooks and Winberry, or Dana and Mantey). The authors use the grammatical language that is found in these kinds of grammars. The details of the grammar of the passage, however, are discussed only when it has a bearing on the interpretation of the text.

The emphasis on this section of the text is to convey the meaning. Commentators examine words and images, grammatical details, relevant OT and Jewish background to a particular concept, historical and cultural context, important text-critical issues, and various interpretational issues that surface.

Theology in Application

This, too, is a unique feature for an exegetical commentary series. We felt it was important for each author not only to describe what the text means in its various details, but also to take a moment and reflect on the theological contribution that it makes. In this section, the theological message of the passage is summarized. The authors discuss the theology of the text in terms of its place within the book and in a broader biblical-theological context. Finally, each commentator provides some suggestions on what the message of the passage is for the church today. At the conclusion of each volume in this series is a summary of the whole range of theological themes touched on by this book of the Bible.

Our sincere hope and prayer is that you find this series helpful not only for your own understanding of the text of the New Testament, but as you are actively engaged in teaching and preaching God's Word to people who are hungry to be fed on its truth.

CLINTON E. ARNOLD, general editor

Author's Preface

Different paths led to the writing of this commentary on two prison letters of Paul. After teaching Colossians for more than ten years as part of the Greek Exegesis sequence at Trinity Evangelical Divinity School, working on this commentary allows me to put in writing the numerous exegetical decisions that came to fruition through the teaching and research process. My interest in Philemon, however, was sparked by a semester-long graduate seminar on this short letter at Harvard University twenty years ago. A number of significant studies on Philemon that were published in the 1980s justified a detailed reexamination of this letter of Paul. I have benefited much from our instructor in that graduate seminar, Allen Callahan, who was gracious to many members of that seminar who remain unconvinced by his final conclusion concerning the circumstances behind this letter.

I am grateful to the general editor of this ZECNT series, Clint Arnold, for his invitation to contribute to the series. Not only did I enjoy wrestling with the various exegetical details of the text, but this series also allows me to reflect on the significance of this text for contemporary believers. As a consulting editor of this series, I passionately share the vision of the Zondervan Exegetical Commentary series that seeks to bridge the gap between a detailed study of the Greek text and the pastoral impact of such a study. I am also grateful to George Guthrie and Karen Jobes, who have provided helpful comments on the commentary proper and the diagrams, and to Verlyn Verbrugge and his team at Zondervan for their excellent editorial work on this commentary.

The Board of Regents and Dean Tite Tienou of Trinity Evangelical Divinity School deserve thanks for their support of this project as well as for the sabbatical granted for the research and writing of this commentary. I am also grateful to my departmental colleagues and fellow contributors to this series, Grant Osborne and Eckhard Schnabel, who shared their experiences with me as we were working on individual volumes in this series.

A number of my research assistants have also contributed to the writing of this commentary. Sandra Storer and Nicholas Bott helped in the construction of the diagrams. Benjamin Sutton, Rui Han Jiao, Stephen Moore, Chi-ying Wang and Cindy Ou have also provided significant assistance at the various stages in the writing of this commentary. Special thanks to Trent Rogers, who has read through the entire manuscript more than once and has provided numerous constructive comments and suggestions.

In not too many years, I hope that my now twelve-year-old twin girls, Charis and Serena, will have the patience to work through this commentary and be convinced of the power of the gospel as contained in these letters of Paul. In their young age, they have already contributed to this writing process through their generous gifts of laughter and numerous written and verbal expressions of love and encouragement.

Above all I thank my wife, Chrystal, who has been my faithful partner in our journeys in faith and in life. Though not a specialist in the Pauline letters, she continues to teach me how I can live out the christocentric gospel embedded in these letters. It is to her that I dedicate this volume.

Soli Deo gloria.

DAVID W. PAO

Abbreviations

Abbreviations for books of the Bible, pseudepigrapha, rabbinic works, papyri, classical works, and the like are readily available in sources such as the *SBL Handbook of Style* and are not included here.

AB	Anchor Bible
ABD	*Anchor Bible Dictionary*. Edited by D. N. Freedman. 6 vols. New York, 1992.
ABR	*Australian Biblical Review*
ABRL	Anchor Bible Reference Library
AGJU	Arbeiten zur Geschichte des antiken Judentums und des Urchristentums
AnBib	Analecta biblica
ANQ	*Andover Newton Quarterly*
ANRW	*Aufstieg und Niedergang der römischen Welt: Geschichte und Kultur Roms im Spiegel der neueren Forschung*. Edited by H. Temporini and W. Haase. Berlin, 1972 – .
ANTC	Abingdon New Testament Commentaries
ASV	American Standard Version
AUSS	*Andrews University Seminary Studies*
b. Ḥag.	Ḥagigah (Babylonian Talmud)
b. Moʿed Qaṭ.	Moʿed Qaṭan (Babylonian Talmud)
b. Yebam.	Yebamot (Babylonian Talmud)
BDAG	W. Bauer, F. W. Danker, W. F. Arndt, and F. W. Gingrich. *Greek-English Lexicon of the New Testament and Other Early Christian Literature*. 3rd ed. Chicago, 2000.
BDF	F. Blass, A. Debrunner, and R. W. Funk. *A Greek Grammar of the New Testament and Other Early Christian Literature*. Chicago, 1961.
BGU	*Aegyptische Urkunden aus den Königlichen Staatlichen Museen zu Berlin, Griechische Urkunden*. 15 vols. Berlin, 1895 – 1983.
Bib	*Biblica*
BIS	Biblical Interpretation Series

BJRL	*Bulletin of the John Rylands University Library of Manchester*
BLG	Biblical Languages: Greek
BN	*Biblische Notizen*
BR	*Biblical Research*
BSac	*Bibliotheca Sacra*
BT	*The Bible Translator*
BTB	*Biblical Theology Bulletin*
BZNW	Beihefte zur Zeitschrift für die neutestamentliche Wissenschaft
CahRB	Cahiers de la Revue biblique
CBET	Contributions to Biblical Exegesis and Theology
CBQ	*Catholic Biblical Quarterly*
CEV	Contemporary English Version
CGTC	Cambridge Greek Testament Commentary
ChrCent	*Christian Century*
ConBOT	Coniectanea biblica: Old Testament Series
CRINT	Compendia rerum iudaicarum ad Novum Testamenum
CTM	*Concordia Theological Monthly*
CurTM	*Currents in Theology and Mission*
DPL	*Dictionary of Paul and His Letters.* Downers Grove, IL, 1993.
EBib	Etudes bibliques
ECC	Eerdmans Critical Commentaries
EFN	Estudios de filología neotestamentaria. Cordova, Spain, 1988 – .
EKKNT	Evangelisch-Katholischer Kommentar zum Neuen Testament
ESV	English Standard Version
ETL	*Ephemerides theologicae lovanienses*
EuroJTh	*European Journal of Theology*
EvQ	*Evangelical Quarterly*
ExAud	*Ex auditu*
ExpTim	*Expository Times*
FRLANT	Forschungen zur Religion und Literatur des Alten und Neuen Testaments
GNB	Good News Bible
GNS	Good News Studies
GTJ	*Grace Theological Journal*
HCSB	Holman Christian Standard Bible
HNT	Handbuch zum Neuen Testament
HTR	*Harvard Theological Review*
HTS	Harvard Theological Studies
ICC	International Critical Commentary
Int	*Interpretation*
ITQ	*Irish Theological Quarterly*

JBL	*Journal of Biblical Literature*
JBMW	*Journal of Biblical Manhood and Womanhood*
JETS	*Journal of the Evangelical Theological Society*
JGRChJ	*Journal of Greco-Roman Christianity and Judaism*
JOTT	*Journal of Translation and Textlinguistics*
JRS	*Journal of Roman Studies*
JSNT	*Journal for the Study of the New Testament*
JSNTSup	Journal for the Study of the New Testament: Supplement Series
JSOT	*Journal for the Study of the Old Testament*
JSOTSup	Journal for the Study of the Old Testament: Supplement Series
JTS	*Journal of Theological Studies*
JTSA	*Journal of Theology for Southern Africa*
KEK	Kritisch-exegetischer Kommentar über das Neue Testament (Meyer-Kommentar)
KJV	King James Version
LCL	Loeb Classical Library
LEC	Library of Early Christianity
LNTS	Library of New Testament Studies
Louw and Nida	*Greek-English Lexicon of the New Testament: Based on Semantic Domains.* Edited by J. P. Louw and E. A. Nida. 2nd ed. New York, 1989.
LSJ	H. G. Liddell, R. Scott, H. S. Jones, *A Greek-English Lexicon.* 9th ed. with revised supplement. Oxford, 1996.
LNTS	Library of New Testament Studies
LXX	Septuagint
m. Ber.	*Berakot* (Mishnah)
m. Ḥul.	*Ḥullin* (Mishnah)
m. Qidd.	*Qiddušin* (Mishnah)
MM	J. H. Moulton and G. Milligan. *The Vocabulary of the Greek Testament.* London, 1930. Reprint, Peabody, MA, 1997.
NA	Nestle-Aland, *Novum Testamentum Graece*
NAB	New American Bible
NASB	New American Standard Bible
NCB	New Century Bible
NEB	New English Bible
Neot	*Neotestamentica*
NET	New English Translation
NewDocs	*New Documents Illustrating Early Christianity.* Edited by G. H. R. Horsley and S. Llewelyn. North Ryde, N.S.W., 1981 – .
NHC	Nag Hammadi Codices
NICNT	New International Commentary on the New Testament

NIDNTT	*New International Dictionary of New Testament Theology.* Edited by C. Brown. 4 vols. Grand Rapids, 1975 – 1985.
NIGTC	New International Greek Testament Commentary
NIV	New International Version
NIVAC	NIV Application Commentary
NJB	New Jerusalem Bible
NKJV	New King James Version
NLT	New Living Translation
NovT	*Novum Testamentum*
NovTSup	Novum Testamentum Supplements
NRSV	New Revised Standard Version
NSBT	New Studies in Biblical Theology
NTL	New Testament Library
NTS	*New Testament Studies*
P.Cair.Zen.	*Zenon Papyri.* Edited by C. C. Edgar et al. Cairo, 1925 – .
P.Eleph.	*Aegyptische Urkunden aus den Königlichen Museen in Berlin.* Edited by O. Rubensohn. Berlin, 1907.
P.Grenf II.	*New Classical Fragments and Other Greek and Latin Papyri.* Edited by B. P. Grenfell and A. S. Hunt. Oxford, 1897.
P.Lond.	London Papyri
P.Mert.	*A Descriptive Catalogue of the Greek Papyri in the Collection of Wilfred Merton.* Edited by H. I. Bell et al. London, 1948 – .
P.Mich.	*Michigan Papyri.* Edited by C. C. Edgar et al. Ann Arbor 1931 – .
P.Oxy.	*Oxyrhynchus Papyri.* Edited by B. P. Grenfell, A. S. Hunt, et al. London, 1898 – .
P.Sarap.	*Les archives de Sarapion et de ses fils.* Edited by J. Schwartz. Cairo, 1961.
P.Tebt.	*The Tebtunis Papyri.* Edited by B. P. Grenfell, A. S. Hunt, J. G. Smyly, et al. London, 1902 – .
PNTC	The Pillar New Testament Commentary
Presb	*Presbyterion*
PRSt	*Perspectives in Religious Studies*
PTMS	Pittsburgh Theological Monograph Series
PzB	*Protokolle zur Bibel*
R&T	*Religion and Theology*
RB	*Revue biblique*
REB	Revised English Bible
ResQ	*Restoration Quarterly*
REV	Revised English Version
RevExp	*Review and Expositor*
RevScRel	*Revue des sciences religieuses*

RSV	Revised Standard Version
RTR	*Reformed Theological Review*
SBLDS	Society of Biblical Literature Dissertation Series
SBLMS	Society of Biblical Literature Monograph Series
SBLSP	*Society of Biblical Literature Seminar Papers*
SBS	Stuttgarter Bibelstudien
SBT	Studies in Biblical Theology
ScEs	*Science et esprit*
SD	Studies and Documents
SE	*Studia evangelica*
Sel.Pap.	*Select Papyri.* Edited by A. S. Hunt and C. C. Edgar. Cambridge, MA, 1871 – .
SJT	*Scottish Journal of Theology*
SNT	Studien zum Neuen Testament
SNTSMS	Society for New Testament Studies Monograph Series
SP	Sacra Pagina
ST	*Studia theologica*
TaJT	*Taiwan Journal of Theology*
TDNT	*Theological Dictionary of the New Testament.* Edited by G. Kittel and G. Friedrich. Translated by G. W. Bromiley. 10 vols. Grand Rapids, 1964 – 1976.
TEV	Today's English Version
THNTC	The Two Horizons New Testament Commentary
TJ	*Trinity Journal*
TNIV	Today's New International Version
TNTC	Tyndale New Testament Commentaries
TTZ	*Trierer theologische Zeitschrift*
TynBul	*Tyndale Bulletin*
UBS	United Bible Society *Greek New Testament*
UNT	Untersuchungen zum Neuen Testament
USQR	*Union Seminary Quarterly Review*
VE	*Vox evangelica*
VTSup	Supplements to Vetus Testamentum
WBC	Word Biblical Commentary
WMANT	Wissenschaftliche Monographien zum Alten und Neuen Testament
WTJ	*Westminster Theological Journal*
WUNT	Wissenschaftliche Untersuchungen zum Neuen Testament
WW	*Word and World*
ZNW	*Zeitschrift für die neutestamentliche Wissenschaft und die Kunde der älteren Kirche*

Introduction to Colossians

The significance of this letter to the Colossians lies in its subject matter, to which Calvin rightly points: "this Epistle ... to express it in one word, distinguishes the true Christ from a fictitious one."[1] In various ways, Paul corrects and challenges his audience's understanding of Christ by insisting on the centrality of the lordship of Christ, through whose death and resurrection God accomplished his salvific plan. Paul labels everyone who adheres to religious practices not centered on Christ as captives to an "empty and deceitful philosophy according to human tradition ... not according to Christ" (2:8).

In this relatively short letter, one finds the use of various literary forms and genres: thanksgiving and prayer reports, hymn, vice and virtue lists, household code, and general exhortation. Through these various literary instruments, the supreme authority of Christ is proclaimed not simply as one who is the Creator of the universe, but as one who accomplishes God's plan of salvation and is therefore the Lord of the new creation as well. As such, he is to be recognized as the Lord of the cosmos as well as every realm of human existence, including people's private practices, their community and households, and their interactions with outsiders. The theoretical and the practical intermingle as Paul affirms the need to live out one's christological confession. This final product provides one of the most significant christological discussions in the NT, and it illustrates the profound interrelationship between Christology, theology, soteriology, ecclesiology, eschatology, and ethics. Though challenging for casual readers, this letter makes a serious theological and practical impact on those who are willing to wrestle with its message.

Before participating in this rich feast, several introductory issues must be dealt with, especially since one's position on these issues will affect how one understands the various aspects of Paul's message here.

---

1. John Calvin, *Commentaries on the Epistles of Paul the Apostle to the Philippians, Colossians, and Thessalonians* (trans. John Pringle; Grand Rapids: Baker, 2003), 134.

People, Place, and Time

Authorship

This letter begins by identifying "Paul, an apostle of Christ Jesus" as its author (1:1),[2] and Pauline authorship had been accepted throughout the early Christian centuries. Challenges to his authorship first surfaced in the early nineteenth century; since the middle of the twentieth century, the authenticity of this letter has been questioned by a growing number of critical scholars. Such challenges are often based on (1) the use of distinct vocabularies and sentence structure, (2) distinct theological emphases that include a relatively more developed Christology and the alleged overemphasis on the realized aspects of eschatology,[3] (3) modern scholars' inability to identify a set of false teachings within the lifetime of the apostle Paul against which the author argues, and (4) the disputed relationship with Ephesians and, to a lesser degree, Philemon.[4]

Many remain unconvinced, however, by these arguments against the authenticity of this letter. First, in reference to vocabulary and sentence structure, it should be noted that "the peculiarities of speech and mode of expression are most evident in those sections of Col in which Paul is polemicizing against the false teaching, or when, with it in view, he sets forth his own ideas in hymnic form (1:10 – 20; 2:16 – 23)."[5] The particular situation within the Colossian church would thus explain the use of a peculiar set of expressions. Moreover, it is questionable whether the size of the Pauline corpus is substantial enough to establish a set of statistical data on which one short letter can be evaluated.[6] Finally, the possible use of an amanuensis

---

2. The letter opening also includes "Timothy" as the coauthor, but the letter body clearly identifies a singular author; see commentary on 1:1.

3. Others have also pointed to the different use of the "body" metaphor in Colossians/Ephesians and in other earlier letters of Paul; see Hanna Roose, "Die Hierarchisierung der Leib-Metapher im Kolosser- und Epheserbrief als 'Paulinisierung': Ein Beitrag Zur Rezeption paulinischer Tradition in Pseudo-paulinischen Briefen," *NovT* 47 (2005): 117 – 41.

4. For a clear summary statement of such challenges, see, in particular, Mark Kiley, *Colossians as Pseudepigraphy* (Biblical Seminar; Sheffield: JSOT, 1986), 37 – 107. To these traditional arguments Kiley further points to the lack of any mention of financial matters in Colossians as Paul did in his earlier (authentic) letters. This, however, fails to take note of the fact that the collection Paul took on his third missionary journey was officially completed with his final return to Jerusalem after the writing of Romans (cf. Rom 15:30 – 32). The absence of simi-

lar references in Philemon (and Ephesians) also weakens this challenge.

5. Werner Georg Kümmel, *Introduction to the New Testament* (rev. ed.; trans. Howard C. Kee; Nashville: Abingdon, 1975), 341.

6. See Kenneth J. Neumann, *The Authenticity of the Pauline Epistles in the Light of Stylostatistical Analysis* (SBLDS 120; Atlanta: Scholars, 1990), 194 – 99, who points to the statistical affinities between Colossians and other authentic letters of Paul. Even those who do not accept the authenticity of Colossians have noted that in Philippians, a letter often accepted to be genuine Pauline, one finds more *hapax legomena* than in Colossians (36 instead of 34) as well as a significant number of words (46) that appear elsewhere in the New Testament but not in the Pauline corpus; Vincent A. Pizzuto, *A Cosmic Leap of Faith: An Authorial, Structural, and Theological Investigation of the Cosmic Christology in Col 1:15 – 20* (CBET 41; Leuven: Peeters, 2006), 20.

in this (cf. 4:18) or other letters of Paul makes it difficult to provide a fair comparison for the judgment in terms of authorship.[7]

In terms of theology, while it is true that Paul does provide a systematic and emphatic presentation of the cosmic significance of Christ in this letter, this presentation is not inconsistent with Paul's statements elsewhere where Christ is depicted as supreme over all spiritual powers (cf. Rom 8:38; 1 Cor 2:6 – 8; 4:9; Phil 2:10). The particular situation in the Colossian community provides the occasion for Paul to provide a systematic presentation of the supremacy of Christ and the finality of his death and resurrection. In terms of eschatology, references to things yet to be fulfilled also play an important role in this letter (cf. 1:23; 2:18 – 19; 3:4, 6, 24).[8] Some would even argue that "eschatological judgment is a central issue in this letter."[9] As in the case of Christology, a certain development in Paul's thought cannot be ruled out.[10] Again, the historical circumstances of this letter must be taken into consideration. As has been noted, realized eschatology is sometimes emphasized when Jewish concerns are at the center of discussion (e.g., Galatians), while future eschatology can often be found when "pneumatic enthusiasm" can be identified (e.g., 1 – 2 Cor, Phil).[11] This may partly explain the emphasis on the present fulfillment of eschatological hope in Colossians.[12]

Concerning the false teaching that Paul is combating, a more detailed discussion will be provided below. Here it is sufficient to note that such false teaching is entirely plausible within the development of late Second Temple Jewish thought in general and first-century Asia Minor in particular. With the limited number of first-century documents that survive for the modern readers, however, one should not expect to have full knowledge of the various types of teachings propagated within the few years of Paul's ministry in the Greek East.

Beyond the identity of the false teachers, several pieces of evidence within the text affirm the authenticity of this letter. First, the author assumes that the audience is aware of the false teaching that he is combating. This fits comfortably within our reading of this letter as an authentic one since "it is characteristic of pseudepigraphical letters … that they must describe the situation of their supposed addressee(s)

---

7. Some, such as Eduard Schweizer, *The Letter to the Colossians* (trans. Andrew Chester; Minneapolis: Augsburg, 1982), 15 – 24, argue for Timothy (cf. 1:1) as the author of this letter. In Rom 16:22, "Tertius" is explicitly noted as the one drafting the letter.

8. See Todd D. Still, "Eschatology in Colossians: How Realized Is It?" *NTS* 50 (2004): 125 – 38. On the relationship between Paul's uses of the baptism metaphor in Rom 6 and in Col 2:12 and 3:1 – 4, see also John W. Yates, *The Spirit and Creation in Paul* (WUNT 2.251; Tübingen: Mohr Siebeck, 2008), 161.

9. Thomas J. Sappington, *Revelation and Redemption at Colossae* (JSNTSup 53; Sheffield: JSOT, 1991), 227.

10. Cf. Leopold Sabourin, "Paul and His Thought in Recent Research (I)," *Religious Studies Bulletin* 2 (1982): 62 – 73, who recognizes these developments without immediately assuming that such developments are not possible in the thought world of an author.

11. George E. Cannon, *The Use of Traditional Materials in Colossians* (Macon, GA: Mercer Univ. Press, 1983), 198.

12. For a further discussion of various theological emphases in this letter, see "The Theology of Colossians," p. 328.

sufficiently for the real readers, who would not otherwise know it."[13] Second, it has been noted that the style of this letter is "characteristic of Asiatic rhetoric,"[14] which also allows this letter to be located comfortably within first-century Asia Minor. Third, while those who assume that this letter is written by a "pseudo-Paul" to a "pseudo-addressee,"[15] it is difficult to explain why this "pseudo-Paul" would pick a city that lay in ruins after the earthquake of AD 60 or 61 (cf. Tacitus, *Annals* 14.27). Moreover, possible veiled references to this earthquake in this letter (cf. 1:23; 2:5, 7, 14, 19; 4:12) may further argue for its pre-AD 70 origin.[16] In short, "nothing in Colossians is demonstrably anachronistic."[17]

Finally, the relationship between this letter and Ephesians and Philemon also needs to be addressed. It is well known that there is significant overlap between the content of Colossians and Ephesians. Some who argue for a "free and creative" dependent relationship between Ephesians and Colossians consider the author of Ephesians as a later imitator of Paul who created a work based on the authentic Pauline letter of Colossians.[18] Others have instead suggested that the relationship between the two goes the other direction, with the author of Colossians copying from Ephesians.[19] Yet others would consider both letters as products of the later "Pauline school."[20] Among those who propose literary dependence, the priority of Colossians receives the strongest support, and the alleged use of Colossians by the author of Ephesians would then testify to the authenticity of Colossians; nevertheless, it does not seem necessary to give up on the authenticity of Ephesians in the affirmation of the Pauline authorship of Colossians. Sufficient differences between the two argue against a mechanical mode of literary dependence between them, and one can easily imagine the same author writing two letters during the same period of time using the same theological language and framework. The fact that scholarly consensus is still lacking concerning their relative priority further testifies to the organic relationship between the two.

As for its relationship with the universally accepted authentic Pauline letter to Philemon, the parallels between the two, especially in their respective greetings sec-

13. Richard Bauckham, "Pseudo-Apostolic Letters," *JBL* 107 (1988): 490.

14. Ben Witherington III, *The Letters to Philemon, the Colossians, and the Ephesians: A Socio-Rhetorical Commentary on the Captivity Epistles* (Grand Rapids: Eerdmans, 2007), 18.

15. Outi Leppä, *The Making of Colossians: A Study on the Formation and Purpose of a Deutero-Pauline Letter* (Publications of the Finnish Exegetical Society 86; Göttingen: Vandenhoeck & Ruprecht, 2003), 13.

16. Thus Larry J. Kreitzer, "Living in the Lycus Valley: Earthquake Imagery in Colossians, Philemon and Ephesians," in *Testimony and Interpretation: Early Christology in Its Judeo-Hellenistic Milieu. Studies in Honour of Petr Pokorý* (ed. Jiří

Mrázek and Jan Roskovec; JSNTSup 272; London: T&T Clark, 2004), 87–89, 92–93.

17. John M. G. Barclay, *Colossians and Philemon* (Sheffield: Sheffield Academic, 1997), 24.

18. See, e.g., Andrew T. Lincoln, *Ephesians* (WBC 42; Dallas: Word, 1990), lv.

19. See the classic presentation in Ernst Theodor Mayerhoff, *Der Brief an die Colosser mit vornehmlicher Berücksichtigung der drei Pastoralbriefe* (Berlin: Hermann Schultze, 1838), 72–106.

20. See, in particular, Ernest Best, "Who Used Whom? The Relationship of Ephesians and Colossians," *NTS* 43 (1997): 72–96.

tions, can best be explained by the hypothesis of a common authorship. Despite the arguments of a vocal minority that the author of Colossians builds his letter on Philemon,[21] internal evidence fails to support an artificial literary dependence between the two.[22] While the status of Onesimus as a slave is a central issue in Philemon, Onesimus is not identified as a "slave" in Col 4:9;[23] this is among the many details that fail to support the hypothesis that Colossians is written by an imitator of Paul.

Among the various possibilities, to consider Paul as the author of Colossians is still the best hypothesis on which our reading can be constructed.

Date and Place of Writing

The place of origin of this letter has direct implications concerning its dating. In light of the overlap between the greetings of Colossians and Philemon, both probably originated from the same place. It is clear that Paul writes as a prisoner (1:24; 4:3, 10, 18; cf. Phlm 1, 9, 10, 13, 23), but he does not specify the precise location of his imprisonment. Three geographical locations have been proposed: Caesarea, Ephesus, and Rome. The presence of Luke in Col 4:14 and Phlm 24 may suggest a Caesarean origin since Luke uses the first person plural in describing presumably his presence with Paul in Caesarea (Acts 27:1 – 2).[24] Nevertheless, Caesarea does not appear in Paul's captivity letters, and this provenance receives no support from ancient evidence.

An Ephesian provenance builds on one reading of 1 Cor 15:32, although an explicit mentioning of his imprisonment is lacking. An Ephesian origin may also be considered to be more probable in light of its proximity with Colossae, thus allowing Onesimus to flee to Paul.[25] This assumes, however, that Onesimus is a runaway slave of limited means and thus unable to travel beyond Asia Minor.[26] Moreover, even if Paul were imprisoned in Ephesus, in light of the travel notes from Acts and from Paul (e.g., Rom 15; 1 Cor 16; 2 Cor 1 – 9), it is unlikely that he would have spent considerable time there as a prisoner.[27]

Paul's Roman imprisonment still provides the best framework for reading these

---

21. Cf. Angela Standhartinger, "Colossians and the Pauline School," *NTS* 50 (2004): 574.

22. Barclay, *Colossians and Philemon*, 24, rightly notes: "If Colossians is by a later Paulinist, it is unparalleled in its sophisticated adaptation of incidental details to camouflage its inauthenticity."

23. For the significance of this observation, see commentary on 4:9.

24. See E. Earle Ellis, *The Making of the New Testament Documents* (BIS 39; Leiden: Brill, 1999), 271 – 72, who also suggests that "Paul's plan to go to Spain via Rome (Rom 15:24), later qualified by an expressed intention to visit Colossae (Phlm 22),

fit a Caesarean better than a Roman provenance of these three prison epistles."

25. See Ralph P. Martin, *Reconciliation: A Study of Paul's Theology* (rev. ed.; Eugene, OR: Wipf & Stock, 1997), 111.

26. For a discussion of this "runaway slave" hypothesis, see "Introduction to Philemon," below. Even those who uphold this hypothesis consider Rome, which is called the "common sink of all nations" (Tacitus, *Ann.* 15.44), a "convenient hiding place" for a runaway slave; J. B. Lightfoot, *St. Paul's Epistles to the Colossians and to Philemon* (London: Macmillan, 1897), 33.

27. See, in particular, Marlis Gielen, "Paulus — Gefangener in Ephesus?" *BN* 133 (2007): 63 – 77.

(two) prison letters. Early manuscript evidence[28] and early church fathers[29] provide the earliest support of this reading, and Paul's relatively lengthy Roman imprisonment with a certain freedom to minister to those around him (cf. Acts 28:30 – 31) is consistent with the evidence contained in these two (and the other two) captivity letters. The appearance of the name "Aristarchus" in Col 4:10 and Phlm 24 is also consistent with Acts 27:2, which mentions his journey with Paul (and Luke) to Rome. While absolute proof for a Roman provenance is lacking, clear and convincing arguments against this traditional identification have yet to surface.

Accepting a Roman provenance, Colossians (and Philemon) can be dated to AD 60 – 62.

Audience

Located 125 miles from the western coast of Asia Minor, Colossae lies in the Lycus Valley eleven miles from the major city of the region, Laodicea. Once "a great city" (Herodotus, *Hist.* 7.30.1), its glory lay in its past during the time of Paul's writing of this letter. After the earthquake of AD 60 or 61 (cf. Tacitus, *Annals* 14.27), this city appears to have suffered significant damages. Commentators have therefore often noted that "Colossae was one of the least important places to which documents that were later canonized were ever sent."[30]

Although Paul was apparently not the founder of the church(es) in Colossae (cf. 2:1), his ministry may have indirectly contributed to the spread of the gospel to the communities in the Lycus Valley. During his three-year ministry in Ephesus (cf. Acts 20:31) "all the Jews and Greeks who lived in the province of Asia heard the word of the Lord" (19:10); among them was possibly Epaphras, the one who brought the gospel to Colossae, Laodicea, and Hierapolis (cf. Col 4:13) after he himself had experienced the power of "the word of truth, the gospel" (1:5). Paul identifies this Epaphras as his and Timothy's "beloved fellow slave, a faithful servant of Christ on [their] behalf" (1:7). He is not only an evangelist, but also a pastor who is "always striving on behalf of you [i.e., the Colossians] in prayers, that you may stand mature and fully assured in all the will of God" (4:12).

After the Colossians had accepted the gospel, apparently they encountered challenges that prompted Epaphras to return to Paul (cf. Phlm 23), who not only told him about their "love in the Spirit" (1:8), but also about the problem among their community. While Epaphras was still with Paul (4:12 – 13; Phlm 23), Paul sent Tychicus

28. The city "Rome" appears in the subscriptions included in some manuscripts of Colossians: B^c K P 82 101 122 431 460 1907 1924; cf. Bruce M. Metzger, *A Textual Commentary on the Greek New Testament* (2nd ed.; Stuttgart: United Bible Societies, 1994), 560.

29. E.g., Jerome, John Chrysostom, Theodoret; see Markus Barth and Helmut Blanke, *Colossians* (trans. Astrid B. Beck; AB 34B; New York: Doubleday, 1994), 127.

30. Barth and Blanke, *Colossians*, 10. Although not explicitly noted, this statement recalls the earlier judgment of Lightfoot, *St. Paul's Epistles to the Colossians and to Philemon*, 16.

(and Onesimus) back to the Lycus Valley. Not only did Tychicus carry this letter with him, but he was also responsible for reporting to them Paul's own situation (4:7).

Since the settlement of two thousand Jewish families in Asia Minor in the third century BC (Josephus, *Ant.* 12.3.4), there was a significant Jewish population in the Lycus Valley and the surrounding areas.[31] Significant Jewish influence in the Colossian community cannot be denied. Nevertheless, in this letter Paul appears to be addressing primarily a Gentile audience. These are the Gentile Christians who are now "to share in the inheritance of the saints in the light" (1:12). The fact that they, the Gentiles, can receive the gospel testifies to the revelation of God's mystery in this eschatological era (1:27). Unlike the Jews, these Christians are "circumcised with a circumcision not performed by human hands" (2:11).

Numerous references to Jewish customs and practices cannot be ignored (cf. 2:16 – 23). These references may point to the presence of Jews whose teachings Paul is combating. It is to such teachings that we must now turn.

Circumstances behind the Text

To discuss the circumstances behind the writing of this letter to the Colossians is to deal with its purpose. Unlike a letter like Romans, Paul's discussion in this letter appears to be more determined by a particular set of situations within the targeted audience. Unlike Philippians, where Paul responds directly to the false teachers abruptly introduced in the second part of the letter (Phil 3:2 – 4), this letter provides a consistent focus on what appears to be a set of false teachings propagated by some unnamed parties. Unlike Galatians, however, Paul's rhetoric is relatively measured; yet compared to the closely related letter in Ephesians, Paul does seem to be combating one particular set of teachings in this letter. This is reflected in statements where Paul warns his audience not to be deceived by people with their "arguments" (2:4) and by their "empty and deceitful philosophy" (2:8), to be judged by things that "are a shadow of things to come" (2:17), or to be condemned by their insistence on certain religious and cultic practices (2:18).

That Paul appears to be dealing with one set of teachings is perhaps reflected in the one solution that he consistently points to: the centrality of Christ and the finality of his authority. Those misleading the Colossian believers are accused of promoting teachings that are "according to human tradition" instead of "according to Christ" (2:8). These teachings are but "a shadow of things to come, but the substance belongs to Christ" (2:17). This explains the intense christocentric focus of this letter that begins with the exalted status of Christ (1:15 – 20). The believers are reminded that

---

31. See the discussion in F. F. Bruce, "Colossian Problems, Part I: Jews and Christians in the Lycus Valley," *BSac* 141 (1984): 5 – 6, who points to the presence of about 9,000 Jewish males in Laodicea alone.

they have already "died with Christ" (2:20; cf. 2:12) and also are "raised with Christ" (3:1; cf. 2:12), thus sharing in his victory over the powers and authorities. Even in the paraenetic section, Paul insists that "Christ is all and in all" (3:11) and that one is to "do everything in the name of the Lord Jesus" (3:17).

Despite these textual clues, however, some scholars have argued against the presence of false teachings in the Colossian community. Some have suggested that Paul's intent is to affirm the faith of the Colossian believers so that they will not be exposed to possible threats from the outside world.[32] Others acknowledge the presence of false teachings but deny that such false teachings are the primary reasons for Paul's writing of this letter,[33] since Paul may be more interested in changing behavior rather than correcting wrong beliefs.[34] The consistency of Paul's interaction with that which challenges the centrality of Christ does argue for the presence of a definite body of teachings that deviates from the gospel that the Colossian believers had received, and this singular focus points also to the interrelationship between ideology and practices among the Colossian believers. Moreover, the fact that unlike the churches in Galatia, Paul is not the founder of the church(es) in Colossae may partly explain the difference in tone between the two letters. Therefore, the existence and influence of this "empty and deceitful philosophy" (2:8) should not be downplayed, although it is more difficult to decide whether those promoting such philosophy are to be considered members of the community. To label this philosophy as "false teaching" would then provide us with a workable framework within which the various parts of this letter can be read.

While many accept the presence of "false teaching" within the Colossian community, its identity is by no means clear. Included in this letter are statements that appear to reflect a Jewish character of this false teaching:

2:11: "you were also circumcised with a circumcision not performed by human hands."

2:16: "do not let anyone judge you in food and in drink, or in regard to a festival, a new moon, or sabbaths"

2:20–21: "Why ... do you submit to its regulations, do not handle, do not taste, do not touch?

---

32. See, e.g., Morna D. Hooker, "Were There False Teachers in Colossae?" in *Christ and Spirit in the New Testament: Studies in Honour of Charles Francis Digby Moule* (ed. Barnabas Lindars and Stephen S. Smalley; Cambridge: Cambridge Univ. Press, 1973), 316: "If false teaching exists, then it cannot be serious, either in character or magnitude; one glance at Galatians reminds us of the way in which Paul reacts when he feels that faith in Christ is being undermined."

33. See, e.g., Thomas H. Olbricht, "The Stoicheia and the

Rhetoric of Colossians: Then and Now," in *Rhetoric, Scripture and Theology: Essays from the 1994 Pretoria Conference* (ed. Stanley E. Porter and Thomas H. Olbricht; JSNTSup 131; Sheffield: Sheffield Academic, 1996), 310–23, who argues that Colossians is closer to 1 Thessalonians than Galatians in this regard.

34. Cf. Harold van Broekhoven, "The Social Profiles in the Colossian Debate," *JSNT* 66 (1997): 73–90, who suggests that Paul is arguing against individualistic behavioral patterns.

Other statements do, however, appear to move beyond the realm of Jewish beliefs and practices:

> 2:15: "When he disarmed the rulers and authorities, he boldly made a spectacle of them, by triumphing over them in him."
>
> 2:18: "Let no one condemn you by insisting on self-humiliation and the worship of angels, entering into these things that he has seen."
>
> 2:23: "These rules have no value … even though they have an appearance of wisdom with their self-imposed worship, self-humiliation, and harsh treatment of the body."

The failure to identify one existing group in first-century Asia Minor that would promote the exact body of teachings reflected in these statements has led some to conclude that the identity of this false teaching is "an unsolved, and insoluble, mystery."[35] For others, these statements suggest that "the author did not have a particular heresy in view,"[36] and if he did, this lack of specificity may be "due in part to the fact that Paul's own knowledge of the situation was limited."[37] To those who doubt the authenticity this letter, this lack of clarity is best explained by the understanding that this is a fictitious problem that reflects the general condition of a post-Pauline church.[38] Before reaching such conclusions, however, it is wise to acknowledge the limitation of our knowledge of first-century Asia Minor in general and the situation in specific local churches. Although an exact parallel from literature from the same geographical and temporal contexts is lacking, many scholars consider the textual clues in this letter sufficient in proposing certain systems of teachings that may lie behind Paul's polemic in this letter.

Pagan Philosophy

Focusing on elements that appear to be outside of the boundaries of typical Jewish practices, a small minority of scholars continues to argue for a predominantly pagan background of this false teaching. The emphases on cosmic speculations and ascetic practices have been taken to reflect a general mixture of Middle Platonic thought and other local traditions that encourage a particular path in the pursuit of wisdom,[39] or a form of Cynic philosophy in particular whose adherents criticize

---

35. Barclay, *Colossians and Philemon*, 54.

36. Charles M. Nielsen, "The Status of Paul and His Letters in Colossians," *PRSt* 12 (1985): 106.

37. Markus Bockmuehl, *Revelation and Mystery in Ancient Judaism and Pauline Christianity* (Grand Rapids: Eerdmans, 1997), 180.

38. Angela Standhartinger, *Studien zur Entstehungsgeschichte und Intention des Kolosserbriefs* (NovTSup 94; Leiden: Brill, 1999), 16 – 25.

39. Richard E. DeMaris, *The Colossian Controversy: Wisdom in Dispute at Colossae* (JSNTSup 96; Sheffield: JSOT, 1994), 16 – 17, 131 – 33. See also George H. van Kooten, *Cosmic Christology in Paul and the Pauline School: Colossians and Ephesians in the Context of Graeco-Roman Cosmology, with a New Synopsis of the Greek Texts* (WUNT 2.171; Tübingen: Mohr Siebeck, 2003), 143, who argues that Colossians "is almost a modification of Middle Platonist doctrine from within."

the ritual and calendrical practices of the Colossian believers.[40] Parallels to Middle Platonic thought can indeed explain certain phrases and expressions in this letter, but we should not ignore the significance of the Jewish elements as noted above. The problem of attempts to identify the specific school of philosophy such as Cynicism[41] is the lack of linguistic parallels that would secure such a link.

Jewish Legalism

On the other end of the spectrum, there are those who argue for a strictly Jewish character of this false teaching, especially the type of Jewish legalism that lies behind other Pauline writings. Insofar as the phrase "the elemental spirits of the world" (τὰ στοιχεῖα τοῦ κόσμου, 2:8; cf. 2:20) had already appeared in Gal 4:3, 9, where "it is clearly linked into the Jewish law, understood as itself a kind of power set in charge over Israel like a slave-custodian or guardian (Gal 3:23 – 25; 4:1 – 3, 9 – 10),"[42] some have suggested that the false teaching Paul is encountering in this letter is similar to what he fought against in Galatians.[43] Additional parallels further strengthen the connection between these two letters: circumcision, Sabbath and feast days, food laws, and the definition of God's people in inclusive terms.[44]

While the significance of the presence of Jewish elements in this false teaching cannot be denied, Jewish legalism is unable to explain other elements in 2:16 – 23 that appear to move beyond this conceptual framework. Moreover, those who "argue *both* that the letter is by Paul *and* that it reacts to the same issues addressed in Galatians adopt the least likely option, since they cannot then explain why the polemic in Colossians is so different from that in Galatians."[45] Equally important is the fact that while the word "law" (νόμος) appears more than thirty times in Galatians, it is not used at all in Colossians. Jewish legalism should not, therefore, be considered the primary target of Paul's discussion in this letter.

Jewish Mysticism

Another form of Jewish influence that has been suggested as behind this false teaching is Jewish mysticism, and this reading has received increasing support in

40. Troy W. Martin, *By Philosophy and Empty Deceit: Colossians as Response to a Cynic Critique* (JSNTSup 118; Sheffield: Sheffield Academic, 1996).

41. See also Schweizer, *Letter to the Colossians*, 126 – 36, who argues for a Pythagorean background; cf. A. J. M. Wedderburn, "The Theology of Colossians," in Andrew T. Lincoln and A. J. M. Wedderburn, *The Theology of the Later Pauline Letters* (Cambridge: Cambridge Univ. Press, 1993), 3 – 12.

42. James D. G. Dunn, *The Epistles to the Colossians and to Philemon* (NIGTC; Grand Rapids: Eerdmans, 1996), 150.

43. Christopher A. Beetham, *Echoes of Scripture in the Let-

ter of Paul to the Colossians* (BIS 96; Leiden: Brill, 2008), 261. See also Gregory K. Beale, "Colossians," in *Commentary on the New Testament Use of the Old Testament* (ed. G. K. Beale and D. A. Carson; Grand Rapids: Baker, 2007), 860, who suggests that the false teaching "appears to be an erroneous Jewish doctrine that focused on the law instead of Christ as the epitome of divine revelation."

44. See, in particular, Allan R. Bevere, *Sharing in the Inheritance: Identity and the Moral Life in Colossians* (JSNTSup 226; London: Sheffield Academic, 2003), 59 – 121.

45. Barclay, *Colossians and Philemon*, 54.

the recent years.[46] For proponents of this view, the ascetic practices in 2:23 are cultic acts in preparation for the "entering" (2:18) into visionary experience where individuals are to worship with the angels. The genitive in the phrase "worship of angels" (θρησκείᾳ τῶν ἀγγέλων) in 2:18 is therefore interpreted as a subjective genitive in reference to the worship of God in the company of angelic beings. The close relationship between wisdom and apocalyptic tradition is also understood as forming the background for the christological hymn in 1:15 – 20.

This reading rightly makes the connection between the traditions concerning angels and ascetic practices,[47] as well as highlights the significance of ascetic practices as cultic acts.[48] This is, however, insufficient in explaining the various elements as related to the false teaching behind this text. First, in focusing on the role of angels as benign spiritual beings who stand in the presence of God, this reading ignores the evil heavenly powers found in 2:15.[49] Even in the christological hymn of 1:15 – 20, a wisdom reading within the framework of Jewish mysticism fails to explain all that is contained in the hymn.[50] More importantly, there is the lack of evidence for understanding the phrase "the worship of angels" in a subjective genitive sense.[51]

For those who affirm a Jewish mystic identification of this false teaching, "Jewish mysticism" is often defined in the broadest sense that would include but not be limited to Jewish apocalyptic thought.[52] Apocalyptic writings are therefore frequently quoted in support for this reading. This transfer is problematic since numerous other significant apocalyptic motifs are missing in later explicitly mystic texts such as those in Jewish *Merkabah* mysticism. Equally important is the fact that Jewish apocalyptic thought is often syncretistic in nature. It is misleading, therefore, to assert that the mysticism behind the Colossian false teaching falls "within Judaism" and that "it is not necessary to look beyond Judaism to find the identity of the errorists,"[53] especially when the one making such an assertion must acknowledge that "although

46. See, e.g., Fred O. Francis, "Humility and Angelic Worship in Col 2:18," in *Conflict at Colossae: A Problem in the Interpretation of Early Christianity Illustrated by Selected Modern Studies* (ed. F. O. Francis and W. A. Meeks; Missoula, MT: Scholars, 1975), 163 – 95; Craig A. Evans, "The Colossian Mystics," *Bib* 63 (1982): 188 – 205; Christopher Rowland, "Apocalyptic Visions and the Exaltation of Christ in the Letter to the Colossians," *JSNT* 19 (1983): 73 – 83; Roy Yates, " 'The Worship of Angels' (Col 2:18)," *ExpTim* 97 (1985): 12 – 15; Sappington, *Revelation and Redemption at Colossae*; Ian K. Smith, *Heavenly Perspective: A Study of the Apostle Paul's Response to a Jewish Mystical Movement at Colossae* (LNTS 326; London: T&T Clark, 2006).

47. See also the helpful discussion in Rachel Elior, *The Three Temples: On the Emergence of Jewish Mysticism* (trans. David Louvish; Oxford: Littman, 2004), 190 – 91.

48. See also Gershom Scholem, *Major Trends in Jewish Mysticism* (New York: Schocken, 1954), 49.

49. Clinton E. Arnold, *The Colossian Syncretism: The Interface between Christianity and Folk Belief at Colossae* (WUNT 2.77; Tübingen: Mohr Siebeck, 1995), 97 – 98.

50. Jarl Fossum, "Colossians 1.15 – 18a in the Light of Jewish Mysticism and Gnosticism," *NTS* 35 (1989): 183 – 201.

51. Arnold, *Colossian Syncretism*, 91: "A survey of the usage of θρησκεία fails to turn up one example of a divine being, or a typical object of worship (e.g. an 'idol'), related to θρησκεία in the genitive case that should be taken as a subjective genitive."

52. Some would prefer this narrower category for the identification of the Colossian false teaching; cf. Robert M. Royalty Jr., "Dwelling on Visions: On the Nature of the So-Called 'Colossians Heresy,'" *Bib* 83 (2002): 329 – 57.

53. Smith, *Heavenly Perspective*, 33, 38.

the background of the Colossian error was clearly Judaism, it was also affected by Hellenism and even Paganism."[54] It is therefore prudent to affirm the significance of Jewish apocalyptic and mystic traditions but allow room for other influences behind this false teaching.

Syncretism

In light of the fact that the Colossian false teaching appears to contain both Jewish elements and those that do not fit comfortably within a traditional Jewish framework, it appears that some sort of syncretism lies behind this false teaching. Even those who argue for a Jewish mysticism background readily admit that "the practices of some of the Jews in Phrygia were syncretistic,"[55] and various forms of Jewish mysticism are often syncretistic in nature: "Cosmogony and cosmology, anthropology and psychology, join magic on the one hand and *halakhah* and the study of the Torah on the other, to become building blocks of this new spiritual enthusiasm."[56] Moreover, the first-century Greco-Roman world is often characterized as syncretistic as eastern cults merged with their western counterparts in the creation of new conglomerations of cultic practices and beliefs. Modern scholars in comparative religions often use this term in light of this Hellenistic-Roman phenomenon,[57] but the term *syncretism* can be used in a variety of ways in reference to various degrees of the inter-influence of two or more systems of thought. In this context, the term is used simply in reference to the presence of elements from different conceptual frameworks in one context without assuming the degree of amalgamation, even though a primary framework can be identified.

Within this broader umbrella of syncretism, two camps can still be identified. The first considers pagan religious beliefs and practices as providing the dominant framework within which Jewish elements can be incorporated. Proponents of this position point to the prominence of Phrygian folk religions[58] or mystery cults[59] in this region, and these scholars highlight pagan elements in these false teachings. Some even consider the clause "entering into these things that he has seen" (2:18) as a specific description of the entry into the initiation rites of these cults. Although pagan elements cannot be denied, the predominantly Jewish character of the false teaching is downplayed in this reading. Moreover, 2:18 is not required to be read as a technical reference to the pagan initiation rites.[60]

54. Ibid., 143.

55. Ibid., 5.

56. Joseph Dan, "The Religious Experience of the Merkavah," in *Jewish Spirituality: From the Bible through the Middle Ages* (ed. Arthur Green; New York: Crossroad, 1986), 306.

57. See, e.g., John B. Carman, "Syncretism: Historical Phenomenon and Theological Judgment," *ANQ* 4 (1964): 30–43.

58. Arnold, *Colossian Syncretism*, 103–244.

59. Barth and Blanke, *Colossians*, 10–16.

60. See also Jerry L. Sumney, "Studying Paul's Opponents: Advances and Challenges," in *Paul and His Opponents* (ed. Stanley E. Porter; Pauline Studies; Leiden: Brill, 2005), 55, who argues against those who argue for both a folk and mystery cult background since those two would attract two different groups of participants.

The evidence, therefore, appears to favor a syncretism with Jewish elements providing the controlling framework. While this general position has been held by many in the past decades,[61] further specificities to the possible outlook of such a system is provided by the proponents of a Jewish mysticism interpretation together with those who emphasize the significance of the local Phrygian cults.[62] This position takes into account the significance of Jewish identity markers such as circumcision (2:11), Sabbath observance (2:16), and ritual purity (2:20–21) as well as the presence of the veneration of angels (2:18) and its related cultic practices (2:23) in this short letter. To call this a syncretistic teaching also acknowledges the reality of first-century Phrygia. A more precise label for such a false teaching may not be possible at the present time, but this general framework is sufficient as we begin our attempt to understand the various elements contained in this letter.

Significance

This letter that addresses a congregation challenged by a form of syncretism has significant contemporary application in a society in which the "virtues" of pluralism and tolerance are exalted as most important. Instead of simply pointing out the errors of the various practices and beliefs promoted by the false teachers, Paul begins and ends with an intense focus on Christ as the foundation of the believers' existence. As a result, one finds powerful theoretical and practical outworkings of a robust Christology. In this letter, the readers encounter a detailed portrayal of the unique identity and final authority of Christ, and this portrayal enriches the high Christology found elsewhere in Paul's letters. In light of this christological confession, practices that compete with the sufficiency of God's work in Christ are challenged and critiqued. Through this process, the contemporary readers should learn to dissect contemporary practices that equally reflect a betrayal of our christological confession.

Just like today!

Definition of worship

In addition to the critique of the practices promoted by the false teachers, Paul also focuses on ways believers can live out their faith in Christ. Paul reminds believers that to worship Christ, who is the Lord of the cosmos, is to live a life that is consistent with our confession (cf. 3:15–17). Through lists of vices (3:5, 8–9) and virtues (3:12–14), Paul reminds believers that Christian ethics consist of a call to abandon a life of idolatry and to participate in the building up of the community of God's people. In a striking way, he also illustrates how an affirmation of the lordship

---

61. See, e.g., Lightfoot, *St. Paul's Epistles to the Colossians and to Philemon*, 73–113; Stanislas Lyonnet, "Paul's Adversaries in Colossae," in *Conflict at Colossae* (ed. F. O. Francis and W. A. Meeks; Missoula, MT: Scholars, 1975), 147–61; Wedderburn, "The Theology of Colossians," 10–11; R. McL. Wilson, *Colossians and Philemon* (ICC; Edinburgh: T&T Clark, 2005), 219.

62. In his more recent writings, Clint Arnold also affirms the significance of Jewish elements behind this false teaching and terms this as "a popular folk Judaism"; cf. Clinton E. Arnold, "Review of *Sharing in the Inheritance: Identity and the Moral Life in Colossians*," *EvQ* 77 (2005): 274–76.

of Christ carries within itself a demand to consider oneself a slave of Christ (cf. 3:15 – 4:1). In an age that worships independence and individual freedom, Paul's message provides a helpful corrective as contemporary believers continue to seek to be faithful to the gospel of the cross.

Finally, Paul reminds the readers of the final consummation of God's act in Christ that is yet to come (cf. 3:1 – 4).[63] Believers who live in the present age are not only urged to be alert (4:2); they are also called to witness to those beyond their own community (4:3 – 6). Missions is therefore properly situated at the intersection of Christology and eschatology. Contemporary believers who have been eagerly waiting for such consummation of God's redemptive history are likewise called to maintain this eschatological urgency. Perhaps nowhere else in Paul does one find such an integration of worship, ethics, soteriology, eschatology, and missions that is built on the work and status of Christ.

Outline

In delineating the line of arguments in Paul's letters, there is an increasing interest in applying ancient rhetorical categories to these letters.[64] It has been suggested that "rhetorical analysis … takes us far closer to the issues that really matter: meaning and significance, intention and strategy."[65] This recognition of Paul's rhetorical skill has served as a helpful corrective from the readings that assume that Paul's letters are simply to be read in light of ancient nonliterary papyri letters.[66] In the case of Colossians, most have suggested that this letter falls within the category of "deliberative rhetoric,"[67] as it aims primarily at dissuading the readers from following the teachings of the false teachers.[68]

It is unclear, however, how useful such a classification would be in our reading of this letter. First, rhetorical analyses that are controlled by the ancient rhetorical handbooks often focus primarily on the body of Paul's letters while ignoring the

---

63. Many would consider the absence of future eschatology as a distinct feature of Colossians (cf. Hans Conzelmann, *An Outline of the Theology of the New Testament* [trans. John Bowden; New York: Harper & Row, 1969], 314 – 15). This, however, is to miss one critical emphasis of Paul in this letter as he argues against the false teachers who dwell on the present age as the locus of their spiritual practices. For a further discussion on this point, see the discussion on eschatology in the Theology of Colossians section at the end of this commentary.

64. For a helpful survey of "the quest of the rhetorical Paul," see Frank W. Hughes, "The Rhetoric of Letters," in *The Thessalonians Debate: Methodological Discord or Methodological Synthesis* (ed. Karl P. Donfried and Johannes Beutler; Grand Rapids: Eerdmans, 2000), 199 – 215.

65. Charles A. Wanamaker, "Epistolary vs. Rhetorical Analysis: Is a Synthesis Possible?" in *The Thessalonians Debate: Methdological Discord or Methodological Synthesis* (ed. Karl P. Donfried and Johannes Beutler; Grand Rapids: Eerdmans, 2000), 286.

66. Cf. Stanley K. Stowers, *Letter Writing in Greco-Roman Antiquity* (LEC 5; Philadelphia: Westminster, 1986), 17 – 26.

67. See, e.g., Ben Witherington III, *Letters to Philemon, the Colossians, and the Ephesians* (Grand Rapids: Eerdmans, 2007), 104.

68. Three types of rhetoric have often been identified: *deliberative* (to exhort or dissuade), *judicial* (to accuse or defend), and *epideictic* (to praise or blame).

significance of the epistolary openings and endings of his letters. The problems with such analyses will be made clear in the commentary as we explore the significance of the opening and closing sections of this letter. In formal terms, the contribution of epistolography to the reading of Paul's letter should also be emphasized in any rhetorical analysis of his work.[69]

Perhaps more importantly, it has been repeatedly noted that while ancient rhetorical handbooks focus on the development of oral arguments, Paul's letters are literary works and are meant to be read as such. One of the early practitioners of NT rhetorical criticism has already noted that "being simply a lifeless piece of paper, [the letter] eliminates one of the most important weapons of the rhetorician, the oral delivery."[70] Moreover, in ancient rhetorical handbooks, the letter form is explicitly contrasted with oratory. This has led some to conclude that "there is, therefore, little if any theoretical justification in the ancient handbooks for application of the formal categories of the species and organization of rhetoric to analysis of the Pauline epistles."[71]

Finally, one wonders if in reality any ancient oratory performance would fit perfectly within the ideal types constructed by the ancient theoreticians. In the case of Pauline letters, many have recognized that these are best understood as mixed types.[72] Rather than considering these as a deviation of ancient practices, it may actually reflect the practices of an accomplished orator who "alters accepted patterns and adjusts them to the particular case and his special intention."[73] In reading the letters of Paul, therefore, one should not be controlled by the categories contained in ancient rhetorical handbooks. Paul's own presentation of the arguments in one particular historical and literary context should be the focus of our analysis.

In this commentary, therefore, we will focus on the development of Paul's argument while noting his rhetorical skill along the way. A detailed discussion of the flow of this letter will be provided at the beginning of our discussion of its various sections. Here, a general outline will allow us to begin in this journey as it highlights

69. For a recent discussion, see Stanley E. Porter and Sean A. Adams, eds., *Paul and the Ancient Letter Form* (Pauline Studies 6; Boston/Leiden: Brill, 2000). A more balanced reading can be found in Hans-Josef Klauck, *Ancient Letters and the New Testament: A Guide to Context and Exegesis* (trans. Daniel P. Bailey; Waco, TX: Baylor Univ. Press, 2006), 225, who recognizes that "rhetorical analysis must not be pursued at the expense of the unique features of the letter genre that epistolograpy has helped us understand."

70. Hans Dieter Betz, "The Literary Composition and Function of Paul's Letter to the Galatians," *NTS* 21 (1975): 377.

71. Stanley E. Porter, "The Theoretical Justification for Application of Rhetorical Categories to Pauline Epistolary Literature," in *Rhetoric and the New Testament: Essays from the 1992*

Heidelberg Conference (ed. Stanley E. Porter and Thomas H. Olbricht; JSNTSup 90; Sheffield: Sheffield Academic, 1993), 115–16. Others have, however, noted that some ancient theoreticians like Cicero (*Att.* 8.14; 9.10; 12.53) and Seneca (*Ep.* 75.1) have recognized the oral character of letters as speech (cf. Brian K. Peterson, *Eloquence and the Proclamation of the Gospel in Corinth* [SBLDS 163; Atlanta: Scholars, 1998], 18).

72. See, e.g., Duane F. Watson, "The Integration of Epistolary and Rhetorical Analysis of Philippians," in *The Rhetorical Analysis of Scripture: Essays from the 1995 London Conference* (ed. Stanley E. Porter and Thomas H. Olbricht; JSNTSup 146; Sheffield: Sheffield Academic, 1997), 398–426.

73. Carl Joachim Classen, *Rhetorical Criticism of the New Testament* (WUNT 128; Tübingen: Mohr Siebeck, 2000), 27.

the movement of Paul's discussion from the Father, to the Son, to the apostle, to the believers, and to the world.[74]

I. Opening Greetings (1:1 – 2)

II. Continuous Work of the Father (1:3 – 14)
  A. Thanksgiving (1:3 – 8)
  B. Intercession for the Colossians (1:9 – 14)

III. Climactic Work of the Son (1:15 – 23)
  A. Supremacy of Christ (1:15 – 20)
  B. Response to the Work of Christ (1:21 – 23)

IV. Apostolic Mission of Paul (1:24 – 2:5)
  A. Paul's Suffering in the Plan of God (1:24 – 29)
  B. Paul's Toil for the Local Churches (2:1 – 5)

V. Faithfulness of the Believers (2:6 – 4:1)
  A. Call to Faithfulness (2:6 – 7)
  B. Sufficiency in Christ (2:8 – 23)
    1. Against Deceptive Philosophy (2:8 – 15)
    2. Against Human Rituals and Regulations (2:16 – 23)
  C. Reorientation of Christian Living (3:1 – 4:1)
    1. Focus on the Risen Christ (3:1 – 4)
    2. Take off the Old Humanity (3:5 – 11)
    3. Put on the New Humanity (3:12 – 17)
    4. Lord of the Household (3:18 – 4:1)

VI. Eschatological Mission to the World (4:2 – 6)
  A. Prayer in Eschatological Alertness (4:2)
  B. Prayer for Paul and His Mission (4:3 – 4)
  C. Witness to Outsiders (4:5 – 6)

VII. Final Greetings (4:7 – 18)
  A. Messengers of the Letters (4:7 – 9)
  B. Greetings from Paul's Coworkers (4:10 – 14)
  C. Greetings to and Instructions for Others (4:15 – 17)
  D. Paul's Signature (4:18)

---

74. Some have detected in this letter the presence of ten microchiastic units that center on 2:6 – 23 and 3:1 – 7 (John Paul Heil, *Colossians: Encouragement to Walk in All Wisdom as Holy Ones in Christ* [Early Christianity and Its Literature 4; Atlanta: Society of Biblical Literature, 2010]). In this commentary, I argue instead for a linear development of thought although chiastic structure can indeed be detected in a smaller scale in passages such as 1:5, 10, 15 – 20; 3:7, 11.

Select Bibliography on Colossians

Aletti, Jean-Noël. *Saint Paul Épître aux Colossiens: Introduction, traduction et commentaire.* EBib 20. Paris: Gabalda, 1993.

Arnold, Clinton E. "Colossians." Pages 370 – 403 in *Zondervan Illustrated Bible Backgrounds Commentary*, vol. 3. Ed. Clinton E. Arnold. Grand Rapids: Zondervan, 2002.

———. *The Colossian Syncretism: The Interface between Christianity and Folk Belief at Colossae.* WUNT 2.77. Tübingen: Mohr Siebeck, 1995.

Barclay, John M. G. *Colossians and Philemon.* Sheffield: Sheffield Academic, 1997.

Barth, Markus, and Helmut Blanke. *Colossians: A New Translation with Introduction and Commentary.* AB 34B. New York: Doubleday, 1994.

Bassler, Jouette M. "Paul's Theology: Whence and Whither? A Synthesis (of Sorts) of the Theology of Philemon, 1 Thessalonians, Philippians, Galatians, and 1 Corinthians." *SBLSP* 28 (1989): 412 – 23.

Bauckham, Richard. *Jesus and the God of Israel.* Grand Rapids: Eerdmans, 2008.

———. "Where Is Wisdom to Be Found? Colossians 1.15 – 20 (II)." Pages 129 – 38 in *Reading Texts, Seeking Wisdom: Scripture and Theology.* Ed. David F. Ford and Graham Stanton. London: SCM, 2003.

Beale, Gregory K. "Colossians." Pages 841 – 70 in *Commentary on the New Testament Use of the Old Testament.* Ed. G. K. Beale and D. A. Carson. Grand Rapids: Baker, 2007.

Beetham, Christopher A. *Echoes of Scripture in the Letter of Paul to the Colossians.* BIS 96. Leiden: Brill, 2008.

Betz, Hans Dieter. "Paul's 'Second Presence' in Colossians." Pages 507 – 18 in *Text and Contexts: Biblical Texts in Their Textual and Situational Contexts: Essays in Honor of Lars Hartman.* Ed. Tord Fornberg and David Hellholm. Oslo/Boston: Scandinavian University Press, 1995.

Bevere, Allan R. *Sharing in the Inheritance: Identity and the Moral Life in Colossians.* JSNTSup 226. London: Sheffield Academic, 2003.

Blumenfeld, Bruno. *The Political Paul: Justice, Democracy and Kingship in a Hellenistic Framework.* JSNTSup 210. London: Sheffield Academic, 2001.

Bock, Darrell L. "'The New Man' as Community in Colossians and Ephesians." Pages 157 – 67 in *Integrity of Heart, Skillfulness of Hands.* Ed. Charles H. Dyer and Roy B. Zuck. Grand Rapids: Baker, 1994.

Bockmuehl, Markus. "A Note on the Text of Colossians 4:3." *JTS* 39 (1988): 489 – 94.

———. *Jewish Law in Gentile Churches: Halakhah and the Beginning of Christian Public Ethics.* Grand Rapids: Baker, 2003.

———. *Revelation and Mystery in Ancient Judaism and Pauline Christianity.* Grand Rapids: Eerdmans, 1997.

Bornkamm, Günther. "The Heresy of Colossians." Pages 123 – 45 in *Conflict at Colossae.* Ed F. O.

Francis and W. A. Meeks. Missoula, MT: Scholars, 1975.

Boyarin, Daniel. "Body Politic among the Brides of Christ: Paul and the Origins of Christian Sexual Renunciation." Pages 459 – 78 in *Asceticism.* Ed. Vincent L. Wimbush and Richard Valantasis. New York: Oxford University Press, 1998.

Bruce, F. F. *The Epistles to the Colossians, to Philemon, and to the Ephesians.* NICNT. Grand Rapids: Eerdmans, 1984.

Campbell, Douglas A. "Unravelling Colossians 3.11b." *NTS* 42 (1996): 120 – 32.

Callow, John. *A Semantic and Structural Analysis of Colossians.* Dallas: SIL International, 2002.

Cannon, George E. *The Use of Traditional Materials in Colossians.* Macon, GA: Mercer University Press, 1983.

Carr, Wesley. *Angels and Principalities: The Background, Meaning and Development of the Pauline Phrase Hai Archai Kai Exousiai.* SNTSMS 42. Cambridge: Cambridge University Press, 1981.

Chester, Andrew. "Jewish Messianic Expectations and Mediatorial Figures and Pauline Christology." Pages 17 – 89 in *Paulus und das antike Judentum.* Ed. Martin Hengel and Ulrich Heckel. WUNT 58. Tübingen: Mohr Siebeck, 1991.

Christopher, Gregory T. "A Discourse Analysis of Colossians 2:16 – 3:17." *GTJ* 11 (1990): 205 – 20.

Clarke, Andrew D. *A Pauline Theology of Church Leadership.* LNTS 362. New York/London: T&T Clark, 2008.

Cohen, Shaye J. D. *The Beginnings of Jewishness: Boundaries, Varieties, Uncertainties.* Berkeley, CA: University of California Press, 1999.

Cole, H. Ross. "The Christian and Time-Keeping in Colossians 2:16 and Galatians 4:10." *AUSS* 39 (2001): 273 – 82.

Cope, Lamar. "On Re-thinking the Philemon-Colossians Connection." *BR* 30 (1985): 45 – 50.

Coppens, Joseph. " 'Mystery' in the Theology of Saint Paul and Its Parallels at Qumran." Pages 132 – 58 in *Paul and the Dead Sea Scrolls.* Ed. J. Murphy-O'Connor and James H. Charlesworth. New York: Crossroad, 1990.

Dan, Joseph. "The Religious Experience of the Merkavah." Pages 289 – 307 in *Jewish Spirituality: From the Bible through the Middle Ages.* Ed. Arthur Green. New York: Crossroad, 1986.

De Boer, Martinus C. "The Meaning of the Phrase τὰ στοιχεῖα τοῦ κόσμου in Galatians." *NTS* 53 (2007): 204 – 24.

DeMaris, Richard E. *The Colossian Controversy: Wisdom in Dispute at Colossae.* JSNTSup 96. Sheffield: JSOT, 1994.

Derrett, J. Duncan M. "Primitive Christianity as an Ascetic Movement." Pages 88 – 107 in *Asceticism.* Ed. Vincent L. Wimbush and Richard Valantasis. New York: Oxford University Press, 1998.

Dibelius, M. "The Isis Initiation in Apuleius and Related Initiatory Rites." Pages 61 – 121 in *Conflict at Colossae.* Ed. F. O. Francis and W. A. Meeks. Missoula, MT: Scholars, 1975.

Dunn, James D. G. *The Epistles to the Colossians and to Philemon.* NIGTC. Grand Rapids: Eerdmans, 1996.

Ehrensperger, Kathy. *Paul and the Dynamics of Power: Communication and Interaction in the Early Christ-Movement.* London: T&T Clark, 2007.

Elior, Rachel. *The Three Temples: On the Emergence of Jewish Mysticism.* Trans. David Louvish. Oxford: Littman, 2004.

Ellis, E. Earle. "Colossians 1:12 – 20: Christus Creator, Christus Salvator." Pages 415 – 28 in *Interpreting the New Testament: Introduction to the Art and Science of Exegesis.* Ed. Darrell L. Bock and Buist M. Fanning. Wheaton, IL: Crossway, 2006.

Fee, Gordon. *God's Empowering Presence: The Holy Spirit in the Letters of Paul.* Peabody, MA: Hendrickson, 1994.

———. *Pauline Christology: An Exegetical-Theological Study.* Peabody, MA: Hendrickson, 2007.

Fitzgerald, John T. "Paul and Paradigm Shifts: Reconciliation and Its Linkage Group." Pages 241–62 in *Paul Beyond the Judaism/Hellenism Divide.* Ed. Troels Engberg-Pedersen. Louisville: Westminster John Knox, 2001.

Flemington, W. F. "On the Interpretation of Colossians 1:24." Pages 84–90 in *Suffering and Martyrdom in the New Testament: Studies Presented to G. M. Styler by the Cambridge New Testament Seminar.* Ed. William Horbury and Brian McNeil. Cambridge: Cambridge University Press, 1981.

Fletcher-Louis, Crispin H. T. "The Image of God and the Biblical Roots of Christian Sacramentality." Pages 73–89 in *The Gestures of God: Explorations in Sacramentality.* Ed. Geoffrey Rowell and Christine Hall. New York: Continuum, 2004.

———. "Wisdom Christology and the Partings of the Ways between Judaism and Christianity." Pages 52–68 in *Christian-Jewish Relations through the Centuries.* Ed. Stanley E. Porter and Brook W. R. Pearson. Sheffield: Sheffield Academic, 2000.

Fraade, Steven D. "Ascetical Aspects of Ancient Judaism." Pages 253–88 in *Jewish Spirituality: From the Bible through the Middle Ages.* Ed. Arthur Green. New York: Crossroad, 1986.

Francis, Fred O. "Humility and Angelic Worship in Col 2:18." Pages 163–95 in *Conflict at Colossae.* Ed. F. O. Francis and W. A. Meeks. Missoula, MT: Scholars, 1975.

Francis, Fred O., and Wayne A. Meeks, eds. *Conflict at Colossae: A Problem in the Interpretation of Early Christianity Illustrated by Selected Modern Studies.* Missoula, MT: Scholars, 1975.

Frank, Nicole. *Der Kolosserbrief im Kontext des paulinischen Erbes: Eine intertextuelle Studie zur Auslegung und Fortschreibung der Paulustradition.* WUNT 2.271. Tübingen: Mohr Siebeck, 2009.

Garland, David E. *Colossians and Philemon.* NIVAC. Grand Rapids: Zondervan, 1998.

Garrett, Susan R. *No Ordinary Angel: Celestial Spirits and Christian Claims about Jesus.* New Haven, CT: Yale University Press, 2008.

Gebauer, Roland. "Der Kolosserbrief als Antwort auf die Herausforderung des Synkretismus." Pages 153–69 in *Die bleibende Gegenwart des Evangeliums. Festschrift für Otto Merk.* Ed. R. Gebauer and M. Meiser. Marburger theologische Studien 76. Marburg: Elwert, 2003.

Gielen, Marlis. "Paulus — Gefangener in Ephesus?" *BN* 133 (2007): 63–77.

Gordley, Matthew E. *The Colossian Hymn in Context: An Exegesis in Light of Jewish and Greco-Roman Hymnic and Epistolary Conventions.* WUNT 2.228. Tübingen: Mohr Siebeck, 2007.

Goulder, Michael D. "The Visionaries of Laodicea." *JSNT* 43 (1991): 15–39.

Gräbe, Petrus J. "Salvation in Colossians and Ephesians." Pages 287–304 in *Salvation in the New Testament: Perspectives on Soteriology.* Ed. Jan G. van der Watt. NovTSup 121. Leiden: Brill, 2005.

Harris, Murray J. *Colossians and Philemon.* Exegetical Guide to the Greek New Testament. Grand Rapids: Eerdmans, 1991.

Hartman, Lars. "Humble and Confident: On the So-Called Philosophers in Colossians." *ST* 49 (1995): 25–39.

Hay, David M. "All the Fullness of God: Concepts of Deity in Colossians and Ephesians." Pages 163–79 in *The Forgotten God: Perspectives in Biblical Theology.* Ed. A. Andrew Das and Frank J. Matera. Louisville: Westminster John Knox, 2002.

———. *Colossians*. ANTC. Nashville: Abingdon, 2000.

———. "Pauline Theology after Paul." Pages 181–95 in *Pauline Theology*, volume 4: *Looking Back, Pressing On*. Ed. E. Elizabeth Johnson and David M. Hay. Atlanta: Scholars, 1997.

Heil, John Paul. *Colossians: Encouragement to Walk in All Wisdom as Holy Ones in Christ*. Early Christianity and Its Literature 4. Atlanta: Society of Biblical Literature, 2010.

Hering, James P. *The Colossian and Ephesian Haustafeln in Theological Context: An Analysis of Their Origins, Relationship, and Message*. American University Studies 7.260. New York: Peter Lang, 2007.

Hooker, Morna D. "Were There False Teachers in Colossae?" Pages 315–31 in *Christ and Spirit in the New Testament: Studies in Honour of Charles Francis Digby Moule*. Ed. Barnabas Lindars and Stephen S. Smalley. Cambridge: Cambridge University Press, 1973.

———. "Where Is Wisdom to Be Found? Colossians 1.15–20 (I)." Pages 116–28 in *Reading Texts, Seeking Wisdom: Scripture and Theology*. Ed. David F. Ford and Graham Stanton. London: SCM, 2003.

Hultin, Jeremy F. *The Ethics of Obscene Speech in Early Christianity and Its Environment*. NovTSup 128. Leiden: Brill, 2008.

Jervis, L. Ann. "Accepting Affliction: Paul's Preaching on Suffering." Pages 290–316 in *Character and Scripture: Moral Formation, Community, and Biblical Interpretation*. Ed. Willam P. Brown. Grand Rapids: Eerdmans, 2002.

Kim, Jung Hoon. *The Significance of Clothing Imagery in the Pauline Corpus*. JSNTSup 268. London: T&T Clark, 2004.

Kleinig, John W. "Ordered Community: Order and Subordination in the New Testament." *Lutheran Theological Journal* 39 (2005): 196–209.

Knight, George W., III. "Husbands and Wives as Analogues of Christ and the Church: Ephesians 5:21–33 and Colossians 3:18–19." Pages 165–78, 492–95 in *Recovering Biblical Manhood and Womanhood: A Response to Evangelical Feminism*. Ed. John Piper and Wayne Grudem. Wheaton, IL: Crossway, 1991.

Knowles, Michael P. " 'Christ in You, the Hope of Glory': Discipleship in Colossians." Pages 180–202 in *Patterns of Discipleship in the New Testament*. Ed. Richard N. Longenecker. Grand Rapids: Eerdmans, 1996.

Kreitzer, Larry J. "Living in the Lycus Valley: Earthquake Imagery in Colossians, Philemon and Ephesians." Pages 81–94 in *Testimony and Interpretation: Early Christology in Its Judeo-Hellenistic Milieu. Studies in Honour of Petr Pokorý*. Ed. Jirí Mrázek and Jan Roskovec. JSNTSup 272. London: T&T Clark, 2004.

Kremer, Jacob. "Was an den Bedrängnissen des Christus mangelt Versuch einer bibeltheologischen Neuinterpretation von Kol 1,24." *Bib* 82 (2001): 130–46.

Lamarche, Paul. "Structure de l'épître aux Colossiens." *Bib* 56 (1975): 453–63.

Lemke, Werner E. "Circumcision of the Heart: The Journey of a Biblical Metaphor." Pages 299–319 in *A God So Near: Essays on Old Testament Theology in Honor of Patrick D. Miller*. Ed. Brent A. Strawn and Nancy R. Bowen. Winona Lake, IN: Eisenbrauns, 2003.

Leppä, Outi. *The Making of Colossians: A Study on the Formation and Purpose of a Deutero-Pauline Letter*. Publications of the Finnish Exegetical Society 86. Göttingen: Vandenhoeck & Ruprecht, 2003.

Lieu, Judith M. *Christian Identity in the Jewish and Graeco-Roman World*. New York: Oxford University Press, 2004.

Lightfoot, J. B. *St. Paul's Epistles to the Colossians and to Philemon*. London: Macmillan, 1897.

———. "The Colossian Heresy." Pages 13–59 in *Conflict at Colossae*. Ed. F. O. Francis and W. A. Meeks. Missoula, MT: Scholars, 1975.

Lincoln, Andrew T. "Liberation from the Powers: Supernatural Spirits or Societal Structures?" Pages 335–54 in *The Bible in Human Society: Essays in Honour of John Rogerson*. Ed. M. Daniel Carroll R., David J. A. Clines, and Philip R. Davies. JSOTSup 200. Sheffield: Sheffield Academic, 1995.

———. *Paradise Now and Not Yet: Studies in the Role of the Heavenly Dimension in Paul's Thought with Special Reference to His Eschatology*. SNTSMS 43. Cambridge: Cambridge University Press, 1981.

Loader, W. R. G. "The Apocalyptic Model of Sonship: Its Origin and Development in New Testament Tradition." *JBL* 97 (1978): 525–54.

Lohmeyer, Ernst. *Die Briefe an die Philipper, an die Kolosser und an Philemon*. KEK 9. Göttingen: Vandenhoeck & Ruprecht, 1964.

Lohse, Eduard. *Colossians and Philemon*. Hermeneia. Philadelphia: Fortress, 1971.

Lorenzen, Stefanie. *Das paulinische Eikon-Konzept: Semantische Analysen zur Sapientia Salomonis, zu Philo und den Paulusbriefen*. WUNT 2.250. Tübingen: Mohr Siebeck, 2008.

Luttenberger, Joram. "Der gekreuzigte Schuldschein: Ein Aspekt der Deutung des Todes Jesu im Kolosserbrief." *NTS* 51 (2005): 80–95.

Lyonnet, Stanislas. "Paul's Adversaries in Colossae." Pages 147–61 in *Conflict at Colossae*. Ed. F. O. Francis and W. A. Meeks. Missoula, MT: Scholars, 1975.

MacDonald, Margaret Y. "Can Nympha Rule This House? The Rhetoric of Domesticity in Colossians." Pages in 99–120 *Rhetoric and Reality in Early Christianities*. Ed. Willi Braun. Waterloo, Ontario: Wilfrid Laurier University Press, 2005.

———. *Colossians and Ephesians*. SP 17. Collegeville, MN: Liturgical, 2000.

———. "Slavery, Sexuality and House Churches: A Reassessment of Colossians 3.18–4.1 in Light of New Research on the Roman Family." *NTS* 53 (2007): 94–113.

Maier, Harry O. "A Sly Civility: Colossians and Empire." *JSNT* 27 (2005): 323–49.

Martin, Ralph P. *Colossians and Philemon*. NCB. London: Oliphants, 1974.

———. *Reconciliation: A Study of Paul's Theology*. Rev. ed. Eugene, OR: Wipf & Stock, 1997.

Martin, Troy. "But Let Everyone Discern the Body of Christ (Colossians 2:17)." *JBL* 114 (1995): 249–55.

———. "Pagan and Judeo-Christian Time-Keeping Schemes in Gal 4.10 and Col 2.16." *NTS* 42 (1996): 105–19.

Meeks, Wayne A. "In One Body: The Unity of Humankind in Colossians and Ephesians." Pages 209–21 in *God's Christ and His People: Studies in Honor of Nils Alstrup Dahl*. Ed. Jacob Jervell and Wayne A. Meeks. Oslo: Universitetforlaget, 1977.

———. "'To Walk Worthily of the Lord': Moral Formation in the Pauline School Exemplified by the Letter to the Colossians." Pages 37–58 in *Hermes and Athena: Biblical Exegesis and Philosophical Theology*. Ed. Eleonore Stump and Thomas P. Flint. Notre Dame, IN: University of Notre Dame Press, 1993.

Merkel, H. "Der Epheserbrief in der neueren exegetischen Diskussion." *ANRW* 2.25.4 (1987): 3156–246.

Moo, Douglas J. *The Letters to the Colossians and to Philemon*. PNTC. Grand Rapids: Eerdmans, 2008.

Moule, C. F. D. *The Epistles of Paul the Apostle to the Colossians and to Philemon*. CGTC. Cambridge: Cambridge University Press, 1957.

Neyrey, Jerome H. "Lost in Translation: Did It Matter if Christians 'Thanked' God or 'Gave God Glory'?" *CBQ* 71 (2009): 1–23.

Nielsen, Charles M. "The Status of Paul and His Letters in Colossians." *PRSt* 12 (1985): 103 – 22.

O'Brien, Peter. *Colossians, Philemon*. WBC 44. Waco, TX: Word, 1982.

Parsons, Michael. "The New Creation." *ExpTim* 99 (1987): 3 – 4.

Pate, C. Marvin. *The Reverse of the Curse: Paul, Wisdom, and the Law*. WUNT 2.114. Tübingen: Mohr Siebeck, 2000.

Pizzuto, Vincent A. *A Cosmic Leap of Faith: An Authorial, Structural, and Theological Investigation of the Cosmic Christology in Col 1:15 – 20*. CBET 41. Leuven: Peeters, 2006.

Pokorný, Petr. *Colossians: A Commentary*. Trans. Siegfried S. Schatzmann. Peabody, MA: Hendrickson, 1991.

Porter, Stanley E. Καταλλάσσω *in Ancient Greek Literature, with Reference to the Pauline Writings*. EFN 5. Córdoba: Ediciones el Almendro, 1994.

———. "Paul's Concept of Reconciliation, Twice More." Pages 131 – 52 in *Paul and His Theology*. Ed. Stanley E. Porter. Pauline Studies 3. Leiden: Brill, 2006.

Reumann, John. "Colossians 1:24 ('What Is Lacking in the Afflictions of Christ'): History of Exegesis and Ecumenical Advance." *CurTM* 17 (1990): 454 – 61.

Roose, Hanna. "Die Hierarchisierung der Leib-Metapher im Kolosser- und Epheserbrief als 'Paulinisierung': Ein Beitrag Zur Rezeption paulinischer Tradition in Pseudo-paulinischen Briefen." *NovT* 47 (2005): 117 – 41.

Roth, Robert Paul. "Christ and the Powers of Darkness: Lessons from Colossians." *WW* 6 (1986): 336 – 44.

Royalty, Robert M., Jr. "Dwelling on Visions: On the Nature of the So-Called 'Colossians Heresy.'" *Bib* 83 (2002): 329 – 57.

Rusam, Dietrich. "Neue Belege zu den τὰ στοιχεῖα τοῦ κόσμου (Gal 4,3.9; Kol 2,8.20)." *ZNW* 83 (1992): 119 – 25.

Sappington, Thomas J. *Revelation and Redemption at Colossae*. JSNTSup 53. Sheffield: JSOT, 1991.

Saunders, E. W. "The Colossian Heresy and Qumran Theology." Pages 133 – 45 in *Studies in the History and Text of the New Testament*. Ed. B. Daniels and J. Suggs. SD 29. Salt Lake City: University of Utah Press, 1967.

Scharlemann, Martin H. "The Scope of the Redemptive Task (Colossians 1:15 – 20)." *CTM* 36 (1965): 291 – 300.

Schnabel, Eckhard J. *Law and Wisdom from Ben Sira to Paul*. WUNT 2.16. Tübingen: Mohr Siebeck, 1985.

Schnackenburg, Rudolf. *Present and Future: Modern Aspects of New Testament Theology*. Notre Dame, IN: University of Notre Dame Press, 1966.

Schnelle, Udo. *Theology of the New Testament*. Trans. M. Eugene Boring. Grand Rapids: Baker, 2009.

Schrage, Wolfgang. *The Ethics of the New Testament*. Trans. David E. Green. Philadelphia: Fortress, 1988.

Schweizer, Eduard. "Slaves of the Elements and Worshippers of Angels: Gal 4:3, 9 and Col 2:8, 18, 20." *JBL* 107 (1988): 455 – 68.

———. *The Letter to the Colossians: A Commentary*. Trans. Andrew Chester. Minneapolis: Augsburg, 1982.

Shogren, Gary S. "Presently Entering the Kingdom of Christ: The Background and Purpose of Col 1:12 – 14." *JETS* 31 (1988): 173 – 80.

Smith, Ian K. *Heavenly Perspective: A Study of the Apostle Paul's Response to a Jewish Mystical Movement at Colossae*. LNTS 326. London: T&T Clark, 2006.

Son, Sang-Won Aaron, "Τὸ σῶμα τοῦ Χριστοῦ in Colossians 2:17." Pages 222–38 in *History and Exegesis: New Testament Essays in Honor of Dr. E. Earle Ellis for His 80th Birthday*. Ed. Sang-Won Aaron Son. New York: T&T Clark, 2006.

Standhartinger, Angela. "Colossians and the Pauline School." *NTS* 50 (2004): 572–93.

———. *Studien zur Entstehungsgeschichte und Intention des Kolosserbriefs*. NovTSup 94. Leiden: Brill, 1999.

———. "The Origin and Intention of the Household Code in the Letter to the Colossians." *JSNT* 79 (2000): 117–30.

Sterling, Gregory E. "From Apostle to the Gentiles to Apostle of the Church: Images of Paul at the End of the First Century." *ZNW* 98 (2007): 74–98.

———. "Prepositional Metaphysics in Jewish Wisdom Speculation and Early Christian Liturgical Texts." Pages 219–38 in *Wisdom and Logos: Studies in Jewish Thought*. Ed. D. T. Runia and G. E. Sterling. Studies in Hellenistic Judaism 9. Atlanta: Scholars, 1997.

Stettler, Christian. "The Opponents at Colossae." Pages 169–200 in *Paul and His Opponents*. Ed. Stanley E. Porter. Pauline Studies. Leiden: Brill, 2005.

Stettler, Hanna. "An Interpretation of Colossians 1:24 in the Framework of Paul's Mission Theology." Pages 185–208 in *The Mission of the Early Church to Jews and Gentiles*. Ed. Jostein Ådna and Hans Kvalbein. WUNT 127. Tübingen: Mohr Siebeck, 2000.

Still, Todd D. "Eschatology in Colossians: How Realized Is It?" *NTS* 50 (2004): 125–38.

Stuckenbruck, Loren T. "Colossians and Philemon." Pages 116–32 in *The Cambridge Companion to St Paul*. Ed. James D. G. Dunn. Cambridge: Cambridge University Press, 2003.

Sumney, Jerry L. *Colossians: A Commentary*. NTL. Louisville: Westminster John Knox, 2008.

———. "Studying Paul's Opponents: Advances and Challenges." Pages 7–58 in *Paul and His Opponents*. Ed. Stanley E. Porter. Pauline Studies. Leiden: Brill, 2005.

———. "The Argument of Colossians." Pages 339–52 in *Rhetorical Argumentation in Biblical Texts: Essays from the Lund 2000 Conference*. Ed. Anders Eriksson, Thomas H. Olbricht, and Walter Übelacker. Harrisburg, PA: Trinity Press International, 2002.

———. "The Function of Ethos in Colossians." Pages 301–15 in *Rhetoric, Ethic, and Moral Persuasion: Essays from the 2002 Heidelberg Conference*. Ed. Thomas H. Olbricht and Anders Eriksson. Emory Studies in Early Christianity 11. New York: T&T Clark, 2005.

Talbert, Charles H. *Ephesians and Colossians*. Paideia Commentaries on the New Testament. Grand Rapids: Baker, 2007.

Thompson, Marianne Meye. *Colossians and Philemon*. THNTC. Grand Rapids: Eerdmans, 2005.

Thornton, T. C. G. "Jewish New Moon Festivals, Galatians 4:3–11 and Colossians 2:16." *JTS* 40 (1989): 97–100.

Thurston, Bonnie. "Paul's Associates in Colossians 4:7–17." *ResQ* 41 (1999): 45–53.

Tomson, Peter J. *Paul and the Jewish Law: Halakha in the Letters of the Apostle to the Gentiles*. CRINT 3.1. Minneapolis: Fortress, 1990.

Trainor, Michael. "The Cosmic Christology of Colossians 1:15–20 in the Light of Contemporary Ecological Issues." *ABR* 53 (2005): 54–69.

Van Broekhoven, Harold. "The Social Profiles in the Colossian Debate." *JSNT* 66 (1997): 73–90.

Van der Watt, J. G. "Colossians 1:3–12 Considered as an Exordium." *JTSA* 57 (1986): 32–42.

Van Kooten, George H. *Cosmic Christology in Paul and the Pauline School: Colossians and Ephesians in the Context of Graeco-Roman Cosmology, with a New Synopsis of the Greek Texts*. WUNT 2.171. Tübingen: Mohr Siebeck, 2003.

———. _Paul's Anthropology in Context: The Image of God, Assimilation to God, and Tripartite Man in Ancient Judaism, Ancient Philosophy and Early Christianity_. WUNT 232. Tübingen: Mohr Siebeck, 2008.

Walsh, Brian J. "Late/Post Modernity and Idolatry: A Contextual Reading of Colossians 2:8 – 3:4." _ExAud_ 15 (1999): 1 – 17.

Walsh, Brian J., and Sylvia C. Keesmaat. _Colossians Remixed: Subverting the Empire_. Downers Grove, IL: InterVarsity Press, 2004.

Wedderburn, A. J. M. "The Theology of Colossians." Pages 3 – 71 in _The Theology of the Later Pauline Letters_. Ed. Andrew T. Lincoln and A. J. M. Wedderburn. Cambridge: Cambridge University Press, 1993.

Wenham, David. _Paul: Follower of Jesus or Founder of Christianity?_ Grand Rapids: Eerdmans, 1995.

Wilson, R. McL. _A Critical and Exegetical Commentary on Colossians and Philemon_. ICC. Edinburgh: T&T Clark, 2005.

Wink, Walter. "The Hymn of the Cosmic Christ." Pages 235 – 45 in _The Conversation Continues: Studies in Paul and John: In Honor of J. Louis Martyn_. Ed. Robert T. Fortna and Beverly R. Gaventa. Nashville: Abingdon, 1990.

Witherington, Ben, III. _The Letters to Philemon, the Colossians, and the Ephesians: A Socio-Rhetorical Commentary on the Captivity Epistles_. Grand Rapids: Eerdmans, 2007.

Witherington, Ben, III, and G. François Wessels. "Do Everything in the Name of the Lord: Ethics and Ethos in Colossians." Pages 303 – 33 in _Identity, Ethics, and Ethos in the New Testament_. Ed. Jan G. van der Watt. BZNW 141. Berlin: de Gruyter, 2006.

Witulski, Thomas. "Gegenwart und Zukunft in den eschatologischen Konzeptionen des Kolosser- und des Epheserbriefes." _ZNW_ 96 (2005): 211 – 42.

Wright, N. T. "Adam in Pauline Christology." _SBLSP_ 22 (1983): 359 – 89.

———. _The Epistles of Paul to the Colossians and to Philemon_. TNTC. Leicester, UK: Inter-Varsity Press, 1986.

Yates, John W. _The Spirit and Creation in Paul_. WUNT 2.251. Tübingen: Mohr Siebeck, 2008.

Yates, Roy. "A Reappraisal of Colossians." _ITQ_ 58 (1992): 95 – 117.

———. "The Christian Way of Life: The Paraenetic Material in Colossians 3:1 – 4:6." _EvQ_ 63 (1991): 241 – 51.

Yinger, Kent L. "Translating καταβραβευέτω ['Disqualify' NRSV] in Colossians 2.18." _BT_ 54 (2003): 138 – 45.

Colossians 1:1 – 8

Literary Context

As in a number of Paul's earlier letters, Colossians begins with the identification of its author, coauthor, recipients, and a brief greeting (1:1 – 2). This introduction not only highlights Paul's authority as an apostle of Christ Jesus; it also points to the public nature of the letter from two leaders to the believers in the church at Colossae. The references to Christ Jesus and God's will also locate the present concerns within the wider salvation-historical plan of God.

It has often been claimed that Paul follows typical Hellenistic epistolary practice in his inclusion of an opening thanksgiving section (1:3 – 8) in many of his letters, and these sections focus on the epistolary situation: "to introduce the main theme of the letter."[1] It is true that such sections provide a preview of the theological emphases of these letters. In the case of Colossians, this one highlights important themes such as "faith in Christ Jesus" (v. 4), "hope stored up ... in heaven" (v. 5), "the gospel" (v. 5), and "love" (v. 8).

It is unclear, however, if such a function is dictated by the convention of the epistolary form. Subsequent studies on the Hellenistic epistolary form have questioned the existence of a typical "thanksgiving section" in Hellenistic papyrus letters.[2] While "health wishes" are often found, the lack of the explicit note of "thanksgiving" in most of these letters argues against seeing thanksgiving in a formulaic or conventional way.[3] An assumption that Paul is here simply following contemporary

---

1. Paul Schubert, *The Form and Function of the Pauline Thanksgivings* (Berlin: Töpelmann, 1939), 180, who also concludes that "the papyri convincingly attest a wide-spread conventional use of an epistolary, religious or non-religious, introductory thanksgiving" (180).

2. See William G. Doty, *Letters in Primitive Christianity* (Philadelphia: Fortress, 1973), 31 – 33; Klaus Berger, "Apostelbrief und apostolische Rede: Zum Formular frühchristlicher Briefe," *ZNW* 65 (1974): 219 – 20.

3. Peter Arzt, "The 'Epistolary Introductory Thanksgiving' in the Papyri and in Paul," *NovT* 36 (1994): 29 – 46. Even Jeffrey T. Reed ("Are Paul's Thanksgivings 'Epistolary'?" *JSNT* 61 [1996]: 87 – 99), who seeks to respond to Arzt's challenge, is forced to conclude that one can no longer speak of the "epistolary introductory thanksgiving" in Hellenistic papyrus letters. The few letters that do contain a thanksgiving section point to actual circumstances where the authors need to acknowledge certain gifts and favors. See, e.g., P.Mich.Inv. 2798. Most often, these notes appear in the body of the letter, e.g., P.Mert. I 12.

epistolary form distracts the readers from noticing the significance of the theme of thanksgiving throughout this letter (cf. 1:12; 2:6 – 7; 3:15 – 17; 4:2).[4]

This thanksgiving section (1:3 – 8) is closely related to the prayer report that follows (1:9 – 14). Both are indirect speeches addressed to God, and in both one finds the introduction to significant themes throughout the rest of this letter. Moreover, both sections point to the acts of God among his people. The focus of the two sections is slightly different, however. The thanksgiving section, comprised of one long sentence, focuses on the power of the gospel among the believers in Colossae, while the prayer report highlights the need to act in a way consistent with the knowledge that the gospel has imparted. The similarities in form and content between the two sections have led some to conclude that they should be considered one section.[5] The parallel ideas between the two sections do, however, point to the existence of two independent, though related, semantic units (see Literary Context on 1:9 – 14 for more on the prayer report).

➡ **I. Opening Greetings (1:1 – 2)**
   II. Continuous Work of the Father (1:3 – 14)
      A. Thanksgiving (1:3 – 8)
      B. Intercession for the Colossians (1:9 – 14)
   III. Climactic Work of the Son (1:15 – 23)

Main Idea

After the opening greetings, the thanksgiving section highlights the centrality of the gospel of Christ Jesus. This gospel points to the hope stored up in heaven, and such hope enables the believers to express their faith in Christ and their love for others.

Translation

(See next page.)

---

4. For a further discussion, see David W. Pao, "Gospel within the Constraints of an Epistolary Form: Pauline Introductory Thanksgivings and Paul's Theology of Thanksgiving," in *Paul and the Ancient Letter Form* (ed. Stanley E. Porter and Sean A. Adams; Pauline Studies 6; Boston/Leiden: Brill, 2010), 101 – 27.

5. Douglas J. Moo, *The Letters to the Colossians and to Philemon* (PNTC; Grand Rapids: Eerdmans, 2008), 73 – 74, 80. See also Jean-Noël Aletti, *Saint Paul épître aux Colossiens: Introduction, traduction et commentaire* (EBib 20; Paris: Gabalda, 1993), 50 – 53.

Colossians 1:1 – 8

1a	Sender	Paul,
b	apposition	an apostle of Christ Jesus,
c	means	by the will of God, and
d	parallel	Timothy,
e	apposition	our brother,
2a	Recipients	to the saints at Colossae,
b	apposition	the faithful brothers in Christ:
c	Desire	Grace to you and peace from God our Father.
3a	Assertion	**We always give thanks to God,**
b	apposition	the Father
c	relationship	of
d	apposition	our Lord Jesus Christ,
e	simultaneous	when we pray for you,
4a	basis (of 3a)	because we have heard of [1] your faith in Christ Jesus and
b	parallel	[2] the love
c	description (of 4b)	that you have for all the saints
5a	basis (of 4a, b)	on account of the hope stored up for you in heaven,
b	identification	which you have previously heard in the word of truth, the gospel,
6a	description	that has come to you,
b	comparison	just as in the whole world it is bearing fruit and growing,
c	comparison	so it has been bearing fruit and growing among you,
d	time	since the day you heard and understood the grace of God in truth,
7a	expansion	as you learned it from Epaphras,
b	apposition	our beloved fellow slave,
c	description	a faithful servant of Christ on our behalf,
8	expansion	who has also told us of your love in the Spirit.

Structure

Paul begins not only by identifying himself as an "apostle" (v. 1b), but also by clarifying the source of his calling (v. 1c). The prepositional phrase "by the will of God" presupposes a verbal idea embedded in the title "apostle" (i.e., "to send, to choose"). Together with Timothy (v. 1d), Paul addresses the believers in Colossae. As in his self-identification, Paul also identifies those in Colossae by means of their relationship with Christ (v. 2b).

The thanksgiving prayer is addressed to "God the Father" (v. 3a-b), but the christological focus in this prayer cannot be missed (cf. vv. 3d, 4a, 7c). The basis of the prayer, as expressed by the causal participle "because we have heard" (ἀκούσαντες),[6] points to the "love" and "faith" manifested in the lives of the believers in Colossae. Unlike elsewhere in Paul where the triad of "love," "faith," and "hope" is expressed in parallel terms (cf. 1 Cor 13:13), here the "hope" that is stored up for the saints in heaven (v. 5a) forms the basis of the "love" and "faith" manifested in the lives of the believers. This paves the way for the later emphasis on the eschatological hope of believers (1:23, 27; cf. 3:4).

In explaining the "hope," Paul introduces the significance and power of the "gospel" (v. 5b). Though tucked in a series of subordinate clauses, the "gospel" becomes the focus for the rest of this thanksgiving section. This "gospel" is portrayed as an active and powerful agent that has "come" to the Colossians (v. 6a), and it is "bearing fruit and growing" among the Colossians (v. 6c) as it is elsewhere in the world (v. 6b). The concluding note introduces Epaphras, the one who brought the gospel to those in Colossae (v. 7) and who had reported to Paul and his coworkers the situation in the church at Colossae (v. 8).

Exegetical Outline

→ **I. Opening Greetings (1:1 – 2)**

II. Thanksgiving for the Continuous Work of the Father (1:3 – 8)

    A. Occasion for the prayer (1:3)

    B. Faith and love manifested in the lives of the recipients (1:4)

    C. Basis of their faith and love (1:5 – 6)

        1. Hope stored up in heaven (1:5a)

        2. Hope as expressed in the powerful gospel (1:5b – 6)

    D. Role of Epaphras (1:7 – 8)

        1. Messenger of the gospel (1:7)

        2. Reporter of the situation in Colossae (1:8)

---

6. Most recent English versions take this as a causal participle (e.g., NET, NLT, NRSV, REB, TNIV, NIV) with the notable exception in NJB, which takes it as a temporal participle.

Explanation of the Text

1:1 Paul, an apostle of Christ Jesus, by the will of God, and Timothy, our brother (Παῦλος ἀπόστολος Χριστοῦ Ἰησοῦ διὰ θελήματος θεοῦ καὶ Τιμόθεος ὁ ἀδελφός). Paul begins this letter by identifying himself and his coauthor. The name "Paul" is likely his Hellenistic *cognomen*, one that is known among the Gentile churches. From Acts, one also learns of his Jewish name, Saul (e.g., Acts 7:58; 8:1; 9:1; 11:25). While an "apostle" (ἀπόστολος) can be merely a "messenger" (2 Cor 8:23; Phil 2:25), in letter openings (Rom 1:1; 1 Cor 1:1; 2 Cor 1:1; Gal 1:1; Eph 1:1; 1 Tim 1:1; 2 Tim 1:1; Titus 1:1) and elsewhere when Paul refers to himself (Rom 11:13; 1 Cor 9:1 – 2; 15:9; 1 Tim 2:7), this word functions as a title that points to his special position in the plan of God. By identifying himself as an "apostle," Paul is not simply explaining his mission as an "apostle to the Gentiles" (Rom 11:13; Gal 2:8); he is also drawing attention to his special status as one who speaks for Christ.[7] This also reflects the Greco-Roman context in which envoys represent and carry the authority of the one who sent them.[8] The following phrase, "of Christ Jesus," points to the authority of the risen Lord, and Paul's unique role is also highlighted in a later section of this letter (1:24 – 2:5).

The genitival construction "of Christ Jesus" (Χριστοῦ Ἰησοῦ) is best taken as a genitive of relationship.[9] This phrase is especially significant in this letter where the supremacy of Christ is the foundation of Paul's response to those who distract the Colossians from the true gospel.[10] The word order "Christ Jesus," instead of "Jesus Christ," seems of no significant theological value since in v. 3 and in the openings of some of his letters (Gal 1:1; 1 Thess 1:1; 2 Thess 1:1) Paul uses "Jesus Christ" instead.[11]

"By the will of God" (διὰ θελήματος θεοῦ) presupposes a verbal idea behind the previous semantic unit. Embedded in the noun "apostle" is the idea of "sending" (ἀποστέλλω), and Paul explicitly noted in 1 Cor 1:17 that Christ "sent" him to preach the gospel. Paul's identity as an apostle cannot be separated from his Damascus experience when he became Christ's "chosen instrument" in the gospel ministry (Acts 9:15; cf. 22:14 – 15; 26:17 – 18). In this context, this phrase highlights God's role behind Paul's ministry, and thus authenticates the gospel he preaches.[12]

"Timothy" accompanied Paul in his missionary journeys (cf. Acts 16:1 – 3; 17:14; 18:5; 19:22), and he was likely converted by Paul (cf. 1 Tim 1:2). His name also appears in the introductory salutations of 2 Corinthians, Philippians, 1 and 2 Thessalonians,

---

7. The origin of the Pauline use of the term "apostle" (ἀπόστολος) is unclear. Since this term was not commonly used in Hellenistic literature as a designation of a special emissary, it seems that the term could reflect a Jewish background, where one finds the explicit note in the rabbinic material that "the one sent by a man is as the man himself" (*m. Ber.* 5:5). Cf. K. H. Rengstorf, *TDNT*, 1:415.

8. See Margaret M. Mitchell, "New Testament Envoys in the Context of Greco-Roman Diplomatic and Epistolary Conventions: The Examples of Timothy and Titus," *JBL* 111 (1992): 644 – 51.

9. See Daniel B. Wallace, *Greek Grammar beyond the Basics: An Exegetical Syntax of the New Testament* (Grand Rapids: Zondervan, 1996), 83 – 84.

10. Cf. 1:2, 3, 4, 7, 24, 27, 28; 2:2, 5, 6, 8, 11, 17, 20; 3:1, 3, 4, 11, 15, 16, 24; 4:3, 12. This also suggests that "Christ" acquires a titular sense and is not simply to be understood as a personal name.

11. One does find the title "Lord" before "Jesus Christ" in v. 3 (and more than forty instances elsewhere in the Pauline letters), but not before "Christ Jesus" (but see "Jesus Christ our Lord" in Rom 1:4; 5:21; 7:25; 1 Cor 1:9). This may highlight the titular significance of "Christ" in the construction "Christ Jesus."

12. The anarthrous "will of God" (θελήματος θεοῦ) does point to the definite "will of God," as the article is often omitted after a preposition; cf. BDF §255.

and Philemon. Such inclusion can be explained in two ways. First, because he is mentioned in three of Paul's four "prison letters," he was likely present with Paul during his Roman imprisonment. Second, in the case of Colossians, Paul's own signature at the end of this letter (4:18) may imply that he employs a secretary for the writing of the rest of the letter. If so, Timothy may have served as his secretary.[13] This is further supported by the fact that Timothy has had no prior contact with the church at Colossae. His appearance in this salutation therefore points to his specific role in the composition of the letter.[14]

The translation "our brother" (ὁ ἀδελφός) takes the article (ὁ) as implying the first person plural pronoun, "our."[15] Unlike 1 Thess 3:2, where Timothy is explicitly called "our brother" (τὸν ἀδελφὸν ἡμῶν), the absence of the personal pronoun here may point to the use of the term "brother" in an absolute sense as a title, "the brother."[16] This would explain the absence of the pronoun whenever a cosender is called a "brother" in salutations of Pauline letters. "Brother," then, may function as a title as "apostle" does.[17]

1:2 To the saints at Colossae, the faithful brothers in Christ: Grace to you and peace from God our Father (τοῖς ἐν Κολοσσαῖς ἁγίοις καὶ πιστοῖς ἀδελφοῖς ἐν Χριστῷ· χάρις ὑμῖν καὶ εἰρήνη ἀπὸ θεοῦ

πατρὸς ἡμῶν). Paul locates his audience in their geographical and theological locations. We begin by exploring the relationship between "saints" (ἁγίοις) and "faithful" (πιστοῖς). At issue is whether ἁγίοις should be rendered simply as an adjectival modifier ("holy") or as a substantive adjective ("saints"). Grammatically, it may appear to be more natural to take both words as adjectival modifiers with "brothers" (ἀδελφοῖς): "to the holy and faithful brothers." The single article (τοῖς) may point to the two adjectives as modifying a single entity, and elsewhere in Colossians Paul exhorts the Colossians to be "holy" (1:22; 3:12).[18]

Nevertheless, in light of the use of this term in other Pauline salutations (Rom 1:7; 1 Cor 1:2; 2 Cor 1:1; Eph 1:1; Phil 1:1), it seems best to take this adjective in a substantive sense: "To the saints and faithful brothers and sisters" (NRSV; cf. NET, NLT, TNIV).[19] This substantival sense is supported by a number of other passages in Colossians (1:4, 12, 26). Even in 3:12, where the Colossians are described as "holy" (ἅγιοι), this adjective is used to explain their status as the "elect of God" (ἐκλεκτοὶ τοῦ θεοῦ), a phrase that explains what it means to be "saints" in the traditions of Israel (cf. Exod 22:30 LXX). Taking the word in a substantival sense also means that the conjunction (καί) that connects the two parts should be taken epexegetically: "To the saints at Colossae, [that is,] the faithful brothers in Christ."

---

13. For a discussion of ancient practices of the use of a secretary in the composition of a letter, see E. Randolph Richards, *The Secretary in the Letters of Paul* (WUNT 2.42; Tübingen: Mohr Siebeck, 1991). The name of one of Paul's secretaries, Tertius, appears in Rom 16:22.

14. Witherington, *Letters to Philemon, the Colossians, and the Ephesians*, 116, further suggests that because Timothy "was from the region just beyond Asia and his father was a Greek … he took a more active role in composing this document in Asiatic since he was familiar with it."

15. See, e.g., Barth and Blanke, *Colossians*, 137–38.

16. Reidar Aasgaard, *"My Beloved Brothers and Sisters!" Christian Siblingship in Paul* (JSNTSup 265; London: T&T Clark, 2004), 297.

17. See also Andrew D. Clarke, *A Pauline Theology of Church Leadership* (LNTS 362; New York/London: T&T Clark, 2008), 93, who notes the function of the term "brother" in Greco-Roman contexts warns against seeing it as a clear indication of egalitarianism in Paul.

18. For a recent defense of this position, see Thomas B. Slater, "Translating ἁγίοις in Col 1,2 and Eph 1,1," *Bib* 87 (2006): 52–54.

19. It is clear in this context that the word "brothers" (ἀδελφοῖς) is to be understood in an inclusive sense: "brothers and sisters."

To call the believers in Colossae "saints" is to remind them of their status as those who have been transferred to the "kingdom of his beloved Son" (1:13). This paves the way for Paul's argument that additional ascetic practices will not contribute to their status in the presence of God (2:16 – 23). To call them "faithful" also reminds them to be faithful to the gospel they have received (2:6). In this letter, Paul will mention three individuals as models of "faithful" brothers: Epaphras, Tychicus, and Onesimus (1:7; 4:7, 9).

The parallel phrases "at Colossae … in Christ" (ἐν Κολοσσαῖς … ἐν Χριστῷ) pave the way for the theological topography constructed in the body of Paul's argument. Historically and geographically, the recipients are "at Colossae," which Herodotus claimed to be "a great city in Phrygia" (*Hist.* 7.30.1) in the fifth century BC. In the Roman imperial period, however, its status and significance are unclear. A passage from Strabo (*Georg.* 12.8.13) seems to group Colossae with other neighboring small cities like Aphrodisias, although a lacuna in the text questions the certainty of this reading. It is clear, however, that Colossae could no longer compete with Laodicea, a major city of the Lycus Valley eleven miles NW of it. This also explains the references to Laodicea in this letter (2:1; 4:13, 15, 16). There is also evidence of the relative inferior status of Colossae even when compared to Aphrodisias, a city that boasted a significant imperial cult dedicated "To Aphrodite, the Divine Augustus and the People."[20]

Equally important is Paul's identification of the Colossians as being "in Christ." First, while "saints" points to God's elect and "brothers" to the new identity within the family of God, "in Christ" highlights the new identity of this people of God under the lordship of Christ. No longer are God's people defined by their blood relationship with their own kin; their identity is now rooted in Christ. Second, the "in Christ" formula paves the way for Paul's discussion of the sufficiency of the work of Christ (cf. 1:27 – 28). The only criterion through which one's spiritual status can be measured is Christ and Christ alone. Third, the parallel construction "at Colossae" and "in Christ" points further to the spatial significance of the "in Christ" formula. In 3:1 – 4, the recipients are reminded that they have been raised with Christ, the one "seated at the right hand of God" (3:1). Seeking "the things above," (3:1) therefore, is not to be understood as the search for additional fulfillment through spiritual exercises; rather, it is to focus on Christ, the one who has accomplished all.[21]

As in Paul's other letters, his greeting is adapted from contemporary Hellenistic epistolary practices. The implied verb "may … be" (εἴη) is often missing in this formulaic greeting, as it is often so in Hellenistic letters.[22] A typical greeting in Hellenistic letters contains a word of greeting and a health wish, with or without the note of prayer. Paul here substitutes the typical Greek word for "greetings" (χαίρειν) with "grace" (χάρις), a significant theological term in his own writings. Jewish letters often contain a prayer of peace as well,[23] and "peace" (εἰρήνη) here reflects such a practice.

---

20. For the influence of Aphrodisias on the neighboring larger cities, see D'Andreia Francesco, "Hierapolis of Phrygia: Its Evolution in Hellenistic and Roman Times," in *Urbanism in Western Asia Minor: New Studies on Aphrodisias, Ephesos, Hierapolis, Pergamon, Perge and Xanthos* (ed. David Parrish; Portsmouth, RI: Journal of Roman Archaeology, 2001), 96 – 115.

21. For a brief but helpful discussion of the significance of the "in Christ" formula in Pauline theology, see Mark Seifrid,

"In Christ," *DPL*, 433 – 36.

22. It could also be expressed in a full sentence, as in, "it would be as I wish" (εἴη ἂν ὡς ἐγώ; cf. P.Eleph. 13 [Sel.Pap. §96] [III BC]).

23. This is the case even in Aramaic letters, see Bezadel Porten, "Address Formulae in Aramaic Letters: A New Collection of Cowley 17," *RB* 90 (1980): 398 – 413.

For Paul, "grace" and "peace" are not merely subjective experiences of kindness and tranquility; rather, they point to the powerful salvific work of God through Christ, (e.g., Rom 3:24; 5:17) and the reconciliation that is already promised for the eschatological era (e.g., Rom 5:1; Eph 2:14 – 18; cf. Isa 52:7; 57:2). Here, Paul again reminds his audience of the foundational significance of the gospel.

The absence of the expected "and our Lord Jesus Christ" has prompted some early scribes to insert this phrase into the text. Most commentators find this omission puzzling,[24] although some have suggested that Paul is reserving this phrase for the next verse.[25] The parallel in 1 Thess 1:1 may further support this reading when Paul's greeting is simply "Grace and peace to you," whereas "God the Father and the Lord Jesus Christ" already appeared in the previous clause when describing the church of the Thessalonians.

1:3 We always give thanks to God, the Father of our Lord Jesus Christ, when we pray for you (Εὐχαριστοῦμεν τῷ θεῷ πατρὶ τοῦ κυρίου ἡμῶν Ἰησοῦ Χριστοῦ πάντοτε περὶ ὑμῶν προσευχόμενοι). Paul now begins a lengthy thanksgiving section (vv. 3 – 8). The principal verb "we give thanks" (εὐχαριστοῦμεν) is following by a participle ("when we pray," προσευχόμενοι). The plural "we" could be an "epistolary plural," where the verb refers to Paul himself,[26] but the switch back to the singular in 1:23 suggests this is not the case. Most commentators see both Paul and Timothy as the subject of this verb, but it remains puzzling as to why the sin-

gular form of the verb is used elsewhere, even when Timothy (among others) is listed as a cosender of the letter (cf. 1 Cor 1:1, 4; Phil 1:1, 3; Phlm 1, 4).[27] With this plural verb, it is at least possible that Paul intends to include his other coworkers as well as witnesses to the work of God among the believers in Colossae. The reference to the work of the gospel in "the whole world" (v. 6) may lend credence to this reading.

"Always" (πάντοτε) can modify either "we ... give thanks" or "when we pray." In light of other Pauline introductory thanksgivings (1 Cor 1:4; 1 Thess 1:2; 2 Thess 1:3; Phlm 4; cf. 2 Thess 2:13), it seems likely that it modifies the former. In Col 3:17, Paul will explain what it means to give thanks to God always, and this in turn supports our reading here: "whatever you do in word or deed, do everything in the name of the Lord Jesus, giving thanks to God the Father through him." That this phrase points to the meaning of "always give thanks" is confirmed by the parallel in Eph 5:20: "always [πάντοτε] giving thanks to God the Father for everything, in the name of our Lord Jesus Christ."

In Paul, thanksgiving is always directed toward God. In line with the OT heritage, this is an act of praise and confession when the mighty acts of God among his people are remembered (cf. Pss 35:18; 100:4; 109:30).[28] It is proper, therefore, for Paul to offer such thanks to God when he prays for the Colossians. Instead of the modern understanding of thanksgiving as a private sentiment, such an act of praise "seeks to persuade others to acknowledge

24. See, e.g., Peter O'Brien, *Colossians, Philemon* (WBC 44; Waco, TX: Word, 1982), 6.

25. Moo, *Letters to the Colossians and to Philemon*, 79.

26. Eduard Lohse, *Colossians and Philemon* (trans. William R. Poehlmann and Robert J. Karris; Hermeneia; Philadelphia: Fortress, 1971), 14.

27. Wilson, *Colossians and Philemon*, 80 – 81, may be right in concluding that this plural is a "real plural," without specifying the intended characters included in this reference.

28. For a discussion of "thanksgiving" as "praise" and "blessings" in postbiblical Jewish contexts, see James M. Robinson, "Die Hodajot-Formel in Gebet und Hymnus des Frühchristentums," in *Apophoreta: Festschrift Ernst Haenchen* (ed. W. Eltester and F. H. Kettler; Berlin: Töpelmann, 1964), 194 – 235. This is not limited to the Jewish background, however. See also H. S. Versnel, "Religious Mentality in Ancient Prayer," in *Faith, Hope and Worship: Aspects of Religious Mentality in the Ancient World* (ed. H. S. Vernel; Leiden: Brill, 1981), 1 – 64.

the deeds of God."[29] As a public act of praise, the content of this thanksgiving prayer draws attention to their "faith" and "love" (v. 4), but the focus is quickly shifted to the power of the gospel in the lives of these believers (v. 6). After all, God alone is the proper object of thanksgiving and worship.

"Our Lord Jesus Christ" (τοῦ κυρίου ἡμῶν Ἰησοῦ Χριστοῦ) is an important formula in both Pauline letters and early Christianity. Variations of this formula include "Jesus Christ our Lord" (e.g., Rom 1:4; 1 Cor 1:9), "Christ Jesus our Lord" (e.g., 1 Tim 1:2; 2 Tim 1:2), and "the Lord Jesus Christ" (e.g., Gal 1:3; Eph 1:2; Phil 1:2). In early Christian proclamation, one finds the confession that "God has made this Jesus, whom you crucified, both Lord and Messiah" (Acts 2:36). The frequent appearance of this title in the openings of Paul's letters may reflect a common liturgical usage (cf. 1 Cor 12:3) that points to Jesus' identity as that of his Father (cf. 1 Cor 8:6). In Colossians, the lordship of Christ is repeatedly affirmed (1:10; 2:6; 3:13, 17, 18, 20, 22, 23, 24; 4:1, 7, 17), and the identity of this Jesus is closely tied with God his "Father" (cf. 1:15 – 20). To reaffirm the significance of this confession in the lives of the believers is precisely the purpose of this letter (cf. 2:6 – 7).

1:4 Because we have heard of your faith in Christ Jesus and the love that you have for all the saints (ἀκούσαντες τὴν πίστιν ὑμῶν ἐν Χριστῷ Ἰησοῦ καὶ τὴν ἀγάπην ἣν ἔχετε εἰς πάντας τοὺς ἁγίους). With a causal circumstantial participle ("because we have heard," ἀκούσαντες), Paul provides the basis

of thanksgiving. Although the verb "to hear" can take a genitive object, here it takes an accusative with no apparent difference in meaning.[30]

"Faith" (τὴν πίστιν) points to the trust in and acceptance of Jesus Christ and his gospel. It is not, however, a virtue about which one can boast. Paul is insistent that faith itself is an act of God, one that enables believers to witness the power of the gospel in one's life (2:12; cf. Rom 5:1 – 2). In this thanksgiving section, the active role of the gospel is explicitly noted, as such a gospel is solely capable and responsible for "bearing fruit and growing" among the Colossians (v. 6). It has been noted that "in" (ἐν) indicates that "Christ Jesus" refers to "the sphere rather than the object of the faith."[31] While the objective sense should not be completely ruled out (cf. 2:5), the use of "in" does point to "Christ Jesus" as the sphere within which faith finds its true fulfillment.

In reference to "love" (τὴν ἀγάπην), however, the preposition "for" (εἰς) clearly points to "all the saints" as the indirect object of the verb "you have." If Paul had intended to highlight the parallelism between their "faith" and "love," he could have written "your love in the Spirit," as he does in v. 8. The fact that only the "love" of these believers is mentioned in v. 8 encourages some to take the "and" (καί) in this verse in an epexegetical sense,[32] and the lack of parallelism between these two phrases may further support this reading: "because we have heard of your faith in Christ Jesus, a faith that is expressed in the love that you have for all the saints."[33] This focus on the "faith" in the sphere

---

29. Jerome Neyrey, "Lost in Translation: Did It Matter if Christians 'Thanked' God or 'Gave God Glory'?" *CBQ* 71 (2009): 23, who further insists on interpreting acts of thanksgiving in Paul in terms of "praise" and "honor," the fundamental cultural values in the Greco-Roman world.

30. Wallace, *Greek Grammar*, 133.

31. C. F. D. Moule, *The Epistles of Paul the Apostle to the Colossians and to Philemon* (Cambridge: Cambridge Univ. Press, 1957), 49.

32. Cf. Barth and Blanke, *Colossians*, 153, who call this "a case of hendiadys." Hendiadys occurs when two words combine to form one concept although sometimes one term is dependent on the other. In this case, it might be rendered "loving faith" or "faith that expresses itself in love." Similarly, in v. 23 only "faith" is mentioned in connection with the "hope of the gospel."

33. Cf. Gal 5:6: "faith expressing itself through love."

of Christ Jesus paves the way for Paul's repeated emphasis that the Colossians should stand firm in their "faith" (1:23; 2:5, 7). "Love," by contrast, is the "perfect bond" manifested in those who hold firm to this "faith" (3:14).

"All the saints" refers to all the believers. As in v. 2, "saints" (ἅγιοι) does not point to the moral achievements of a selected group of believers but to those who are the elect of God. Some have therefore preferred simply to render this phrase "all of God's people" (NLT). The idea of "holiness" is important, however, though not as an attribute of believers; it refers to the accomplished work of Christ; who died on the cross: "now he has reconciled you in his body of flesh through death, in order to present you holy [ἁγίους], without blemish, and blameless before him" (1:22). It is tempting to see the all-inclusive "all the saints" as anticipating the arguments against a certain type of elitism among the false teachers (2:16 – 23; cf. 3:11), but the phrase often appears in Paul's writings, especially the prison letters, so it is better understood in a nonpolemical way as a general reference to believers (cf. Eph 1:15; 3:18; 6:18; Phil 1:1; 4:21, 22; Phlm 5).

1:5a On account of the hope stored up for you in heaven (διὰ τὴν ἐλπίδα τὴν ἀποκειμένην ὑμῖν ἐν τοῖς οὐρανοῖς). Paul now turns to the basis of the "faith" and "love" of the Colossians. The mentioning of "hope" (τὴν ἐλπίδα) completes the triad of "love," "faith," and "hope" (cf. Rom 5:1 – 5; 1 Cor 13:13; 1 Thess 1:3; 5:8). The origin of this triad is unclear, and its use is not limited to Paul (Heb 10:22 – 24; 1 Pet 1:21 – 22).[34] For Paul, "faith" is often understood as the foundation of "hope" (Rom 5:2; Gal 5:5) and "love" (1 Cor 13:2; 1 Tim

1:5), and when all three terms appear together the focus is often on the social manifestation of the gospel message (1 Cor 13:13; 1 Thess 1:3).[35] In this verse, however, the focus is on the fundamental significance of "hope," and the series of subordinate clauses that follow testifies to the emphasis placed on "hope."

The readers should expect the phrase introduced by the preposition "on account of" (διά) to provide the grounds of a verbal act, but the basis of the preceding verb "we … give thanks" has already been stated in v. 4 with the causal participle "because we have heard." This prepositional phrase can modify the verbal noun "love" or both "faith" and "love" (as taken by most English versions): "the faith and love that spring from the hope stored up for you in heaven" (TNIV, NIV). The choice between "love," the immediate antecedent, and "faith and love" is less of a pressing issue when one takes the "and" in v. 4 as epexegetical — "love" as the manifestation of "faith." In any case, "faith" and "love" flow from "hope." Syntactically, the three terms are not strict parallels, as "hope" becomes the source of "faith" and "love."

In Paul, "the hope" is not primarily a subjective sentiment of optimism. Hope is rooted in the promises of the faithful God, the one "who raises the dead" and the one who "will deliver us" (2 Cor 1:9 – 10). Based on God's acts in the past, this hope points forward to the consummation of his work in Christ (Titus 2:13). As such, this hope "does not disappoint" (Rom 5:5 NRSV). In Colossians, this "hope" is the reality proclaimed in the gospel (1:23) and centered on the work of Christ (1:27). Instead of the subjective sentiment, therefore, this hope is the object that provides grounds for one's confidence in God's continuous acts in history.

---

34. See the discussion in Thomas Söding, *Das Trias Glaube, Hoffnung, Liebe bei Paulus: Eine exegetische Studie* (SBS 150; Stuttgart: Katholisches Bibelwerk, 1992), 38 – 64. While recognizing the contribution of Hellenistic Jewish paraenetic traditions, Söding concludes that Paul was ultimately the one responsible for this formulation.

35. Cf. David M. Bossman, "Paul's Mediterranean Gospel: Faith, Hope, Love," *BTB* 25 (1995): 71 – 78.

Paul further specifies that this hope is "stored up for you in heaven." The implied subject of the attributive participle "stored up" (τὴν ἀποκειμένην) is God himself. This verb emphasizes the security and certainty of this hope because God is the actor (cf. Luke 19:20; 2 Tim 4:8; Heb 9:27). While Paul in Colossians often emphasizes the realized aspects of God's eschatological acts (cf. 2:12 – 15; 3:1), in this verse Paul makes it clear that this hope awaits future consummation. When Paul later explicitly identifies the "hope of glory" with "Christ" himself (1:27), it becomes clear that this "hope" that is "stored up … in heaven" will be revealed "when Christ is revealed" at the end of time (3:4).

The fact that this hope is stored up "in heaven" (ἐν τοῖς οὐρανοῖς)[36] is important for a number of reasons. First, this spatial imagery adds certainty to the "hope" that will be revealed in the future.[37] Second, possibly in anticipating the suggestions of the false teachers who promote the "worship of angels" (2:18), Paul is asserting that such ascents into the heavens through visionary experiences are not necessary because that which is in heaven has been secured for us and is to be revealed at the end of time. By defining a temporal concept ("hope") with a spatial one ("heaven"), Paul may therefore be providing a critique of individual mystical practices that ignore the wider salvation-historical plan of God.

1:5b Which you have previously heard in the word of truth, the gospel (ἣν προηκούσατε ἐν τῷ λόγῳ τῆς ἀληθείας τοῦ εὐαγγελίου). Further explicating on hope, this relative clause clearly points

to Paul's emphasis on the content of "hope," not on the act of hoping. The aorist verb "you have heard" (προηκούσατε) points to their hearing "beforehand."[38] In this context, it probably refers to the time when they learned of the gospel from Epaphras (v. 7).

The exact relationship between "the word" (τῷ λόγῳ), "truth" (τῆς ἀληθείας), and "the gospel" (τοῦ εὐαγγελίου) is not clear. Among the various options, three might fit the context. The first takes "truth" as an attributive genitive modifying "the word," and "the gospel" as an epexegetical genitive in apposition to "the word": "the true message, the Good News" (TEV).[39] This does not acknowledge the independent significance of "truth." Elsewhere in Paul, one finds a repeated emphasis on "truth," and a close parallel can be found in 2 Tim 2:15, where "the word of truth" clearly points to "the word of the Truth." The second takes both "truth" and "the gospel" as epexegetical genitives modifying "the word": "the word that is the truth and the gospel."[40] It is unusual, however, in a chain of multiple genitives for the last item to modify the first. The final option is to understand "truth" as an independent entity, and "the gospel" as an epexegetical genitive in apposition to "truth": "the word of the truth, the gospel" (NRSV).[41] This reading best captures the sense of the verse in this context, as it both emphasizes truth as the content of the proclamation, and the apostolic gospel as one that is identified with truth. This paves the way for Paul's argument against the false teachers who have deviated from this gospel.

---

36. The plural Greek verb reflects the Hebrew plural, "heavens" (שָׁמַיִם).

37. This reflects Jewish apocalyptic background, where promises that will be realized in the future are often said to have already existed in heaven; cf. Andrew T. Lincoln, *Paradise Now and Not Yet: Studies in the Role of the Heavenly Dimension in Paul's Thought with Special Reference to His Eschatology* (SNTSMS 43; Cambridge: Cambridge Univ. Press, 1981), 118.

38. BDAG, 865.

39. Cf. Murray J. Harris, *Colossians and Philemon* (Exegetical Guide to the Greek New Testament; Grand Rapids: Eerdmans, 1991), 18.

40. Or: "the message that is [or contains, or reveals] the truth, the message, that is, of the gospel" (Moo, *Letters to the Colossians and to Philemon*, 87).

41. This reading is also supported by the parallel in Eph 1:13: "the word of truth, the gospel of your salvation" (NRSV; τὸν λόγον τῆς ἀληθείας, τὸ εὐαγγέλιον τῆς σωτηρίας ὑμῶν).

Often translated simply as "the message" (NAB, REB, TEV, NET), "the word" (ὁ λόγος) is an important term in early Christian writings and Paul's theology.[42] In Colossians, it is to be identified as "the word of God" (τὸν λόγον τοῦ θεοῦ, 1:25) or even "the word of Christ" (ὁ λόγος τοῦ Χριστοῦ, 3:16). As such it is not to be reduced to mere human speech; rather, it refers to the entirety of the proclaimed gospel. "Truth" in this context points to "the content of Christianity as the ultimate truth."[43] It reflects the OT background, where "truth" is not simply that which conforms to reality; it is also God's truth as it reflects on the true object that demands full submission and worship (e.g., Pss 86:11 [85:11]; 96:13 [95:13]; cf. Rom 15:8).

In Paul, "truth" often appears in polemical contexts, where one finds an argument against false gospels and wickedness (cf. Rom 1:18, 25; 2:8; 1 Cor 5:8; Gal 2:5; 2 Thess 2:10 – 13). In this thanksgiving section, Paul twice emphasizes "truth" (see also v. 6), highlighting the contrast between the gospel and the message of the false teachers. Finally, while among the recipients "the gospel" may evoke the good news claimed by Roman imperial propaganda, Paul's use of the term more likely reflects an OT background, where one finds the promise of the eschatological message of salvation (cf. Isa 40:9; 41:27; 52:7).[44] For Paul, this promise finds its fulfillment in the death and resurrection of Jesus Christ (cf. 2:12 – 13).

1:6a That has come to you (τοῦ παρόντος εἰς ὑμᾶς). Paul now turns his attention to the power of "the gospel." The neuter attributive participle "that has come" (τοῦ παρόντος) modifies "the gospel" (τοῦ εὐαγγελίου), the focus of the rest of this thanksgiving section. The translation "that has come" accurately draws attention to the proclamation of the gospel among the Colossian believers, a point made more than once in this section (vv. 5, 7). The meaning of this verb, however, is often "to be present,"[45] although this translation is less often adopted perhaps because the preposition "to" (εἰς) points to the movement of the subject.[46]

It should be noted, however, that this verb may also evoke a motif also present in other Hellenistic letters. The discussion of the presence/absence of the author can often be found in Hellenistic letters especially when letters represent his or her presence.[47] While some have argued against seeing this as an epistolary convention, most would recognize this as at least an important literary *topos*.[48] In Paul's letters, the verb "to be present, come" (πάρειμι, 1 Cor 5:3; 2 Cor 10:2, 11; 13:2, 10; Gal 4:18, 20) and the related noun "presence" (παρουσία, Phil 1:26; 2:12) have also been used in depicting his presence. In Colossians, however, instead of focusing on his presence/absence, his emphasis is on the gospel "that has come" to the Colossians.[49] Historically, Paul had never been to

---

42. For the portrayal of "the word" (ὁ λόγος) as the powerful gospel, see the discussion on v. 6b-c.

43. BDAG, 42.

44. Peter Stuhlmacher, *Die paulinische Evangelium, 1: Vorgeschichte* (FRLANT 95; Göttingen: Vandenhoeck & Ruprecht, 1968), 109 – 79, 218 – 25.

45. BDAG, 773 – 74.

46. Moo, *Letters to the Colossians and to Philemon*, 87. But see Judg 19:3 [LXX], where the preposition "to" (εἰς) simply points to intention rather than movement.

47. Robert W. Funk, "The Apostolic *Parousia*: Form and Significance," in *Christian History and Interpretation: Stud-*

ies Presented to John Knox (ed. W. R. Farmer, C. F. D. Moule and R. R. Niebuhr; Cambridge: Cambridge Univ. Press, 1967), 249 – 68.

48. Terrence Y. Mullins, "Visit Talk in New Testament Letters," *CBQ* 35 (1973): 350 – 58; Lee A. Johnson, "Paul's Epistolary Presence in Corinth: A New Look at Robert W. Funk's Apostolic Parousia," *CBQ* 68 (2006): 481 – 501.

49. Elsewhere, Paul also directs the attention away from his absence/presence, and points to the (future) "presence" (παρουσία) of Jesus (1 Cor 15:23; 1 Thess 2:19; 3:13; 4:15; 5:23; 2 Thess 2:1, 8).

Colossae. Theologically, the presence of the gospel is that on which he wants to focus.

1:6b-c Just as in the whole world it is bearing fruit and growing, so it has been bearing fruit and growing among you (καθὼς καὶ ἐν παντὶ τῷ κόσμῳ ἐστὶν καρποφορούμενον καὶ αὐξανόμενον καθὼς καὶ ἐν ὑμῖν). In these two clauses, the power of the gospel among the Colossians is compared with its effect elsewhere. The periphrastic participles "it is bearing fruit and growing" that appear in the first clause are implied in the second. The metaphor of "bearing fruit and growing" may evoke Gen 1:28,[50] and some have further suggested that this points to Paul's use of the Last Adam typology,[51] although the linguistic parallels are not exact. Paul's usage here is consistent with other early Christian depictions of the spread of the gospel. Luke, for example, uses the metaphor of fruit-bearing in the parable of the sower in relation to the word (καρποφοροῦσιν, Luke 8:15), and he also uses the metaphor of growing in the depiction of the spread of the word (ηὔξανεν, Acts 6:7; 12:24; 19:20). Moreover, the word of God is powerful and active in building up believers (20:32). Paul here is likewise emphasizing the power of the gospel/word to accomplish the salvific will of God.

The note on the power of this gospel "in the whole world" likewise emphasizes the universality of the impact of the word, unlike the local aberrations of the gospel message among some in Colossae. It should not be taken simply as a hyperbole because Paul's emphasis is on the continued progress of the gospel throughout humankind (cf. 1 Tim 3:16).[52] Moreover, Paul is not stating that every individual will accept the gospel message; rather, he emphasizes that the gospel is effective not simply among one race or one social class (3:11) because Christ is the cosmic Lord of all (1:15 – 20).

1:6d Since the day you heard and understood the grace of God in truth (ἀφ᾽ ἧς ἡμέρας ἠκούσατε καὶ ἐπέγνωτε τὴν χάριν τοῦ θεοῦ ἐν ἀληθείᾳ). "Since the day" (lit., "from which day") is a formulaic expression where the antecedent of the relative pronoun "which" (ἧς) actually appears after the pronoun ("day," ἡμέρας). "Since the day you heard and understood" expands on "you have previously heard" in v. 5. The verb "understood" does not simply point to a mental act, but an appropriation of the gospel in one's personal life and community.[53]

Most recent versions supply a different object ("the word" or "the gospel") for the verb "you heard" (ἠκούσατε) and take "the grace of God in truth" as the object of "[you] understood" (ἐπέγνωτε) alone: "since the day you heard it and truly understood God's grace" (TNIV, NIV; cf. KJV, NAB, NASB, NRSV, NET, ESV). If the two verbs are taken as a hendiadys (two verbs to describe the one act of receiving the grace), however, "the grace of God in truth" can serve as the object for both: "since the day you heard and knew the grace of God in truth" (NKJV; cf. REV, NJB, NLT). The mentioning of "truth" in relation to "the grace of God" may point to a common reference behind "the grace of God" and "the word/gospel." Given this association between "grace" and "word," it is unnecessary to supply a different object for "to hear."

For Paul, "the grace of God" (τὴν χάριν τοῦ θεοῦ) is at the center of the gospel message (cf. Rom 4:16; 5:2; Gal 1:6). It often points to the gracious gift bestowed by God (cf. Rom 3:24; 5:15, 17;

---

50. Cf. Beetham, *Echoes of Scripture*, 53 – 54, who also suggests that Paul uses his own translation of the Hebrew text.

51. See Beale, "Colossians," 844, who further points to the eschatological promises in Jer 3:16; 23:3; Ezek 36:10 – 11, 29 – 30.

52. See also comments on 1:23f-g.

53. Cf. Jerry L. Sumney, *Colossians* (NTL; Louisville: Westminster John Knox, 2008), 39, who calls this "experiential knowledge, knowledge that comes from having participated in the experience of God's presence that the gospel mediates."

Eph 2:8), and as this gift is realized by the death and resurrection of his Son, it also points to his power and might (cf. 2 Cor 12:9; Eph 3:7; see also Acts 20:32). This focus on the powerful work of God is particularly relevant in this context, where the focus is on the fruit-bearing and growth of the gospel throughout the world. Grammatically, "in truth" can modify the verb "understood" (i.e., "truly comprehended," NRSV; cf. TNIV, NIV), but in light of v. 5 it is best taken to modify the verbal idea embedded in the word "grace": "the grace of God in truth" (cf. NJB, REB, CEV).[54] The truthfulness of the gospel is again affirmed over against the falsehood spread by those who misunderstood and misinterpreted the power of God's work.

1:7a As you learned it from Epaphras (καθὼς ἐμάθετε ἀπὸ Ἐπαφρᾶ). Concluding his discussion of the movement of the gospel, Paul identifies its messenger. Although the adverb "as" (καθώς) often carries a comparative sense in the New Testament (as it does twice in v. 6), the lack of a corresponding comparative clause[55] here argues against this. Though less common, this word can also carry a temporal sense ("when") or even depict the "manner" ("this is how") in which an act is carried out.[56]

The understood object of the aorist indicative verb "you learned" (ἐμάθετε)[57] is the "gospel" (v. 5), which in turn is identified in the preceding clause as "the grace of God in truth" (v. 6). In Paul, the close relationship of this verb ("to learn," μανθάνω) with "to hear" (ἀκούω) and "to receive" (παραλαμβάνω), all of which are applied to the re-

ception of the gospel in Colossians (cf. 1:6, 23; 2:6), is illustrated by Phil 4:9, where one finds all three verbs being used in Paul's call to imitate him as he imitates Christ (Phil 3:17; cf. 1 Cor 11:1). In this context, therefore, "to learn" the gospel is not simply to be intellectually enlightened; it also points to the reception of the gospel. This understanding is confirmed by a similar use in Eph 4:20, where the expression "learned [Christ]" also points to the reception of the gospel.[58]

"Epaphras" may be a shortened form of Epaphroditus, which means "honored by Aphrodite." A certain Epaphroditus was mentioned by Paul in Phil 2:25; 4:18, but this is a common name especially among slaves. There is nothing in either letter to suggest they are the same person. Epaphras is probably the founder of the church at Colossae. He is apparently also influential in the churches of the surrounding area that includes Laodicea and Hierapolis (4:13). He is the one who informs Paul of the faithfulness of the Colossians (v. 8), and likely also of the problems with the false teachers there (2:4). His name surfaces again in the closing greeting of this letter (4:12). His prominent position in the greeting in Phlm 23 also suggests he is one of the closest associates of Paul.[59] His title there as Paul's "fellow prisoner" also indicates his relationship with Paul, who described himself as "a prisoner of Christ Jesus" (Phlm 1).

1:7b-c Our beloved fellow slave, a faithful servant of Christ on our behalf (τοῦ ἀγαπητοῦ συνδούλου ἡμῶν, ὅς ἐστιν πιστὸς ὑπὲρ ἡμῶν

---

54. Or: "the grace of God untravestied" (cf. Moule, *Epistles to the Colossians and to Philemon*, 51).

55. Such clauses are often introduced by one of the comparative conjunctions "just as" (ὡς, καθώς, οὕτως, or even καί); BDF §453.

56. BDAG, 493 – 94; LSJ, 857.

57. For a discussion of the use of this word group (including μαθητής, "disciple") in Greco-Roman and Jewish literature, see Michael J. Wilkins, *Discipleship in the Ancient World and Mat-*

thew's Gospel (2nd ed.; Grand Rapids: Baker, 1995), 11 – 125.

58. Cf. Harold W. Hoehner, *Ephesians: An Exegetical Commentary* (Grand Rapids: Baker, 2002), 594, who understands the aorist as an "inceptive aorist" that points to the time of conversion.

59. For a discussion of the status of Epaphras within the network of coworkers of Paul, see Michael Trainor, *Epaphras: Paul's Educator at Colossae* (Paul's Social Network; Collegeville, MN: Liturgical, 2008), 25 – 35.

διάκονος τοῦ Χριστοῦ). Paul identifies Epaphras by noting his role in the gospel ministry. The first person plural "our" refers to Paul and Timothy. "Beloved" is a term of endearment that appears in the greetings (4:7, 9, 14). The rendition "fellow slave" (συνδούλου) highlights the significance of the prefix συν in this word. This prefix is a favorite of Paul, and it reinforces the close relationship as established by the word "beloved."

To call Epaphras his "fellow slave" is important for several reasons. First, it highlights the lordship of Christ, as the next relative clause asserts. In a letter that focuses on the supremacy of Christ, this word becomes an implicit christological statement. Second, this title identifies both Paul himself and Epaphras as merely instruments of the powerful God.[60] The previous note on the powerful work of the gospel (v. 6) has already relativized the role of Paul and Epaphras in the success of the gospel mission. With this title, Paul makes it clear that their mission is simply to serve the one they are serving. Third, it should also be noted that "fellow slave" can serve as an affirmation of one's status and authority, especially when the one whom they are serving is "seated at the right hand of God" (3:1).[61] Affirming Epaphras as a "fellow slave," then, secures his position as the authoritative delegate of the gospel of Jesus Christ.

The title "faithful servant of Christ" reflects Epaphras's work for the gospel ministry. The genitive "of Christ" (τοῦ Χριστοῦ) can be a possessive genitive (cf. NLT: "Christ's faithful servant"); but it is probably an objective genitive (cf. REB: "a trusted worker for Christ") identifying Christ as the object of Epaphras's faithful service, especially when the verbal idea behind "servant" is highlighted through the prepositional phrase "on our behalf" (ὑπὲρ ἡμῶν).[62] In Paul, "servant" (διάκονος) is often used for a minister of the gospel ministry, but rarely as a formal title for an office.[63] The distinctive Christian background of this term rests in the imitation of Jesus, who is "the one who serves," Luke 22:27).[64]

1:8 Who has also told us of your love in the Spirit (ὁ καὶ δηλώσας ἡμῖν τὴν ὑμῶν ἀγάπην ἐν πνεύματι). After discussing the role of Epaphras in bringing the gospel to the Colossians, Paul now focuses on his role as a messenger who provides a report on the work of the Colossians. This shift corresponds to the two-part focus of the first section of the thanksgiving section:

A Faith and love of the Colossians (v. 4)
  B Powerful work of the gospel (vv. 5 – 6)
  B′ Epaphras as the messenger of the gospel (v. 7)
A′ Epaphras as the messenger of the love of the Colossians (v. 8)

While the note on Epaphras as the messenger of the gospel (v. 7) establishes his authority as the founder of the church at Colossae, the focus on his role as the one who reports on the good work of

---

60. In secular Greek, the word is often used by those who shared the same master. It is also used interchangeably with ὁμόδουλοι, a word that is also used in reference to those who suffer the same fate as a slave. Cf. D. J. Kyrtatas, "The Vocabulary of Slavery," in *A History of Ancient Greek: From the Beginnings to Late Antiquity* (ed. A. F. Christidis; trans. D. Whitehouse; New York: Cambridge Univ. Press, 2007), 1059.

61. For a general discussion of the historical reality of slavery in the Roman times as well as the metaphor of slavery, see the introduction to Philemon.

62. Against UBS⁴-NA²⁷ (see also KJV, NLT, NRSV, ESV), this translation adopts the reading supported by the earliest and most reliable witnesses (𝔓⁴⁶ ℵ* A B D* F G 326* 1505), and is followed by most recent English versions (NAB, NASB, NJB, REB, TEV, NKJV, NET, TNIV, NIV). This reading also fits the context where the emphasis is on Epaphras's ministry in extending the ministries of the apostles.

63. With the notable exceptions in Rom 16:1; Phil 1:1; 1 Tim 3:8, 12.

64. See the discussion in Clarke, *A Pauline Theology of Church Leadership*, 65.

the Colossians establishes his credibility among the Colossians. This provides the transition to the next section, where Paul begins to address the concerns among the Colossians. Not to be missed is the implicit role of Paul in relation to the Colossians.[65] The fact that Epaphras has to report to Paul concerning the church he had founded also points to Paul as the apostle responsible for the Colossians, and such authority ultimately rests on Christ, who called him to be an apostle.

The attributive participle "who has … told" provides further information about Epaphras. The verb "tell" (δηλόω) can be used for the revelation of hidden knowledge, but it can also refer simply to the reporting of information (cf. 1 Cor 1:11). The object of their "love" (τὴν … ἀγάπην) is not explicitly stated. Although the intended object of this "love" could have been limited to Paul (and Timothy), in light of v. 4 it most likely refers to all the believers and to one another within the church at Colossae. In 2:2, Paul again expresses his wishes that the Colossians be "united in love," as "love" is the virtue that is able to provide the perfect bond (cf. 3:14). Compared with v. 4, which mentions the "faith" and "love" of the Colossians, Epaphras only provided a report of their "love." This confirms our understanding of their "love" as an expression of their "faith in Christ Jesus."

In the prepositional phrase "in the Spirit," one finds the first and only explicit reference to the Holy Spirit in Colossians.[66] Paul does not emphasize the work of the Spirit in this letter, probably because Christology, not pneumatology, is at the center of his dispute with the false teachers. A much stronger emphasis on the Holy Spirit in Ephesians (Eph 1:13, 17; 2:18, 22; 3:5, 16; 4:3, 4, 30; 5:18; 6:17, 18), a letter that bears many parallels to Colossians, supports this reading. In this context, the preposition "in" (ἐν) takes on an instrumental sense that points to the Spirit as the agent through whom the manifestation of genuine love is possible: "the love for others that the Holy Spirit has given you" (NLT).[67] This use is consistent with the use of this formula elsewhere in Paul, with or without the preposition, as is the association of the Spirit with love (Rom 5:5; 15:30; Gal 5:22 – 23).[68]

Intentional or not, one finds references to all three persons of the Godhead in this thanksgiving section: "God, the Father" (v. 3; cf. v. 6), "our Lord Jesus Christ" (v. 3; cf. v. 4, 7), and "the Spirit" (v. 8). While the relationship between the three is not explicitly noted here, it is passages like these that contribute to the fully developed doctrine of Trinity.

---

65. Aletti, *Saint Paul Épître aux Colossiens*, 65.

66. The "spirit" in 2:5 is most likely a reference to the human spirit. See also the implicit references to the Holy Spirit in the word "spiritual" (πνευματικός) in 1:9; 3:16.

67. Cf. REB: "the love the Spirit has awakened in you." Others, however, have taken it in a locative sense, and the point "is only that a spiritual love is to be distinguished from one that is purely worldly" (Schweizer, *Letter to the Colossians*, 38).

68. For a further discussion, see Gordon Fee, *God's Empowering Presence: The Holy Spirit in the Letters of Paul* (Peabody, MA: Hendrickson, 1994), 21 – 24.

Theology in Application

Paul, His Coworkers, and the People of God

As in his other letters, Paul begins with a self-identification as "an apostle of Christ Jesus" (v. 1). This designation not only establishes his authority among the churches, but it also points to the public and official nature of this document. This is not a private letter expressing the author's personal opinion on certain matters. As Paul is appointed "by the will of God" (v. 1), this letter is an authoritative and reliable expression of God's will for the Colossians. Mentioning Timothy, his coworker, likewise confirms the nature of this document as one written from the leaders of the early Christian movement.

The way the cosender, the recipients, and the messenger are introduced provides a glimpse of the symbolic universe created by Paul within which his message to the Colossians should be received. Timothy and the recipients are identified as "brothers." Epaphras is not only a "faithful servant" (v. 7), but also a "fellow slave," a term that allows Paul to be included in this identification. Such labels are meaningful only when they are related to God "our Father" (v. 2) and his Son "Christ Jesus/Jesus Christ" (vv. 1, 4, 7). The use of this household language may reflect the reality of early Christian communities that centered on Christian households (cf. 4:15).[69] For Paul, however, this household setting also provides a new identification for its members, where they are no longer to be related by their race or class (3:11); they have become parts of a new humanity related to one another only through their relationship with Christ, who is "all … in all" (3:11). It is not surprising, therefore, that a discussion of household relationships appears in Colossians, where the lordship of Christ is repeatedly noted (3:18, 20, 22, 23, 24; 4:1).[70]

For modern readers situated in a very different temporal, cultural, and historical setting, the conversation between Paul and the Colossians is still relevant because we too are part of this household insofar as we are reconciled to God by the death of Christ (1:22). If we consider our churches to be nothing more than interest groups or community organizations, we must be reminded that we belong to a family that submits to the authority of Christ. This letter will challenge us to reevaluate the way that we see the church and fellow believers. They are not just other people with whom we share an interest; they are our brothers and sisters in Christ to whom we have obligations to love, support, rebuke, and encourage. Moreover, viewing the church as

---

69. See also Acts 2:46; 5:42; 8:3; 20:20; Rom 16:5; 1 Cor 16:19; 1 Tim 3:5; Phlm 2.

70. Cf. 1 Pet 4:17, where believers are called "God's household." In the ancient world, as in many modern societies, household often serves as the context within which one's social

and political relationships are defined with reference to both diachronic (i.e., blood) concerns as well as synchronic (i.e., contextual) factors; cf. Jean Kellerhals, Cristina Ferreira, and David Perrenoud, "Kinship Cultures and Identity Transmission," *Current Sociology* 50 (2002): 213 – 28.

a family highlights the obligations we have to each other and to the family as a whole; we share the name of Christ and we work for his glory.

Letters and the Maintenance of Relationships

Compared to the opening section of Hellenistic papyrus letters, the specific focus on God in Paul's thanksgiving sections becomes all the more striking.[71] Beyond the repeated mentioning of God (vv. 3, 6, 10), this theocentric focus is also manifested here in a number of ways. First, the lack of focus on Paul and his personal well-being is noteworthy. While he does mention later his role in God's plan (1:24 – 2:5), this thanksgiving section draws attention away from his accomplishments. The focus is rather on the powerful work of the gospel (vv. 5 – 6).

Second, the opening health wishes of Hellenistic letters are often concerned with the physical well-being of the recipients (and the author). In this thanksgiving section, however, Paul is concerned with the relationship between the Colossians and "Christ Jesus" (v. 4).

Finally, in terms of function, the opening section of Hellenistic letters aims at securing the "horizontal" relationship between the author and the recipient, thus providing the basis for the requests made in the body of the letter. In this section, however, Paul is far more concerned with the "vertical" relationship between the readers and their God.[72]

The emphasis on their "faith in Christ Jesus" (v. 4) and "love in the Spirit" (v. 8) that are built on the "hope" as expressed in the gospel they had received (v. 5 – 6) becomes a significant statement on the purpose of this letter. Rather than maintaining the relationship between himself and the Colossians, this letter aims at securing the Colossians in the gospel. This provides a powerful model of ministry for all generations of Christian leaders. Instead of drawing people to ourselves, the ministry of the gospel demands that we shift the focus to God and his work alone.

In contemporary terms, the pressure to please those around us should be replaced by the passion to worship God and him alone. Modern social networking tools provide ingenious ways of maintaining and restoring relationship among friends, but such tools can easily disguise themselves as providing that which only a relationship with God can provide. Perhaps even more dangerous are houses of worship that

---

71. In those Hellenistic letters that do evoke God in the act of thanksgiving, the gods are never the subject of verbs and noted acts. See, e.g., P.Cair.Zen. III 59426 (260 – 250 BC) lines 1 – 3: "I give thanks to all the gods, if you yourself are well and if all your other affairs have been in order."

72. Cf. Helmut Koester ("1 Thessalonians — Experiment in Christian Writing," in *Continuity and Discontinuity in Church History: Essays Presented to George Huntston Williams on the*

Occasion of his 65th Birthday [ed. E. F. Church and T. George; Leiden: Brill, 1979], 36), further argues that the Pauline introductory thanksgiving "establishes a situation for the addressee that is independent of the writer." One should not deny the importance of personal relationship in Pauline writings, however (e.g., Abraham Malherbe, *The Letters to the Thessalonians* [AB 32B; New York: Doubleday, 2000], 125).

focus more on the interrelationship among believers at the expense of their relationship with God. This letter promises to correct such tendencies as Paul demonstrates the primary significance of understanding the work of God through Christ and how such understanding affects the lives of believers in the community of God's people.

The Power of the Word

The shift away from the work and accomplishments of Paul allows the attention to be drawn to the power of "the word of truth, the gospel" (v. 5). Paul portrays this word as coming to the Colossians, "bearing fruit and growing" (vv. 5 – 6). The focus on this active word may reflect the historical reality that the spread of the gospel to that area was independent of Paul's direct effort at evangelizing the area (cf. v. 7). This focus also reflects Paul's wider focus on the power of the gospel message despite human weaknesses and failures. In the OT, one finds not only the power of the creative word (cf. Ps 33:6, 9), but also the power of the faithful word of God that is able to accomplish his salvific act (cf. Isa 40:8; 55:10 – 11). The understanding of God's word as the creative word continues in the NT (cf. John 1:1; Heb 11:3; 2 Pet 3:5), and this creative word is identified as one that accomplishes God's eschatological act in history as this is "the message God sent to the people of Israel, announcing the good news of peace through Jesus Christ" (Acts 10:36).[73] Even for the writer of Revelation, the spread of the gospel is understood as the conquest of the word (Rev 19:13).

For Paul, this "word" centers on the cross and therefore points to "the power of God" (1 Cor 1:18). Paul's focus on the word is best seen in Colossians, as introduced in this thanksgiving section. This word is not only powerful in one community (v. 5), but its impact can be felt throughout "the whole world" (v. 6). This focus allows Paul to see himself merely as its servant, one whose task is "to fulfill the word of God" (1:25). For the believers, their dependence also rests on this word as noted in Paul's exhortation for them: "Let the word of Christ dwell in you richly" (3:16).

For the contemporary audience, this emphasis on the Word of God bears a timely message. First, preachers can often be confused with a "cult of personality," where their audiences are fed with a gospel filtered through their own lenses.[74] A focus on the Word allows the gospel to strengthen the authority of these agents as they become faithful and powerful guardians of the word of life. Paul's message reminds us of the central role of the active Word, to which we should all submit. The success of one's ministry is likewise attributed to God's work in history rather than to techniques and strategies of the servants of the Word.

---

73. See also Acts 6:7; 12:24; 19:20; 20:32. For the appropriation of the Isaianic Word of God in the early Christian kerygma, see David W. Pao, *Acts and the Isaianic New Exodus* (WUNT 2.130; Tübingen: Mohr Siebeck, 2002), 147 – 80.

74. John S. McClure, *The Roundtable Pulpit: Where Lead-

ership and Preaching Meet* (Nashville: Abingdon, 1995), 21: "leader-follower and preacher-hearer relationships can become *symbiotic*. When this happens, leaders and preachers tend to assume that everyone in their congregations are extensions of their personalities."

Equally important is the focus on the Word in the discussion of one's relationship with God. In an era when discussion of "spirituality" often begins with one's experience and context, we are reminded of the centrality of the gospel of Jesus Christ.[75] The relationship between one's belief and one's behavior will occupy much of the remaining parts of this letter.

Theory and Praxis

In this introductory section, Paul does not separate theology and ethics or belief and behavior; on the contrary, the theological framework provides the basis of proper action. The presence of the triad of faith, love, and hope best illustrates this point. Paul does not present the three as parallel Christian virtues here. Instead, "faith" points to one's relationship with Jesus ("in Christ Jesus," v. 4), while "love" is the outward manifestation of this "faith." Both are in turn based on the "hope" identified as the gospel message (v. 5). The interrelationship between faith and practice is again noted at the end of this section, when the "gospel" (vv. 5 – 7) that the Colossians received is linked with the "love" (v. 8) manifested in their acts to others. Paul clearly reminds his readers that one's relationship with Jesus will affect one's relationship with others, and one's behavior reflects one's belief system. To emphasize one without the other is not only misleading; it is to misunderstand the demands of the gospel message.

To focus on the interrelationship between faith and practice can often be used as an excuse to downplay the fundamental significance of the content of the gospel message. In this section, however, Paul reminds us that the content of the objective gospel serves as the basis for both "faith" and "love."[76] It is to be "heard" and "understood" (v. 6). As such, it is not a subjective truth that can be manipulated, either by the false teachers at Colossae or by their modern counterparts who attempt to strip the gospel of any objective content. The personification of the word as one that "has come to you" (v. 6) and one "bearing fruit and growing" (v. 6) can then be understood as an intentional rhetorical strategy whereby the objective reality of the gospel message is emphasized.[77]

The cognitive significance of this gospel forms the basis of this letter. In the next

---

75. For a helpful discussion of Christian spirituality in terms of the exposition of the gospel message and its impact, see Alister McGrath, *Beyond the Quiet Time: Practical Evangelical Spirituality* (Grand Rapids: Baker, 1995). For a further discussion of spirituality, see the Theology in Application section of 1:9 – 14.

76. In his discussion of faith, hope, and love, Augustine (*Faith, Hope and Charity* [trans. Louis A. Arand; New York: Newman, 1947], 33 – 112) provides a survey of God's mighty

acts from the fall of human beings to the redemptive work of Jesus Christ. This salvation-historical analysis is often missing in contemporary analyses of these "virtues."

77. One can point to the parallel development in Second Temple Judaism, where the hypostasized wisdom is identified with Torah (cf. Sir 1:25 – 27; 6:37; 19:17; 24:23; Bar 4:1). In Paul, this mediatorial role is clearly fulfilled in Jesus Christ, who represents the climactic and final revelation of the will of God.

section, for example, one again finds Paul reminding the Colossians of "the knowl-edge of his will" (1:9) so that they may "walk in a manner worthy of the Lord" (1:10). In the body of his argument, Paul argues against questionable practices (2:16 – 23) again by reminding the Colossians of the gospel they had received (2:6 – 15). Even the "ethical" section (3:1 – 4:1) begins with a strong christological affirmation of the status and authority of the risen Christ (3:1 – 4).

This connection between theory and praxis is important as we begin to appre-ciate the power of Paul's message. First, instead of dealing with particular acts and patterns of behavior, Paul reaches to the roots of such practices and seeks to correct the belief system that gives rise to these practices. For Paul, therefore, ethics are not simply the implications of his gospel exposition; they are rather the reason that prompts him to remind his audience of the true gospel of Jesus Christ.

Second, to be reminded of the gospel is part of the "application" of Paul's mes-sage in this letter. "Application" can no longer be defined narrowly as the superficial prescription of a series of ethical commands. When wrong practices point to wrong beliefs, to have one's belief system challenged anew by the gospel message is to begin the process of appropriating this gospel in our lives in the most practical and sig-nificant way.

Finally, in a culture that craves quick and immediate solutions,[78] this letter calls for patience as we are asked to substitute our reading of reality with one that is in-formed and empowered by the true gospel. It is only by being armed with this under-standing of reality that one can begin to live a consistent and faithful life under the lordship of Christ. For pastors who are often pressured into functioning primarily as therapists, Paul reminds us to train our flocks to understand the wider framework within which individual acts and practices are to be understood. For example: "tith-ing" is not simply a matter of financial management but fundamentally a matter of stewardship and a response to prior gracious acts of God; "divorce" is not simply a matter of marital relationship but one that involves issues of covenantal faithfulness and obedience to the lordship of Christ; "career choice" is not a matter of professional development but one that cannot be discussed apart from an understanding of one's place within the wider plan of God.

---

78. In a previous generation "easy believism" may be mani-fested in the failure to appreciate the demands of the gospel message (cf. Gary R. Collins, *Beyond Easy Believism* [Waco, TX: Word, 1982], 17 – 29). In Generation X or Y, this "easy be-lievism" is also manifested in the refusal to acknowledge the transformative significance of this gospel for both the minds and the lives of believers (cf. Steve Rabey, *In Search of Authentic Faith: How Emerging Generations Are Transforming the Church* [Colorado Springs, CO: Waterbrook, 2001], 15 – 46).

CHAPTER 2

Colossians 1:9 – 14

Literary Context

After the thanksgiving section, where Paul has provided an account of the gospel's power in the lives of the Colossians (1:3 – 8), he proceeds with a prayer report, where he exhorts them to continue being faithful to God. The thanksgiving section thus provides the basis for this further discussion (cf. "for this reason" in v. 9).

There is no consensus on the exact delineation of this section. Some consider vv. 9 – 14 as one "single complex sentence,"[1] while others point to a shift in emphasis in v. 12.[2] In light of the relative pronoun at the beginning of v. 15 ("who," ὅς), some consider vv. 15 – 16[3] or even vv. 15 – 20[4] as part of this long sentence. Because of the syntactical parallelism among the four participial phrases in vv. 10 – 12, it is unnatural to introduce a sentence break between v. 11 and v. 12. This break would be especially awkward since the participle "giving thanks" (εὐχαριστοῦντες, v. 12) should not be considered as the main verb of a syntactical unit. Furthermore, vv. 15 – 20 have a distinctive style as hymnic material, so a break is more likely after v. 14. Moreover, the use of the relative pronoun in v. 15 can be explained by the literary convention that allows such a relative pronoun to introduce a hymnic section (see comments on v. 15). Therefore, it seems best to consider vv. 9 – 14 as a distinct section.

The common themes of the first two sections have often been noted: thanksgiving (vv. 3, 12), prayer (vv. 3, 9), hearing (vv. 4, 9), bearing fruit (vv. 6, 10), growing (vv. 6, 10), and "saints" (vv. 4, 12). But these themes should not mask the progression of thought in vv. 9 – 14, where unique emphases are placed on a number of points. First, Paul repeatedly draws attention to the significance of the act of knowing. The phrases "knowledge of his will" (v. 9), "spiritual wisdom and understanding" (v. 9), and "knowledge of God" (v. 10) pave the way for his discussion of the correct understanding of the gospel that the Colossians have received (vv. 5 – 6) and for his urging these believers not to be deceived by the false teachers (cf. 2:4).

Second, Paul also focuses here on the powerful work of God. While he has al-

---

1. Moo, *Letters to the Colossians and to Philemon*, 92; cf. Harris, *Colossians and Philemon*, 28.

2. E.g., Schweizer, *Letter to the Colossians*, 40.

3. E.g. Barth and Blanke, *Colossians*, 173.

4. E.g., Charles H. Talbert, *Ephesians and Colossians* (Paideia; Grand Rapids: Baker, 2007), 185.

ready introduced the active work of the "gospel" as one that is "bearing fruit and growing" (v. 6), the emphasis on God's power here is reflected in words and phrases such as "being strengthened" (v. 11), "with all power" (v. 11), "his glorious might" (v. 11), "delivered us from the dominion of darkness," (v. 13), and "kingdom" (v. 13). For Paul, to misunderstand the gospel is not simply a deficient mental act; it is a denial of God's power on behalf of his own people.

These emphases converge on the proper knowledge of that power as manifested in the climactic act of his "Son" (v. 13). In a sense, then, this prayer report introduces the foundational argument of this letter in the next section, where Paul presents the powerful work of this unique Son in both creation (1:15 – 17) and redemption (1:18 – 20). To live in light of this knowledge is one of the central demands of this letter.

That Paul frames his wishes for the Colossians in the form of a prayer report reflects his conviction that even their obedience is part of God's powerful work. This is consistent with other prayer reports where Paul focuses on the power of the gospel.[5] Moreover, in terms of epistolary function, to begin his argument with a prayer report also suggests that the entire letter should be understood as one that evokes God's power on behalf of his own people.[6] The arguments presented are, therefore, not simply directed to the audience to achieve a self-initiated change of behavior; they are also a plea to the merciful God who remains faithful to those whom he has redeemed through his Son.

I. Opening Greetings (1:1 – 2)

II. Continuous Work of the Father (1:3 – 14)

   A. Thanksgiving (1:3 – 8)

➡   **B. Intercession for the Colossians (1:9 – 14)**

III. Climactic Work of the Son (1:15 – 23)

Main Idea

The Colossians are to be filled with the knowledge of God so that they can live lives worthy of the gospel they have received. This knowledge centers on the powerful redemptive work of God through his beloved Son.

---

5. See, e.g., Rom 15:30 – 33; Eph 1:15 – 23; 3:14 – 21; Phil 1:9 – 11; 1 Thess 3:11 – 13. Cf. D. A. Carson, "Paul's Mission and Prayer," in *The Gospel to the Nations* (ed. Peter Bolt and Mark Thompson; Downers Grove, IL: InterVarsity Press, 2000), 175 – 84.

6. In the case of 1 Thessalonians and Ephesians, it is not incorrect to say that the entire letter is "swallowed up in prayer" (M. C. Dippenaar, "Prayer and Epistolarity: The Function of Prayer in the Pauline Letter Structure," *TaJT* 16 (1994): 147 – 88.

Translation

Colossians 1:9-14

9a	Basis (of 9c)	For this reason
b	time	since the day we heard,
c	assertion	**we also . . .**
d	restatement	**. . . have not ceased praying for you** and **asking God**
e	content	that you may be filled with the knowledge of his will in all spiritual wisdom and understanding,
10a	purpose (of 9d)	in order that you may walk in a manner worthy of the Lord, and please him in every way,
b	series (means)	[1] bearing fruit in every good work,
c	series	[2] growing in the knowledge of God,
11a	series	[3] being strengthened with all power according to his glorious might for all endurance and patience,
b		
c		with joy*
12	series	[4] giving thanks to the Father, who has qualified you to share in the inheritance of the saints in the light.
13a	description	He delivered us from the dominion of darkness
b	progression	and transferred us into the kingdom of his beloved Son,
14a	means	in whom we have redemption,
b	apposition	the forgiveness of sins.

*In traditional verse division, "with joy" belongs to v. 11, but it should best be taken as modifying the clause that follows. See comments on v. 11.

Structure

This long sentence begins with "for this reason" (v. 9a), which connects it with the previous section. The main clause points to Paul's incessant prayer on behalf of the Colossians (v. 9c-d). He prays that they might be filled with the proper knowledge (v. 9e) in order to live properly in the Lord (v. 10a).

The four participial clauses introduced by four adverbial participles ("bearing fruit," v. 10b; "growing," v. 10c; "being strengthened," v. 11a; "giving thanks," v. 12a) modify the verb "walk" in 10a, but the exact relationship between the participles and the verb is not clear. They might characterize ways to "walk in a manner worthy of the Lord," but they might also specify the means through which such a "walk" is possible. The parallelism among these four clauses is further reinforced by the presence of an adverbial modifier within each of these clauses.

In the lengthier, fourth participial clause (v. 12a), Paul discusses the work of God in the relative clause (v. 13a-b). This clause in turn leads to the introduction of "his beloved Son" (v. 13b) and the redemptive work accomplished through him (v. 14). This "Son," who appears here only in a subordinate clause, will become the main subject of the following section (1:15 – 20), which extols his supremacy both in status and in his work in and beyond history.

Exegetical Outline

→ I. Occasion for Paul's Intercession for the Colossians (1:9a-d)

II. Content: They Should Be Filled with the Knowledge of God's Will (1:9e)

III. Purpose: So That They Can Walk in the Lord (1:10a)

IV. Means of Walking in the Lord (1:10b – 12)

    A. By means of bearing fruit (1:10b)

    B. By means of growing (1:10c)

    C. By means of being strengthened (1:11)

    D. By means of giving thanks (1:12)

V. The Work of the Father (1:13)

VI. The Mediation of the Son (1:14)

Explanation of the Text

1:9a-b For this reason we also, since the day we heard (Διὰ τοῦτο καὶ ἡμεῖς, ἀφ᾽ ἧς ἡμέρας ἠκούσαμεν). Paul begins this prayer report by connecting it with the words of thanksgiving in vv. 3 – 8. "For this reason" points back to the report of Epaphras concerning the Colossians (vv. 4 – 8). The translation "also" (καί) reflects the adjunctive use of this conjunction,[7] marking a transition from Epaphras (vv. 7 – 8) back to Paul and Timothy.[8] In addition to giving thanks to God, Paul (with Timothy) is now interceding for the Colossians (cf. Eph 1:15). Moreover, the Pauline uses of the phrase "for this reason ... also" elsewhere point to the introduction of a new act rather than a change of the subject of a verb (cf. Rom 13:6; 1 Thess 2:13; 3:5). It is significant that Paul's exhortation for the Colossians to stand firm in their faith is grounded in the power of the gospel they have already experienced.

"Since the day we heard" recalls a similar phrase in v. 6d ("since the day you heard"). This further stresses that the basis of Paul's request is not simply on the challenge of the false teachers, but on God's work already evident in their lives.

1:9c-d Have not ceased praying for you and asking God (οὐ παυόμεθα ὑπὲρ ὑμῶν προσευχόμενοι καὶ αἰτούμενοι). Paul begins this prayer report by highlighting his constant concern for the Colossian believers. The main clause of this long sentence is the negated verb "have not ceased," with the two complementary participles, "praying" and "asking." "Have not ceased" (παυόμεθα) in the middle voice

means "to cease doing something."[9] The thought parallels "always" in v. 3 and refers to Paul's deep concern for the Colossians. It may have the sense of "regularly,"[10] and in reference to prayer may refer to Paul's remembering the Colossians during his regular prayer time.[11]

"Praying" and "asking" form a hendiadys — that is, two words expressing one complex idea, with the second item often subordinate to and specifying the first: "we have not ceased to pray for you, asking that ..." (ESV).[12] In this case, Paul specifies that he is now involved in intercession for the Colossians.[13] In other words, while vv. 3 – 8 provide an example of a thanksgiving prayer, vv. 9 – 14 provide an intercessory prayer. "God" in this translation is inserted for the sake of clarity, because "asking" in the context of prayer naturally refers to God as the object of Paul's intercession.

1:9e That you may be filled with the knowledge of his will in all spiritual wisdom and understanding (ἵνα πληρωθῆτε τὴν ἐπίγνωσιν τοῦ θελήματος αὐτοῦ ἐν πάσῃ σοφίᾳ καὶ συνέσει πνευματικῇ). Paul now turns to the content of his prayer as it relates to the circumstances of the Colossian believers. "That" (ἵνα) indicates the content of the prayer.[14] The passive verb "may be filled" (πληρωθῆτε) is a divine passive, where God is the implied subject and is therefore also the reference behind the possessive pronoun "his." The use of the verb "to fill" (πληρόω) is perhaps prompted by the use of the noun "fullness" by the false teachers (1:19; 2:9;

---

7. See Wallace, *Greek Grammar*, 671.

8. For the reference behind the "we," see the discussion on 1:3.

9. BDAG, 790.

10. See esp. Acts 5:42, where the verb used together with "day after day" stresses regularity and consistency.

11. Cf. Peter T. O'Brien, *Introductory Thanksgivings in the Letters of Paul* (NovTSup 49; Leiden: Brill, 1977), 21 – 22.

12. Others have, however, considered the two as synonyms: "We have not stopped praying for you.... In fact, we always pray that ..." (CEV).

13. Cf. Mark 11:24: "whatever you ask for in prayer ..." (πάντα ὅσα προσεύχεσθε καὶ αἰτεῖσθε).

14. BDAG, 476 (though some consider this a purpose clause; Sumney, *Colossians*, 45).

cf. 1:25; 2:10), even though this word group also appears elsewhere in Paul's letters.[15] Moreover, "knowledge" also paves the way for Paul's argument that full knowledge can be found only in the gospel of Jesus Christ (2:2; 3:10; cf. 2:3). In this context, to "be filled with the knowledge" is to obtain both a "fullest knowledge" (NJB; cf. 1:6) as well as to be "completely certain" (TNT; cf. 2:2 – 5) of God's will. Moreover, what Paul emphasizes in this prayer report is that this knowledge must come from God, not from human traditions.

"The knowledge of his will" is the knowledge of what God has done through Jesus Christ. This "will" is not concerned primarily with God's private plan for individual believers; it is rather his salvific will as he accomplishes his plan of salvation. Paul later defines this "knowledge of his will" as "the knowledge of God" (v. 10) and "the knowledge of the mystery of God, Christ" (2:2).

"In" (ἐν) should probably be taken in an instrumental sense modifying "you may be filled": "through all the wisdom and understanding" (TNIV, NIV; cf. NAB, NJB).[16] Both the adjectives "all" and "spiritual" modify "wisdom and understanding." "Spiritual" (πνευματικῇ) can have a general "possessive" sense: it belongs to the sphere of the Spirit. It is then contrasted with the wisdom of this world (cf. 1 Cor 2:1 – 13).[17] This adjective can also point to the Spirit as the source of such "wisdom and understanding."[18] The parallel in Eph 1:17 supports this reading: "the Spirit of wisdom and revelation."

"Knowledge," "wisdom," and "understanding" are often found in Jewish traditions (Exod 31:3; 35:31; Isa 11:2; Sir 1:19; 1QS 4:4; 10:9, 12; 1QSb 5:21; 1QH 2:18; 11:17 – 18; 12:11 – 12). Most significant is the reference to the Spirit linked with "wisdom" and "understanding" in Exod 31:3; 35:31; Isa 11:2.[19] In light of the eschatological context, the allusion to Isa 11:2 is particularly possible, especially since with the "Spirit of wisdom and of understanding" there is also the "Spirit of knowledge," which becomes the agent of the new creation. Also noteworthy is the idea of fullness, although a different word group is used: "the [whole] earth will be filled [ἐνεπλήσθη] with the knowledge of the LORD" (Isa 11:9). In any case, Paul's prayer is not that the messianic figure in Isa 11 will come, but that God's own entire people may likewise be filled with this "spiritual wisdom and understanding."

1:10a In order that you may walk in a manner worthy of the Lord (περιπατῆσαι ἀξίως τοῦ κυρίου). This verse begins with an infinitive (περιπατῆσαι) that expresses the purpose of the prayer for the Colossians to be filled with "the knowledge of his will" (v. 9).[20] As in v. 9, where "knowledge" and "spiritual wisdom and understanding" reflect Paul's indebtedness to Jewish uses, the metaphor of walking likewise points to a Jewish background in which "to walk" (*hālak*) means to act in a certain way.[21] Thus it is true that this metaphor can rightly be rendered as to "live a life" (TNIV, NIV) or to "lead a life" (NJB, NAB, NRSV), though to "walk" (ESV)

---

15. Especially in Romans (1:29; 8:4; 11:12, 25; 13:8, 10; 15:13, 14, 19, 29) and Ephesians (1:10, 23; 3:19; 4:10, 13; 5:18).

16. Some (e.g., N. T. Wright, *The Epistles of Paul to Colossians and to Philemon* [TNTC; Grand Rapids: Eerdmans, 1986], 38; Moo, *Letters to the Colossians and to Philemon*, 94) take this as modifying "knowledge": "*manifested in/with* all spiritual wisdom and understanding."

17. Fee, *God's Empowering Presence*, 641.

18. Cf. BDAG, 837.

19. Beale, "Colossians," 846 – 47; Beetham, *Echoes of Scrip-*

ture, 73 – 76. These references in turn support the understanding that the Spirit is the source of "wisdom and understanding."

20. Some take this infinitive as denoting result rather than clause: "Then the way you live will always honor … the Lord" (NLT). The difference between purpose and result here is not significant especially when this is an intended result of the prayer.

21. As Heinrich Seesemann (*TDNT*, 5:944) has noted, "there are no parallels in classical Greek." For possible exceptions, see LSJ, 1382.

evokes OT commandments where the Israelites are "to love the LORD your God, to walk [*hālak*] in obedience to him and to hold fast to him" (Deut 11:22).

To lead a life in a manner "worthy of the Lord" (ἀξίως τοῦ κυρίου) is to act and behave in a way consistent with their status as the "saints" (v. 2). In the NT, "worthy" is mostly confined to Paul's letters,[22] where one finds references to being worthy "of the saints" (Rom 16:2 ESV), "of the calling" (Eph 4:1), "of the gospel of Christ" (Phil 1:27); and "of God, who calls you" (1 Thess 2:12). Believers are called to have the proper response in light of the mighty acts of God in their lives. In this context, to "walk in a manner worthy of the Lord" is to lead a life consistent with their deliverance "from the dominion of darkness" (v. 13).

The connection between "wisdom and understanding" (v. 9) and "to walk" in the Lord alludes to the book of Proverbs:

Get wisdom, get understanding;
   do not forget my words or turn away from
      them.
Do not forsake wisdom, and she will protect you;
   love her, and she will watch over you....
When you walk, your steps will not be hampered;
   when you run, you will not stumble.
Hold on to instruction, do not let it go;
   guard it well, for it is your life.
Do not set foot on the path of the wicked
   or walk in the way of evildoers.
              (Prov 4:5–6, 12–14).

Already in the LXX, the "wisdom" and "under-standing" in Prov 4:5 is identified with the Torah as the call, "get wisdom, get understanding," is replaced simply by "keep the commandments" (φύλασσε ἐντολάς). In Second Temple Jewish wisdom traditions, "wisdom" is explicitly identified as the Torah: "in all wisdom there is the fulfillment of the law" (Sir 19:20), and "if you desire wisdom, keep the commandments, and the Lord will lavish her upon you" (Sir 1:26). It is also in postbiblical wisdom books that one finds the use of the word "worthy" (Wis 7:15; 16:1; Sir 14:11).

In this context, therefore, Paul may be indebted to the wisdom traditions, but what is equally important is that "the knowledge of his will" in v. 9 is no longer identified with the Torah, but with Christ (2:2), and to "walk in the manner worthy of the Lord" is to lead a life that focuses on Christ when "Lord" (κύριος) is identified as Christ himself. This is explicitly noted in 2:6: "Therefore, just as you received Christ Jesus the Lord, continue to walk in him." The reuse of wisdom traditions within this christocentric framework may also pave the way for Paul's argument in 1:15–20, where Christ is to fulfill the role of the Wisdom figure.[23]

1:10a And please him in every way (εἰς πᾶσαν ἀρεσκείαν). This prepositional phrase parallels "walk in a manner worthy of the Lord" in providing yet another purpose of "being filled with the knowledge of his will" (v. 9): "that you may ... please him in every way."[24] In light of its parallel with the previous phrase, the implied object of "please" (ἀρεσκείαν)[25] should be "the Lord," not

---

22. The only exception is 3 John 6.

23. Cf. Morna D. Hooker, "Where Is Wisdom to Be Found? Colossians 1.15–20 (I)," in *Reading Texts, Seeking Wisdom: Scripture and Theology* (ed. David F. Ford and Graham Stanton; London: SCM, 2003), 123–24.

24. Others (e.g., Harris, *Colossians and Philemon*, 31) consider this phrase "as a second qualification of περιπατῆσαι." Elsewhere in Paul, however, to "walk" in righteousness is not

considered simply as a penultimate purpose of Paul's exhortation (cf. Rom 6:4; 8:4; Gal 5:16; Eph 4:1). It is best, therefore, to see "please him in every way" as explicating the meaning of "walk in a manner worthy of the Lord."

25. This feminine singular verbal noun refers to "the desire to please" (cf. "unto all pleasing," KJV) but is better translated as a verb in English in this context.

other human beings. In the NT, the nominal form of "please" only appears here, but Paul often uses the corresponding verb (ἀρέσκω) both for pleasing human beings (e.g., Rom 15:1, 2; 1 Cor 7:33; 10:33; 2 Tim 2:4) and for pleasing God (e.g., Rom 8:8; 1 Cor 7:32; 1 Thess 2:4, 15). The parallel in 1 Thess 4:1 is especially helpful since it points to the parallel between walking in the Lord and pleasing him; it explicitly makes God the object of the act of pleasing. In this context, therefore, inserting the personal pronoun "him" is justified.

"In every way" (εἰς πᾶσαν) emphasizes the total obedience demanded by the gospel. The ways to please the Lord "in every way" are listed in the four participial clauses in vv. 10b–12.

1:10b Bearing fruit in every good work (ἐν παντὶ ἔργῳ ἀγαθῷ καρποφοροῦντες). As with the next three participial phrases, this clause modifies the understood subject of "walk" (περιπατῆσαι) and therefore also provides an illustration of the ways in which one can please God. Grammatically, these can be taken in an instrumental sense, but in context, these phrases describe ways to live in a manner worthy of the Lord.

"Bearing fruit" (καρποφοροῦντες) points to the work of the gospel in v. 6,[26] but here it is applied to the Colossian believers.[27] This is consistent with the nature of these two sections: the thanksgiving section points back to the work of God among the Colossians, and this intercessory prayer report points forward to their responsibility as believers. "In every good work" may also point back to the "love that [they] have for all the saints" (v. 4), although elsewhere in Paul "good work" often denotes a way to witness to those outside of the

church (cf. Rom 13:3; Gal 6:10; Titus 3:1). In any case, "good work" should not be understood in a legalistic sense, especially in a letter that emphasizes the final and complete work of Christ (cf. also Phil 1:6).

1:10c Growing in the knowledge of God (καὶ αὐξανόμενοι τῇ ἐπιγνώσει τοῦ θεοῦ). In Greek, the chiastic structure between this clause and the previous is clear:

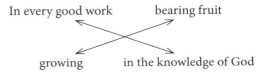

Basing on this structure, some have suggested that "in every good work" and "in the knowledge of God" modify both participles.[28] This may further be supported by v. 6, where "growing" and "bearing fruit" form a hendiadys. Nevertheless, in light of vv. 11 and 12, where one also finds the alternate positions of the participles in relation to their modifiers, one should probably see these as separate clauses conveying distinct ideas.

The dative "in the knowledge" (τῇ ἐπιγνώσει) is a dative of respect, expressing the realm within which one is expected to find this growth (cf. v. 9). The genitive "of God" (τοῦ θεοῦ) is then an objective genitive.[29] It refers to knowing who God is and what he has done through his Son (cf. vv. 12–14). Characterizing the means to "walk in a manner worthy of the Lord," Paul again points to the necessary relationship between knowledge and behavior.

1:11a Being strengthened with all power according to his glorious might (ἐν πάσῃ δυνάμει δυναμούμενοι κατὰ τὸ κράτος τῆς δόξης αὐτοῦ).

---

26. In v. 6, Paul uses a middle voice, but here he uses an active voice with no apparent change of meaning.

27. The metaphor of "bearing fruit" is often used in reference to the "practical conduct as the fruit of inner life" (Philo, *Cherubim* 84; *Odes Sol.* 11.23; Margaret Y. MacDonald, *Colossians and*

Ephesians (SP 17; Collegeville, MN: Liturgical, 2000), 49).

28. Lohse, *Colossians and Philemon,* 29 n. 48; Barth and Blanke, *Colossians,* 179.

29. In Colossians, all three genitives that follow the noun "knowledge" (ἐπίγνωσις) are objective genitives (1:9, 10; 2:2).

This third participial clause further explains how believers can "walk in a manner worthy of the Lord" (v. 10). The passive participle "being strengthened" points again to God as the actor. The focus on the need for the believers to be strengthened may be due to the fact that "the standards set before the Colossians were far higher than those of the false teachers."[30] Yet the focus on God as the source of the believers' strength may also aim at the reliance of the false teachers on their own efforts to obtain superior knowledge or unique spiritual experiences (cf. 2:8 – 10, 16 – 19).

The phrase "with all power" reinforces Paul's focus on God's power in two ways. First, "all" (πάσῃ), as in its previous instances (cf. vv. 6, 9), emphasizes the completeness and sufficiency of God's power. Second, the use of "power" (δυνάμει), a cognate dative of content,[31] highlights God's act of empowerment (δυναμούμενοι).

The focus on God's power continues with the phrase, "his glorious might." The distinction between "power" (δύναμις) and "might" (κράτος) is not clear, but in Greek literature "power" often points to "the potentiality to exert force in performing some function" while "might" points to "the power to rule or control."[32] This distinction may also be applicable here, where "power" points to God's strength in enabling us to accomplish his will, while "might" points to his authority established through his mighty acts in history. This "might" of God is manifested "when he raised

Christ from the dead and seated him at his right hand in the heavenly realms" (Eph 1:20; see also 6:10).[33]

The translation "his glorious might" takes "glorious" (τῆς δόξης) as a qualitative genitive, although some see it as a possessive genitive: "the strength that God supplies his people is in accordance with (and is the expression of) his own intrinsic glory."[34] This rightly draws attention to "glory" as an attribute of God. Nevertheless, the clear qualitative use of this genitive in the Ephesian parallel (Eph 1:17) argues against this reading.

1:11b For all endurance and patience (εἰς πᾶσαν ὑπομονὴν καὶ μακροθυμίαν). This prepositional phrase points to the purpose of being strengthened by God: "so that you may have great endurance and patience" (TNIV, NIV).[35] The adjective "all" echoes the earlier use of this word (vv. 9, 10, 11a). The exact nuance is not specified although grammatically it modifies "endurance" and "patience": "you will have all the endurance and patience you need" (NLT).[36] In this context, however, it also points to the comprehensive realm within which the act of enduring and being patient is to be performed: "to endure everything with patience" (NRSV). Given the fact that "endurance" and "patience" are both verbal nouns, we may also translate this adjective as an adverb specifying the comprehensive temporal aspect: "always to persevere and endure" (NJB). In any case, being strengthened by God will bring

---

30. O'Brien, *Colossians, Philemon*, 24.

31. A cognative dative or accusative of content is a noun that shares the same stem of the verb. While found often in Semitic material, it also appears in Greek literature. Cf. BDF §153.

32. Louw and Nida, §76.3.

33. Incidentally, apart from these references in Colossians and Ephesians, the word "might/power" (κράτος) only appears in the doxology of 1 Tim 6:16 in the works of Paul. In light of the tautological nature of these formulas ("his glorious might," "his mighty power"), Bruno Blumenfeld (*The Political Paul: Justice, Democracy and Kingship in a Hellenistic Framework*

[JSNTSup 210; London: Sheffield Academic, 2001], 165) has suggested that this might reflect the polemical use of magical invocations. This, however, remains a speculation.

34. Moo, *Letters to the Colossians and to Philemon*, 98; cf. Moule, *Epistles to the Colossians and to Philemon*, 54; Lohse, *Colossians and Philemon*, 30.

35. Thus most modern versions. In some renderings, however, this purpose clause is considered to parallel the call to be strengthened: "may you be prepared to …" (NRSV).

36. Cf. "great endurance and patience" (TNIV, NIV).

about every "endurance" and "patience" in every way and in everything.

The distinction between "endurance" (ὑπομονὴν) and "patience" (μακροθυμίαν) is not clear in this context. While the two terms have appeared together in several passages (e.g., Rom 2:4, 7; 2 Tim 3:10), a clear distinction can be found in 2 Cor 6:4 – 6, where "endurance," grouped with "troubles," "hardships," and "distresses" (6:4), points to the ability to stand in the midst of persecutions and difficulties. "Patience," however, grouped with "purity," "understanding," and "kindness" (6:6), points to a general state of calmness and control.

In Colossians, "endurance" may point to afflictions the believers are suffering as they are challenged by the false teachers, but "patience" is a virtue to be practiced within the community of God's people (see 3:12). Moreover, in Gal 5:22, this term is considered one of the aspects of the fruit of the Spirit. This in turn may suggest that the "strengthening" these believers receive is the work of the Spirit, as made explicit in a similar prayer report in Eph 3:16: "I pray that ... he may strengthen you with power through his Spirit."[37]

1:11c With joy (μετὰ χαρᾶς). This prepositional phrase is included in v. 11, and some versions see this phrase as modifying "endurance and patience" (KJV, NAB, CEB, RSV, ESV). Most, however, consider this as modifying the participle that follows in v. 12: "giving joyful thanks to the Father" (TNIV, NIV).[38] While in the NT "joy" often appears in "circumstances calling for both ὑπομονή and μακροθυμία,"[39] Paul has noted elsewhere that

he gives thanks to God while praying "with joy" (Phil 1:4). Moreover, since the previous three participial phrases contain a prepositional phrase, it is best to consider this one as part of the fourth participial phrase. Elsewhere in Paul, "joy" is often considered a manifestation of the power of the Spirit (Rom 15:13; cf. 15:32; Gal 5:22; 1 Thess 1:6). Here, Paul also considers giving thanks "with joy" as paralleling "being strengthened with all power according to his glorious might." If so, just as "bearing fruit" (v. 10b) and "growing" (v. 10c) form a closely related pair, "being strengthened" (v. 11) is closely related to "giving thanks" (v. 12).

1:12 Giving thanks to the Father (εὐχαριστοῦντες τῷ πατρί). The final item of this series describing the means through which believers can "walk in a manner worthy of the Lord" (v. 10), calls believers to give thanks to God the Father. Such a call is somewhat surprising in this context in which Paul is concerned with the proper behavior of believers. But Paul is not simply calling for thanksgiving as an emotional state; his call reflects the Jewish tradition, where giving thanks to God means to praise him and confess him as one's Lord.[40] Through remembering the mighty acts of God for his people, one submits to him as one's deliverer. This becomes an act of worship, where God's authority is acknowledged.[41]

It is not surprising, therefore, to find the call to give thanks to God as another means through which one can "walk in a manner worthy of the Lord." Later in this letter, Paul again notes the ethical implications of thanksgiving when he urges

---

37. This may also explain the appearance of yet another fruit of the Spirit in this context: joy. Cf. Fee, *God's Empowering Presence*, 644.

38. UBS4 and NA27 also consider this phrase as part of the following participial clause.

39. Moule, *Epistles to the Colossians and to Philemon*, 55, who points to Matt 5:12; Acts 5:41; Jas 1:2 – 3; 1Pet 4:13.

40. See comments on 1:3.

41. This also explains why Paul considers "ingratitude" as an act of idolatry (cf. Rom 1:21; Eph 5:3 – 5). For a further discussion of the Pauline understanding of thanksgiving as "God-centeredness," see David W. Pao, *Thanksgiving: An Investigation of a Pauline Theme* (NSBT 13; Downers Grove, IL: InterVarsity Press, 2002), 15 – 38.

the Colossians "to walk" in Jesus Christ whom they have received as "Lord," and to do so with "thanksgiving" (2:6 – 7; see also 3:17). "Giving thanks" is thus also closely connected with "being strengthened" (v. 11), for one submits to the lordship of Christ and asks for the power of the Spirit in one's life. The lordship of Christ is the focus of Paul's discussion in the next section (vv. 15 – 20).

1:12 Who has qualified you to share in the inheritance of the saints in the light (τῷ ἱκανώσαντι ὑμᾶς εἰς τὴν μερίδα τοῦ κλήρου τῶν ἀγίων ἐν τῷ φωτί). Paul now provides an important statement on the significance of God the Father. Grammatically, this clause is introduced by an adjectival participle (τῷ ἱκανώσαντι)[42] that modifies "the Father," to whom one gives thanks. But in terms of syntactic function, this adjectival clause provides the reason for thanksgiving: the Father is the one who has qualified you to share in the inheritance of the saints in the light. Consistent with the focus of Paul's call to thanksgiving elsewhere (cf. Rom 7:25; 1 Cor 15:56 – 57), this call points to the work of God on behalf of his own people. Particularly relevant is the note of thanksgiving in 2 Thess 2:13 – 14, which points to the object of thanksgiving as the one who has allowed his people to participate in the salvation that he has provided:

> We ought always to thank God for you, brothers and sisters loved by the Lord, because God chose you as firstfruits to be saved.... He called you to this through our gospel, that you might share in the glory of our Lord Jesus Christ.

The translation "to share in the inheritance" (εἰς τὴν μερίδα τοῦ κλήρου) provides one possible rendering of this prepositional phrase, which contains two nouns that have overlapping semantic ranges. There are two ways to understand the relationship between these nouns. First, the second noun ("the inheritance") can be a genitive of apposition; if so, this word aims at explaining the first: "for the share that is the inheritance." Second, "the inheritance" can be a partitive genitive: "the share in the inheritance." This second option justifies the translation of the first word of the pair as a verb as in most versions: "to share in the inheritance."

The motif of the "share" and the "inheritance," together with the dualism between "light" and "darkness" (v. 13), has prompted some to read this section in light of Qumran material (e.g., 1QS 11.7 – 8; 1QH 3.19 – 22). This would in turn affect the way one understands the reference behind "the saints" (τῶν ἀγίων) since in these Qumran references "the saints" are understood as "the angels."[43] Against this reading, however, is the use of "saints" already in vv. 2 and 4, which clearly points to the believers. Even in the Qumran material the word does not refer to "the angels."[44]

More importantly, this verse should be read in light of the exodus traditions in the OT.[45] First, the use of both "share" (μερίς) and "inheritance" (κλῆρος) points to the apportionment of the land of Canaan in the exodus/conquest tradition (Deut 32:9; Josh 19:9). The concept of "deliverance" and "transfer" in v. 13 also points to this past salvific act of God. Moreover, in evoking the exodus traditions in describing the eschatological act of God, Isaiah also uses the same ideas: light/glory, deliv-

---

42. In Paul, this verb is only used elsewhere in 2 Cor 3:6, where it also has the sense of "to be qualified for."

43. See, e.g., Lohse, *Colossians and Philemon*, 35 – 36. Lincoln (*Paradise Now and Not Yet*, 119) has further pointed to other Pauline uses where "the saints" could also refer to "the angels" (e.g., 1 Thess 3:13; 2 Thess 1:7, 10).

44. Cf. Sappington, *Revelation and Redemption at Colossae*, 199, who sees this as a reference to the property of being holy, rather than as a special designation of a selected group of persons/beings.

45. Cf. Cannon, *Use of Traditional Materials in Colossians*, 12 – 19; Beale, "Colossians," 848 – 50; Beetham, *Echoes of Scripture*, 81 – 95.

erance, inheritance, and holiness (Isa 63:15 – 19).[46] Therefore, "the saints" here should likewise be understood within this tradition where it is applied to God's chosen people (e.g., Num 15:40; 16:3; Deut 14:2; cf. Isa 4:3).

This use of this term not only points to God's deliverance of his people through his Son as a new exodus; it also points to believers as the true people of God — those who are set apart for his own purpose. These believers will receive their share of "the inheritance" as promised by God, just as the Israelites were meant to do: "I will bring you to the land I swore with uplifted hand to give to Abraham, to Isaac and to Jacob; I will give it to you as a possession [i.e., as an inheritance]. I am the LORD" (Exod 6:8; cf. Deut 1:8). The understanding of "inheritance" as the eschatological promise of God is noted in Isa 49:8: "In the time of my favor I will answer you, and in the day of salvation I will help you; I will keep you and will make you to be a covenant for the people, to restore the land and to reassign its desolate inheritances."

"In the light" (ἐν τῷ φωτί) can modify the "saints,"[47] but it most likely modifies "the inheritance." This prepositional phrase, then, distinguishes this inheritance from the earthly inheritance promised to Israel of old. In light of its contrast with "the dominion of darkness" in v. 13, the NIV has rightly translated this phrase as "in the kingdom of light." For Paul, believers should rest secure in the promise of the inheritance in the kingdom of light. Moreover, in view of the polemical use of the imagery of light in Eph 5:6 – 14, where light is defined as "goodness, righteousness

and truth" (Eph 5:9), it is also possible that Paul is here affirming the significance of "the word of truth" (Col 1:5) that the Colossians have received, and they should not be persuaded by the message preached by the false teachers.[48]

1:13a He delivered us from the dominion of darkness (ὃς ἐρρύσατο ἡμᾶς ἐκ τῆς ἐξουσίας τοῦ σκότους). This relative clause further describes the salvific work of the Father and leads to the introduction of the Son in v. 13b. For clarity's sake, most versions choose to begin with a new sentence here. Just as the previous clause points to the reason for Paul's call to give thanks to God, this clause elaborates on the reason why God "has qualified [us] to share in the inheritance of the saints in the light"; that is, he delivered us from the dominion of darkness and transferred us into the kingdom of his beloved Son.

The shift from the second person plural pronoun (ὑμᾶς, v. 12) to the first person plural pronoun (ἡμᾶς) may simply be a stylistic shift to enhance the rhetorical force of the argument,[49] but the use of this pronoun may also reflect the traditional confessional nature of vv. 13 – 14. In terms of content, v. 12 obviously points to the conversion of the Gentiles as they share the inheritance that was thought to have been reserved for the Jews; in v. 13, Paul is pointing to the universal impact of God's salvific act through his Son. It is therefore natural for him to include himself in this claim.[50]

The verb "delivered" (ἐρρύσατο) together with the term "redemption" (τὴν ἀπολύτρωσιν) in v. 14 points again to God's deliverance of Israel in the

---

46. See Gary S. Shogren, "Presently Entering the Kingdom of Christ: The Background and Purpose of Col 1:12 – 14," *JETS* 31 (1988): 175 – 77, who also points to the use of similar material in Paul's description of his own call by the risen Lord (Acts 26:17 – 18).

47. Cf. NLT: "He has enabled you to share in the inheritance that belongs to his people, who live in the light."

48. See also 2 Cor 4:3 – 6, a passage that contains numerous parallels to Col 1: "gospel," "glory," "Christ," "image of God," "light," "darkness," and "knowledge."

49. Cf. Harris, *Colossians and Philemon*, 35, who suggests that this shift "is not uncommon in Paul" (cf. 2:13 – 14; Rom 6:14 – 15).

50. Cf. Wilson, *Colossians and Philemon*, 115 – 16.

Exodus narrative: "I am the Lord. I will bring you out from the control of the Egyptians, and I will deliver [ῥύσομαι] you from slavery, and I will redeem [λυτρώσομαι] you by an outstretched arm and great judgment" (Exod 6:6 LXX).[51] This tradition has also been evoked in the prophets in pointing to the eschatological salvation: "I will rescue [ῥύσομαι] them from the hand of Hades, and I will redeem [λυτρώσομαι] them from death" (Hos 13:14 LXX; cf. Mic 4:10). The combination of redemption and darkness can also be found in Isaiah, who portrays God's eschatological act of salvation as the new exodus (cf. Isa 41:14; 42:7, 16; 43:1, 14; 44:22 – 23).[52]

The phrase "dominion of darkness" (τῆς ἐξουσίας τοῦ σκότους) assumes that "darkness" is a personal force able to exert its rule on its subjects (see Eph 5:11). The contrast with "the kingdom of his beloved Son" that follows this phrase further supports this reading. Nevertheless, "dominion" can also acquire "personal" attributes, as is made clear in Eph 6:12, where it is paralleled with the "powers of this dark world."[53] "Dominion of darkness" also anticipates Paul's argument in Col 1:16, where Christ is superior to "thrones," "dominions," "rulers," and "authorities" (v. 16; cf. 2:10, 15), which are personified manifestations of the evil one. Therefore, it is tempting to see the genitive "of darkness" as an epexegetical genitive, explaining the nature of this "dominion." But at this point of Paul's argument, this should be taken as a possessive genitive because of its parallel with "the kingdom of his beloved Son." Perhaps Paul's use of this phrase here is constrained by the confessional nature of this statement rather than by the arguments that he will launch (cf. Acts 26:18).

1:13b And transferred us into the kingdom of his beloved Son (καὶ μετέστησεν εἰς τὴν βασιλείαν τοῦ υἱοῦ τῆς ἀγάπης αὐτοῦ). This clause continues to explain how God "has qualified you to share in the inheritance of the saints in the light" (v. 12). In contemporary Greek literature, the verb "transferred" (μετέστησεν) could refer to the action of a king who transplanted a people group in another country or region.[54] Here, Paul points to the accomplishment of God's mighty act of salvation in transferring those who belong to him from darkness into light.

"The kingdom of his beloved Son" describes the realm "in the light" (v. 12). The genitive "of … Son" (τοῦ υἱοῦ) is a possessive genitive (i.e., the kingdom that belongs to the Son), while "beloved" (τῆς ἀγάπης) is a qualitative genitive that modifies "Son."[55] Many see behind this phrase an allusion to the promise to David and his descendents in 2 Sam 7:8 – 17, a passage that contains references to "son/offspring" (v. 12), "kingdom" (vv. 12, 13, 16), and "love" (v. 15).

The reference to "the kingdom of his beloved Son" (i.e., the kingdom of Christ) is uncommon in Pauline writings (cf. 1 Cor 15:24 – 28; 2 Tim 4:1, 18). The use of this phrase can be explained in a number of ways. First, to focus on the "Son"

---

51. The verb "to redeem" (λυτρόω) itself often appears in exodus traditions in reference to God's deliverance of his people; see comments on v. 14.

52. Beale, "Colossians," 848, suggests that the Isaianic contrast between "light" and "darkness" can also be traced back to the exodus traditions (Exod 10:21 – 23; 14:20).

53. In the NT, the semantic range of "dominion" (ἐξουσία) includes freedom of choice, right, capability, might, power, authority, domain, as well as a means of exercising power (cf. BDAG, 352 – 53).

54. Jos. *Ant.* 9.235; Lohse, *Colossians and Philemon*, 37; BDAG, 625. This imagery may also have reminded the Colossians of Antiochus III's transplantation of 2,000 Jewish families from Mesopotamia to Asia Minor (223 – 187 BC; Jos. *Ant.* 12.146 – 53); cf. Clinton E. Arnold, "Colossians," in *Zondervan Illustrated Bible Backgrounds Commentary* (ed. Clint E. Arnold; Grand Rapids: Zondervan, 2002), 3:378 – 79.

55. Some versions make explicit the verbal idea embedded in this adjective: "the kingdom of the Son he loves" (TNIV, NET, NIV; cf. NJB).

is to affirm the unique authority of Christ, whose work parallels that of his Father (cf. 1:15 – 20). This unique title therefore anticipates the christological argument that follows (cf. also Eph 5:5, where the phrase "the kingdom of Christ and of God" equates the authority of the Son with that of the Father).

Second, in light of the allusion to 2 Sam 7:8 – 17, some have suggested the "Son" in this context points not to Jesus' relationship with his Father, but it is "a royal title for the kings of the promised Davidic lineage."[56] In other words, this phrase highlights the messianic status of Jesus, who naturally is the one sitting on the throne in his messianic kingdom.

Third, in light of the note concerning the impotence of the "dominion of darkness" (v. 13a), the affirmation of the reign of Christ is not unexpected.

Finally, the title "his beloved Son" points back to God the Father as the ultimate actor in the drama of salvation: "the Son who redeems through his own blood is the ultimate expression of God's love for us, as Paul says emphatically in Rom 5:5 – 9."[57] Thus, the distinction between the "kingdom of his beloved Son" and the "kingdom of God" should not be overstressed.

Some are also surprised because "kingdom" in Paul often refers to a future reality (cf. 1 Cor 15:50; Gal 5:21). One finds here a "note of realized eschatology,"[58] but elsewhere in Paul kingdom language is also used in describing the present reality (Rom 14:17; 1 Cor 4:20; 15:24; 1 Thess 2:12).[59] Moreover, the tension between realized and futurist eschatology can also be found in Colossians, as elsewhere in Paul.[60]

1:14a In whom we have redemption (ἐν ᾧ ἔχομεν τὴν ἀπολύτρωσιν). Only in the Son can one find true salvation. The antecedent of the relative pronoun ("whom") is the "Son," and it points to a significant shift of focus in Paul's argument. The instrumental "in" (ἐν), therefore, points to the critical means by which God accomplishes his plan of salvation. While the thanksgiving and prayer are addressed to God, Paul here introduces the center of his argument in this letter. This focus on the Son leads naturally to the christological hymn in vv. 15 – 20.

The shift from the aorist tense of the verbs in vv. 12 and 13 to the present tense "we have" (ἔχομεν) here has often been understood as pointing to the "ongoing and permanent result of the Father's threefold action" as noted in vv. 12 – 13.[61] This shift also signals the opening of a discourse unit — in this case the shift from the work of the Father to that of the Son.[62]

As noted above (cf. comments on v. 13), the word group of "redemption" (τὴν ἀπολύτρωσιν) points to the exodus traditions as well as to the new exodus in Isaiah. The word "redemption" is rare in secular Greek, but a "ransom" is almost always implied with this term.[63] While some have suggested that "the primary emphasis of v. 14a is on the fact of emancipation rather than on the

56. Beetham, *Echoes of Scripture*, 109. Cf. Pss 2:7; 110:1 – 2. For an attempt to read this title in light of the exodus traditions, see Bevere, *Sharing in the Inheritance*, 144.

57. Gordon Fee, *Pauline Christology: An Exegetical-Theological Study* (Peabody, MA: Hendrickson, 2007), 297.

58. Dunn, *Epistles to the Colossians and to Philemon*, 77.

59. Moo, *Letters to the Colossians and to Philemon*, 105.

60. See, in particular, Still, "Eschatology in Colossians," 125 – 38. See "Theology of Colossians" in the final section of this commentary.

61. Harris, *Colossians and Philemon*, 37.

62. Grammatically, vv. 9 – 14 constitutes one long sentence, but the shift of tense points to a shift in the focus (or "prominent features" of the discourse); cf. Stanley E. Porter, *Idioms of the Greek New Testament* (2nd ed.; BLG 2; Sheffield: Sheffield Academic, 1994), 301 – 2.

63. E.g., Plutarch, *Pompey* 24; Josephus, *Ant.* 12.24; *Let. Aris.* 12.33; Philo, *Good Person* 114. Cf. Nigel Turner, *Christian Words* (Edinburg: T&T Clark, 1980), 397.

means by which it was brought about,"[64] the atoning death of Jesus is clearly assumed in light of the following phrase ("the forgiveness of sins") as well as the explicit mentioning of the cross in 1:20 and 2:13 – 15. In the parallel in Ephesians, the blood of Jesus is also included in this description: "in him we have redemption through his blood" (Eph 1:7). Even in this context in Colossians, the redemption language together with the note on the deliverance "from the dominion of darkness" (v. 13) clearly assumes "a previous bondage from which [believers] have been ransomed."[65]

1:14b The forgiveness of sins (τὴν ἄφεσιν τῶν ἁμαρτιῶν). This accusative phrase stands in apposition to "redemption," explicating the meaning of this term. This phrase points again to the new exodus tradition in Isaiah, where the word "forgiveness," also translated as "release," characterizes God's eschatological deliverance of his people (Isa 58:6; 61:1 – 2).[66] Equally relevant is Isaiah's declaration that Israel's "sin has been paid for" (40:2)[67] and the linkage between the act of redemption and the forgiveness of "sins": "I have swept away your offenses like a cloud, your sins like the morning mist. Return to me, for I have redeemed you" (44:22).

In Colossians, "the forgiveness of sins" appears only here, but this phrase anticipates the note on reconciliation "through the blood of his [Jesus'] cross" (v. 20; cf. v. 23). In 2:13, with a different vocabulary, Paul does note that God has "forgiven us all our transgressions" when he asserts that believers should no longer be judged by those who insist on the importance of ascetic practices and visionary experiences (2:16 – 23). To affirm the significance of "the forgiveness of sins" is therefore to anticipate the discussion of the significant implications of this climactic act of God through his Son.

Theology in Application

A Pauline Model of Prayer

While Paul is not intentionally providing us with a systematic teaching on how to pray properly, this prayer report nonetheless becomes a powerful model of prayer. First, this prayer begins and ends with the confession of what God has done for his people. The phrase "for this reason" (v. 9) points to the thanksgiving section (vv. 3 – 8) as providing the foundation for Paul's intercession as he prays that believers continue to live out the gospel they have received. Perhaps not coincidentally, the call to prayer in 4:2 is also grounded in thanksgiving as one appeals to God with the clear conviction of what God has already done for his people.[68] At the end of this prayer

---

64. Sappington, *Revelation and Redemption at Colossae*, 202.

65. E. Earle Ellis, "Colossians 1:12 – 20: Christus Creator, Christus Salvator," in *Interpreting the New Testament: Introduction to the Art and Science of Exegesis* (ed. Darrell L. Bock and Buist M. Fanning; Wheaton, IL: Crossway, 2006), 424. Cf. "who purchased our freedom" (NLT).

66. Both passages were explicitly quoted in Jesus' sermon

at Nazareth in Luke 4:18 – 19. Elsewhere in the Lukan writings, this word always carries the sense of "forgiveness of sins." Particularly relevant is Acts 26:18 where one finds both the contrast between light and darkness, and the "forgiveness of sins" (ἄφεσις ἁμαρτιῶν).

67. Not to be missed are the numerous references to "sins" in the Servant Song of Isa 52:11 – 53:12 (cf. 53:4, 5, 6, 10, 11, 12).

68. For the connection between the prayer report in 1:9 – 14

report, Paul returns to the heart of the gospel when he affirms God's deliverance of his people through his Son (vv. 12 – 14). Paul reminds us that our confidence in approaching God rests in the mighty acts he has performed in history.

Recalling the acts of God in the past, Paul demonstrates that the focus of our prayer should also be on God himself and his people. It has been noted that our prayers often reflect our self-centeredness: "Left to ourselves, we are never more selfish than when we pray. With God as the Great Sympathizer, the Great Giver, the Great Promiser, we go to our knees and indulge every impulse for gratification."[69] In this prayer, however, Paul does not pray for his own concerns but for those of the Colossians. And the focus is not primarily on their physical well-being, but on their knowledge of God and his will (v. 9).[70]

Yet even the spiritual well-being of the believers is only the penultimate concern because the goal of acquiring such knowledge is to "walk in a manner worthy of the Lord, and please him in every way" (v. 10). The center of this intercessory prayer lies, therefore, in their role in the salvific plan of God. In one's practice of prayer, the fundamental distinction is not primarily the one between physical versus spiritual concerns, but between the focus on oneself and the focus on God.[71] After all, Jesus himself asserted that one should "seek first his kingdom and his righteousness" (Matt 6:33).

Equally important is the scope of Paul's intercession. The prayer is directed to the entire church, and it provides a redefinition of God's people by including the Gentiles among those who are now able "to share in the inheritance of the saints" (v. 12).[72] Moreover, Paul prays that God will provide them with the full blessings: "*all* spiritual wisdom and understanding" (v. 9), "please him in *every* way" (v. 10), "bearing fruit in *every* good work" (v. 10), "being strengthened with *all* power" (v. 11), and "for *all* endurance and patience" (v. 11). Paul's bold petition rests on God's accomplished act of deliverance (vv. 13 – 14). These petitions also encourage believers to claim the fullness that had already been made available to them.

Do our prayers reveal that we worship no one but ourselves? Are we praying simply to "use" God to accomplish our will? Do such prayers reveal that we are nothing but materialists who care only about our well-being in this earthly existence?

---

and the call to prayer in 4:2 – 6, see Karl-Heinrich Ostmeyer, *Kommunikation mit Gott und Christus: Sprache und Theologie des Gebetes im Neuen Testament* (WUNT 197; Tübingen: Mohr Siebeck, 2006), 124 – 25.

69. Eugene H. Peterson, *Answering God: The Psalms as Tools for Prayer* (San Francisco: Harper & Row, 1989), 91.

70. The parallel in the prayer report of Epaphras affirms this focus: "He is … always striving on behalf of you in prayers, that you may stand mature and fully assured in all the will of God" (Col 4:12; cf. Phil 1:9).

71. For Paul, however, one's spiritual well-being should be grounded precisely in one's desire to fulfill the purpose of God. The fulfillment of God's purpose will in turn fulfill our deepest desires (cf. 2 Thess 1:11).

72. This is a consistent feature in Paul's prayer (cf. Rom 15:33; 2 Cor 13:14; Gal 6:16; Phil 1:4; 1 Thess 1:2; 3:12); Gordon P. Wiles, *Paul's Intercessory Prayers: The Significance of the Intercessory Prayer Passages in the Letters of St Paul* (SNTSMS 24; Cambridge: Cambridge Univ. Press, 1974), 60.

Christian "Spirituality"

The four participial phrases that characterize the means through which one can "walk in a manner worthy of the Lord" (v. 10) point to four seemingly unrelated aspects of Christian life: "bearing fruit" (1:10), "growing" (1:10), "being strengthened" (1:11) and "giving thanks" (1:12). The way these four phrases modify one's walk with the Lord do, however, point to critical aspects of a proper understanding of "spirituality."

First, the phrase "walk in a manner worthy of the Lord" itself argues against the false dichotomy between knowledge and behavior. This is reinforced by the notes on "bearing fruit" and "growing" (1:10). In the previous section, "bearing fruit and growing" (v. 6) can be considered a hendiadys that describes the power of the gospel in the lives of the believers. In this section, however, the two terms describe two sides of Christian maturity. "Bearing fruit" is qualified by "in every good work," while "growing" points to "the knowledge of God" (v. 10). To know God, therefore, is not to be involved in a private search for the esoteric communion with the deity but to witness the impact of God's salvific plan in history. To do "good deeds" is likewise not to follow general ethical principles, but to live out the particularistic gospel of Jesus Christ within a community of believers.

Second, the passive participle "being strengthened" (v. 11), with God as the implied agent, points to the source of one's walk in the Lord.[73] Arguing against those who rely on their own ability in approaching God, Paul again emphasizes human impotence and the redemptive activity of God (v. 14).[74] Elsewhere in Paul, this redemption is explicitly linked with the "grace" given by God: "and all are justified freely by his grace through the redemption that came by Christ Jesus" (Rom 3:24). Here, Paul points to the paradox of the Christian life as he calls believers to strive to please God, but in doing so to recognize fully that one's strength to do so lies beyond oneself. In relying on God, Paul also reminds believers that this act of worship will invite rejection and persecution, and this reminder is embedded in the reference to "endurance and patience" (v. 11). Instead of proposing general spirituality, the particularistic gospel that Paul preaches includes the acceptance of an exclusivistic truth claim that will separate those who do and those who do not follow Jesus.

Finally, the call to thanksgiving (v. 12) makes explicit the content of the gospel message in the confession that points to the climax of God's redemptive activity in

---

73. As noted in the exegetical discussion above, God often strengthens his people through the power of the Holy Spirit (cf. Eph 3:16). The relevance of this verse becomes more apparent when "Spirituality" is understood as experiencing the power of the Spirit.

74. Contra the recent trend that "confuses spirituality with the actualization of divinity supposedly lurking in one's own being and life" (Carl H. Henry, "Spiritual? Say It Isn't So," in *Alive to God: Studies in Spirituality Presented to James Houston* [ed. J. I. Packer and Loren Wilkinson; Downers Grove, IL: InterVarsity Press, 1992], 9).

his Son.[75] Instead of a general sense of gratitude and optimism, thanksgiving becomes the vehicle through which the acts of God are remembered. In the OT, one finds an explicit call to remember God's acts on behalf of his people (Exod 3:15). To forget is to fail to worship God, and thus to commit idolatry (cf. Deut 4:23 – 24; 2 Kings 17:38 – 39; Isa 46:9; Ezek 6:9) and to violate God's covenant with his people (cf. Ps 44:17). In this confession (vv. 13 – 14), Paul reminds believers to be faithful to the one who is their Redeemer and Savior. Spirituality, therefore, cannot be separated from the concerns of the past that provide the basis for both our present relationship with God and our future, which rests in the faithful God who will work again in history. The author of the *Epistle of Barnabas* rightly reminds us "to give great thanks to the Lord that he has given us knowledge of the past, and wisdom for the present, and that we are not without understanding for the future" (*Barn.* 5.3).

In modern Western culture, spirituality is often defined simply as a way to be in touch with one's inner voice. Consider, for example, the message "preached" in the finale of a popular talk show in 2011, where the person often considered to be one of the most popular "spiritual" figures of the late twentieth and early twenty-first century provides a good summary of her view of spirituality: "So what I know is, God is love and God is life, and your life is always speaking to you."[76] Paul reminds us that this God is manifested in Christ, and believers are called to live in light of what God did through this Christ. A spirituality that caters to everyone regardless of his or her particular religious beliefs is but an act of idolatry.

Exodus and Liberation

As noted in our discussion, one finds numerous allusions to the exodus/new exodus traditions in this prayer report; these include: "to share in the inheritance" (v. 12), "delivered" (v. 13), "light"/"darkness" contrast (vv. 12 – 13), "redemption" (v. 14), and "forgiveness of sins" (v. 14). While none of these by itself necessarily points to these traditions, together this cluster can best be explained in light of these traditions. For the modern readers, as for the ancient audience, the significance of this observation moves beyond issue of textual relationships. Understanding the work and identity of Jesus Christ within this tradition affects how believers understand their own mission and identity.

First, in evoking the exodus/new exodus traditions, the concern for the salvation and eternal destiny of an individual is situated within God's larger drama of salvation. Possibly in combating the tendencies of the Colossian mystics who focused on the elevation of one's own spiritual self, Paul redirects our attention to the work of God

---

75. Cf. Clement of Alexandria, *Miscellanies* 7.3, "Confession is thanksgiving."

76. See www.oprah.com/oprahshow/The-Oprah-Winfrey-Show-Finale_1/8 (accessed June 1, 2011).

since the time when he called Israel for the sake of his own name. The introduction of this wider salvific plan of God forces believers to realize that the center of his salvific act is his own glory. In Exodus 15, one already finds this theocentric emphasis:

> Who is like you, O LORD, among the gods?
>> Who is like you, majestic in holiness,
>> awesome in splendor, doing wonders?
> You stretched out your right hand,
>> the earth swallowed them.
> In your steadfast love you led the people whom you redeemed;
>> you guided them by your strength to your holy abode. (Exod 15:11 – 13 NRSV)

This emphasis resurfaces in the new exodus narrative of Isaiah, where God's redemption of his people serves to testify to his power and glory:

> Turn to me and be saved,
>> all the ends of the earth!
>> For I am God, and there is no other.
> By myself I have sworn,
>> from my mouth has gone forth in righteousness
>> a word that shall not return:
> "To me every knee shall bow,
>> every tongue shall swear." (Isa 45:22 – 23 NRSV)

In evoking these traditions, Paul is reminding the believers of the centrality of the glory of God. In much of modern religious discourse, individual deliverance and transcendence have replaced God as the center of our concerns.[77] Thanksgiving, confession, and praise cease to be meaningful acts within such a framework. Paul, however, insists on the primary significance of this act of worship. His evocation of the exodus/new exodus traditions paves the way for the christological hymn that follows (vv. 15 – 20), where God and his beloved Son reclaim the proper place in Christian discourse.

Liberation is often understood as one of the significant goals of the exodus event as God delivered his people from the hand of Pharaoh. Often ignored, however, is the fact that those delivered by God became a people who were to serve him: "For the Israelites belong to me as servants. They are my servants, whom I brought out of Egypt. I am the LORD your God" (Lev 25:55).[78] Submission to the one true God of all

---

77. As prayers can be selfish acts, spiritual exercises wrongly conceived can also mask one's selfish desire to use the power of the Spirit to fulfill one's agenda. In doing so, we become like those who are "lovers of themselves ... rather than lovers of God" (2 Tim 3:2 – 4).

78. In reacting against those who see the exodus as a model of liberation, Jon D. Levenson ("Liberation Theology and the Exodus," *Midstream* 35 [1989]: 30 – 36) rightly emphasizes that the exodus signifies instead the transfer of ownership.

is also the focus of the new exodus: "Remember these things, Jacob, for you, Israel, are my servant. I have made you, you are my servant" (Isa 44:21). For Paul, God's redemptive act likewise transforms those who are delivered by him into those who are to serve him. The calls to "walk in a manner worthy of the Lord" and to "please him in every way" (v. 10) are therefore to be understood as acts of worship and submission in response to God's act of deliverance through his beloved Son. Moreover, the numerous calls to submit to this Lord are also grounded in this act of deliverance (cf. 2:6; 3:17, 23, 24; 4:1). As we attempt to appropriate Paul's message in this letter, we must first be reminded of the basis on which such appropriation is to be carried out.

CHAPTER 3

Colossians 1:15 – 23

Literary Context

Paul has thanked God for his work among the Colossians (vv. 3 – 8) and prayed on their behalf so that they can be filled with the knowledge of his will to live lives worthy of the Lord (vv. 9 – 14). The final section of that prayer ended with a statement on the climactic work of God through his Son (vv. 13 – 14); that conclusion introduces the hymn that follows (vv. 15 – 20), in which Paul points to the unique status of Christ as both "the firstborn of all creation" (v. 15) and "the firstborn from the dead" (v. 18). As such, he is the one in whom "all things are held together" (v. 17). For those who consider vv. 3 – 14 as one long thanksgiving prayer, this hymn provides the ultimate grounds for such thanksgiving as Paul emphasizes the fulfillment of God's plan for creation in general and his people in particular.[1]

In terms of focus, this section consists of the hymn (vv. 15 – 20) and its appropriation for the specific situation among the Colossians (vv. 21 – 23). It signifies the shift from God the Father to Christ the Son as the one through whom God's salvific plan is fulfilled. This christological section serves as the basis for the arguments that follow.[2] Terms and phrases in this hymn that reappear in the rest of Colossians include "the image" (v. 15; cf. 3:10), "all" (vv. 15, 16 [2x], 17 [2x], 18, 19, 20, 23; cf. v. 28; 2:2, 3, 9, 10, 13 … etc.), "created" (v. 16; cf. 3:10), "heaven" (vv. 16, 20; cf. 4:1), "earth" (vv. 16, 20; cf. 3:2, 5), "ruler … authorities" (v. 16; cf. 2:10, 15), "the head" (v. 18; cf. 10, 2:19), "the body," (v. 18; cf. v. 24; 2:11, 17, 19; 3:15), "the church" (v. 18; cf. v. 24), "from the dead" (v. 18; cf. 2:12, 13), "fullness" (v. 19; cf. 2:9, 10), "to dwell" (v. 19; cf. 2:9; 3:16), "peace" (v. 20; cf. 3:15), and "cross" (v. 20; cf. 2:14).[3]

The more immediate application of the Colossian hymn appears in vv. 21 – 23. Here, Paul picks up the idea of reconciliation "through the blood of his cross" from

---

1. James Robinson, "Die Hodajot-Formel in Gebet und Hymnus des Frühchristentums," in *Apophoreta: Festschrift Ernst Haenchen* (ed. W. Eltester and F. H. Kettler; Berlin: Töpelmann, 1964), 231 – 33.

2. In rhetoric terms, this section serves as a *narratio*. Cf. Witherington, *Letters to Philemon, the Colossians, and the Ephesians*, 128: "The requirements for a narratio … were that it be short and lucid, saying no more than was sufficient and

necessary, and that it describe the problem that has generated the discourse (Quintilian, *Inst.* 4.2.45)."

3. Matthew E. Gordley, *The Colossian Hymn in Context: An Exegesis in Light of Jewish and Greco-Roman Hymnic and Epistolary Conventions* (WUNT 2.228; Tübingen: Mohr Siebeck, 2007), 265 – 66, who also lists other thematic connections between this hymn and the rest of Paul's argument in this letter.

the hymn (v. 20) and applies it to the Colossian believers who are now "reconciled … in his body of flesh through death" (v. 22). This section does not simply extend the confessional material in the hymn, however, for Paul points to the necessary response of the believers through a conditional clause in v. 23. The work of Christ has indeed been completed (v. 21 – 22), but believers must continue to stand firm in the gospel. The declaration therefore calls for a proper response by those who have been confronted by the power of the gospel message.

It is unclear exactly how Paul intends to use this hymn to respond directly to the false teachers. Some have insisted that "the hymn is not the writer's weapon with which he refutes a heresy. Rather, the hymn belongs to both the rivals and the writer and constitutes the common ground for their debate."[4] Others, however, have noticed the focus on Jesus' death both in the hymn (vv. 18, 20) and the immediate appropriation of the hymn (v. 22), and suggest that Paul intends to downplay Jesus' exaltation in his argument against the visionaries who might have overly focused on heavenly matters.[5] What is clear is that believers should be mindful of what God has accomplished through his Son, as stated in this hymn.

The final phrase in this section points to Paul as a "servant" of the gospel (v. 23). This paves the way for 1:24 – 2:5, which focuses on the role of Paul and his apostolic authority. The universal gospel that "has been proclaimed in all creation under heaven" (v. 23) is mediated through a particular envoy who is able to provide the faithful interpretation of such a gospel.

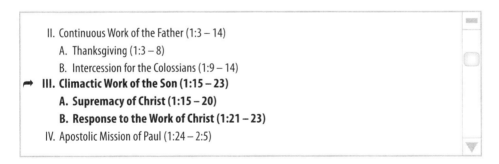

   II. Continuous Work of the Father (1:3 – 14)
      A. Thanksgiving (1:3 – 8)
      B. Intercession for the Colossians (1:9 – 14)
➡ **III. Climactic Work of the Son (1:15 – 23)**
      A. Supremacy of Christ (1:15 – 20)
      B. Response to the Work of Christ (1:21 – 23)
   IV. Apostolic Mission of Paul (1:24 – 2:5)

Main Idea

Jesus Christ, the agent and goal of God's act of creation, is the one through whom God reconciles all things through his death on the cross. Through this reconciliation, God will present believers as acceptable to himself if they continue to stand firm in the gospel they have received.

---

4. Van Broekhoven, "The Social Profiles in the Colossian Debate," 74 – 75. See also Sappington, *Revelation and Redemption at Colossae*, 175 – 76.

5. Cf. Pizzuto, *A Cosmic Leap of Faith*, 264 – 65. One can of course point to the phrase "the firstborn from the dead" in v. 18 as obviously pointing to Jesus' resurrection, but explicit exaltation language that one finds elsewhere in similar confessional material (e.g., Phil 2:9) is missing here.

Translation

Colossians 1:15 – 23

15a	Assertion	**He is the image of the invisible God,**
b	expansion	the firstborn of all creation,
16a	Basis (of 15)	for in him all things were created,
b	sphere	in heaven and
c	sphere	on earth,
d	content	visible and
e	content	invisible,
f	explanation	whether thrones or
g	list	dominions or
h	list	rulers or
i	list	authorities;
j	expansion	all things were created
k	agency	through him and
l	advantage	for him.
17a	Expansion (of 15a)	**He is before all things,** and
b	expansion	**in him all things are held together;**
18a	expansion (of 17a)	**he is the head of the body, the church.**
b	Assertion	**He is the beginning,**
c	expansion	the firstborn from the dead,
d	result (of 18c)	so that in all things he may become supreme,
19	basis (of 18b)	for in him all the fullness was pleased to dwell and
20a	expansion	through him to reconcile all things to him,
b	means	by making peace through the blood of his cross,
c	sphere	[through him] whether things on earth, or
d	sphere	things in heaven.
21	Problem	And you were once alienated and hostile in mind through evil deeds,
22a	Resolution	but **now he has reconciled you in his body of flesh**
b	means	through death,
c	purpose (of 22a)	in order to present you [1] holy,
d	list	[2] without blemish, and
e	list	[3] blameless before him,
23a	condition	if indeed you continue in your faith,
b	means	established and
c	parallel	steadfast,
d	contrast	not shifting from the hope of the gospel,
e	identification	which you heard,
f	description	which has been proclaimed
		in all creation under heaven, and
g	description	of which I, Paul, became a servant.

Structure

Scholarly consensus is lacking when it comes to the structure of this hymn.[6] Those who propose a two-part structure are right in pointing to the clear parallelism between the two sections that begin with the phrase "he is ... the firstborn" (ὅς ἐστιν ... πρωτότοκος, vv. 15b, 18c), contain two clauses that point to the basis of this declaration ("for [ὅτι]," vv. 16a, 19a), and conclude with notes on the cosmic dimension of Christ's rule (vv. 16b-j, 20c-d).[7] The problem with this two-part structure is its inability to account for the central section of this hymn: "He is before all things, and in him all things are held together; he is the head of the body, the church" (vv. 17 – 18a).

Because of that central section, some have opted for a three-part structure, with vv. 17 – 18a being the second stanza.[8] Most of those who adopt a three-part structure also recognize that this second stanza differs from the first and third in both length and style. Some have identified this second stanza as "the central matrix and nexus of both stanzas,"[9] and this hymn can therefore be understood as a two-stanza hymn with a central focus.

To call the second stanza of a three-part hymn its central focus is to suggest a chiastic structure for this hymn.[10] Even those who propose a five-part chiastic structure recognize the parallelism between vv. 15 – 16 and vv. 18b – 20 as well as the centrality of vv. 17 – 18a:

> A He is the image of the invisible God,
>> the firstborn of all creation.... (vv. 15 – 16)
>> B He is before all things (v. 17a)
>>> C In him all things are held together (v. 17b)
>> B′ He is the head of the body, the church (v. 18a)
> A′ He is the beginning,
>> the firstborn from the dead.... (vv. 18b – 20)[11]

This five-part chiastic structure best explains the structure and arrangement of this hymn, and the focus clearly points to Christ as the sustainer of all things. Moreover, it also takes into the account the shift of focus from creation in general (vv. 15 – 17a) to the church in particular (vv. 18a – 20). Without insisting that this is

---

6. See, e.g., John F. Balchin, "Colossians 1:15 – 20: An Early Christian Hymn? The Arguments from Style," *VE* 15 (1985): 86 – 87, who lists twenty proposed structures for this hymn.

7. See, e.g., Lohse, *Colossians and Philemon*, 44 – 45; Schweizer, *Letter to the Colossians*, 57.

8. See, e.g., Ralph P. Martin, *Colossians and Philemon* (NCB; London: Oliphants, 1974), 55.

9. Luis Carlos Reyes, "The Structure and Rhetoric of Colossians 1:15 – 20," *Filologia Neotestamentaria* 12 (1999): 139 – 54.

10. Thus Michel Gourgues, "La foi chrétienne primitive face à la croix: le témoignage des formulaires pré-pauliniens," *ScEs* 41 (1989): 49 – 69.

11. Pizzuto, *A Cosmic Leap of Faith*, 203 – 5. Cf. van Kooten, *Cosmic Christology in Paul*, 119. Wright ("Poetry and Theology in Colossians 1.15 – 20," 447), who argues for a four-part chiastic structure, can be considered as a variation of this five-part structure: A (vv. 15 – 16), B (v. 17), B′ (v. 18a), A′ (vv. 18b – 20).

the final and perfect reconstruction of Paul's mind in writing this hymn, this structure can become a useful hermeneutical tool for our reading of this section.

Within this broad structure, Paul provides details in his portrayal of Christ as the supreme Son of God. He begins with a relative clause that describes the work of "his beloved Son" (v. 13). After asserting Christ's status through his relationship with God and his supremacy over all creation (v. 15), Paul provides the basis for that assertion by providing a list to illustrate how he is above "all things," because they were created through him (v. 16). This assertion leads to the reassertion that Christ's supremacy is over all (v. 17a-b) while the focus is shifted to his supremacy over "the church" in particular (v. 18a). The final section begins with the supremacy of the resurrected Christ (v. 18b-d) because of his full deity (v. 19) and his role in the reconciliation of all things through his death on the cross (v. 20).

In applying this hymn to the context of the Colossian believers, Paul emphasizes how these believers are part of those being reconciled to God (vv. 21 – 22). The final conditional clause (v. 23) reminds them to be faithful to the gospel message so that they can experience the consummation of this reconciliation that has already been accomplished for them.

Exegetical Outline

→ **I. Supremacy of Christ (1:15 – 20)**

    A. Christ and the first creation (1:15 – 16)

        1. Christ the image of God, the firstborn of all creation (1:15)

        2. All things were created by him (1:16a-i)

        3. All things were created through him and for him (1:16j-l)

    B. In Christ all things are held together (1:17 – 18a)

    C. Christ and the new creation (1:18b – 20)

        1. Christ is the beginning, the firstborn from the dead (1:18b-d)

        2. All the fullness of God is in him (1:19)

        3. All things are reconciled through him (1:20)

II. Response to the Work of Christ (1:21 – 23)

    A. Believers are reconciled in Christ (1:21 – 22)

    B. Believers are to stand firm in the gospel (1:23)

IN DEPTH: The Colossian Hymn

Several interrelated issues concerning 1:15 – 20 will affect our discussion of the individual phrases. These issues have attracted a considerable amount of scholarly attention,[12] and a brief survey will allow readers to navigate this complex yet significant section.

Genre

Most scholars consider this section a "hymn," a conclusion that is based on a number of features in this section: the use of relative clauses (vv. 15, 18), parallelism (vv. 15 – 16 and vv. 18b – 20) and balance, the use of relative and personal pronouns as connectives, the self-contained nature of this unit, the presence of *hapax legomena*, similarities of style and subject matter with other early christological "hymns" in Paul (Phil 2:6 – 11; 1 Tim 3:16), and references to "hymns" in this letter (Col 3:16; cf. 1 Cor 14:26; Eph 5:19 – 20).

It is unclear, however, as to the criteria against which a section can qualify as a "hymn." For those who insist on "meter" as a necessary condition for a hymn, the strophic arrangement of this section is not sufficient for this label.[13] Even with parallelism, the structure is not as tightly organized as some would have expected.[14] Some therefore prefer to label this section as "elevated prose" or "some kind of poem."[15] But to replace the label "hymn" with that of "elevated prose" or "poem" is simply to replace one group having clear ancient literary examples with ambiguous titles that bear no such parallels.[16]

More fruitful is making a distinction between various types of hymns. With meter being a prominent characteristic in Greek hymns, some have pointed rather to Jewish hymns, where chiastic structure and parallelism rather than meter are more significant features.[17] Moreover, hymnic material in the Greco-Roman world is often not defined by formal characteristics but by its content. In an earlier study, Stephen Fowl defined hymns as "poetic accounts of the nature and/or activity of a divine figure,"[18] but the more recent work of Matthew

---

12. See the recent surveys of scholarship in Christian Stettler, *Der Kolosserhymnus: Untersuchungen zu Form, traditionsgeschichtlichem Hintergrund und Aussage von Kol 1,15 – 20* (WUNT 2.131; Tübingen: Mohr Siebeck, 2000), 1 – 35; and Gordley, *Colossian Hymn in Context*, 3 – 26.

13. Cf. Balchin, "Colossians 1:15 – 20," 86 – 87, who further concludes that there is "no actual parallel anywhere in ancient literature, Christian, Jewish or pagan, which justifies our using the description of 'hymn' for the passage."

14. J. C. O'Neill, "The Source of the Christology in Colossians," *NTS* 26 (1979): 87 – 88.

15. N. T. Wright, "Poetry and Theology in Colossians 1.15 – 20," *NTS* 36 (1990): 448.

16. Cf. Pizzuto, *A Cosmic Leap of Faith*, 225.

17. Steven M. Baugh, "The Poetic Form of Col 1:15 – 20," *WTJ* 47 (1985): 237.

18. Stephen E. Fowl, *The Story of Christ in the Ethics of Paul: An Analysis of the Hymnic Material in the Pauline Corpus* (JSNTSup 36; Sheffield: Sheffield Academic, 1990), 45.

Gordley provides a more elaborate defense of this view with a detailed definition of a "hymn":

> A hymn is a self-contained composition of relatively short length (most are between 4 and 35 lines, though longer hymns are attested as well) whose contents are primarily centered on praise of the divine in a descriptive or declarative style, which may be expressed in direct address (e.g., You alone are …) or in the third person (e.g., She shows mercy …), whether in poetry or prose, and whose primary purpose may have been liturgical or instructional (i.e., cultic or didactic).[19]

This definition accounts for the hymnic sections contained in various types of material; this definition also allows one to examine this section in Colossians without necessarily positing a Jewish versus Greco-Roman dichotomy since it is able accommodate samples from both traditions.

To label this section as a hymn is, therefore, not simply a conclusion concerning its style; it also highlights the significance of the subject discussed. Moreover, within the context of contemporary Jewish traditions where hymnic material often becomes the vehicle in the expression of the eschatological hope of Israel,[20] this hymn becomes a useful instrument through which the climax of God's acts in history is expressed.

Origin

In identifying this section as a "hymn," many have also assumed that this is an existing hymn incorporated into this letter. The significant presence of *hapax legomena*,[21] together with the assumed liturgical setting of the hymn, appears to indicate an earlier use of this hymn. Others have argued that "the circumstances of the writer as a prisoner is another factor which militates against the production *currente calamao* of a rhythmical passage, in liturgico-hymnic vein, as he dictates a pastoral letter."[22] For those who insist on the pre-Pauline nature of the hymn, many further suggest that Paul endows this hymn with unique words and phrases. Scholars cannot agree on the form of the "original hymn," however,

---

19. Gordley, *Colossian Hymn in Context*, 32 – 33, who further notes, "The distinction between a hymn and other specimens of a particular genre is observed primarily in the question of who is praised" (39). See Schweizer, *Letter to the Colossians*, 56, who defines "hymn" above all as material with "doxological intent."

20. Cf. Jdt 16; Tob 13; 1QH[a]; Maurya P. Horgan and Paul J. Kobelski, "The Hodayot (1QH) and New Testament Poetry," in *To Touch the Text: Biblical and Related Studies in Honor of Joseph A. Fitzmyer, S.J.* (ed. M. P. Horgan and P. J. Kobelski; New

York: Crossroad, 1989), 179 – 93; and Steven Weitzman, *Song and Story in Biblical Narrative: The History of a Literary Convention in Ancient Israel* (Indiana Studies in Biblical Literature; Bloomington: Indiana Univ. Press, 1997), 65 – 70.

21. See, e.g., Lohse, *Colossians and Philemon*, 42, who points to other words that have appeared elsewhere in Paul but "are used … with a different meaning."

22. Ralph P. Martin, "An Early Christian Hymn (Col. 1:15 – 20)," *EvQ* 36 (1964): 199.

and most can only agree that vv. 15 – 16a and 19 – 20a should be considered to be part of this "original hymn" with "the church" (v. 18a) and "through the blood of his cross" (v. 20b) as obvious Pauline insertions.[23]

The arguments for Paul's use of an existing hymn are not decisive, however. The fact that Paul is able to provide a well-crafted argument elsewhere in this letter suggests that he is equally capable of creating a structured piece even though he might be in a less than ideal situation. As far as theological and linguistic consistency is concerned, the content of this hymn is not sufficient evidence against Pauline authorship.[24] First, since confessional material often uses traditional expressions, it is not surprising to find Paul using language that belongs to an earlier tradition. The significance of the *hapax legomena* in this hymn should be considered in light of the fact that most of these terms appear in the LXX.[25] Paul may therefore be simply drawing from the sacred tradition of Israel in expressing his thoughts. Moreover, perhaps Paul is drawing from the false teachings in his composition of this hymn to respond to such teachings.[26]

In any case, we would expect Paul to use a different set of expressions in hymnic material.[27] The fact that nothing in this hymn contradicts Paul's teaching elsewhere should serve as cautionary note for those who insist on the pre-Pauline nature of this hymn.[28] While remaining evidence may not be able to confirm that this hymn originated from Paul, clearly everything included in this section should be considered as significant parts of Paul's wider argument in this letter.

Conceptual Framework

In examining the individual phrases in this hymn, Second Temple Jewish traditions provide a fruitful framework within which its unique emphases can be appreciated. It has been noted that "one could quote the parallels to the first stanza word by word in the wisdom literature."[29] These common concepts and expressions include "image" (v. 15), "firstborn" (vv. 15, 18), "created" (v. 16), "all

23. Cf. Balchin, "Colossians 1:15 – 20," 65 – 94. Some have also attempted to delineate the various stages in the composition of this hymn; see Roy Yates, "A Reappraisal of Colossians," *ITQ* 58 (1992): 98.

24. As Leppä argues, *Making of Colossians*, 257 – 65.

25. Balchin, "Colossians 1:15 – 20," 74.

26. Smith, *Heavenly Perspective*, 152.

27. Judging from Paul's own writings, one should also not downplay his creativity when identifying pre-Pauline material in Paul's letters. See Martin Hengel, *Between Jesus and Paul: Studies in the Earliest History of Christianity* (trans. John Bowden; London: SCM, 1983), 32 – 44, who criticizes the very concept of "pre-Pauline."

28. Beyond this claim, one can argue that most of the concepts embedded in this hymn can be found in other Pauline writings. The cosmic role of Christ, one feature often claimed to be unique in this hymn, can also be found elsewhere in Paul (Gal 4:4 – 5; 1 Cor 1:3; 2:7; 8:6; 10:4; Phil 2:6 – 11; 1 Tim 1:15); see Larry R. Helyer, "Cosmic Christology and Col 1:15 – 20," *JETS* 37 (1994): 235 – 46.

29. Eduard Schweizer, "The Church as the Missionary Body of Christ," *NTS* 8 (1961): 7.

things" (v. 17), "are held together" (v. 17), "beginning" (v. 18), and "in all things …
supreme" (v. 18).[30] These parallels allow Paul to highlight the significance of the
work and status of Jesus. As the ultimate Wisdom figure, Jesus is considered to
be the agent and sustainer of creation; as such, he is above all creation. He is
the preexistent one who became the mediator of God's eternal plan. In light of
the identification of the Torah with the Wisdom figure, Jesus also becomes the
final revelation of the will of God.

Read in light of the wisdom traditions, the unique emphases of the cosmological, soteriological, ontological, and revelatory significance of Christ become
even more apparent.[31] Cosmologically, Christ is not simply the agent of creation,
but the goal of creation (all things are created "for him," v. 16). Paul also makes
it explicit that Christ is therefore above all "visible and invisible … authorities"
(v. 16). Soteriologically, the climax of God's acts in history is not located in the
creation of the physical world but in the death of Jesus on the cross (v. 20). It is
striking to find two references to Jesus' death in this hymn, which focuses on his
exalted status (vv. 18, 20). Although his resurrection is alluded to in v. 18, it is his
death that becomes the focus when Paul appropriates this hymn for his argument in v. 22.[32] Ontologically, it is equally striking to find the unprecedented
identification of Wisdom with a historical figure who is also the preexistent Son.
Jesus is the Son in whom full deity can be found (v. 19). Finally, in terms of revelation, Jesus becomes the one and final revelation of the "invisible God" (v. 15).
As such, he fulfills the Torah in providing humanity access to God.

In these ways, it becomes clear that while wisdom traditions may provide
lenses through which the significance of this hymn (and other passages in Colossians) can be appreciated, Paul also makes it clear that Jesus is not simply to
be identified as Wisdom since he supersedes those ideas contained in such traditions.[33] As the perfect and personal embodiment of God's will (v. 15), whose

---

30. See comments on the individual verses for a discussion
of these parallels in Jewish wisdom literature. For a notable
example of those who deny any influence from the Jewish
wisdom traditions, see Gordon D. Fee, "Wisdom Christology
in Paul: A Dissenting View," in *The Way of Wisdom: Essays
in Honor of Bruce K. Waltke* (ed. J. I. Packer and S. K. Soderlund; Grand Rapids: Zondervan, 2000), 257 – 60; idem, *Pauline
Christology*, 317 – 25.

31. For a discussion of the relationship between Jewish
wisdom traditions and Pauline Christology through these four
categories, see Eckhard J. Schnabel, *Law and Wisdom from Ben
Sira to Paul* (WUNT 2.16; Tübingen: Mohr Siebeck, 1985),
262 – 63.

32. For a discussion of the cultic context of Jewish wisdom
traditions, see Crispin H. T. Fletcher-Louis, "Wisdom Christology and the Partings of the Ways between Judaism and Christianity," in *Christian-Jewish Relations through the Centuries* (ed.
Stanley E. Porter and Brook W. R. Pearson; Sheffield: Sheffield
Academic, 2000), 52 – 68, who nonetheless emphasizes that
"Jesus' atoning self-sacrifice … is a qualitatively new sacrifice
and ultimately a cause of the partings of the ways between Judaism and Christianity" (68).

33. Karen H. Jobes's comment on the Johannine prologue
would also apply here: "Jesus was not a child of Wisdom-
Sophia as some theologians would claim; rather, the preexistent
Christ created the Wisdom-Sophia found in Prov 8 and all that

death (v. 18) presents the eschatological climax of God's act among his people (v. 16), Jesus brought about the final reconciliation (v. 20) that transcends all expectations contained in these traditions.

To identify wisdom traditions as a prominent framework does not rule out the presence of other motifs and themes. In the discussion of creation, Gen 1 becomes the most natural source of influence. Some have even considered this hymn as a "midrash" on Gen 1:1, where the hymn explicates the four meanings of the word "beginning": firstborn, supreme, head, and beginning.[34] The connection with the wisdom traditions is paved by the paradigmatic wisdom passage in Prov 8:22, which already builds on Gen 1:1. The connection with Genesis also leads to the possibility of identifying an Adam Christology behind this hymn, especially when Adam Christology and Wisdom Christology are often connected. Jesus is "that which Adam ought to be."[35] In Jesus, one finds the beginning of a new humanity. For Paul, this humanity constitutes his "body, the church" (v. 18).

Others argue for the prominence of a royal Christology here, though they also acknowledge the presence of wisdom motifs "especially as it related to Christ's involvement in creation."[36] Such royal Christology points to a significant strand of Jewish messianic traditions, and its presence behind Paul's emphasis on Jesus as the "Son" cannot be denied (cf. 1:13). Such a Christology does not compete with the portrayal of Christ as the true "wisdom" of God, especially in a letter flooded with wisdom language (cf. 1:9, 28; 2:3, 23; 3:16; 4:5).

she represents" ("Sophia Christology: The Way of Wisdom?" in *The Way of Wisdom: Essays in Honor of Bruce K. Waltke* [ed. J. I. Packer and S. K. Soderlund; Grand Rapids: Zondervan, 2000], 241).

34. C. F. Burney, "Christ as the APXH of Creation," *JTS* 27 (1926): 160 – 77. Cf. Martin H. Scharlemann, "The Scope of the Redemptive Task (Colossians 1:15 – 20)," *CTM* 36 (1965): 291 – 300; Frédéric Manns, "Col. 1,15 – 20: Midrash chrétien de Gen. 1,1," *RevScRel* 53 (1979): 100 – 110; Wright, "Poetry and Theology in Colossians 1.15 – 20," 456 – 57; and P. Lefebvre, "Les mots de la Septante, ont-ils trois dimensions? *Phosteres eis archas* (Gn 1, 16)," in *Selon les Septante: trente études sur la Bible grecque des Septante, en hommage à Marguerite Harl* (ed. G. Dorival and O. Munnich; Paris: Éditions du Cerf, 1995), 301 – 3.

35. N. T. Wright, "Adam in Pauline Christology," *SBLSP* 22 (1983): 385, who also notes that both Adam Christology and Wisdom Christology are basically "Israel-Christologies" as they point to "what Israel ought to be." See also James D. G. Dunn, *The Theology of Paul the Apostle* (Grand Rapids: Eerdmans, 1998), 275 – 76.

36. John Anthony Dunne, "The Regal Status of Christ in the Colossian 'Christ-Hymn': A Re-Evaluation of the Influence of Wisdom Traditions," *TJ* 32 (2011): 7. While pointing to the presence of royal christological language and motifs in this christological hymn, Dunne further argues for the presence of an anti-imperial polemic in this hymn. Nevertheless, this polemic, if present, does not appear to be the focus of this hymn especially within Paul's argument in this letter.

Explanation of the Text

1:15a He is the image of the invisible God (ὅς ἐστιν εἰκὼν τοῦ θεοῦ τοῦ ἀοράτου). Paul begins this christological statement by pointing to Christ's true representation and revelation of God and his will. The relative pronoun rendered "he" (ὅς) points back to "the Son" in v. 13.[37] Some consider this as a typical feature in hymnic and confessional material (Phil 2:6; 1 Tim 3:16; Heb 1:3).[38] Others suggest that the use of the relative pronoun "allows the hymn to move immediately to its content in the space of just one syllable."[39] In the context of Colossians, this use of this relative pronoun parallels a similar use in 1:13 that introduced the work of the Father. The present pronoun then signifies the shift of focus from the Father to the Son.

"Image" (εἰκών) is anarthrous because of its predicate position and should be translated as a definite noun ("the image"), as do all modern versions, in light of its context that highlights the unique status of Christ. Despite uses of this word in Greek philosophical traditions where "image" is considered inferior to that which is real, the word in the context "is not to be understood as a magnitude which is alien to the reality and present only in the consciousness."[40] In the canonical context, the word evokes Gen 1:27, where one reads, "God created humankind in his own image" (NET).[41] In other Pauline references to "the image of God," one also finds clear allusions to Genesis (Rom 8:29; 1 Cor 11:7; 15:45 – 49; 2 Cor 4:4).[42] In the Genesis context, to be created in God's image is not to resemble God in all aspects and attributes, but to represent him as the authority over his created realm (Gen 1:28).[43] The focus on the preeminence of Christ in this hymn also points to this emphasis on his unique authority.

In this context, however, the Genesis passage cannot fully account for the "image of God" reference. More prominent is the use of this imagery in the wisdom traditions, which in turn reflect the influence of the Genesis creation account (cf. Wis 7:26; Philo, *Alleg. Interp.* 1.43; *Migration* 175; *Unchangeable* 142 – 43). First, in this hymn the basis for claiming the Son to be "the image of the invisible God" is that "in him," "through him," and "for him" all things were created (v. 16). This points to the role of Wisdom, rather than the Adam of the Genesis account.[44] Moreover, the first Adam is one who was created "in" or "after" the image of God, but he is not identified as the image.[45] Finally, the genitival qualifier, "of the invisible God,"[46] focuses on the revelatory function of this "image." This

---

37. Cf. TNIV, NIV: "The Son is the image of the invisible God."

38. Schweizer, *Letter to the Colossians*, 56. Cf. Dunn, *Epistles to the Colossians and to Philemon*, 77, who points to the exact parallel phrase in 2 Cor 4:4: "who is the image of God" (ὅς ἐστιν εἰκὼν τοῦ θεοῦ).

39. Gordley, *Colossian Hymn in Context*, 180.

40. Kleinknecht, *TDNT*, 2:389.

41. This inclusive translation is justified by Gen 5:1 – 2, where both men and women are said to be created in the image/likeness of God. It is also worth noting that the same Greek word (εἰκών) is used in the LXX.

42. See Beale, "Colossians," 851 – 52, who sees an Adam typology behind this imagery. He further points to the connection between Adam's sonship and the image of God in Sec-

ond Temple Jewish traditions (*LAE* 35; Philo, *Planting* 18 – 19; *Worse* 86 – 87, *Moses* 2.65).

43. For a helpful survey of scholarship up to the 1980s, see Gunnlaugur A. Jónsson, *The Image of God: Genesis 1:26 – 28 in a Century of Old Testament Research* (trans. Lorraine Svendsen; ConBOT 26; Stockholm: Almqvist and Wiksell, 1988), who considers this reading the consensus of OT scholarship.

44. Beetham, *Echoes of Scripture*, 132. It should be noted, however, that Christ transcends Wisdom in being also the "goal" of all creation.

45. This prompted some to identify the context of this imagery in the later gnostic material (NHC II.5, 108.7 – 9; cf. Fossum, "Colossians 1.15 – 18a in the Light of Jewish Mysticism and Gnosticism," 185), but the early Jewish wisdom traditions provide a more plausible context for this hymn.

46. The notion of "the invisible God" finds its roots in the

again points to the function of Wisdom as the intermediary being that provides access to the transcendent God. For Paul, Jesus as the true Wisdom is and always has been the image of God, and through him God's nature and will are made known.

1:15b The firstborn of all creation (πρωτότοκος πάσης κτίσεως). This phrase provides an additional description of the Son by pointing to his supreme status above all created beings. "Firstborn" (πρωτότοκος) can denote temporal priority (cf. Luke 2:7; Heb 11:28), which in itself already often points to the rank or supremacy of an individual. This word can, however, be used in a metaphorical sense where rank rather than temporal priority is the primary if not the only focus. In Ps 89:27 (LXX 88:28), for example, one reads: "I will appoint him [David] to be my firstborn [πρωτότοκον], the most exalted of the kings of the earth." David (and the messianic Davidic ruler) is considered to be the "firstborn," although David himself was the youngest among his brothers (1 Sam 16:11). Just as Israel is considered to be the "firstborn" of God (Exod 4:22; Jer 31:9), this Davidic ruler will become the exalted and honored king who will rule over all nations. In the Greco-Roman context, "firstborn" is also used as a legal term to refer to one who is the legal heir of his father's inheritance.[47] As the heir, this person also inherits the power and authority of his father over his household.

The genitival modifier, "of all creation" (πάσης κτίσεως),[48] must be considered before the full meaning of the verse can be understood. This modifier can hardly be a partitive genitive ("firstborn among all creation")[49] because in v. 16 Christ is clearly distinguished from all creation since all things were created through him. Christ is therefore different from Wisdom, who was created as the "first of his works" (Prov 8:22).[50] It is more likely either a genitive of comparison ("firstborn before all creation") or an objective genitive ("firstborn over all creation"),[51] although these are not exclusive categories especially when the parallel phrase in v. 18 ("firstborn from the dead") again points to both temporal priority and supremacy in rank. The title "firstborn," therefore, points to the unique and incomparable identity of Jesus Christ.[52]

1:16a-e For in him all things were created, in heaven and on earth, visible and invisible (ὅτι ἐν αὐτῷ ἐκτίσθη τὰ πάντα ἐν τοῖς οὐρανοῖς καὶ ἐπὶ τῆς γῆς, τὰ ὁρατὰ καὶ τὰ ἀόρατα). Paul again affirms the supremacy of Christ by describing his role as the unique agent of creation. This clause introduced by "for" (ὅτι) provides the basis of v. 15. It does not acquire a strong or full causal force,[53] however, since this statement merely provides the basis or explanation for the *assertion* in v. 15.

The exact sense of the prepositional phrase "in him" (ἐν αὐτῷ) is not clear. For those who take this in an instrumental sense, "Christ is God's means of creating the world."[54] Many modern versions adopt

---

consistent prohibition against the making of images of God (cf. Exod 20:4); cf. Gregory K. Beale, *We Become What We Worship: A Biblical Theology of Idolatry* (Downers Grove, IL: InterVarsity Press, 2008), 91.

47. Cf. Francis Lyall, "Roman Law in the Writings of Paul — Adoption," *JBL* 88 (1969): 458 – 66. See also Heb 12:23, where the term applies to believers who inherit God's promises.

48. This phrase most likely points to the collective sense ("all creation") instead of the distributive sense ("every creation") in light of similar uses of "all" (πᾶς) in this hymn (vv. 16 [2x], 17 [2x], 18, 19, 20).

49. Cf. "firstborn among many any brothers and sisters" (Rom 8:29).

50. See Bevere, *Sharing in the Inheritance*, 128, who sees an allusion to Prov 8:22 behind this verse.

51. Cf. Harris, *Colossians and Philemon*, 44. See also Wallace, *Greek Grammar*, 103 – 4, who labels this a "genitive of subordination."

52. See also the absolute use of this title in Heb 1:6; 12:23.

53. See BDAG, 31 – 32, for the semantic range of this conjunction.

54. Sumney, *Colossians*, 66; cf. Lohse, *Colossians and Philemon*, 49 – 50; Wilson, *Colossians and Philemon*, 137 – 38.

this view: "all things … were created by him" (NET; cf. KJV, NASB, NLT, NKJV, TEV, ESV). This preposition is then connected with "through him" (δι᾽ αὐτοῦ) and "for him" (εἰς αὐτόν) in the second part of the verse. Some have considered these three prepositional phrases as the basis for "prepositional metaphysics" that can be traced to Aristotle's discussion on causes (*Phys.* 2.3 – 9 [194b – 200b]).[55] If so, then, these three phrases point to the three causes that are involved in the act of creation: "in him" points to efficient causation, "through him" to instrumental causation, and "for him" to final causation.[56]

In the context of this hymn, however, one wonders if this "prepositional metaphysics" can fully explain the presence of these prepositions. First, these philosophical traditions fail to provide the exact parallel to these three phrases, especially the coexistence of "in him" and "through him." The instrumental reading of the first forces one to explain the presence of "through him," which is clearly instrumental. Moreover, while "efficient cause" may explain the presence of "in him," the three phrases are not strictly parallel. It is best to see "through him" and "for him" as explicating the meaning of "in him." The all-encompassing nature of "in him" is confirmed by the parallel in the other two parts of this hymn (vv. 17, 19). In vv. 19 – 20, in particular, one finds the presence of all three prepositional phrases, but "in him" (ἐν αὐτῷ) in v. 19 clearly should not be limited to an instrumental sense. Some have suggested that this is a "dative of sphere,"[57] although in light of the prominence of the "in Christ" formula in Paul (cf. v. 2), it is probably best to see this as a wider category that denotes a certain organic association, one that contains locative reference and possibly causal relationship as well.

In the passive "were created" (ἐκτίσθη), one finds an explicit focus on God's act of creation, one that is embedded in the presence of its nominal form in v. 15 ("creation"). In the biblical times, discussion of creation can often be found in contexts where power relationships are defined (e.g., 1 Chr 29:10 – 19; Ps 89:9 – 14; Isa 40:18 – 24; 1 Cor 10:26; Rev 4:11).[58] The Creator is the Supreme Being to whom all creatures are to submit and worship. It is not surprising, therefore, to find the focus on creation in a hymn that highlights the power and status of Christ.

The following two phrases, "in heaven and on earth, visible and invisible," utilize opposing polarities in denoting totality (merisms). All creatures must submit to him. "In heaven and on earth" may again evoke the creation context (Gen 1:1), but in the present context this pair may also pave the way for Paul's argument against the worship of angels (2:18),[59] and for his argument for focusing on Christ and "not things on the earth" (3:2).[60] The second pair, "visible and invisible," is far less common in canonical literature. But in Colossians, this phrase may acquire special significance when Paul criticizes those who claim to have seen spe-

---

55. Gregory E. Sterling, "Prepositional Metaphysics in Jewish Wisdom Speculation and Early Christian Liturgical Texts," in *Wisdom and Logos: Studies in Jewish Thought* (ed. David T. Runia and G. E. Sterling; Studies in Hellenistic Judaism 9; Atlanta: Scholars, 1997), who further points to Middle Platonism and Stoicism that inherit this tradition, as exemplified by the note on "nature" by Marcus Aurelius: "All things are from you [ἐκ σοῦ], all things are in you [ἐν σοί], and all things are for you [εἰς σέ]" (Marcus Aurelius 4.23).

56. Cf. Richard Bauckham, "Where Is Wisdom to Be Found? Colossians 1.15 – 20 (II)," in *Reading Texts, Seeking*

Wisdom: Scripture and Theology (ed. David F. Ford and Graham Stanton; London: SCM, 2003), 134.

57. Fee, *Pauline Christology*, 302. See, also, TNIV, NIV: "in him all things were created" (cf. NAB, REV, NJB, NRSV).

58. Cf. Stephen Lee, "Power Not Novelty: The Connotations of ברא in the Hebrew Bible," in *Understanding Poets and Prophets: Essays in Honour of George Wishart Anderson* (ed. A. Graeme Auld; Sheffield: JSOT, 1993), 199 – 212.

59. Or "angelic worship"; see comments on 2:18a-c.

60. Embedded in 3:1 – 4 is also an argument against focusing on anything else "above" but Christ himself (cf. 3:1).

cial visions or received revelation (2:18). Here, Paul makes it clear that Christ is above all these. This reading assumes, of course, that this hymn is not simply a pre-Pauline hymn that reflects the common liturgical traditions of the early church.

1:16f-1 Whether thrones or dominions or rulers or authorities; all things were created through him and for him (εἴτε θρόνοι εἴτε κυριότητες εἴτε ἀρχαὶ εἴτε ἐξουσίαι· τὰ πάντα δι᾽ αὐτοῦ καὶ εἰς αὐτὸν ἔκτισται). "Thrones," "dominions," "rulers," and "authorities" provide specific examples of what are subordinated to Christ. In the Jewish traditions, "thrones" (θρόνοι) can refer to beings connected with the divine council and are best understood as angelic beings (cf. *2 En.* 20.1; *T. Levi* 3.8). The term "dominions" (κυριότητες) does not appear in LXX and may belong to the unique early Christian vocabulary (cf. Eph 1:21; 2 Pet 2:10; Jude 8), although the phrase "lordship over many" (κυριότης πολλῶν) does appear in contemporary literature.[61] "Rulers" (ἀρχαί) and "authorities" (ἐξουσίαι) appear often in Pauline letters in reference to spiritual powers (1 Cor 15:24; Eph 1:21; 3:10; 6:12), although this vocabulary likely derives from analogies in secular government (cf. Luke 12:11; 20:20; Titus 3:1).[62]

While these four terms are derived from different traditions, here they all point to spiritual beings,[63] although the extant literature fails to support the claim that these are "four classes of angelic powers."[64] In light of the attempt to emphasize Christ's universal rule, it is possible that Paul uses these four terms as inclusive of all spiritual beings, without necessarily distinguishing between good and evil beings.[65] The fact that only "rulers" and "authorities" are among those criticized by Paul in this letter (2:10, 15) may support this reading.

"All things were created through him and for him" provides a fitting conclusion to this part of the hymn, further explicating the meaning of the earlier prepositional clause, "in him all things were created." "Through him" points to Jesus as the intermediate agent through whom God accomplishes his creative acts,[66] and "for him" points to Christ as the goal of creation. While "through him" may evoke the role of Wisdom in God's act of creation (Ps 104:24; Prov 3:19; 8:27 – 30; cf. Prov 24:3), "for him" "exceeds anything predicated for divine Wisdom and now conceives of Christ in an eschatological sense."[67] The change from the aorist (ἐκτίσθη) at the beginning of the verse to the perfect tense (ἔκτισται) here may draw attention to the continued purpose of creation. As the goal of creation, Christ restores creation to its intended state. This phrase then anticipates the final section of this hymn that points to the reconciliation achieved through the work of Christ (vv. 18 – 20).

1:17 He is before all things, and in him all things are held together (καὶ αὐτός ἐστιν πρὸ πάντων καὶ

---

61. Memnon, *Hist.* 434, frags. 1, 4, 6; BDAG, 579.

62. This pair can also be found in secular Greek literature (Plato, *Greater Alcibiades* I, 135 A-B; Dionysius of Halicarnassus 11.32), but not in LXX; cf. Jennifer Dines, "Light from the Septuagint on the New Testament — or Vice Versa? Genesis 1,16 and Colossians 1,16," in *Voces Biblicae: Septuagint Greek and Its Significance for the New Testament* (ed. Jan Joosten and Peter J. Tomson; Leuven: Peeters, 2007), 22.

63. These terms have also been understood as referring to impersonal powers, ideologies, and systemic evil embedded in societal and political structure; see, e.g., Brian J. Walsh and Sylvia C. Keesmaat, *Colossians Remixed: Subverting the Empire* (Downers Grove, IL: InterVarsity Press, 2004), 91 – 93. For a critique of this position, see Andrew T. Lincoln, "Liberation from the Powers: Supernatural Spirits or Societal Structures?" in *The Bible in Human Society: Essays in Honour of John Rogerson* (ed. M. Daniel Carroll R., David J. A. Clines, and Philip R. Davies; JSOTSup 200; Sheffield: Sheffield Academic, 1995), 335 – 54, who sees Paul as referring to spiritual beings, but he suggests that such *applications* on ideologies and sociopolitical structures are valid in the contemporary context.

64. O'Brien, *Colossians, Philemon*, 46.

65. Smith, *Heavenly Perspective*, 165; Wilson, *Colossians and Philemon*, 140 – 41.

66. Wallace, *Greek Grammar*, 433 – 34; cf. BDF §223.

67. Arnold, *Colossian Syncretism*, 257.

τὰ πάντα ἐν αὐτῷ συνέστηκεν). Christ is supreme in both time and rank, but he is also the sustainer of all things. The pronoun "he" (αὐτός) ties this new section with the previous verses where the three prepositional phrases ("in him," "through him," "for him") emphasize the role of Christ in creation. In its nominative form, moreover, this emphatic pronoun[68] ties this part of the verse with the following two clauses (v. 17b, 18a). Depending on the accentuation, the pronoun with the verb (ἐστιν) can be translated either "he exists" (αὐτός ἔστιν, REB, NJB, NLT) or "he is" (αὐτός ἐστιν, NAB, NASB, NKJV, NRSV, TNIV, ESV, NET, NIV). In light of the use of this verb in the parallel in v. 18a, it seems best to see the verb functioning simply as a copula linking the subject with the prepositional phrase that follows: "he is before all things."

Adding to the confusion is the fact that the prepositional phrase used here (πρὸ πάντων) can denote time ("he is before all things") or rank ("he is above all things"). In light of the consistent temporal use of this preposition elsewhere in Paul, a temporal sense cannot be denied.[69] Christ's preexistence is thus clearly affirmed. At the same time, as in the earlier case of the "firstborn" (v. 15), the focus is on the supremacy of Christ. Moreover, elsewhere in the NT when the exact phrase (πρὸ πάντων) is used, this is always a marker for rank and supremacy (Jas 5:12; 1 Pet 4:8).[70] In the context of this hymn, even the temporal sense of this prepositional phrase ultimately serves to denote his supremacy. It seems best, therefore, to see both senses embedded in this phrase: as Christ is the goal of all

creation (v. 16), he is likewise prior to all creation, and as such he is supreme over all creation.

The exact sense of "in him" (ἐν αὐτῷ) is again in dispute (cf. v. 16a). Many take it in an instrumental sense, a reading supported by the wisdom traditions in reference to the Divine Logos: "by his word all things hold together" (Sir 43:26).[71] In light of the parallel in v. 16a, however, the instrumental sense does not exhaust the meaning of this prepositional phrase. All things are indeed sustained "by him," because all things owe their continuous existence to him. The locative idea is also present, especially in light of the portrayal of the cosmic unity provided by Christ (cf. 2:19).[72] Perhaps the ambiguity and complexity of the Pauline "in Christ" formula is again operating here behind this phrase.

The verb translated "are held together" (συνέστηκεν) carries various shades of meaning. In Paul, it is often used in the sense of commendation (Rom 16:1; 2 Cor 3:1; 4:2; 5:12; 6:4; 10:12, 18; 12:11), although it can also denote demonstration (Rom 3:5; 2 Cor 7:11; Gal 2:18). In philosophical traditions, this verb has the sense of existence and coherence (2 Pet 3:5).[73] In this context, this verb can point to the existence of all things; if so, this verse repeats what has been asserted in vv. 15–16 in providing the conclusion to the first half of the hymn.[74]

In light of the wisdom context, however, the idea of cohesion and sustenance is more appropriate. The conceptual parallel in the confession in Heb 1:3 supports this reading ("sustaining all things by his powerful word"),[75] although here in Colossians the implied subject of συνέστηκεν is

---

68. Cf. NRSV, NET: "He himself."

69. Cf. Rom 16:7; 1 Cor 2:7; 4:5; 2 Cor 12:2; Gal 1:17; 2:12; 3:23; Eph 1:4; 2 Tim 1:9; 4:21; Titus 1:2; Moo, *Letters to the Colossians and to Philemon*, 125.

70. This use is also found in extracanonical literature (cf. *Let. Aris.*, 9, 2; Justin, *Dial.* 7, 3; P.Oxy. 292, 11; 294, 30; BDAG, 864).

71. Lohse, *Colossians and Philemon*, 52.

72. See also 2:9–10, which has been taken to refer to the

cosmic body of Christ; cf. van Kooten, *Cosmic Christology in Paul*, 22–23.

73. Cf. Plato, *Rep.* 7, 530a; *Tim.* 61a; BDAG, 973.

74. Thus Wilhelm Kasch, *TDNT*, 7:897, who suggests that this note of the existence of all things in Christ "forms the climax and conclusion of a train of thought which bases the saving significance of Christ on His cosmic significance."

75. Lightfoot, *St. Paul's Epistles to the Colossians and to Philemon*, 156.

God even when the focus is on Christ. This verse, therefore, points to the progression of thought as Christ is not only the Creator, but also the one who sustains all creation. If we read this against the ancient concept of creation, however, the distinction between existence and cohesion may be less pronounced when the act of creation is also the act of subduing the forces of chaos in bringing about and sustaining order.[76]

1:18a He is the head of the body, the church (καὶ αὐτός ἐστιν ἡ κεφαλὴ τοῦ σώματος, τῆς ἐκκλησίας). As Paul affirms Christ's supremacy over the community of believers, the attention shifts from the cosmos to the church, and from creation to redemption. Because Christ is supreme over all creation (vv. 15 – 17), he is also the head of the church.

"The head" (ἡ κεφαλή) stands in the predicative position and is marked by an article, which indicates "absolute identification"[77] with the subject: Christ and Christ alone is to be identified as "the head." In this context, "the head" clearly points to the position of authority and power as Christ is supreme over all creation, as he is over the church. Although it is debatable whether "the head" can be taken as the source for growth and sustenance,[78] in Colossians even such emphasis on growth and sustenance aims at affirming the authority of

Christ (v. 17; cf. 2:19). A notable parallel in Greek literature can be found in *Orphic Frag.* 21a, where "Zeus is the head [κεφαλή]" on which all things are dependent. Note also that some manuscripts of this fragment include the appellation "beginning" (ἀρχή) in describing Zeus,[79] which thus points to the relationship between these two terms, as is evident in this hymn (v. 18b).

The genitival modifier "of the body" (τοῦ σώματος) can be a possessive genitive ("the head that belongs to the body"), but the focus is on the authority of the head over the body, rather than the dependence of a part upon the entire body. In context, this should be taken rather as an objective genitive: "the head that is sovereign over the body." The origin of this metaphor is likely the common observation of the relationship between the physical head and the body, and the earlier Pauline discussion of the human body with various parts can be considered as anticipating this discussion (Rom 12:4 – 5; 1 Cor 12:12).[80]

"The church" (τῆς ἐκκλησίας) is an epexegetical genitive[81] that provides further definition to "the body": "He is the Head of the Body, that is, the Church" (NJB).[82] In this context, this "church" is the "universal church," which includes all who belong to Christ. In the earlier writings of Paul, the church is portrayed as the body of Christ (Rom

---

76. Cf. Jon D. Levenson, *Creation and Persistence of Evil* (New York: Harper & Row, 1988), 3 – 50.

77. Harris, *Colossians and Philemon*, 47.

78. Cf. Wayne A. Grudem, "Does κεφαλή Mean 'Source' or 'Authority over' in Greek Literature?: A Survey of 2,336 Examples," *TJ* 6 (1985): 38 – 59; Philip Barton Payne, "Response," in *Women, Authority and the Bible* (ed. Alvera Mickelsen; Downers Grove, IL: InterVarsity Press, 1986), 118 – 32; Wayne A. Grudem, "The Meaning of κεφαλή ('Head'): An Evaluation of New Evidence, Real and Alleged," *JETS* 44 (2001): 25 – 65.

79. Cf. Otto Kern, *Orphicorum Fragmenta* (2nd ed.; Berlin: Weidmannsche Verlagsbuchhandlung, 1963), 91 – 92. In the LXX, both "head" (κεφαλή) and "beginning" (ἀρχή) were also used to translate Hebrew term for "head" (rō's); cf. Turner, *Christian Words*, 201.

80. Cf. Clinton E. Arnold, "Jesus Christ: 'Head' of the Church (Colossians and Ephesians)," in *Jesus of Nazareth: Lord and Christ: Essays on the Historical Jesus and New Testament Christology* (ed. Joel B. Green and Max Turner; Grand Rapids: Eerdmans, 1994), 346 – 66; Gottfried Nebe, "Christ, the Body of Christ, and Cosmic Powers in Paul's Letters and the New Testament as a Whole," in *Politics and Theopolitics in the Bible and Postbiblical Literature* (ed. Henning Graf Reventlow, Yair Hoffman, and Benjamin Uffenheimer; JSOTSup 171; Sheffield: JSOT, 1994), 100 – 18.

81. Also known as genitive of apposition, Wallace, *Greek Grammar*, 99.

82. See also the similar phrase in v. 24 ("his body, which is the church," τοῦ σώματος αὐτοῦ, ὅ ἐστιν ἡ ἐκκλησία), which confirms the epexegetical genitive reading.

12:4 – 5; 1 Cor 12:12 – 30), but it is only in Colossians and Ephesians that one finds Christ as the head of the church (cf. Eph 4:15; 5:23). Nevertheless, the hierarchical structure in 1 Cor 11:3 already paves the way for the portrayal of Christ as the head of the body.[83] Moreover, in 1 Cor 12:27, the description of the various members of the church and members of the body naturally leads one to see Christ as the head of these members.

We should note the significance of identifying the body as the church in this context. First, by identifying the head of the church as the one who is also supreme over all creation, Paul is affirming that the church holds a crucial position in the redemptive plan of God. Salvation can be found in the gospel that the church preaches, and the church becomes the context through which God's redemptive act can be fulfilled. Second, since Christ is the head of the church, the church takes on the mediatorial role through which one can approach God. Perhaps in reaction to the individualism embedded in a mystical view of salvation and spirituality, Paul points to the importance of this community within which a new reality is to be experienced (cf. 3:9 – 11).[84] Through this discussion, however, Paul is not affirming the significance of the church as an "institution." His focus is on how individual members can rely on this head in overcoming all spiritual and cosmic forces (cf. 2:19).

1:18b-d He is the beginning, the firstborn from the dead, so that in all things he may become supreme (ὅς ἐστιν ἀρχή, πρωτότοκος ἐκ τῶν νεκρῶν, ἵνα γένηται ἐν πᾶσιν αὐτὸς πρωτεύων). Pointing to Christ's resurrection, Paul moves to the final sec-tion of this hymn that highlights Christ's supremacy over the new creation. As in v. 15, this section begins with a relative clause (ὅς ἐστιν ἀρχή) and reference to the "firstborn" (πρωτότοκος). To label Christ as "the beginning" (ἀρχή) is again to refer to his supreme status with a temporal reference.[85] The different uses of ἀρχή in the LXX may help to illuminate its significance here. First, it is used in the Genesis creation account (Gen 1:1). In light of the focus on creation in this hymn, this usage is the primary one. Second, the term often refers to the head of a group, such as the chief cupbearer and the head of the bakers (Gen 40:20), or the head of the household (Exod 6:25; cf. also the sense of rank in Job 40:19). Elsewhere in the LXX ἀρχή implies both rank and temporal priority. Particularly significant is the reference to Wisdom in Prov 8:22 – 23:

> The Lord created me as the first [ἀρχήν] of his
>   works,
> Before his works of old
> From eternity he established me,
> From the beginning [ἀρχῆς].

If "the beginning" reflects the language of the wisdom traditions, "firstborn from the dead" moves beyond these traditions in affirming the unique redemptive work of the Son. In v. 15, "firstborn" signifies Christ's status in relation to his role in the creation of all things. In the present verse, "firstborn" points to the new creation. Between the first and second creation is the unstated assumption of the fall, which necessitated this "re-creation."

The verb "raised" is implied in the phrase "from

---

83. The relevance of 1 Cor 11:3 in this discussion is supported by Eph 5:23, where Paul combines the idea of the Christ as the head of the church (Col 1:18) with that of the husband as the head of the wife (1 Cor 11:3); cf. Leppä, *Making of Colossians*, 94.

84. See Blumenfeld, *The Political Paul*, 215, who points to the significance of the portrayal of mediation through political instead of mystical terms in this christological hymn.

85. Most translations render this term "beginning," while REB uses the word "origin" in drawing out the significance behind this temporal reference.

the dead" (cf. 2:12), and Christ's being "raised from the dead" lies at the center of early Christian proclamation (cf. Luke 24:46; Acts 3:15; 4:10; 13:30, 34; 17:3, 31; Rom 6:4, 9; 7:4; 10:9; 1 Cor 15:12; Gal 1:1; 2 Tim 2:8). To be "the firstborn from the dead" is to affirm that he is "the first to rise from the dead" (Acts 26:23a). Elsewhere Paul stresses the significance of this fact for those who belong to him: "But Christ has indeed been raised from the dead, the firstfruits of those who have fallen asleep" (1 Cor 15:20).[86] As in other titles in this hymn, the reference to "the firstborn of the dead" not only points to the temporal priority of Jesus' resurrection, but also to his status as one who brings about the eschatological era. The fact of Jesus' resurrection ultimately testifies to the power of his death on the cross (cf. v. 20).

"So that in all things he may become supreme" shows the result of Jesus' being raised from the dead.[87] In contrast to the verb "is" (ἐστιν) in v. 17a, which affirms Jesus' supremacy in eternity, "he may become" (γένηται) may point to the particular moment when he became supreme in the new creation. The participle "being supreme" (πρωτεύων) is best taken with the verb "he may become" as a periphrastic construction, and "in all things" specifies the universality of Christ's supremacy. The note on the resurrection as well as the cross reappears in yet another passage in the NT, one that also serves to affirm Christ's supremacy: "Jesus Christ, who is the faithful witness, the firstborn from the dead, and the ruler of the kings of the earth. To him who loves us and has freed us from our sins by his own blood ..." (Rev 1:5).

1:19 For in him all the fullness was pleased to dwell (ὅτι ἐν αὐτῷ εὐδόκησεν πᾶν τὸ πλήρωμα κατοικῆσαι). Paul now points to the full deity of Christ, while in v. 20 he explains the function of this fact. Just as v. 16 provides the basis for the assertion in v. 15, so vv. 19 – 20 provide the basis for v. 18b.

The difficulties in understanding this verse lie in the ambiguity of subject of the verb "was pleased" (εὐδόκησεν), as well as the presence of the neuter nominative/accusative phrase, "all the fullness" (πᾶν τὸ πλήρωμα). This leads to a number of proposed readings. (1) Christ or the Son is the subject of the verb, and the verb introduces an indirect discourse: "For Christ was pleased that all the fullness dwells in himself."[88] This option is the least probable because this would have to turn the dative pronoun "him" (αὐτῷ) into a reflexive pronoun.[89] Moreover, it is best to take "God" as the subject of the verb "to reconcile" in v. 20 (see comments below).

(2) God as the implied subject of the verb, with the accusative phrase as the subject of the indirect discourse: "For God was pleased to have all his fullness dwell in the Son" (NET; cf. NJV, NASB, NKJV, TEV, NJB, NLT, TNIV, NIV). In favor of this view is that "was pleased" often takes a personal subject, and in the LXX the subject is often God himself (cf. Pss 40:13 [LXX 39:14]; 51:16 [50:18]; 85:1 [84:2]; Jer 2:19; 14:10, 12; Jdt 15:10; 2 Macc 14:35; Sir 34:19; 45:19). The masculine participle "by making peace" (εἰρηνοποιήσας, v. 20) also suggests a masculine personal subject. Moreover, God is likely the implied subject of the act of reconciliation in v. 20.

---

86. The significance of this verse for v. 18 not only lies in the confession of Jesus being raised from the dead, but the title "the beginning" (ἀρχή) in this verse may also evoke "the firstfruits" (ἀπαρχή) as in 1 Cor 15:20; cf. Leppä, *Making of Colossians*, 95.

87. For the conjunction "so that" (ἵνα) to introduce a result clause, see Wallace, *Greek Grammar*, 665.

88. Cf. Tertullian, *Against Marcion* 5.19.

89. This would also turn the pronouns in v. 20 into reflexives. Although it is possible for the accusative form to be a contracted reflexive form, contracted genitive and dative forms are rare in Hellenistic Greek; cf. Stanley E. Porter, Καταλλάσσω in *Ancient Greek Literature, with Reference to the Pauline Writings* (EFN 5; Córdoba: Ediciones el Almendro, 1994), 173.

(3) A simple solution that alleviates the need to supply a subject is one that takes "all the fullness" (πᾶν τὸ πλήρωμα) as the subject of the verb: "For in him all the fullness of God was pleased to dwell" (ESV; cf. RSV, NAB). This reading assumes that "all the fullness" refers to "God in all his fullness" (REB) or "all the fullness of God" (NRSV), and the masculine participle that follows in v. 20 "may be explained as a construction according to sense."[90]

The factors that favor "God" as the implied subject of the verb also support this reading, but a number of additional considerations add credence to this third option. First, in the conceptually parallel statement in 2:9, "all the fullness" is clearly the subject of the verb: "For in him all the fullness of deity dwells bodily." Second, in the LXX, the verbal (πληρόω) and adjectival forms (πλήρης) of "fullness" (τὸ πλήρωμα) often point to the presence of God (Isa 6:1; Ezek 43:5; 44:4; Hag 2:7).[91] The understanding of "all the fullness" as referring to God is further supported by the possible allusion to Ps 68:16 (LXX Ps 67:17): "at the mountain which God was pleased [ὃ εὐδόκησεν ὁ θεός] to dwell in it."[92] It seems best, therefore, to see "all the fullness" as a periphrasis for God; to insert God as the implied subject is thus redundant.

By using the phrase "all the fullness" as referring to God, Paul keeps the emphasis on the Son, to whom the phrase "in him" refers.[93] In the wisdom tradition, God's act of filling the earth signifies his

dominion and authority (cf. Wis 1:7; Philo, *Alleg. Interp.* 1.44).[94] Paul's use of "in him" therefore emphasizes again the supreme authority of Christ. This point is reinforced by the "dwell" (κατοικέω) word group, one that evokes the presence of God in both his heavenly (1 Kgs 8:39, 43, 49; 2 Chr 6:30, 33, 39) and earthly (2 Chr 6:18, 21) abodes. Christ fulfills the role of the temple in which one finds the full presence of God. This points to the reality of the incarnation.[95] "Fullness" becomes a technical term in later Gnostic writings, and it might have been used in a similar way in certain circles in the first century AD.[96]

This note on incarnation reminds the readers that the christological point acquires a soteriological function here.[97] All fullness dwells in Christ, so that through him universal reconciliation can be accomplished (v. 20). What is striking, however, is the focus on Christ as the embodiment of full deity in a section that begins with a reference to his own death (v. 18c). Instead of resting his arguments on the abstract assurance of Christ's exalted status, Paul shows how Christ's exalted status is relevant for those who are alienated from God, particularly in his work on the cross.

1:20a And through him to reconcile all things to him (καὶ δι᾽ αὐτοῦ ἀποκαταλλάξαι τὰ πάντα εἰς αὐτόν). The purpose of God's fullness in Christ (v. 19) is to reconcile the entire created realm to Christ. "To reconcile" (ἀποκαταλλάξαι) makes it

---

90. Moule, *Epistles to the Colossians and to Philemon*, 70.

91. Cf. Arnold, *Colossian Syncretism*, 263, who suggests that this is a "circumlocution of the Spirit."

92. Psalm 68 points to the transfer of God's presence from Sinai to Zion. If Paul indeed alludes to this psalm, he may be pointing to yet another transfer, now from Zion to Christ himself (cf. Beetham, *Echoes of Scripture*, 155).

93. Fee, *Pauline Christology*, 311.

94. See Suzanne Watts Henderson, "God's Fullness in Bodily Form: Christ and Church in Colossians," *ExpTim* 118 (2007): 169–73, who further suggests that God's act of filling extends his authority from creation to the present age.

95. Dunn, *Theology of Paul*, 276, recognizes the presence of the concept of "incarnation" in this passage, but emphasizes that it is the "incarnation" of the fullness of God, and not a separate "being." While this distinction rightly maintains Paul's affirmation of monotheism, this distinction may be foreign to Paul as he affirms the unique status of Christ, who, unlike his Father, assumes an earthly existence.

96. Cf. C. F. D. Moule, "'Fulness' and 'Fill' in the New Testament," *SJT* 4 (1951): 79–86.

97. Cf. David Tripp, "ΚΑΤΟΙΚΗΣΑΙ, ΚΑΤΟΙΚΕΙ (Colossians 1:19, 2:9): Christology, or Soteriology Also?" *ExpTim* 115 (2004): 78–79.

clear that the new creation noted in v. 18 becomes a necessity (for humanity) because of the rift between the Creator and his creation. The act of reconciliation points to the restoration of this broken relationship.

In Paul, this specific verb occurs only in Col 1:20, 22 and Eph 2:16, but the related word group ("to reconcile," καταλλάσσθω; "reconciliation," καταλλαγή) also occurs in Paul's earlier writings (Rom 5:10, 11; 11:15; 1 Cor 7:11; 2 Cor 5:18, 19, 20). This word group finds its roots in a Hellenistic political background, where it was used in the realm of diplomatic relationships.[98] But Paul transforms this concept. Instead of the guilty party initiating the process of reconciliation, Paul emphasizes that it is God, the offended party, who took the initiative while humans were still sinners (Rom 5:8, 10). Equally striking is Paul's emphasis on the death of Christ, which accomplished this act of reconciliation, rather than on reparations made by the offending humanity.[99] Paul's addition of the preposition ἀπό to this verb should be taken simply as an intensified form of the stem, not as an attempt to emphasize the idea of returning to the original state. After all, Paul "is speaking not of merely restoring the world before the fall and the introduction of sin, making Christ's death avoidable, but of the work of Christ as necessary to overcome alienation."[100]

"All things" (τὰ πάντα) parallels the references to "all things" in vv. 16 and 17. In light of this parallelism, it most likely refers to both animate and inanimate entities. The neuter phrases that follow, "things on earth ... things in heaven," are consistent with this reading.[101] Nevertheless, "all things" is a formulaic phrase that focuses on the distinction between the Creator and the created realm.[102] Moreover, the parallelism between this section and the first section of the hymn does not point to a strict identification between the two, especially when one finds the transition from the cosmic creation to the church in v. 18a. The references to the resurrection in v. 18c and reconciliation here should therefore be understood in personal (though universal) terms. The context of this hymn (vv. 13 – 14) as well as its application (vv. 21 – 22), where the same verb ("he has ... reconciled," ἀποκατήλλαξεν) points to a personal focus, likewise supports this reading. Therefore, while a cosmic reading cannot be ruled out, the primary focus is on personal relationships that can be restored.

This personal focus should not, however, limit the object of reconciliation to those who have and will accept Christ's work on the cross. The references to "things on earth ... things in heaven" certainly include those forces that continue to oppose him. This verse should therefore be read in light of 2:15, where Christ's triumph over "rulers and authorities" is noted. Many rightly see this act of "reconciliation" as one that includes the idea of "pacification."[103] This idea was not foreign to the first-century Colossians. In the nearby Aphrodisias, there were panels in the North Portico that boasted about Augustus and the Roman Empire pacifying various people groups.[104]

---

98. Cf. Cilliers Breytenbach, *Versöhnung: Eine Studie zur paulinischen Soteriologie* (WMANT 60; Neukirchen-Vluyn: Neukirchener, 1989), 40 – 83.

99. Cf. John T. Fitzgerald, "Paul and Paradigm Shifts: Reconciliation and Its Linkage Group," in *Paul Beyond the Judaism/Hellenism Divide* (ed. Troels Engberg-Pedersen; Louisville: Westminster John Knox, 2001), 241 – 62, 316 – 25.

100. Porter, *Καταλλάσσω in Ancient Greek Literature*, 184.

101. Lohse, *Colossians and Philemon*, 59; Moo, *Letters to the Colossians and to Philemon*, 135.

102. See Richard Bauckham, *God Crucified: Monotheism and Christology in the New Testament* (Grand Rapids: Eerdmans, 1998), 31 – 32, who suggests that this phrase "belongs to the standard rhetoric of Jewish monotheism" (e.g., Isa 44:24; Jer 10:16; 51:19).

103. See, in particular, Peter O'Brien, "Col. 1:20 and the Reconciliation of All Things," *RTR* 33 (1974): 45 – 53.

104. R. R. R. Smith, "*Simulacra Gentium*: The Ethne from the Sebasteion at Aphrodisias," *JRS* 78 (1988): 50 – 77. For the influence of this Aphrodisian Sebasteion structure and

Like the first section of the hymn, this one also contains the three prepositional phrases: "in him" (ἐν αὐτῷ, vv. 16, 19), "through him" (δι' αὐτοῦ, vv. 16, 20), and "for/to him" (εἰς αὐτόν, vv. 16, 20). In light of the consistent usage of the pronoun "him" (αὐτός) in reference to Christ in this hymn, "to him" (εἰς αὐτόν) here should best be taken as also referring to Christ. Most versions prefer to translate this personal pronoun as a reflexive ("to himself")[105] because elsewhere the one to whom the created order is reconciled is always God himself (Rom 5:10; 2 Cor 5:18 – 19).[106] In context, however, the strength of other Pauline usages fails to supersede the clear context where Christ is the agent and the goal of both the original and new creation.[107] The striking departure from these other usages achieves its intended purpose to highlight the close identification between God and Christ. This high Christology provides the critical foundation for Paul's subsequent arguments in this letter.

1:20b-d By making peace through the blood of his cross, [through him] whether things on earth, or things in heaven (εἰρηνοποιήσας διὰ τοῦ αἵματος τοῦ σταυροῦ αὐτοῦ, [δι' αὐτοῦ] εἴτε τὰ ἐπὶ τῆς γῆς εἴτε τὰ ἐν τοῖς οὐρανοῖς). The instrumental circumstantial participle "by making peace" (εἰρηνοποιήσας) provides the means through which the divine act of reconciliation can be accomplished, while the means through which such peace can be accomplished is the death of Christ himself. The idea of "making peace" evokes the OT portrayal of the eschatological restoration:

I am present ...

Like the feet of one bearing the gospel of peace,
Like one bearing the gospel of good tidings,
Because I will make your salvation heard,
Saying to Zion, "Your God will reign!"

(Isa 52:6b – 7 LXX)

And again,

And all your descendants will be taught by God,
And your children will be in great peace.

(Isa 54:13 LXX)

In these passages, the cosmic merges with the political in the portrayal of the fulfillment of God's promises to his people. This portrayal allows Paul to move from the cosmic significance of Christ as emphasized in the hymn to the community being reconciled to him (vv. 21 – 23).

To the Gentile audience in Colossae, "making peace" may also evoke the political propaganda of the early imperial period, where the title "peacemaker" was applied to Roman emperors and generals who established peace by military pacification (Dio Cassius 44.49.2; 72.15.5).[108] Paul's subsequent reference to Jesus' death on the cross thus provides a critique of such power because his reign is established through humility instead of might. This may also explain the absence of explicit references to Jesus' exaltation and enthronement (cf. Phil 2:9).

As "making peace" provides the means for reconciliation, "through the blood of his cross" provides the means for "making peace." The reference to "the blood of his cross" brings the cosmic drama down to the earthly plane where a particularly shameful death accomplishes that which will have cosmic significance. In the context of Colossians,

its Roman imperial ideology in the surrounding regions, see D'Andreia Francesco, "Hierapolis of Phrygia: Its Evolution in Hellenistic and Roman Times," in *Urbanism in Western Asia Minor: New Studies on Aphrodisias, Ephesos, Hierapolis, Pergamon, Perge and Xanthos* (ed. David Parrish; Portsmouth, RI: Journal of Roman Archaeology, 2001), 103.

105. Notable exceptions include NAB ("for him") and NJB ("to him").

106. Lightfoot, *St. Paul's Epistles to the Colossians and to Philemon*, 160.

107. Porter, Καταλλάσσω *in Ancient Greek Literature*, 174, 180.

108. Cf. Harry O. Maier, "A Sly Civility: Colossians and Empire," *JSNT* 27 (2005): 323 – 49.

the graphic portrayal of Jesus' death may also aim at reminding the audience about the significance of the earthly realm in God's salvific purposes.[109] This would then prevent the audience from being preoccupied with the heavenly realm as their retreat from earthly community through ascetic practices.

In his earlier writings, Paul's discussions of reconciliation also contain references to Jesus' death or his shedding of blood, because it is only through his atoning death that the sinful humanity can be reconciled with God (cf. Rom 5:9 – 13; 2 Cor 5:14 – 21). The full ecclesiological significance of this reference to the "blood of his cross" is explicated in Eph 2:13 – 16, a passage that contains references to "blood" and "cross," as well as "peace," "reconcile," and "death."[110] In the context of Ephesians, the focus is on the creation of the new humanity, where Jews and Gentiles can become one. In Colossians, one finds both the focus on the atoning death of Christ (Col 2:13 – 14; 3:13) and the creation of the new humanity (3:11, 15). In any case, in light of the presence of the same conglomeration of ideas elsewhere in Paul, "through the blood of his cross" should not be considered as an "interpretive phrase"[111] interrupting the flow of the original hymn.

"Through him" (δι' αὐτοῦ) is absent in some early manuscripts,[112] but its presence is supported by external evidence of equal strength.[113] Its omission may result in a smoother text, but this may also explain why it was omitted in some manuscripts. In light of the support by the earliest papyrus and the longer reading being the more difficult reading, the phrase should probably be considered as original to the hymn. If so, Christ's role is again emphasized at the end of this hymn.

"Whether things on earth, or things in heaven" again points to the universal scope of Christ's redemptive activity as it parallels the reference to the "heaven – earth" pair in v. 16. As the reconciliation of all things does not point to the willful and enthusiastic submission of all things to Christ, the universal scope of Christ's peacemaking act on the cross should not be considered as affirming the reception of salvation by all humanity. This explains the presence of the call to be faithful to the gospel in the section that immediately follows (v. 23; cf. 3:5, 6).

1:21 And you were once alienated and hostile in mind through evil deeds (Καὶ ὑμᾶς ποτε ὄντας ἀπηλλοτριωμένους καὶ ἐχθροὺς τῇ διανοίᾳ ἐν τοῖς ἔργοις τοῖς πονηροῖς). From Christ's status, Paul now switches to the former sinful state of the readers prior to being reconciled to Christ. This verse introduces the next subsection, which constitutes one long sentence (vv. 21 – 23), which accomplishes two functions. First, it provides an application of the Colossian hymn (vv. 15 – 20) for the situation of the Colossians. The most obvious link lies in the reference to reconciliation in v. 22. As the final section of the hymn points to God's act of reconciliation through Christ, this section applies this reconciliation to one particular community. The universal sovereignty of Christ also provides the basis for Paul's affirmation of the universal claim of the gospel, "which has been proclaimed in all creation under heaven" (v. 23). This brief subsection in turn provides a way to read the preceding hymn as dealing with the consequence of the fall, which makes such an act of reconciliation necessary, as explicitly noted in terms such as "alienated," "hostile," and "evil deeds" (v. 21).

---

109. See Jerome Murphy-O'Connor, *Paul: A Critical Life* (Oxford: Clarendon, 1996), 240, who rightly notes that the earthly focus of Christ's death is at least as striking as the high Christology in this hymn.

110. See Gourgues, "La foi chrétienne primitive face à la croix," 49 – 69.

111. Lohse, *Colossians and Philemon*, 60.

112. B D* F G I 0278 81 1175 1739 1881 2464.

113. 𝔓⁴⁶ ℵ A C D¹ Ψ 046ᵛⁱᵈ 33 𝔐.

Moreover, the reference to Christ's "death" (v. 22) also reinforces the centrality of Christ's humiliation in the hymn.

The second function for this subsection is to pave the way for Paul's arguments in the rest of this letter. In rhetorical terms, some have considered this section the *partitio* in which three themes are identified: (1) the work of Christ for the believers (vv. 21 – 22), (2) the call to be faithful to the gospel (v. 23a-f), and (3) Paul as the one who proclaims this gospel (v. 23g). This corresponds to the main arguments in the *probatio* (1:24 – 4:1) in reverse order: (1) the role of the apostle Paul (1:24 – 2:5), (2) the call to faithfulness (2:6 – 23), and (3) the response of the believers to the work of Christ (3:1 – 4:1).[114] Others have pointed to the unique significance of vv. 21 – 22 as setting out the "thesis" for this letter: the Colossians are to be convinced of the new reality they find in Christ, as they are now reconciled to him and so are holy, spotless, and blameless before him.[115]

The main clause in this long sentence lies in v. 22a, and this verse provides a description of the object of the act of reconciliation in v. 22. "You" (ὑμᾶς) is the object of the verb "he has reconciled" (ἀποκατήλλαξεν, v. 22). The two participles translated as "were ... alienated" (ὄντας ἀπηλλοτριωμένους) form a periphrastic construction that "illustrates the emphatic weight the author gives to the state of alienation."[116] The first participle (ὄντας), which governs both the participle "alienated" (ἀπηλλοτριωμένους) and the adjective "enemies" (ἐχθρούς), can be taken as a concessive circumstantial participle ("although you

were ... alienated and hostile," NASB), but it may also include a temporal sense as suggested in the word "once" (ποτε).[117]

A genitive of separation is often expected after the verb "alienated" (cf. Eph 2:12; 4:18). In light of the preceding verse, where reconciliation assumes the hostility between Creator and the created, "alienated" can only refer to alienation *from God*.[118] The parallel that follows, "hostile in mind through evil deeds," further supports this reading. "And" (καί), which connects "alienated" and "hostile in mind," is best taken as epexegetical, so that the latter expression explains the alienation. The mention of "mind" and "deeds" points to the alienation of the entire person and thus also the predicament of humanity apart from the redemptive act of God.

Paul does not provide the reasons for their alienation from God here because the focus is on the Colossians' present status as having been reconciled. The parallel in Eph 4:18 – 19, however, is helpful here, especially when one also finds the notion of alienation and evil behavior:

> They are darkened in their understanding and separated from the life of God because of the ignorance that is in them due to the hardening of their hearts. Having lost all sensitivity, they have given themselves over to sensuality so as to indulge in every kind of impurity, and they are full of greed.

1:22a-b But now he has reconciled you in his body of flesh through death (νυνὶ δὲ ἀποκατήλλαξεν ἐν τῷ σώματι τῆς σαρκὸς αὐτοῦ διὰ τοῦ θανάτου).

Because of the death of Christ, believers are now reconciled to Christ. "But now" is contrasted with the

---

114. Thus Aletti, *Saint Paul Épître aux Colossiens*, 39, who classifies the rhetorical genre of this letter as deliberative.

115. Cf. Jerry L. Sumney, "The Argument of Colossians," in *Rhetorical Argumentation in Biblical Texts: Essays from the Lund 2000 Conference* (ed. Anders Eriksson, Thomas H. Olbricht, and Walter Übelacker; Harrisburg, PA: Trinity International, 2002), 346.

116. Porter, Καταλλάσσω *in Ancient Greek Literature*, 94; cf. BDF §352.

117. Cf. Rom 5:8: "While we were still sinners, Christ died for us." The same ambiguity exists in a similar construction in Col 2:13 (see comments there).

118. Cf. "You who were once far away from God" (NLT; cf. REB).

"once" in the previous verse. This "once … now" contrast appears often in Paul in the description of the radical change in the lives of the believers (cf. Rom 11:30; Gal 1:23; 4:8–9; cf. Rom 3:21) as "the gravity of their previous condition serves to magnify the wonder of God's mercy."[119]

While it is clear that "he has reconciled" (ἀποκατήλλαξεν) points back to the act of reconciliation already noted in v. 20, the subject of this verb is less clear.[120] In light of v. 20, many see "God" as the subject: "by Christ's death in his body of flesh and blood God has reconciled you to himself" (REB). In this context where the focus is consistently on Christ, however, the implied subject of an unspecified third person singular verb should be Christ himself: "Yet now he has reconciled you to himself through the death of Christ in his physical body" (NLT). As noted above, "all the fullness" (v. 19) is used as a periphrasis for God precisely to have the focus remain on Christ. Again, this ambiguity may be intentional as Christ now assumes the role of his Father in accomplishing his redemptive will.

The relationship between the two prepositions in the phrase "in his body of flesh through death" (ἐν τῷ σώματι τῆς σαρκὸς αὐτοῦ διὰ τοῦ θανάτου) is not clearly defined. While "through" (διά) denotes the means through which the act of reconciliation is accomplished, "in" (ἐν) can point to the general circumstances through which

the act is accomplished. Yet it seems best to take ἐν as also indicating the means of reconciliation: "he has reconciled you by Christ's physical body through death" (TNIV, NIV). "In his body of flesh" may point to the necessity of his incarnation, and "through death" may point to the necessity of his atoning death.[121] In light of the frequent use of the phrase "in him" (ἐν αὐτῷ) in the hymn (vv. 16, 17, 19), however, "in his body of flesh" may also evoke those references and specify the earthly reality of Christ's existence. Moreover, ἐν may then point to personal or direct agency,[122] while διά is used to express impersonal or intermediate means.

"Body of flesh" refers to the physicality of the body. "Body" (σῶμα) here is different from the "body" of v. 18.[123] Nevertheless, it is the shift from the universal to the earthly existence that Paul is emphasizing. The church that is his body originated from this particular body that was the object of both rejection and vindication. Elsewhere in Paul, "flesh" (σάρξ) often refers to one's sinful nature (Col 2:13, 23; cf. Rom 6:19; 7:18, 25; Gal 5:13, 24). In this context, however, it is used without negative connotations and refers to Christ's physical existence.[124]

"Through death" (διὰ τοῦ θανάτου) constitutes the first reference to Jesus' death in this section (cf. vv. 18, 20). The climactic act of salvation is accomplished at the end of Jesus' earthly existence,[125] a note that may pave the way for Paul's argument

---

119. O'Brien, *Colossians, Philemon*, 66.

120. This problem is less pronounced if we adopt the passive form (ἀποκατηλλάγητε) as supported by a few important manuscripts (𝔓[46] B). But in light of the infinitive that follows, this reading does not fit well into this context: "you were reconciled … to present you." Precisely because of the difficulty of this reading, many see this as the original reading; see Metzger, *Textual Commentary*, 554–55; Moo, *Letters to the Colossians and to Philemon*, 141; Sumney, *Colossians*, 84.

121. O'Brien, *Colossians, Philemon*, 68. Cf. "his Son became a human and died" (CEV).

122. Unlike the "in him" (ἐν αὐτῷ) references in the hymn that are not limited to the instrumental function, this function is clear here in light of this specific context.

123. Elsewhere in Paul, however, the two can be used together without significant difference in meaning (cf. 1 Cor 15:38–39).

124. This use is common in both Greek and Jewish literature. For an account of the development of the particular Pauline use of the "flesh" (σάρξ) in contrast to the "spirit" (πνεῦμα), see Robert Jewett, *Paul's Anthropological Terms: A Study of Their Use in Conflict Settings* (AGJU 10; Leiden: Brill, 1971), 95–166 (cf. also REB: "his body of flesh and blood").

125. Cf. John 6:51: "This bread is my flesh [σάρξ], which I will give for the life of the world." Notably, John has already used this term in reference to Jesus' incarnation (1:14).

against those who focus on heavenly visions while denigrating their earthly bodies (cf. 2:18 – 23).

1:22c-e In order to present you holy, without blemish, and blameless before him (παραστῆσαι ὑμᾶς ἁγίους καὶ ἀμώμους καὶ ἀνεγκλήτους κατενώπιον αὐτοῦ). The goal of the atoning death of Jesus is made clear with this purpose clause as believers become acceptable in his sight. In LXX, the verb "to present" (παραστῆσαι) is often used in reference to human beings standing before God (cf. Deut 18:5, 7; 21:5; Job 1:6; 2:1; Jer 42:19 [LXX; Eng. 35:19]; Dan 7:10, 13). In Paul, this verb can point to either one's present status before God (Rom 6:16, 19; 12:1) or one's standing before him during the time of the final judgment (Rom 14:10; 2 Cor 4:14). The transitive sense may evoke a cultic or sacrificial context, as in Rom 12:1: "I urge you … to offer [παραστῆσαι] your bodies as a living sacrifice, holy and pleasing to God."

The sacrificial reading is supported by the reference to Jesus' death in v. 22, and his "blood" in particular in v. 20. As in Rom 12:1, this presentation may point to the present status of believers, who have already gained access to God: "he has brought you into his own presence, and you are holy and blameless as you stand before him without a single fault" (NLT).[126] This progressive reading that does not downplay the present reality is confirmed by the use of the same verb in v. 28.

The words "holy," "without blemish," and "blameless" provide further support to reading this verse in light of a sacrificial context. In the Old Testament, the word "holy" often appears in cultic contexts especially in reference to the "holy place" (Exod 26:33; 28:43; Lev 14:13; 1 Kgs 8:8; Isa 63:18), "holy altar" (Exod 29:37; 40:10; Lev 10:12), or even "holy offerings" (Lev 2:3; Num 18:8, 9, 19, 32; Neh 10:33; Ezek 42:13; 44:13). "Without blemish"

likewise points to a sacrificial victim that must be without defect (Exod 29:1; Lev 1:3; Num 6:14; Ezek 43:22). "Blameless," however, is found primarily in moral discourse (cf. 3 Macc 5:31).[127] In Paul, this term refers both to the present behavior of believers (1 Tim 3:10; Titus 1:6 – 7) as well as to their status before Christ in the final judgment (1 Cor 1:8). This combination of terms may then point to both cultic and ethical aspects, especially when a strict separation between the cultic and the ethical cannot be made in Paul (cf. Eph 5:2; Phil 4:18).

The essence of this verse is well expressed through the mouth of a different biblical author: "we have been made holy through the sacrifice of the body of Jesus Christ once for all.… For by one sacrifice he has made perfect forever those who are being made holy" (Heb 10:10, 14). Both authors, while not denying the present reality of sinful struggle, emphasize the power and finality of Jesus' atoning death.

In applying these terms to the believers, Paul may also have in mind Jesus, who is himself the holy and perfect sacrifice. Paul refers to Christ as the "fragrant offering and sacrifice to God" (Eph 5:2), but perhaps this is best stated in 1 Pet 1:18 – 19: "you were redeemed … with the precious blood of Christ, a lamb without blemish or defect." In Colossians, Paul is likewise moving from the perfect atoning death of Christ (v. 20) to the effect of this sacrifice in the lives of the believers here. This anticipates Paul's further identification of the believers with the death and resurrection of Christ in 2:20 and 3:1.

As in the previous uses of the pronoun αὐτός in reference to Christ, "before him" (κατενώπιον αὐτοῦ) also refers to Christ. This phrase can refer to the present age (cf. "before his sight," KJV, NKJV, TNIV, NIV) or the final judgment (cf. "into his own presence," REB). In light of the frequent uses

---

126. Cf. Moule, *Epistles to the Colossians and to Philemon*, 76.

127. Cf. "irreproachable" (BDAG, 76), and "above reproach" (ESV).

of the related word "before" (ἐνώπιον) elsewhere in Paul in the sense of "in the sight of" or "in the opinion of" (Rom 3:20; 12:17; 14:22; 1 Cor 1:29; 2 Cor 4:2; 7:12; 8:21; 1 Tim 2:3; 5:4), a future reference is not necessary.

1:23a-e If indeed you continue in the faith, established and steadfast, not shifting from the hope of the gospel, which you heard (εἴ γε ἐπιμένετε τῇ πίστει τεθεμελιωμένοι καὶ ἑδραῖοι καὶ μὴ μετακινούμενοι ἀπὸ τῆς ἐλπίδος τοῦ εὐαγγελίου οὗ ἠκούσατε). Paul now calls the believers to stand firm in the gospel that has already been working among them. "If indeed" introduces a conditional clause, modifying the infinitive "to present" in v. 22. The believers' continuous walk in the gospel is the condition of, but not the basis for, Christ's presentation of them.

The emphatic particle "indeed" (γε) "often becomes no more than a meaningless appendage,"[128] but when used with "if" (εἰ) it can point to a more "definite condition."[129] In the NT, the phrase "if indeed" appears only in Paul, and it can denote both more probable (2 Cor 5:3; Eph 3:2; 4:21) and less probable (Gal 3:4) conditions. In this case, the focus should not be on the probability of the condition, although elsewhere in this letter one does find Paul affirming the likelihood of this condition being fulfilled (cf. 1:3 – 6; 2:5). The focus is rather on the conditionality of the statement as it functions as a call for the Colossian believers to be faithful to the gospel they have received (cf. 2:6 – 7).[130]

In Greek, a personal pronoun is lacking in the phrase "your faith" (τῇ πίστει), one that can refer to either the objective gospel (cf. "the faith," KJV, NAB, NASB, NKJV, NRSV, NJB, NET, ESV, and "this truth," NLT) or the personal faith[131] of the believers (cf. "your faith," CEV, TNIV, NIV). The objective sense is present in this letter (2:7), but Paul often refers to their faith/faithfulness (1:4; 2:5, 12). In this context, however, in light of the reference to the objective gospel introduced in the second part of this verse, a subjective reference is more likely (cf. also Rom 11:23).

The phrase "established and steadfast" refers to their own conviction and persistence in the act of believing or being faithful. As such, these two terms also support the reading of "your faith." The perfect passive participle ("established") is paired with the adjective "steadfast" in the description of the kind of faith required of the believers. "Established" possibly draws on the building metaphor in stressing the strength of the foundation of faith (cf. Matt 7:25).[132] But in light of the preceding hymn where creation is the focus, the word "established" may share this conceptual framework in evoking the foundation of the world,[133] as noted in Ps 102:25 (LXX 101:26): "In the beginning you laid the foundations [ἐθεμελίωσας] of the earth, and the heavens are the work of your hands" (cf. Heb 1:10). In response to God's new creative acts in Christ, Paul calls his audience to provide a proper response by standing firm and secure in their faith.

Although "not shifting" (μὴ μετακινούμενοι)[134]

---

128. BDF §439.

129. BDF §454(2).

130. Some have denied the true conditionality of this clause because "Paul does not convey doubt with the words … but expects that the Colossians will do so" (Judith M. Gundry Volf, *Paul and Perseverance: Staying In and Falling Away* [Louisville: Westminster John Knox, 1990], 197 n. 231). The nature of the simple conditional sentence does not, however, support this condition (cf. Wallace, *Greek Grammar*, 690 – 91). See also Robert A. Peterson, "The Perseverance of the Saints: A Theological Exegesis of Four Key New Testa-

ment Passages," *Presb* 17 (1991): 95 – 112.

131. Or "faithfulness" (cf. "faithful," TEV).

132. Cf. the translation of the two terms "established and steadfast," with the phrase "firm on your foundations" (REB).

133. This, of course, can also be considered an extension of the building metaphor.

134. This translation takes this verb as a middle participle. For those who take it as a passive participle, a reference to the false teachers may be implied: "are not moved away" (NKJV; cf. KJV, NASB, REV).

may be particularly relevant for an audience that
would not be surprised by seismic activity,[135] this
word group together with the reference to "steadfast" has already appeared in Paul's earlier writings:
"be steadfast, do not be moved" (ἑδραῖοι γίνεσθε,
ἀμετακίνητοι, 1 Cor 15:58).

"The hope of the gospel" (τῆς ἐλπίδος τοῦ
εὐαγγελίου) likely refers to "the hope generated by
the gospel," with "the gospel" being a genitive of
source. The gospel is understood as an active agent
that can grow and bear fruit (1:5 – 6). As in 1:5, this
hope is not a subjective sentiment but the object
on which such sentiment rests. "Which you heard"
likewise recalls 1:5, and in this instance it modifies "the gospel." Here, Paul is again reminding his
readers to stand firm in a gospel that has already
begun to work among them and has proven to be
effective among them.

**1:23f-g Which has been proclaimed in all cre-
ation under heaven, and of which I, Paul, became
a servant** (τοῦ κηρυχθέντος ἐν πάσῃ κτίσει τῇ ὑπὸ
τὸν οὐρανόν, οὗ ἐγενόμην ἐγὼ Παῦλος διάκονος).
This verse not only points to the universal scope
of the gospel; it also provides the transition to a
section that focuses on Paul as its messenger. The
attributive participle "which has been proclaimed"
provides further definition to "the gospel." The
claim that the gospel has been preached "in all creation under heaven" (cf. NASB, REB, NET, ESV)
is a bit surprising because it appears to be a claim
that is yet to be fulfilled in Paul's time. While some
translations have "to every creature" (KJV, NAB,
NJB, NKJV, NRSV, TNIV, NIV), the Greek term
behind "creature" (κτίσις) is more often used in
the sense of "creation" elsewhere in Paul (Rom

1:20; 8:19, 20, 21, 22; 2 Cor 5:17; Gal 6:15). More
importantly, this is how the word is used in the
preceding hymn (v. 15), and the focus is on the
universal claim of the gospel rather than its individual distributive reception. Therefore, as Christ
is the "firstborn of all creation" (v. 15), his gospel
demands the submission of all creation.

Second, it should not be assumed that Paul
is referring to the preaching of the gospel to the
"great centers of the Empire"[136] since a particular
geographical reading is insufficient in this context.
Instead of simply labeling this claim as a "hyperbole,"[137] the eschatological, cosmic, and confessional nature of this note must be understood. As
in the preceding hymn where "firstborn from the
dead" (v. 18) points to the beginning of the new eschatological era in which one finds the fulfillment
of God's redemptive act, this phrase may focus on
the universal impact of the power of the cross that
is yet to be fully revealed.

In cosmic terms, the universality emphasized
here should not simply be understood in geo-
graphical/horizontal terms ("every person everywhere"), but in cosmic/vertical terms ("every realm
of beings"). A possible parallel can be identified in
Rev 5:13:

> Then I heard every creature in heaven and on
> earth and under the earth and on the sea, and all
> that is in them, saying: "To him who sits on the
> throne and to the Lamb be praise and honor and
> glory and power, for ever and ever!"

The focus is on the cosmic submission to God and
his Son, not simply on the geographical expansion
of the gospel proclamation.

Finally, as this section seeks to apply the christo-

---

135. Cf. Larry J. Kreitzer, "Living in the Lycus Valley:
Earthquake Imagery in Colossians, Philemon and Ephesians,"
in *Testimony and Interpretation: Early Christology in its Judeo-
Hellenistic Milieu: Studies in Honour of Petr Pokorý* (ed. Jiří
Mrázek and Jan Roskovec; JSNTSup 272; London: T&T Clark,
2004), 81 – 94.

136. Moule, *Epistles to the Colossians and to Philemon*, 73.
137. Cf. "in every place"; Lightfoot, *St. Paul's Epistles to the
Colossians and to Philemon*, 163.

logical confession in vv. 15 – 20, the nature of such a confession needs to be noted. Universal claim often finds its place in such confessional material. See, for example, the confession in 1 Tim 3:16:

> He appeared in the flesh,
> > was vindicated by the Spirit,
> was seen by angels,
> > was preached among the nations,
> was believed on in the world,
> > was taken up in glory.

In confessions, universal claims are to be expected. These are not exaggerated claims, however, because they do point to a reality guaranteed by God's act through his Son.

"Of which I, Paul, became a servant" points ahead to the next section, where Paul describes his apostolic role in God's redemptive plan. With this verse, one also finds the implicit claim that the gospel that Paul preaches is the one and only universal gospel. The label "servant" (διάκονος) has already been introduced in v. 7, where it refers also to a minister of the gospel ministry (cf. v. 25). This title emphasizes both Paul's submission to his calling from the risen Lord as well as his authority as one who represents this gospel ministry.

Theology in Application

The Universal and the Particular Christ

To many, Christology may not be the most pragmatic of all topics, but it forms the basis for Paul's attempt to alter the behavior of the Colossian believers. Instead of being directed to Christ, this hymn depicts the status and work of Christ for the sake of the readers. In doing so, Paul provides a christocentric framework within which all beliefs and practices are to be evaluated. In seeking to apply this material, therefore, one must begin with the content of this confession.

The exalted status of Christ is affirmed through his identity with God the Creator. The power of God as Creator is consistently affirmed in the OT (cf. Gen 14:19, 22; Pss 96:5; 121:2; 146:5 – 6; Isa 40:12 – 31; 51:13); thus, to consider Christ as the agent of creation is to identify him as someone who shares the essence of his Father. In early Christian confessions, the present (Acts 2:34, 36; Col 3:17; 1 Thess 4:1 – 2) and future (Acts 3:19; Phil 2:11; 1 Thess 4:17) lordship of Christ is repeatedly noted, but the emphasis on the eternal lordship of Christ does not appear to have the same immediate utility for the Christian life. It is therefore remarkable to find Paul emphasizing Christ as the unique agent of creation. In this remarkable inclusion of Jesus "in the unique divine sovereignty not only eschatologically but also protologically,"[138] one finds the essential identification of Jesus with his Father. This "participation of Christ in the creative work of God is necessary, in Jewish monotheistic terms, to complete the otherwise incomplete inclusion of him in the divine identity."[139] If worship is considered a legitimate "application" of this hymn, the worship of Christ as the one and only Son is to be our first and immediate reaction to reading this text.

---

138. Baukham, *God Crucified*, 35.   139. Ibid., 36.

The emphasis on the universal submission of all things flows directly out of the confession of Christ as the Lord of all. The repeated reference to "all things" (vv. 16, 17, 18, 20), the all-encompassing description "in heaven and on earth, visible and invisible" (v. 16; cf. v. 20), as well as the rhetorically powerful list in v. 16, "thrones or dominions or rulers or authorities," all serve to underline the universal sovereignty of Christ.

Read against this emphasis on Christ's sovereignty, the particular themes noted in this text are all the more noteworthy. Moving beyond wisdom traditions, the affirmation of the fact of incarnation (v. 19) redirects one's attention to the earthly reality of Christ as the universal Lord who manifests himself in one earthly individual. The striking coexistence of the universal and the particular is matched by the appearance of the theology of suffering in the midst of the theology of glory. Shifting his attention from creation to the particularity of the "cross" and the physicality of the "blood" (v. 20), Paul challenges the dualism between heaven and earth, between the material and the spiritual. It is precisely because of his universal significance that his death can bring about universal restoration (v. 20; cf. v. 22).

It is also because of his role as the Lord of all that his resurrection becomes a sign for the future deliverance of believers (v. 18). In this text, therefore, one searches in vain to find a general model of liberation.[140] Instead, one finds the Son of God, whose atoning death on the cross brings about reconciliation and whose resurrection from the dead points to eternal glory. The striking paralleling of the two sections (vv. 15 – 16, 18b – 20) of this hymn confirms this point when the new creation parallels that of the first, but the power is no longer manifested by the act of creating, but by the death that conquers all.

In the context of Colossians, the coexistence of the universal and the particular is a peculiar feature of NT Christology.[141] To emphasize one over against the other is to cease to be faithful to the true gospel. To the Colossian believers, to emphasize the cosmic Christ apart from the power of his atoning death is to lead to the thirst for visionary experience and the misled insistence on ascetic behavior. In the modern context, one also finds the temptation to emphasize the universality of the power of the gospel while ignoring its particular demands. By contrast, for those who emphasize only the particularities of the historical Jesus, one finds the refusal to acknowledge him to be the Lord of all. As the NT witnesses remind us, only a healthy Christology can allow us to appropriate fully the gospel message.

In Colossians, Paul begins by establishing the theological framework in which Christians are to worship. From a rich understanding of who Christ is and what he has done on our behalf, Christian worship flows naturally. Thus it is imperative

---

140. For a critique of those who replace the particularity of death and resurrection with the general notion of liberation, see the helpful discussion in Marva J. Dawn, *Powers, Weak-ness, and the Tabernacling of God* (Grand Rapids: Eerdmans, 2001), 16 – 17.

141. Cf. Bauckham, "Where Is Wisdom to Be Found?" 134.

that we understand more fully the person of Christ to enrich our worship of him. But Paul is also combating improper worship, which includes people who seek to worship a Christ who conformed to their legalistic and mystic structures. Against this, Paul presents the unique Son, Creator, and incarnate Redeemer. Christology undergoes a similar assault today. People try to merge the Christian Redeemer with the principles of the Tao or propose a kind of liberation apart from Christ. Paul's message of the unique Son combats this syncretistic tendency, and it pronounces the exclusive sufficiency of the gospel for salvation because it rests on the incomparable and singular Christ. Only a high Christology can combat the modern claims of pluralism and inclusivism.

Paul considers this high Christology to be an essential aspect of the gospel message of which the main parts are in this section. Thus, this section can serve as an effective evangelistic tool. Paul covers the sinfulness of human beings by describing them as under the dominion of darkness; they are separated from God by nature. The transference from the kingdom of darkness to the kingdom of light occurs only through the redemption that Paul describes as the forgiveness of sins accomplished by the Son. Paul then sees it necessary to describe the weightiness of the sacrifice, and by implication the sinfulness of humanity, by describing the exaltedness of the one who is sacrificed. Verses 15 – 17 show how great the Son is, and v. 18 relates the greatness of the Son to the redeemed as his resurrection is prototypical for humans.

This great redemption is similarly described as an act of peacemaking in v. 20, where the hostility of humanity toward God and God toward humanity is placated through his blood. Verse 21 reemphasizes the fallen state of humanity in their rebellion against God, and v. 22 further describes the reconciliation as accomplished through the physical death of Christ. There are a few other places in the NT where the gospel is summarized in a nutshell. I suggest that 1:13 – 23 can be a useful way for Christians to work through their understanding of the gospel message and use it as a profitable text for the evangelization of the unbelievers.

Christ and the Church

Some have been surprised by the appearance of "the church" (v. 18) in this hymn, but the move from God's creation of the world and the creation of his people is one that is not unexpected in the biblical context. Already in Genesis, the climax of the creation can be considered to be the call of Abraham in Gen 12, an act that begins the process of the creation of God's own people. In remembering the exodus account, which signifies a significant step in the relationship between God and his people, one also finds the psalmists evoking God's power in his creative acts (cf. Pss 74:12 – 17; 77:12 – 20; 89:5 – 37; 114:1 – 8; 136:4 – 17). Even in the prophetic traditions, where one finds God's promise concerning the restoration of his people in the new exodus, the creative act of God is again repeatedly noted (cf. Isa 40:12 – 31; 42:5; 44:24;

45:9 – 18; 48:12 – 13; 51:12 – 16).[142] This is possible because the Creator of the world is "Israel's Creator" (cf. Isa 43:15). In Paul's depiction of the fulfillment of the new exodus promises, therefore, one should not be surprised to find that God's original creative act culminates in the creation of his true people in the end times. The explicit note of the "church" (v. 18) in the central section, therefore, should not be considered an afterthought or an interpolation in this christological confession.

A healthy doctrine of the church must be rooted in God's redemptive act in history. Without drawing out a full Pauline ecclesiology from this brief section, a few points need to be highlighted in light of the context of the hymn. First, as the head of the church, the lordship of Christ over the church is affirmed. For Paul, this is not an abstract statement that points simply to Christ as the head of the organizational chart of the church. Christ is the ground and purpose of the existence of this church. As creation discourse often aims at unmasking the false claims of idols (Pss 96:3 – 6; 115:2 – 16; 135:5 – 18; Isa 40:18 – 24; 41:4 – 7; 46:1 – 4), to claim that Christ is the agent of the new creation and the head of the church is to identify him as the sole object of worship. To replace Christ with other means in approaching God becomes an idolatrous act.

Second, when the church is connected to Christ, believers who "have been filled in him" (2:10) share in his lordship over all powers and authorities.[143] Believers are no longer threatened by other spiritual forces because of the work of Christ. As the "firstborn from the dead" (v. 18), believers can also claim victory against the final enemy, death. Although not fully consummated, the salvation Christ provides is already a present reality that points toward the final restoration of all things.

Third, the community of God's people as the earthly representative of God/Christ is also important. Some have considered the phrase "the image of the invisible God" (v. 15) "deliberately subversive,"[144] as it points to the concrete manifestation of the Creator God in the earthly realm, thus challenging all other means of divine representation. The affirmation of Christ's human body as shedding blood on the cross also challenges the assumption that ascension is the way through which God can be known.[145] Moreover, in light of the reappearance of this concept in 3:10, it is clear that the church is also called to carry on the task of being the "image of God"

---

142. See Richard J. Clifford, *Fair Spoken and Persuading: An Interpretation of Second Isaiah* (New York: Paulist, 1984), 23, who notes that in modern understanding, "the historic type is called redemption and the cosmogonic type is called creation. They are however the same event — the emergence of Israel as a people before Yahweh."

143. See Fee, *Pauline Christology*, 307. As discussed above, these powers and authorities should be taken primarily as referring to spiritual and cosmic realities, rather than particular earthly political systems.

144. Crispin H. T. Fletcher-Louis, "The Image of God and

the Biblical Roots of Christian Sacramentality," in *The Gestures of God: Explorations in Sacramentality* (ed. Geoffrey Rowell and Christine Hall; New York: Continuum, 2004), 75.

145. For a recent discussion of Paul's understanding of the "image of God" against Second Temple Jewish Wisdom traditions, see Stefanie Lorenzen, *Das paulinische Eikon-Konzept: Semantische Analysen zur Sapientia Salomonis, zu Philo und den Paulusbriefen* (WUNT 2.250; Tübingen: Mohr Siebeck, 2008), 139 – 256, who emphasizes that the significant novelty of Paul's use of this phrase lies in his focus on the perfected physical body of Christ (cf. 1 Cor 15:49) (156).

through its proclamation of the gospel in words and in deeds. Believers therefore assume the dignity of being an instrument of divine revelation, through whom "the invisible God" can be made known.

Christ and Creation

Despite a strong focus on God's creation, the precise way such a focus should be applied to the contemporary contexts needs to be articulated carefully. Some have suggested that this hymn affirms a sacred cosmology, which in turn provides a Christology that contributes to current ecological concerns:

> The Sophia-nature of this ancient early Christian hymn and the language of creation that permeates it reinforce what we might anachronistically call an ecologically sensitive, creation-tempered christology.[146]

This reading fails to be supported by a close reading of this hymn, however. First, instead of affirming the sacred nature of the cosmos, this hymn actually insists on the distinction between the Creator and the created. Instead of aiming at providing "an ecologically sensitive" Christology, this hymn emphasizes the submission of all things to Christ (v. 16). Moreover, the need for a new creation (v. 18b) as well as the notion of reconciliation (v. 20) presupposes the fall, an event that has affected "things on earth" and "things in heaven" (v. 20). Therefore, the mere presence of creation language does not support a "sacred cosmology."

This hymn does, however, provide a proper understanding of creation. The "christological monotheism"[147] allows Paul to affirm that the restoration of all things is possible only because of God's redemptive act through Christ. The singular act of Christ's death on the cross affects all creation and brings about the renewal of all things. The restoration of all things rests, however, in the future with the consummation of God's redemptive plan: "the creation itself will be liberated from its bondage to decay and brought into the freedom and glory of the children of God" (Rom 8:21).

Even in reference to the redeemed creation, the role of the incarnated Christ and the focus of God's people in this new creation should be noted. Calvin's discussion of these critical ingredients, as summarized by a modern synthesis of his doctrine of creation, provides a more helpful discussion even for our contemporary audience:

> ... the *Logos* who orders existence and its intelligibility, and the Word incarnate through whom alone life reaches its goal; the providence which preserves all life, even after the perfidy of human sin, and the providence which especially guards the community of the elect; a humanity which bears God's image as qualities of excellence

---

146. Michael Trainor, "The Cosmic Christology of Colossians 1:15 – 20 in the Light of Contemporary Ecological Issues," *ABR* 53 (2005): 69.

147. Bauckham, "Where Is Wisdom to Be Found?" 134.

engraved by a loving hand, and a humanity which can truly mirror God's excellence and goodness only as remade in the image of Christ.[148]

Calvin's reading points to the resources Paul provides in articulating a healthy doctrine of creation. Read in light of the wider redemptive plan of God, concerns for creation can find their place in our attempt to be faithful to the gospel of Jesus Christ.

Christ's Work and Human Responses

The brief section (vv. 21 – 23) that follows the christological hymn points to a response required in light of God's redemptive work through Christ. The conditional statement embedded in this section highlights the urgency for a proper response. Consistent with the teachings of Paul elsewhere (cf. Rom 8:12 – 17; 1 Cor 15:1 – 2) and of the other NT witnesses (cf. John 8:31 – 32, 51; Heb 2:1 – 18; 4:11 – 16; 5:11 – 6:20; 1 John 2:20 – 25), the sovereign and mighty acts of God are mentioned together with the emphasis on human responsibility. In this context, Paul is also calling believers to be faithful to Christ and his gospel while at the same time insisting on the finality of Christ's atoning death, through which eschatological restoration becomes a reality.

Paul's emphasis on reconciliation (v. 20, 22) forces one to realize that the perceived freedom and autonomy that one assumes to possess is but a deceptive ploy imposed by the spiritual powers and forces (v. 16). Rather than focusing on the liberation of the self and the attainment of individual autonomy, Paul points to the existence of true freedom "in Christ" (cf. vv. 16, 17, 19).[149] In labeling one's existence prior to Christ's act of reconciliation as "hostile in mind" (v. 21), Paul reminds his audience that one can either remain faithful in Christ or fight against him. Not only should one take off "the old humanity with its practices" (3:9) as one repents from one's evil behavior; even reliance on one's self as one approaches God becomes an idolatrous act that rejects the power of Christ and his cross (2:18 – 19).

Finally, in situating the story of humanity's redemption within the wider story of the cosmos, Paul reminds his readers that "the choice to become a follower of Jesus involves more than simply a different lifestyle, attitude, or understanding. Far more profoundly, choosing to follow Jesus involves a choice between different visions of reality itself."[150] Within this vision of reality, one finds the ontological identity of Christ, the significance of the church, the lordship of Christ over all, and God's

---

148. Peter Wyatt, *Jesus Christ and Creation in the Theology of John Calvin* (PTMS 42; Allison Park, PA: Pickwick, 1996), 81.

149. Cf. Richard L. Christensen, "Colossians 1:15 – 28," *Int* 61 (2007): 318 – 20, who provides a critique of modern notions of individualism and autonomy. One should be reminded, however, that Paul's does not deny the significance of an individual's standing before God, and individual responsibility is

repeatedly emphasized before the focus on the significance of the redeemed community.

150. Michael P. Knowles, "'Christ in You, the Hope of Glory': Discipleship in Colossians," in *Patterns of Discipleship in the New Testament* (ed. Richard N. Longenecker; Grand Rapids: Eerdmans, 1996), 186.

redemptive plan for the entire cosmos. Paul is not content to provide a quick solution to the problems among the Colossian believers; instead, he traces problematic behavior to a false perception of reality. Discipleship is therefore understood as no less than the transformation of the mind, and only through such transformation can the will of God be discerned (Rom 12:2).

For the contemporary audience, this section reminds us that christological discussions are not simply theoretical speculations. The doctrine of Christ leads to doctrines of soteriology, sanctification, missions, and eschatology. The remaining sections of this letter will demonstrate how these doctrines find their roots in Christ.

4

Colossians 1:24 – 2:5

Literary Context

This section follows the christological confession in 1:15 – 20, which has provided the critical foundation for this entire letter. In the form of a hymn, the exalted status of Christ is affirmed through a description of both his role in creation (vv. 15 – 16) and his death and resurrection (vv. 18b – 20), which climaxes in his role as the sustainer of all things (vv. 17 – 18a). Paul emphasizes how the death of Jesus in his physical body has completed the act of reconciliation through which believers can approach God. In response to this act, Paul also urges the Colossians to stand firmly in the gospel that they had received.

The status of Paul as Christ's "servant," noted at the end of the previous section (1:23), becomes the focus of this next section. The gospel now centers on the ministry of one particular apostolic bearer of this gospel. This connection between the cosmic Christ and the particular servant explains a number of parallels that exist between these two sections: suffering (1:24, 29; 2:1; cf. 1:18, 20), physical body (1:24; cf. 1:22), church (1:24; cf. 1:18), and Christ (1:24, 27, 28; 2:5; cf. 1:15 – 20).

Although this section focuses on Paul's unique role as an apostle, he first makes it clear that he is not the center of the gospel message. His role within God's wider plan is to be the "servant of the church" (v. 25). Second, in a section flooded with the first person singular, the appearance of the first person plural pronoun "we" (ἡμεῖς, v. 28) must not be missed. Rather than simply a "stylistic variation,"[1] this pronoun emphasizes that Paul is not the only one proclaiming the gospel of Christ. Third, the emphasis in this section is on his "suffering" (vv. 24, 29; 2:1), not on his "power," since that power only comes from Christ (v. 29).

Just as the previous section contains both a summary of the gospel (1:15 – 20) and an appropriation of such a gospel (1:21 – 23), this section also contains two subsections. The first one (1:24 – 29) introduces Paul's own mission and role, and he draws attention to the "mystery" that has now been revealed (vv. 26, 27). In the second subsection, Paul explains that his apostolic call and mission allows believers to be assured of their knowledge of and commitment to this "mystery" (2:2). At the end (2:5), Paul refers to his absence, which reminds his audience that this letter represents

---

1. Moo, *Letters to the Colossians and to Philemon*, 148.

his presence and authority.[2] This leads into the next major section (2:6 – 15), where Paul addresses the specific concerns the Colossians are facing in their own context.

This section that focuses on the role of Paul is not simply an excursus; instead, it forms an integral part of his argument. First, in light of Paul's emphasis on God's plan, the progression from God the Father (1:3 – 14) to Christ the Son (1:15 – 23) that leads to the present section on Paul the servant of Christ (1:24 – 2:5) becomes understandable. In the next section, the focus is then shifted to the recipients of the gospel that the apostles are preaching (2:6 – 4:1). Second, in emphasizing his unique role in God's plan, Paul also reminds his audience to submit to the gospel for which he has labored (1:29; 2:1). This then prepares for the strong critique of the false teachers in the next section. Third, in emphasizing his own "suffering" and "struggles" (1:24, 29; 2:1), Paul may also be preparing the Colossians to participate in this struggle as they seek to be faithful to the gospel (2:16; 4:2). Finally, some have also detected a subtle reaction against the false teachers in this section.[3] Instead of speculations and misleading visionary reports, Paul reminds the audience that they should rely on the secure "knowledge" that is anchored in Christ himself (2:2).

At the end of this section, the reference to Paul's absence also reminds his audience that this letter represents his presence and authority (2:5).[4] Though absent in flesh, Paul as the mediator of the gospel message continues as he urges the Colossians to stand firm in their "faith in Christ" (2:5). This urge becomes powerful precisely because his absence testifies to his own faithfulness to the gospel as he repeatedly reminds his audiences that he is faithful to this gospel for which he is "in chains" (4:3, 18).

III. Climactic Work of the Son (1:15 – 23)
    A. Supremacy of Christ (1:15 – 20)
    B. Response to the Work of Christ (1:21 – 23)
➡ **IV. Apostolic Mission of Paul (1:24 – 2:5)**
    A. Paul's Suffering in the Plan of God (1:24 – 29)
    B. Paul's Toil for the Local Churches (2:1 – 5)
    V. Faithfulness of the Believers (2:6 – 4:1)

Main Idea

As a servant of Christ and his church, Paul labors as a steward of the plan of God, a plan that reveals the glorious mystery that is relevant for all humanity. For those in Laodicea and Colossae in particular, Paul points to the urgent need to be grounded in the knowledge that is in Christ so that they will not be deceived by false teachings.

---

2. See comments on 1:6a and 2:5a.

3. See, for example, Sumney, "The Argument of Colossians," 346.

4. See comments on 1:6 and 2:5.

Translation

Colossians 1:24 – 2:5

24a	Assertion	**Now**	**I rejoice in my sufferings for your sake,**
b	Explanation	**and**	**I fill up … that which is lacking of the afflictions of Christ**
c	means		in my flesh
d	advantage		for the sake of his body,
e	identification		which is the church,
25a	description		of which I became a servant
b	cause		according to the commission from God given to me for you,
c	purpose		to fulfill the word of God,
26a	apposition		the mystery hidden for ages and generations, but
b	contrast		now revealed to his saints,
27a	Expansion		those to whom God desired to make known the glorious riches of this mystery
b	sphere		among the Gentiles,
c	identification		which is Christ in you,
d	apposition		the hope of glory.
28a	Identification		Him we proclaim,
b	means		admonishing everyone and
c	means		teaching everyone
d	means		with all wisdom,
e	purpose		so that we may present everyone mature in Christ.
29a	Explanation		For this I toil,
b	expansion		striving with his energy that powerfully works in me.

2:1a	Desire	**For I desire you to know**
b	content	how great a struggle I have for you and
c	list	those in Laodicea and
d	list	those who have not seen my face in the flesh,
2a	purpose	so that their hearts may be comforted
b	expansion	as they are united in love,
c	purpose	to obtain all the wealth of full assurance of understanding, and
d	purpose (content of 2c)	the knowledge of the mystery of God,
e	apposition	Christ,
3a	explanation	in whom all the treasures of wisdom and knowledge are hidden.
4a	Explanation	**I say this**
b	purpose	so that no one may deceive you through speculative arguments.
5a	Concession	For **though I am absent in body,**
		I am with you in spirit,
b	contra-expectation	rejoicing to see your order and the firmness of your faith in Christ.

Structure

Various proposals have been offered in mapping the development of Paul's thought in this section. These include a single or double chiastic structure.[5] While a consensus may not be possible, three structural markers are clear. First, the recurrence of rejoicing (χαίρω/χαίρων) and physicality (τῇ σαρκί) in both 1:24 and 2:5 serve as an inclusio to delineate this section, which focuses on Paul's apostolic mission.

Second, in both subsections (1:24 – 29 and 2:1 – 5), the focus is on the "mystery" of God (1:26 – 27; 2:2 – 3). This points to both the center of Paul's mission as well as the urgency of his message for his audience.

Third, in light of the parallelism between the two subsections that deal with Paul's struggles (1:24 – 25; 2:1), the mystery of God (1:26 – 27; 2:2 – 3), and the mission of Paul among the apostles (1:28 – 29; 2:4 – 5), one difference is also clear: 1:24 – 29 focuses on Paul's general stewardship of the gospel, and 2:1 – 5 focuses on Paul's specific labor for the Colossians and Laodiceans. These two related subsections recall the previous section, where one also finds a general christological confession (1:15 – 20) and a specific application particularly relevant in one local context (1:21 – 23).

Paul begins by noting the role of his suffering in the wider plan of God (1:24 – 25). Through these difficult verses, the eschatological significance of Paul's mission is clarified. He then shifts the attention to the mystery of God, one that is particularly relevant in his mission to the Gentiles (1:26 – 27). With a shift to the plural pronoun in 1:28, Paul identifies himself with other servants of the gospel whose mission is to present everyone mature in Christ (1:29). Paul concludes by noting the source of his power, which can be found in Christ.

In the second subsection, Paul likewise begins with his struggles, but he now focuses on his labor for those in Colossae and Laodicea (2:1). The goal of such labor is that they may be united in love and understanding so that they can fully comprehend the mystery of God (2:2 – 3). With a firm grasp of that mystery, Paul expresses his wish that they withstand the challenges of the false teachings (2:4 – 5).

Exegetical Outline

➡ **I. Paul's Suffering in the Plan of God (1:24 – 29)**

    A. Paul's suffering for the sake of the church (1:24 – 25)

    B. Mystery of God revealed (1:26 – 27)

    C. Apostolic mission (1:28 – 29)

II. Paul's Toil for the Local Churches (2:1 – 5)

    A. Paul's struggles for the Colossians and Laodiceans (2:1)

    B. Full understanding of the mystery of God (2:2 – 3)

    C. Epistolary mission of Paul (2:4 – 5)

---

5. Single: see Moo, *Letters to the Colossians and to Philemon*, 148; double: see Aletti, *Saint Paul Épitre aux Colossiens*, 134 – 48.

Explanation of the Text

1:24a Now I rejoice in my sufferings for your sake (Νῦν χαίρω ἐν τοῖς παθήμασιν ὑπὲρ ὑμῶν). Paul here shifts his attention to his apostolic role as one who suffers for the Gentile believers. "Now" (νῦν) may simply signify the logical progression of Paul's argument (1 Cor 5:11; 12:20),[6] although in this context with the reference to his "sufferings" Paul may have his present imprisonment in mind (cf. 4:3, 10, 18). In light of the emphasis on his involvement in the unfolding of the eschatological plan of God, this "now" may also point to the realization of the age of fulfillment. This reading is supported by the reappearance of "now" (νῦν) in v. 26 in reference to the revelation of God's mystery.

"I rejoice in my sufferings" points to Paul's practicing of what he teaches in 1:11 – 12, where he encourages the Colossians to give thanks to the Father joyfully even when they need to be patient and steadfast. The note on "rejoicing" reappears at the end of this section in 2:5, where Paul shifts the focus to the life and behavior of the audience. These two notes bracket the intervening material that centers on the relevance of Paul's suffering for the Colossians.

Although the Greek text does not specify that Paul is referring to his own suffering,[7] the context makes it clear that he is the implied subject of this verbal noun ("my sufferings"). The coexistence of joy and suffering can be found elsewhere in Paul (cf. 2 Cor 6:10), especially when this suffering is related to his proclamation of the gospel (cf. Phil 1:18 – 19). This reference to suffering highlights its importance in his apostolic ministry (cf. Rom 5:3;

2 Tim 1:12; 3:11). It also points to Paul's imitation of Christ's suffering (cf. 1 Thess 1:6) and to his authority as an apostle called to this path of suffering (cf. Acts 9:26).

In this context, Paul's rejoicing is not simply because he is suffering, but because he is suffering "for your sake" (i.e., for the sake of the Colossians; cf. also 2 Cor 1:6). But this connection is still surprising here because it is not immediately clear as to how Paul's suffering will affect a community that he had neither founded nor visited. The end of this verse, which identifies the audience as part of the "body" of Christ, helps to alleviate the initial shock of this verse.[8] Moule, who accepts this identification, further suggests that Paul is referring to the Gentiles in particular, of which the Colossians are a part, and "Paul's sufferings were incurred largely as a result of his apostleship to them."[9] The parallel in Eph 3:13 further supports this reading. The second part of this verse, therefore, serves to explain how Paul's suffering affects the Gentiles.

1:24b-c And I fill up in my flesh that which is lacking of the afflictions of Christ (καὶ ἀνταναπληρῶ τὰ ὑστερήματα τῶν θλίψεων τοῦ Χριστοῦ ἐν τῇ σαρκί μου). Paul now specifies that he is completing that which remains to be filled up in the predetermined messianic afflictions that are taking place in the eschatological era. While this clause is meant to explain Paul's suffering for the sake of the Colossians,[10] the difficulties embedded in this verse have often limited the explicatory power of this clause. Before providing various

---

6. Cf. BDAG, 681.

7. Most contemporary versions make it explicit that it is Paul's own suffering to which he is referring. A notable exception can be found in the intentionally ambiguous rendering in the earlier editions of NIV (1973 – 84): "Now I rejoice in what was suffered for you." TNIV and the most recent edition of

NIV (2011), however, follow the majority rendering: "Now I rejoice in what I am suffering for you."

8. O'Brien, *Colossians, Philemon*, 76 – 77.

9. Moule, *Epistles to the Colossians and Philemon*, 79.

10. This interpretation takes "and" (καί) as an epexegetical conjunction; cf. BDF §442 (9).

options in understanding this entire clause, the various elements should first be analyzed.

The verb "I fill up" (ἀνταναπληρῶ) appears only here in the NT, but the related form, with only one prepositional prefix, "to fill up/to complete" (ἀναπληρόω), has appeared together with the references to "that which is lacking" (τὰ ὑστερήμα[τα]) in 1 Cor 16:17; Phil 2:30.[11] Whether the second prepositional prefix ἀντί ("instead of," "on behalf of") adds anything to this verb is unclear. Taking into account the full force of this preposition, some have translated the verb as "to fill up or complete for someone else."[12] But others have considered the two verbs as synonymous ("fill up," NKJV, TNIV, NIV).[13] In light of Paul's earlier reference to "for your sake" (ὑπὲρ ὑμῶν) and the phrase that follows, "for the sake of his body" (ὑπὲρ τοῦ σώματος αὐτοῦ), a certain sense of representation is likely present although an exclusive vicarious significance cannot be deduced from the presence of this prefix.

In the Greek text, "in my flesh" (ἐν τῇ σαρκί μου) follows "the afflictions of Christ," and this word order has encouraged some to take this prepositional phrase as modifying Christ's afflictions: "I am completing what is lacking in Christ's-afflictions-in-my-flesh for the sake of his body."[14] With the absence of a definite article (τῶν) before this prepositional phrase, however, it is best to take this phrase in an adverbial sense modifying the verb "is lacking" (as most contemporary versions do). Moreover, the placement of this phrase is probably dictated by the next phrase in the Greek text, "for the sake of his body" (ὑπὲρ τοῦ σώματος αὐτοῦ), as

the two phrases together aim at evoking the earlier reference to "his [Christ's] body of flesh" (τῷ σώματι τῆς σαρκὸς αὐτοῦ, 1:22). In focusing on his own physical suffering, not only does Paul point to the importance of the continuation of Christ's work on the historical plane; he also points to the proper way to use one's body within the greater salvation plan of God. This emphasis may in turn anticipate his criticism of the false teachers, who encourage the misuse and mistreatment of one's "body" and "flesh" (2:23).

"That which is lacking of the afflictions of Christ" (τὰ ὑστερήματα τῶν θλίψεων τοῦ Χριστοῦ) is perhaps one of the most difficult phrases to interpret in this letter. "That which is lacking" can point to a relative degree of insufficiency or a definite gap that has to be filled. Linking this deficiency with the "afflictions of Christ" causes confusion with the exact sense of this phrase. The function of the genitival phrase "of Christ" (τοῦ Χριστοῦ) lies at the center of this debate. The possible renderings include "Christ's own afflictions" (possessive genitive), "afflictions for Christ" (objective genitive), "afflictions in regard to Christ" (genitive of reference), or "messianic afflictions" (attributive genitive). Most contemporary commentators choose either the possessive genitive or attributive genitive.

(1) *Christ's own afflictions.* For those who consider this phrase as referring to Christ's own afflictions, some have suggested that the suffering of Christ was indeed insufficient for the salvation of his followers.[15] This interpretation, however, is unlikely in light of the repeated references to the suf-

11. Cf. προσαναπληρόω (2 Cor 9:12; 11:9).

12. Wilson, *Colossians and Philemon*, 170.

13. Barth and Blanke, *Colossians*, 256; Sumney, *Colossians*, 99.

14. Jerome Murphy-O'Connor, *Paul*, 239; cf. W. F. Flemington, "On the Interpretation of Colossians 1:24," in *Suffering and Martyrdom in the New Testament: Studies Presented to G.*

M. Styler by the Cambridge New Testament Seminar (ed. William Horbury and Brian McNeil; Cambridge: Cambridge Univ. Press, 1981), 87; Aletti, *Saint Paul Épître aux Colossiens*, 135.

15. Hans Windisch, *Paulus und Christus: Ein biblisch-religionsgeschichtlicher Vergleich* (UNT 24; Leipzig: Hinrichs, 1934), 244 – 45.

ficient and final salvific work of Christ (1:18 – 20, 22; 2:9 – 10, 14 – 15).

Others see this as an exaggerated statement that aims at exalting the role of Paul by one his disciples or admirers. This portrayal of Paul becomes a "mirror-image of the portrait of Christ,"[16] and it appears only after Paul's own martyrdom, which prompted some "to interpret Paul's death theologically."[17] This reading assumes that the author is a poor student of Paul's own theology who ends up with a portrayal that is in conflict with the rest of this letter with its emphasis on the final sufficiency of Christ.

Others distinguish between the various types of sufferings of Christ. While the final "sacrificial efficacy" of Christ's suffering cannot be doubted, the "ministerial utility" of such suffering remains an object of imitation.[18] It is unclear, however, whether any ancient examples can be cited for the coexistence of the two types of the suffering within the same text, and whether the audience would be able to detect such a subtle distinction.

Noticing the word order in the Greek text, some take the phrase "in my flesh" (ἐν τῇ σαρκί μου) as modifying "the afflictions of Christ" (τῶν θλίψεων τοῦ Χριστοῦ). Therefore, it is not Christ's suffering that is deficient: "the defect that St. Paul is contemplating lies not in the afflictions of Christ as such, but rather in the afflictions of Christ as they are

reflected and reproduced in the life and behavior of Paul, his apostle."[19] As noted above, this reading of the Greek text is problematic. Moreover, while in Phil 3:10 – 11 Paul does express his conviction to participate in the suffering of Christ,[20] the parallel with our present verse is not exact especially in light of the absence of the critical reference to Paul's filling up "that which is lacking" in Christ's afflictions.

Finally, some who take the phrase "of Christ" as a possessive genitive nevertheless see the believers as standing behind this reference to Christ. This can be understood as a case of corporate identity, where the community of Christ is represented by Christ himself.[21] Others point to the mystical union between Christ and his followers.[22] This reading is again problematic in light of the clear distinction made between Christ and both the creation and the church in the preceding hymn (1:15 – 20) and in the rest of the present verse.

(2) *Messianic afflictions.* To take the genitival phrase as an attributive genitive and thus see "Christ" as a title ("Messiah") that modifies the noted afflictions allows Paul to affirm the presence of a deficiency that is related to Christ the Messiah, but not one for which Christ is responsible.[23] Jewish texts testify to the belief in the time of Paul that tribulations and sufferings would precede the arrival of the end of times (Dan 7:21 – 27; 12:1; *Jub.*

16. Hans Dieter Betz, "Paul's 'Second Presence' in Colossians," in *Text and Contexts: Biblical Texts in Their Textual and Situational Contexts: Essays in Honor of Lars Hartman* (ed. Tord Fornberg and David Hellholm; Oslo/Boston: Scandinavian Univ. Press, 1995), 516. See also Nielsen, "The Status of Paul and His Letters in Colossians," 112; Yates, "A Reappraisal of Colossians," 107; Leppä, *Making of Colossians*, 105

17. Standhartinger, "Colossians and the Pauline School," 572 – 93. Cf. Günther Bornkamm, *Paul* (trans. D. M. G. Stalker; New York: Harper, 1969), 171.

18. Lightfoot, *St. Paul's Epistles to the Colossians and to Philemon*, 166. See also Leppä, *Making of Colossians*, 665: "What is lacking in Christ's afflictions is the more immediate and accessible example that Paul's sufferings give the readers."

19. Flemington, "On the Interpretation of Colossians 1:24," 87.

20. Cf. Andrew Perriman, "The Pattern of Christ's Sufferings: Colossians 1:24 and Philippians 3:10-11," *TynBul* 42 (1991): 68 – 77.

21. Wedderburn, "The Theology of Colossians," 39.

22. Schweizer, *Letter to the Colossians*, 101.

23. This reading is supported by many contemporary commentators: Moule, *Epistles to the Colossians and to Philemon*, 76 – 77; O'Brien, *Colossians, Philemon*, 78 – 80; Dunn, *Epistles to the Colossians and to Philemon*, 114 – 16; Witherington, *Letters to Philemon, the Colossians, and the Ephesians*, 144. See also Victor C. Pfitzner, *Paul and the Agon Motif: Traditional Athletic Imagery in the Pauline Literature* (NovTSup 16; Leiden: Brill, 1967), 111.

23:13; *4 Ezra* 4:36 – 37; 13:16 – 19; cf. also NT texts, such as Mark 13:20; Rev 7:14; 12:13 – 17). The idea of a definitive amount of sufferings to take place during this period is also assumed in Rev 6:9 – 11. In Paul, the language of "birth pangs" is also used to refer to the suffering that precedes the final consummation of God's salvation among his people (Gal 4:19), and the relationship between his mission and the parousia is also noted in his earlier letters (cf. Rom 11:25 – 32; 2 Thess 2:6 – 7). In light of this background, Paul's reference to "that which is lacking of the afflictions of Christ" may then point to the amount that remains to be filled up in the predetermined sufferings that are to take place in the end times.[24]

This reading is further supported by a number of observations: (a) the reference to "that which is lacking" may presuppose a predetermined quota; (b) the word for "afflictions" (θλίψεων) is never used by Paul for Christ's own atoning suffering; (c) the presence of a definite article (τῶν) before "afflictions" may point to a precise kind of suffering that Paul has in mind; (d) the note on the necessity of Paul's suffering as related to his calling as an apostle suggests the idea of a quota (1 Cor 4:9; 2 Cor 2:14; 4:11);[25] (e) this present paragraph is flooded with eschatological references, especially in v. 26;[26] (f) while many concede that "Colossians does not specify how Paul's suffering benefits the church,"[27] this reading provides at least one possible link when his suffering fulfills this quota, thus hastening the fulfillment of God's work in history and benefitting even those whom he had never met.[28]

The purpose of evoking such messianic afflictions may be twofold. First, Paul seeks to establish his authority as an apostle to the Gentiles who suffers for them in proclaiming the powerful gospel. This allows him to provide the warnings and encouragements that follow. Second, perhaps in anticipating the false teachers who emphasize immediate eschatological experience through spatial ascent, Paul emphasizes the significance of the temporal framework of salvation history. Ultimate fulfillment and union with Christ await when the promised final consummation is realized. A similar strategy can also be detected in 3:1 – 4 (see comments there).

1:24d-e For the sake of his body, which is the church (ὑπὲρ τοῦ σώματος αὐτοῦ, ὅ ἐστιν ἡ ἐκκλησία). This phrase recalls "for your sake" (ὑπὲρ ὑμῶν) in 1:24a as it identifies the audience as part of the universal church. In the christological hymn, Paul has already identified Christ as "the head of the body, the church" (v. 18). The reappearance of this description therefore also connects Paul's ministry with Christ's, while emphasizing that Christ is the authority under which he serves. This phrase also links this section with the conclusion of the

---

24. The prevalence of this concept in Second Temple Jewish literature and in the NT may explain why Paul does not make explicit reference to the messianic woes in this context; cf. Dale C. Allison Jr., *The End of the Ages Has Come: An Early Interpretation of the Passion and Resurrection of Jesus* (Philadelphia: Fortress, 1985), 63 – 64.

25. Hanna Stettler, "An Interpretation of Colossians 1:24 in the Framework of Paul's Mission Theology," in *The Mission of the Early Church to Jews and Gentiles* (ed. Jostein Ådna and Hans Kvalbein; WUNT 127; Tübingen: Mohr Siebeck, 2000), 206. The idea of divine necessity in regards to Paul's suffering is explicitly noted in Luke's account of his conversion and call (Acts 9:16).

26. For the significance of the term "mystery," see comments on v. 26a. For a discussion on the eschatological character of Paul's suffering, see also L. Ann Jervis, "Accepting Affliction: Paul's Preaching on Suffering," in *Character and Scripture: Moral Formation, Community, and Biblical Interpretation* (ed. William P. Brown; Grand Rapids: Eerdmans, 2002), 290 – 316.

27. Jerry L. Sumney, "The Function of Ethos in Colossians," in *Rhetoric, Ethic, and Moral Persuasion: Essays from the 2002 Heidelberg Conference* (ed. Thomas H. Olbricht and Anders Eriksson; Emory Studies in Early Christianity 11; New York: T&T Clark, 2005), 312.

28. See Richard Bauckham, "Colossians 1:24 Again: The Apocalyptic Motif," *EvQ* 47 (1975): 170.

previous section, where Paul affirms his role as a "servant" of the gospel (v. 23), an affirmation that will be reiterated in the next verse. Both the unique status of Paul the apostle and his subordinating role to the authority of Christ are emphasized throughout this section.

1:25a Of which I became a servant (ἧς ἐγενόμην ἐγὼ διάκονος). The relative pronoun "of which" refers back to "the church" and points to Paul's self-portrayal as one who is not only subservient to the gospel but also carries the distinct honor to speak on its behalf. This section (vv. 25 – 29) provides significant elaboration on the purpose of the suffering noted in v. 24. Note also the presence of two phrases that point back to the previous discussions: "of which I became a servant" recalls v. 23, and "to fulfill the word of God" at the end of v. 25 parallels Paul's mission as just noted in v. 24.

In v. 23, Paul claims to be "a servant" (διάκονος) of the gospel; here, however, Paul is "a servant" of the church. The connection between the gospel and the church has already been established in v. 6, where it is stated that the gospel bears fruit and grows "in the whole world." The existence of the universal church testifies to the power of this gospel. In this context, since the church is considered to be "the body" of Christ (v. 24), to be a servant of this body is to serve the "head" of this body (v. 18). Elsewhere in this letter, Paul also names Epaphras (1:7) and Tychicus (4:7) as "fellow slaves" (σύνδουλος) of Christ. In all three cases, servitude may be implied, but the word may also point to the honor of one who serves as the spokesperson for one in power.[29]

1:25b-c According to the commission from God given to me for you, to fulfill the word of God

(κατὰ τὴν οἰκονομίαν τοῦ θεοῦ τὴν δοθεῖσάν μοι εἰς ὑμᾶς πληρῶσαι τὸν λόγον τοῦ θεοῦ). Paul continues his self-portrayal by locating himself within the wider plan of God. "The commission" (τὴν οἰκονομίαν) can refer to an office, and some have taken the phrase "the commission from God" as referring to "the office of God," thus the "divine office" (RSV) of the apostle Paul.[30] The parallel in 1 Cor 9:16 – 17 is important, however, especially when the word is used in both contexts to refer to the call and responsibility of Paul as one who must proclaim the gospel to the Gentiles. Therefore, "the commission" is perhaps the best translation, understood as "the commission God gave me" (TNIV, NIV).[31] The word οἰκονομία originated in a household context (cf. Luke 16:1 – 4), and it became a particularly relevant term when the early Christians found their roots by gathering around the "household" (οἶκος), as noted in this letter (4:15; cf. Rom 16:5; 1 Cor 11:34; 16:19; 1 Tim 3:5).

The parallel in Eph 3:2 further explains that this commission is "the commission of God's grace" (pers. trans.). In Colossians, the close connection between the powerful "word" (ὁ λόγος), "gospel" (τὸ εὐαγγέλιον), and "grace" (ἡ χάρις) in Col 1:5 – 7 has already paved the way for Paul's description of his own mediatorial role in the outworking of God's plan in history. The prepositional phrase "for you" (εἰς ὑμᾶς) anticipates v. 27, where Paul points to the revelation of the mystery of God to the Gentiles. Reading vv. 25 and 27 together, Paul is reiterating the fact that he is an "apostle to the Gentiles" (Rom 11:13; cf. Gal 2:8), "appointed a herald and an apostle … and a true and faithful teacher of the Gentiles" (1 Tim 2:7).

The clause "to fulfill the word of God" is similar to Paul's description of his own mission in v. 24.[32]

---

29. Cf. John N. Collins, *Diakonia: Re-interpreting the Ancient Sources* (New York: Oxford Univ. Press, 1990), 77 – 191.

30. BDAG, 697; Lohse, *Colossians and Philemon*, 72. For Lohse, Paul is affirming that he is "the one and only Apostle."

31. This is to take the genitive "of God" (τοῦ θεοῦ) as a genitive of source.

32. See, in particular, Michael Cahill, "The Neglected Parallelism in Colossians 1,24 – 25," *ETL* 68 (1992): 142 – 47.

The word "fulfill" (πληρῶσαι) has been taken in various ways. Some take it in an adjectival sense as modifying "the word of God" ("proclaiming his entire message to you," NLT). Perhaps closer to the intention of Paul, others take it in an adverbial sense in the depiction of the full reception of the word ("to make the word of God fully known," ESV), or in the portrayal of the mission to preach the word ("so that I might fully carry out the preaching of the word of God," NASB; cf. NET). But in light of the use of a related term in v. 24 ("I fill up," ἀνταναπληρῶ), the full force of this infinitive has to be recognized especially in reference to that which needs to be filled up.

Paul is not simply aiming to fill the audience with the word of God; instead, Paul is focusing on the need to fulfill the mission of God's word. As that word is destined to grow and bear fruit "in the whole world" (v. 6), Paul, as the bearer of this word, is to participate in fulfilling its mission. In v. 27, he further explains that this fulfillment is to be found in proclaiming the gospel among the Gentiles. This is similar to Paul's christological confession in 1 Tim 3:16, which portrays the mission of the Son:

> He appeared in the flesh,
>   was vindicated by the Spirit,
> was seen by the angels,
>   was preached among the nations,
> was believed on in the world,
>   was taken up in glory.[33]

In language closer to this particular verse, one can also point to Rom 15:19: "From Jerusalem all the way around to Illyricum, I have fully proclaimed [from πληρόω] the gospel of Christ." This comment is not to boast about the effectiveness of Paul's own ministry; the focus is rather on the inherent power embedded in the mission of the word.

The significance of the parallels between Paul's need to "fill up" that which is lacking in the afflictions of Christ in v. 24 and his commitment to fulfill the word of God in this verse should not be downplayed. To suffer is part of the proclamation of the word of God. This suffering for the gospel is, after all, the content of Paul's call as conveyed through Ananias: "This man is my chosen instrument to proclaim my name to the Gentiles and their kings and to the people of Israel. I will show him how much he must suffer for my name" (Acts 9:15 – 16).

1:26a The mystery hidden from ages and generations (τὸ μυστήριον τὸ ἀποκεκρυμμένον ἀπὸ τῶν αἰώνων καὶ ἀπὸ τῶν γενεῶν). Paul now describes his ministry in relation to the mystery in the eschatological promises of God. "The mystery" (τὸ μυστήριον) stands in apposition to "the word of God" (τὸν λόγον τοῦ θεοῦ) in the preceding clause, and as such it explains the content of this "word." "The mystery" may evoke the "mystery cults" in the mind of the Gentile audience, but most scholars are now convinced that the context clearly points to the Jewish background of the term.[34] Moreover, if Paul intends to refer to the "mystery cults," he would have used the plural instead. For the ancient audience, however, it is possible that some may have seen this word as acquiring a polemical sense as this new "mystery" is to replace the mystery cults with which they were familiar.[35]

To appreciate the richness and complexity of this term, one must begin with its use in the Old

---

33. On the understanding of this confession as a Pauline hymn, see Philip H. Towner, *The Letters to Timothy and Titus* (NICNT; Grand Rapids: Eerdmans, 2006), 276 – 85.

34. Günther Bornkamm, "Μυστήριον κτλ.," *TDNT*, 4:802 – 28; Raymond E. Brown, *The Semitic Background of the*

Term *"Mystery" in the New Testament* (Philadelphia: Fortress, 1968).

35. Cf. Rosalind Kearsley, "Mysteries of Artemis at Ephesus," in *NewDocs*, 6:201 – 2.

Testament apocalyptic traditions. In Daniel, in particular, the "mystery" refers to the plan of God that will find its fulfillment in the future (Dan 2:18, 19, 27, 28, 29, 30, 47). This use can also be identified in the later Jewish literature.[36] In light of this background, Paul's use of this term here highlights both the continuity with the prophetic traditions as well as the discontinuity that this gospel of the eschatological age signifies.[37] This mystery thus affirms the consistency of God's plan for his people as well as the surprising elements that can only be revealed with the arrival of the climax of salvation history in the life and death of Jesus Christ.

A close parallel to Paul's description of this "mystery" can be found in 1 Cor 2:6 – 7, where one finds references to wisdom (cf. v. 28), maturity (cf. v. 28), the ages, and the hiddenness of the mystery in the context of the revelation of God's glory in an eschatological age: "We … speak a message of wisdom among the mature, but not the wisdom of this age or of the rulers of this age, who are coming to nothing. No, we declare God's wisdom, a mystery that has been hidden and that God destined for our glory before time began."

In Paul, the "mystery" can refer to the entire gospel (Rom 16:25) or one aspect of it (1 Cor 15:51).[38] In the present context, this "mystery" centers on the inclusion of the Gentiles (v. 27) as Paul presents "everyone" mature in Christ (v. 28). This aspect of the "mystery" can also be found in Rom 11:25 and is elaborated in Eph 3:1 – 9. For Paul, this "mystery" is one aspect of the gospel, but it draws from its center as it points to the powerful work of God in

the death of Christ that breaks down ethnic and cosmic barriers in the creation of the one people.

"Hidden" is a concept inherent in the term "mystery," but it also anticipates the time of revelation. "For ages and generations" can have a temporal sense or a personal sense. In the LXX, "ages" and "generations" are often synonymous, referring to a lengthy period of time (cf. Exod 40:15; Lev 3:17). In this context, however, some point to the possible parallel in Eph 2:2 and the reference to the "rulers of this age" in 1 Cor 2:6 – 13 and suggest that the "ages" and "generations" are to be understood as the personified Aeons.[39] The translation "from ages and from generations" (KJV, NKJV) leaves room for this personified reading. The temporal particle "now" that follows, however, supports a temporal reading.

1:26b But now revealed to his saints (νῦν δὲ ἐφανερώθη τοῖς ἁγίοις αὐτοῦ). The contrast between the past and the present is made clear with this verse, which announces the revelation of God's eschatological mystery. In light of the reference to the "ages" and "revelation," "now" (νῦν) likely points to the entire messianic era initiated by the death and resurrection of Christ (vv. 18, 20) and actualized in the proclamation of the gospel (v. 25). God is the implied agent of the passive verb "revealed" (ἐφανερώθη). This verb means "disclosed" (TNIV, NIV), but it is closely related to a similar term "revealed" (ἀποκαλύπτω)[40] and therefore can justifiably be translated as such in this context (cf. NKJV, NRSV, ESV, NLT).

Unlike some recent attempts to interpret "his

---

36. In such literature that has apparently drawn from Dan 2, the revelation of this "mystery" is often associated with the arrival of the messianic age (cf. *4 Ezra* 12:37 – 38; *1 En.* 46, 52, 71); Beale, "Colossians," 857.

37. See D. A. Carson, "Mystery and Fulfillment: Toward a More Comprehensive Paradigm of Paul's Understanding of the Old and the New," in *Justification and Variegated Nomism*, vol. 2: *The Paradoxes of Paul* (ed. D. A. Carson, Peter

T. O'Brien, and Mark A. Seifrid; Grand Rapids: Baker, 2004), 412 – 25.

38. The same distinction can also be identified in 1 Cor 2:1, 7; cf. Bockmuehl, *Revelation and Mystery*, 186.

39. See BDAG, 33, 192, which takes the "ages" in a personified sense but the "generations" in a temporal sense.

40. Cf. Rom 1:17//3:21; 16:25//26; O'Brien, *Colossians, Philemon*, 85; Moo, *Letters to the Colossians and to Philemon*, 156.

saints" (τοῖς ἁγίοις αὐτοῦ) as "those to whom the Gospel was first revealed and entrusted,"[41] this term most likely refers to all believers in light of the consistent use of this term elsewhere in this chapter (vv. 2, 4, 12). Moreover, Paul later argues against the focus on private and selective revelatory experience (2:18) while affirming that all believers are the beneficiaries of such eschatological acts of revelation (2:6 – 15; 3:3 – 4). To Paul, therefore, the revelation of mystery is not simply "an essentially religious experience,"[42] but the act of God in history for all who respond to the proclamation of God's word.

1:27a-b Those to whom God desired to make known the glorious riches of this mystery among the Gentiles (οἷς ἠθέλησεν ὁ θεὸς γνωρίσαι τί τὸ πλοῦτος τῆς δόξης τοῦ μυστηρίου τούτου ἐν τοῖς ἔθνεσιν). Paul further identifies the recipients of the revelation of the mystery. "Those" (οἷς) goes back to the "saints" who receive this revelation (v. 26). The verb "desired" (ἠθέλησεν) indicates "the freedom of the divine will"[43] and points back to 1:1, where the cognate nominal form occurs in the description of the foundation of Paul's apostolic mission: "the will of God" (θελήματος θεοῦ). This emphasis on God's active will again highlights the significance of his plan throughout history. Here Paul stresses that the inclusion of the Gentiles into God's elect ones is not a historical accident; instead, it is within the predetermined plan of a God who is actively working in history. Some versions have chosen to make this idea explicit by translating the clause "God desired" as "it was God's purpose" (NJB). This entire verse, with its references to

the sovereign will of God, the glorious richness of the mystery, and the centrality of Christ, is similar to Eph 1:4 – 7.

"To make known" (γνωρίσαι) is another word often used in relation to the revelation of God's mystery. The object clause after this infinitive is in indirect discourse and is introduced by an interrogative pronoun (τί), variously translated as "what" (KJV, ASV, NASB, REB), "what sort of,"[44] and "how great" (NRSV, ESV) in this context. Although this pronoun can accentuate the quality or quantity of that which it introduces,[45] here it functions primarily as an object marker (cf. 1 Thess 1:8; 1 John 3:2) and can therefore be omitted in translation.[46]

"The glorious riches" (τὸ πλοῦτος τῆς δόξης) literally reads "the riches of the glory." In light of v. 11, where "the glory" is to be taken as a qualitative genitive, the genitive here takes on an adjectival sense, thus "the riches of his glorious inheritance" (CEV, TEV, TNIV, NET).[47] The "riches" refers to the amazing plan of God that includes both Jews and Gentiles; Paul goes on to note explicitly that the object of God's act of revelation is "the Gentiles." In Eph 1:18, where one also finds the use of the phrase "the glorious riches," Paul makes it clear that he has the "inheritance in his holy people" in mind — that is, the sharing of the inheritance among the Jews and Gentiles, both of which are now to be considered as God's chosen ones.

1:27c-d Which is Christ in you, the hope of glory (ὅ ἐστιν Χριστὸς ἐν ὑμῖν, ἡ ἐλπὶς τῆς δόξης). While the previous relative clause identifies the recipients of the revelation of the mystery, this relative clause

---

41. Bockmuehl, *Revelation and Mystery*, 184.

42. Joseph Coppens, " 'Mystery' in the Theology of Saint Paul and Its Parallels at Qumran," in *Paul and the Dead Sea Scrolls* (ed. J. Murphy-O'Connor and James H. Charlesworth; New York: Crossroad, 1990), 150.

43. Schweizer, *Letter to the Colossians*, 108.

44. So also BDAG, 1007.

45. Cf. Harris, *Colossians and Philemon*, 70.

46. Cf. NAB, TNIV, NET, NIV; others chose simply to use the object marker "that" (NLT).

47. In the light of "his glory" in Rom 9:23, the significance of "glory" as an attribute of God should not be downplayed.

explains the content of such mystery. Grammatically, the relative pronoun "which" (ὅ) can refer either to "the … riches" or "this mystery" in the preceding clause. In light of 2:2 ("the mystery of God, Christ"), however, it is best to take "the mystery" as the antecedent of this pronoun. This relative clause explains the content of the mystery and explicitly identifies it with the indwelling of "Christ." Taking "in you" (ἐν ὑμῖν) as referring to the Gentiles,[48] Lightfoot is probably correct in claiming that "not Christ, but Christ given freely to the Gentiles is the 'mystery' of which St Paul speaks."[49]

"The hope of glory" stands in apposition to Christ, who is the basis of this eschatological hope (cf. v. 23; 1 Tim 1:1). The genitive "of glory" (τῆς δόξης) is best taken as an objective genitive, thus, "the hope for glory" (NAB).[50] This hope is "the blessed hope — the appearing of the glory of our great God and Savior, Jesus Christ" (Titus 2:13). In Jewish traditions, "glory" often accompanied the Torah, and the full "glory" will be restored at the end of time to those who are faithful to the law (2 Esd 7:95, 97; *1 En*. 38:4; 50:1).[51] To identify Christ as "the hope of glory" may then highlight his role as the fulfillment of the Torah, an assumption that lies behind the claim that in Christ, the mystery of God, one finds "all the treasures of wisdom and knowledge" (Col 2:3).

1:28a Him we proclaim (ὃν ἡμεῖς καταγγέλλομεν). "Him" translates the relative pronoun (ὅν) that points back to "Christ" (v. 27) as the center of Paul's proclamation. This clause is important in providing critical corrections to possible misconceptions

concerning the focus of this section. First, the self-description of Paul's own suffering (vv. 24, 29) may give the impression that he is emphasizing his own role as the apostle. While his unique role is not to be doubted, Paul here emphasizes that it is "Christ" who is the object of all proclamation. With this relative pronoun, the reader is reminded not only of the grammatical antecedent in the previous verse, but all the previous mentions of "Christ" as the center and sole focus of Paul's gospel (cf. vv. 1, 2, 3, 4, 7, 15 – 20, 24). The role of Paul is a derivative one, and his status is relative to the absolute claim of Christ and his gospel that cannot be compromised.

Second, the appearance of the first person plural pronoun "we" (ἡμεῖς) is surprising, especially in light of the use of first person singular verbs before and after this verse (cf. vv. 24, 25, 29). Reading in light of first person plural verbs in v. 3, many assume that Paul is primarily referring to his specific coworkers (see vv. 1, 7 – 8; cf. 4:12 – 13),[52] while others entertain the possibility of Paul's use of the "editorial we" in this context.[53] But both readings fail to explain the sudden appearance of this plural pronoun. It is more likely that Paul is intentionally including all who participate in the proclamation of the gospel message with this pronoun, and this group cannot be limited to those noted in this letter. The awkward repeated emphasis on "everyone" in the subordinate clauses that follow together with the note on "all wisdom" confirms that Paul is making a universal claim. This is also consistent with the reference to "the Gentiles" in the v. 27, a group not limited to the Colossians. This universal

---

48. The direct reference of this second person plural pronoun is, of course, the Colossians, but only as they represent the other Gentiles to be included in God's people.

49. Lightfoot, *St. Paul's Epistles to the Colossians and to Philemon*, 169. Note that in Ephesians, one finds Paul again speaking of "the mystery of Christ" (Eph 3:4) and Paul's mission "to preach to the Gentiles the boundless riches of Christ" (3:8).

50. Cf. "This gives you assurance of sharing his glory" (NLT).

51. Hooker, "Where Is Wisdom to Be Found?" 124.

52. See, e.g., O'Brien, *Colossians, Philemon*, 87; Aletti, *Saint Paul Épître aux Colossiens*, 144; MacDonald, *Colossians and Ephesians*, 82.

53. Moo, *Letters to the Colossians and to Philemon*, 159; cf. Lohse, *Colossians and Philemon*, 76.

claim thus reminds one of early Christian confessions where the universal and absolute claim of the gospel is made (Rom 6:4; 1 Cor 8:6; 2 Cor 4:13 – 14; 2 Tim 1:9 – 10; Titus 3:4 – 7; cf. 1 Cor 1:23). In using this pronoun, Paul is situating himself within all those who confess Jesus to be the Christ.

The verb "we proclaim" (καταγγέλλομεν) belongs to missionary discourse, and the object of such proclamation is often "Jesus" (Acts 17:3), "Christ" (Phil 1:17 – 18), "the gospel" (1 Cor 9:14), or "the word of God/the Lord" (Acts 13:5; 15:36). As such, its uses overlap with that of "to proclaim" (κηρύσσω; cf. v. 23) and "to evangelize" (εὐαγγελίζω).[54] This note on proclamation points to the concrete ways in which "the mystery" is able to be "revealed to his saints" (v. 26). Though those who proclaim are not the objects of such proclamation, they all play a critical role in fulfilling God's plan in the historical plane.

1:28b-d Admonishing everyone and teaching everyone with all wisdom (νουθετοῦντες πάντα ἄνθρωπον καὶ διδάσκοντες πάντα ἄνθρωπον ἐν πάσῃ σοφίᾳ). Paul further identifies the means of proclamation in the acts of admonishing and teaching. These two adverbial participles can be taken either in an instrumental sense ("by admonishing ... and by teaching")[55] or as participles of accompanying circumstances ("as we admonish ... and teach").[56] It is unclear, however, whether such a distinction is a meaningful one here. Moreover, in light of the use of the verbs "to proclaim" and "to teach" as parallel terms in Acts 4:2, a fine distinction between "proclaiming," "admonishing," and

"teaching" should not be made especially in reference to the early Christian missionary activity.[57]

"Admonishing" (νουθετοῦντες) may imply that an error needs to be corrected. In the NT, however, this word can also refer to the general instruction and proclamation of the word. In Rom 15:14, for example, the word denotes mutual encouragement: "I myself am convinced, my brothers and sisters, that you yourselves are full of goodness, filled with knowledge and competent to instruct [νουθετεῖν] one another." Some have therefore preferred the rendering, "to lay at one's heart"[58] — a rendering supported by 3:16. If so, "teaching" (διδάσκοντες) may denote an activity that need not be distinguished from "admonishing," both of which are intimately related to the act of proclamation. In 2:6 – 7, being taught is equated to receiving the traditions concerning Jesus Christ.

In this context, Paul uses "admonishing" and "teaching" perhaps not to elaborate on the act of proclamation but to highlight the subsequent phrase "with all wisdom," which illustrates its content.[59] This phrase recalls "in all spiritual wisdom and understanding" of v. 9. The connection between v. 9 and this context is important. In the prayer report of v. 9 Paul points to God being the one who is able to fill the Colossians "with the knowledge of his will in all spiritual wisdom and understanding." In this verse, however, Paul and the other gospel messengers become the agents through whom the recipients can receive "all wisdom." This points to the emphasis on both divine acts and human mediation in this letter. In

---

54. Cf. Julius Schniewind, "ἀγγελία, κτλ.," *TDNT*, 1:71 – 72.

55. Cf. Lohse, *Colossians and Philemon*, 77; Moule, *Epistles to the Colossians and to Philemon*, 74.

56. Cf. Harris, *Colossians and Philemon*, 72. It is also possible to take these two participles as pointing to two aspects in the proclamation of the gospel; cf. Wright, *Colossians and Philemon*, 93.

57. See also Acts 5:42 ("teaching and proclaiming the good

news that Jesus is the Messiah") and 28:31 ("proclaimed the kingdom of God and taught about the Lord Jesus Christ").

58. Barth and Blanke, *Colossians*, 266.

59. This takes the phrase as a reference to the content of "admonishing" and "teaching" (KJV, ASV, NRSV, NJB, NKJV, REB) rather than the means through which such acts could be accomplished (i.e., "with all wisdom," NAB, NASB, ESV, TNIV, NLT, NIV).

2:2 – 3 Paul will again emphasize that this "wisdom" is hidden in Christ himself. This emphasis on "wisdom" anticipates Paul's critique of the false teachers, who only acquire "an appearance of wisdom" (2:23).

In comparing 1:9 with this verse, another point becomes apparent. In the section where v. 9 belongs (vv. 3 – 14), Paul focuses on the particular situation of the Colossians and their faithfulness to God; in this context, however, Paul focuses on the power of the gospel among the Gentiles and uses the Greek term "all" (πᾶς) three times: "admonishing everyone [πάντα ἄνθρωπον]," "teaching everyone [πάντα ἄνθρωπον]," and "with all [πάσῃ] wisdom." The reference to "everyone" (πάντα ἄνθρωπον) in v. 28e confirms this emphasis. Against the elitists, Paul is again emphasizing the universal scope and power of this gospel. In this verse, Paul points to both Jews and Gentiles as recipients of God's work through Christ.

1:28e So that we may present everyone mature in Christ (ἵνα παραστήσωμεν πάντα ἄνθρωπον τέλειον ἐν Χριστῷ). This clause points to the purpose of the act of proclamation. As in v. 22, one again finds the use of the cultic term "to present" (παρίστημι), in reference to the proclamation of the power of Christ's sacrificial death. While some translations chose to render τέλειον as "perfect" (KJV, ASV, NAB, NKJV, NJB, NLT),[60] "(fully) mature" (RSV, NRSV, REB, ESV, TNIV, NET, NIV) is a more appropriate translation since Paul does not downplay the process of sanctification as he argues against those who claim perfection in their religious and ascetic practices (2:18, 23).

Nevertheless, this rendering should not deflect one from focusing on the finality of that which is required of believers as they stand before God. Paul emphasizes that this maturity is grounded in the unfolding of God's will (Rom 12:2), which can be achieved only by the act of God in an eschatological era (1 Cor 13:10) when the believers find themselves in final and complete union with Christ (Eph 4:13). The "in Christ" (ἐν Χριστῷ) reference here is sufficient to highlight this salvation-historical, eschatological, and christocentric aspect in reference to Christian maturity. David Peterson is therefore correct in asserting that this maturity "is not some vague notion of 'spiritual growth' or 'moral progress,' but actualization of the redemption in Christ in personal and corporate Christian living."[61] In v. 22, Paul noted that Christ is to present believers as "holy, without blemish, and blameless before him"; this description helps us understand what is implied by the term "mature."

1:29a For this I toil (εἰς ὃ καὶ κοπιῶ). With this clause, Paul returns to a discussion of his struggles for the sake of the gospel. The relative pronoun "this" (ὅ) is best taken to refer back to Paul's attempt to "present everyone mature in Christ" (v. 28). Nevertheless, since such presentation is the goal of his act of proclaiming the gospel, Paul's struggle ultimately points back to his wider apostolic mission. "For this" thus introduces the purpose for Paul's toil, which can be made explicit in renderings such as "for this purpose" (NASB) and "to this end" (NKJV, REB, TNIV, NIV).

With "I toil," Paul returns to his first person narration as he highlights his personal involvement in the spread of the gospel. Paul often uses this verb to describe his work for the Christian communities (1 Cor 15:10; Gal 4:11; Phil 2:16; cf. 1 Thess 2:9; 3:5; 2 Cor 6:5; 11:23). Although some consider this portrayal of Paul as authored by one of his admirers who was attempting to highlight his unique and

---

60. Cf. "complete" (NASB).

61. David G. Peterson, "Maturity: The Goal of Mission," in *The Gospel to the Nations: Perspectives on Paul's Mission* (ed. Peter Bolt and Mark Thompson; Downers Grove, IL: InterVarsity Press, 2000), 193.

exalted status,[62] this reading is problematic. First, "since the verb and its cognate noun can both be used for common manual labor, the writer's use of *kopiaō* suggests that he has not exalted Paul's sufferings and work to the degree that they are in a completely different category from the suffering and work of other leaders."[63] Related to this is the fact that Paul himself often uses this term in his generally accepted letters to describe the labor of others (Rom 16:6, 12; 1 Thess 5:12). In highlighting his personal involvement, therefore, it is not his unique role that is emphasized here.

1:29b Striving with his energy that powerfully works in me (ἀγωνιζόμενος κατὰ τὴν ἐνέργειαν αὐτοῦ τὴν ἐνεργουμένην ἐν ἐμοὶ ἐν δυνάμει). Paul further qualifies his previous clause with a note on the source of his labor. The participle "striving" (ἀγωνιζόμενος) can indicate manner ("I toil strenuously," REB; cf. TNIV, NIV) or attendant circumstances ("I labor, striving").[64] This verb may have belonged to the athletic imageries from which Paul often draws (cf. 1 Cor 9:25; 2 Tim 4:7),[65] and it highlights a sustained effort for a particular goal. In this context, however, we cannot make a clear distinction between the previously noted toiling and the striving here. Some translations have therefore rendered the two as parallels terms, "I toil and struggle" (NRSV; cf. NAB; NLT; cf. 1 Tim 4:10).

The use of a participle ("striving") that shares its semantic range with the verb it modifies ("I toil") indicates that Paul is not introducing a new act; instead, he is attempting to explain the power that lies behind his toiling. This emphasis

on being empowered by God's power provides a critical balance to his earlier claim concerning his own work and labor. "His energy [ἐνέργειαν] that … works [ἐνεργουμένην]" reflects the Semitic use of a verb and its cognate noun.[66] In Paul, ἐνέργεια often points to the power of God (Eph 1:19; 3:7; Phil 3:21; Col 2:12; 2 Thess 2:11), and it is often found together with other words denoting "power" (κράτος, Eph 1:19; ἰσχύς, Eph 1:19; δύναμις, Eph 3:7; 2 Thess 2:9; δύναμαι, Phil 3:21). The presence of "powerfully" (ἐν δυνάμει; lit., "with/in power") is therefore not unusual.

Equally important is the connection between "energy" and the theologically significant term "grace," especially illustrated in Eph 3:7: "I became a servant of this gospel by the gift of God's grace given me through the working [ἐνέργεια] of his power." For Paul and other NT authors, "grace" is a manifestation of the working and power of God.[67] On God's working through Paul's own toil, a paraphrase of our present clause can also be found in 1 Cor 15:10: "I worked [ἐκοπίασα] harder than all of them — yet not I, but the grace of God that was with me." Paul never allows the readers to consider him as the center of God's work in history.

2:1a-b For I desire you to know how great a struggle I have for you (Θέλω γὰρ ὑμᾶς εἰδέναι ἡλίκον ἀγῶνα ἔχω ὑπὲρ ὑμῶν). While the previous subsection (1:24 – 29) provides a general statement on Paul's stewardship of the gospel, this subsection (2:1 – 5) centers on Paul's specific labor for the Colossians and Laodiceans. The previous subsection opened with the direct address to the audience

---

62. Many consider the toiling language together with the "agon" vocabulary in the next clause as evidence of non-Pauline authorship. See, e.g., Kiley, *Colossians as Pseudepigraphy*, 96.

63. Sumney, *Colossians*, 110; see 1 Cor 4:12; cf. 1 Thess 2:9; 2 Thess 3:8. Building on this observation, MacDonald (*Colossians and Ephesians*, 84) also argues against a clear distinction between the use of this verb in ministry and "secular" contexts because for Paul, the understanding of the growth of his gospel

ministry cannot be separated from its social contexts.

64. BDAG, 17.

65. Paul's use of the nominal form (ἀγών; 1 Thess 2:2; Phil 1:30) indicates that this term is often used simply in reference to any fight or struggle.

66. The two terms are similarly found in Eph 1:19 – 20 and 2 Thess 2:7 – 11.

67. See comments on vv. 2 and 1:6. See also Acts 6:8.

through a second person plural personal pronoun "you" (vv. 24 – 25), and this pronoun was defined by the subsequent references to "the church" (vv. 24, 25), the "saints" (v. 26), "the Gentiles" (v. 27), and "everyone" (v. 28). In this subsection, however, the reference to "you" (ὑμῶν) is followed by specific references to the local audiences. This allows Paul to speak about his own absence from their midst (v. 5) — hence the need for this letter. More importantly, this shift from the general statement to the specific context situates the audience within the wider salvation-historical plan of God as they become the beneficiaries of God's work through his Son.

"I desire you to know" highlights the significance of what follows (cf. 1 Cor 11:3).[68] In terms of function, this is comparable to the formula "you know that" (3:24; 4:1), where Paul reminds his audience of what is important.[69]

"How great a struggle I have for you" indicates the intensity of the struggle Paul has endured. In English, "how great a struggle" could be rendered "I struggle very much indeed."[70] "A struggle" (ἀγῶνα) relates back to participle in v. 29 ("striving," ἀγωνιζόμενος); although Paul did not make it clear as to the kind of "struggle" he had undergone for the sake of the readers, the connection with v. 29 provides some hints. In vv. 27 – 29, Paul connects his "striving" with his mission as an apostle to the Gentiles who is faithful in proclaiming the gospel message. In light of 4:3, where Paul states that he is "bound" in chains because of the proclamation of "the mystery of Christ," the "struggle" should

therefore include his imprisonment, which is a direct consequence of his faithfulness to his call and mission.[71] In the verses that follow, Paul likewise points to his proclamation (vv. 2 – 3) and alludes to his absence, presumably a result of his imprisonment (v. 5). If we read 2:1 – 5 in light of 1:24, Paul's "struggle ... for you" is also to be understood in light of his participation in the eschatological suffering. This helps explain how he is able to suffer on behalf of those whom he had never met.

2:1c-d And those in Laodicea and those who have not seen my face in the flesh (καὶ τῶν ἐν Λαοδικείᾳ καὶ ὅσοι οὐχ ἑόρακαν τὸ πρόσωπόν μου ἐν σαρκί). Assuming that "for you" in the previous phrase refers to the Colossians, Paul points to other groups who have benefited from his ministry of proclamation. Laodicea was located eleven miles northwest of Colossae. The Jewish population in Laodicea can probably be traced back to third century BC when 2,000 Jewish families were settled in Asia Minor under the policy of Antiochus III. The significant contribution of the Laodicean Jews to the temple tax was documented before the first Jewish revolt.[72] Students of the NT have often considered the message to the Laodiceans in Rev 3:14 – 22 as providing critical information concerning the first-century city of Laodicea, especially in the area of water supply (cf. Rev 3:15 – 16), finances (cf. 3:17 – 18a), textile industry (cf. 3:18b), and medicine (3:18c). More recent examination of the archaeological and textual data suggests, however, that these phrases evoke images understandable for the entire local region.[73]

---

68. The negative formulation ("I do not want you to be ignorant") appears more often in Paul (cf. Rom 1:13; 11:25; 1 Cor 10:1; 12:1; 2 Cor 1:8; 1 Thess 4:13).

69. The negative formulation of this formula ("don't you know that") also appears throughout Paul (cf. Rom 6:16; 1 Cor 3:16; 5:6; 6:2, 3, 9, 15, 16, 19; 9:13; 9:24).

70. Louw and Nida, §78.13. Cf. "how much I am struggling for you" (NRSV; cf. TNIV, NLT, NIV).

71. In Acts, Paul's imprisonment is also explicitly con-

nected with his mission to the Gentiles (cf. Acts 21:21 – 22, 28; 22:21 – 22; 26:23).

72. See Cicero, *Pro Flacco* 68 – 69, who mentions that more than twenty pounds of gold were seized from the Laodicean Jews; much of it appears to have been collected for the half-shekel temple tax.

73. See, in particular, Craig R. Koester, "The Message to Laodicea and the Problem of Its Local Context: A Study of the Imagery in Rev 3.14 – 22," *NTS* 49 (2003): 407 – 24.

Together with Hierapolis, Laodicea and Colossae are the notable cites in the Lycus Valley, and they are mentioned together in 4:13. It is unclear why Hierapolis is not also mentioned here,[74] but it is possible that Laodicea is mentioned because the Laodiceans also received a letter from Paul, one that Paul encourages to be read aloud to the Colossians as well (4:16). Another possibility is that the Laodiceans are facing the same false teachings that plague the Colossians.[75] Paul's letters to the Colossians would then be of particular significance to the Laodiceans.

"And those who have not seen my face in the flesh" can refer to all those in Colossae and Laodicea who had not met Paul personally. If so, "and" (καί) is to be taken in an epexegetical sense. While some consider this phrase as referring to those whom he has not met, thus "universaliz[ing] Paul's place in the church,"[76] the shift from the universal language of 1:24 – 29 to the local references in 2:1 – 5 suggests that this group is likely referring to those who resided in the Lycus Valley.[77] Paul's discussion of his absence from them in v. 5 lends further support to this local reading.

2:2a-b So that their hearts may be comforted as they are united in love (ἵνα παρακληθῶσιν αἱ καρδίαι αὐτῶν, συμβιβασθέντες ἐν ἀγάπῃ). With this clause, Paul points to the purpose of his struggles for the Colossians, Laodiceans, and the others in the Lycus Valley. The "heart" is to be considered as the center of one's will and emotions. In this

case, Paul is pointing to one's inner self: he wants them to "be comforted."

The verb "comforted" (παρακληθῶσιν) is often translated as "encouraged" (NASB, NAB, NKJV, NRSV, NLT, TNIV, ESV, NIV), but this translation may focus too heavily on the emotional state of a person and is therefore unable to convey the significance of this term in this context. The verb can also be translated "strengthened,"[78] which would relate to Paul's activity of reaffirming the gospel message in this letter. The connection between this verb and the act of instruction is further supported by 1 Cor 14:31: "For you can all prophesy in turn so that everyone may be instructed [μανθάνωσιν] and encouraged [παρακαλῶνται]."

Our translation, "comforted," understood properly,[79] points to yet another layer in the significance of this term in this context. In the LXX, this verb evokes the eschatological comfort that will come from God in the time of salvation (cf. Isa 40:1, 2, 11; 51:3).[80] The "comfort" that Paul's eschatological suffering (cf. 1:24, 2:1) brings about is not simply the emotional and intellectual support for his readers; rather, his suffering will bring about the comfort that comes from God himself. The passive voice of this verb (a "divine passive") supports this reading, and the relationship between Paul's suffering and the comfort that is to come through God's salvific act is made clear in 2 Cor 1:6: "If we are distressed, it is for your comfort and salvation; if we are comforted, it is for your comfort."

---

74. A few manuscripts (104 424) do include "Hierapolis" in this verse.

75. See, e.g., M. D. Goulder, "The Visionaries of Laodicea," *JSNT* 43 (1991): 15 – 39, who further suggests that Ephesians is an authentic Pauline letter written to the Laodiceans.

76. Sumney, *Colossians*, 114. Thus: "for *all* who have not seen me face to face" (NRSV, italics mine; cf. TNIV, NIV).

77. O'Brien, *Colossians, Philemon*, 92; Harris, *Colossians and Philemon*, 79

78. O'Brien, *Colossians, Philemon*, 92 – 93.

79. Cf. Lightfoot, *St. Paul's Epistles to the Colossians and to Philemon*, 172 – 73, "'comforted' in the older and wider meaning of the word ('confortati'), but not with its modern and restricted sense."

80. For an examination of the semantic field of the term "comfort" that points to both divine actions and human responses, see also Klaus Baltzer, "Liberation from Debt Slavery after the Exile in Second Isaiah and Nehemiah," in *Ancient Israelite Religion: Essays in Honor of Frank Moore Cross* (ed. Patrick D. Miller Jr., Paul D. Hanson, and S. Dean McBride; Philadelphia: Fortress, 1987), 477 – 84.

The question concerning the function of the participle "as they are united" (συμβιβασθέντες) in this context is related to the wider question concerning the relationships between the various pieces in this verse. Some have divided the verse into four clauses as the "fourfold purpose of the struggle" of Paul:[81]

> that their hearts may be comforted
> and they may be united in love,
> also that they may gain the full wealth of
>   assurance...
> and that they may gain the knowledge of the
>   mystery of God.

This parallel structure does not, however, reflect the construction of this verse. The first clause, introduced by a "marker to denote purpose" (ἵνα),[82] should be understood as the main purpose clause of the paragraph. The participial clause that follows ("united in love") is best taken as modifying the act of comforting.[83] The final two units, introduced twice by another purpose marker (εἰς), are purpose phrases, but it is unclear if they are to be seen as parallel with the ἵνα clause. Some take these phrases as the result of being "united in love,"[84] but the presence of καί before these two phrases separates them from the participle and is best taken as modifying the entire purpose clause as introduced by "comforted" (παρακληθῶσιν):[85]

> that their hearts may be comforted
> as they are united in love
> to obtain all the wealth of full assurance ... and
> the knowledge....

"As they are united in love" (συμβιβασθέντες ἐν ἀγάπῃ) introduces the theme of unity in this letter. Although in Greek the word "united" could acquire the sense of "instructed" especially in the LXX (cf. Exod 4:12, 15; Isa 40:13, 14),[86] the use of this term in Col 2:19 and Eph 4:16 suggests that it should be understood in the sense of "being united."[87] Arguing against individual and elitist spiritual practices (2:16 – 23), Paul points to the significance of the unity of God's people as they experience his redemption. This unity is explicitly noted in 3:11, where traditional barriers can no longer define their identity. Here in 2:2, "in love" points to the means through which such unity can be achieved. After the affirmation of the unity of God's people in 3:11, one likewise finds the focus on "love" as the "bond" for perfect unity (3:14).

2:2c To obtain all the wealth of full assurance of understanding (καὶ εἰς πᾶν πλοῦτος τῆς πληροφορίας τῆς συνέσεως). With this prepositional phrase, Paul points further to the purpose of the comfort that the Colossians (and others) would receive. In Greek, "all the wealth" (πᾶν πλοῦτος) is followed by two genitives, "of full assurance" and "of understanding." Two notable options are (1) taking "of full assurance" as a genitive of source and "of understanding" as objective genitive: "the wealth that comes from the full assurance of understanding" (NASB); and (2) taking "of full assurance" as a genitive of content and "of understanding" as genitive of source: "the wealth consisting of full assurance that springs from understanding."[88] What is clear

---

81. Harris, *Colossians and Philemon*, 78.

82. BDAG, 475.

83. Moreover, one would not typically expect an aorist participle as we have it here; cf. Wallace, *Greek Grammar*, 636.

84. See, e.g., Sumney, *Colossians*, 115.

85. Barth and Blanke, *Colossians*, 278 – 79. In English, this conjunction is best left untranslated. Others (e.g., Moo, *Letters to the Colossians and to Philemon*, 165) consider the conjunction as indicating parallelism with the previous purpose

clause(s), but this downplays the adverbial function of the participle that breaks the parallelism in these clauses.

86. Cf. BDAG, 957; O'Brien, *Colossians, Philemon*, 93.

87. Lightfoot, *St. Paul's Epistles to the Colossians and to Philemon*, 173.

88. Cf. Moule, *Epistles to the Colossians and to Philemon*, 86. See also REB: "the full wealth of conviction which understanding brings."

is that Paul is providing an emphatic statement that highlights complete conviction and understanding as the purpose of one's being comforted by the gospel message. The translation provided by NJB, though cumbersome, reflects Paul's emphasis and passion here: "until they are rich in the assurance of their complete understanding."

This purpose phrase provides a critical definition of the significance of the act of comfort. Instead of simply providing emotional support for his readers, Paul focuses on the need to have full conviction that is not to be separated from a complete understanding of the salvific plan of God. It is for their understanding of this gospel that Paul is willing to go through hardships and suffering.

2:2d-e And the knowledge of the mystery of God, Christ (εἰς ἐπίγνωσιν τοῦ μυστηρίου τοῦ θεοῦ, Χριστοῦ). Syntactically this purpose phrase, introduced by the same preposition (εἰς), parallels the previous phrase, but in terms of function this phrase further explains the content of the "understanding" noted in the previous clause. The connection between "knowledge" (ἐπίγνωσιν) and "understanding" (τῆς συνέσεως) has already been made in Paul's prayer report (1:9), where he also considers the readers' growth "in the knowledge of God" (1:10) as the goal of his prayer. This focus on "knowledge" continues in Paul's ethical exhortation below (3:10). In this context, Paul's discussion of this "knowledge" is explicitly linked with "the mystery of God" — a theme introduced in 1:26 – 27.

In the textual tradition, more than ten possible readings can be identified after "the mystery" (τοῦ μυστηρίου).[89] The reading accepted by most

translations, "of God, Christ" (τοῦ θεοῦ, Χριστοῦ), is supported by two of the best manuscripts[90] and best explains the origin of the other variants.[91] The genitive "of the mystery" is an objective genitive that functions as the object of the verbal noun, "knowledge." "Of God" can also be taken as an objective genitive ("[mystery] about God"), but it is best taken as a possessive genitive in light of a similar construction in 1:9. Finally, "Christ" has often been taken as a genitive of apposition that defines "mystery" ("mystery, that is, Christ," NRSV; cf. NASB, REB, NLT, ESV).[92] This reading is supported by the early connection between "Christ" and "mystery" (1:27). Since "the mystery of God" can be identified with the gospel that centers on Christ,[93] to know the mystery of God is to know Christ.

2:3 In whom all the treasures of wisdom and knowledge are hidden (ἐν ᾧ εἰσιν πάντες οἱ θησαυροὶ τῆς σοφίας καὶ γνώσεως ἀπόκρυφοι). With the relative pronoun "whom" (ᾧ) referring to Christ (v. 2), this prepositional phrase provides further description of the significance of Christ. The construction points back to the prepositional Christology of the christological hymn, where two references to "in him" (ἐν αὐτῷ, 1:16, 19) bracket the climactic and central affirmation: "in him [ἐν αὐτῷ] all things are held together" (1:17). Just as the hymnic affirmation points to the critical role of Christ, the present affirmation also points to his unique status. In light of the emphasis that "all [πάντες] the treasures of wisdom and knowledge" are contained in him, one is justified in rendering the phrase as "in him *alone* are hidden all the treasures of wisdom and knowledge."[94]

---

89. See, in particular, Pierre Benoit, "Colossiens 2:2 – 3," in *The New Testament Age: Essays in Honor of Bo Reicke* (ed. William C. Weinrich; Macon, GA: Mercer Univ. Press, 1984), 1:41 – 51.

90. 𝔓⁴⁶ B.

91. Metzger, *Textual Commentary*, 555.

92. This is reflected in the textual reading that makes this reading explicit ("that is, Christ," ὅ ἐστιν Χριστός; D* ar vg^mss).

93. Similarly, for Paul to preach "the gospel" is to preach "Christ" (1 Cor 1:23; 15:12; Gal. 2:2; Phil 1:15; Col 1:23); Bockmuehl, *Revelation and Mystery*, 188.

94. Cf. Lohse, *Colossians and Philemon*, 82.

"The treasures" (οἱ θησαυροί) denote "that which is stored up."[95] The two genitives that follow ("of wisdom and knowledge," τῆς σοφίας καὶ γνώσεως) should be considered as genitives of content, thus providing the description of "all the treasures." The focus here is on "all," which stresses that the readers possess such richness and thus have no need to seek that which is only an illusion of such wisdom and knowledge (cf. 2:4, 23).[96]

"The treasures" rarely appears in the Pauline corpus,[97] although the pair "wisdom and knowledge" does appear elsewhere (Rom 11:33; 1 Cor 12:8; cf. Eph 1:17; Col 1:9). All three word groups, however, appear in the same context in the LXX. Many have pointed to the significance of Prov 2:1 – 8, where one finds the following claim: "For the LORD gives wisdom [σοφίαν]; from his mouth come knowledge [γνῶσις] and understanding. He holds success in store [θησαυρίζει] for the upright" (Prov 2:6 – 7a).[98] Most scholars affirm the influence of wisdom traditions in both canonical (Dan 2:19 – 22)[99] and extracanonical material (Sir 1:24 – 25; Wis 6:22; 7:13 – 14; Bar 3:15).[100] Paul is clearly portraying Christ as the embodiment of wisdom, and through Christ and him alone can one understand the divine will and plan.[101]

The notion of hiddenness (ἀπόκρυφοι) provides yet another dimension of Paul's description of Christ as the embodiment of wisdom. In 1:26 – 27, Paul speaks of the revelation of the mystery to "the saints," but the public revelation remains in the future, when these saints will appear with him in glory (3:4).[102] This hiddenness does not point to the need for further revelation for those in Christ precisely because these saints are already "hidden with Christ in God" (3:3). Paul's focus on hiddenness in this context points rather to the significance of the unfolding of the salvation plan of God. The mere use of the term "hidden," therefore, anticipates the point of full and complete revelation.[103]

2:4 I say this so that no one may deceive you through speculative arguments (τοῦτο λέγω ἵνα μηδεὶς ὑμᾶς παραλογίζηται ἐν πιθανολογίᾳ). Here Paul shifts from the unique status of Christ, whom he preaches, to the deceptiveness of the false teachers whom the Colossians may be encountering. Some have therefore considered this verse as the beginning of a new section, with "this" (τοῦτο) pointing forward to the words that follow: "I tell you, then, do not let anyone deceive you ..." (GNB).[104] This reading is, however, problematic.

First, "I say this" in this concluding part recalls "I desire you to know" at the beginning of this paragraph (v. 1), as Paul expresses concerns for his readers. While vv. 1 – 3 focus on the positive note of encouragement, this verse points to the warning that must be issued. The reappearance of the direct address to the readers ("you," ὑμᾶς) in this verse and in v. 1 provides coherence for this paragraph.

Second, while Paul can use "I say this" to refer to something that follows (cf. Gal 3:17; 1 Cor 1:12), with "so that" (ἵνα) the phrase should be understood to refer to what precedes:[105] "My aim in

---

95. BDAG, 456.

96. Barth and Blanke, *Colossians*, 283.

97. The only other occurrence can be found in 2 Cor 4:7.

98. See, e.g., Martin, *Colossians and Philemon*, 75 – 76; Wright, *Colossians and Philemon*, 96; Moo, *Letters to the Colossians and to Philemon*, 170.

99. Beale, "Colossians," 859.

100. Dunn, *Epistles to the Colossians and to Philemon*, 131 – 32.

101. Schnabel, *Law and Wisdom from Ben Sira to Paul*, 259 – 60.

102. Bockmuehl, *Revelation and Mystery*, 189.

103. See the other uses of the term "hidden" (ἀπόκρυφος) in the New Testament (Mark 4:22; Luke 8:17), where "hiddenness" anticipates "revelation."

104. F. F. Bruce, *The Epistles to the Colossians, to Philemon, and to the Ephesians* (NICNT; Grand Rapids: Eerdmans, 1984), 92. See also the paraphrase in Moule, *Epistles to the Colossians and to Philemon*, 88: "What I mean is, nobody is to talk you into error by specious words...."

105. See, e.g., Sappington, *Revelation and Redemption at Colossae*, 177, who points to the fact that "for" (γάρ) in v. 5 "is more difficult to explain when the ἵνα is taken imperatively, since v. 5 picks up the thought of v. 1 and so binds 2.1 – 5 together."

telling you all this is that…."[106] Paul is providing the rationale and a concluding note concerning what he just said. This statement highlights the urgency of Paul's previous comments concerning the gospel he is commissioned to preach.

Behind the reference of "no one" (μηδείς) lies the false teachers whom Paul is criticizing (cf. v. 18), as are the references to "no one" and "anyone" in 2:8, 16. Some consider these references as indicating "that the philosophers were not a large group, but actually a minority from a numerical point of view."[107] It is equally possible, however, that Paul uses such references to downplay the significance of the false teachers rather than their number, by rhetorically stripping them of influence and identity.

The verb "deceive" (παραλογίζηται) should most likely be taken in the middle voice to refer to the act of deception through false reasoning (cf. "talks you into error," REB).[108] This definition is supported by papyri usages where the verb can be applied for the "wrong use" of particular documents.[109] In this context, deception is carried out through the means of "speculative arguments" (πιθανολογίᾳ), a word not easily translated by an English word. In Classical Greek, this word is used in reference to speculative arguments as opposed to empirical demonstration.[110] "Speculative arguments" is thus justifiably rendered as "fine-sounding arguments" (TNIV, NIV), "well-crafted arguments" (NLT), "specious arguments" (NAB, NJB, REB), or even "fancy talk" (CEV). In any case, this verse anticipates 2:8, where Paul likewise warns his audience of the misleading arguments posed by the unnamed false teachers, though he uses stronger and more explicit language: "See to it that no one takes you captive by means of empty and deceitful philosophy."

2:5a For though I am absent in body, I am with you in spirit (εἰ γὰρ καὶ τῇ σαρκὶ ἄπειμι, ἀλλὰ τῷ πνεύματι σὺν ὑμῖν εἰμι). Paul's unique role in the plan has already been established (1:24 – 29), and his work for the Colossians in particular (2:1 – 3) further establishes his position as one who has the authority to remind them of the gospel they have received. Now Paul deals directly with his absence and thus introduces the significance of this letter.

"For" (γάρ) provides the grounds for Paul's issuing his warnings in v. 4, and they will find fuller development in what follows. Some have taken this sentence as pointing to the very danger caused by Paul's absence: "the danger at hand is not to be underestimated, because the Apostle is distant and cannot be on hand to speak directly to the community."[111] "For" thus points to the reason for Paul's urgent words of warning. While the reality and the potential peril of Paul's absence cannot be denied, Paul's focus here is not the severity of the situation but his unique authority as an apostle.

"Absent in body" can literally be rendered as "absent in the flesh" (KJV, ASV, NKJV); in light of this context it is clear that Paul is simply referring to his physical presence. His choice of the word "flesh" (σάρξ) instead of "body" (σῶμα) here and in v. 1 may be due to the use of this pair at the beginning of this section (1:24). There Paul uses the term "flesh" in reference to his own body, but he reserves the term "body" for the church, the "body" of Christ. Elsewhere in a similar context, Paul uses the word "body" instead: "For though I am absent in body [τῷ σώματι], I am present in

---

106. Harris, *Colossians and Philemon*, 94.

107. Lars Hartman, "Humble and Confident: On the So-Called Philosophers in Colossians," *ST* 49 (1995): 26.

108. The CEV takes this as a passive verb: "I tell you these things to keep you from being fooled by fancy talk."

109. P.Oxy. I 34; MM, 487.

110. Cf. Plato, *Theatetus* 162E; LSJ, 1403.

111. Lohse, *Colossians and Philemon*, 83.

spirit" (lit. trans. of 1 Cor 5:3; cf. 2 Cor 10:10). Elsewhere Paul could also talk about his absence "in face" (προσώπῳ, 1 Thess 2:17; cf. also Col 2:1). In any case, the flexibility of Paul's use of these related terms is to be recognized.[112]

Some have, however, suggested that "I am with you in spirit" refers not to Paul's spirit/heart but to the Holy Spirit, who is present with the readers as they read Paul's own written words.[113] In light of Paul's reference to his physical presence, however, this phrase seems primarily to refer to Paul's own self, though one cannot deny that "this self is connected with the divine Spirit which grants strength to the apostle to unite with the community in common action, despite the distance."[114] Moreover, consistent with the epistolary practices of his time, Paul's use of the absence-presence formula also sheds light on this verse.[115] His physical absence provides the urgent necessity for writing this letter. His words thus represent the very words of Paul the apostle, and in this manner he is present among them "in spirit."

2:5b Rejoicing to see your order and the firmness of your faith in Christ (χαίρων καὶ βλέπων ὑμῶν τὴν τάξιν καὶ τὸ στερέωμα τῆς εἰς Χριστὸν πίστεως ὑμῶν). With this description of his expectation of the Colossian believers, Paul concludes this section before addressing directly the false teachings that those believers face. In Greek, "re-joicing to see" consists of two participles connected with a conjunction, rendered literally by the KJV as "joying and beholding." In this context, it is best to consider the two participles as expressing one complex verbal act,[116] and this is adopted by almost all modern English translations: "rejoicing to see."

"Order" (τάξιν) and "firmness" (στερέωμα) could evoke a military context: "your orderly formation and the firm front which your faith in Christ presents."[117] But in Paul, "order" has only appeared elsewhere in 1 Cor 14:40 in reference to proper and orderly behavior.[118] "Firmness" only appears here in the NT, but related forms have been used in the description of the strengthening (Acts 16:5; cf. 3:7, 16) and firmness (1 Pet 5:9; cf. 2 Tim 2:19) of one's faith.[119] While "of your faith" (πίστεως ὑμῶν) can conceivably modify both "order" and "firmness," in light of the first appearance of the same personal pronoun ("your") earlier in the clause, it is best to take that first ὑμῶν as modifying "order," and "of your faith" as modifying "firmness." Taking the conjunction "and" (καί) as having an epexegetical function, the interrelationship between the two parts of the sentence becomes clear: "rejoicing to see your order that is reflected in the firmness of your faith in Christ." In this context, the focus is not simply on their order or the strength of their faith; it is on the anchor of their lives "in Christ," which points to Christ as the object of their faith.

Paul's note of joy and praise has several possible

---

112. This is to challenge Betz's conclusion that the use of the term "flesh" (σάρξ) in this context points the work of a post-Pauline author who is alluding to Paul's own death; Hans Dieter Betz, "Paul's 'Second Presence' in Colossians," in *Text and Contexts: Biblical Texts in Their Textual and Situational Contexts: Essays in Honor of Lars Hartman* (ed. Tord Fornberg and David Hellholm; Oslo/Boston: Scandinavian Univ. Press, 1995), 513. See also Angela Standhartinger, "Colossians and the Pauline School," *NTS* 50 (2004): 582 – 83.

113. Fee, *God's Empowering Presence*, 646.

114. Lohse, *Colossians and Philemon*, 83.

115. Heikki Koskenniemi, *Studien zur Idee und Phraseologie des griechischen Briefes bis 400 n Chr.* (Helsinki: Suomal-aisen Kirjallisuuden Seura, 1956), 177.

116. Cf. BDF §471(5), which considers this as the use of parataxis in hypotactic syntactic structure.

117. Moule, *Epistles to the Colossians and to Philemon*, 89. See also REB, which follows closely this reading: "rejoice to see your unbroken ranks and the solid front which your faith in Christ presents."

118. In this context, "order" has also been rendered as "good discipline" (NASB), "living as you should," (NLT), "morale" (NRSV), and "well-ordered" (NJB).

119. See also Kreitzer, "Living in the Lycus Valley," 88 – 89, who sees behind this word an allusion to the earthquake-prone region where Colossae is located.

functions here. First, these words of praise have been considered a rhetorical device through which the goodwill of the audience is secured.[120] Second, the note of "rejoicing" points back to the beginning of this section, where the same verb (χαίρω) appears in reference to Paul's rejoicing over his own sufferings for the sake of the Colossians (1:24). This second note provides closure for this section while providing transition to the next section, which focuses intently on the strength of the faith of the Colossians. Third, and perhaps most importantly, the reference to "in Christ" paves the way for his arguments where he reaffirms the centrality of Christ in the faith of the believers. In combating the false teachings that the Colossians are facing, Paul insists that nothing less than a christocentric faith is sufficient for one to stand firm in the gospel they have received. It is for this gospel, after all, that Paul is willing to undergo great sufferings and afflictions.

Theology in Application

Identity and Self-Understanding

It may surprise some that we begin a section that deals with eschatology, gospel, mystery, wisdom, and apostolic suffering with a section on one's self-understanding. Within the structure of Colossians, however, this section that focuses on Paul's identity and mission does have a special role. After the discussion of the work and significance of Christ (1:15 – 23), and before dealing directly with the issues the Colossians are facing (2:6 – 23), one finds the critical bridge in the self-portrayal of Paul the apostle. While it can be dangerous to pull this aspect out of its theological and rhetorical contexts, certain elements of what Paul affirms here are relevant for all believers who seek to find their identity properly grounded in the gospel they have received.

Paul's autobiographical details begin with the account of his call from God to become one who serves the word of God (1:25). In response to this call, Paul commits himself to proclaiming that word to all people as he is empowered by God (1:29). What is missing in Paul's self-portrayal here is worth noting. Paul does not comment on his educational background in both Jewish and Greco-Roman centers of learning,[121] nor does he emphasize his experience as a teacher of the Torah and one who must have had considerable power within the Jewish religious and political system.[122] He focuses solely on his call from God, the source of his power. This is ultimately grounded in his understanding of the powerful grace of God, which is able to transfer sinners despite their unworthiness.

---

120. Sumney, "The Function of Ethos in Colossians," 306 – 37.

121. Cf. Acts 21:39; 22:3. It should be noted that even in Acts when Paul was first introduced, his credentials are not listed. Instead, he is simply introduced as an opponent of the Word (Acts 7:58; 8:1 – 3).

122. This is reflected in his involvement in the judicial procedures of the stoning of Stephen (Acts 7:58) as well as his connection with the high priest, which allowed him to obtain permission to persecute the Christians (9:1 – 2).

One noteworthy element in this self-portrayal is the importance of the "mystery" of God, which is revealed now at the end of times when God works through Christ in this climax of salvation history (1:26). Paul not only grounds his mission within this significant unfolding of salvation history, but his mission is also to be the instrument through which such "mystery" can be revealed to those who encounter the gospel (2:2). Throughout this self-portrayal, therefore, Paul identifies his life and ministry within the wider salvation plan of God. Writing in prison as he looks back at his ministry, Paul finds meaning neither in his accomplishments nor in the exotic episodes in his numerous journeys,[123] but in his participation in the unfolding of God's purpose. This purpose centers on "Christ," who is, after all, "the mystery of God" (2:2). Before encouraging his readers to lead a Christ-centered life, he first demonstrates what such a life looks like.

In our contemporary culture, where greatness is often defined by one's popularity, income, or social and political status, this section serves as a powerful reminder for the church to create a different culture, where significance is to be measured in a radically different way. In the early church, one can point to numerous "minor characters," such as Matthias (Acts 1) and Ananias (Acts 9), who must be considered as "great" since they accomplish their call within the redemptive history of God. For us, our identity and worth are to be measured by our faithfulness to God's wider plan of redemption and our specific calls within that plan.

Struggles and Afflictions

Both Paul's focus on the call of God, who empowers him, and his role as the proclaimer of the gospel within the wider plan of God are grounded in his understanding of God's grace, which does not allow for any boasting: "For when I preach the gospel, I cannot boast, since I am compelled to preach" (1 Cor 9:16). The achievement in which Paul does boast, however, is his own struggles: "If I must boast, I will boast of the things show my weaknesses" (2 Cor 11:30; cf. 12:9). It is not surprising, therefore, to find Paul discussing his own struggles and sufferings whenever he talks about his own identity and mission.

In his discussion of his suffering here, it is important to note that Paul does not provide a general theology of suffering, nor does he exhaust all types of suffering a believer may encounter. Rather, Paul's focus is on his own suffering in the ministry of the gospel. To recognize this does not limit the power of this discussion, however, as it points to several important elements that are relevant for those who suffer for the sake of the gospel. First, to suffer for the sake of Christ is at the center of his mission as an apostle. The reference to "the commission from God given to me for

---

123. The focus on the exotic is frequently the focus of the travel reports in both travelogues and ancient Greco-Roman novels; cf. Neil Rennie, *Far-Fetched Facts: The Literature of* *Travel and the Idea of the South Seas* (Oxford: Clarendon, 1995), 1 – 29; Bryan P. Reardon, *The Form of Greek Romance* (Princeton: Princeton Univ. Press, 1991), 15 – 45.

you" (1:25) clearly points to the relationship between suffering and the ministry of "the word of God" (1:25). This is consistent with the Lukan account of Paul's call and conversion in Acts 9:16 through the words of the risen Lord: "He must [δεῖ] suffer for my name."

This reference to divine necessity points to the relationship between Paul's suffering and Christ's own suffering. In Luke 9:22, for example, one finds the same term for Jesus' prediction concerning his own death: "The Son of Man must suffer [δεῖ] many things and be rejected … and he must be killed." Regardless of how the expression "the afflictions of Christ" (Col 1:24) is to be understood, the numerous references to Christ in this section (cf. 1:27, 28; 2:2, 5) point to the relationship between Paul's suffering and Christ's own death, which was the center of the previous section (1:18, 20, 22).[124] To be an apostle of Christ means, therefore, that one must be willing to "take up their cross" and follow him (Luke 9:23). In focusing on a lifelong ministry of walking on the path of the cross, Paul provides an alternative to those who are involved in ascetic practices (2:20 – 23) without fully realizing the demands of the cross that involve a total reorientation of one's life in response to what was accomplished on the cross.

The reference to divine necessity also points to the wider plan of God within which the suffering of both Jesus and Paul has to be understood.[125] Paul identifies his suffering with the revelation of Christ as "the mystery hidden for ages and generations" (1:26). This suffering is not an end in and of itself, but it points forward to Christ, who is also identified as "the hope of glory" (v. 27). For Paul, therefore, to align his suffering with Christ is to experience living in light of the climax of salvation history, which centers on the death and resurrection of Jesus Christ with the hope for the fulfillment of such history in the full revelation of Christ's glory.

This is consistent with Paul's affirmation elsewhere that "we share in his [Christ's] sufferings in order that we may also share in his glory" (Rom 8:17), and that "our present sufferings are not worth comparing with the glory that will be revealed in us" at the end of times (8:18). Within such a wider perspective, suffering in Christ's name is to experience fully the tension between the "already" and the "not yet." Perhaps Paul emphasizes his own suffering at this point to reintroduce this temporal perspective into a community that seeks to transcend this tension in achieving the experience of the consummated age.

Finally, Paul does not suffer for suffering's sake. Instead, he considers his suffering as contributing to the body of Christ. Paul begins by noting that his suffering is

---

124. This christological identification is often understood as a unique Pauline contribution to the discussion of Christian suffering, one that is picked up by later authors within the circle of Paul; cf. Barry D. Smith, *Paul's Seven Explanations of the Suffering of the Righteous* (SBT 47; New York: Peter Lang, 2002), 183.

125. This would also explain the identification of Jesus and Paul as that of a "missiological" nature rather than an "ontological" one; see Scott J. Hafemann, "The Role of Suffering in the Mission of Paul," in *The Mission of the Early Church to Jews and Gentiles* (ed. Jostein Ådna and Hans Kvalbein; WUNT 127; Tübingen: Mohr, 2000), 174.

"for your sake" and "for the sake of his body, which is the church" (1:24). Turning his attention to his immediate readers, Paul again emphasizes "how great a struggle" he has for them (2:1). In light of the emphasis on the efficacy and sufficiency of Christ's death in 1:15 – 20, Paul's notes on his suffering for the church aim not at exalting himself as the great benefactor of the church. Instead of reaffirming a martyr mentality, Paul is emphasizing his solidarity with those who are also looking forward to the fulfillment of "the hope of glory" (1:27). It is not surprising, therefore, to find his statement that his suffering is to build up the community of God's people "in love" (2:2). Transforming an individualistic view of spirituality, Paul points to the community through which the mystery of God can be fully made manifest. Suffering, then, becomes the means through which community can be built as God's people share in the weaknesses that create the space of the powerful acts of God.

Suffering and persecution are very much a reality for believers in many parts of the world. Paul reminds these believers that their suffering is not in vain and that it often serves to build up the churches. It may perhaps seem surprising to believers in other parts of the world when these suffering brothers and sisters are not always envious of the life of the churches in the "free" world since they fully understand the sanctifying power of suffering in creating an alert community that thirsts for the final consummation of God's kingdom. In a meeting with pastors of underground churches in a "closed" society, I was struck by the response they gave when asked of the greatest worries they have for their churches: "the end of the persecution of our churches." Their response reflects a realization that the lack of suffering and affliction can often lead to a lazy church that is no longer alert in her existence between the times. For those in the "free" world, we are called to be alert as faithful witnesses in our own contexts. We are also called to identify with the suffering believers through prayer, financial support, and short-term and long-term mission work.

It is not that faithfulness to the gospel necessarily entails suffering in every instance — even Paul occasionally garnered a decent reception. But we might question our faithfulness if we never suffer for Christ and the gospel in ways Paul did. We should recall the words of Jesus:

> If the world hates you, keep in mind that it hated me first. If you belonged to the world, it would love you as its own. As it is, you do not belong to the world, but I have chosen you out of the world. That is why the world hates you. Remember what I told you: "A servant is not greater than his master." If they persecuted me, they will persecute you also. If they obeyed my teaching, they will obey yours also. They will treat you this way because of my name, for they do not know the one who sent me. (John 15:18 – 21)

If the world is giving us a far better reception than they gave our Lord and his faithful servant Paul, we may have to consider whether we are accommodating the gospel too much.

Caring in a Christian Community

It is with this understanding of the community of sufferers that the theology of caring can be articulated. In the discussion of his suffering, Paul's note of the Colossians' being "comforted" by God (2:2) recalls the extensive discussion in 2 Cor 1:3 – 7, which concludes in Paul's definition of the community of God's people who await the full revelation of God's glory: "just as you share in our sufferings, so also you share in our comfort" (2 Cor 1:7). In suffering, we recognize our common humanity as those who anticipate the full redemption of our bodies. This recognition allows Paul to affirm that comfort can only come from God. This comfort is not caused by a temporary elevation of one's emotional state; it is anchored rather in the work of God through Jesus Christ himself (Col 2:2 – 3). In demonstrating the proper role of a "carer," Paul labors in bringing the full knowledge of God's work through Christ to those who need to be comforted. Recognizing that God is the ultimate comforter, we can be freed from the impossible burden of providing true care to those who are drawn in the common human predicament brought about by the effects of sin in the present age.[126]

The recognition that God is the only one who can offer comfort to those who suffer will also impede the projected sense of superiority for the ones who offer care. Any act of caring can become an occasion that fosters selfishness, betrayal, ambition, greed, and even cruelty.[127] To affirm that God is the one on whom we all depend reminds us that we share the common human predicament as we all await his final redemptive act. Instead of a competitive act, to care is to be involved in a community where vulnerability and weaknesses become the bond.

The connection between christological affirmation and a vibrant theology of caring is found in another letter of Paul probably written during the same imprisonment. Prior to the christological hymn in Phil 2:6 – 11, Paul argues against competition among the followers of Christ as they experience the "comfort" (παράκλησις) that comes from God (Phil 2:1). The act of caring and compassion is then defined by imitating Christ, and in doing so a community of caring is formed. As it has been noted, "Paul stresses that the compassionate life is a life in community."[128] This is particularly true when this community is defined by their sharing in the life in the body of Christ, a body that is "united in love" (Col 2:2).

---

126. See William Beniah Willis, *Caring Is God: A Systematic Pastoral Theology* (Macon, GA: Smyth and Helwys, 1993), 123 – 33.

127. Mike W. Martin, *Love's Virtues* (Lawrence, KA: Univ. Press of Kansas, 1996), 33 – 35.

128. Donald P. McNeill, Douglas A. Morrison, and Henri J. M. Nouwen, *Compassion: A Reflection on the Christian Life* (New York: Doubleday, 1982), 50.

Mystery of God

In this section, Paul introduces the "mystery of God" for the Colossians, a concept that appears three times here (1:26, 27; 2:2). Although not a concept that easily lends itself to "application," in a section that focuses on having the right "knowledge," acquiring the right perspective and the right framework of thought is perhaps the intended course of action for this section. This emphasis is confirmed by vocabularies and phrases such as "revealed" (1:26), "make known" (1:27), "proclaim" (1:28), "admonishing" (1:28), "teaching" (1:28), "with all wisdom" (1:28), "know" (2:1), "full assurance of understanding" (2:2), "knowledge" (2:2), and "all the treasures of wisdom and knowledge" (2:3). In this section emphasizing the acquisition of the right knowledge, Paul's focus on the "mystery of God" becomes all the more important.

First, "the mystery hidden for ages and generations" (1:26) points to the continuity of the gospel with God's previous work in history. The fact that the time of the proclamation of Christ's death and resurrection is finally the moment for God "to make known the glorious riches of this mystery" (v. 27) also points to the discontinuity of this moment from the past.[129] This uniqueness is further highlighted by the identification of this "mystery" as "Christ" himself (2:2). A proper understanding of the significance of the gospel is to appreciate both the continuity and the discontinuity of this climax of history. Within this tension is the one truth that cannot be compromised: all reality must be understood through the lens of "Christ," who is both the goal and the fulfillment of God's promises.

Second, the christological identification of this "mystery" has an ecclesiological aspect. Paul points to inclusion of "the Gentiles" as something that is revealed in this age of fulfillment. The point is developed in Ephesians (cf. Eph 3:1 – 11), but the significance of the gospel that brings together both Jews and Gentiles is also noted in Col 3:11. The power of this gospel is not limited to the individual; it also creates a new community through which the revelation of this mystery is made manifest. Paul also offers helpful descriptions of what should characterize this new community. It is a place in which the mystery about Christ is proclaimed and explained, so that Christians may mature in Christ (1:28). We must question whether our churches have this same focus on proclaiming the Word so that Christians develop in maturity. Or do we get sidetracked by programs and functions and lose sight of the central issues?

Furthermore, Paul desires that the community be a place where the love of Christ is expressed (2:2) and the community functions in an orderly manner (2:5). This difficult balance is hard to achieve and maintain in a local church, but we must reflect

---

129. This description would remind the Jewish audience of the former role of the Torah. One can therefore speak of "a fundamental shift in the approach to revelation, in which the Torah has become (not 'replaced' by Christ and the gospel, but) the attendant witness to the surpassing end-time revelation of God's righteousness and saving design" (Bockmuehl, *Revelation and Mystery*, 225).

properly the work of the gospel in believers' lives. Paul's description of the community of Christians serves as a challenge to our churches to align ourselves with the positive qualities he lists. While the list is far from exhaustive, it is instructive in how the gospel is manifested in the community.

Third, since "Christ" is the "mystery," he becomes the criterion through which all arguments must be evaluated (2:4). In transitioning to a direct refutation of the arguments of the opponents in the next section, Paul does not present a series of propositions on which he builds his case. Instead, he points back to Christ himself, who is the anchor of all truth. As Paul repeatedly points to the sufficiency of Christ, we must also emphasize this point even when we are commenting on this text.

In our times, many searching for spiritual enlightenment treasure the term "mystery" as that which is private/esoteric, individualistic/existential, and immediate/unmediated.[130] Modern preachers ought to spend some time introducing this concept to their audience since for Paul this mystery points to a historical event, one that has an impact for the entire community of God's people and one that, mediated through the gospel of Jesus Christ, must be lived out between the cross and the parousia. In the time of Paul, this challenges the religious practices in Asia Minor; in our time, this continues to challenge us as we are tempted by false gospels.

---

130. See, e.g., Andrew Schneider, *The Mysteries Revealed: A Handbook of Esoteric Psychology, Philosophy and Spirituality* (Las Vegas, NV: New Falcon, 1995).

Colossians 2:6 – 15

Literary Context

In the previous sections, Paul has set down the foundation for his argument in this main body of the letter. In the christological hymn of 1:15 – 20, Paul focused on the supremacy of Christ as manifested both in creation (1:15 – 16) and in his death and resurrection, which gave rise to a new created order (1:18b – 20). At the center is his affirmation that in Christ all things are held together (1:17 – 18a). In light of the completed work of Christ, Paul urged the Colossians to remain faithful to this gospel (1:21 – 23).

From this christological confession, Paul shifted his attention to his own role as one suffering on behalf of the body of Christ. After locating his role as a proclaimer of the mystery hidden for ages (1:24 – 29), he focused on his particular concerns for those in Colossae and the surrounding area (2:1 – 5). As in the previous section, Paul concluded this one too with a note on the firmness of the faith of the Colossians.

With 2:6 – 7, Paul moves into the main body of the letter as he focuses on the problems that appear in Colossae. The concerns expressed in the previous two sections are clearly alluded to in this brief section. The note on the reception of "Christ Jesus the Lord" (v. 6) alludes to the christological confession of 1:15 – 20, and the call to remain firm in the faith as they "were taught" (2:7) points to the description in 2:1 – 5 of Paul's apostolic ministries.[1]

Paul then confronts directly the problems the Colossians are facing (2:8 – 23). He begins with the imperative "see to it" (βλέπετε, v. 8), which draws attention to what Christ has already accomplished for those who belong to him (2:8 – 15). This restatement of the gospel message that challenges the ideological foundation of the false teachings paves the way for 2:16 – 23, where Paul challenges the behavior and practices imposed by the false teachers. The connection between these two sections is confirmed by the word, "therefore" (οὖν) in v. 16, a connective particle that draws out the implications of what has been affirmed. Since salvation has been accomplished

---

1. Some have therefore considered 2:6 – 7 as a conclusion to the previous sections (1:1 – 2:5); cf. MacDonald, *Colossians and Ephesians*, 88.

by Christ in his death and resurrection, the believers should not be convinced to act in a way that contradicts this belief.

Paul then moves to positive exhortation in 3:1 – 4:1, where he explains the vision of proper Christian living. He is deeply concerned to encourage the believers to be faithful to Christ and the gospel. This call to faithfulness has been explicitly noted in 1:23; 2:6 – 7.

As Paul moves through the various stages of his arguments, he repeatedly reminds his readers to be thankful to God, who accomplished his mighty acts of salvation through Christ. After the thanksgiving section of 1:3 – 8, Paul again issues a call to thanksgiving at the beginning of this main section (2:7) and repeats it in 3:15 – 17. The final section is likewise introduced by a call to thanksgiving (4:2). In other words, Paul reminds his readers that this is not a presentation of an abstract theory; rather, it is a call to worship the one and true Creator, who has brought about an era of new creation.

IV. Apostolic Mission of Paul (1:24 – 2:5)
  A. Paul's Suffering in the Plan of God (1:24 – 29)
  B. Paul's Toil for the Local Churches (2:1 – 5)
➡ **V. Faithfulness of the Believers (2:6 – 4:1)**
  A. Call to Faithfulness (2:6 – 7)
  B. Sufficiency in Christ (2:8 – 23)
    1. Against Deceptive Philosophy (2:8 – 15)
    2. Against Human Rituals and Regulations (2:16 – 23)
  C. Reorientation of Christian Living (3:1 – 4:1)

Main Idea

The Colossian believers are called to be faithful to Christ and the gospel they have received. They are reminded of the death and resurrection of Christ, who has delivered them from their sins and the powers that threaten them. Rather than following the human traditions, these believers must place their trust in Christ, in whom the fullness of deity resides.

Translation

(See pages 152 – 53.)

Structure

The main thesis of this letter is laid out in a well-structured sentence in 2:6 – 7, in which Paul calls the Colossian believers to be faithful to the gospel they have received. The first clause, "just as [ὡς] you received Christ Jesus the Lord" (v. 6a), is balanced by "just as (καθώς) you were taught" in v. 7d;[2] both point to the reception of the traditions of Jesus Christ as the Lord of all. The main clause appears with the imperative to "continue to walk in him" (v. 6b), which is qualified by four participles in v. 7: "rooted," "built up," "established," and "abounding."

These four participles are not to be understood in strictly parallel terms, however. While the first three clearly describe various components of walking in Christ, the active participle at the end is separated from the first three by an intervening comparative clause ("just as you were taught") and summarizes the previous three passive participles. To abound in thanksgiving is the goal of being "rooted" and "built up" in him and "established in the faith" (cf. a similar thanksgiving function in 3:17).

With v. 8, one enters the main section where Paul directly challenges his audience as they face the false teachings. The imperative "see to it" alerts the readers of the danger they are facing. Before providing substantial arguments against these teachings, Paul rhetorically reduces the status of false teachers by criticizing their teaching as "empty and deceitful philosophy," "according to human tradition ... [and] the elemental spirits of the world," and most importantly, "not according to Christ." Building on this final criticism, Paul reaffirms the sufficiency and centrality of Christ as the critical principle of any version of the gospel message (v. 9).

Moving from this christocentric principle, Paul then emphasizes the reality in which the believers already find themselves: they are filled in Christ (v. 10), they have died and been raised with him (vv. 11 – 12), and they share in his victory over all competing moral and cosmic forces (vv. 13 – 15). This affirmation of the supremacy of Christ and of the finality of his salvific work is, therefore, not simply an abstract truth; it affects the very self-understanding of believers, who find their true identities in what Christ has done for us.

---

2. Both "just as" (ὡς) and "just as" (καθώς) are comparative conjunctions familiar to most Hellenistic authors; BDF §453.

Colossians 2:6 – 15

6a	accordance	Therefore,
		just as you received Christ Jesus the Lord,
b	Exhortation	**continue to walk in him,**
7a	means	[1] rooted and
b	list	[2] built up in him and
c	list	[3] established in the faith,
d	accordance	just as you were taught,
e	list: summary/goal	[4] abounding in thanksgiving.
8a	Warning	**See to it that no one takes you captive**
b	means	by means of empty and
		deceitful philosophy
c	source	according to human tradition,
d	expansion	according to the elemental spirits of the world and
e	contrast (to 8d)	not according to Christ.
9	basis	For in him all the fullness of deity dwells bodily, and
10a	expansion	you have been filled in him,
b	description	who is the head of every ruler and authority.

11a	Assertion	**In him you were also circumcised with a circumcision not performed by human hands,**
b	means	in the putting off of the body of flesh,
c	explanation	by the circumcision of Christ,
12a	time	when you were buried with him in baptism,
b	progression	in whom you were also raised
c	means	through faith in the work of God,
d	description	who raised him from the dead.
13a	concession	And you, who were once dead in your transgressions and in the uncircumcision of your flesh,
b	Contra-expectation	**God made alive with him,**
c	cause	having forgiven us all our transgressions,
14a	expansion	by expunging the written decree that is against us,
b	association	together with its regulations,
c	description (of 14a)	which opposed us, and
d	event	this he took from among us,
e	means	nailing it to the cross.
15a	time	When he disarmed the rulers and authorities,
b	Event	**he boldly made a spectacle of them,**
c	means	by triumphing over them in him.

Exegetical Outline

→ **I. Call to Faithfulness (2:6 – 7)**

    A. Continue to walk in Christ (2:6)

    B. Being established and giving thanks (2:7)

II. Sufficiency in Christ (2:8 – 23)

    A. Against deceptive philosophy (2:8 – 15)

        1. Call to be alert (2:8a)

        2. Identification of the false teachers (2:8b-e)

            a. Empty and deceitful philosophy (2:8b)

            b. Human tradition (2:8c)

            c. Principles of the world (2:8d)

            d. Not according to Christ (2:8e)

        3. Full deity of Christ (2:9)

        4. Believers' participation in Christ (2:10 – 15)

            a. Being filled in Christ (2:10)

            b. Died and raised with Christ (2:11 – 12)

            c. Share in the victory of Christ (2:13 – 15)

Explanation of the Text

2:6a Therefore, just as you received Christ Jesus the Lord (Ὡς οὖν παρελάβετε τὸν Χριστὸν Ἰησοῦν τὸν κύριον). Paul begins this section by reminding the Colossian believers of their reception of the traditions concerning Christ Jesus. "Therefore" (οὖν) links this passage with the previous sections, which focused on the supreme status and identity of Christ (1:15 – 23) and the apostolic gospel that has been faithfully transmitted (1:24 – 2:5).[3] "Just as" (ὡς) provides the grounds for the imperative clause that follows.

The verb "you received" (παρελάβετε) belongs to a pair of verbs ("to transmit," παραδίδωμι; "to receive," παραλαμβάνω) that is often used to describe the transmission and reception of traditions and teachings in both Classical Greek (Plato, *Theaet.* 198b, Polybius, 7.1.1) and Hellenistic Jewish (Jos., *Ag. Ap.* 1.60) writings.[4] In Paul's letters, this use is best illustrated in his description of the transmission and reception of the core gospel message:

> For what I received [παρέλαβον] I passed on [παρέδωκα] to you as of first importance: that Christ died for our sins according to the Scriptures, that he was buried, and that he was raised on the third day according to the Scriptures. (1 Cor 15:3 – 4)[5]

In light of these usages, it seems appropriate to take the verb here as referring to the Colossians' reception of "the content of that which had been

---

3. While this particle can function simply as a transition maker (e.g., "and now," NLT), in this context it clearly points to the logical consequence of the previous affirmations.

4. BDAG, 762 – 63, 768; G. Delling, "λαμβάνω, κτλ.," *TDNT*, 4:11 – 14.

5. See also 1 Cor 11:2, 23; Gal 1:9, 12; 1 Thess 4:1; 2 Thess 3:6.

communicated to the community."[6] In other words, Paul is not primarily referring to receiving Christ Jesus as one's personal Lord,[7] but to the reception of the traditions concerning Christ Jesus the Lord. This reading is further supported by its immediate context. In the previous section, Paul has emphasized that Christ is the one whom "we proclaim, admonishing everyone and teaching everyone with all wisdom" (1:28). Moreover, the parallelism with a similar phrase that follows also highlights the act of teaching as an act of transmitting the reliable tradition:

> just as you received … (v. 6)
> just as you were taught … (v. 7)

The point Paul is establishing here is not that the Colossians have not submitted to the lordship of Christ, but that they need to be reminded that they have received the authentic gospel of Christ Jesus, who is the Lord of all. Therefore, they should not be deceived by the "empty and deceitful philosophy" that finds its roots in "human tradition" and the "elemental spirits of the world" (v. 8). In other words, Paul is referring to the Colossians' reception of "Christ Jesus the Lord" (KJV, NASB, NKJV, NRSV, ESV), and not "Christ Jesus as Lord" (REB, TEV, NET, TNIV, NIV) or even "Christ Jesus as your Lord" (NLT).

It should be emphasized, however, that for Paul the reception of the gospel of "Christ Jesus the Lord" is not merely to provide an intellectual consent to a set of propositions. Elsewhere in Paul,

a reminder of the tradition is always followed by a proper response that includes both a belief system (e.g., 1 Cor 15:12 – 13) and a behavioral pattern (e.g., 11:27 – 32; 1 Thess 4:1). In this verse, the note on the Colossians' reception of the gospel is immediately followed by the call for his readers to "continue to walk in him."

In light of the definite article before "Christ" (τὸν Χριστὸν Ἰησοῦν), "Christ" should be taken as a title rather than as a personal name.[8] The phrase therefore could be taken as "the Messiah, Jesus, the Lord," or even "Jesus as Lord and Christ" (NJB). This formulation may be intended as a confession against the mystics who deny the lordship of the earthly Jesus.[9] Others see behind this formulation "a sort of double creed":[10] "Jesus is the Messiah/Christ" (Acts 5:42; 9:22; 18:5, 28; 1 John 5:1) and "Jesus is Lord" (Rom 10:9; 1 Cor 12:3).

2:6b   Continue to walk in him (ἐν αὐτῷ περιπατεῖτε). The affirmation of Jesus as Christ and Lord should lead to changed behavior. The Greek verb "continue to walk" can be either an indicative or an imperative according to morphology, but in this context it is clearly an imperative that exhorts the Colossians to lead lives consistent with their confession. The impact of such a christological confession is also implied in 1:10 and 3:13, where Paul affirms how the lordship of Christ should affect every aspect of one's life.

The verb "to walk" (περιπατέω) in 1:10 in particular points to its affinity to 2:6. Colossians 1:10

---

6. Lohse, *Colossians and Philemon*, 93; cf. Dunn, *Epistles to the Colossians and to Philemon*, 138 – 39; Barth and Blanke, *Colossians*, 299 – 300.

7. Thus Moo, *Letters to the Colossians and to Philemon*, 177. Some have also considered this a reference to the "baptism" or the "whole process of resocialization into the Christian community of which baptism is the symbolic center"; Wayne A. Meeks, "'To Walk Worthily of the Lord': Moral Formation in the Pauline School Exemplified by the Letter to the Colossians," in *Hermes and Athena: Biblical Exegesis and Philosophical The-*

ology (ed. Eleonore Stump and Thomas P. Flint; Notre Dame, IN: Univ. of Notre Dame Press, 1993), 44.

8. Some consider the mere placement of "Christ" before "Jesus" as an indication of the use of "Christ" as a title rather than a personal name; Oscar Cullmann, *The Christology of the New Testament* (rev. ed.; trans. Shirley C. Guthrie and Charles A. M. Hall; Philadelphia: Westminster, 1963), 134.

9. Lightfoot, *St. Paul's Epistles to the Colossians and to Philemon*, 176.

10. Moule, *Epistles to the Colossians and to Philemon*, 90.

emphasizes the need to act in light of the reception of "the knowledge of his will in all spiritual wisdom and understanding" (1:9), and in 2:6, the call to "continue to walk in him" is also built on the reception of the knowledge and affirmation of Jesus as Lord and Christ. If so, "continue to walk in him" can also be understood in light of the purpose clause in 1:10: "in order that you may walk in a manner worthy of the Lord, and please him in every way." The list that follows in 1:10b – 12 is similar to the list here in 2:7. In both lists, Paul makes it clear that "to walk" should not be defined simply in pragmatic and behavioral terms, for it involves both living in faith and in the worship of the true Lord of all.

"In him" (ἐν αὐτῷ) again points to the christocentric principle that lies at the center of Paul's argument in this letter. As Paul continues with this line of argument, he will once again stress that proper behavior is grounded in the fact that believers "have been filled in him [ἐν αὐτῷ], who is the head of every ruler and authority" (2:10). Here one finds a clear statement of the purpose of this letter as Paul aims at reforming the confessional, ethical, and cultic lives of those who have received the gospel of Christ Jesus the Lord. It is not an overstatement to consider this "the key verse for understanding the letter."[11]

2:7a-b Rooted and built up in him (ἐρριζωμένοι καὶ ἐποικοδομούμενοι ἐν αὐτῷ). Paul now outlines the means through which believers can live a faithful life in Christ. This list (a series of participles) resembles the list that appears earlier in reference to the means through which one can walk in a manner that pleases God:

1:10b – 12a	2:7
bearing fruit in every good work	rooted [in him]
growing in the knowledge of God	built up in him
being strengthened with all power …	established in the faith …
giving thanks to the Father …	abounding in thanksgiving

Both lists begin with a horticultural metaphor, and both end with a note on thanksgiving. In light of an intervening section that focuses on the supremacy of Christ (1:15 – 20), this second list makes it more explicit that the believers are now to be grounded "in him."

The metaphors in v. 7 shift from the field of horticulture ("rooted") to that of architecture ("built up").[12] It is possible, however, that Paul is not arbitrarily combining different metaphors. Both kinds of metaphors can be found in the description of the Jerusalem temple, and this connection may shed light on the significance of these metaphors here.

First, in using the verb "built up" (ἐποικοδομούμενοι), Paul likely has the community of God's temple in mind, especially when "the building metaphor assumed by Paul is, as almost everywhere, the people of God as the new-covenant temple of God."[13] The two other instances where this verb appears in Paul's writings both point to this temple imagery. In 1 Cor 3:10, 12, 14, where the verb is used three times, Paul explicitly notes that the believers are "God's temple" (3:16). Similarly, in Eph 2:19 – 21, Paul writes:

> [God's] household [is that which is] built [ἐποικοδομηθέντες] on the foundation of the apostles and prophets, with Christ Jesus himself as the chief cornerstone. In him the whole build-

11. Wayne A. Meeks, "In One Body: The Unity of Humankind in Colossians and Ephesians," in *God's Christ and His People: Studies in Honor of Nils Alstrup Dahl* (ed. Jacob Jervell and Wayne A. Meeks; Oslo: Universitetsforlaget, 1977), 210.

12. See, e.g., Lightfoot, *St. Paul's Epistles to the Colossians*

and to Philemon, 176; Moule, *Epistles to the Colossians and to Philemon*, 90; O'Brien, *Colossians, Philemon*, 107; Wilson, *Colossians and Philemon*, 193; Moo, *Letters to the Colossians and to Philemon*, 180 – 81.

13. Fee, *Pauline Christology*, 327.

ing is joined together and rises [or grows, αὔξει] to become a holy temple in the Lord.

Notably, both sets of metaphors appear in the same context in reference to the temple of God.[14] This Ephesian passage can also explain the parallel between Col 1:10 and 2:7, where one finds "growing [αὐξανόμενοι] in the knowledge of God" paralleled by "built up [ἐποικοδομούμενοι] in him."[15]

Second, horticulture imageries by themselves are also not foreign to biblical depictions of the temple. In Ps 52:8, for example, one finds the worshiper compared to an "olive tree flourishing in the house of God," and 92:12 – 14 describes the righteous who "flourish like a palm tree … planted in the house of the LORD"; they will "bear fruit in old age." Moreover, in the portrayal of the ideal temple in Ezek 47, one likewise encounters "a great number of trees on each side of the river" (47:7). Finally, the depiction of the righteous as "a tree planted by the water" in Jer 17:8 is likewise situated in the context of the discussion of the presence of God (cf. 17:12).

In light of this background, the depiction of those who meditate on the law of God in Ps 1 as those who are like "a tree planted by streams of water, which yields its fruits in season and whose leaves do not wither" (Ps 1:3), becomes important as it points to the Torah as taking the role of the temple through which the presence of God can be felt.[16] This may also explain the emphasis in this psalm on cultic separation as one approaches the law (v. 1).

If both the horticultural and architectural images here point to the temple or even the Torah, Paul's selection of this imagery received added significance. As the Torah takes the place of the temple as an instrument through which one can approach God, to be "rooted and built up in him" points to the central role of Christ as the mediator between God and human beings.[17] This also paves the way for Paul's argument in 2:8 – 15 as he emphasizes that no human traditions or decree can diminish the completed work of God in Christ.

The perfect participle "rooted" (ἐρριζωμένοι) may point to a past act, while the three present participles ("built up," ἐποικοδομούμενοι; "established," βεβαιούμενοι; "abounding," περισσεύοντες) that follow point to "the ongoing process of edification."[18] Others, however, see the shift in tenses not in a temporal sense, but in the shift in "markedness" as Paul focuses on selected acts of the believers as they respond to the reception of the gospel message.[19]

2:7c-e And established in the faith, just as you were taught, abounding in thanksgiving (βεβαιούμενοι τῇ πίστει καθὼς ἐδιδάχθητε, περισσεύοντες ἐν εὐχαριστίᾳ). "Established" (βεβαιούμενοι) can be used in a variety of contexts; in Paul, it is often used in the sense of "strengthening" (Rom 15:8; 1 Cor 1:8) or "confirming" (1 Cor 1:6; 2 Cor 1:21). Modern versions are divided here in rendering this verb either as "established" (ASV, NASB, NAB, NKJV, NRSV, ESV; cf. KJV) or "strengthened" (TNIV, NIV).[20] In light of the previous two participles that emphasize the firmness of the believers in their walk in Christ, "established"

---

14. See, in particular, Derwood C. Smith, "Cultic Language in Ephesians 2:19 – 22: A Test Case," *ResQ* 31 (1989): 201 – 17.

15. See also 1 Cor 3:6 – 12, where Paul clearly switches metaphors in v. 9b: "you are God's field, God's building."

16. See Robert Cole, "An Integrated Reading of Psalms 1 and 2," *JSOT* 26 (2002): 75 – 88.

17. The parallel clause in 1:10, "growing in the knowledge of God," also alludes to the role of the Torah as the vehicle

through which God's will is made known. In this context, however, it is Christ who fulfills that role.

18. Harris, *Colossians and Philemon*, 90.

19. Cf. Stanley E. Porter, *Verbal Aspect in the Greek of the New Testament* (New York: Lang, 1989), 249.

20. Some versions chose to render this passive verb in an active sense: "grow strong" (NLT, REB).

appears preferable. This participle builds on the previous two and emphasizes the significance of their stability in the gospel that they had received.

"The faith" (τῇ πίστει) can refer to one's personal faith ("your faith," ASV, NASB, NLT, NET), but in a context that emphasizes the reception of the gospel message (v. 6) and their being "taught" (v. 7), it more likely points to the content of their act of belief: "the faith" (KJV, NAB, NKJV, NJB, NRSV, REB, ESV, NIV). This dative phrase should therefore be understood in the locative sense ("in the faith"), not an instrumental sense ("by your faith").

"Just as you were taught" (καθὼς ἐδιδάχθητε) is an adverbial clause modifying either the immediately preceding clause ("established in the faith") or all three preceding participial clauses; the difference between the two is minimal. In terms of structure and content, this phrase recalls a similar comparative note in v. 6: "just as you received Christ Jesus the Lord."

Paul shifts from the three passive participial clauses to an active one, "abounding in thanksgiving," which functions as a concluding call to lead a Christ-centered life. As the act of thanksgiving is an act of confession,[21] this phrase points to a need to be involved in a continuous act of worship through which one reaffirms the lordship of Christ. As the previous note on thanksgiving (1:12) led to the christological confession (1:13 – 14) and the christological hymn (1:15 – 20), this note on thanksgiving recalls such affirmations as it provides the transition into Paul's main arguments against the false teachings (2:8 – 23).

2:8a See to it that no one takes you captive (Βλέπετε μή τις ὑμᾶς ἔσται ὁ συλαγωγῶν). Paul now

opens the *refutatio* (2:8 – 15)[22] as he argues against the false teachers. Moving from a call to remain firm in the faith (2:6 – 7), Paul now directly warns his readers not to drift away on account of those who challenge the sufficiency and supremacy of Christ.

The construction used here — "see to it that no one" (βλέπετε μή) — appears several times in Paul's letters as readers are warned to take note of the danger they are facing (1 Cor 8:9; 10:12; Gal 5:15; cf. Eph 5:15). Paul is again pointing to the danger the false teachers pose (cf. "no one" in 2:4). This expression may point to the undefined group of disciples, but "this indefinite τις is frequently used by St Paul, when speaking of opponents whom he knows well enough but does not care to name."[23]

"Takes you captive" (ὁ συλαγωγῶν) provides a dramatic imagery of the power of those who spread the false teachings. Some have considered Paul's use of the Greek verb behind this phrase as a "contemptuous pun" with the word "synagogue" (συναγωγή): "see to it that no-one snatches you as a prey ... from the flock of Christ, to lock you up instead within Judaism."[24] Even if the Colossian heresy is to be identified as falling entirely within Jewish teachings, Paul appears to be directing his attention to the mystic tradition within Judaism, a tradition that does not necessarily identify the synagogue as the center of their ritual and activities. It seems unlikely, therefore, that Paul aims at the synagogue with this participle.

In light of the combat and military metaphors in this section (see v. 15), the appearance of "take captive" is not entirely surprising. Such imagery is similar to the sayings of Jesus when he describes the binding of the strong man and robbing him of his possessions (Matt 12:29; Mark 3:27; Luke

---

21. See comments on 1:3, 12.

22. *Refutatio* can be defined as "an elaborated argument from the contrary;" Sumney, "The Argument of Colossians," 347.

23. Lightfoot, *St. Paul's Epistles to the Colossians and to Philemon*, 178, who refers to Gal 1:7.

24. Wright, *Colossians and Philemon*, 100.

11:21 – 22).[25] In this case, Paul is applying the imagery to the false teachers taking the believers away from the gospel "into the slavery of error."[26]

2:8b By means of empty and deceitful philosophy (διὰ τῆς φιλοσοφίας καὶ κενῆς ἀπάτης). This prepositional phrase describes the weapon through which believers could be taken captive. This phrase literally reads "through philosophy and empty deception" (NASB, NKJV, NRSV, ESV; cf. KJV, ASV), but the conjunction "and" most likely carries an epexegetical function, with "empty deceit" describing "philosophy" — thus, "hollow and deceptive philosophy" (TNIV, NIV; cf. REB). "Philosophy" (τῆς φιλοσοφίας) is a general term used to refer to a general love of knowledge (Plato, *Phaed.* 61a), philosophical traditions or teachings (Josephus, *Ag. Ap.* 1.14), sects (Josephus, *Ant.* 18.11), and even religions (4 Macc 5:11). While Paul may not be arguing against philosophy in general, it should not be forgotten that this discipline finds its origin in the attempt to establish elemental principles and causal relationships (cf. Aristotle, *Metaph.* 1.3).[27]

The labels attached to philosophy here as well as reference to "human tradition" may point to a negative evaluation of the entire enterprise especially when practiced by those who refused to work within a theocentric or christocentric framework. This should not, however, be considered an indictment for the practitioners of the modern discipline, especially when many today carry out their task as theists in exposing the epistemic basis of systems that exclude all religious claims.

The description "empty and deceitful" sets up a contrast with Christ — "in him all the fullness was pleased to dwell" (1:19)[28] and "in whom all the treasures of wisdom and knowledge are hidden" (2:3) — and with the gospel that is "the word of truth" (1:5). This call to beware of those who would take them captive through such philosophy recalls Paul's earlier warning that they should not be deceived "through speculative arguments" (2:4). In the verses that follow, Paul makes it clear that this philosophy is "empty and deceitful" not because it is void of ideology or pragmatic rules and regulations, but because it is based on "human tradition" rather than on "Christ" and him alone.

2:8c According to human tradition (κατὰ τὴν παράδοσιν τῶν ἀνθρώπων). Paul uses three prepositional phrases, all governed by the preposition "according to" (κατά), to indicate the basis of such worldly philosophy. It seems best to consider the first prepositional phrase as providing a general statement, while the second and third provide further expansion of this statement:[29]

> According to human tradition,
> [that is] according to the elemental spirits
>   of the world
> and not according to Christ.

"According to human traditions" recalls Jesus' criticism of the Pharisees and the teachers of the law in Mark 7:8 ("You have let go of the commands of God and are holding on to human traditions"), a verse that immediately follows a quote from Isa 29:13, where God's people are accused of false

---

25. In his use of this imagery, Jesus may also be drawing from the exodus tradition (Exod 3:21 – 22; 12:34 – 35; cf. Isa 49:25; 53:12); Susan R. Garrett, *The Demise of the Devil: Magic and the Demonic in Luke's Writings* (Minneapolis: Fortress, 1989), 45 – 46.

26. BDAG, 955.

27. In the time of Paul, however, the term is also applied to magic and religious practices. See Günther Bornkamm, "The Heresy of Colossians," in *Conflict at Colossae* (ed. F. O. Francis

and W. A. Meeks; Missoula, MT: Scholars, 1975), 139.

28. This note on emptiness also anticipates the depiction of the "fullness of deity" that dwells in Christ (v. 9).

29. Some consider the first phrase as indicating source, while the second and third phrases indicate content (Lightfoot, *St. Paul's Epistles to the Colossians and to Philemon*, 177 – 78; Harris, *Colossians and Philemon*, 92 – 94). This does not, however, take sufficient account of the use of the same preposition in introducing all three phrases.

worship.[30] A contrast between divine initiative and human constructs appears elsewhere in the description of the worship of idols (Isa 40:18 – 24; 41:4 – 7; 44:9 – 11; 46:6 – 7; Acts 17:24 – 31; cf. Acts 7:39 – 41, 48 – 50),[31] and "empty and deceitful" reminds one of prophetic anti-idol polemic (cf. Isa 44:9; Jer 2:4 – 8; Pss 97:7; 115:4 – 7; 135:15 – 18).[32] In this passage, therefore, Paul is not simply accusing the false teachings of being merely human teachings, but that these teachings represent a false worship that cannot be tolerated. The severity of this warning is underlined by the next two prepositional phrases as the worship of those who compete with God is contrasted with the true worship of the Creator.

2:8d-e According to the elemental spirits of the world and not according to Christ (κατὰ τὰ στοιχεῖα τοῦ κόσμου καὶ οὐ κατὰ Χριστόν). Paul now sets up a contrast between the worship of created beings and that of the Creator. The exact meaning of the phrase "the elemental spirits of the world" (τὰ στοιχεῖα τοῦ κόσμου) is subject to debate. Major options include:

(1) *Elements of the physical world.* This reading has the strongest lexical support since the word "elements" (στοιχεῖα) in extracanonical Greek literature refers almost exclusively to the four or five elements of the physical earth.[33] What Paul would be warning against, then, is that one should not be "enslaved to earthly, physical things, which are destined to pass away."[34]

(2) *Elemental teachings of the world.* Extending on the first category, some consider this phrase as referring to the rudimentary teachings of the world.[35] Drawing on the only parallel in the Pauline corpus in Gal 4:3 (cf. 4:9), some have suggested that this phrase points primarily to the Torah and the Jewish teachings that focus on the Torah. The phrase would then point to "a 'materialistic' teaching bound with 'this world' alone, and contrary to the freedom of the Spirit."[36]

(3) *Elemental spirits of the world.* In light of the context of Colossians, some have suggested that this phrase refers instead to spiritual beings. In some documents in the traditions of magic and astrology that can be dated as early as the first century AD, "the term *stoicheia* was indeed used of personalized spiritual forces that have significant influence over the affairs of day-to-day existence."[37]

In light of numerous references to the angelic powers in Colossians (1:13, 16; 2:10, 15, 18), option (3) provides the best reading of the phrase and is adopted by a number of modern versions: "elemental spirits of the world" (ESV, NET; cf. NRSV, REB), "elemental spiritual forces of this world" (TNIV, NIV), and "spiritual powers of this world" (NLT; cf. NAB).

This understanding is supported by a number

---

30. This same verse is alluded to in Col 2:22.

31. See, in particular, Rémi Lack, *La symbolique du livre d'Isaïe* (AnBib 59; Rome: Biblical Institute, 1973), 95 – 99.

32. Brian J. Walsh, "Late/Post Modernity and Idolatry: A Contextual Reading of Colossians 2:8 – 3:4," *ExAud* 15 (1999): 8 – 9.

33. See Gerhard Delling, "Στοιχέω, κτλ.," *TDNT*, 7:670 – 83; and the examination of nine more occurrences of the word that confirms this conclusion in Dietrich Rusam, "Neue Belege zu den στοιχεῖα τοῦ κόσμου (Gal 4,3.9; Kol 2,8.20)," *ZNW* 83 (1992): 119 – 25; cf. KJV and ASV: "rudiments of the world."

34. Christian Stettler, "The Opponents at Colossae," in *Paul and His Opponents* (ed. Stanley E. Porter; Pauline Studies; Leiden: Brill, 2005), 192.

35. Sappington, *Revelation and Redemption at Colossae*, 164 – 70; see NASB, "elementary principles of the world" (cf. NJKV; NJB).

36. Moule, *Epistles to the Colossians and to Philemon*, 92. Some see behind Galatians and Colossians a Jewish tradition that focuses on calendrical practices, and the reference to these elements are then tied with the operation of the physical earth; Martinus C. de Boer, "The Meaning of the Phrase τὰ στοιχεῖα τοῦ κόσμου in Galatians," *NTS* 53 (2007): 204 – 24.

37. Arnold, *Colossian Syncretism*, 173. See also Smith, *Heavenly Perspective*, 84 – 86.

of observations. First, even in Galatians, the references to the "principles" (στοιχεῖα) as "weak and miserable" (ἀσθενῆ καὶ πτωχά, Gal 4:9) point to the likelihood that such "principles" are not simply religious teachings but personal and spiritual forces.[38] Second, the physical elements of the earth are objects of fear,[39] and the division between the physical and the spiritual seems less pronounced in the ancient cosmological worldview. Third, it is also possible that Paul is attacking primarily the false teachings by characterizing them as instruments of evil spiritual forces. This polemical intent allows him to use the phrase in ways not paralleled by ancient Greek literature.[40] In this verse, in contrast to "Christ," this empty and deceitful philosophy is clearly understood as a force that must be denied.

"Not according to Christ" provides the strongest argument against this false teaching. This phrase also brings us back to the center of Paul's argument: any teachings that challenge the supremacy and sufficiency of Christ are to be unmasked to reveal their true nature as personal spiritual forces that threaten the Christian community. These forces, bound with this "world," cannot be compared to Christ, through whom "all things were created, in heaven and on earth, visible and invisible, whether thrones or dominions or rulers or authorities" (1:16).

2:9 For in him all the fullness of deity dwells bodily (ὅτι ἐν αὐτῷ κατοικεῖ πᾶν τὸ πλήρωμα τῆς θεότητος σωματικῶς). Paul now provides the grounds for the previous warning: because "all the fullness" can be found in the incarnated Christ,

one should not be deceived by "empty and deceitful philosophy" (v. 8). Moreover, this verse explains why a teaching that is not "according to Christ" (v. 8) is to be rejected.

The placement of "in him" (ἐν αὐτῷ) at the beginning of the clause emphasizes the significance of this christological principle. This is reinforced by the seemingly superfluous "all" (πᾶν), which modifies a term that in itself indicates the idea of totality and completeness: "the fullness" (τὸ πλήρωμα). The reference to "all the fullness" provides "an explanatory repetition of 1:19"[41] as it makes explicit that the fullness is in reference to "deity."

In this context, the genitive "of deity" (τῆς θεότητος) is best taken as a genitive of content: Jesus is filled with the full deity.[42] But if "all the fullness" is to be considered as the subject of the verb in 1:19, then one finds God identified as "all the fullness." In that case, "of deity" could also be understood as an epexegetical genitive: "all the fullness, that is, God himself."[43] The word "deity" has been variously understood as referring to "God" (NLT), "Godhead" (KJV, ASV, REB, NKJV), "divinity" (NJB), "deity" (NRSV, ESV, NET), and "the Deity" (TNIV, NIV), but it is clear that the word together with the reference to "all the fullness" points to God himself in his full essence.

As in 1:19, the idea that God "dwells" (κατοικεῖ) in Christ may allude to Ps 68:16 (LXX Ps 67:17), where God is said to reside in his own abode on the holy mount. Because of the various uses of the noun "body" (σῶμα) in Colossians, various proposals have been offered for the reading of the adverbial form, "bodily" (σωματικῶς).

(1) *The church.* With the use of "body" as a

---

38. Edward Adams, *Constructing the World: A Study in Paul's Cosmological Language* (Edinburgh: T&T Clark, 2000), 230.

39. See, in particular, Eduard Schweizer, "Slaves of the Elements and Worshippers of Angels: Gal 4:3, 9 and Col 2:8, 18, 20," *JBL* 107 (1988): 455 – 68.

40. Ernst Percy, *Die Probleme der Kolosser- und Epheserbriefe* (Lund: Gleerup, 1946), 156 – 70.

41. Lohse, *Colossians and Philemon*, 99.

42. Wallace, *Greek Grammar*, 94.

43. Petr Pokorný, *Colossians: A Commentary* (trans. Siegfried S. Schatzmann; Peabody, MA: Hendrickson, 1991), 121.

reference to the church in 1:18 and 1:24, some have suggested that Paul aims at forging an "unmistakable bond between Christ and 'his body, the church.'"[44] The next verse (2:10), which emphasizes the fullness in the believers, may also lend support to this reading. Although the ecclesiological import cannot be denied, the focus of this verse is to provide justification for the claim in v. 8, and the focus is undeniably christological. Moreover, the wider parallel of this verse with 1:19 also argues against this reading.

(2) *Cosmic body.* Noting the various cosmic forces behind the reference to "the elemental spirits of the world" in v. 8, some argue that "bodily" here refers to "the cosmic body which is constituted by the principles, powers, and other cosmic forces."[45] In preceding references to the "body" as it relates to Christ himself, however, the idea of a cosmic body is not dominant (cf. 1:18, 22, 24; see comments). Moreover, Paul's emphasis here is Christ's supremacy over all spiritual powers, not his containment of them in his own body.

(3) *Reality.* In light of the use of the nominal form in 2:17 in reference to the reality that is contrasted with the shadow of things to come, some have taken "bodily" as a reference to the "reality" of God's dwelling in Christ: "In Christ all the fullness of the Deity lives in solid reality."[46] This reading can be traced back to Augustine, who understood it as "really, as opposed to shadowy" (*Epist.* 149, 25).[47]

(4) *Incarnated body.* The reading that poses the fewest problems is the one that takes "bodily" as a reference to the incarnated body of Christ, as seems to be the case in 1:19 though without the use of this adverb. This is adopted by most English transla-

tions: "bodily" (KJV, ASV, NAB, NRSV, NKJV, ESV), "in bodily form," (NASB, NJB, TNIV, NET, NIV), "embodied" (REB), or even "in a human body" (NLT). This reading builds on option (3) as the reality of the incarnated Christ is emphasized over against those who claim that Christ's earthly existence is but an illusion.

This emphasis of the body of Christ "underscores the accessibility (come-at-ableness) of the divine epiphany,"[48] as Christ's presence is already a historical reality that requires no special visionary experience as one gains access to him and the deity with whom he is filled. This note may also argue against the ascetic practices promoted by the false teachers (cf. 2:16 – 23) since Christ's own body was an instrument of God's redemption and deliverance.[49] As the exalted christological hymn finds its climax in the death and resurrection of Jesus Christ (1:18, 20), Paul's arguments against the false teachings also build on this material reality, one that has profound spiritual and cosmological significance.

2:10a And you have been filled in him (καὶ ἐστὲ ἐν αὐτῷ πεπληρωμένοι). With the conjunction "and" (καί), Paul moves from the christological affirmation to its ecclesiological implications. The combination of a present verb "to be" (ἐστέ) with the perfect participle (πεπληρωμένοι) makes a perfect periphrastic construction.[50] Two peculiar features of the use of this verbal form have led to various renderings. First, while God is clearly the implied agent of this passive participle, it has often been translated as a stative ("you are complete in him," NKJV; cf. KJV, ASV, NLT) or as an active verb ("you share in this fullness in him," NAB; "in him you find your own fulfillment," NJB). These rendi-

---

44. Henderson, "God's Fullness in Bodily Form," 170.

45. See van Kooten, *Cosmic Christology in Paul*, 25.

46. David E. Garland, *Colossians and Philemon* (NIVAC; Grand Rapids: Zondervan, 1998), 146.

47. Lohse, *Colossians and Philemon*, 100.

48. Dunn, *Epistles to the Colossians and to Philemon*, 152.

49. Wedderburn, "The Theology of Colossians," 37.

50. Some, however, consider this as a reference to two separate verbal acts: "and you are in him, being fulfilled" (Lightfoot, *St. Paul's Epistles to the Colossians and to Philemon*, 182).

tions distract readers from Paul's intense focus on God and more specifically on Christ as the proper subject who can bring about true fulfillment. This intense theocentric and christocentric emphasis reaches its climax in the immediately preceding verse, which provides the contrast between "according to human tradition" and "not according to Christ" (v. 8).

Second, the lack of a clear second object to indicate that with which the believers are filled has also led to other creative renderings (e.g., "in Christ you have been brought to fullness," TNIV, NIV), including one that supplies a second object, "life" ("you have been given full life in union with him," GNB).[51] While this verb could be understood in terms of "certainty" and thus without an explicit second object (cf. 4:12), in this context this divine passive participle likely points back to three preceding passive participles as explicating the full meaning of this divine act of filling: "rooted and built up in him, established in the faith" (v. 7).

The connection with v. 9 is clear as both verses use the same word group: believers are to be satisfied fully because they "have been filled" in the one who contains "all the fullness" of deity. This connection cannot be pressed, however, since believers are not filled with the full deity as Christ is. Rather, it is because of Christ's full deity that believers, having been filled in him, can experience full salvific assurance and benefits.

2:10b Who is the head of every ruler and authority (ὅς ἐστιν ἡ κεφαλὴ πάσης ἀρχῆς καὶ ἐξουσίας). After a note on believers, Paul returns to the supremacy of Christ over all created beings. The christological hymn again makes its presence

felt here. The reference to Christ as "the head" (ἡ κεφαλή) points back to 1:18, while his power over "every ruler and authority" (πάσης ἀρχῆς καὶ ἐξουσίας) points back to the reference to "rulers" (ἀρχαί) and "authorities" (ἐξουσίαι) in 1:16.

The metaphor of "the head" points to supremacy and authority, with "of every ruler and authority" being objective genitives: "head over every ruler and authority" (NLT, NET). Some versions make explicit the idea of supremacy embedded in the metaphor: "He is supreme over every spiritual ruler and authority" (GNB). This portrayal of Christ echoes the Stoic conception of the deity as "the world's own commanding faculty" (Cicero, *Nat. d.* 1.39),[52] but what is striking in the case of Christ is that this supreme power of the universe is also one that is filled with the fullness of deity in "bodily" form (v. 9). Unlike the use of the same metaphor in 1:18, the rulers and authorities are not perceived as belonging to the body of Christ;[53] instead, they are powers that are now "disarmed" and subjected to him (v. 15). The metaphor of "head" should, therefore, not be pressed into a full-blown portrayal of Christ as the cosmic body.

"Every" recalls the "all" in the previous verse in emphasizing the supreme status of Christ as well as the comprehensiveness of his reign. Together with 2:15, one finds a progressive depiction of Christ's power in relations to such spiritual powers: they are created through him (1:16), subjected to him (2:10), and disarmed and defeated by him (2:15). The intensity of the polemic against these powers through Paul's arguments cannot be missed.

2:11a In him you were also circumcised with a circumcision not performed by human hands

---

51. Perhaps the use of the lone verb reflects the awareness of the readers of the fuller reference; as Paul is "using a slogan which the false teachers were adopting when they promised 'fullness of life' to their followers at Colossae" (Martin, *Colossians and Philemon*, 81).

52. Van Kooten, *Cosmic Christology in Paul*, 24.

53. This general use of the metaphor is consistent with OT and Jewish usage; cf. Arnold, "Jesus Christ: 'Head' of the Church," 364; Nebe, "Christ, the Body of Christ," 115.

(Ἐν ᾧ καὶ περιετμήθητε περιτομῇ ἀχειροποιήτῳ). Paul continues to focus on the effects of Christ's work on believers, who are now "in him" (ἐν ᾧ). While v.10 uses the positive metaphor of filling up, this verse focuses on the negative metaphor of stripping off. The connection of these two aspects is provided by the adverbial use of the conjunction "also" (καί).

The reference to circumcision here is unexpected. In the OT, circumcision is the covenantal sign of God's people as they were separated from those around them (Gen 17:9 – 14). In Second Temple Judaism, circumcision became an identity marker, symbolizing the Jews' self-understanding as the unique elect people of God (cf. 1 Macc 1:60). In light of the reference to baptism in v. 12, some have argued that Paul is evoking this Jewish rite by suggesting that Christian baptism fulfills the ancient Jewish covenantal entry rite. If so, "this is the first place where circumcision appears as a symbol for baptism in extant early Christian writings."[54] The absence of other NT witnesses with a connection between baptism and circumcision argues against this identification here.[55] Moreover, the passive verb "you were ... circumcised" (περιετμήθητε) points to God as the implied subject; thus, it seems more likely that this circumcision refers to the conversion of the believers as they experience the powerful deliverance and salvific act of God (cf. Rom 2:25 – 29). The further reference to a circumcision "not performed by human hands" also points to the unique and sovereign act of God in the lives of the believers.[56]

Regardless of its relation to the Christian baptism, the introduction of the imagery of circumcision needs further explanation. The possibility that circumcision is an important element of the false teachings that Paul is combating cannot be dismissed.[57] Some have argued against this possibility because the argument against physical circumcision is not elaborated in this letter,[58] but this downplays the intense emphasis on circumcision in this verse and its significance as a power symbol among the Jews in the ancient world.[59]

Moreover, the nature of the problems Paul is encountering here seems very different from those he had encountered in Galatia. One should therefore not expect the same focus on this issue. Even if circumcision does not lie at the center of the teachings Paul is combating, the Jewish nature of such teachings seems clear. This does not rule out the syncretistic nature of these teachings, but to introduce this significant symbol at the beginning of Paul's critique of these teachings forces one to examine the material that follows through the lens of at least a form of Diaspora Judaism in the first century.

"A circumcision not performed by human hands" literally reads, "a circumcision made without hands" (NASB, ESV). This phrase reflects two related OT traditions. First, already in the OT one finds circumcision imagery as referring to God's disobedient people, who are circumcised in their flesh but not in their hearts (cf. Lev 26:41 – 42; Deut 10:16; Jer 4:3 – 4; 9:24 – 25; Ezek 44:6 – 9), their ears (Jer 6:10), or their lips (Exod 6:12, 30).[60] The posi-

---

54. Sumney, *Colossians*, 136; cf. MacDonald, *Colossians and Ephesians*, 99.

55. Roy Yates, "Colossians 2:15: Christ Triumphant," *NTS* 37 (1991): 587.

56. For a detailed argument against the identification of "circumcision" here with the baptismal rite, see J. P. T. Hunt, "Colossians 2:11 – 12, the Circumcision/Baptism Analogy, and Infant Baptism," *TynBul* 41 (1990): 227 – 44.

57. Barth and Blanke, *Colossians*, 317.

58. See, e.g., Moo, *Letters to the Colossians and to Philemon*, 199 – 200.

59. See, in particular, Judith M. Lieu, *Christian Identity in the Jewish and Graeco-Roman World* (New York: Oxford Univ. Press, 2004), 108 – 26.

60. Werner E. Lemke, "Circumcision of the Heart: The Journey of a Biblical Metaphor," in *A God So Near: Essays on Old Testament Theology in Honor of Patrick D. Miller* (ed. Brent A. Strawn and Nancy R. Bowen; Winona Lake, IN: Eisen-

tive use can also be found when God promises to work among his people: "The LORD your God will circumcise your hearts and the hearts of your descendants, so that you may love him with all your heart and with all your soul, and live" (Deut 30:6). Here Paul points to the fulfillment of such promises as God is able to cleanse the hearts of his restored people through the death and resurrection of his Son.

Second, the Greek word rendered "not performed by human hands" (ἀχειροποιήτῳ) may also evoke the long anti-idol tradition in Israel. The related term "made by human hands" (χειροποίητος) in the LXX is almost always used in reference to the idols made by human hands (Lev 26:1, 30; Isa 2:18; 10:11; 16:12; 19:1; 21:9; 31:7; 46:6; Dan 5:4, 23; 6:28; cf. Wis 14:8). This use reappears in the anti-idol polemic in Acts, when Paul challenges the Athenians of their worship of the false deities (Acts 17:24 – 25). What is surprising is how similar language is also applied to those abusing the Jerusalem temple as Stephen accuses the Jewish leaders of limiting God's work by works of their own hands (Acts 7:48).[61] Here, in noting the circumcision that is "not performed by human hands," therefore, Paul is indirectly accusing those who emphasize physical circumcision of worshiping false gods.

2:11b-c In the putting off of the body of flesh, by the circumcision of Christ (ἐν τῇ ἀπεκδύσει τοῦ σώματος τῆς σαρκός, ἐν τῇ περιτομῇ τοῦ Χριστοῦ). The second part of the sentence points to the means through which the true circumcision

of the believers is performed. The exact meaning of this part of the verse depends on the relationship between the two prepositional phrases: To whose "body of flesh" Paul is referring, and what is the function of the genitive "of Christ"? Among the possible readings, three stand out as being the most probable readings, and two render the two prepositional phrases as parallel in function.

(1) The prepositional phrases are parallel and describe that which was done to the believers when they were "circumcised": "Your whole self ruled by the flesh was put off when you were circumcised by Christ" (NIV; cf. TNIV).

(2) The first prepositional phrase describes the experience of the believers, but the second phrase describes the experience of Christ: "Your sinful nature was put off in Christ's own 'circumcision.'"[62]

(3) Both phrases are parallel and describe Christ's own experience when he was "circumcised": "when (Christ) stripped off his physical body, that is, in Christ's own 'circumcision.'"[63]

In light of the parallel use of the same preposition ("in/by," ἐν) with the dative article ("the," τῇ), most consider the two phrases as parallel; thus the above options are reduced to (1) and (3). Many who argue for (1) point to 3:9, where the verbal form of the noun "putting off" (τῇ ἀπεκδύσει) refers to the putting off of the old nature: "for you have taken off [ἀπεκδυσάμενοι] the old humanity with its practices."[64] Moreover, the lack of a personal pronoun in reference to "the body of flesh" (τοῦ σώματος τῆς σαρκός) may indicate that Paul has a wider reference in mind. Finally, Paul often

---

brauns, 2003), 299 – 319. For the use of this metaphor in Second Temple Jewish literature, see also R. Le Déaut, "Le thème de la circoncision du coeur (Dt. xxx 6; Jér. iv 4) dans les versions anciennes (LXX et Targum) et à Qumrân," in *Congress Volume: Vienna, 1980* (ed. J. A. Emerton; VTSup 32; Leiden: Brill, 1981), 187 – 203.

61. In the same context one also finds the description of Israel rejoicing over the "works of their hands" (Acts 7:41) as they made and worshiped the golden calf. For a further discus-

sion of these passages in light of the wider anti-idol polemic in Acts, see Pao, *Acts and the Isaianic New Exodus*, 181 – 216.

62. Few versions explicitly adopt this reading, although the ambiguous "of Christ" could accommodate this reading: "in putting off the body of the sins of the flesh by the circumcision of Christ" (KJV).

63. Moule, *Epistles to the Colossians and to Philemon*, 96.

64. See the representative statement in Lightfoot, *St. Paul's Epistles to the Colossians and to Philemon*, 183 – 84.

uses "flesh" to refer to one's sinful nature (e.g., Rom 6:19; 7:5, 18; 8:4, 5, 6; Gal 5:13).

In context, however, option (3) provides a better reading.[65] First, instead of the subsequent reference in 3:9, one should look to the previous reference in 1:22, where "[the] body of flesh" (τῷ σώματι τῆς σαρκός) clearly points to Christ's own body that suffered on the cross. Thus, the readers would bring the understanding of the body of flesh from 1:22 to 2:11.

Second, the absence of a personal pronoun ("his") can be explained by the already numerous references to Christ in this section and especially the phrase "in him" (ἐν ᾧ) at the beginning of this verse.

Third, the verbal form of "putting off" has a wider usage even in Colossians, as shown in 2:15, where the disarming (ἀπεκδυσάμενος) of the rulers and authorities is noted. In other words, the mere appearance of this word group does not necessarily point to the stripping of one's sinful nature.[66]

Fourth, all of the previous references to "flesh" in Colossians carry a neutral meaning rather than a negative one (1:22, 24; 2:1, 5).

Fifth, it has been shown that in every use of "circumcision" (περιτομή) with a genitive in the Jewish literature, the genitive is always understood as an objective genitive (LXX Exod 4:25 – 26; Jer 11:16; Rom 2:25, 29; Josephus, *Ant.* 1.192; 8.262; Philo, *Spec. Laws* 1.2).[67]

Finally, in our discussion of circumcision as a metaphor of Christ's death, the relevance of Rom 6:3 – 4 should also be noted as Paul there speaks of the death, burial, and resurrection of Jesus,

and here Paul speaks of circumcision, burial, and resurrection.[68]

In this passage, therefore, Paul is speaking of two circumcisions: believers are circumcised by Christ's own circumcision (i.e., his death). This imagery is particularly powerful because the traditional circumcision involves the cutting off of a piece of flesh, while Christ's circumcision involves the sacrifice of his entire body. With this complete sacrifice, no longer is the bodily identity marker important, nor does one need to rely on ascetic practices to curb the desires of one's flesh (cf. 2:20 – 23).

2:12a When you were buried with him in baptism (συνταφέντες αὐτῷ ἐν τῷ βαπτισμῷ). This verse is connected with the previous one in a number of ways. First, this participial phrase explains what happens in the "circumcision" of the believers. Second, this verse emphasizes the significance of the death and resurrection of Christ for the believers. Third, while the previous note focuses on God's work through the death of Christ, the end of this verse also takes note of the way human beings can participate in this divine salvific act through the response of faith.

Though the participle used here ("when you were buried [συνταφέντες] with him") is aorist, it should be considered as a contemporaneous act with the verb noted above ("you were circumcised," v. 11).[69] The prepositional prefix "with" (συν-), attached to both verbs in this verse, carries special theological weight as it points to the participation of believers "in Christ." The pronoun αὐτῷ, therefore, denotes "not simply spatial proximity

---

65. See, e.g., O'Brien, *Colossians, Philemon*, 117; Barth and Blanke, *Colossians*, 364 – 65.

66. The concept of the stripping off of one's body in reference to one's death is also present in 2 Cor 5:2 – 4; cf. Smith, *Heavenly Perspective*, 95.

67. Beetham, *Echoes of Scripture*, 177.

68. See Hunt, "Colossians 2:11 – 12," 241 – 42, who points

further to the close parallels between Eph 2:11 – 13 and Col 2:11 – 12; thus, it confirms our understanding of "the circumcision of Christ" as a reference to his death.

69. Most take the participle, "you were buried with [him]" (συνταφέντες) as a temporal participle, although it is conceivable to take it in the causal sense: "for you were buried with [him]" (REB).

to Christ but active communion with Christ" (cf. 1 Thess 4:17; Phil 1:23).[70] To define further this communion as indicating that believers are "covered by his protective power"[71] may not do justice to the richness and complexity involved in this association.

The significance of the believers' participation in the death, burial, and resurrection of Christ is discussed in Rom 6:5 – 11, which emphasizes that "death no longer has mastery over" those who belong to him (6:9). In 6:5, however, resurrection with Christ is a future event, but here the emphasis is on the accomplished act of God (cf. 3:1 – 4). Even those who deny the authorship of Paul for Colossians recognize that Paul's focus on the future resurrection in Rom 6 has a distinct purpose, as he is arguing "against an enthusiastic evaluation of baptism which would conceive of it as a pledge of accomplished resurrection."[72] Here in Colossians, Paul's emphasis on the present reality of one's resurrection with Christ is to combat those who deny the finality of Christ's salvific act and its significance for believers.[73] This "already but not yet" tension should not surprise contemporary readers familiar with the writings of Paul.

In this reference to the rite of "baptism," one would expect a different word (βαπτίσματι rather than βαπτισμῷ).[74] If a distinction between the two can be made, "βαπτισμός denotes the act in process and βάπτισμα the result."[75] In this verse, the relationship between circumcision and baptism cannot be denied, but the latter is not meant to replace the former. To understand Paul as referring primarily to the external rite of baptism would contradict his argument in the previous verse, where the internal transformation brought about by the death of Christ is emphasized. "Baptism" here can only refer to the "spiritual reality"[76] that this metaphor symbolizes as the immersion points to the participation in the death and burial of Jesus Christ. Moreover, "baptism" here is not something that human beings can perform; it points rather to the prior act of God that allows the external rite to be of significance.

2:12b-d In whom you were also raised through faith in the work of God, who raised him from the dead (ἐν ᾧ καὶ συνηγέρθητε διὰ τῆς πίστεως τῆς ἐνεργείας τοῦ θεοῦ τοῦ ἐγείραντος αὐτὸν ἐκ νεκρῶν). It is unclear what/who the intended antecedent of the relative pronoun (ᾧ) is. Many prefer to see the immediately preceding term "baptism" as the antecedent ("in which you were also raised up with Him," NASB; cf. NAB, NKJV, REB, GNB, NJB, TNIV, ESV, NIV), a reading that claims to alleviate the awkwardness caused by the double reference to Christ: "you were also raised with him in him."[77]

In light of the constant focus on Christ, however, this relative pronoun should be understood as also referring to him. In the preceding passages in Colossians, every reference to "in whom/which (ἐν ᾧ, 1:14; 2:3, 11) or "in him" (ἐν αὐτῷ, 1:16, 17, 19; 2:6, 7, 9, 10) refers to Christ, and this christological focus is especially pronounced in this section (vv. 6 – 15). In these two verses (vv. 11 – 12) in

---

70. Murray J. Harris, "Prepositions and Theology in the Greek New Testament," *NIDNTT*, 3:1207.

71. Kenneth Grayston, *Dying, We Live: A New Enquiry into the Death of Christ in the New Testament* (New York: Oxford Univ. Press, 1990), 18.

72. Lohse, *Colossians and Philemon*, 103. The present emphasis is not entirely missing in the description of the resurrected life in Rom 6 either, as noted in the formula in 6:11: "count yourselves dead to sin but alive to God in Christ Jesus."

73. It should again be noted that a futuristic eschatology is not missing in this letter (cf. 3:4, 6, 24); cf. Still, "Eschatology in Colossians," 125 – 38.

74. This may explain why some manuscripts (ℵ* A C D² Ψ 33 𝔐) read βαπτίσματι.

75. Lightfoot, *St. Paul's Epistles to the Colossians and to Philemon*, 184.

76. Cf. James D. G. Dunn, *Baptism in the Holy Spirit* (Philadelphia: Westminster, 1970), 154.

77. Cf. Moo, *Letters to the Colossians and to Philemon*, 203.

particular, where Paul explicitly refers to Christ by noting his death (i.e., "circumcision") and burial, one should also expect Christ to be mentioned in relation to his own resurrection. Moreover, the awkwardness of this reading noted above, with the double reference to Christ, exists only in English, since in Greek "with him" is embedded in the prefix of the verb "you were … raised" (συνηγέρθητε) while "in him" is explicitly noted. As the believers' pasts are buried with him, their new life in Christ provides the power through which competing claims are rendered impotent.

"Through faith in the work of God" points to the means through which believers can appropriate the power of Christ's resurrection. The translation "in the work" (τῆς ἐνεργείας) takes this as an objective genitive, and "of God" (τοῦ θεοῦ) is therefore a possessive genitive. Earlier Paul noted his appropriation of God's power in his powerful ministry (1:29). Here, this power is extended to those who put their trust in this power of God. Elsewhere, Paul notes that "if you … believe in your heart that God raised him from the dead, you will be saved" (Rom 10:9). Here, however, Paul specifies the object of one's faith as "the work of God," probably to draw attention to God's power and initiative when describing human responses to his mighty acts.[78] Even in the act of appropriating God's power in one's life, one must rely on God's power for such a receptive act.

In light of Paul's previous affirmation of Christ as the object of one's faith (1:4; 2:5), one can also consider "the work of God" as another appellation of Christ as he symbolizes the climax of God's revelatory power in history. If Christ is defined as the climax and ultimate revelation of God's power, God in turn is also defined by his work in Christ since

he is the one "who raised him from the dead." As noted in the christological hymn, the resurrection of Jesus "from the dead" (1:18) represents God's new creative act, an act that accomplishes universal reconciliation (1:20). Through faith, believers can participate in this universal reconciliation not simply as those who are pacified by God's power but as those who can participate in God's creative power.[79]

2:13a And you, who were once dead in your transgressions and in the uncircumcision of your flesh (καὶ ὑμᾶς νεκροὺς ὄντας [ἐν] τοῖς παραπτώμασιν καὶ τῇ ἀκροβυστίᾳ τῆς σαρκὸς ὑμῶν). After noting the believers' participation in the death, burial, and resurrection of Christ, Paul explains the implications of such participation for the life of believers as well as for the challenges they are facing. In terms of their status, they are now freed from the sinful nature that dominated them (v. 13). In terms of the challenges they are facing, Paul reminds them that they should no longer be threatened by the evil forces that may claim to have power over them (v. 14).

The shift of attention to the believers in Colossae is dramatically highlighted by the presence, placement, and case of the personal pronoun "you" (ὑμᾶς) in this clause. With this personal pronoun at the beginning of the clause, Paul highlights his move from God's accomplishments in Christ to the benefits of such accomplishments for these believers. Grammatically, this accusative pronoun is repeated as the object of the next clause ("God made you alive together with him," συνεζωοποίησεν ὑμᾶς σὺν αὐτῷ) as it provides further information on the "you" who were made alive with Christ.

The anarthrous participle "who were" (ὄντας) can be considered an adverbial participle modify-

---

78. This emphasis also qualifies the previous reference to baptism since "circumcision comes to an end not because of baptism, but 'through your faith in the act of God'" (Bevere, *Sharing in the Inheritance*, 70).

79. See also Rom 8:11: "if the Spirit of him who raised Jesus from the dead is living in you, he who raised Christ from the dead will also give life to your mortal bodies because of his Spirit who lives in you."

ing the main verb (lit., "he made alive") in the next clause. If so, it expresses either a temporal ("when you were dead," NAB, NASB, NRSV, TNIV, NIV) or a concessive ("although you were dead," REB; cf. NET) sense. But this participle could also an attributive participle modifying the preceding "you": "you, who were dead" (ESV).[80] In the present case, the adverbial and the attributive sense may both be present, as in our translation: "you, who were once" (see also comments on a similar construction in 1:21).

"You" (ὑμᾶς) stands in contrast with "us" (ἡμῖν) in the final clause of this verse, and thus it should best be taken as referring to the Gentile readers (cf. 3:7, 8).[81] "Once dead in your transgressions and in the uncircumcision of your flesh" would then refer to the condition of these Gentiles. In this context, "dead" refers to the absence of relationship with God. In the OT, to be dead is to be cast out from the presence of God (Gen 3:17, 23 – 24). In Ephesians, Paul explicitly notes that when the Gentiles were in the state of sin, they were "separate from Christ" (Eph 2:12). As the previous verse is similar to Romans 6, this reference to "dead in your transgressions" may also remind one of Rom 6:11: "count yourselves dead to sin but alive to God in Christ Jesus." The difference between Rom 6:11 and this verse is clear, however, since in Romans Paul is talking about the status of believers while here he is describing the preconversion state. Some have therefore understood the preposition "in" (ἐν)

as acquiring a causal sense here: "you were dead because of your sins" (NLT; cf. REB, NJB).[82] This reading is supported by yet another parallel in Romans, where the use of a different preposition (διά) makes this causal sense clear: "your body is subject to death because of sin" (Rom 8:10).

"The uncircumcision of your flesh" draws on the physical reality of the uncircumcised state of the Gentiles in their former status as excluded from God's people.[83] Thus, "uncircumcision" carries both a literal and metaphorical sense. Similarly, "flesh" refers to their physical state,[84] although one should not exclude an implicit reference to their "sinful nature," especially in light of the reference to "transgressions" in the preceding phrase.

2:13b-c God made alive with him, having forgiven us all our transgressions (συνεζωοποίησεν ὑμᾶς σὺν αὐτῷ, χαρισάμενος ἡμῖν πάντα τὰ παραπτώματα). Elsewhere Paul talks about Christ's death for us while we were sinners (Rom 5:8); here Paul emphasizes the believers' participation in Christ's resurrection, but the phrase "having forgiven us all our transgressions" does point forward to v. 14, where Christ's death on the cross forms the basis of such forgiveness.

"God made [you] alive with him" continues to focus on the Gentiles,[85] but in the second part, Paul points to the universal significance of Christ's death on the cross.[86] The verb with the συν-prefix, "made alive [with]" (συνεζωοποίησεν) links this

---

80. Lohse, *Colossians and Philemon*, 107, who considers "and you" as reflecting early Christian preaching style. Some (Harris, *Colossians and Philemon*, 105) object to this reading because of the lack of an article before the participle. Nevertheless, with "you" (ὑμᾶς) being definite in meaning, an article is not necessary for the participle to be attributive.

81. See also Eph 1:13; 2:1, 11, 13, 17, 22; 3:2; 4:17; Lightfoot, *St. Paul's Epistles to the Colossians and to Philemon*, 185.

82. See also O'Brien, *Colossians, Philemon*, 122; Moo, *Letters to the Colossians and to Philemon*, 206. This use of the preposition, though unusual, can also be found in Paul (Rom 1:24; 8:3; 1 Cor 4:4; 7:14; 2 Cor 5:2); BDAG, 329. Others have

considered this preposition as indicating the circumstances in which the Gentiles found themselves: "you were dead when they were in the state of sin;" Moule, *Epistles to the Colossians and to Philemon*, 97.

83. This expression also alludes to Gen 17:11, 14, 23, 24, 25; see Beale, "Colossians," 862; Beetham, *Echoes of Scripture*, 189.

84. See comments on "flesh" in v. 11, above.

85. "You" (ὑμᾶς) is left untranslated because of its appearance in the previous clause.

86. Others have detected behind this change of pronoun the use of traditional material; Cannon, *Use of Traditional Materials in Colossians*, 39 – 40, 46.

clause with "you were buried" (συνταφέντες) and "you were raised" (συνηγέρθητε) in v. 12. "Made alive [with]" reverses the state of "dead" and points to a new existence. The implied subject of this verb is God, while "with him" (σὺν αὐτῷ) refers clearly to Christ. This double συν-reference points to the believers' participation in Christ's resurrection, which in turn brings about new life in them. In this sense, one again finds the connection between the physical and the spiritual as Christ's physical resurrection brought about the believers' spiritual resurrection.

The adverbial participle "having forgiven" (χαρισάμενος) can convey a temporal ("when he forgave us all our trespasses," NRSV; cf. CEV) or a causal ("for he forgave all our sins," NLT; cf. REB) sense. Both senses could be present here; what is important is that the reception of the new life is impossible without God's initiative in restoring people to himself. Later in this letter, Paul also urges his readers to imitate this act of God: "just as the Lord forgave you … forgive one another" (3:13).[87]

2:14a-b   By expunging the written decree that is against us, together with its regulations (ἐξαλείψας τὸ καθ' ἡμῶν χειρόγραφον τοῖς δόγμασιν). Paul continues to emphasize the salvific work of God through Christ. The participle "expunging" (ἐξαλείψας) can point to the means through which divine forgiveness is carried out

("by canceling," ESV), although it can also serve to explicate further the grounds or the process of such acts of forgiveness ("having canceled out," NASB; cf. ASV, NKJV, NRSV, TNIV, NIV). The meaning of this participle is "to cause something to cease by obliterating any evidence,"[88] and relevant parallels to this verb refer to the wiping out of one's sins (Acts 3:14) and the blotting out of one's name from the book of life (Rev 3:5). With this verb, Paul highlights the complete destruction of that which was against believers.

The exact meanings of the words "written decree" (χειρόγραφον) and "regulations" (δόγμασιν) remain a subject of scholarly debate. Most agree that "written decree" is taken from the fields of commerce and law in reference to a "certificate of debt" (NASB; cf. ESV, NLT, TNIV, NET, NIV),[89] and in this context would refer to an IOU from human beings to God.[90] This meaning is supported by the widespread use of this term in contemporaneous papyri[91] and would be immediately understood as such by the ancient readers. The two other major interpretations are derived from this primary use. Reading in light of Jewish apocalyptic writings, some have pointed to "the heavenly book" as the intended reference for this term.[92] This heavenly book "contains a record of humanity's sins,"[93] and Christ's redemption includes the destruction of this record as he forgives the sins of all. Others see this IOU as a reference to the Mosaic law,[94]

---

87. Although "the Lord" in 3:13 refers to Christ, the forgiveness of God cannot be separated from that of Jesus himself as illustrated by the parallel in Eph 4:32: "forgiving each other, just as in Christ God forgave you."

88. Louw and Nida, §13.102.

89. See Joram Luttenberger, "Der gekreuzigte Schuldschein: Ein Aspekt der Deutung des Todes Jesu im Kolosserbrief," *NTS* 51 (2005): 80 – 95. Kreitzer, "Living in the Lycus Valley," 92, further suggests that this "image of debt-cancellation may be a deliberate allusion to the tax relief granted by the Roman state following the earthquake of 60 CE."

90. This derivative meaning finds its parallel in inscriptional evidence from Asia Minor that points to an "autographed

self-condemnation" (Wesley Carr, "Two Notes on Colossians," *JTS* 24 [1973]: 494).

91. MM, 687.

92. Cf. Dan 12:1 – 3; *As. Mos.* 10; *Jub.* 23.27 – 31; *T. Jud.* 20, 25; Smith, *Heavenly Perspective*, 98.

93. See, in particular, Sappington, *Revelation and Redemption at Colossae*, 215 – 17, who points to the particular relevance of *Apoc. Zeph.* 7 for the reading of Col 2:14 – 15.

94. Lightfoot, *St. Paul's Epistles to the Colossians and to Philemon*, 187. See the translation in NJB that combines the two words ("the record of our debt" and "the Law"): "the record of our debt to the Law."

although it is difficult to understand how Christ is "nailing ... to the cross" this Mosaic Torah.

Even though a strict identification with the Mosaic Torah cannot be made, this "record of debt" should be understood in relation to the Mosaic law. First, in some Jewish references to the heavenly book, the Mosaic law is not far from the mind of their authors.[95] Second, there may have been a play on words with the use of ἀχειροποιήτῳ ("not performed by human hands," v. 11) and χειρόγραφον ("written decree").[96] If so, the circumcision that is considered to symbolize one's faithfulness to the Torah is related to this "written decree" (cf. Rom 2:25 – 27). Third, the idea of the Torah as the certificate of debt should not surprise those familiar with Paul's writings. Elsewhere, Paul states that "through the law we become conscious of our sin" (Rom 3:20) and in this sense "the law brings wrath" (4:15). Although "the law is holy" (7:12), it testifies to one's failure to fulfill God's will. It can therefore be considered a "record of debt," and as it testifies against us, in this sense the "record" is "against us" (καθ' ἡμῶν).

This reading is consistent with the consideration of the use of the word for "regulation" (δόγμα) in its only other occurrence in Paul's letters, where he points directly to the Mosaic law: "For he himself ... has destroyed the barrier, the dividing wall of hostility, by setting aside in his flesh the law with its commands and regulations [δόγμασιν]" (Eph 2:14 – 15a).[97] In Ephesians, Paul focuses on the barrier between Jews and Gentiles, while in Colossians, Paul focuses on the spiritual forces that stand between God and humanity. In both letters, Paul challenges the reliance on the regulations associated with the written law.

While the "written decree" should not be identified entirely with the Torah, the "regulations" (δόγμασιν) may refer to the rules imposed by those who consider themselves to be faithful to the Torah. The use of the verbal cognate (δογματίζεσθε) in v. 20 points to these "regulations" as ascetic practices imposed by the false teachers.[98] The same word group appears in Greco-Roman philosophers in reference to ascetic practices.[99] Paul is therefore not suggesting that the Torah is nailed to the cross; what he is combating is a misuse of the Torah for such practices.

2:14c-e Which opposed us, and this he took from among us, nailing it to the cross (ὃ ἦν ὑπεναντίον ἡμῖν, καὶ αὐτὸ ἦρκεν ἐκ τοῦ μέσου προσηλώσας αὐτὸ τῷ σταυρῷ). Paul expands on God's destruction of those things that were against the believers. Both the neuter singular relative pronoun "which" (ὅ) and the pronoun "this" (αὐτό) point back to "the written record." It opposes believers by testifying against them before God and by condemning them with the deception that their guilt will never be erased by God's own redemptive acts through his Son. In response to such condemnation, Paul again alludes to the power of the death of God's Son on the cross.

"He took from among us" acquires a sense of elimination: "[he] did away with it completely" (GNB).[100] The participle "nailing" indicates the means through which the written decree is obliterated: "by nailing it to the cross" (NJB, NLT, NET). The reference to "the cross" points back to

---

95. See, e.g., the emphasis of the "Law of the Lord" (*T. Jud.* 26; cf. *T. Jud.* 24) in relation to the note on the written record in the presence of the Lord (*T. Jud.* 20).

96. Bevere, *Sharing in the Inheritance*, 140.

97. See also the reference to the "cross" that ends all hostility in Eph 2:16.

98. See Roy Yates, "Colossians 2,14: Metaphor of Forgiveness," *Bib* 71 (1990): 256 – 59, who further suggests that these regulations are part of the program to prepare believers for their mystical visionary experiences.

99. See Schweizer, "Slaves of the Elements," 464 – 65.

100. See the similar construction in 1 Cor 5:2 on being separated from those who live in sin.

"the blood of his cross" in the christological hymn (1:20). The thought that Jesus' death on the cross cancelled that which is against us recalls a similar note concerning one's deliverance from God's wrath: "Since we have now been justified by his blood, how much more shall we be saved from God's wrath through him!" (Rom 5:9).

2:15a When he disarmed the rulers and authorities (ἀπεκδυσάμενος τὰς ἀρχὰς καὶ τὰς ἐξουσίας). In the final verse of this section, Paul provides the climactic note on God's victory through Christ on the cross. Having urged the Colossians not to be taken captive (v. 8), Paul now focuses on the disarming of the forces that oppose Christ and his followers. As Christ rules over "every ruler and authority" (v. 10), here God is said to have disarmed them through Christ. Finally, in the stripping off of Christ's body on the cross (v. 11), one finds the rulers and authorities in turn being stripped of their power. Crucified on the cross, "the one who had died the death of a slave was exalted to be the Lord of the whole creation and bearer of the divine name Kyrios."[101] The followers of this Lord of all should no longer subject themselves to the power of what had been subdued.

The adverbial participle (ἀπεκδυσάμενος), a rare verb that means "stripping off" (cf. 3:9), should be taken as a temporal participle: "when he disarmed" (cf. NASB). It is more difficult, however, to determine the sense of this middle participle and therefore also the subject of this participle. Most English versions adopt an active sense with God being the implied subject: "having disarmed the powers and authorities" (NIV, et al.),[102] but the minority voice is reflected in a reading that takes this as a middle participle with Christ being the subject: "Christ freed himself from the power of the spiritual rulers and authorities" (GNB; CEV). This latter reading is supported by many of the Greek fathers, and "it is commended by the parallel uses of the substantive in v. 11"[103] when Paul discusses Christ's "putting off [τῇ ἀπεκδύσει] of [his] body of flesh."

Nevertheless, in this context, God should be considered the subject of this participle. The subject of the verbs since v. 13b has been God, so it is fitting to see Paul as continuing this pattern. Second, the following note on the triumphal processions requires not simply Christ's freeing himself from the evil powers, but these powers have been stripped of their power.[104] Finally, if "in him" (ἐν αὐτῷ) at the end of this verse refers to "Christ" (cf. "through/in him," NASB, ESV),[105] as in all the repeated appearances of this phrase in this section (cf. vv. 6, 7, 9, 10), it is more natural to see God performing the action.

The objects of God's act of disarming are "the rulers and authorities" (τὰς ἀρχὰς καὶ τὰς ἐξουσίας). These should be understood as demonic spiritual powers (cf. 2:10),[106] and this usage is clearly paralleled by the description of divine warfare in Eph 6:12, where believers are called to fight "against the rulers, against the authorities ... and against the spiritual forces of evil" (cf. also Eph 2:2). Here, Paul

---

101. Martin Hengel, *Crucifixion in the Ancient World and the Folly of the Message of the Cross* (trans. John Bowden; Philadelphia: Fortress, 1977), 62.

102. See BDF §316(1), which considers this participle as an example of the use of the middle verb when an active is expected.

103. Lightfoot, *St. Paul's Epistles to the Colossians and to Philemon*, 191.

104. Cf. Arnold, *Colossian Syncretism*, 279. Some, however, consider these "rulers and authorities" as benign beings, thus requiring no need of disarmament. See discussions on 2:15b-c for the image of triumphal procession.

105. Some consider "the cross" (TNIV, NET, NIV) as the intended reference behind this phrase; Yates, "Colossians, 2:15," 588 – 91.

106. Contra Wesley Carr, *Angels and Principalities: The Background, Meaning and Development of the Pauline Phrase Hai Archai Kai Exousiai* (SNTSMS 42; Cambridge: Cambridge Univ. Press, 1981), 61 – 66.

notes the "disarming" of these powers; thus, he emphasizes that these powers can no longer threaten those who believe in Christ.

2:15b-c He boldly made a spectacle of them, by triumphing over them in him (ἐδειγμάτισεν ἐν παρρησίᾳ, θριαμβεύσας αὐτοὺς ἐν αὐτῷ). In Roman military practices, victory was followed by the public demonstration of the glory of the victor as well as the shame of the defeated. The verb "made a spectacle" is followed by a prepositional phrase (ἐν παρρησίᾳ, lit., "in public/boldness") that functions adverbially (cf. Mark 8:32; John 7:26; 18:20; Acts 4:13, 29; 28:31; 2 Cor 3:12; Eph 3:12).[107] Here the prepositional phrase most likely intensifies the public nature of making a spectacle; thus "he boldly made a spectacle" — although most translations prefer simply to make explicit the "public" nature of such an act: "he made a public display" (NASB; cf. NAB, REB, NLT, NKJV, NRSV, NJB, TNIV, NET, NIV).

In ancient literature, the word translated "triumphing" (θριαμβεύσας) is often used to describe the victory parade in which victorious Roman generals would lead captives in a public procession.[108] Some, therefore, have chosen to make this explicit: "leading them as captives in his triumphal procession" (REB; cf. GNB). Others have suggested that this participle refers to the victory celebration of those who may even have aligned themselves with the victor: "The emphasis is then on the glorification of Christ following his death and the public

celebration of the victor by the hosts of angels as well as the company of the redeemed."[109] This reading lacks the lexical support that points to a "triumphal procession." Moreover, this would require the "rulers and authorities" to be benign spiritual powers, a reading that is inappropriate here.

What is worth noting is that in a traditional Roman triumphal procession, captives are led to their death.[110] This may be implied in this passage, but the focus of Paul's discussion is not the fate of these "rulers and authorities," but on the believers, who should not be deceived by these spirits whose powers have been stripped by the climactic act of God through his Son.

"In him" (ἐν αὐτῷ) points again to the critical role Christ plays in this divine warfare. In light of the previous reference to "the cross" (v. 14), some consider this moment of public display of the honor of the victor and the shame of the captives to lie in Jesus' death on the cross.[111] In light of the sequence of the death, burial, and resurrection noted above (vv. 11 – 12), however, one would have expected the reference to the resurrection after the note on "the cross" (v. 14). It seems probable that this public display takes place during Jesus' exaltation. This sequence is attested in Eph 1:20 – 21, where Christ's exaltation is depicted in terms of his supreme glory and authority over "all rule and authority, power and dominion."[112] To the believers who are "dead" in their transgressions, they can likewise receive power to be "made alive with him" (Col 2:13).

---

107. "Public" and "boldness" should not be considered as two separate senses of this word. Both senses are often found together, especially in a political context where free citizens of a polis claim the right to participate in the political discourse; cf. LSJ, 1344; A. Missiou, "The Vocabulary of Democracy," in *A History of Ancient Greek: From the Beginnings to Late Antiquity* (ed. A. F. Christidis; trans. A. Missiou; Cambridge: Cambridge Univ. Press, 2007), 1063.

108. See, in particular, Lamar Williamson Jr., "Led in Triumph: Paul's Use of *Thriambeuō*," *Int* 22 (1968): 317 – 32.

109. Yates, "A Reappraisal of Colossians," 105; see also his "Colossians 2:15," 573 – 91.

110. Smith, *Heavenly Perspective*, 108.

111. Wright, *Colossians and Philemon*, 116.

112. Cf. Moo, *Letters to the Colossians and to Philemon*, 215. See also Schweizer, *Letter to the Colossians*, 152, who points to Eph 4:8, where one finds the exalted Christ leading the captives in a triumphal procession depicted through the quotation from Ps 68:18.

Theology in Application

Deception of the Idols

This section begins with the reminder that Jesus is to be recognized as "Lord" (2:6),[113] and its detailed arguments draw out the implications of such a confession. A visible thread can be identified behind the criticisms launched against the false teachings: in affirming Jesus as Lord, any teaching that contradicts this central confession must be considered idolatry.[114] "Empty and deceitful philosophy" (v. 8) recalls OT anti-idol polemic that labels idols as "worthless" and those who worship them as "ignorant" (Isa 44:9; cf. 44:18). More explicit is the claim that "idols speak deceitfully" (Zech 10:2). "According to human tradition" (v. 8) points to the portrayal of idols as human fabrications (Isa 40:18 – 24; 41:4 – 7; 44:9 – 11). "Not according to Christ" (v. 8) is the definition of idolatry because idols are "no god" (Deut 32:21), and they cannot be compared to the one who creates all things (1 Chr 16:26; Ps 96:5; cf. 1:16). "Not performed by human hands" (v. 11) is contrasted to the idols that are "made with human hands"; and unlike impotent idols that cannot "rescue you" (1 Sam 12:21; cf. Isa 46:6 – 7; 57:13; Jer 14:22), God is able to deliver his people from their transgressions (v. 13). Finally, just as the idols and their makers will be put to shame (Ps 97:7; Isa 42:17; 45:16; Hos 10:6), the "rulers and authorities" that oppose God will be put to shame (v. 15).

If such anti-idol polemic can be detected behind Paul's discussion in this section, one can immediately point to two implications for those who claim to worship Christ the Lord. First, these believers who have "received Christ Jesus the Lord" (v. 6) should not "exchange their glorious God for worthless idols" (Jer 2:11), especially because these idols cannot rescue them from their predicament. Second, those who follow these worthless idols likewise turn into worthless beings because they can no longer respond to God's salvific act (cf. 2 Kgs 17:15; Pss 115:5 – 8; 135:15 – 18; Isa 6:9 – 10). The urgency of Paul's message, therefore, becomes evident. He is not simply warning the Colossian believers to resist a teaching that may supplement that which they have received; he is making it clear that if they follow such teachings, they will be led to worship false gods that cannot deliver what has been promised to their followers. When Paul reminds the believers of the gospel they have received (v. 6), he is therefore calling them to be faithful to the one and true God.[115]

While "idols" may evoke that which is strange and foreign, even in the OT idols

---

113. Although this is the only appearance of this christological title in the central sections (2:6 – 23) of this letter, Jesus as Lord is undoubtedly the focus of these sections.

114. See, in particular, Walsh, "Late/Post Modernity and Idolatry," 1 – 17. For a helpful survey of the biblical theological theme of idolatry, see also Beale, *We Become What We Worship*.

115. In covenantal terms, to forget the mighty acts of God is to reject him and his covenant (cf. Deut 8:18 – 19; Prov 2:17); cf. Brevard S. Childs, *Memory and Tradition in Israel* (London: SCM, 1962), 49 – 51.

are defined as the objects of one's trust. In Isa 2, for example, idols are mentioned together with objects on which one's security rests:

> You, LORD, have abandoned your people,
>> the descendants of Jacob.
> They are full of superstitions from the East;
>> they practice divination like the Philistines
>> and embrace pagan customs.
> Their land is full of silver and gold;
>> there is no end to their treasures.
> Their land is full of horses;
>> there is no end to their chariots.
> Their land is full of idols;
>> they bow down to the work of their hands,
>> to what their fingers have made. (Isa 2:6 – 8; cf. Mic 5:10 – 15)

Contemporary readers may not readily recognize the idols we worship, but "divination," "silver," "gold," "horses," and "chariots" are still apt descriptions of the obsessions of modern men and women. This prophetic message is brought alive by Eugene Peterson's paraphrase:

> God, you've walked out on your family Jacob
>> because their world is full of hokey religion,
> Philistine witchcraft, and pagan hocus-pocus,
>> a world rolling in wealth,
> Stuffed with things,
>> no end to its machines and gadgets,
> And gods — gods of all sorts and sizes.
>> These people make their own gods and worship what they make.
>
> *(The Message*, Isa 2:6 – 8)

Peterson's paraphrase reminds the modern reader that the concept of idolatry is immediately relevant. While few of us would bow before a statue, many of us place our trust and hope in things other than God. This emphasis — idols as anything in which we put our trust instead of God — explains why Isa 2:6 – 8 and Mic 5:10 – 15 condemn horses and chariots along with idols. They both represent areas of Israel's unbelief in God and their trust in other possessions. Many of us hunger more for things, success, security, and position than we do for God. For the readers of Isaiah's text, idols represented an alternative security to belief in God. Are our modern gods any different?

In this context, Paul not only identifies the danger of idols; he also points to how the worship of such beings denies the power and sufficiency of the death and resurrection of Christ (vv. 11 – 13). Such false worship not only exalts the created to the level of the Creator, but it also distorts the image of the Creator as the one and only deserving object of worship. This distortion is, after all, the root of idolatry as it is to be understood "first and foremost as an improper conception of God in the mind of the worshiper, thereby internalizing the sin."[116]

Sin and Guilt

In this section, Paul shifts from the status and supremacy of Christ to the relevance of such christological affirmations for the struggles of the Colossian believers. Instead of providing a series of ethical imperatives, Paul begins by noting that all that is required of the believers has been accomplished by Christ. While not minimizing the moral implications of such a declaration, Paul nonetheless begins with the sufficiency of Christ's work. The deceptiveness of the false teaching in Colossae lies in the claim that more needs to be done as one seeks to stand before God. Paul responds by noting that such claims deprive Christ of his glorious victory in his death and resurrection.

Paul takes seriously the consequences of sin, but he also focuses intensely on the striking power of the solution God has provided through his Son. The note on the death, burial, and resurrection of Christ (vv. 11–12) points to the seriousness of sin, and the need to mention the death of Christ in connection with God's act of forgiveness (v. 13) points to the atoning significance of his death: "While we were still sinners, Christ died for us" (Rom 5:8). Because Christ bore our sins in his death, our participation in his death becomes the only viable way to live: "The life I now live in my body, I live by faith in the Son of God, who loved me and gave himself for me" (Gal 2:20).

It is only because of Christ's atoning death and his victorious resurrection that one can be freed from the bondage of sin. In modern society, which downplays the notion of sin, one finds a sense of guilt that continues to plague even those who do not claim to have any use for religions. In a classic work that points to the disappearance of the concept of sin as the root of the resurgence of human despair and guilt, Karl Menninger, well-known psychiatrist and founder of the Menninger Clinic, laments that "sins had become crimes, and now crimes were becoming illnesses."[117] He further points to what lies beyond the power of the medical professional:

> Psychiatrists have finally demonstrated that there is an effective treatment for certain conditions which doctors formerly ignored or mistreated. But do we not repeat the error if we ignore appropriate help available for some individuals whose sins are greater than their symptoms?[118]

Building on such an observation, Menninger urges ministers of the gospel to resist

---

116. Moshe Halbertal and Avishai Margalit, *Idolatry* (trans. Naomi Goldblum; Cambridge, MA: Harvard Univ. Press, 1992), 2.

117. Karl Menninger, *Whatever Became of Sin?* (New York: Hawthorn, 1973), 45.

118. Ibid., 49.

the temptation to bypass the difficult doctrine of sin; rather, they must proclaim the gospel as the solution that deals with sin, which is the root of guilt.[119]

Recognizing the serious consequences of sin, Paul turns to the power of Christ's death and resurrection. Since Christ has "disarmed the rulers and authorities" (v. 15), believers will no longer be threatened by such forces as they stand righteous in God's presence because of their identification with the victorious Christ. "The written decree that is against us" (v. 14) has been nailed to the cross, and one can experience the power of divine forgiveness that reaches to the depth of one's soul and cures the disease that defies human therapists.

Challenging the moral teachers of his time, Paul insists on the relevance of the prior act of Christ, "who gave himself as a ransom for all people" (1 Tim 2:6). For contemporary preachers who claim to proclaim the good news, we are also called to point first and foremost to the divine solution to the human predicament. This freedom from guilt is built on an act that is external to the human predicament, and it is a freedom that the true gospel promises:

> No condemnation now I dread,
> Jesus, and all in Him, is mine.
> Alive in Him, my Living Head,
> And clothed in Righteousness Divine.
> Bold I approach the Eternal Throne,
> And claim the Crown, through Christ my own.[120]

Circumcision and the New Community

The unexpected appearance of the notes on "circumcision" (v. 11) and "uncircumcision" (v. 13) demands further comments. As discussed above, circumcision was a significant identity symbol for the Jews. Proselytes who converted into Judaism were to be circumcised (Jdt 14:10), and many Jews would give up their lives rather than leave their children uncircumcised (1 Macc 1:60 – 61; 2 Macc 6:10; 4 Macc 4:25). The significance of circumcision is grounded in the Abrahamic narrative, when it became "a sign of the covenant" between God and Israel (Gen 17:11). This physical act that makes a mark on the male body symbolizes a radical discontinuity in the line of ancestry:

> The circumcision of Abraham and his descendants introduces a break in the genealogy, which distinguishes Abraham from his forbearers and presents him as a founder of a new lineage. The action of cutting suggests this break: there is separation from the past and the start of something new. This new thing includes change in identity — as expressed in the change of names — and taking on a new status.[121]

119. Ibid., 192 – 203.

120. Charles Wesley, "And Can It Be," final stanza, *Wesley Hymn Book* (ed. Franz Hildebrandt; London: A. Weekes, 1958), 88.

121. Athena E. Gorospe, *Narrative and Identity: An Ethical Reading of Exodus 4* (BIS 86; Leiden/Boston: Brill, 2007), 135.

As the physically violent act of circumcision established a new starting point in the identity of God's chosen, Christ's violent death on the cross is understood as his "circumcision" (v. 11) and provides the final starting point for the building up of God's people. This new lineage is grounded in the believers' identification with his death and resurrection (vv. 12 – 13). The clear break with the past is accomplished by the destruction of the "written decree" and the disarming of the forces of the former age (v. 14). Believers are called to live a life that does not betray that which has already been accomplished for them (v. 6). As the Jews grounded their identity in the mark that separated them from other ethnic entities, believers in Christ are to ground their identities in the person of Christ, in whom we find our roots and future. To ground one's identity in the person of Christ also allows the Gentiles who were physically uncircumcised to participate in this people of God.[122] This paves the way for the argument that follows, when Paul again uses the metaphor of the shedding of one's flesh that allows putting on the new humanity that includes both "Greek" and "Jew" (3:9 – 11).

In light of this redefinition of God's people, it is no longer surprising to find Paul's use of the metaphor of "a circumcision not performed by human hands" (v. 11). The link between the physical act of circumcision and the spiritual act can also be found in Rom 2:25 – 29, where Paul identifies a "Jew" as one who has experienced the "circumcision of the heart" instead of that of "the written code" (2:29). This reading not only presupposes the discussion of the physical circumcision of Gen 17 and that of the heart in Deut 30, but it also assumes the note on the circumcision of the "heart of flesh" in Ezek 36:26, as that which provides the link that allows later Jewish exegetical traditions to suggest that "circumcision of the heart *is* the circumcision of the flesh."[123] More importantly, in these traditions, spiritual circumcision is an act of God that will be carried out at a future point: "The LORD your God will circumcise your hearts and the hearts of your descendants, so that you may love him with all your heart and with all your soul, and live" (Deut 30:6).

In Ezekiel, this future act is understood in eschatological terms when God will pour out his Spirit among his people, and it is with this Spirit that one can resist the temptation to worship idols:

> I will sprinkle clean water on you, and you will be clean; I will cleanse you from all your impurities and from all your idols. I will give you a new heart and put a new spirit in you; I will remove from you your heart of stone and give you a heart of flesh. (Ezek 36:25 – 26)

---

122. Already in the OT one finds Israel, "uncircumcised in heart," compared to the Gentiles, who are "uncircumcised [in flesh]" (Jer 9:26). See also the description of Israel as "uncircumcised [in] hearts" in Lev 26:41, although this description could also apply to the Gentiles (cf. Ezek 44:7, 9).

123. Timothy W. Berkley, *From a Broken Covenant to Circumcision of the Heart: Pauline Intertextual Exegesis in Romans 2:17 – 29* (SBLDS 175; Atlanta: Society of Biblical Literature, 2000), 145, italics his.

In this passage in Colossians, which unveils the deceptive nature of the idolatrous philosophy, Paul points to the fulfillment of such promises in Christ, who is able to provide this circumcision of the heart to those who believe in him because of the shedding of his own body of flesh. For those who have experienced this eschatological blessing, to return to a life that is governed by "human tradition" (v. 8) will itself be an idolatrous act.

What are the modern equivalents to the rite of circumcision? In some circles, certain acts are considered to be "identity-markers" that aim at identifying a group as those true to the gospel message. In the previous generation, the avoidance of drinking, smoking, dancing, and movie attendance were considered to be such markers. While avoiding such acts is often consistent with aspects of NT teachings, it is tempting to highlight them at the expense of the renewal of the heart.

This has not been missed by those observing from the outside. A notable example can be found from 1950 when a striking spiritual revival took place in a prominent Christian college. An editor from *Time* magazine noted that this was a college where one could find "no movies, smoking, card-playing, dancing or drinking."[124] Despite such practices, it was questioned whether these students were following Christ in their personal and spiritual lives. In 1950, however, the Spirit worked in a powerful way on this campus. As a result, the hearts of many of these students were turned to God. This turn was evidenced by a comment by one of those present: "Of that senior class, one-third of us became foreign missionaries. That's the only class in the history of the school with such a percentage. Other classes had one missionary or two or three. We had one hundred. And I think that's a very telling fact."[125] Not only were these students "circumcised in flesh"; they are now also "circumcised in heart."

---

124. This article "42 Hours of Repentance," originally appeared in the Feb. 20, 1950, issue of *Time* and is now available online: www.time.com/time/magazine/article/0,9171,81 2008,00.html.

125. Online: http://fcov.blogspot.com/2005/08/wheaton-college-revival – 1950.html.

Colossians 2:16 – 23

Literary Context

Although a bit distanced from the christological confession in 1:15 – 20, the christocentric focus of Paul's arguments can still be felt in the remaining sections of this letter. After providing a strong critique of the "empty and deceitful philosophy" (2:8) in the previous section, Paul now tackles the practices and behavior such a philosophy might have encouraged. In his critique of the false teaching, Paul has already established a few critical points: (1) in Christ one finds the fullness of deity, and he is therefore the head of every ruler and authority (vv. 8 – 10); (2) in participating in Christ's death, burial, and resurrection, believers can now participate in the victory that is in him alone (vv. 11 – 12); and (3) that victory points to the freedom of the believers from the "written decree against us" (v. 14) since Christ has already disarmed the powers behind such a record (v. 15).

Building on these three points, 2:16 – 23 discusses the behavior and practices that should reflect on the believers' participation in Christ's victory. (1) Believers should not be judged concerning dietary customs and calendrical practices dictated by human tradition (vv. 16 – 17); (2) they should not be disqualified by those who insist on various types of visionary experiences (vv. 18 – 19); and (3) they should not submit to ascetic practices as dictated by human tradition (vv. 20 – 23). Although details are provided concerning the practices promoted by these false teachings, clarity is lacking concerning to what the various terms refer. Nevertheless, Paul makes it clear that these practices are "according to human tradition" and "not according to Christ" (cf. v. 8). After his critique of these practices, Paul turns to the positive exhortation, beginning with "seek the things above" (3:1). In these exhortation sections, Paul continues to emphasize the central role of Christ (cf. 3:1, 3, 4, 15, 16, 17).

The shift from the aorist indicatives and participles in 2:13 – 15 to the present imperative in 2:16 points to the development of another stage of Paul's argument, and some have suggested that beginning with 2:16, one finds the beginning of the "practical" or "paraenetic" section.[1] Others have simply labeled this section as the

---

1. Paul Lamarche, "Structure de l'épître aux Colossiens," *Bib*
56 (1975): 460.

"consequence" of the prior christological affirmations[2] or even the "conclusion" of such affirmations.[3] What is clear is that this section builds on the previous ones. To separate it strictly from the previous does not do justice to the intricate relationship between this section and its preceding and following contexts. First, the appearances of "therefore" (οὖν) in 2:6 as well as 3:1 suggests that Paul is building his arguments step by step, and the presence of οὖν in 2:16 points to another stage of his argument.

Second, in the preceding and following sections, one also finds the combination of the theoretical and the practical. This is most apparent in the several references to Jesus' death and resurrection. In the previous section, the call to be "rooted and built up in him" (2:7) is based on the believers' participation in the death and resurrection of Jesus (vv. 11 – 14). In this section, the call to resist the practices imposed by the false teachers is also grounded in the same series of events (v. 20). This focus on the climactic events in salvation history likewise provides the grounds for Paul's arguments in the sections that follow (3:1 – 4, 5 – 9, 12 – 14). It is therefore clear that a theoretical/practical distinction is insufficient to delineate the arguments of Paul in this letter. He is, however, intensely focused on the relevance of the death and resurrection of Christ for those who believe in him in the context of the false teachers.

V. Faithfulness of the Believers (2:6 – 4:1)
   A. Call to Faithfulness (2:6 – 7)
   B. Sufficiency in Christ (2:8 – 23)
      1. Against Deceptive Philosophy (2:8 – 15)
➡   **2. Against Human Rituals and Regulations (2:16 – 23)**
   C. Reorientation of Christian Living (3:1 – 4:1)
VI. Eschatological Mission to the World (4:2 – 6)

Main Idea

In light of the death and resurrection of Christ, Paul urges the Colossian believers not to submit themselves to ethnic and religious rituals, visionary experiences, and ascetic practices. Unlike the reality of the victory accomplished by God through Christ, these regulations and practices provide only false promises that distract one from God's powerful work.

Translation

(See next page.)

---

2. Aletti, *Saint Paul Épître aux Colossiens*, 39.   3. Sumney, "The Argument of Colossians," 349.

Colossians 2:16 – 23

16a	Exhortation	Therefore, **do not let anyone judge you**
b	realm	[1] in food and in drink, or
c	list	[2] in regard to a festival,
d	list	[3] a new moon, or
e	list	[4] sabbaths.
17a	description (16b-e)	These are a shadow of things to come, but
b	contrast	the substance belongs to Christ.
18a	Exhortation	**Let no one condemn you**
b	means	[1] by insisting on self-humiliation and
c	means	[2] the worship of angels,
d	description	entering into these things that he has seen,
e	description	conceited without reason by his carnal mind, and
19a	description	not holding fast to the head,
b	source	from which the entire body,
c	means	nourished and
		united through the joints and ligaments,
d	action	grows with a growth from God.
20a	condition	If you have died with Christ
b	separation	to the elemental spirits of the world,
c	Question	**why,**
		as though you were still alive to this world,
21a	illustration	**do you submit to its regulations:**
		[1] do not handle,
b	list	[2] do not taste,
c	list	[3] do not touch,
22	description	all these, related to things that are destined to perish with use,
	description	according to human commands and teachings?
23a	description	These rules have no value in restraining the gratification of the flesh,
b	concessive	even though they have an appearance of wisdom
c	cause	with their [1] self-imposed worship,
d	list	[2] self-humiliation, and
e	list	[3] harsh treatment
		of the body.

Structure

After revealing the deceptiveness of the false teachings in 2:8 – 15, Paul shifts his attention to the practices promoted by those who are spreading such false teachings. This section is divided into three subsections, each of which begins with a critique of a set of practices. After listing the questionable practices, Paul provides the grounds on which such practices are to be critiqued. Although specific terms are provided in describing the targeted practices, the significance of many of these terms is not readily comprehensible to the contemporary readers. These terms might have been used by the false teachers themselves, or at least they appear to belong to a set of vocabulary shared by Paul and the Colossian believers. But the precise nuance becomes unclear for us who stand in considerable historical and cultural distance from first-century Asia Minor.[4]

In vv. 16 – 17, Paul urges the Colossians not to be judged concerning selected dietary and calendrical practices. While we cannot pinpoint the specific nature of the false teachings, the practices noted are at least not foreign to those who are familiar with Jewish customs and observances. Paul's critique of these practices centers on the incomparable status of Christ, compared to whom these practices are but a "shadow."

In vv. 18 – 19, Paul focuses on self-humiliation and the worship of angels. These two items possibly point to ascetic practices and claims of visionary experiences; these are experiences shared by more than one religious tradition. To Paul, these not only point to the empty and carnal minds of the practitioners, but more importantly, they point to the failure to be connected with Christ the head.

In the final section (vv. 20 – 23), Paul returns to a critique of selected regulations. These are transitory and merely products of human creation. They are of "no value"; this expression not only applies to the regulations listed here, but it also serves as the concluding remark of all three sections (vv. 16 – 17, 18 – 19, 20 – 23) as Paul provides a succinct and final evaluation of these practices.

The relationship between the first (vv. 16 – 17) and second (vv. 18 – 19) sections is clear: both begin with a subtle reference to the false teachers together with an imperative verb ("do not let anyone judge"; "do not let anyone condemn"). Verses 20 – 23, however, begin with a conditional clause (v. 20), and the regulations critiqued are related to both the dietary practices noted in the first section (v. 16) and the ascetic practices noted in the second (v. 18).

The relationship between the first two sections and the final one, therefore, needs further comment. Some see in the final section a move from "religious and cultic demands" to "ethical and ascetic requirements,"[5] while others see a move from "motives

---

4. Of course, one can also argue that these are simply general terms that point to the pagan and Jewish environment in which the early Christians found themselves. This would, however, assume that no specific heresy can be identified within this text (cf. Hooker, "Were There False Teachers in Colossae?" 329). For a further discussion, see "Circumstances behind the Text" in the introduction.

5. Schweizer, *Letter to the Colossians*, 154.

and results" to "regulations and practices."[6] Neither of these, however, is adequate. One should begin by focusing on the conditional clause in the final section that points to the death of Christ: "if you have died with Christ" (v. 20). This provides a transition to 3:1: "if you have been raised with Christ."[7] Reading in light of these two references, we can see the final section summarizes the first two in claiming that the noted practices and claimed experiences are worthless, and they should have been abandoned when believers died with Christ. This final section, therefore, serves both as the conclusion of 2:6 – 23 as well as the introduction to 3:1 – 4:1.

Exegetical Outline

➡ **I. Against Human Rituals and Regulations (2:16 – 23)**

    A. Critique of false practices (I) (2:16 – 17)

        1. Against dietary and calendrical practices (2:16)

        2. Because they are mere shadows of things to come (2:17)

    B. Critique of false practices (II) (2:18 – 19)

        1. Against ascetic practices and visionary experiences (2:18a-c)

        2. Because they are empty, carnal, and not connected to the head (2:18d – 19)

    C. Critique of false practices (III) (2:20 – 23)

        1. Against legalistic regulations (2:20 – 21)

        2. Because they are transitory, human, and worthless (2:22 – 23)

Explanation of the Text

2:16 Therefore, do not let anyone judge you in food and in drink, or in regard to a festival, a new moon, or sabbaths (Μὴ οὖν τις ὑμᾶς κρινέτω ἐν βρώσει καὶ ἐν πόσει ἢ ἐν μέρει ἑορτῆς ἢ νεομηνίας ἢ σαββάτων). With "therefore" (οὖν), Paul moves to another stage of his critique of the false teachings (cf. 2:6; 3:1). As the preceding section focused on the theoretical underpinnings of the false teachings, this section tackles specific practices demanded by the false teachers. This exhortation is connected directly with the previous assertion of the defeat of the evil powers and with the general discussion of the sufficiency of the believers' shar-

ing in the death, burial, and resurrection of Christ (vv. 11 – 15).

"Anyone" (τις) is another way of rhetorically suppressing the identity of the false teachers.[8] "Judge" (κρινέτω) here carries the sense of passing "an unfavorable judgment upon" a person.[9] This negative use of the verb is consistent with Paul's usage elsewhere; it is best illustrated by Rom 2:1, where "judge" is paralleled by "condemn": "for at whatever point you judge [κρίνεις] another, you are condemning [κατακρίνεις] yourself." Particularly relevant is the repeated use of this verb in a negative sense in Rom 14, where Paul forbids believers

---

6. Sumney, *Colossians*, 159.
7. Cf. Wright, *Colossians and Philemon*, 124.

8. See comments on 2:4.
9. BDAG, 567.

to judge one another in their dietary (14:3, 10) and calendrical practices (14:5). It is, therefore, justifiable to translate the phrase, "do not let anyone condemn you" (NRSV; cf. NLT).[10]

"In food and in drink" means "in matters of food and drink" (NRSV; cf. NASB, TNIV, ESV, NIV).[11] This probably reflects the dietary practices of eating and drinking in a pagan context (cf. Rom. 14). The avoidance of "food and drink" refers to the abstention "from meat" and "from wine and strong drink" in preparation for the participation in cultic and religious rituals.[12] In light of the following reference to feast and "sabbaths" in particular, however, a Jewish background cannot be excluded. In Rom 14:14, 21, "meat" and "wine" are the subject of disputes where one finds disagreements concerning issues of "clean" and "unclean" (v. 14), and such issues became important in contexts where the interaction between Jews and Gentiles was prominent. A similar context seems likely for the Colossian believers.

In the OT, fasting is also considered a preparatory act for an encounter with God (Exod 34:28; Deut 9:9; Judg 20:26; Jer 36:6; Dan 9:3; 10:2 – 3, 12). Restrictions concerning drinks appear less often, however, except in a few special cases related to regulations applied to priests (Lev 10:9; cf. Lev 11:34, 36) and Nazirites (Num 6:3).[13] Later rabbinic sources testify to certain dietary restrictions concerning drinks (e.g., *m. Ḥul.* 8.1),[14] and these restrictions are particularly relevant when Jews

find themselves living among the Gentiles. In this context, these dietary regulations should be understood in light of both the discussions of ethnic identity of Jewish Christians and the preparatory rites for visionary experiences.

"In regard to" (ἐν μέρει) is a "stylistic variation of the previous simple ἐν, used to avoid a succession of five datives."[15] "Festival" (ἑορτῆς), "new moon" (νεομηνίας), and "sabbaths" (σαββάτων) point clearly to a Jewish context. These three terms appear together in a number of OT passages (e.g., 1 Chr 23:31; 2 Chr 2:4; 31:3; Ezek 45:17; cf. 2 Kgs 4:23; Neh 10:33; Isa 66:23; Ezek 46:1; Amos 8:5). Some consider these terms here simply as the imposition of a "religious calendar" on the Colossian believers.[16] It should be noted, however, that when these terms are listed together in the OT, it often refers to cultic rituals linked with these festal days. If so, Paul is not opposed to the Jewish calendar per se but to the imposition of practices related to these feasts.[17] As in the reference to dietary restrictions noted above, these practices may also remind the Gentile audiences of pagan religious observances especially in relation to astrological observations and speculations. If so, Paul is further suggesting that their submission to the (Jewish) calendrical practices can be considered a return to their past when they were involved in idolatrous worship.[18]

2:17a These are a shadow of the things to come (ἅ ἐστιν σκιὰ τῶν μελλόντων). Paul continues his critique of "these" customs and regulations related

---

10. For a more neutral rendering, cf. CEV: "do not let anyone tell you...."

11. "In" (ἐν) would then indicate "sphere;" Wallace, *Greek Grammar*, 372.

12. Lohse, *Colossians and Philemon*, 115.

13. O'Brien, *Colossians, Philemon*, 138, has therefore argued against an OT background for these terms. These references do, however, point to general issues of ritual purity; cf. Beetham, *Echoes of Scripture*, 196 – 200.

14. Bevere, *Sharing in the Inheritance*, 86.

15. Harris, *Colossians and Philemon*, 118.

16. Troy Martin, "Pagan and Judeo-Christian Time-Keeping Schemes in Gal 4.10 and Col 2.16," *NTS* 42 (1996): 111.

17. H. Ross Cole, "The Christian and Time-Keeping in Colossians 2:16 and Galatians 4:10," *AUSS* 39 (2001): 273 – 82.

18. See also T. C. G. Thornton, "Jewish New Moon Festivals, Galatians 4:3 – 11 and Colossians 2:16," *JTS* 40 (1989): 100, who further suggests that the astronomical bodies that determine times and seasons "were aspects of the στοιχεῖα τοῦ κόσμου from which Christians had been freed."

to dietary and calendrical practices in v. 16 by noting its insignificance when compared to the accomplished work of God in Christ. While "shadow" (σκιά) can refer simply to the shade cast by a source of light (Plato, *Phaed.* 101d, 239c), an inferred use of this term is implied here. Three particular uses of this metaphor could have been implied with the use of this word. First, in Greek philosophical traditions (esp. Plato), "shadow" (σκιά) is contrasted with "reality" (πρᾶγμα) or "form" (εἰκών), and the "shadow" represents that which only acquires the appearance of what is real.[19] Paul's use of a different term for the contrasted "substance" (σῶμα) in v. 17b may be dictated by his agenda in this letter, although the contrast between these two terms does appear in Hellenistic Jewish writers.[20]

Second, "shadow" is also often used to describe fleeting and transitory representation, as contrasted to that which is permanent and stable.[21] This is related to the first use of the metaphor, but this use emphasizes the temporal nature of what is depicted. The genitive modifier, "of the things to come" (τῶν μελλόντων), may point to this background.

Third, in light of the connection between the words "shadow" and "image" (εἴδωλον) across the various Greek writers,[22] it is also possible that Paul has "idols" in the back of his mind when he uses this term. This is made all the more possible with the anti-idol polemic in 2:6 – 15. If so, the "shadows" represent that which is "not according to Christ" as contrasted to that which is "according to Christ" (v. 8).

Contextually, the third use would fit this context well, but in Greek writers "shadow" is hardly connected with the worship of the idols. The first two uses would come close to Paul's argument here. If the contrast between "shadow" and "reality," especially in the Platonic sense, is to be assumed, then Paul's usage here is striking in that he is replacing the ontological distinction between appearance and reality with the temporal one.[23] This temporal perspective is highlighted by the genitival phrase, "of the things to come."

"Of the things to come" refers to the acts of God through Christ that have already been accomplished, thus justifying a translation that makes this temporal aspect explicit: "these are a shadow of the things that were to come" (TNIV, NIV). In the NT, the participle μελλόντων often acquires an explicitly eschatological sense as it can refer to the eschatological figure (Matt 11:14), the age to come (Eph 1:21; 1 Tim 6:19), or eternal life (1 Tim 4:8). In this context, the climactic eschatological event has already taken place in the death and resurrection of Christ (vv. 11 – 15), and the reference to the relative future "is to be interpreted from the period when the restrictions of verse 16 were enjoined."[24] This imagery of the "shadow of the things to come" is best paralleled by the description of the law in Heb 10:1a: "The law is only a shadow of the good things that are coming — not the realities themselves." This strengthens our understanding of the significance of the Jewish context of the false teachings plaguing the Colossian believers.

2:17b But the substance belongs to Christ (τὸ δὲ σῶμα τοῦ Χριστοῦ). In contrast to shadowy existence of the customs and practices promoted by the false teachers, the reality belongs to Christ.

---

19. Plato, *Rep.* 514a – 518b; Cf. Plato, *Crat.* 391b, 432b.

20. Philo, *Migration* 12; *Confusion* 190; Josephus, *J. W.* 2.28; Beetham, *Echoes of Scripture*, 201.

21. Pindar, *Pythian Odes* 8.95 – 96; Sophocles, *Antigone* 1170; Euripides, *Medea* 1224.

22. Aeschylus, *Agamemnon* 839; Sophocles, *Fragment*

598.6. This is consistent with the OT portrayal of idols as those of a fleeting existence (cf. Isa 40:18 – 24).

23. For Plato this ontological distinction is, of course, derived from the epistemological one, as the issue of knowledge serves as the starting point of his discussion of reality.

24. O'Brien, *Colossians, Philemon*, 140.

The conjunction "but" (δέ) is a coordinating conjunction, which normally connects two similar clauses. Here, however, it connects the previous relative clause with this independent clause. Some have therefore questioned if this clause is intended to serve as a contrast to the previous one. Various other constructions have been suggested,[25] but the contrast between "the shadow of the things to come" and "the substance [that] belongs to Christ" is still the least problematic reading. First, while δέ is a coordinating conjunction, "the equivalence required between coordinating clauses is that of their position within the hierarchy of the sentence, not that of their clause type."[26] Second, this contrast between the inadequacy of the human tradition and the finality and sufficiency of Christ fits well with Paul's wider argument here. Third, this contrast is not foreign to NT writers, as testified by Heb 10:1.

The use of σῶμα to refer to the "substance" is unexpected. Elsewhere in Colossians, this word refers to either a "physical body" (1:22; 2:11, 23) or the metaphorical "body of Christ" (1:18, 24; 2:19; 3:15). Some have therefore considered this term here as also referring to the "body of Christ," with the concept of "reality" only implied in the Greek text: "the reality is the body of Christ" (NJB).[27] This reading is possible because what is modified by the genitival phrase ("of Christ") is left unspecified. One could, therefore, assume that σῶμα carries the sense of "substance" or "reality" while "the body of Christ" is implied by the genitival phrase. In any case, the fact that "it is not altogether certain … whether it is Christ or the church that is set as reality in contrast to the shadow"[28] may point to

an intentional ambiguity as Paul tries to emphasize the incorporation of the believers "in Christ."

2:18a-c Let no one condemn you by insisting on self-humiliation and the worship of angels (μηδεὶς ὑμᾶς καταβραβευέτω θέλων ἐν ταπεινοφροσύνῃ καὶ θρησκείᾳ τῶν ἀγγέλων). Paul now focuses his critique of false teachings by warning the Colossian believers not to be misled by ascetic practices and cultic acts of worshiping angels. The negated imperative, "let no one condemn," introduces the second part of this section. As 2:16 began with a reference to the false teachers through the indefinite τις, Paul points to the same people group through the indefinite "no one" (μηδείς). In extending his arguments from v. 16, however, one finds Paul using terms and expressions even more puzzling to us. The various possibilities in translating each of these terms and expressions create myriads of possible interpretations concerning the nature of the false teachings that Paul is combating. Nevertheless, before unpacking this verse, we should be reminded that Paul's response to the false teachers is unequivocal and clear even if we may not be able to understand fully the exact nature of the false teachings.

The verb "let … condemn" (καταβραβευέτω) has often been understood in a narrower meaning of "robbing of a prize" (cf. ASV, NKJV; NJB) or "disqualifying" (cf. NAB, NRSV, REB, TNIV, NIV), which has been assumed to signify the presence of an athletic metaphor. This reading is often built on an etymological analysis of the word: "βραβεύω has the primary meaning of 'award a prize' … hence

---

25. See, e.g., Troy Martin, "But Let Everyone Discern the Body of Christ (Colossians 2:17)," *JBL* 114 (1995): 249 – 55; Sang-Won Aaron Son, "Τὸ σῶμα τοῦ Χριστοῦ in Colossians 2:17," in *History and Exegesis: New Testament Essays in Honor of Dr. E. Earle Ellis for His 80th Birthday* (ed. Sang-Won Aaron Son; New York: T&T Clark, 2006), 222 – 38.

26. Cole, "The Christian and Time-Keeping in Colossians

2:16 and Galatians 4:10," 271, who further points to 3:7 – 8, where an independent clause introduced by δέ (v. 8a) is again contrasted with a relative clause (v. 7a).

27. See also Son, "Τὸ σῶμα τοῦ Χριστοῦ in Colossians 2:17," 236, who, denying the presence of a contrast, considers "the body of Christ" in apposition to "the things to come."

28. Schweizer, *Letter to the Colossians*, 158.

καταβραβεύω ... means 'decided against' as an umpire."[29] Although this verb appears only here in the NT and rarely in extracanonical material, the few contemporary parallels in both literary and non-literary sources point to the use of this term in a general sense without any allusion to the athletic context.[30] In this context, therefore, it is best to take this in the general sense of "condemn" (NLT) or "pass judgment" (NET). If so, "let no one condemn you" builds on the similar call in v. 16 with a greater sense of urgency.

The translation "by insisting on" (θέλων) takes the participle as an adverbial participle of means, although this use has been debated. Some see Hebraic influences behind the use of this participle with the preposition (ἐν) as expressing the idea of "delighting in" (NAB; cf. NKJV),[31] thus modifying "no one": "do not let anyone who delights in ... " (TNIV, NIV; cf. NET). In this context, however, it is best to take the participle as modifying "condemn" with the sense of "by insisting on,"[32] articulating the means through which the believers are being condemned by the false teachers (cf. NLT, NASB, RSV, NRSV, GNB, ESV).[33] This is supported by its proximity to the imperative and the parallel in v. 16, where the preposition "in" introduces the means through which the believers are being judged/condemned. The final part of this section (vv. 20 – 23), which argues against ascetic practices, also suggests that the false teachers are not simply being content with such practices among themselves; they are also imposing them on the Colossian believers.

"Self-humiliation" (ταπεινοφροσύνη) retains the ambiguity of the use of the Greek term in this context. In the NT, this term is almost always used in reference to the positive virtue of "humility" (Acts 20:19; Eph 4:2; Phil 2:3; Col 3:12; 1 Pet 5:5), and this use appears later in this letter (Col 3:12). Here, however, Paul is clearly not endorsing the practices of the false teachers. This can therefore be labeled generally as "wrongly directed" humility[34] or even "false humility" (NKJV, TNIV, NIV).

It is possible to understand this noun as referring to "asceticism" (ESV) or "self-abasement" (NAB, NASB, NRSV). First, in the LXX the cognate verbal form appears in connection with the act of fasting (e.g., Ezra 8:21; Ps 34[35]:13; Isa 58:3, 5). Elsewhere, the term is also used to refer to other ascetic practices.[35] This "humility" can therefore denote the self-humiliation or self-discipline of one's body. Second, in v. 23 this noun indicates the "harsh treatment of the body." Third, certain ascetic practices are connected with heavenly ascent (*Apoc. Ab.* 9.7 – 10; 12.1 – 2; *T. Isaac* 4 – 5; *2 Bar.* 5.7).[36] If the following phrase ("worship of angels") is to be understood as referring to heavenly ascent, "self-humiliation" is then a practice that prepares for this visionary experience. Or if "worship of angels" points to the invocation of angels, these ascetic practices would also point to rituals that accompany the encounter of angelic beings.

The second act imposed on the Colossian believers is the "worship of angels" (θρησκείᾳ τῶν ἀγγέλων). The understanding of this phrase depends on whether "of angels" is a subjective genitive

29. Dunn, *Epistles to the Colossians and to Philemon*, 177.

30. See esp. Kent L. Yinger, "Translating καταβραβευέτω ['Disqualify' NRSV] in Colossians 2.18," *BT* 54 (2003): 140 – 41.

31. Cf. 1 Sam 18:22; 2 Sam 15:26; 1 Kgs 10:9; Ps 146[147]:10; Mal 1:10; Lightfoot, *St. Paul's Epistles to the Colossians and to Philemon*, 195; Schweizer, *Letter to the Colossians*, 158; Moo, *Letters to the Colossians and to Philemon*, 225.

32. Though rarely, this is an attested use of the verb: CPR 20.17 (LSJ, 479).

33. Harris, *Colossians and Philemon*, 121; Garland, *Colossians and Philemon*, 176.

34. BDAG, 989.

35. Tertullian, *On Fasting* 12.2; 13.4; 16.4 – 6; Francis, "Humility and Angelic Worship in Col 2:18," 168.

36. Smith, *Heavenly Perspective*, 122.

or an objective genitive. Recent interest in under-standing the Colossian false teachings in light of a predominantly Jewish background has prompted many to understand this phrase within the back-ground of Jewish mysticism; those who adopt this reading argue for a subjective genitive reading, where "worship of angels" is interpreted as "wor-shiping with angels" in one's heavenly ascent.[37] Note also certain texts that point to the participa-tion in heavenly worship with celestial beings (Isa 6:2 – 3; *Apoc. Ab.* 17 – 18; *Apoc. Zeph.* 8.3 – 4; *T. Levi* 3.4 – 8; *T. Job* 48 – 50; *Asc. Isa.* 7 – 9; 1QS 11.8).

Nevertheless, an objective genitive reading pro-vides the best reading. First, note that Paul appears to be arguing against a worship initiated by human beings. This is already noted in v. 8, where Paul ar-gues against such "human tradition." Moreover, the note on "self-imposed worship" in v. 23 "specifi-cally characterizes the concept 'worship' [θρησκεία] as performed by men."[38]

Second, the strongest argument is one of lexical evidence: "A survey of the usage of θρησκεία fails to turn up one example of a divine being, or a typical object of worship (e.g. an 'idol'), related to θρησκεία in the genitive case that should be taken as a sub-jective genitive."[39] The Jewish texts cited in support of a subjective genitive reading merely point to a general sense of heavenly worship but lend no sup-port for the reading of this particular genitive.

Third, instead of locating the Colossian false teaching in a general trajectory within mystical Ju-

daism, angel veneration has been shown to have existed in Phrygian Judaism.[40] Few would argue against a syncretism in the Judaism of first-century Asia Minor,[41] and it is also possible that the Jew-ish angelology was influenced by the Hellenistic demonology.[42]

Finally, the negative evaluation of spiritual be-ings in 1:16 and 2:15 also argues against reading angels in this context simply as benign beings in the heavenly court.

Yet even with the adoption of an objective geni-tive, the precise meaning of this act of worship re-mains unclear. Against those who suggest that Paul would have provided a stronger argument against such idolatrous worship, it should be noted that an anti-idol polemic can indeed be identified behind Paul's argument.[43] Moreover, the "worship of an-gels" noted here may point simply to the "venera-tion"[44] or the "invocation"[45] of angels. We know, for example, of a connection between angels and the Jewish Torah found elsewhere in the NT (cf. Acts 7:53; Gal 3:19; Heb 2:2). Although an established angel cult cannot be deduced from these refer-ences,[46] it is at least possible that this "worship of angels" is related to the rules and regulations re-peatedly noted in this section (vv. 16, 20, 21, 23).

The oddity of this reference to the "worship of angels" may also be another example of an ironic note in this letter: "the people he is opposing spend so much time in speculations about angels, or in celebrating the fact that the law was given by them,

37. See, in particular, Francis, "Humility and Angelic Wor-ship in Col 2:18," 163 – 95; Sappington, *Revelation and Redemp-tion at Colossae,* 158 – 61; Bevere, *Sharing in the Inheritance,* 101 – 114; Smith, *Heavenly Perspective,* 122 – 27; Stettler, "The Opponents at Colossae," 186.

38. Lohse, *Colossians and Philemon,* 119.

39. Arnold, *Colossian Syncretism,* 91.

40. See the extensive discussion in ibid., 8 – 102.

41. Images from (later) Jewish synagogues in Asia Minor do point to a certain degree of syncretism in this general area; cf. A. Thomas Kraabel, "Social Systems of Six Diaspora Syna-

gogues," in *Diaspora Jews and Judaism: Essays in Honor of, and in Dialogue with, A. Thomas Kraabel* (ed. J. A. Overman and R. S. MacLennan; Atlanta: Scholars, 1992), 79 – 91.

42. DeMaris, *The Colossian Controversy,* 58 – 63.

43. See comments on vv. 6 – 15.

44. Pokorný, *Colossians,* 119.

45. Arnold, *Colossian Syncretism,* 101 – 2.

46. Crispin H. T. Fletcher-Louis, *Luke-Acts: Angels, Chris-tology and Soteriology* (WUNT 2.94; Tübingen: Mohr Siebeck, 1997), 99.

that they are in effect worshipping them instead of God."[47] The following phrase, however, suggests that Paul is not simply referring to Torah observance; a certain element of syncretism has to be assumed when Paul further discusses the religious experiences encouraged by the false teachers.

2:18d Entering into these things that he has seen (ἃ ἑόρακεν ἐμβατεύων). Paul continues to criticize the false teachers for their promotion of visionary experiences in the worship of angels. The difficulties involved in making sense of v. 18d are reflected by the insertion of a negative particle in some manuscripts[48] by early scribes, and this emendation is reflected in some modern versions: "intruding into those things which he has *not* seen" (NKJV, italics added). The various interpretations of this difficult clause depend on the way the participle "entering" (ἐμβατεύων) is understood.

(1) Many versions translate this participle as "entering into details": "such a person also goes into great detail about what they have seen" (NIV; cf. NET, TNIV). Others have made it explicit that "what he has seen" are the visions: "dwelling on visions" (NRSV; cf. ESV).[49] While this meaning of the participle is not without precedent (cf. 2 Macc 2:30), such a usage is rare. Moreover, this reading "is very tame, where the context seems to require something more assertive."[50]

(2) Understanding "entering" as a technical term for part of the entry rites into mystery cults, some see this Hellenistic cultic background as explaining the meaning of this clause: "as he has had visions of them during the mystery rites."[51] While this view may explain the significance of the act of "entering," it is difficult to explain "self-humiliation" and "the worship of angels" as that which the initiated see when they enter the cult. Moreover, "entering" acquires a technical sense only when it is used with other related vocabularies.[52] Finally, the references to Jewish regulations and customs elsewhere in this section also question this connection even when a syncretistic Judaism is assumed.

(3) The best reading takes the participle ἐμβατεύων in the sense of entry into an inheritance to take possession of it. Together with the legal term "written record" (χειρόγραφον) in v. 14, this term points to the acquisition of property.[53] The LXX usage is particularly relevant here, where "entering" and "inheritance" appear together in reference to taking possession of the Promised Land (Josh 19:49), and both terms appear in Colossians (cf. Col 1:12). This reading retains the usual meaning of the verb while allowing the additional significance to be carried by this verb as demanded by the context in which it appears.

If we read it this way, this section refers to visionary experiences while worshiping the angels, and "entering into these things that he has seen" is an attempt to enter into the heavenly realm through visionary experiences to gain possession of that which escapes mere mortals. Instead of gaining possession of the heavenly realm, however, they are only able to encounter what they see in their futile minds.[54] The Colossian believers are called to resist

---

47. Wright, *Colossians and Philemon*, 122.

48. Some manuscripts insert μή (ℵ[2] C D[1] Ψ 075 0278 1881 𝔐), while others οὐκ (F G).

49. For a recent defense of this view, see Moo, *Letters to the Colossians and to Philemon*, 227 – 29.

50. Moule, *Epistles to the Colossians and to Philemon*, 105.

51. Lohse, *Colossians and Philemon*, 114. For the evidence for the presence of mystery cults in Asia Minor, see Arnold, *Colossian Syncretism*, 109 – 20.

52. See Arthur D. Nock, "The Vocabulary of the New Testament," *JBL* 52 (1933): 132 – 33; Sappington, *Revelation and Redemption at Colossae*, 155.

53. Fred O. Francis, "The Background of EMBATEUEIN," in *Conflict at Colossae* (ed. F. O. Francis and W. A. Meeks; Missoula, MT: Scholars, 1975), 197 – 207; Beetham, *Echoes of Scripture*, 206 – 7.

54. This contrast between reality and the illusion of their minds is implied with the presence of the final clause of this verse.

such practices because all promises to them have already been provided through Christ, in whom "all the fullness of deity dwells" (v. 9). Again, while the specific problem may remain unclear to modern readers, the solution is clear and unmistakable.

2:18e Conceited without reason by his carnal mind (εἰκῇ φυσιούμενος ὑπὸ τοῦ νοὸς τῆς σαρκὸς αὐτοῦ). This description of the false teachers confirms the reading of the difficult clause that precedes it. "Conceited without reason" (εἰκῇ φυσιούμενος)[55] points to the baseless assertions of the false teachers who claim superior visionary experience while not being able to experience anything but their illusions. Assumed to be humble through their ascetic practices (v. 18), they are actually consumed by pride that prompts them to be involved in false worship.

The ironic nature of their claims is further illustrated by the phrase "his carnal mind" (lit., "the mind of his flesh"). Here Paul is accusing the false teachers of claiming to transcend their physical bodies in their involvement in visionary experiences but ending up becoming preoccupied by a mind that is controlled by the flesh (cf. Rom 7:25). This phrase then points forward to v. 23 concerning the futility of the "harsh treatment of the body" in controlling the desires of "the flesh."

2:19a And not holding fast to the head (καὶ οὐ κρατῶν τὴν κεφαλήν). This participial clause further defines the false teachers as those who do not focus solely on Christ. This clause not only points to the critical deficiency of the false teaching, but it also identifies the shaky ground on which the false teachings are built. The false teachers can be criticized for their particular practices and their focus on visionary experiences, but these practices and

experiences are to be criticized primarily because they do not find their roots in Christ. This section again builds on Paul's earlier call for the Colossian believers to be "rooted and built up in him" (v. 7), and not to be deceived by a philosophy that is based on "human tradition" instead of being "according to Christ" (v. 8).

"Not holding fast" (οὐ κρατῶν) assumes that the false teachers were at least once connected with Christ or his body in some ways, but they have ceased to do so. Some versions make this explicit: "lose their hold upon the head" (REB). But this phrase has also been translated as "not connected to": "has no connection to the Head" (NJB); this assumes that the false teachers never were part of the body of Christ. This issue cannot be settled by the examination of this short phrase alone.[56] What is clear, however, is that a continued connection with Christ is critical for the growth of the believers.

"The head" is an appropriate metaphor here in that it points both to the final authority of Christ as emphasized above (vv. 8 – 10, 15) and to the source on which the body is dependent (see the following clause). These two are parallel ideas, however, since the derivative idea of dependence draws on the understanding of the head as the determinative part of the body.

2:19b-d From which the entire body, nourished and united through the joints and ligaments, grows with a growth from God (ἐξ οὗ πᾶν τὸ σῶμα διὰ τῶν ἁφῶν καὶ συνδέσμων ἐπιχορηγούμενον καὶ συμβιβαζόμενον αὔξει τὴν αὔξησιν τοῦ θεοῦ). The dependence of the believers on Christ is illustrated with this physiological metaphor of the body. The antecedent of the masculine relative pronoun "which" (οὗ) is apparently the feminine

---

55. The passive participle "conceited" (φυσιούμενος), takes on an active sense of becoming "puffed up or conceited" (BDAG, 1069; cf. 1 Cor 4:18, 19; 5:2; 13:4).

56. On this issue, see "Introduction to Colossians".

noun "head" (κεφαλήν). This gender of this relative pronoun is likely constructed by sense and refers back to "Christ" (v. 17), who is the "head."[57] The christological focus is again unmistakable.

This section apparently draws from the physiological metaphor of the body, although the participles "nourished" and "united" move beyond medical terminology.[58] With this use of the "body" metaphor, one finds both the emphases on Christ as the head (1:18) and the church as the unified body of Christ (3:15). Rather than borrowing from the Greco-Roman concept of the cosmic body,[59] Paul most likely begins his reflection on the death of the physical body of Christ (1:22) and the believer's participation in his death and resurrection (2:11–13). The physiological understanding of the body provides further fuel for the emphasis on both the significance of the "head" and the intimate connection between the various parts of the body. In this verse, therefore, one finds a link between the earlier Pauline discussion of the unity of the various parts of the body of Christ (cf. 1 Cor 12:12–26) and the later Pauline emphasis on the love that holds this body together (cf. Eph 4:1–16).

With this clause, a subtle shift of focus in Paul's argument begins: from the emphasis on Christ as the head, Paul is preparing his readers for the ecclesiological impact of such an affirmation. This focus will dominate the discussion in the sections that follow (3:1–14). Here, however, Paul focuses on the danger of the false teachings: they not only draw one's attention away from Christ, but they also disrupt the unity of the church that finds her foundation on Christ and him alone. The emphasis on "the entire body" likewise points both to the need of every member to be dependent on Christ and to the unity of this body under this head.

"Grows with a growth from God" identifies the ultimate source behind the growth of the body. The accusative "a growth" (τὴν αὔξησιν) should be considered as an accusative of content,[60] and the genitive "from God" (τοῦ θεοῦ) is a subjective genitive.[61] This seemingly awkward construction can partly be explained by the presence of the intransitive verb "grows" (αὔξει), where God is considered to be the ultimate subject: "grows as God causes it to grow" (TNIV, NIV). Another reason for this awkward construction is the presence of two sources of growth. Christ the head provides nourishment for the entire body, but the ultimate source of this growth can be found in God himself. The presence of God and Christ as dual agents are already found in Paul's description of the first (1:15–16) and second (1:18–20) creations.

The "growth" of the body of Christ involves the spiritual growth of the individual members (3:5–8), the growth of the unity among these various members (3:9–14), and the outreach to those outside the body (4:5–6). Paul's emphasis on this growth is polemical in intent with each of these areas. The false teachers who focus on themselves instead of Christ fail to bring about spiritual growth in their followers. Their focus on individual visionary experiences destroys the community of God's people. Their obsession with their own superior knowledge and with their own exclusivist practices prevents them from bringing the gospel to the outsiders. For Paul, members of the body

---

57. It is also possible to take this relative pronoun as a neuter pronoun ("which," NJB), which points to the generic reference to the head.

58. See Arnold, "Jesus Christ: 'Head' of the Church," 361, who suggests that the first participle draws from marital imagery, where the husband is to provide for the wife, and the second emphasizes unity.

59. Van Kooten, *Cosmic Christology in Paul*, 53.

60. Harris, *Colossians and Philemon*, 124.

61. As it modifies "growth," a clear distinction between a subjective genitive and a genitive of source cannot be made.

of Christ do not need to look beyond the gospel of Christ to find ultimate fullness and fulfillment.

2:20a-b If you have died with Christ to the elemental spirits of the world (Εἰ ἀπεθάνετε σὺν Χριστῷ ἀπὸ τῶν στοιχείων τοῦ κόσμου). Paul now turns to the absurdity of following that which Christ had already conquered. Unlike the previous two subsections that began with an imperative (vv. 16, 18), this one begins with a conditional sentence, followed by a question addressed to the readers. Recognizing the connection between the notes on the death of Christ in this section (vv. 20–23) and his resurrection in the next (3:1–4), some have considered 2:20–3:4 as a unit.[62] Nevertheless, the listing of a sample of regulations in vv. 20–21 seems to be a continuation of the discussion of customs and regulations imposed by the false teachers in v. 16. It is best, therefore, to consider this final subsection as one that bridges the previous discussion with the paraenetic sections that follow.

This subsection can be understood as providing "counterdefinition."[63] Verses 20–21 label regulations that prepare for heavenly visionary experiences as those that belong to "this world," and vv. 22–23 challenge the wisdom of the ascetic practices by claiming that they are of "no value" especially in combating the desires of the flesh.

The conditional sentence beginning with εἰ points to a first-class conditional sentence that can be used in stating what is perceived to be real.[64] In light of the previous discussion of the believer's identification with Christ in his death (cf. vv. 11–13), this protasis is assumed to be true. Moreover, Louw suggests that when the protasis

of a first-class conditional clause is followed by a question, the resulting construction "functions (semantically) as a speech act to emphasize that the condition is a claimed fact."[65] If so, it is justifiable to translate "if" (εἰ) as "since" (TNIV, NIV; cf. NLT), although this protasis does force the audience to reconsider the reality they had experienced.

As in v. 8, "the elemental spirits of the world" (τῶν στοιχείων τοῦ κόσμου) refer to evil spiritual forces that fight against God's work through Christ. In this section that challenges the claims of the false teachers, this phrase becomes important as it qualifies the previous reference to the "worship of angels" (v. 18). While the false teachers may consider their visionary experience of the worship of benign spiritual beings as being allies of God, Paul is saying that they are actually submitting to the evil forces at enmity with God. The awkward presence of the preposition "from" (ἀπό, translated here as "to")[66] is important because for Paul, death is not the final event, but it leads to resurrection (vv. 12–13; 3:1). Death is therefore not a state of impotence; rather, it foreshadows the coming victory. "Died with Christ to the elemental spirits of the world," therefore, contains the idea of victory and liberation, as is made explicit in some versions: "You have died with Christ, and he has set you free from the spiritual powers of this world" (NLT; cf. TEV, CEV).

2:20c Why, as though you were still alive to this world, do you submit to its regulations (τί ὡς ζῶντες ἐν κόσμῳ δογματίζεσθε;). In this apodosis, one finds the question that illustrates the irrational choices of those who claim to belong to Christ. "As

---

62. See, e.g., J. P. Louw, "Reading a Text as Discourse," in *Linguistics and New Testament Interpretation: Essays on Discourse Analysis* (ed. David Alan Black; Nashville: Broadman, 1993), 17–30.

63. Sumney, "The Argument of Colossians," 350.

64. BDF §3721. See, however, the cautionary note in Wallace, *Greek Grammar*, 690.

65. Louw, "Reading a Text as Discourse," 26.

66. To avoid this awkwardness, most versions avoid "from" and use "to" instead, but see: "if you died with Christ from the basic principles of the world" (NKJV).

though you were still alive" translates an adverbial participle (lit., "living," ζῶντες), which, together with the marker "as" (ὡς), denotes a concessive idea. "To this world" refers to "the world of their old life."[67] The literal translation "in the world" (KJV, NASB, NKJV, NJB, NET, ESV) may give the false impression that Paul is arguing for an escapist mentality, but Paul is arguing for the freedom from the control of the spiritual forces of this world. This sense is best expressed with creative renderings of the clause: "as though you still belonged to the world" (NRSV, TNIV, NIV; cf. GNB), and "as if you were still living the life of the world" (REB). The rendering "you were still alive to this world" is not only able to capture the sense of the clause, but it also retains the emphasis on one's death to this world in the previous clause.

"Submit to its regulations" (δογματίζεσθε) translates a Greek verb that can be taken as a middle ("submit to [its] regulations") or a passive voice ("allow yourselves to be controlled by [these] regulations").[68] In both cases, the regulations are imposed by an external force, and those who adopt them do so willingly (although with the middle sense the responsibility of the believers is more apparent). What is not clear is whether the believers have already submitted to these regulations. Those who consider the Colossians believers as not yet having fallen away from the true gospel argue for a slightly different translation: "Why subject yourselves to regulations?"[69] Regardless of how one comes down on this issue of apostasy, Paul is presenting a real danger, and it is entirely possible that some have already believed these false teachers.

A conceptual parallel to this discussion can be found in Rom 6, where Paul argues that since sin and death no longer rule over Christ (6:9), believers who identify with Christ should no longer submit to sin as their master (v. 14).[70] For Paul, to follow a set of regulations is to submit to a master. In this case, to submit to the regulations of the world is to reject Christ as the Lord of the universe, one who has already "disarmed" the evil spiritual forces (Col 2:15).

2:21 Do not handle, do not taste, do not touch (μὴ ἅψῃ μηδὲ γεύσῃ μηδὲ θίγῃς). This verse provides a sample of the content of the "regulations" of the world mentioned above. Of the three terms, the meaning of "do not taste" is clear as it apparently points back to "food" and "drink" in v. 16. The meaning of the first and third items and the relationship between them remains unclear. Several readings are possible:

(1) In light of the possible distinction between "handle" and "touch," some have suggested that Paul may be referring to different degrees of the same general decree against defilement, with "touching" representing a weaker sense of "handling."[71] The ironic tone can also be detected behind this sequence as this "downward sliding scale ... corresponds to the upward rise in absurd scrupulosity."[72] Without denying the ironic nature of this sequence, however, it is questionable if we can clearly distinguish between "handle" and "touch."[73] The place of "taste" is also unclear within this sequence.

(2) With the use of "handle" (ἅπτομαι) in 1 Cor 7:1 (often translated "touch") in reference to a sexual act, some have considered "do not handle" here

---

67. Wilson, *Colossians and Philemon*, 226.

68. This is an example of the permissive use of the passive voice; cf. BDF §314; Harris, *Colossians and Philemon*, 128.

69. Stettler, "The Opponents at Colossae," 174 – 75.

70. Knowles, " 'Christ in You, the Hope of Glory,' " 191.

71. Lightfoot, *St. Paul's Epistles to the Colossians and to Philemon*, 203 – 4.

72. Wright, *Colossians and Philemon*, 126.

73. Diachronically, "to touch" (θιγγάνω) is foreign to the Attic dialect and can be considered as roughly equivalent to "to handle" (ἅπτομαι); cf. LSJ, 801.

as referring to abstention from sexual relation-ships.[74] Paul's further statement that this "has no value in restraining the gratification of the flesh" (v. 23) may lend support to this reading. But when the term is used in a sexual sense, one expects to find "woman" (1 Cor 7:1) or "her" (Gen 20:4, 6 LXX) after the verb. The lack of such references weakens this reading.

(3) Some have considered all three terms as nothing "more than an emphatic expression for the food regulations addressed in 2:16."[75] While possible, this view ignores other aspects of the false teachings as noted in vv. 16, 18, and 23 (i.e., calendrical practices, visionary experiences, and other ascetic practices).

(4) Perhaps the best way to understand these items is to read them within a general framework of cultic concerns. In LXX, "to touch" (θιγγάνω) appears only once in a context where one also finds the word "to handle" (ἅπτομαι), where the holiness of the presence of God on Mount Sinai is to be safeguarded (Exod 19:12 – 13).[76] Elsewhere "to handle" often appears in cultic context (e.g., Exod 30:29; Lev 5:2, 3; 6:18, 27 [LXX 6:11, 20]; 11:24 – 39), and this is extended to the gospel narratives when Jesus challenges the cultic boundaries of Israel (cf. Matt 8:3; Luke 5:13). The dietary practices noted above in v. 16 appear with calendrical discussions, and they are both situated in a cultic context of "the worship of angels" (v. 18). Instead of a thoroughgoing asceticism, therefore, the regulations imposed on the Colossian believers aim at preparing them for an encounter with the angels.[77]

This cultic reading explains the diversity of the regulations in this section as they center on cul-

tic purity in the worship of heavenly beings. For Paul, therefore, these practices are not to be condemned because of the rigorous treatment of the body. They are to be condemned because they look to other beings as the objects of worship instead of Christ himself, to whom these beings have been submitted (v. 15).

2:22 All these, related to things that are destined to perish with use, according to human commands and teachings? (ἅ ἐστιν πάντα εἰς φθορὰν τῇ ἀποχρήσει, κατὰ τὰ ἐντάλματα καὶ διδασκαλίας τῶν ἀνθρώπων;). In this apodosis (beginning in v. 20c), Paul further provides reasons for the Colossian believers to reject the regulations imposed by the false teachers. This verse can be rendered literally as: "These are all destined to perish with use, founded as they are on human commands and teachings" (NET). Grammatically, the antecedent of the relative pronoun translated here as "these" (ἅ) appears to be the regulations noted in the previous verse. The content of this verse, however, complicates this simple identification. Those who argue against this identification find it difficult to understand how rules and regulations can "perish with use." "All" should then refer to "the material things with which the rules 'handle not', etc., are concerned."[78]

It is difficult, however, to reconcile this reading with the second part of the verse because it seems evident that "according to human commands and teachings" refers to the regulations and not to the targeted objects behind these regulations. It seems best, therefore, to consider the two parts as referring to separate antecedents, with "destined to

---

74. MacDonald, *Colossians and Ephesians*, 116, 121.

75. Pokorný, *Colossians*, 153.

76. Also worth noting is the call to abstain from sexual activities in Exod 19:15 in preparation for the encounter with the holy God.

77. Sumney, *Colossians*, 162. For a discussion of asceticism and divine-human encounter in Jewish traditions, see also Steven D. Fraade, "Ascetical Aspects of Ancient Judaism," in *Jewish Spirituality: From the Bible through the Middle Ages* (ed. Arthur Green; New York: Crossroad, 1986), 253 – 88.

78. Moule, *Epistles to the Colossians and to Philemon*, 108.

perish with use" referring to the material things, and "all these" referring to rules. Without following strictly the word order in Greek, the following rendering makes this clear: "Such rules are mere human teachings about things that deteriorate as we use them" (NLT).

"Destined to perish with use" points to the lack of any permanent value of the regulations that guard such material things. In Paul, "perish" (φθορά) is often used in reference to that which belongs to this age instead of the age to come (Rom 8:21; 1 Cor 15:42, 50). The contrast between legalistic practices that are destined to perish and the life-giving promises of Christ (v. 13) also reminds one of a similar contrast between "flesh" and "Spirit" in Gal 6:8: "Whoever sows to please their flesh, from the flesh will reap destruction (φθοράν); whoever sows to please the Spirit, from the Spirit will reap eternal life."

"According to human commands and teachings" alludes to Isa 29:13 (LXX):

> The Lord said:
> These people draw near to me,
> with their lips they honor me,
> but their hearts are far from me,
> and in vain they worship me,
> teaching human commands and teachings
>   [ἐντάλματα ἀνθρώπων καὶ διδασκαλίας,
>   pers. trans.].

This passage is one of Isaiah's critiques of the idolatrous acts of God's people. The phrase "far from me" is often used explicitly for Israel's departure from her God in worshiping idols (cf. Jer 2:5; Ezek 44:10).[79] Jesus also evoked this prophetic tradition against those who follow the "traditions of the elders" in insisting on legalistic practices (Matt 15:9;

Mark 7:7), though it is not clear if Paul is aware of this gospel tradition. Paul's use here is consistent with his earlier critique of the false teaching as "according to human tradition" (v. 8).

While most recognize the allusion to Isa 29:13 here, the verse that follows this statement from Isaiah also needs to be noted:

> Therefore, I will proceed to remove this people.
> I will remove them and destroy the wisdom [τὴν
>   σοφίαν] of the wise,
> and I will hide the understanding [τὴν σύνεσιν]
>   of the intelligent. (Isa 29:14 LXX, pers. trans.)

While not an exact parallel, Paul's subsequent note on the false teachers having "an appearance of wisdom [σοφίας]" (v. 23)[80] may also evoke this Isaianic tradition. If so, Paul is identifying these false teachers with those who misled Israel into a departure from the worship of the one and true God. In both, the urgency of such a critique is unmistakable.

2:23a These rules have no value in restraining the gratification of the flesh (ἅτινά ἐστιν ... οὐκ ἐν τιμῇ τινι πρὸς πλησμονὴν τῆς σαρκός). Paul continues to ridicule the "regulations" of the world by noting their impotence in combating the desires of the flesh. The translation adopted here demands a discussion of the structure of the entire verse: "These rules have no value in restraining the gratification of the flesh, even though they have an appearance of wisdom with their self-imposed worship, self-humiliation, and harsh treatment of the body." Considered "almost impossible to translate,"[81] the difficulties of this verse lie in the possible meanings of the various parts of the verse and the lack of clarity concerning the relationship between these parts. The basic difference among the proposals centers on the decision concerning

---

79. Beale, "Colossians," 861 – 62.

80. Also worth noting is the fact that both "wisdom" and "understanding" appear in Isa 29:14 and also appear together in Col 2:2 – 3.

81. Schweizer, *Letter to the Colossians*, 168.

the main clause and therefore what is to be taken together with the first two words (lit., "which are"; ἅτινά ἐστιν).

(1) In light of its close proximity, some consider the participle "having" (ἔχοντα) to be linked with "are" (ἐστιν), thus forming a periphrastic: "Such rules indeed appear wise…."[82] The placement of the contrastive marker (μέν) between the finite verb and the participle is unusual, however, especially when it is expected to appear as the second word of a clause.

(2) Some take "are" (ἐστιν) with the final prepositional phrase, "result in the indulgence of the flesh" (πρὸς πλησμονὴν τῆς σαρκός),[83] with the two clauses in between, the second subordinating to the first: "Even though they have the appearance of wisdom with their self-imposed worship and false humility achieved by an unsparing treatment of the body — a wisdom with no true value — they in reality result in fleshly indulgence" (NET). While this does take into account of the postpositive position of the particle μέν, it seems difficult to have two subordinate clauses interrupting the flow of the sentence, especially when the second subordinate clause modifies the first.

(3) Although not without difficulties, the best reading is to consider "no value in restraining the gratification of the flesh"[84] as completing the thought introduced by the finite verb "are" (ἐστιν), with the intervening clause as a concessive clause, as in NAB: "While they have a semblance of wisdom in rigor of devotion and self-abasement [and]

severity to the body, they are of no value against gratification of the flesh." This reading takes advantage of reading (2) in treating the particle μέν in the postpositive position, but without assuming the presence of two complex subordinating clauses in between. Moreover, the negative particle "not" (οὐκ) can function as a particle that provides the contrast to the statement introduced by the particle μέν.[85] The contrast set up by the phrases "the appearance of wisdom" and "no value" also fits well within the flow of Paul's argument here.[86] Finally, this reading also recognizes the contrast between the two clauses that contain the preposition "by means of/in" (ἐν).

"Have no value" (οὐκ ἐν τιμῇ τινι) literally reads "not in any honour" (KJV), and those who take this word in the sense of "honor" would suggest that "the 'honor' (τιμή), which they claim for themselves, cannot be conferred on them."[87] In this context the word commonly rendered as "honor" can acquire the sense of "value" or "price" (Matt 27:9; Acts 4:34; 1 Cor 6:20; 7:23).[88] Most versions therefore translate this phrase as "are of no value" (ASV, NASB, NRSV, NKJV, ESV; cf. NET, TNIV, NIV). Taking the preposition πρός in the sense of "against," Paul is affirming that the ascetic rules and regulations have no value in combating the desires of "the flesh." This reference to the failure of their practices recalls Paul's critique of the false teachers as "conceited without reason by his carnal mind" (v. 18). Paul's rhetoric here points to his sustained attempt in this section to unmask

---

82. Harris, *Colossians and Philemon*, 131.

83. See the influential study of Bruce Hollenbach, "Col. ii. 23: Which Things Lead to the Fulfillment of the Flesh," *NTS* 25 (1978–79): 254–61.

84. This is to take the preposition πρός in the sense "against."

85. Moule, *Epistles to the Colossians and to Philemon*, 105. For the absence of the expected δέ after μέν, see BDF §447(4).

86. See Lightfoot, *St. Paul's Epistles to the Colossians and to Philemon*, 206.

87. Lohse, *Colossians and Philemon*, 127, who identifies a mystery cult background to this phrase as "τιμή signifies the divine election and deification which the initiate experiences." See also MacDonald, *Colossians and Ephesians*, 123 who likewise prefers the translation "honor," but reads this in light of the honor-shame of the first-century Greco-Roman world.

88. For the possibility of this usage as a Latinism, see BDAG, 1005.

the claims of the false teachers as their seemingly spiritual practices simply reflect their denial of the sufficiency of Christ.

2:23b-e Even though they have an appearance of wisdom with their self-imposed worship, self-humiliation, and harsh treatment of the body (λόγον μὲν ἔχοντα σοφίας ἐν ἐθελοθρησκίᾳ καὶ ταπεινοφροσύνῃ καὶ ἀφειδίᾳ σώματος). In these clauses, Paul unveils the true nature of the cultic and ascetic practices promoted by the false teachers. "Even though they have" takes the participle ἔχοντα as a concessive adverbial participle, which thus sets up a contrast between the appearance of the wisdom of the imposed practices and their actual uselessness. To translate λόγον as "appearance" has been adopted by most versions although it is difficult to pinpoint the exact sense of this Greek word, which has a wide semantic range.

Paul characterizes the false teachings and their related practices in three ways.[89] First, "self-imposed worship" (ἐθελοθρησκίᾳ) can refer to the general system embraced by the false teachers ("self-made religion," NASB, ESV) or a general spiritual orientation ("self-imposed piety," NRSV). Both senses are certainly present, but this word should be understood in light of "the worship of angels" in v. 18. If so, this act of worshiping angels is now considered to be "self-imposed worship," which is contrasted with a growth that is initiated by God (v. 19); as such, it is "according to human tradition ... and not according to Christ" (v. 8).

"Self-humiliation" (ταπεινοφροσύνη) has already appeared in v. 18, and this connection with ascetic practices is clearer as it appears together with "harsh treatment of the body" (ἀφειδίᾳ σώματος).[90] "Harsh treatment of the body" includes but is not limited to the dietary, calendrical, and cultic practices noted above (vv. 16, 20 – 21). In light of the "worship of angels" in v. 18 and "self-imposed worship" in this verse, this asceticism is not simply the disciplining of the body; it is also preparation for an act of worship and is thus a cultic act. This understanding of asceticism can be identified across various ancient ascetic traditions, as it is "not simply the cutting off or destroying of the lower but, much more profoundly, the refinement and illumination of the lower and its transfiguration into something higher."[91] For Paul, the question is whether such "illumination" and "transfiguration" are grounded in the salvific act of God through Christ or are simply self-imposed acts of worship, the object of which are forces that had already been pacified by Christ.

---

89. The preposition translated "with" (ἐν) has been taken in a locative ("in the realm of," cf. NJB), instrumental ("by promoting," HCSB), result ("to make you," CEV), or causal sense ("because," NLT). This is best translated with a preposition in English that can express association, means, as well as content: "with" (NET, TNIV).

90. The connection is clearer in some manuscripts that lack "and" before this final item: 𝔓[46] B 1739 b m vg[mss]. But the inclusion of the conjunction is supported by geographically diverse manuscript traditions; cf. Metzger, *Textual Commentary*, 556 – 57.

91. Kallistos Ware, "The Way of the Ascetics: Negative or Affirmative?" in *Asceticism* (ed. Vincent L. Wimbush and Richard Valantasis; New York: Oxford Univ. Press, 1998), 12.

Theology in Application

Rules and Regulations

In the previous section, Paul pointed to the problems with the rules and regulations imposed by the false teachers (v. 14). In this section, he provides several lists with specific regulations and practices noted (vv. 16, 21, 23). This critique reminds readers of the NT of Jesus' criticism of the Pharisees and the scribes for ignoring the "commands of God" while holding fast to "human traditions" (Mark 7:8). Elsewhere in his letters, Paul notes that those who "rely on the works of the law are under a curse" (Gal 3:10). Reading such statements may seem to suggest that Christian traditions are unequivocally against all rules and regulations.

This conclusion must be qualified, however, by other statements in both the gospels and in Paul. In Luke 1:6, for example, Zechariah and Elizabeth are both favorably depicted as people who were "observing all the Lord's commands and decrees blamelessly." Likewise Paul also affirms that "the law is holy, and the commandment is holy, righteous and good" (Rom 7:12). Even in the following sections in Colossians, Paul will advocate specific patterns of behavior to which the Colossian believers should conform (esp. 3:5 – 4:1). It is thus misleading to assert that Paul and other NT writers have no concern for rules of conduct.

The question then is: Why are Jesus and his followers so critical of a certain set of regulations or certain groups that follow such traditions? Without providing a comprehensive survey of Jesus' and Paul's view of the law,[92] a few points should be noted when one probes into the rationale behind such critique. The first and most obvious basis of such a critique lies in the contrast between external practice and the condition of the heart. In the midst of Jesus' critique of the Pharisees and the scribes, one finds the same Isaianic passage that Paul uses in v. 22, although Paul only alludes to a part of it:

> These people honor me with their lips,
> > but their hearts are far from me.
> They worship me in vain;
> > their teachings are merely human rules.
> > (Mark 7:6 – 7; Isa 29:13; cf. Matt 15:8 – 9)

Second, the arrival of the messianic era brings about necessary changes. In response to questions concerning fasting, for example, Jesus uses the parable of the old and new wineskins to illustrate the drastic changes brought by the arrival of a new era in salvation history (Mark 2:18 – 22; par. Matt 9:14 – 17; Luke 5:33 – 39). Certain

---

92. For helpful surveys, see William R. G. Loader, *Jesus' Attitude Towards the Law: A Study of the Gospels* (Grand Rapids: Eerdmans, 2002); and Frank Thielman, *Paul and the Law: A* *Contextual Approach* (Downers Grove, IL: InterVarsity Press, 1994).

regulations that are specific for the time of promise may not be applicable in the time of fulfillment.

Third, many of the rules and regulations imposed by the Jews of the first century are at best a secondary application of the Torah. Both the content and intent of such application seem to deviate from the original purpose of the foundational Mosaic precepts. This can at least partly explain some of the criticisms directed against the teachers of the law. This is also the reason why those teachers were criticized for "setting aside the commands of God in order to observe [their] own traditions" (Mark 7:9).

Fourth, the ethnic component should also be noted. Many of the laws and regulations targeted by Jesus and especially by Paul are related to particular Jewish practices that seek to consolidate their ethnic identity. The identity markers of Sabbath observances, circumcision, and ritual purity laws in particular were efficient vehicles through which the identity of the Jewish community could be protected. In response to those who insisted that "Gentiles must be circumcised and required to keep the law of Moses" (Acts 15:5), Peter emphasized that God "did not discriminate between us and them" (15:9). Ethnic identity should not be the basis of one's salvation.

Peter's further response led to the final and most important point, that rules and regulations cannot take on soteriological significance because "it is through the grace of our Lord Jesus that we are saved, just as they are" (Acts 15:11). If such rules distract one from recognizing that one "is not justified by the works of the law, but by faith in Jesus Christ" (Gal 2:16),[93] following such rules can be considered an idolatrous practice as one fails to worship the God who alone can provide salvation for human beings.

In this section of Colossians, Paul's critique of the false teachings contains all of these reasons. The focus on the external fails to deal with the desires of the heart (v. 23), and to follow specific regulations reflects the failure to realize that they are "a shadow of things to come" (v. 17). Claimed to be of special value, they are but "human commands and teachings" (v. 22). Moreover, the particular dietary regulations and calendrical practices (v. 16) point to a specific ethnic focus, and with the reference to "circumcision" in the previous section (v. 11), the distinct Jewish focus cannot be ignored. The most critical deficiency of such regulations is that they distract one from the work of God in Christ, who has freed us from the evil forces that formerly ensnared us (v. 20).

To reduce this passage to a polemic against an ethical import of the Christian gospel is therefore unjustifiable. Instead of attacking the general rules and regulations that aim at promoting godly living for the community of God's people, Paul is

---

93. Translations that take the genitive as a subjective genitive (e.g., "faithfulness of Jesus Christ," NET) do not affect our argument here.

targeting those traditions that deprive Christ of the glory that belongs to him alone. To Paul, those traditions violate "the first ethical response" that is required of one who should worship God and him alone.[94]

Moreover, if our interpretation is correct, the specific rules noted in this section should be considered as cultic rules that prepare one for entering into the "worship of angels" (v. 18). If so, Paul's focus is not on Christian ethics in general, but on the false object of worship that plagued the practices of these false teachers. Even so, this is not even an act of worshiping "the other" when one assumes that one's power resides in oneself in accomplishing what can be accomplished only by God. This is perhaps our greatest temptation — one that results in the creation of objects of worship that are but "the illusions created by our false self-expansion."[95] At the end, therefore, this "worship of angels" can be nothing but the worship of oneself, or in the language of Paul, a worship that is "according to human tradition … not according to Christ" (v. 8).

From Rules and Regulations to Spiritual Disciplines: Fasting as a Case Study

Paul's critique of the particular rules and regulations imposed by the false teachers naturally leads one to reconsider the positive roles of spiritual disciplines, especially when some of those named rules and regulations can be and have been useful instruments in the development of God's people. In contemporary contexts, references to terms such as "food" and "drink" (v. 16), and the commandment "do not taste" (v. 21) in the context of a discussion of "rules" that seek to restrain "the gratification of the flesh" (v. 23), remind one of the Christian practice of fasting. While Paul's words do not address the issue of fasting, principles provided here may be relevant in discussing this practice and other related spiritual disciplines.

Should Christians practice the discipline of fasting? The varied interpretations that one can draw from the different NT passages should alert us to the difficulties in formulating a simple answer to this question. That Jesus fasted (Matt 4:2; Luke 4:2) and taught his disciples to do so (Matt 6:16 – 18) makes it clear that he does not object to this practice inherited from the OT traditions. This practice is affirmed by Christ's followers at various significant moments in their Christian lives (Acts 9:9; 13:2 – 3; 14:23).

Several cautionary notes concerning this practice can, however, be identified in both Jesus' teachings and the rest of the NT. First, those who fast should not consider this practice as one that elevates their spiritual status (Matt 6:16, 18; Luke 18:9 – 14). Second, fasting should not be considered as an act that rejects the creation of God,

---

94. Cf. Waldo Beach, *Christian Ethics in the Protestant Tradition* (Atlanta: John Knox, 1988), 32.

95. Diogenes Allen, *Temptation* (Cambridge, MA: Cowley, 1986), 68.

which includes one's own body (1 Tim 4:3). Third, even in the midst of fasting, believers should recognize the arrival of the climax of salvation history in the person of Jesus Christ (Matt 9:14 – 17; Mark 2:18 – 20; Luke 5:33 – 35; cf. Luke 2:36 – 38).

While the topic of fasting is never the focus of Paul's discussion in his letters, one should not assume that he entirely rejects this practice.[96] Paul here echoes the cautionary notes that appear elsewhere. The issue of conceit lies at the center of his critique of those who impose this discipline on believers (v. 18). His affirmation of the significance of the "body" has been repeatedly noted in Colossians (1:22, 24; 2:11) since creation belongs to God and his Son (1:15 – 20), and this affirmation forms the foundation for Paul's critique of the "harsh treatment of the body" (2:23). Most importantly, the arrival of the eschatological age relativizes the efficacy of such disciplines (v. 17), and those who practice them apart from a recognition of one's inadequacy apart from the work of God through Christ are involved in the worship of a false god (vv. 18 – 19).

Recognizing the profound significance of these practices, contemporary Christians should be reminded that practices such as fasting can be understood wrongly as instruments to manipulate God and others. It is therefore important to emphasize that "fasting is a response to a sacred moment, not an instrument designed to get a desired result."[97] Those who fast should also resist the urge to consider this as "an inevitable sign of piety."[98] We should not deny, however, that among other practices, fasting can prepare one to recognize one's impotence and dependence on the grace of God (cf. Lev. 16:29 – 31; 23:26 – 32). Yet such recognition must be coupled with an understanding that points to the completed and final sacrifice in the death of Jesus Christ (Heb 9:23 – 28).

Stubborn Christocentricism

The focus on Christ and his work has been the subject of previous sections.[99] In this section, the reader again finds Paul focusing on Christ and on the need of believers to appreciate the implications of participating in his body. In seeking ways to apply this passage, one may be hesitant in repeatedly returning to the same message. For Paul, however, this christocentric emphasis lies at the core of the gospel, and he is unashamedly repetitive in drawing attention to the center of God's redemptive plan for humanity.

In this section of Colossians, which discusses the false teachings, the significance of Christ is portrayed not primarily through the use of specific christological titles. Instead, one finds the attention focused on the narrative of Christ's death and

---

96. See, e.g., Keith Main, *Prayer and Fasting: A Study in the Devotional Life of the Early Church* (New York: Carlton, 1971), 48 – 54.

97. Scot McKnight, *Fasting* (Nashville: Nelson, 2009), xxi.
98. Ibid., 134.
99. See the Theology in Application section on 1:15 – 23.

resurrection.[100] This narrative ties the various sections together and thus forms an underlying story through which the problems facing the Colossian believers can be resolved. The participation of the believers in the death and resurrection of Christ is introduced already in 2:11 – 13 through the metaphor of circumcision. This is unpacked in 2:16 – 23, where Paul focuses on the freedom that believers experienced when they died with Christ, whose death liberates us from the power of the evil forces. Moving from death to resurrection, the next section focuses on the exaltation of Christ, whose resurrection guarantees a new life for believers, a life that will find its consummation when Jesus appears again in glory (3:1 – 4).

In the sections that follow, Paul returns to the believers' participation in Jesus' death when they are called to "put to death" the evil practices of their past (3:5 – 9); this act of stripping off reminds one of the death of Christ (cf. 2:11) and is followed by the putting on of the new nature, which is characterized by a community of unity and righteousness (3:10 – 14). This continued unpacking of the relevance of Christ's death and resurrection for the believers illustrates what it means to "continue to walk in him" (2:6).

From cultic practices in the worship of a false deity to the behavior of the believers, and to the formation of a new community that is not separated by ethnic, social, and economic barriers, one finds the impact of one's participation in the death and resurrection of Christ. This narrated gospel should affect every part of Christian existence. It provides the foundation for one's identity, and it dictates the behavior of an individual and of a community. To allow one aspect not to be affected by this story of Christ is to challenge the cosmological and final significance of God's new creative act (1:18 – 20).

---

100. For the significance of narrative in christological expressions throughout the NT, see also Richard A. Burridge, "From Titles to Stories: A Narrative Approach to the Dynamic Christologies of the New Testament," in *The Person of Christ* (ed. Murray Rae and Stephen R. Holmes; London: T&T Clark, 2005), 37 – 60.

Colossians 3:1 – 11

Literary Context

Many consider 3:1 – 4 as signifying the shift from the theoretical to the practical.[1] This reading is correct in noting the shift in focus from the polemic to the hortatory as Paul encourages his audience to "set your minds on the things above, not things on the earth" (v. 2). The paragraphs that follow, which include vice (vv. 5, 8 – 9) and virtue (vv. 12 – 14) lists, a call to lead a life of worship (vv. 15 – 17), and a discussion of behavior within the household (3:18 – 4:1), confirm this reading.

It is incorrect, however, to consider 2:23 as the conclusion of Paul's theoretical arguments or that Paul does not have the false teachers in mind in the remaining sections. First, the connection with the previous section is unmistakable. Paul's discussion of the believers' participation in the death of Christ, introduced by a conditional clause in 2:20, finds its counterpart in 3:1, which likewise begins with a conditional clause as he discusses the significance of their participation in Christ's resurrection (3:1).[2] Putting to death evil desires in v. 5 also points to the continued relevance of the arguments presented in 2:20 – 23.

Second, this section begins with a call to "seek the things above" (3:1). This is not an abstract call to follow Christ; rather, it comes after the extensive polemic against the false teachers, who apparently were promoting the "worship of angels" (2:18) and related cultic practices (2:20 – 21, 23). Paul here challenges such visionary experiences. Instead of seeking what is exotic and alien in the realm "above," Paul specifies that the one who should be worshiped is "Christ," who is "seated at the right hand of God" (3:1). The call to "seek the things above" and the expansion of this call in

---

1. See, e.g., John Callow, *A Semantic and Structural Analysis of Colossians* (Dallas: SIL International, 2002), who sees in 3:1 "a change of topic from the previous section, and indeed there is, the previous section being concerned with warnings against the false teaching." Some have further made a distinction between the practical moral imperatives and the theoretical discussion of the legal matters as this section is considered to focus primarily on the "ethical," without "reflections or

implications of actual halakha" (Peter J. Tomson, *Paul and the Jewish Law: Halakha in the Letters of the Apostle to the Gentiles* [CRINT 3.1; Minneapolis: Fortress, 1990], 91).

2. These two sections that build around the death and resurrection of Christ remind one of a similar set of arguments presented in Rom 6:1 – 14; see Louw, "Reading a Text as Discourse," 29.

3:5 – 11 are thus a polemical note against those who seek private visions in an attempt to obtain superior religious experiences.[3]

Third, the introduction of a note on eschatology in the appearance of Christ at the end of time (v. 4) also provides a strong response to the false teachers at Colossae. Instead of focusing on the present, private consummation of one's communion with the divine, Paul emphasizes the coming public display of the glory of Christ, when every believer "will be revealed with him in glory" (v. 4). As in 2:20 – 23, therefore, this section should also be considered a transitional paragraph that combines theoretical discussions with Paul's paraenetic concerns.

In 3:5 – 11, Paul moves further to the concerns of Christian living, though this section is also clearly built on the foundation of the previous sections. Concern for Christian living reflects the affirmation in 1:15 – 20, where the church, which symbolizes the new creation, is compared to the creation of the universe. As such, "the church becomes the microcosm for cosmic reconciliation."[4] The concern for the behavior of the believers is therefore a concern closely related to the discussion of Christ as the Lord of the cosmos.

The discussion that follows this section continues Paul's concern to establish the right pattern of behavior for the Christian community. As 3:5 – 11 points to the stripping off of the old nature as one participates in the community of God's people, 3:12 – 14 points to the putting on of the new nature. This leads to the reaffirmation of the lordship of Christ through thanksgiving (3:15 – 17), a theme concretely illustrated in Paul's discussion of household relationships (3:18 – 4:1). Thus, Paul continues to explain the centrality of Christ as the necessary basis for one's worship and moral life.

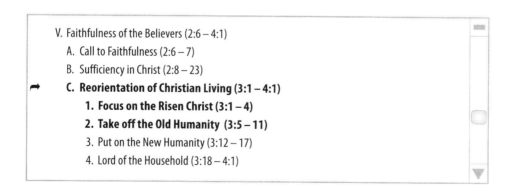

V. Faithfulness of the Believers (2:6 – 4:1)

   A. Call to Faithfulness (2:6 – 7)

   B. Sufficiency in Christ (2:8 – 23)

➡   **C. Reorientation of Christian Living (3:1 – 4:1)**

      1. Focus on the Risen Christ (3:1 – 4)

      2. Take off the Old Humanity (3:5 – 11)

      3. Put on the New Humanity (3:12 – 17)

      4. Lord of the Household (3:18 – 4:1)

---

3. The sections that follow, which explicate that which is "above," also make clear that "attending to heavenly things is not an otherworldly fixation on spiritual matters" (Michael Barram, "Colossians 3:1 – 17," *Int* 59 [2005]: 189).

4. Wedderburn, "The Theology of Colossians," 41. This connection is explicitly secured with the allusion to 1:20 in 3:15.

Main Idea

Believers should focus on Christ alone, the exalted one who will be revealed in glory at the end of times. Identified with this exalted Christ, believers are to live lives that are not controlled by the earthly desires, and they are to participate in a unified community that finds its foundation in nothing but Christ himself.

Translation

(See pages 208 – 9.)

Structure

After a critique of the false teachers who were promoting the worship of heavenly beings (2:16 – 19), Paul reminds his readers that their proper object of worship is Christ, who is seated at the right hand of God (3:1 – 4). In this section, therefore, Paul returns to his intense focus on Christ as the only acceptable object of worship. Since believers have been raised with Christ, they are to "seek the things above" (v. 1). These "things above" are not lofty heavenly visions, however, but "Christ," whose body exists in the earthly realm (cf. 3:5 – 4:1). To "seek the things above" is, therefore, to live a life worthy of Christ, who died on the cross and was raised from the dead (vv. 2 – 3a).

The present reality of sharing in Christ's death and resurrection anticipates the glory to come (vv. 3b – 4). Instead of the benefit for a few who are able to obtain superior knowledge in their private religious experiences, Paul emphasizes the full revelation of glory in the public return of Christ at the end of times. The eschatological consummation of salvation history that centers on the mighty acts of God through Christ becomes the foundation of Paul's critique of those who focus on self-centered religious experiences.

In vv. 5 – 11, Paul illustrates the implications of the worship of the exalted Christ for believers struggling in their earthly existence. It is significant that Paul starts with their identity in the exalted Christ (vv. 1 – 4) and only then proceeds to their pattern of behavior (vv. 5 – 11). Unlike the false teachers, who insist on their own works as they attempt to participate in the heavenly experiences, "Paul moves in the reverse direction, since he sees the starting-point and source of the believer's life in the resurrected Christ in heaven, from where it works itself out into the earthly life (3:5ff)."[5]

---

5. Lincoln, *Paradise Now and Not Yet*, 127.

In the call to take off the old self, Paul begins with two vice lists that sandwich the grounds for rejecting such vices (vv. 5 – 8). The first vice list contains a catalogue of sinful desires (v. 5), several of which remind one of the Ten Commandments. The final explanatory phrase, "which is idolatry" (v. 5g), is important because it points to the central concern behind these vices. Paul is not simply randomly listing the vices that believers should avoid; he is rather describing selected manifestations of hearts that worship idols and is more concerned with the ultimate object of worship, Christ. Criticizing the false teachers of false worship, Paul points to a life that manifests the worship of the true God.

The grounds of Paul's exhortation provided in vv. 6 – 7 further confirm this reading as he urges the (Gentile) believers to abandon a pattern of behavior that characterized their life before they participated in Christ's death and resurrection. Consistent with his emphasis in vv. 1 – 5, Paul again points to the eschatological judgment as the reality that faces those who refuse to worship the one true God.

The second vice list contains a catalogue of sins related to speech and violent offenses in interpersonal relationships (v. 8). While the previous list in v. 5 may point to the sins of one's heart, this list may point to those actions that interrupt the harmonious life of the community of God's people. While the exhortation "do not lie to one another" (v. 9a) introduces the final paragraph of this section, it also serves as a concluding remark for this second vice list. Its function is comparable to the explanatory phrase in v. 5g ("which is idolatry"). In other words, the sins listed in v. 8 are actions of lying to one another. They point to a life in falsehood that refuses to acknowledge the truth and reality of the death and resurrection of Christ. This therefore corresponds to the sin of idolatry.

This reading of the vice list in v. 8 is confirmed by 3:9b – 11. In 3:9b – 10, Paul points directly to the putting on of the "new humanity" according to the image of its Creator. The notes on the new humanity bring up the issue of living according to one's confession. In 3:11, Paul defines this "new humanity" in communal terms. Instead of focusing simply on individual virtues, Paul defines this "humanity" as a community that is not to be divided along ethnic, cultural, or social lines. This focus on community is also a response to the false teachers, who have erected barriers in their focus on private experiences for a few. Instead, Paul points to "Christ" (v. 11e) as the sole foundation of this community. The "new humanity" is the "body of Christ" (1:18, 24; 2:19; cf. 3:15), which reflects the power of God's work in Christ's death and resurrection.

Colossians 3:1 – 11

1a	condition	Therefore,
		if you have been raised with Christ,
b	Exhortation	**seek the things above,**
c	place	where Christ is,
d	description	seated at the right hand of God.
2a	Exhortation	**Set your minds on the things above,**
b	contrast	not things on the earth.
3a	basis	For **you have died,**
b	result	and **your life is hidden with Christ in God;**
4a	time	when Christ is revealed,
b	apposition	who is your life,
c	sequence	then
		you also will be revealed with him in glory.
5a	Exhortation	**Put to death,** therefore, **your earthly parts,**
b	example	[1] sexual immorality,
c	list	[2] impurity,
d	list	[3] lust,
e	list	[4] evil desires, and
f	list	[5] covetousness,
g	description	which is idolatry.
6	expansion	Because of these the wrath of God is coming
		[upon the sons of disobedience].
7a	explanation	In these you once walked,
b	time	when you were living in them.

8a	Exhortation	But **now you also must put all these away:**
b	example	[1] anger,
c	list	[2] rage,
d	list	[3] malice,
e	list	[4] slander, and
f	list	[5] abusive speech
		from your mouth.
9a	Exhortation	**Do not lie to one another,**
b	basis	for you have taken off the old humanity with its practices and
10a	progression	have put on the new humanity, being renewed in knowledge
b	basis	according to the image of their Creator,
11a	description	where there is neither Greek nor Jew,
b	series	circumcised nor uncircumcised,
c	series	barbarian, Scythian,
d	series	slave nor free,
e	contrast	but Christ is all and in all.

Exegetical Outline

→ **I. Focus on the Risen Christ (3:1 – 4)**

    A. Having been raised with him, seek things above (3:1)

    B. Having died with him, do not focus on the things below (3:2 – 3a)

    C. Having been hidden with him, you will be revealed in glory (3:3b – 4)

II. Take Off the Old Humanity (3:5 – 11)

    A. Put to death the earthly nature (3:5 – 8)

        1. Catalogue of the sins of desire (3:5)

        2. Warning to those who live in their past (3:6 – 7)

        3. Catalogue of the sins of speech (3:8)

    B. Resist The Life In Falsehood (3:9 – 11)

        1. Do not lie to one another (3:9a)

        2. Because you have put on the new nature (3:9b – 10)

        3. New nature defined as the new community in Christ (3:11)

Explanation of the Text

3:1a Therefore, if you have been raised with Christ (Εἰ οὖν συνηγέρθητε τῷ Χριστῷ). Paul reminds the Colossian believers of their new lives and identities in Christ. As in previous sections (cf. 2:6, 16), "therefore" (οὖν) marks the transition into another stage of Paul's argument. In his discussion of baptism in 2:12, Paul has already noted how believers were raised in Christ. Closer to this section, the protasis of the conditional clause ("if you have been raised with Christ") here naturally completes the thought of 2:20 ("if you have died with Christ"). In both clauses, the participation of the death and resurrection of Christ is not in doubt, and these notes serve rather as the grounds for Paul's further argument concerning the appropriate behavior of the believers. As with 2:20, it is justifiable to translate this protasis as an assumed fact: "since … you have been raised with Christ" (NIV, TNIV).[6]

The passive verb "you have been raised"

(συνηγέρθητε) points to God's actions, which serves as a corrective to the false teachings that emphasize human efforts in approaching the divine. While the previous note on dying "with Christ" (σὺν Χριστῷ) uses the pronoun "with" (σύν) in emphasizing the believer's identification with Christ, a similar effect is accomplished here with the prepositional prefix ("with," σύν-) attached to the verb "to raise" (see comments on 2:12). To be raised "with Christ" is to be raised "to new life with Christ" (NLT). Although 2:12 pointed directly to baptism as the context of the believers' participation in the resurrection of Christ, baptism is but "the symbolic center"[7] of the believer's participation in an entire new pattern of life that involves spiritual, mental, physical, and cultic aspects. In the discussion that follows, Paul makes clear what this new life in Christ entails.

3:1b-d Seek the things above, where Christ is, seated at the right hand of God (τὰ ἄνω ζητεῖτε, οὗ ὁ Χριστός ἐστιν ἐν δεξιᾷ τοῦ θεοῦ καθήμενος).

---

6. See comments on 2:20.

7. Meeks, " 'To Walk Worthily of the Lord,' " 46.

In light of the believers' sharing in the resurrection of Christ, they are called to "seek the things above." With the definite article τά), the adverb "above" (ἄνω) takes on a substantive sense: "the things above." Since this adverb is used substantivally only here (and in v. 2) in the NT, some scholars argue that "this is another of the catchwords of the philosophy."[8] If so, what is striking is not Paul's call to "seek the things above," but his further explication of that which is above. While the false teachers encourage their followers to focus on the heavenly realm (2:18), Paul makes it clear that the center of such heavenly attention is nothing but Christ himself.

"Where Christ is, seated at the right hand of God" can be taken in two ways, and each option depends on the relationship between the indicative verb "is" (ἐστιν) and the participle "seated" (καθήμενος). Some take both together as a periphrastic construction, expressing one verbal idea: "where Christ is seated at the right hand of God" (TNIV; cf. KJV, NAB, NLT, TEV). In light of the intervening prepositional phrase ("at the right hand of God"), which can modify either the auxiliary verb or the participle,[9] it is more plausible that Paul is expressing two verbal ideas: "where Christ is, seated at the right hand of God" (NRSV, NIV; cf. ASV, NASB, NJB, NKJV, REB, NLT, NET, HCSB, ESV).

This separation of the two clauses also allows them to contain independent though related concepts. To identify Christ in heaven is to situate him where the throne of God is situated (see 2 Chr 18:18; Pss 11:4; 103:19; Isa 6:1; 66:1; Dan 7:9).[10] This affirmation attests to the power and glory of one who has participated in God's creative act (cf. 1:15 – 20), and this is consistent with the high Christology exhibited throughout the previous sections.

"Seated at the right hand of God" furthers this christological affirmation with an allusion to Ps 110:1 (109:1 LXX): "Sit at my right hand until I make your enemies a footstool for your feet." The lack of exact parallel has caused some to question this allusion, but the widespread use of this psalm in early Christianity makes this connection more probable than not (Acts 2:34 – 35; Heb 1:13; 8:1; 10:12 – 13; 12:2; 1 Pet 3:22). Moreover, this allusion also fits the context of Paul's arguments: since Christ has defeated all the spiritual powers and forces (2:10, 15; cf. 1:16), he alone should be worshiped. With the allusion to Ps 110:1, therefore, one finds affirmation of the beginning of Christ's sovereign rule.[11] The consummation of such rule is again dependent on Christ's return in glory (cf. v. 4).

The participation of Christ in God's glory is further illustrated by the metaphor of "seating." In Jewish traditions, God alone sits in the heavens, while the other subordinating angelic beings stand beside him.[12] Christ's being seated at the right hand of God, therefore, points to his sharing of God's sovereign rule. The allusion to Ps 110:1 is a striking departure from Jewish traditions, which find little use of this verse. This "difference simply reflects the fact that early Christians used the text to say something about Jesus which Second Temple Jewish literature is not interested in saying about anyone: that he participates in the unique divine sovereignty over all things."[13]

8. Lincoln, *Paradise Now and Not Yet*, 123. Cf. Sumney, "The Argument of Colossians," 350.

9. A prepositional phrase that modifies the auxiliary verb rules out the possibility of this being a periphrastic participle.

10. Beetham, *Echoes of Scripture*, 226.

11. Cf. Beale, "Colossians," 864.

12. E.g., Dan 7:10; *1 En.* 14:22; 39:12; *2 En.* 21:2; *2 Bar.* 21:6; *4 Ezra* 8:21; see Richard Bauckham, *Jesus and the God of Israel* (Grand Rapids: Eerdmans, 2008), 163 – 64, who further points to the saying, "on high there is no sitting" (*b. Ḥag.* 15a; *Gen. Rab.* 65:1).

13. Bauckham, *God Crucified*, 31.

The affirmation of Christ's status and his participation in God's sovereignty do not simply aim at responding to the false teachers. They also provide the foundation for a pattern of Christian earthly living that should reflect this heavenly reality. In the remaining sections, Paul draws out the practical implications that flow from the common Christian confession that "Jesus is Lord" (Rom 10:9; 1 Cor 12:3).

3:2a Set your minds on the things above (τὰ ἄνω φρονεῖτε). This clause completes the thought of "seek the things above" in v. 1. "Set your minds" goes beyond "seek" in emphasizing the need to dwell intently on the things above, and this translation is adopted by most modern versions.[14] NLT's more dramatic rendering may further bring out the nuance of this verb in this context: "Think about the things of heaven." This involves the transformation of one's mind in the obedient submission to God's will as manifested in both thoughts and actions (cf. Rom 12:1 – 2).[15]

The significance of this verb is best illustrated by its uses in another of Paul's prison letters, written most likely during the same period of time. In Philippians, after the call for believers to being "like-minded" (τὸ αὐτὸ φρονῆτε) since they have "one mind" (ἓν φρονοῦντες; Phil 2:2), Paul criticizes those whose "mind is set on earthly things" (οἱ τὰ ἐπίγεια φρονοῦντες, 3:19). Instead, believers' "citizenship is in heaven" (3:20a).

This reminder of the heavenly orientation of the believers in Philippians is likewise framed within the expectation of the final revelation of Christ: "we eagerly await a Savior from there, the Lord

Jesus Christ, who, by the power that enables him to bring everything under his control, will transform our lowly bodies so that they will be like his glorious body" (Phil 3:20b – 21). While Paul focuses on the future subjection of all things to Christ in Philippians, in Colossians he emphasizes Christ's inaugurated rule, as Christ has already defeated his enemies on the cross and through his resurrection (2:14 – 15). In both contexts, the call to focus on heavenly things is grounded on the lordship of Christ, the consummation of which lies in the future when all believers will be glorified with Christ (3:4).

3:2b Not things on the earth (μὴ τὰ ἐπὶ τῆς γῆς). The second way this verse goes beyond v. 1 is the presence of the polarity between "above" and "earth." Not only is Paul calling believers to focus intently on the things above, but he also urges them to reject "things on the earth." This contrast is meaningful in various ways. First, the contrast is comparable to that of the "flesh" and the "spirit" elsewhere. If so, to reject the "things on the earth" is to reject the earthly desires.[16] This reading is supported by the note on "earthly parts" in v. 5, which introduces the vice lists that follow (vv. 5, 8; see comments below).

Second, if "above" is defined as the place "where Christ is, seated at the right hand of God" (v. 1), the "things on the earth" are practices that refuse to acknowledge Christ as the sovereign Lord of all. The contrast between "above" and "earth" can then be compared to that of "human tradition" and "Christ" (2:8), and even of "shadow" and "substance" (2:17). The use of this polarity is then polemical in intent,

---

14. Cf. BDAG, 1065 – 66. Although "keep thinking about things above" (NET; cf. NAB) may be a more literal translation, this rendering may give the false impression that Paul is focusing simply on the mental act.

15. The call to submit to God's will with a transformed mind in Rom 12:1 – 2 is followed by calls "to think" (φρονεῖν)

through the mind of Christ (12:3, 16).

16. This use of "the earth" (τῆς γῆς) may draw ultimately from Gen 3:17 (LXX ἐπικατάρατος ἡ γῆ), where "the earth" is seen as "the primary setting of fallen creation" (Lincoln, *Paradise Now and Not Yet*, 126).

as Paul argues against any practices that distract one from worshiping the one and only rightful object of worship.

Finally, the use of this polarity may also be an intentional critique of the dualistic framework assumed by the false teachers. Their ascetic practices may assume a body-soul dualism as they seek to transcend the constraints of the material world. Earlier in this letter, however, Paul has already noted that in Christ "all things were created, in heaven and on earth" (1:16). Moreover, through his death on the cross, all things were reconciled to him, "whether things on earth, or things in heaven" (1:20). In this context, therefore, Paul is not assuming the same metaphysical dichotomy; he is rather using such categories in an attempt to transform the perspective of his audience. Believers are not to escape from this material world; rather, they are to focus on Christ as they live faithfully on earth: "It is in their corporeal body that the community should be oriented toward God's will, and thus, as v 4 goes on to say, toward God's future consummation."[17] As such, believers can acknowledge Christ to be both creator and sustainer of both the heaven and the earth.

3:3 For you have died, and your life is hidden with Christ in God (ἀπεθάνετε γάρ, καὶ ἡ ζωὴ ὑμῶν κέκρυπται σὺν τῷ Χριστῷ ἐν τῷ θεῷ). Providing the grounds for the call to focus on the things above, Paul again points to the believers' death with Christ. In light of 2:20, "you have died" here points to both their identification with Christ and their liberation from the evil powers. Mentioned together with their being "raised with Christ" (3:1), this death is not a sign of weakness but a sign of empowerment in Christ as he defeated the power of death in his resurrection.

With the plural pronoun "your" (ὑμῶν), the sin-gular "life" (ἡ ζωή) should be considered as a "distributive singular," where the individual person among the wider group is in view.[18] This "life" is the present existence of believers as they participate in the resurrection of Christ. The continuity of this "life," which bridges the present experience of God's salvation and the future consummation, reappears in the final revelation of Christ's glory in v. 4.

That this life "is hidden with Christ" is significant in a number of ways. First, the verb "to hide" (κρύπτω) can signify close association (cf. Luke 13:21),[19] and this meaning is certainly present in light of Paul's identification of Christ as "your life" (ἡ ζωὴ ὑμῶν). To be "hidden with Christ" reaffirms the believers' participation in Christ's death and resurrection as they anticipate the final consummation of God's salvific act at the end of time.

Second, to be "hidden with Christ" necessarily implies the security that one finds in Christ.[20] The following verse explains the purpose of this hiddenness as it guarantees the final participation of believers in the revelation of God's glory. This security from the evil powers is also implied in the reference to their dying with Christ, an act that points to the freedom of the threats posed by the opposing spiritual powers (2:20).

Third, in light of 2:3, where Paul asserts that in Christ "all the treasures of wisdom and knowledge are hidden," Paul is here affirming that the lives of believers are also contained in Christ. This may serve a polemical purpose as Paul argues against those who continuously seek to get access to the heavenly mysteries. Paul's response is that believers are already hidden with all the treasures in Christ. The sufficiency of Christ cannot be challenged, and to seek for these treasures elsewhere is to betray the true gospel.

---

17. Schweizer, *Letter to the Colossians*, 175.
18. Cf. BDF §140.

19. BDAG, 571.
20. See, in particular, O'Brien, *Colossians, Philemon*, 166.

Related to this polemical purpose is the redefinition of this hiddenness in historical rather than mystical terms.[21] This redefinition can already be found in 1:26, where the "the mystery [that is] hidden" is defined in historical terms as it is "now revealed to his saints." In the present context, this hiddenness likewise anticipates the final revelation of glory (3:4). This hope not only explains the lack of full manifestation of divine power and glory in believers who live in the present age; this anticipated manifestation of the full glory of God also obviates the need to focus on the present attainment through ascetic practices and visionary experiences.

Finally, this association with Christ may reveal the true identity of believers that can be found only in Christ. This reading finds its parallel in Rom 2:28 – 29, where the "hidden" word group is used in the definition of the true people of God: "someone is a Jew who is one inwardly" (NET).[22] When the lives of believers are identified with Christ in v. 4, therefore, it is not simply association but also identity that is at issue. Instead of identity markers that provide external identification of those who follow the false teachers (2:11, 16, 20 – 21), the Colossian believers are called to identify themselves simply in reference to Christ.

Although translated as "in God" (ἐν τῷ θεῷ) in most modern versions, it is possible to take this phrase in an instrumental sense: "your life is hidden in Christ by God"[23] (cf. Eph 3:9). Nevertheless, one does not find an instrumental use of ἐν in this letter when final agency in reference to God the Father is in view. Some have taken it in a locative sense and have made it explicit in their translation: "your life is hidden with Christ, who sits beside God" (CEV). It is perhaps best to see this prepositional phrase as indicating close identification since Christ is to be identified as God; as such, "its christological weight is wholly of a piece with the Wisdom Christology of the hymn in 1:15 – 20."[24] The unbreakable bond between believers, Christ, and God the Father is here established. It is this bond that provides the security for believers as they await the final fulfillment of God's plan in history.

3:4a-b When Christ is revealed, who is your life (ὅταν ὁ Χριστὸς φανερωθῇ, ἡ ζωὴ ὑμῶν). The note on the hiddenness of an object demands a discussion about its revelation. Here, Paul adopts a temporal framework that accommodates this polarity. The intense christocentric focus is again reflected as Paul describes the destiny of believers in terms of the consummation of God's salvific plan in Christ.

The verb "is revealed" (φανερωθῇ) is unexpected in the description of the return of Christ at the end of times, and this word choice has led some to conclude that Paul is not referring to Christ's second coming here. According to this reading, since dying and being hidden do not refer to the physical death and burial of believers, neither should "is revealed" refer to the physical return of Christ with his followers. Instead, one should read the verse in the following sense: "If you let it become visible that Christ is your life, then to his glory it will also become manifest that you have been raised to a new life with him."[25] The discussion that follows (3:5 – 4:1) then points to this manifestation of Christ's glory in the daily living.

This noneschatological reading is unlikely, however, and a response to this reading sheds light on the function and significance of this verse. This reading downplays the references to the future in this letter. "The hope of glory" in 1:27 clearly points

---

21. Thus Lincoln, *Paradise Now and Not Yet*, 129; Smith, *Heavenly Perspective*, 182.

22. MacDonald, *Colossians and Ephesians*, 128.

23. Cf. Barth and Blanke, *Colossians*, 396.

24. Dunn, *Epistles to the Colossians and to Philemon*, 207.

25. Gerhard Swart, "Eschatological Vision or Exhortation to Visible Christian Conduct? Notes on the Interpretation of Colossians 3:4," *Neot* 33 (1999): 175.

to the consummation of glory at a future point in time. An eschatological emphasis is also apparent in this section, where Paul points to "the wrath of God" in 3:6, a phrase often found in eschatological contexts. The call to be "alert" in 4:2 likewise evokes a similar context. Therefore, a reference to the revelation of Christ cannot be limited to present Christian living.

The choice of the verb "is revealed" (φανερωθῇ) is anticipated by the reference to hiddenness in v. 3, and should therefore not be used as an argument against an eschatological reading (cf. 1:26). Hiddenness itself is a concept familiar in eschatological contexts as it "reflects the apocalyptic conviction that what will be revealed in glory is hidden for the duration of the present age (e.g., 2 Bar. 48.49; 52.7)."[26] Although not a technical term in reference to the parousia, the verb "to reveal" has been used in reference to the manifestation of all deeds in eschatological judgment (2 Cor 5:10).

Finally, the significance of the pair "when" (ὅταν) and "then" (τότε) must not be missed. This pair points to a reality that has not been realized — a pair that naturally follows the death and resurrection/exaltation of Christ. Elsewhere in Paul, one also finds references to the death, resurrection, and return of Christ mentioned together (esp. 1 Cor 15, where Paul discusses the identification of believers with Christ in his death and resurrection, which thus provides the basis of the future hope when he returns in glory):

> But Christ has indeed been raised from the dead, the firstfruits of those who have fallen asleep. For since death came through a man, the resurrection of the dead comes also through a man. For as in Adam all die, so in Christ all will be made alive. But each in turn: Christ, the firstfruits; then, when he comes, those who belong to him. Then the end will come, when he hands over the kingdom to God the Father after he has destroyed all dominion, authority and power. (1 Cor 15:20 – 24)

In this context, the return of Jesus likewise justifies the hope that believers place in his resurrection. Although our present living out of the power of the risen Lord is the emphasis of the following verses, this life is grounded in the historical events that have and will take place according to the salvific plan of God.

"Who is your life" (ἡ ζωὴ ὑμῶν)[27] renders the phrase literally translated as "your life." This phrase stands in apposition to "Christ." Paul moves here from association to identification: "It is not enough to have said that the life is shared *with* Christ. The apostle declares that the life *is* Christ."[28] This identification is critical to Paul's argument and should not be limited to one particular set of relationships, as is illustrated in CEV: "Christ gives meaning to your life." One's identification with Christ in the context of the outworking of his death and resurrection can also be found elsewhere in Paul:

> We always carry around in our body the death of Jesus, so that the life of Jesus may also be revealed in our body. For we who are alive are always being given over to death for Jesus' sake, so that his life may also be revealed in our mortal body. So then, death is at work in us, but life is at work in you. (2 Cor 4:10 – 12; cf. Gal 2:20; Phil 1:21)

In this section in Colossians, however, Paul extends this identification to the final revelation of Christ's glory.

3:4c Then you also will be revealed with him in glory (τότε καὶ ὑμεῖς σὺν αὐτῷ φανερωθήσεσθε ἐν δόξῃ). This final clause draws out the implication

---

26. Talbert, *Ephesians and Colossians*, 226; cf. Bevere, *Sharing in the Inheritance*, 153 – 61.

27. Some manuscripts read "our" (ἡμῶν) instead of "your" (ὑμῶν), but the later reading is supported by the earliest (𝔓⁴⁶)

and the more diverse manuscript traditions; cf. Metzger, *Textual Commentary*, 557.

28. Lightfoot, *St. Paul's Epistles to the Colossians and to Philemon*, 210, italics his.

of the believers' identification with Christ. The reuse of the verb "reveal" in "you will be revealed" (φανερωθήσεσθε), together with the phrase "with him" (σὺν αὐτῷ), points to the ultimate goal of our identification with Christ. This appearance in glory justifies our present hiddenness.

Paul does not explain the significance of the reference to "in glory" (ἐν δόξῃ) in this context, except that this is the fulfillment of the longings of believers. Elsewhere in Paul, this glory often consists of Christ's ultimate victory over death when believers will be clothed with an immortal body (1 Cor 15:53–54; cf. Rom 2:7; 6:4; 1 Thess 4:16–17). This fits this context well, although earlier in this letter, Paul also pointed to the glory in the ultimate manifestation of the power of God through Christ (1:11) and the fulfillment of God's plan in history (1:27). This glorious note becomes a significant anchor for the Colossians as they seek to be faithful to the gospel in which they are called. After all, these "insignificant ex-pagans from a third-rate country town"[29] will participate in a glory that encompasses all creation, and it is to this cosmic vision that their identities are to be grounded.

IN DEPTH: Vice and Virtue Lists

The appearance of the two vice lists (3:5, 8–9) and a corresponding virtue list in 3:12–14 point to the importance of these lists in Paul's argument. Before exploring these lists in their contexts, a general discussion on their conceptual background as well as their general functions may help.

Origin

Numerous other vice (e.g., Rom 1:25–31; 13:13; 1 Cor 5:10–11; Eph 5:3–4; 1 Tim 1:9–10; 6:4–5; 1 Pet 4:3) and virtue (e.g., 2 Cor 6:6–7; Gal 5:22–23; Eph 4:2–3; Phil 4:8; 1 Tim 3:2) lists can be found in NT letters,[30] and many have suggested that one can speak of a distinct literary form here. Since the influential study by Burton Scott Easton in the 1930s,[31] many have read NT vice and virtue lists against similar lists in the Hellenistic authors. These lists play a prominent role in Stoic philosophers, and drawing from such Hellenistic traditions Philo provides extensive lists that delineate the vices of those who follow their carnal desires (*Sacrifices* 32). In contrast, although the OT does contain a few vice lists (e.g., Prov 6:17–19; Jer 7:9; Hos 4:2), they "do not appear to be a well-developed literary form"; this suggests that NT authors "borrowed from Hellenistic literature and rhetoric."[32] This reading is followed by many, including commentators working through Colossians.[33]

While the existence of the numerous lists in Hellenistic literature argues for

---

29. Wright, *Colossians and Philemon*, 133.

30. Outside of NT letters, only a few vice (e.g., Mark 7:21–22) and virtue (e.g., Matt 5:3–11) lists can be identified.

31. Burton Scott Easton, "New Testament Ethical Lists," *JBL* 51 (1932): 1–12.

32. James L. Bailey and Lyle D. Vander Broek, *Literary Forms in the New Testament: A Handbook* (Louisville: Westminster John Knox, 1992), 65–66.

33. Schweizer, *Letter to the Colossians*, 188.

the significance of this literary form, the content of the NT lists is often quite different from their Hellenistic counterparts.[34] Instead of the four cardinal virtues emphasized in the Stoic traditions, for example, the emphasis in the NT lists often lies elsewhere. Even those who acknowledge the influence of such traditions point to other significant differences between the Hellenistic lists and NT lists, especially Paul's. Paul focuses on the prior act of God rather than the self-generation of human beings; Paul focuses on community rather than on virtues that exemplify the individual self; and Paul focuses not simply on state of mind but also on action.[35] If one insists on Paul's use of such traditions, one must also recognize the radical transformation of such traditions in his writings.[36]

The content of these lists points rather to Jewish traditions. In the OT, one can point to the Ten Commandments as providing the content of some of the NT lists.[37] Here, the note on "idolatry" in 3:5 as a summary of the vice list and some of the listed vices support this reading.[38] Other Pauline lists also show special interest in this foundational set of commands (cf. 1 Cor 5:9, 10; 1 Tim 1:9, 10).[39] Beyond the Ten Commandments, one can also point to the Holiness Code of Lev 17 – 26.[40] Paul's notes on sexual immorality (v. 5), anger, wrath, malice (v. 8), and love (v. 14) can all be found in Leviticus. The note on "idolatry" (v. 5; cf. Rom 1:25; Gal 5:19 – 21; Eph 5:5) may also remind the readers of the anti-idol polemic in OT (e.g., Isa 40:18 – 24; 41:4 – 7, 10; 44:9 – 11; Jer 10:1 – 16) and Jewish traditions (Wis 13:1 – 15:19; *Sib. Or.* 3.11 – 6). These traditions all serve to provide boundaries for the covenantal people of God.[41]

Function

Various functions can be detected behind the NT lists. Some deal with certain general patterns of behavior that challenge the integrity of the churches (e.g., 1 Cor 5:9 – 10; 6:9 – 10; 2 Cor 12:20) while others focus on the lifestyle imposed

---

34. Based on formal considerations that both the vice and virtue lists in Colossians contain a fivefold enumeration, some (e.g., Lohse, *Colossians and Philemon*, 137) have further pointed to an Iranian tradition that emphasizes five good and five evil deeds.

35. Troels Engberg-Pedersen, "Paul, Virtues and Vices," in *Paul in the Greco-Roman World: A Handbook* (ed. J. Paul Sampley; Harrisburgh, PA: Trinity International, 2003), 608 – 9. For the influence of Stoic thoughts on Paul, see also his *Paul and the Stoics* (Louisville: Westminster John Knox, 2000).

36. Engberg-Pedersen, "Paul, Virtues and Vices," 628: "He did radicalize what he found by extending it to what may well be called its logical end: now was the time, not only when what should be done could be done, but also when it could be done in such a way that any relic of the individual, bodily person would be wiped out completely by an exclusive directedness toward Christ."

37. Robert M. Grant, "The Decalogue in Early Christianity," *HTR* 40 (1947): 1 – 17.

38. See comments on v. 5 for a discussion of the individual vices in this list.

39. Cannon, *Use of Traditional Materials in Colossians*, 63.

40. See Bevere, *Sharing in the Inheritance*, 190 – 93, who further points to the Jewish two-way tradition (Deut 30:15 – 16; Ps 1:6; Prov 2:12 – 13; 4:18 – 19; Jer 21:8; cf. *Did.* 1 – 6).

41. Sexual immorality, a vice that tops a number of the lists (v. 5; cf. Rom 1:26 – 27; 13:13; 1 Cor 5:10 – 11; Eph 5:3; 1 Tim 1:10), often symbolizes the sins of the Gentiles. These sexual rules therefore reflect a concern to preserve "social boundaries" (Mary Douglas, *Natural Symbols: Explorations in Cosmology* [London: Routledge, 1996], 74).

by the false teachers (e.g., 1 Tim 1:9 – 10; 6:4 – 5; Titus 3:1 – 3).[42] For those who may have misunderstood his gospel of grace, Paul uses such lists in emphasizing the need to live in the Spirit (Gal 5:19 – 23).

In Colossians, these lists acquire a number of functions. As in other lists, Paul is perhaps using these lists in view of the challenges posited by the false teachers. In response to their emphasis on visionary experience and the worship of heavenly beings, these lists point to the need to focus on faithful obedience in everyday living.[43] Moreover, the individualistic emphasis of such religious experiences may also have prompted Paul to focus on the community as the context for faithful living. The second vice list (3:8) and the virtue list (3:12 – 14) clearly reflect this emphasis on interpersonal relationships. It is no exaggeration to assert that in these lists the church "is the real ethical subject."[44]

Beyond a response to elements of the false teachings, these lists also reflect their origin in the OT and Jewish traditions. As the Ten Commandments are grounded in the confession of God as the one and only God of Israel (Exod 20:2 – 6; Deut 5:6 – 8), the summary of the first list in terms of "idolatry" (v. 5) reflects this concern. Instead of supplying yet another set of new commandments, therefore, Paul is more concerned with the manifestations that point to the worship of the false deity. The affirmation of the final authority of Christ in 1:15 – 20 is now explicated by the encouragement of a pattern of behavior that reflects such an affirmation.

Reflecting the concerns of the Holiness Code, Paul's discussion here is also concerned with the identity of the people of God. The description of the "new humanity" replaces ethnic, cultural, and social criteria with the one that centers on Christ and points to a new identity for those who accept God's climactic act in history: "there is neither Greek nor Jew, circumcised nor uncircumcised, barbarian, Scythian, slave nor free, but Christ is all and in all" (v. 11). Some have further suggested that these vice and virtues lists reflect a baptismal liturgy.[45] Such a context would also explain Paul's notes on "the old humanity" (v. 9) and "the new humanity" (v. 10). He focuses on replacing old identity markers with new ones that center on Christ and him alone.[46] Believers have a new identity that lives out the grace and forgiveness they receive from God's mighty act through Christ on the cross and in his resurrection.

---

42. Some consider the lists of "qualifications" for church leaders noted in the Pastoral Letters (1 Tim 3:1 – 7, 8 – 13; Titus 1:6 – 16) as a reaction to the lifestyle of those threatening the church; cf. William D. Mounce, *Pastoral Epistles* (WBC 46; Nashville: Nelson, 2000), 155 – 60.

43. Cannon, *Use of Traditional Materials in Colossians*, 244.

44. Wolfgang Schrage, *The Ethics of the New Testament* (trans. David E. Green; Philadelphia: Fortress, 1988), 250.

45. See also Gal 5:17 – 24; Eph 5:3 – 14; David E. Aune, *The New Testament in Its Literary Environment* (LEC 8; Philadelphia: Westminster, 1987), 195.

46. It is in this sense that these lists point to the sectarian nature of the early church as it distinguishes itself from the wider world; cf. Wayne A. Meeks, *The Moral World of the First Christians* (LEC 6; Philadelphia: Westminster, 1987), 79 – 80.

3:5a Put to death, therefore, your earthly parts
(Νεκρώσατε οὖν τὰ μέλη τὰ ἐπὶ τῆς γῆς). This verse begins with the particle "therefore" (οὖν), which signals another stage of Paul's argument (cf. 2:6, 16; 3:1) as it builds on the previous call to focus on the risen Christ (3:1) and "the things above, not things on the earth" (3:2) while awaiting the full revelation of Christ's glory (3:4). The list of vices to be avoided represents the "things on the earth."

"Put to death" (νεκρώσατε) is built on the previous assertion that "you have died" (v. 3). The relationship between the previous indicative statement and the present aorist imperative must be noted. In the preceding discussion, Paul has emphasized the active work of God through Christ on behalf of those who believe in him. God is the one who "delivered us from the dominion of darkness and transferred us into the kingdom of his beloved Son" (1:13), and this is accomplished through "the blood of his [Christ's] cross" (1:20). While believers are called to participate in Christ's death and resurrection (2:11 – 12), Paul makes it clear that God has destroyed all opposing forces through Christ's death on the cross (2:14 – 15). In this context, therefore, the call to "put to death" the old practices is to be balanced by the recognition that Christ's death allows such an imperative to be a possibility. Moreover, this call is also based on the fact that believers were already "dead in [their] transgressions" (2:13). This call to "put to death" the old self is the living out of the victory that has already been won.

This call, therefore, means: "let the old man, who has already died in baptism, be dead."[47] This relationship between the indicative and the imperative is best explicated in an earlier Pauline letter:

For we know that our old self was crucified with him so that the body ruled by sin might be done away with, that we should no longer be slaves to sin — because anyone who has died has been set free from sin.... Count yourselves dead to sin but alive to God in Christ Jesus. Therefore do not let sin reign in your mortal body so that you obey its evil desires. (Rom 6:6 – 7, 11 – 12)

To "put to death" means to live with a recognition that one is already freed from the power of sin. This relationship between the imperative and the indicative is reflected in versions that translate the imperative as "consider ... as dead" (NASB) or "don't be controlled by" (CEV).

The direct object of putting to death is "your earthly parts" (τὰ μέλη τὰ ἐπὶ τῆς γῆς). The second article followed by the prepositional phrase functions as an adjectival modifier, thus "earthly." "Your ... parts" is commonly used in reference to body parts (see esp. 1 Cor 12:12 – 16). Since in Jewish traditions evil deeds are often related to the various parts of the body, some have taken "your earthly parts" as referring to these various parts doing various types of sins. "Your earthly parts" then refers to "your limbs as put to earthly purposes."[48] The translation adopted here assumes this background. Nevertheless, since the vice list that follows focuses primarily on sexual sins, it is also possible to read this phrase as referring to the general sinful nature of unredeemed humankind — thus, "whatever belongs to your earthly nature" (TNIV, NIV; cf. NET), or even "the sinful, earthly things lurking within you" (NLT).

3:5b-g Sexual immorality, impurity, lust, evil desires, and covetousness, which is idolatry
(πορνείαν, ἀκαθαρσίαν, πάθος, ἐπιθυμίαν κακήν, καὶ τὴν πλεονεξίαν ἥτις ἐστὶν εἰδωλολατρία). This

---

47. Lohse, *Colossians and Philemon*, 137.

48. Moule, *Epistles to the Colossians and to Philemon*, 115. A NT example can be found in Matt 5:29 – 30, and Rom 6:13 can also be understood in such terms. Barth and Blanke, *Co-*

lossians, 399, further point to the later rabbinic assertion that the various commandments correspond to the 248 members of the human body.

list provides examples of the believers' past unredeemed nature.[49] The first four items are directly related to sins of a sexual nature. "Sexual immorality" refers to various kinds of sexual transgressions; in the OT, it is also connected with idolatrous practices (Isa 47:10; Jer 3:9; Ezek 23:8; Mic 1:7; cf. Exod 34:15 – 16; Deut 31:16).[50]

"Impurity" is often used in reference to cultic impurity in the OT (Lev 5:3; 15:3, 30 – 31; 16:16; 22:4 – 5; Num 19:13; Judg 13:7; 2 Chr 29:5, 16), but it also appears in contexts where sexual immorality (Hos 2:10 [LXX 2:12]) and idolatry (Jer 19:13; 32:34 [LXX 39:34]; Ezek 7:20; 36:25) are discussed. In Paul, it is also often used in relation to sexual immorality (Rom 1:24; 2 Cor 12:21; Gal 5:19)[51] although it can refer to the general rejection of the holiness of God (1 Thess 4:7).

"Lust" (πάθος) literally reads "passion" (ASV, NAB, NASB, NRSV, NKJV, ESV), but in this context it most likely refers to "shameful passion" (NET) of a sexual nature.[52] This is confirmed by its use elsewhere in Paul, especially when this is used to characterize "the pagans, who do not know God" (1 Thess 4:5; cf. Rom 1:26).

"Evil desires" (lit., "evil desire," ἐπιθυμίαν κακήν) can refer to sinful desires in general (e.g., Rom 6:12; 7:8; 13:14; Gal 5:16) but in this context also likely refers to illicit sexual passion (e.g., Rom 1:24;

1 Thess 4:5). This term serves as a transition to the last vice, as the relationship between "evil desires" and "covetousness" is made clear in Rom 7:7: "I would not have known what coveting [ἐπιθυμίαν] really was if the law had not said, 'You shall not covet'" (Rom 7:7; cf. Exod 20:17; Deut 5:21).[53]

The final item, "covetousness" (πλεονεξίαν), together with the descriptive phrase, "which is idolatry," points to the background of this list in the Ten Commandments. The general background of the Ten Commandments to NT vice and virtue lists has already been noted,[54] and this is particularly clear in here.[55] Following various expressions of sexual transgressions, Paul ends with the command against covetousness (cf. Exod 20:17; cf. Deut 5:21). In the OT, this tenth commandment properly concludes the Ten Commandments in two ways. First, it is obviously different from the previous ones in that it "deals with motivation rather than action," especially "motivations behind the crimes … of commandments six through nine."[56] Second, it points back to the first set of commandments since all the crimes reflected in these commandments find their roots in their refusal to worship the one true God and thus are forms of idolatrous practices.

Although grammatically the phrase "which is idolatry" modifies only "covetousness," "covetous-

---

49. One should not expect any vice list to provide a comprehensive catalogue of vices, but only those that characterize certain aspects of one's moral inclinations; cf. Abraham J. Malherbe, *Moral Exhortation: A Greco-Roman Sourcebook* (LEC 4; Philadelphia: Westminster, 1986), 138.

50. See also Gal 5:19, where "sexual immorality" also tops the list for "acts of the flesh" (cf. Eph 5:3).

51. In light of the use of the term in Rom 1:24, Ed. L. Miller ("More Pauline References to Homosexuality?" *EvQ* 77 [2005]: 131) has further suggested that this term is to be distinguished from "sexual immorality," as "impurity" is used instead "as a condensed and perhaps euphemistic expression" in reference to homosexual behavior as described in 1 Cor 6:10. The wider use of this term in both the OT and NT does not support this reading, however.

52. BDAG, 748.

53. While the Greek verb "covet" (ἐπιθυμήσεις) recalls the tenth commandment in the LXX, "covetousness" (πλεονεξίαν) in this Colossian list uses a different word group.

54. See comments in "In Depth: Vice and Virtue Lists," above.

55. For a further discussion of allusions to the Ten Commandments in Col 3, see also Lars Hartman, "Code and Context: A Few Reflections on the Parenesis of Col 3:6 – 4:1," in *Tradition and Interpretation in the New Testament: Essays in Honor of E. Earle Ellis for His 60th Birthday* (ed. Gerald F. Hawthorne and Otto Betz; Grand Rapid: Eerdmans, 1988), 240 – 41.

56. David Noel Freedman, *The Nine Commandments: Uncovering the Hidden Pattern of Crime and Punishment in the Hebrew Bible* (ABRL; New York: Doubleday, 2000), 155.

ness" reflects the motive behind all the preceding vices. Paul instructs believers to avoid the various sexual vices because they are manifestations of covetousness, a general and comprehensive vice that points to the refusal to submit to the lordship of Christ. Paul is not randomly imposing a new list of selected regulations; rather, he is calling the believers to reject their idolatrous past and to worship the one Lord of all.

3:6 Because of these the wrath of God is coming [upon the sons of disobedience] (δι᾽ ἃ ἔρχεται ἡ ὀργὴ τοῦ θεοῦ [ἐπὶ τοὺς υἱοὺς τῆς ἀπειθείας]).

Paul uses the phrase "the wrath of God" to underline the significance of the above call to faithful living. Although the present manifestation of God's wrath is not foreign to Paul's thought (e.g., Rom 1:18 – 32), in light of the reference to the final revelation of Christ's glory in v. 4, it seems best to take this as a reference to the eschatological wrath of God to be revealed at the final judgment (cf. Rom 2:5; 5:9; 9:22; 1 Thess 1:10).[57] The contrast between participation in the final revelation of glory and the experience of God's wrath is illustrated in Rom 2:7 – 8:

> To those who by persistence in doing good seek glory, honor and immortality, he will give eternal life. But for those who are self-seeking and who reject the truth and follow evil, there will be wrath and anger.

Although one's evil deeds precipitate the final manifestation of God's wrath, one's good deeds cannot deliver that person from that wrath. Elsewhere, Paul makes it clear that for those who turn from idols, Jesus delivers them from God's coming wrath:

> They tell how you turned to God from idols to serve the living and true God, and to wait for his

Son from heaven, whom he raised from the dead — Jesus, who rescues us from the coming wrath. (1 Thess 1:9 – 10)

Therefore, one should not downplay God's salvific act through Christ (1:12 – 14, 20 – 23; 2:11 – 15) when the evil deeds to be avoided by believers are listed.

The authenticity of the prepositional phrase "upon the sons of disobedience" (ἐπὶ τοὺς υἱοὺς τῆς ἀπειθείας) is uncertain, and it is not included in some modern versions.[58] The appearance of this phrase in Eph 5:6 may have prompted some early scribes to insert it into this context, and it is not found in two of the earliest and most reliable manuscripts.[59] Both the internal and external evidence seem to provide a slightly stronger case for its omission. Thus, it is best to include it in parentheses (see UBS4 and NA27).

Regardless of whether the phrase comes from the parallel in Eph 5:6, Eph 2:2 – 3 is equally relevant as Paul describes the believers as those who formerly belong to "the sons of disobedience" and were "by nature the children of wrath" (NASB). Here in Colossians, Paul is likewise calling believers to reject their former lives as those who were "once alienated and hostile in mind" (1:21). The notes on "the wrath of God" and "the sons of disobedience" point again to the function of the vice list as providing the definition of God's people and thus consolidating the boundary between those who belong to Christ and those who refuse to submit to his lordship. The distinction is not simply a sociological one, for Paul emphasizes the eternal relevance for one's faithful submission to Christ.

3:7 In these you once walked, when you were living in them (ἐν οἷς καὶ ὑμεῖς περιεπατήσατέ ποτε

---

57. This is made explicit by the use of the future tense in some versions: "For it is because of these things that the wrath of God will come" (NASB; cf. NLT).

58. "The sons of disobedience" is a Semitic way of turn-

ing a noun into an adjectival modifier of another noun: "the disobedient ones."

59. 𝔓⁴⁶ B.

ὅτε ἐζῆτε ἐν τούτοις). Paul now makes it explicit that in the vice list above, he is characterizing the former life of the (Gentile) believers. Taken as a neuter relative pronoun, "these" (οἷς) most likely refers to the sins listed in v. 5.[60] Paul is criticizing the believers for participating in the sinful practices that characterized unbelievers.

The significant change in one's way of living has already been noted in 2:6, where Paul likewise adopted the metaphor of walking: "just as you received Christ Jesus the Lord, continue to walk in him." The contrast between their former lives and their present existence in Christ is highlighted by the temporal indicator "once" (ποτε), which has already appeared in 1:21: "you were once [ποτε] alienated and hostile in mind through evil deeds." The list in 3:5 has elaborated on such "evil deeds." In Paul, vice lists are often used to describe the former pattern of those now redeemed by Christ, and the content of the two vice lists here (vv. 5, 8) merges in Paul's later writings to make the same point (see Titus 3:3; cf. 1 Cor 6:9–11).[61]

The second part of the verse ("when you were living in them") seems redundant.[62] Word order in Greek, however, points to a chiastic structure with "then" and "when" at the center, highlighting the former pattern of behavior of these believers:

A   In these (ἐν οἷς)
  B   you walked (καὶ ὑμεῖς περιεπατήσατε)
    C   once (ποτε)
    C′   when (ὅτε)
  B′   you were living (ἐζῆτε)
A′   in them (ἐν τούτοις)

This emphasis on the past ("once" and "when") paves the way for the next verse, which begins with yet another temporal particle, "but now" (νυνὶ δέ). The contrast between the former life and the present status as followers of Christ becomes clear.

Others have also attempted to make sense of this apparent tautology by noting a development from the first to the second half of the verse. Drawing on the difference in nuances between "you … walked" and "you were living," some see the first part as focusing on "actual conduct" while the second describes a "general lifestyle,"[63] while others see the first as "the condition of their life" and the second as the "character of their practice."[64] While a semantic analysis of the two words may not justify such a distinction, in context a progression of thought seems clear. In light of 2:6, the metaphor of walking provides a general context in reference to lifestyle and behavior, while "living" points back to 2:20, where Paul makes a distinction between living in the world and dying to it with Christ. "Living" thus points more specifically to the life-death-resurrection metaphor used throughout this letter (1:18–20; 2:11–12, 13–14, 20). In any case, Paul is clearly calling believers to die to their former life as they participate in the worship of the risen Christ (3:1).

3:8 But now you also must put all these away: anger, rage, malice, slander, and abusive speech from your mouth (νυνὶ δὲ ἀπόθεσθε καὶ ὑμεῖς τὰ πάντα, ὀργήν, θυμόν, κακίαν, βλασφημίαν, αἰσχρολογίαν ἐκ τοῦ στόματος ὑμῶν). With this

---

60. Grammatically, it could be read as a masculine pronoun if "upon the sons of disobedience" is adopted as part of the text: "among whom you once walked" (cf. Wilson, *Colossians and Philemon*, 248). But even if this were the reading, the relative pronoun should be taken to refer to the sinful behavior of their former lives in light of the parallel in Eph 2:1–2.

61. In Ephesians, the contrast between the former and present lives is marked by references to light and darkness: "For you were once [ποτε] darkness, but now you are light in the Lord.

Live [lit., walk] as children of light" (Eph 5:8).

62. Many label the two parts of this verse as "tautology"; cf. Pokorný, *Colossians*, 167. See also Sumney, *Colossians*, 194, who sees this as serving an emphatic purpose.

63. Harris, *Colossians and Philemon*, 149. See also Wright, *Colossians and Philemon*, 136, who sees "the actual conduct" as revealing "the settled state of existence."

64. Lightfoot, *St. Paul's Epistles to the Colossians and to Philemon*, 213.

second list of vices, Paul shows how believers should act in building up their community in unity and love. "Put ... away" (ἀπόθεσθε) can refer to the general action of "to get rid of" (NLT), but in this context it may be related to the specific metaphor of putting away one's clothing. Elsewhere in Paul, this word is always used with the contrastive verb "to put on" (ἐνδύω, Rom 13:12 – 14; Eph 4:22 – 25), a verb also used by Paul in the arguments that follow (vv. 10, 12).[65] In other NT writings, however, the verb is also used in the general sense of getting rid of evil practices (Jas 1:21; 1 Pet 2:1).

The meaning of this verb depends on whether the various vices are to be considered as a group or whether the final phrase ("from your mouth") modifies all the members of this group. Defining the phrase "from your mouth" more narrowly, many understand it as attaching "to the end of the last as a way to reinforce the last two sins."[66] This reading is explicit in some versions: "But now you must get rid of all these things: anger, passion, and hateful feelings. No insults or obscene talk must ever come from your lips" (GNB).

In this context, however, it is best take "from your mouth" as referring to the entire group of vices: "But now have done with rage, bad temper, malice, slander, filthy talk — banish them all from your lips" (REB). First, since the final phrase in the previous list ("which is idolatry") modifies all the items, this last modifying phrase should likewise be understood that way. Elsewhere in Paul, evil speech out of one's mouth can also be understood as symbolizing a general refusal to worship God (Rom 3:10 – 18). Moreover, the "mouth" is portrayed as the primary vehicle through which one can submit to the lordship of Christ: "If you declare with your mouth, 'Jesus is Lord,' and believe in your heart that God raised him from the dead, you will be saved" (Rom 10:9). The various vices listed here are but expressions of one whose mouth refuses to confess Jesus as one's Lord.

This understanding is confirmed by Paul's subsequent arguments when he suggests that one should ground one's behavior in thanksgiving and praise (vv. 15 – 17). This contrast between sinful behavior as symbolized by one's evil speech and a life of worship is best illustrated by two other NT passages. First, in the parallel passage in Eph 5, after a list of sexual sins (Eph 5:3), Paul turns to a list of vices all related to speech: "obscenity, foolish talk [and] coarse joking" (Eph 5:4). This not only lends support to reading the second vice list in Col 3 as one that focuses on speech, but the alternate behavior Paul recommends also sheds light on the reasons behind his mentioning of such vices: "but rather thanksgiving" (Eph 5:4). This call to "thanksgiving" is a call to worship and confess God and his mighty deeds on behalf of his people.[67] The underlying problem behind those involved in evil speech is a refusal to worship God and submit to the lordship of his Son.

A second passage (one outside of Paul's letters) further confirms this reading. After a critique of those who cannot control their tongues (Jas 3:1 – 6), James provides the basis of such a critique in the need to choose between praising God with one's mouth and cursing others with the same mouth:

> With the tongue we praise our Lord and Father, and with it we curse human beings, who have been made in God's likeness. Out of the same mouth come praise and cursing. My brothers and sisters, this should not be. Can both fresh water and salt water flow from the same spring? (Jas 3:9 – 11)

---

65. See also Schweizer, *Letter to the Colossians*, 193, who considers the verb as marking the "transition to the image of clothing (vv 9 – 12)."

66. Moo, *Letters to the Colossians and Philemon*, 263.

67. See comments on 1:3 and 1:12. See also Pao, *Thanksgiving*, 86 – 118.

In Col 3, Paul appears to be making a similar argument. From a mouth that refuses to confess the singular lordship of Christ, one finds various kinds of evil acts and patterns of behavior. As such, this list is related to the previous catalogue in v. 5 in that both lists point to manifestations of acts of idolatry; and even though "from your mouth" modifies the entire list, the individual vices noted in this list are not limited to explicit verbal sins.

"Anger" (ὀργή) and "rage" (θυμός) have overlapping semantic fields. In the LXX, they often refer to the wrath of God (e.g., Num 12:9; 14:34; 32:14; Deut 13:17 [LXX 13:18]; Josh 7:26; 2 Chr 28:11; Isa 5:25), and in Paul they also appear with other vice lists (Eph 4:31). Although in certain contexts "anger" can denote "a more or less settled feeling of hatred" while "rage" refers to "a tumultuous outburst of passion,"[68] this distinction is not obvious in the biblical texts when the two terms are used together. If the manifestation of "anger" and "rage" in the OT is primarily the right of the sovereign and holy God, such behavior among human beings usurps divine right while assuming that one can function similarly as the ultimate judge.

"Malice" (κακία) also appears in NT vice lists (cf. Rom 1:29; Eph 4:31; Titus 3:3; 1 Pet 2:1). It can refer to evil disposition or even "malicious behavior" (NLT) that results from such a disposition. In Greco-Roman literature, the term often contrasts to "virtue" (ἀρετή) and can refer to the general "quality or state of wickedness."[69]

"Slander" (βλασφημία) can acquire the specific sense of "blasphemy" (KJV, NKJV) against God (Matt 12:31; 26:65; Mark 14:64; Luke 5:21; John 10:33; Rev 13:1, 5–6; 17:3), but it also appears in other vices for defamatory speech against others (Matt 15:19; Mark 7:22; Eph 4:31; 1 Tim 6:4). It is possible, however, that speaking against others should be understood as an act of blasphemy because to do so is to "curse human beings, who have been made in God's likeness" (Jas 3:9).

Finally, "abusive language" (αἰσχρολογία) can refer more specifically to "obscene language" (NAB) or even "dirty talk" (NJB; cf. NLT). In light of a related word in Eph 5:4 (αἰσχρότης, "obscenity," NIV) in the context of coarse and inappropriate speech, this narrower definition is not impossible. Nevertheless, since all previous vices are related primarily to displays of anger, a more general reference to "abusive language" is more likely. Although occurring only here in the NT, this term appears in extracanonical vice lists for abusive speech.[70] If so, this list points to expressions of anger that prevent one from participating in the community of God's people, which is characterized by unity and love (vv. 12–14).

3:9a Do not lie to one another (μὴ ψεύδεσθε εἰς ἀλλήλους).[71] Concluding his discussion on vices, Paul urges the believers to live a life in truth. This isolated call is often considered as yet another command that grows from the concerns expressed above: "The same concerns for relationships of mutual confidence and respect continue in a warning against lying to one another."[72] It is best to

68. Lightfoot, *St. Paul's Epistles to the Colossians and to Philemon*, 214.

69. BDAG, 500; cf. Xenophon, *Mem.* 1, 2, 28; Aristotle, *Rhet.* 2, 6.

70. Epictetus, *Diatr.* 4.4.46. For a discussion of this word group especially in relation to slander, see also Jeremy F. Hultin, *The Ethics of Obscene Speech in Early Christianity and Its Environment* (NovTSup 128; Leiden: Brill, 2008), 157–60, 166, 208.

71. Instead of the well-supported reading of the negated present imperative (μὴ ψεύδεσθε), the early and usually reliable 𝔓46 has the negative present subjunctive instead (μὴ ψεύδησθε). This use is attested in at least one other early papyrus and may well represent the original reading (cf. Stanley E. Porter, "P.Oxy. 744.4 and Colossians 3,9," *Bib* 73 [1992]: 565–67). This does not affect the meaning of this verse, however.

72. Dunn, *Epistles to the Colossians and to Philemon*, 219; cf. O'Brien, *Colossians, Philemon*, 188.

consider this call as summarizing the previous list that involves primarily the sins "from your mouth" (v. 8).[73]

The act of lying should not be considered simply as a verbal act of making a false statement. In the biblical material, to lie is to deny the Truth as represented by God himself. This is best illustrated in Paul's own statement in Romans: "They exchanged the truth about God for a lie, and worshiped and served created things rather than the Creator — who is forever praised. Amen" (Rom 1:25). Significantly, this verse also appears in a vice list that depicts the sinful behavior of the Gentiles (1:26 – 30), and it mentions the act of lying as these Gentiles worship idols instead of the Creator God. This accusation reappears in Rom 2:8: "But for those who are self-seeking and who reject the truth and follow evil, there will be wrath and anger." To Paul, therefore, the act of lying is an active denial of the truth that can only be found in God. "Do not lie," therefore, provides the proper conclusion to the vice list in v. 8, and the fact that lying is to be equated to idolatry also links this second list with the first (v. 5).

"To one another" provides the link between offenses directed against God and those against others. As lying is understood as an idolatrous act, lying "to one another" is to act within a community that denies the truth of God. The same connection between vertical and horizontal relationships is also expressed by this reciprocal pronoun in v. 13, where Paul urges believers to "forgive one another" as they have been forgiven by God. This pronoun

points to the community as the context through which vices are to be avoided and virtues to be practiced (cf. vv. 10 – 12).

3:9b For you have taken off the old humanity with its practices (ἀπεκδυσάμενοι τὸν παλαιὸν ἄνθρωπον σὺν ταῖς πράξεσιν αὐτοῦ). Paul now grounds the previous exhortation with a note on their new identity in Christ. Although considered by some to be an imperatival participle,[74] "for you have taken off" is best taken as a causal adverbial participle providing the grounds for the previous all-encompassing call to recognize and acknowledge the truth. This distinction is important because the act of taking off the old humanity is already an accomplished fact, and Paul is pointing instead to the implications of that act.[75]

In light of 2:11 – 15, where one also finds the metaphor of taking off clothing (ἀπεκδυσάμενος, v. 15), this participle likely reflects the background of baptism, when believers participate in the death and resurrection of Christ. Together with the call to "put on" (ἐνδύσασθε) in v. 12, however, this pair also points to the use of the clothing metaphor.[76] Some have understood the coexistence of these two metaphors as rooted in OT practice, where the priest washed himself with water before clothing himself with the sacred garment as he approached God (cf. Exod 29:4 – 9; Lev. 16:3 – 4).[77]

This clothing metaphor also likely alludes to the Adam account in Genesis. As God provided a new set of clothing for the fallen humans (Gen 3:7, 21), here Paul uses this change of clothing to signify the believers' "inaugurated new-creation relationship

---

73. Thus Schweizer, *Letter to the Colossians*, 193.

74. Roy Yates, "The Christian Way of Life: The Paraenetic Material in Colossians 3:1 – 4:6," *EvQ* 63 (1991): 247.

75. Cf. Rudolf Schnackenburg, *Present and Future: Modern Aspects of New Testament* Theology (Notre Dame, IN: Univ. of Notre Dame Press, 1966), 90.

76. Some have argued for an either/or option here and deny the significance of the baptismal imagery because of Paul's re-

jection of ritualism; cf. Ben Witherington III and G. François Wessels, "Do Everything in the Name of the Lord: Ethics and Ethos in Colossians," in *Identity, Ethics, and Ethos in the New Testament* (ed. Jan G. van der Watt; BZNW 141; Berlin: de Gruyter, 2006), 311.

77. See Jung Hoon Kim, *The Significance of Clothing Imagery in the Pauline Corpus* (JSNTSup 268; London: T&T Clark, 2004), 158.

with God."[78] The reference to the new creation ("according to the image of their Creator") in v. 10 confirms this allusion. Elsewhere in Paul, "the old humanity" refers to "the body ruled by sin" (Rom 6:6). In the present context, Paul points not only to the regeneration of one's nature, but also to the new community that is created, a community that bears the image of God. For those reading through the lens of individualism, the climactic statement in v. 11 is surprising since it defines not one's inner being but the new community of God's people: "where there is neither Greek nor Jew, circumcised nor uncircumcised, barbarian, Scythian, slave nor free" (v. 11).

Paul's assertion here is a natural progression of his arguments begun in 1:15 – 20, where the church is identified as the body of Christ in the new creation (1:18). Unlike the false teachers, who seem to have focused on private religious experience, Paul focuses on a community of regenerated persons who testify to God's work through Christ in the new created order. In this reading, "the old humanity" refers to those who belong to the old lineage of the first Adam, while "the new humanity" belongs to Christ (cf. 1 Cor 15:22, 45). Though these phrases have often been rendered as "the old/new man" (KJV, ASV, NKJV, NET, HCSB) or "the old/new self" (NAB, NASB, NRSV, NJB, GNB, TNIV, ESV, NIV), in light of Paul's emphasis on the creation of a new community, "the old/new humanity"[79] best captures Paul's intention here as these phrases "derive their force not simply from some individual change of character, but from a corporate recreation of humanity."[80]

3:10 And have put on the new humanity, being renewed in knowledge according to the image of their Creator (καὶ ἐνδυσάμενοι τὸν νέον τὸν ἀνακαινούμενον εἰς ἐπίγνωσιν κατ' εἰκόνα τοῦ κτίσαντος αὐτόν). Corresponding to the act of taking off "the old humanity" (v. 9), Paul calls the believers to "put on the new humanity."[81] Like the participle "taken off," "put on" is also a causal adverbial participle providing further grounds for Paul's previous call to avoid behavior that reflects the "old humanity." Clearly, Paul has fully shifted to the clothing metaphor as he points to a decisive and drastic change brought by the cross and resurrection.

The presence of the attributive participle "being renewed" (ἀνακαινούμενον), which modifies the substantive "the new [humanity]" (τὸν νέον), may appear to be a paradox: "the new being renewed again."[82] The juxtaposition of these terms is important for a number of reasons. First, "the new humanity" points to the decisive incorporation of believers in Christ, while the participle "being renewed" points to the ongoing participation of believers as they become what they are already. This is consistent with Paul's emphasis on the daily involvement of believers in this process: "our inner self is being renewed day by day" (2 Cor 4:16 ESV).[83] This tension points again to the "already but not yet" tension typical of Pauline theology. For those who only see a realized eschatology in Christian existence, this offers a corrective note.

Second, the passive voice of this participle points to God as the ultimate agent. The temporal

---

78. Beale, "Colossians," 866.

79. Or at least "the old/new nature" (REB, NLT).

80. Moule, *Epistles to the Colossians and to Philemon*, 119. See also Darrell L. Bock, "'The New Man' as Community in Colossians and Ephesians," in *Integrity of Heart, Skillfulness of Hands* (ed. Charles H. Dyer and Roy B. Zuck; Grand Rapids: Baker, 1994), 157 – 67.

81. Elsewhere, Paul calls the believers to put on Christ himself (Rom 13:14; Gal 3:27).

82. Cf. Harris, *Colossians and Philemon*, 152.

83. This is the only other appearance of "to renew" (ἀνακαινόω) in the NT. But see the related verb (ἀνακαινίζω) in Heb 6:6 in reference to the possibility of those who have fallen away being renewed. The nominal form (ἀνακαίνωσις) occurs in Rom 12:2 and Titus 3:5.

tension between God's past act through Christ and the present Christian involvement is therefore supplemented by the tension between divine agency and human responsibility.

Third, the use of the verb "to renew" (ἀνακαινόω) may also be important in revealing the work of the triune God. In Paul, the renewal of believers is often the work of the Holy Spirit (Titus 3:5; cf. Eph 3:16).[84] If so, God calls believers to put on the new humanity created by his new creative act through his Son, and the Spirit continues to work through them as they grow into what has been prepared for them. This tension, therefore, sheds light on the unfolding of God's plan for humanity through his Son and the Holy Spirit.

"In knowledge according to the image of their Creator" again alludes to the Genesis creation account.[85] "Knowledge" may echo the centrality of "knowledge" in the account of the fall in Gen 2 – 3, so that "being renewed in knowledge" points to the reversal of the effect of the fall through God's new creative act in Christ. "The image of their Creator"[86] clearly alludes to Gen 1:26 – 27.

In light of the previous reference to Christ's role in both the old and new creations (1:15 – 20), it is not impossible to take this "Creator" as Christ himself.[87] In this context, however, it is better to take it as a reference to God the Father. In light of the allusion to Gen 1:26 – 27, a reference to God the Father is to be assumed. Since Christ himself was "the image of the invisible God" in Col 1:15, the christocentric emphasis is retained here, where

Paul is urging believers to conform to Christ, who is the perfect image of the Creator. "When God recreates Man, it is in the pattern of Christ, who is God's absolute Likeness."[88] As such, the process of renewal is also a christocentric one: "Since man has been created after the image of God, i.e., Christ, assimilation to God must also take place via Christ."[89]

3:11 Where there is neither Greek nor Jew, circumcised nor uncircumcised, barbarian, Scythian, slave nor free, but Christ is all and in all (ὅπου οὐκ ἔνι Ἕλλην καὶ Ἰουδαῖος, περιτομὴ καὶ ἀκροβυστία, βάρβαρος, Σκύθης, δοῦλος, ἐλεύθερος, ἀλλὰ [τὰ] πάντα καὶ ἐν πᾶσιν Χριστός). The climax of this discussion of the "new humanity" comes with this verse, which provides definition for this community. Paul makes it clear that he is not focusing narrowly on the behavior of an individual; rather, his concerns center on the upbuilding of the community of God's people.

"Neither Greek nor Jew" is a familiar contrastive pair in Paul's letters.[90] It can refer to the different stages in God's redemptive plan (Rom 1:16; 2:10), and as the basic categories that divide humanity in the eyes of the Jews, this pair can also point to the universal human predicament (Rom 3:9) and the corresponding universal lordship of Christ (10:12; 1 Cor 1:24). Thus, the word "Greek" is not a narrow ethnic label pointing simply to those who are "Greek" by birth; it applies to anyone influenced by Greek culture or, even more broadly, to anyone who is not identified as a Jew (e.g., John 7:35).

---

84. Fee, *God's Empowering Presence*, 647.

85. See, in particular, Beale, "Colossians," 865.

86. This phrase with the singular third person masculine pronoun literally reads "the image of the one who creates him." Nevertheless, in light of our reading of τὸν νέον as the "new humanity," and in light of Paul's understanding of this phrase in community terms, it is best to translate the pronoun as a third person plural pronoun.

87. Thus Fee, *Pauline Christology*, 304; cf. Rom 8:29, where one finds the conformation to "the image of his Son."

88. Moule, *Epistles to the Colossians and to Philemon*, 120.

89. George H. van Kooten, *Paul's Anthropology in Context: The Image of God, Assimilation to God, and Tripartite Man in Ancient Judaism, Ancient Philosophy and Early Christianity* (WUNT 232; Tübingen: Mohr Siebeck, 2008), 217.

90. It is also a pair that appears often in Acts (14:1; 18:4; 19:10, 17; 20:21) in the context of early Christian missionary activities.

Some versions have, therefore, justifiably chosen to translate the term "Greek" as "Gentile" (NLT, TNIV, NIV).[91]

"Circumcised nor uncircumcised" often refers to "Jews" and "Gentiles" respectively, and they also appear elsewhere in contrastive terms (Rom 2:25 – 27; 3:30; 4:9 – 12; 1 Cor 7:19; Gal. 2:7; 5:6; Eph 2:11). The point here is well expressed in Gal 6:15, a verse that also refers to the community of God's new creative act: "Neither circumcision nor uncircumcision means anything; what counts is the new creation." The presence of a contrastive pair that essentially repeats the preceding phrase, "neither Greek nor Jew," may be explained by the ethnic barrier set up by the false teachers, who were insisting on certain elements of Jewish identity markers (cf. 2:16 – 23). The notes on "circumcision" (2:11) and "uncircumcision" (2:13) mentioned above may also have prompted Paul to emphasize this contrastive pair.

The pair "barbarian, Scythian" is more difficult to explain. "Barbarian" often refers to those who do not speak Greek,[92] and it is thus considered to be someone who is not only a "foreigner"[93] but also "uncivilized."[94] "Scythian" points to the inhabitants north of the Black Sea. The Scythians were often considered to be an extreme example of "barbarian" (i.e., "the lowest type of barbarian").[95] But then this pair appears out of place since the other pairs are clearly contrastive in nature.[96] Presupposing a Cynic background of the Colossian false teachers,

who may have identified themselves as Scythians, Troy Martin has suggested that this pair should be understood from a Scythian perspective: "From a Scythian viewpoint, the term barbarian means anyone who is a non-Scythian."[97] Paul is then directly reacting against this Cynic perspective in breaking down barriers between different people groups. Attractive though this proposal may be, it is difficult to explain how "Scythian" should be paired with "barbarian" instead of "Greek."[98]

A more plausible case has been proposed by Douglas Campbell, who suggests that Scythians are to be understood as "slaves," and they are opposed to the free "barbarians."[99] This proposal not only maintains the contrasting nature of this pair, but it also explains the relationship between the first and second pair, and thus the third and fourth:

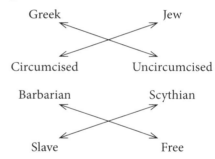

Paul is therefore arguing against the distinction between circumcised Jews and uncircumcised Greeks, and also that between free barbarians and Scythian slaves. Although this theory may lack extensive literary support,[100] this would at least

---

91. Thus also BDAG, 318.

92. See esp. Rom 1:14, where the term βάρβαρος is contrasted with "Greeks."

93. For this use, see 1 Cor 14:11; see also Acts 28:2, 4.

94. Louw and Nida, §41.31.

95. Lightfoot, *St. Paul's Epistles to the Colossians and to Philemon*, 218 – 19, who provides ancient examples for this usage. Cf. "savages" (GNB).

96. Those who deny the contrastive nature of the other pairs ("Greek, Jew, barbarian, Scythian") point to people groups in the West, East, South, and North (cf. Otto Michel,

"Σκύθης," *TDNT*, 7:449). This, however, lacks support in both extracanonical literature and is inconsistent with the use of at least some of these terms in Paul's own writings.

97. Troy Martin, "The Scythian Perspective in Col 3:11," *JBL* 114 (1995): 253.

98. Cf. Douglas A. Campbell, "The Scythian Perspective in Col. 3:11: A Response to Troy Martin," *NovT* 39 (1997): 81 – 84.

99. Douglas A. Campbell, "Unraveling Colossians 3.11b," *NTS* 42 (1996): 120 – 32. This is based on Pliny (*Nat.* 4.80 – 81), who uses "Scythian" to refer to slaves near the Black Sea.

100. See the response by Troy Martin, "Scythian Perspective

explain both the structure and the content of this series.

The final pair, "slave nor free," is an obvious pair that points to contrastive social status; it has appeared both in Paul in a literal (1 Cor 12:13; Gal 3:28) and a metaphorical sense (Rom 6:20; 1 Cor 7:21 – 22; Eph 6:8), and elsewhere in the NT (1 Pet 2:16; Rev 6:15; 13:16; 19:19). A discussion of the relationship between master and slave also appears in 3:22 – 4:1. Paul grounds his critique of the social division of his time in the theological affirmation that we have all been slaves to sin, and freedom can only be found in Christ: "For the one who was a slave when called to faith in the Lord is the Lord's freed person; similarly, the one who was free when called is Christ's slave" (1 Cor 7:22; cf. Gal 4:21 – 31).

These contrasts are consistent with Paul's statement elsewhere when he affirms the unity brought by God's redemptive work through Christ: "There is neither Jew nor Gentile, neither slave nor free, nor is there male and female, for you all are one in Christ Jesus" (Gal 3:28; cf. 1 Cor 12:13). The lack of the gender pair in Col 3:11 list may be explained by the subsequent discussion of husband and wife in 3:18 – 19,[101] though this would not explain the presence of the slave-free pair in spite of its reappearance in 3:22 – 4:1. More likely Paul formulates this structure in light of the challenges the Colos-

sian believers are facing. It seems that ethnic and class distinction played a part in the formulation of the false teachings, but gender seems less of an issue.[102]

The portrayal of the unity of this new humanity is important for Paul as he points to the impact of the universal reconciliation achieved by Christ's death and resurrection (1:18 – 20; cf. 2:15). This is expressed in the final clause: "Christ is all and in all." Here, however, the "all" moves from cosmological affirmations to its ecclesiological significance: since Christ has conquered all, all peoples now can participate in this one body. As such this gospel, which centers on Christ's work, is proclaimed all over the world (1:6, 23). Behind this affirmation of the unity of God's people is also the recognition of the diversity found in this new humanity,[103] and each group will play a part as they live out Christ's lordship.

Finally, this cosmological and ecclesiological reality also carries its own ethical impact, and this present section points precisely to a new heavenly perspective even for earthly living (cf. 3:1 – 4).[104] In further unpacking this "all and in all," Paul will continue to demonstrate the relevance of this confession for both the community of God's people (3:12 – 4:1) and those presently outside this community (4:2 – 6).

---

or Elusive Chiasm: A Reply to Douglas A. Campbell," *NovT* 41 (1999): 256 – 64.

101. Dennis R. MacDonald, *There Is No Male and Female: The Fate of a Dominical Saying in Paul and Gnosticism* (Philadelphia: Fortress, 1987), 128.

102. See, e.g., the appearance of only one pair in Rom 10:12, a letter that focuses on the issue of Jews and Gentiles: "For there is no difference between Jew and Gentile — the same Lord is Lord of all and richly blesses all who call on him." The comprehensive list in Gal 3:28 may in turn be emphatic as Paul points

to the three possible widespread distinctions among people groups. Others (Bevere, *Sharing in the Inheritance*, 120) prefer to see behind these lists a pre-Pauline formula from which he formulates statements appropriate to each context.

103. This has been aptly labeled as "christological pluralism" (Tomson, *Paul and the Jewish Law*, 93).

104. Some have also detected "utopian associations" here, thus highlighting the realized eschatology of Paul as he responds to the false teachers; cf. Maier, "A Sly Civility," 341 – 44.

Theology in Application

Spirituality and Eschatology

Reading through Col 2, where one finds Paul criticizing the false teachers for their promotion of the worship of heavenly beings (2:18), the readers may be surprised to find the call to "seek the things above" (v. 1) at the beginning of a section that contains exhortation for the believers (vv. 1 – 4). In numerous ways, however, Paul makes it clear that he is not calling his readers to return to the search for spiritual fulfillment in their particular experiences as they seek to encounter those heavenly beings.

First, instead of esoteric experiences, Paul points to Christ alone, who is "seated at the right hand of God." This distinct christocentric perspective is consistent with his arguments earlier (cf. 1:15 – 20; 2:8, 13 – 15, 16 – 17) as Paul emphasizes that the only proper goal of any spiritual journey is Christ and he alone.

Second, while this section begins with the call for believers to act, the focus quickly shifts to the act of Christ himself. As one's "life is hidden with Christ in God" (v. 3), one's fulfillment depends only on God's further work in and through Christ.

Third, since one's fulfillment is dependent on the act of Christ and not one's ability or achievement, all who have been "buried with him in baptism" (2:12) are able to gain access to this fulfillment, which can be found in Christ. Instead of a private and elitist experience, therefore, Paul emphasizes the universal accessibility of the powerful work of the cross, one that brings reconciliation to all things, "whether things on earth, or things in heaven" (1:20).

Finally, and perhaps most striking of all, Paul introduces the eschatological perspective, when he mentions the future participation of the revelation of Christ's glory at the end times. The glory that one seeks in one's private religious experiences through either heavenly ascent or the worship of heavenly beings is to be superseded by the public revelation of Christ's glory, when all who have died and have been raised in him can find true fulfillment in this consummation of God's work in Christ.

In numerous ways, this eschatological perspective is critical for appreciating a spirituality that is faithful to the gospel message. The reference to the revelation of "Christ … in glory" in the end times is but the consummation of God's work in Christ through his death and resurrection. For believers, the death, resurrection, and return of Christ form the basis of any call to faithful living. Again, one finds the indicative as the basis of the imperative, which is "just the reverse of Aristotelian and indeed all human religious approaches to holiness."[105]

In repeatedly emphasizing the mighty acts of God through Christ, Paul calls believers to abandon their self-centered preoccupation with their statuses, even their

---

105. Robert Paul Roth, "Christ and the Powers of Darkness: Lessons from Colossians," *WW* 6 (1986): 344.

spiritual statuses, as they participate in the metanarrative with Christ at the center of this drama of salvation. This is then another call to abandon an idolatrous life and turn to a life that centers on the one who alone deserves all honor and worship. Any discussion of spirituality that is not attentive to God's promise to complete his work through Christ can easily become a trap that ironically lures one away from the true worship of God.

To acknowledge the reality of the fulfillment of God's promise in the future complete redemption of the body is to realize the need to be faithful in one's present existence. The failure to affirm this objective reality leads to a false understanding of the significance of Christ's death and resurrection. An example can be found in a recent treatment on spirituality that adopts an existential reading of the meaning of Christ in which dying to Christ is interpreted as death to an insistence of "a heterosexual orientation" and "a judgmental image of God," while resurrection becomes the awakening "to a gay or lesbian identity, a God of unconditional love, or the realization that the church is a fallible and, at times, oppressive and damaging institution."[106] One wonders if this understanding of spirituality is precisely the kind that Paul is seeking to correct when he insists on the sovereignty of Christ, who is not only the liberator of the oppressed but the one who challenges all forces that distract one from conforming "to the image of their Creator" (v. 10). Moreover, the note on "the wrath of God" in v. 6 reminds one that the glorious Christ is also the holy God, who demands full obedience.

An eschatological spirituality is, therefore, not an escapist ideology that allows its followers to downplay the significance of the present, earthly existence. This point is already implicitly noted in the tension between the singular "Christ," who is in heaven (v. 1), and the plural "things above," on which one is supposed to focus (v. 2). These "things" are further explicated as Paul urges believers to lead a faithful life precisely because they are focused on the exalted Christ. For Paul, then, "believers should (to adapt a modern idiom) be so heavenly minded that they do more earthly good."[107]

Finally, this critical eschatological spirituality unmasks all present imposters who claim to be the realization of God's kingdom on earth. To identify the consummation of God's work in the present age without sufficient attention to the glorious future can easily lead to "enslavement to current ideology, be it liberal democracy, feminism or green politics."[108] Since God is the one who brings about this new creation through Christ, he is the only one who can complete this new creative act when Christ returns

---

106. Jean Stairs, *Listening for the Soul: Pastoral Care and Spiritual Direction* (Minneapolis: Fortress, 2000), 99.

107. Craig S. Keener, "Heavenly Mindedness and Earthly Good: Contemplating Matters Above in Colossians 3.1 – 2," *JGRChJ* 6 (2009): 185. See also Keener's discussion in this article of the challenge of Paul's call in 3:1 – 4 for an ancient audience whose vision of the transcendent was often abstract and transcendent, as testified by the writings of philosophers, mystics, and apocalyptic visionaries.

108. Simon Chan, *Spiritual Theology: A Systematic Study of the Christian Life* (Downers Grove, IL: InterVarsity Press, 1998), 186.

in glory. To downplay the future only leads to a false perception of God's work in the present age. Certainly, God works through the church to redeem people and incidentally culture today. Historically, however, some groups have attempted to inaugurate heaven on earth through ascetic communities or other cloisters. This self/ human-generated attempt misses the point of Colossians. Paul emphasizes that the church must live in light of the accomplished new reality even though things are not yet consummated and physically perceptible. Paul is focused on right action in light of God's work in Christ, not the bringing about a new kingdom on earth. Christ accomplished a new reality, and he alone will bring it to consummation.

Put to Death the Earthly Parts

In our previous discussion, we offered cautionary notes concerning the function of the ethical imperatives in Paul.[109] In this section, however, one cannot ignore the clear and direct call to avoid certain vices. Without taking the two lists (vv. 5, 8) as comprehensive, they do sufficiently represent behaviors that betray one's identity as God's redeemed people. Both lists directly lend themselves to application, and numerous examples can be cited in bringing to life these vices.

The significance of the first list is noted with the final item linked with an explanatory phrase: "covetousness, which is idolatry" (v. 5). As noted in the exegetical discussion, this final note connects the list to the Ten Commandments. Lust and illicit sexual behavior are expressions of covetousness, which are considered to be idolatrous acts because of the displacement of God as the proper object of worship. Beyond marital infidelity and other immoral acts, contemporary readers should also be reminded that pornography, which is so prevalent among Christians and even clergy, does not simply involve a "two-dimensional artifact" but is itself "a series of activities" that reduces the person (often a woman) to a subordinate tool devoid of the dignity as one created in the image of God.[110]

Often considered as belonging to a different category, premarital sexual acts that glorify the supremacy of love often loom large in church youth programs, but a repressive strategy is often imposed without a proper positive focus on the need to divert one's energy in the pleasure of worshiping God. Paul reminds us that the root of these vices lies in covetousness, which can be defined as "the loss of contentment in Christ so that we start to crave other things to satisfy the longings of our heart."[111] As sexual desires touch on the deepest cravings of one's soul, their manifestation reflects whether one is able to lead a christocentric life through faith in God's redemptive act in Christ. This in turn explains why sexual vices often appear in vice lists in Paul (Rom 1:26–27; 13:13; 1 Cor 5:10–11; Eph 5:3; 1 Tim 1:10).

---

109. See Theology in Application for previous chapter.

110. Susan G. Cole, *Pornography and the Sex Crisis* (Toronto: Amanita, 1989), 22.

111. John Piper, *Future Grace* (Sisters, OR: Multnomah, 1995), 224.

In the second list (v. 8), one finds various forms of vices related to the untamed tongue. The connection with James 3 has already been established insofar as violent verbal acts are considered acts that contradict the confession of the lordship of Christ. Notes on anger and wrath (v. 8) in the context of a reference to "the image of their Creator" (v. 10) point to the relevance of a book that contains an intense focus on speech ethics (Jas 1:19, 26; 3:1 – 12; 4:11 – 12; 5:9, 12), and where speech is considered "the index of a person's whole moral being."[112] In 3:9, James makes it clear that to insult a person is to insult the Creator in whose image the person had been created: "With the tongue we praise our Lord and Father, and with it we curse human beings, who have been made in God's likeness." To insult a person is therefore to take on the posture of the Creator, who alone has the right to judge his creation. Instead, believers are called to the humble worship of the Creator God — a point that is well made by Jeremy Taylor in the classic work, *The Rule and Exercises of Holy Living and Holy Dying*:

> Humility is the most excellent natural cure for anger in the world; for he that by daily considering his own infirmities and failings makes the error of his neighbour or servant to be his own case, and remembers that he daily needs God's pardon and his brother's charity, will not be apt to rage at the levities, or misfortunes, or indiscretions, of another.[113]

In the context of Colossians, this vice list should also be understood in light of the repeated affirmation of the final authority of Christ. To be involved in violent speech acts is to refuse to submit to the lordship of Christ and is thus an idolatrous act. Moreover, as in James 3, where abusive speech is an act of denying the truth (Jas 3:14), Paul concludes the list with a call to acknowledge the truth in one's daily living (v. 9). His exhortation is therefore one that centers on the integrity of faithful living that is consistent with the confession of believers.

Put on Christ, the New Uniform

In adopting the clothing metaphor with the call to "put ... away" (v. 8) and "put on" (v. 10), Paul draws attention to the need to shed one's identity and put on a common identity that conforms to the reality one finds in Christ. This uniformity, which results in the conformity to "the image of their Creator" (v. 10), creates a new social self within a community that is to be distinguished by nothing else but "Christ," who is "all and in all" (v. 11).

The significant social and political implications are highlighted by Paul's

---

112. Richard Bauckham, "James and Jesus," in *The Brother of Jesus: James the Just and His Mission* (ed. Bruce Chilton and Jacob Neusner; Louisville: Westminster John Knox, 2001), 127.

113. Jeremy Taylor, *The Rule and Exercises of Holy Living and of Holy Dying* (London: Longman, Brown, Green, and Longmans, 1850), 197.

definition of the new humanity in communal terms: "where there is neither Greek nor Jew, circumcised nor uncircumcised, barbarian, Scythian, slave nor free" (v. 11). Although the Jews were not distinguished by their clothing, the Greeks and Romans did notice the distinct clothing practices of various people groups.[114] To suggest that believers put on a distinct set of clothing is to call the believers to participate in a "communion of the different"[115] as they distinguish themselves as those belonging to Christ alone.

The power of this clothing metaphor is well illustrated by a sociocultural analysis of clothing practices:

> Clothing functions to indicate personal identities, social and cultural positions and roles. For example, garments worn may indicate that one is male, female, young, old, wealthy, poor, monarch, peasant, priest, minister, civilian, soldier, athlete, prisoner, judge, academic or many other things. A redressed person may be a re-formed or re-presented person, one who has a changed identity and a changed social role.[116]

Not only does the clothing of a person reflect on his or her social and political identity; the wearing of a specific type of clothing also aids in transforming the self-understanding of a person: "Constant wearing of official costume can so transform someone that it becomes difficult or impossible for him or her to react normally."[117] In the case of a uniform, when the entire community follows the same clothing practices, it transforms the individual's personality into a social identity where one acts within the boundaries within a code of behavior dictated by the wider community.

In light of the significance of clothing practices, therefore, Paul's use of the clothing metaphor takes on added significance. To outsiders, believers are to be identified as those belonging to Christ. To the believers, this act of adopting a new set of clothing will affect their behavioral pattern as they externalize their confession under the lordship of Christ. Though no longer unique within the group, this group is to be different from the rest of humanity as it transcends social, cultural, and ethnic barriers in testifying to the transformative power of the gospel of the cross.

In our times, communities of God's believers still need to be called to witness this new social and cultural identity. It has been noted that "at 11:00 on Sunday morning when we stand and sing and Christ has no east or west, we stand at the most segre-

---

114. Cf. Shaye J. D. Cohen, *The Beginnings of Jewishness: Boundaries, Varieties, Uncertainties* (Berkeley, CA: Univ. of California Press, 1999), 30 – 34, who also notes that although the OT describes two distinct items for the Israelites (*ṣîṣit* and *pātîl*; Num 15:37 – 41; cf. Deut 22:12), the absence of any reference to these items in Gentile sources suggest they were not followed at least by Jews in Diaspora communities.

115. Daniel Migliore, *Faith Seeking Understanding* (Grand Rapids: Eerdmans, 1991), 200 – 205.

116. Roy R. Jeal, "Clothes Makes the (Wo)man," *Scriptura* 90 (2005): 686. For an insightful analysis of the change in clothing practices as reflecting social and historical changes of a community as it interacts with foreign elements, see Eileen Chang, "A Chronicle of Changing Clothes," *Positions* 11 (2003): 427 – 41.

117. Alison Lure, *The Language of Clothes* (New York: Random House, 1981), 18.

gated hour in this nation."[118] In other parts of the world, similar observations can be made in Christian communities, whether it is the remnant of a colonial past or the result of more recent labor movements where different people groups converge in one locale.

Those preaching or teaching on this text may want to take the opportunity to encourage their audience to wrestle with ways in which the unity of God's people can be lived out in their own contexts. The disunities are not exclusively racial as Paul indicates, and they often involve economic, educational, and social stratifications and biases imported from the larger culture. Some have attempted to merge different ethnic congregations,[119] while other creative solutions may be more appropriate in different contexts.[120] In any case, we are called to demonstrate our unity in Christ as one new humanity in concrete ways. This unity will testify to the power of the gospel message even in the present age.

118. This precise quotation appears in a 1963 interview with Martin Luther King Jr. at Western Michigan University (www.wmich.edu/library/archives/mlk/q-a.html).

119. For a discussion of the problems and promises of such an approach, see the helpful case study in Kersten Bayt Priest and Robert J. Priest, "Divergent Worship Practices in the Sunday Morning Hour: Analysis of an 'Interracial' Church Merger Attempt," in *This Side of Heaven: Race, Ethnicity, and Christian Faith* (ed. Robert J. Priest and Alvaro L. Nieves; Oxford: Oxford Univ. Press, 2007), 275 – 91.

120. In some contexts, ethnic churches are effective instruments to address the need of immigrant communities; see, e.g., Carolyn Chen, *Getting Saved in America: Taiwanese Immigration and Religious Experience* (Princeton, NJ: Princeton Univ. Press, 2008), 38 – 76.

Colossians 3:12 – 17

Literary Context

This section contains two subsections. Verses 12 – 14 can be considered an independent section because they provide the positive counterpart to the prohibition in vv. 5 – 11. Nevertheless, vv. 15 – 17 should not be considered a separate section because they provide the climax to the positive exhortation of vv. 12 – 14, although they also serve to introduce the household discussion in 3:18 – 4:1.[1] As will be noted in our discussion on structure, vv. 15 – 17 also provide a suitable conclusion to the vice and virtue lists of vv. 5 – 14, especially since vv. 15 – 17 echo some of the themes introduced in vv. 1 – 4.

This larger section begins with a call to "seek the things above" (v. 1), and this general exhortation is expanded into a pair of related commands: "set your minds on the things above, not things on the earth." Vv. 5 – 11 contain two vice lists (vv. 5, 8 – 9) and illustrate to what "things on the earth" refer; vv. 12 – 17 expand on "the things above." Just as vv. 5 – 11 began with the conjunction "therefore" (οὖν), this section also begins this way. The relationship between vv. 5 – 11 and vv. 12 – 17 is best illustrated by the parallel between the call to "put away" in v. 8 and the corresponding call to "put on" in v. 12.[2]

The affirmation of the exalted status of the risen Christ in v. 1 is further expanded in vv. 15 – 17, where the lordship of Christ is again affirmed. The reference to being "called in one body" (v. 15) points back to the new humanity that believers are to put on, "where there is neither Greek nor Jew, circumcised nor uncircumcised, barbarian, Scythian, slave nor free" (v. 11). The call to teach and admonish one another with songs of worship (v. 16) also finds its counterpart in the previous call to put away the vices that originate "from your mouth" (v. 8). Finally, to "do everything in the name of the Lord Jesus" (v. 17) provides a fitting conclusion to both the vice and

---

1. In some versions, vv. 12 – 17 are taken as one paragraph: NAB, NRSV, NEB, TEV, HCSB, NET.

2. The verb "to put on" has already appeared in v. 10 in participial form, but the imperative in v. 12 should be considered as the proper counterpart to the imperative in v. 8.

virtue lists; Paul is calling believers to live a christocentric life characterized by the worship of the one Creator God.

Verses 15 – 17 also introduce the section that follows. The call to "do everything in the name of the Lord Jesus" (v. 17) again affirms the lordship of Christ, a theme that reappears through Paul's numerous uses of the christological title "Lord" in 3:18 – 4:1 on household relationships (3:18, 20, 22, 23, 24; 4:1),[3] which illustrates what affirming the lordship of Christ means in a concrete manner. The connection between 3:17 and the household discussion that follows is further secured by the parallel between v. 17 ("whatever you do in word or in deed, do everything in the name of the Lord Jesus, giving thanks to God the Father through him"), and v. 23 ("whatever you do, do it wholeheartedly, as to the Lord and not to people").

V. Faithfulness of the Believers (2:6 – 4:1)

  A. Call to Faithfulness (2:6 – 7)

  B. Sufficiency in Christ (2:8 – 23)

  C. Reorientation of Christian Living (3:1 – 4:1)

    1. Focus on the Risen Christ (3:1 – 4)

    2. Take off the Old Humanity (3:5 – 11)

➡   **3. Put on the New Humanity (3:12 – 17)**

    4. Lord of the Household (3:18 – 4:1)

VI. Eschatological Mission to the World (4:2 – 6)

Main Idea

After putting off earthly practices, believers must put on a new set of behaviors that reflects the reality of the new humanity, characterized by unity and love. This call rests on the prior act of grace by Jesus Christ, and it culminates in the submission to the lordship of this Christ through words and deeds of worship.

Translation

(See next page.)

---

3. The emphasis on the lordship of Christ is precisely the point of Paul's discussion of the household relationships. See comments on 3:18 – 4:1.

Colossians 3:12 – 17

12a	Exhortation	**Put on,** therefore,
b	basis	as elect of God,
c	basis	holy and beloved,
d	example	[1] compassion,
e	list	[2] kindness,
f	list	[3] humility,
g	list	[4] meekness, and
h	list	[5] patience,

13a	means	bearing with one another and
		forgiving one another,
b	expansion	if anyone has a complaint against another;
c	accordance	just as the Lord forgave you,
d	inference	so also forgive one another.

14a	Expansion	Above all these put on love,
b	description	which is the perfect bond.
15a	Exhortation	And **let the peace of Christ rule in your hearts,**
b	purpose	to which indeed you were called in one body.
c	Exhortation	And **be thankful.**
16a	Exhortation	**Let the word of Christ dwell**
		in you richly,
b	means (of c)	in all wisdom
c	means (of a)	teaching and
		admonishing one another
d	means (of c)	with [1] psalms,
e	list	[2] hymns,
f	list	[3] and spiritual songs,
g	means (of h)	with gratitude
h	means (of a)	singing
i	sphere	in your hearts
j	direction	to God.
17a	condition	And
		whatever you do in word or in deed,
b	Exhortation	**do everything in the name of the Lord Jesus,**
c	means	giving thanks to God the Father through him.

Structure

After the call to "put away" the practices that disrupt the life of the one body of Christ (v. 8), Paul now urges the believers to "put on" a new set of behaviors consistent with their identity as the "elect," "holy," and "beloved" people of God (v. 12). In his catalogue of virtues, Paul focuses on those that are community-oriented as they seek to build up relationships among members of God's people. This focus on community is consistent with the preceding call to "put on the new humanity," where this "new humanity" is likewise defined not in terms of social and cultural markers but by Christ and him alone (vv. 10 – 11).

The means through which such virtues can be practiced are explicitly identified in the act of forgiving, an act grounded in the prior act of forgiveness by Jesus the Lord (v. 13). This recalls 2:13 – 14, where Paul pointed to the believer's participation in the resurrection of Christ made possible by God's act of forgiveness through Christ's death on the cross. This note is important as it points to the virtues not simply as benevolent acts of kindness by a neutral ethical subject, but acts made possible by God's act in Christ.

The call to practice these virtues culminates in the call to "love" one another.[4] The relationship between this call to love one another and the christological affirmations emphasized in the first half of this letter is made clear in 2:2: "[My purpose is] that their hearts may be comforted as they are united in love, to obtain all the wealth of full assurance of understanding, and the knowledge of the mystery of God, Christ." Only when united in love can the community of God's people apprehend and testify to the mighty acts of God through Christ as he creates a new people through the death of the Son whom he loves (1:13).

The final verses of this section (vv. 15 – 17) have been understood as a "self-contained" unit that has "only a loose and somewhat arbitrary connection with the context."[5] This conclusion fails to note, however, both the unifying theme behind these verses and the prominence of this theme throughout Colossians. In these three verses, one finds the emphasis on thanksgiving: "be thankful" (v. 15), "with gratitude" (v. 16), and "giving thanks" (v. 17). Earlier Paul made the connection between thanksgiving and the submission to the lordship of Christ (2:6 – 7) because to give thanks to God is to acknowledge him to be the Creator and the source of all goodness. In this context, Paul is again calling the believers to submit to the lordship of Christ through a constant practice of acts of thanksgiving.

In v. 15, to be ruled by "the peace of Christ" is to "be thankful." In v. 16, to be filled with "the word of Christ" is to worship "with gratitude … in your hearts to God." Finally, in v. 17, to "do everything in the name of the Lord Jesus" is to give "thanks to God the Father through him." This emphasis on the lordship of Christ provides a fitting conclusion to the previous discussion of vices and virtues (vv. 5 – 11, 12 – 14). It points back to the affirmation of the exalted status of Christ in vv. 1 – 4, and it also paves the way for a discussion of the lordship of Christ in 3:18 – 4:1, a section that concludes with yet another call to thanksgiving in 4:2.

---

4. The presence of δέ ("and/but") together with the phrase "above all" (ἐπὶ πᾶσιν) suggests that this call points to "a climax rather than simply the end of a list" (Callow, *Semantic and Structural Analysis*, 128).

5. Yates, "A Reappraisal of Colossians," 111.

Exegetical Outline

➡ **I. Put on the New Humanity (3:12 – 17)**

    A. In unity and harmony (3:12 – 14)

        1. Catalogue of the virtues of love (3:12)

        2. Forgive one another (3:13)

        3. Supremacy of love (3:14)

    B. Thanksgiving and the lordship of Christ (3:15 – 17)

        1. Rule of peace (3:15)

        2. Indwelling of the Word through worship (3:16)

        3. Do everything for the Lord Jesus (3:17)

Explanation of the Text

3:12 Put on, therefore, as elect of God, holy and beloved, compassion, kindness, humility, meekness, and patience (Ἐνδύσασθε οὖν ὡς ἐκλεκτοὶ τοῦ θεοῦ, ἅγιοι καὶ ἠγαπημένοι, σπλάγχνα οἰκτιρμοῦ, χρηστότητα, ταπεινοφροσύνην, πραΰτητα, μακροθυμίαν). In 3:10 – 11 Paul defined the act of putting on the new humanity; now he elaborates on this new humanity. The imperative "put on" (ἐνδύσασθε) completes the clothing metaphor that began with the call to "put ... away" (ἀπόθεσθε, v. 8),[6] and this imperative is further anticipated by the appearance of the participial form in v. 10 ("[for you] have put on," ἐνδυσάμενοι). The connection to the previous paragraph is further emphasized by "therefore" (οὖν).

Before listing the virtues that believers are to embrace, Paul again points to the basis for these actions. He calls believers the "elect of God." This description, used for the Israelites in the OT (Ps 105:6, 43 [LXX 104:6, 43]; Isa 43:20; 45:4; 65:9, 15), is particularly important since it is now applied to Gentile believers in Colossae. Because of redemp-

tion brought by Christ's death on the cross, all who participate in his death and resurrection can now be identified as his own people. This application of election language to Gentiles further explicates the definition of the new humanity as "neither Greek nor Jew, circumcised nor uncircumcised" (v. 11); this application is consistent with his rhetorical strategy elsewhere in this letter, where he repeatedly applies election vocabulary to these believers as they are called "the saints" (1:2, 12) — "the holy ... and blameless" people (1:22)[7] who have been "circumcised" (2:11) and are now heirs of "the inheritance" promised by God for his own people (1:12; cf. 3:24).

The phrase "holy and beloved" (ἅγιοι καὶ ἠγαπημένοι) stands in apposition to "elect of God" and further expresses the believers' status as God's chosen people. In this context, "holy" does not describe moral accomplishment but the act of God's setting them apart as his people for his own purpose.[8] This reading is confirmed by the passive participle "beloved," which points to God as the im-

---

6. Some versions justifiably make explicit this clothing metaphor by translating the imperative as "clothe yourselves" (NRSV, NLT, NET, NIV). Cf. REB: "put on ... garments."

7. For the connection between God's sanctifying act and the call for believers to be holy, see 1 Cor 1:2.

8. Cf. TEV's translation of the word "holy" with the phrase, "his own special people."

plied agent. In the OT, to be chosen by God is to be separated and thus be "holy" in his sight: "For you are a people holy to the LORD your God. The LORD your God has chosen you out of all the peoples on the face of the earth to be his people, his treasured possession" (Deut 7:6). The prior salvific act of God is assumed in the call to be a holy people:

> You yourselves have seen what I did to Egypt, and how I carried you on eagles' wings and brought you to myself. Now if you obey me fully and keep my covenant, then out of all nations you will be my treasured possession. Although the whole earth is mine, you will be for me a kingdom of priests and a holy nation. (Exod 19:4 – 6a)

The connection between God's election and his love for his people, especially for Gentiles, is best illustrated by Paul's quotation from Hos 2:23 in Rom 9:25: "I will call them 'my people' who are not my people; and I will call her 'my loved one' who is not my loved one."[9] Note too that God's love is not contingent on human response, but is a prior act that forms the basis for such response. The use of the participle "beloved" paves the way for the following virtue list, which culminates in "love" (τὴν ἀγάπην) among believers (v. 14).

Paul will soon offer a number of imperatives, which instruct believers to behave in a manner consistent with their new identity. The use of election language before his exhortation "brings the tension to a climax" as the imperatives become "the final and most effective attempt to change the behavior of the readers."[10]

The virtue list[11] that follows points to concrete ways believers can respond to God's grace of election.[12] Compared to other NT virtue lists that include virtues such as "purity" (2 Cor 6:6; cf. Phil 4:8; 1 Tim 4:12), "joy" (Gal 5:22), "righteousness" (1 Tim 6:11; 2 Tim 2:22), "faith" (1 Tim 6:11; 2 Tim 2:22; 3:10), and "knowledge" (2 Pet 1:5 – 6), this list is singularly focused on building and maintaining a community characterized by "love" (v. 14). This is undoubtedly a set of virtues to counter the vices listed in v. 8. This reading is confirmed by Eph 4:31 – 32, where a similar pair of vice and virtue lists are placed next to each other. Moreover, this list emphasizing humility and mutual submission paves the way for the reaffirmation of the lordship of Christ in vv. 15 – 17. This similar connection occurs in 1 Pet 3:8, where a virtue list ("be like-minded, be sympathetic, love one another, be compassionate and humble") also leads to a call to "revere Christ as Lord" (v. 15).[13]

"Compassion" (σπλάγχνα οἰκτιρμοῦ) literally reads "bowels of mercies" (KJV). Taking "bowels" as the "seat of the emotions,"[14] some have rendered this phrase "heart of compassion" (ASV, NASB), "heart of mercy" (NET), or even "tenderhearted mercy" (NLT). By itself, "bowels" can point to compassion or kind acts, in both the OT (Prov 12:10) and NT (2 Cor 6:12; 7:15), and it has also been used in parallel with "mercy" elsewhere in Paul (Phil 2:1). The noun οἰκτιρμός (Rom 12:1; 2 Cor 1:3) and the related noun ἔλεος (Rom 9:23; 11:31; 15:9; Eph 2:4; 1 Tim 1:2; Titus 3:5) almost

---

9. The use of the "love" word group in reference to election is also highlighted by the variation in the heavenly voice in the transfiguration scene between Mark 9:7 ("This is my Son, whom I love [ὁ ἀγαπητός]. Listen to him," 9:7 NIV; cf. Matt 17:5) and Luke 9:35 ("This is my Son, whom I have chosen [ὁ ἐκλελεγμένος]; listen to him").

10. Gregory T. Christopher, "A Discourse Analysis of Colossians 2:16 – 3:17," *GTJ* 11 (1990): 218, who considers 3:12 as the "discourse peak" of the chiastic structure of 2:16 – 3:17.

11. For a discussion of the genre of vice and virtue lists, see "In Depth: Vice and Virtue Lists" at 3:5.

12. The call of God as the basis of action is explicitly noted in Gal 5:13; Eph 4:1; 1 Tim 6:12. Outside of the Pauline corpus, 2 Pet 1:5 – 7 is particularly relevant as a virtue list that points to ways to confirm one's calling (v. 10).

13. In Eph 4, the vice and virtue lists also lead to a similar confession as the basis of the unity of believers: "one Lord, one faith, one baptism" (v. 5).

14. BDAG, 939.

always point to the mercies of God.[15] In this verse, therefore, this genitive (οἰκτιρμοῦ) is best taken as an attributive genitive that functions in an adjectival sense;[16] it reminds readers that they are to imitate God in being merciful and compassionate.

"Kindness" (χρηστότητα), a word that can refer to any benevolent act in extracanonical writings,[17] is also often used for God's merciful acts for his people (Pss 25:7; 31:19 [LXX 30:20]; 68:10 [LXX 67:11]; Rom 2:4; 11:22; Eph 2:7; Titus 3:4).[18] Paul is again calling believers to live out the kindness they have already experienced from the compassionate God.

"Humility" (ταπεινοφροσύνην) is the posture of one who submits to the lordship of Christ. It represents the opposition to a self-centered will (Phil 2:3), and it points to the virtue of mutual submission (cf. 1 Pet 5:5). The related word group is used particularly in reference to those who await God's salvific act in the eschatological reversal to come (Matt 18:4; 23:12; Luke 1:52; 14:11; 18:14; 2 Cor 7:6; Jas 4:6, 10; 1 Pet 5:5). In light of the previous virtues and the call to imitate Christ in the next verse, the example of Christ in Phil 2:8 becomes especially relevant: "And being found in appearance as a man, he humbled [ἐταπείνωσεν] himself by becoming obedient to death — even death on a cross" (Phil 2:8). Paul is calling the believers to follow Christ's example and exhibit true humility, unlike the false humility promoted by the false teachers (2:18, 23).

In the LXX, "meekness" (πραΰτητα) can refer to

the state of being humiliated (Pss 89:10; 131:1), but in later writings it often points the virtue of being humble and gentle (LXX Esth 15:8; Sir 4:8; 10:28; 36:23; 45:4; cf. Ps 45:4 [LXX 44:5]). In the NT, it is used in reference to Christ (2 Cor 10:1).[19] As the opposite of acting in anger, it is the opposite of the behavior in the vice list of v. 8.

Finally, "patience" (μακροθυμίαν) points to God's forbearance for his people (cf. Isa 57:15 LXX) as noted also by Paul's description of God in a rhetorical question: "What if God, although choosing to show his wrath and make his power known, bore with great patience [μακροθυμίᾳ] the objects of his wrath — prepared for destruction?" (Rom 9:22; cf. 2:4). As God is patient with his people, believers are called to be patient with those around them. Some have considered the difference between "meekness" and "patience" to be best illustrated by their opposites: "meekness" is the opposite of "rudeness, harshness," while "patience" is the opposite of "resentment, revenge, wrath."[20] The note on forgiveness (v. 13) is particularly relevant after this call to be patient and not seek revenge.

3:13a-b Bearing with one another and forgiving one another, if anyone has a complaint against another (ἀνεχόμενοι ἀλλήλων καὶ χαριζόμενοι ἑαυτοῖς ἐάν τις πρός τινα ἔχῃ μομφήν). After listing the virtues that are to characterize the new humanity, Paul provides the means through which such virtues can be practiced. The syntactical function of these two participial phrases is twofold: they modify the main clause in the previous verse ("put on

---

15. Knowles, "'Christ in You, the Hope of Glory,'" 197–98, points more specifically to the influence of Exod 33:19 and 34:6–7, two passages considered to be the source of a tradition that emphasizes God's gracious and merciful acts (Neh 9:17; Pss 86:15; 103:8; Joel 2:13; Jonah 4:2; Rom 9:15–18; *4 Ezra* 7:132–39).

16. Thus "a compassionate heart;" Harris, *Colossians and Philemon*, 161.

17. See, e.g., Philo, *Spec. Laws* 1.284; 2.104; *Virtues* 182; Jose-

phus, *Ant.* 2.149; 9.133; Bevere, *Sharing in the Inheritance*, 205.

18. In light of these references to God's merciful acts, the rendering adopted by NJB is acceptable: "generosity."

19. See also the use of the related word πραΰς ("gentle") in reference to Christ in Matt 5:5; 11:29; 21:5.

20. Lightfoot, *St. Paul's Epistles to the Colossians and to Philemon*, 221, followed by Wright, *Colossians and Philemon*, 142. The translation of these terms in *The Message* best reflects this distinction: "quiet strength" and "discipline."

...."), and they form the apodosis ("then-clause") of the protasis ("if-clause") that follows, even though normally the protasis precedes the apodosis.

Though often translated as imperatives (e.g., "Bear with one another and ... forgive each other," NRSV; cf. NLT, TNIV, NIV), these participles should be taken as circumstantial participles of means.[21] Modifying the imperative "put on," they demonstrate how the virtues listed above can be used in constructing a community of love. "Bearing" (ἀνεχόμενοι) carries the sense of tolerance (e.g., Matt 17:17; Mark 9:19; Luke 9:41; 2 Cor 11:4, 19, 20) or "endurance" (e.g., 1 Cor 4:12; 2 Thess 1:4). It seems particularly related to the virtue of "patience" (v. 12; cf. Eph 4:2), but it can also be used in a broader sense with reference to interpersonal relationships in general. "Forgiving [χαριζόμενοι] one another" points to actively accepting those who have wronged them; it manifests virtues such as "compassion," "kindness," "humility," and "meekness" (v. 12).[22]

Drawing from the general conditional clause as reflected in the protasis ("if anyone has a complaint against another," ἐάν τις πρός τινα ἔχῃ μομφήν), many consider this note expresses "something that is universally valid for the community's life together" with "no reference to a specific situation in the community."[23] Nevertheless, this note is particularly relevant in the context of Paul's argument in this letter. For a community where some are seeking other means to approach God and be reconciled to him, Paul has repeatedly emphasized that through the death of his Son, "God made [us] alive with him, having forgiven us all our transgressions" (2:13; cf. 1:13–14, 21–22; 2:14–15). More-

over, the word "forgiving" (χαριζόμενοι) may also remind the readers of the nominal form, "grace" (χάρις), the word that denotes the gospel of God in truth (1:6). For Paul, then, to live out the practice of forgiveness is to live out the gospel as embodied in Christ's death on the cross.

3:13c-d Just as the Lord forgave you, so also forgive one another (καθὼς καὶ ὁ κύριος ἐχαρίσατο ὑμῖν οὕτως καὶ ὑμεῖς). The relationship between the believers' practice of forgiveness and the divine act of grace is explained here. The comparative conjunctions "just as ... so" (καθὼς ... οὕτως) often depict two similar scenarios (e.g., Luke 11:30; 17:26; John 3:14; 12:50; 15:4). In Paul, this pair of conjunctions has also been used to ground the believers' behavior in Christ's prior act (e.g., 2 Cor 1:5). In light of the connection between Paul's use of the clothing metaphor and his use of the death-resurrection paradigm in this letter, the call to "put on" (v. 12) naturally leads Paul to refer to putting on the new life that is in Christ. The structure of this verse, therefore, reflects a wider structure in Paul's ethics, one that can already be found in Romans: "We were therefore buried with him through baptism into death in order that, just as [ὥσπερ][24] Christ was raised from the dead through the glory of the Father, [so, οὕτως] we too may live a new life" (Rom 6:4).

Paul characterizes this new life by the imitation of divine forgiveness. In the preceding context, "the Lord" has been explicitly identified as "Christ Jesus" (2:6; cf. 1:3, 10), and at the end of this section, this title is also explicitly applied to Jesus (3:17). Therefore, it seems clear that Paul is

---

21. Cf. Aletti, *Saint Paul Épître aux Colossiens*, 237. On imperatival participles, see Wallace, *Greek Grammar*, 652. In light of the second half of the verse, however, the imperatival force cannot be denied, but it is context that determines that nuance.

22. In papyri, one of the most common usages of this term is in reference to the act of showing "kindness"; MM, 684. In

Eph 4:32, the discussion of forgiveness also follows the virtues of kindness and compassion.

23. Lohse, *Colossians and Philemon*, 147–48.

24. For the discussion of the various comparative conjunctions, see BDF §453.

referring to Christ's act of forgiveness here. This is consistent with Paul's usage elsewhere as the title "Lord" is always applied to Christ (except in OT quotations).

In light of the reference to "the word of Christ" in v. 16, it is tempting to identify the source of this exhortation about forgiveness in the sayings of Christ recorded in the gospels. Besides the general call to forgiveness (e.g., Matt 5:21 – 26), one also finds a correlation between divine and human acts of forgiveness, but these parallels often consider human acts of forgiveness as the condition for divine forgiveness (cf. Matt 6:12, 14 – 15; 18:23 – 35; Mark 11:25; Luke 6:37; 11:4).[25] Here, however, Christ's forgiveness serves as the basis of human forgiveness.[26] As noted above, the priority and finality of divine forgiveness is emphasized repeatedly in this letter as Paul corrects the false teachers, whose acts challenge the sufficiency of God's work through Christ. As a response, Paul emphasizes the need to imitate Christ in the creation of a community based on the divine grace manifested on the cross.

3:14 Above all these put on love, which is the perfect bond (ἐπὶ πᾶσιν δὲ τούτοις τὴν ἀγάπην, ὅ ἐστιν σύνδεσμος τῆς τελειότητος). After the virtue list, Paul points to the supreme significance of love. "Above all" is a formulaic phrase often used in the sense of "in addition to" (cf. NET)[27] or in the elative sense, "above all" (KJV, ASV, NASB, NKJV, NRSV, HCSB, ESV) — thus, "more important than anything else" (CEV). In light of the use of the clothing metaphor, however, some suggest that "love is the outer garment which holds the others in their places"[28] and therefore argue for the translation, "on top of all the other 'articles of clothing.' "[29] Even the proponents of this reading admit, however, that "clear syntactical parallels for this … sense are lacking."[30] It seems best, therefore, to retain the clearly attested meaning of "above all" while allowing room for the contextual significance of the clothing metaphor.

The supremacy of love is reflected in Paul's statement elsewhere that "love is the fulfillment of the law" (Rom 13:10; cf. Gal 5:6; 1 Tim 1:5), and that of "faith, hope and love … the greatest of these is love" (1 Cor 13:13). In this context where God's act of grace is noted (Col 3:13), this love points back to the salvific love revealed on the cross as noted in the Ephesian parallel: "walk in the way of love, just as Christ loved us and gave himself up for us as a fragrant offering and sacrifice to God" (Eph 5:2; cf. Rom 5:8).

As noted earlier in this letter, believers who are "united in love" can in turn receive "the knowledge of the mystery of God, Christ" (2:2). In light of this christological focus, one can appreciate the significance of love in NT virtue lists (2 Cor 6:6; 8:7; Gal 5:22; Eph 4:2; Phil 2:1; 1 Tim 6:11; Titus 2:2; 2 Pet 1:7), a virtue that leads directly into a discussion of thanksgiving in vv. 15 – 17: "Christian morality is distinctly the morality of charity … whereby one gives evidence of an internal work of grace, demonstrating gratitude through one's actions."[31]

---

25. Apart from these examples of the correlation between divine and human acts of forgiveness, one can also find the emphasis on the priority of unconditional divine grace (e.g., Mark 2:7; Luke 7:41 – 42; 17:10). In the NT, the tension between the two is not considered an irreconcilable one, however: "God's forgiveness, although it cannot be merited, must be received, and it cannot be received by those without the will to forgive others" (W. D. Davies and Dale Allison, *A Critical and Exegetical Commentary on the Gospel According to Saint Matthew* [ICC; Edinburgh: T&T Clark, 1988 – 97], 1:611).

26. In Paul, the closest parallel can be found in Gal 6:1 – 2, where acts of forgiveness and restoration "fulfill the law of Christ."

27. BDAG, 365.

28. Lightfoot, *St. Paul's Epistles to the Colossians and to Philemon*, 222.

29. Moule, *Epistles to the Colossians and to Philemon*, 123. Cf. "over all these" (NIV).

30. Moo, *Letters to the Colossians and to Philemon*, 279.

31. J. Daryl Charles, *Virtue amidst Vice* (JSNTSup 150; Sheffield: Sheffield Academic, 1997), 145.

"The perfect bond" (σύνδεσμος τῆς τελειότητος) literally reads "a bond of perfection"; our translation takes the genitive "of perfection" as an attributive genitive modifying "bond," although it can also be taken as an objective genitive (thus, "the bond that produces perfection").[32] More problematic is the object of those things bound together by this love. Those who take the previous phrase in the sense of "over all" argue for the individual virtues noted in vv. 12 – 13 as that which is bounded by love: "over all these virtues put on love, which binds them all [i.e., all these virtues] together in perfect unity" (TNIV, NIV).[33] For those who do not insist on seeing love as the outer garment, this "perfect bond" binds together all believers into one unified community: "love … binds us all together in perfect harmony" (NLT; cf. NASB, HCSB).[34]

In this context, the latter reading is preferable. First, "bond" (σύνδεσμος) was used earlier for the unity among the body of Christ when Paul accused the false teachers of "not holding fast to the head, from which the entire body, nourished and united through the joints and ligaments [συνδέσμων], grows with a growth from God" (2:19). Paul's exhortation here continues that line of argument by calling the believers to be united in love in Christ.

Second, the parallel in Eph 4:3, which calls believers to be unified in the Spirit through "the bond [τῷ συνδέσμῳ] of peace," also follows a listing of the virtues. There, the unity of the believers is clearly in view.[35]

Third, in the present context, the unity of believers is the dominant theme. Note v. 11, where the definition of the unified new humanity is provided. This emphasis resurfaces in v. 15, where Paul reminds the believers that they "were called into one body." Therefore, it seems best to consider love, as well as the virtues listed above, as the sustaining force that binds believers together.

This reading may also explain the appearance of the word "perfection." In defining "perfection" or "completeness" in terms of a community, Paul may be challenging the false idea of perfection promoted by the false teachers, who emphasized individual accomplishment as they sought to achieve a higher spiritual status through their own efforts.[36]

3:15a And let the peace of Christ rule in your hearts (καὶ ἡ εἰρήνη τοῦ Χριστοῦ βραβευέτω ἐν ταῖς καρδίαις ὑμῶν). Paul now moves to the climactic exhortation that affirms the significance of the lordship of Christ through a grateful heart in the life of worship (vv. 15 – 17). Often considered to be "without any apparent connection" to the previous discussion,[37] this verse actually provides the critical christological lens through which the above-mentioned virtues are to be understood. Instead of general exhortations that lead to a virtuous life, the above discussion points to a way of life that acknowledges God's prior acts of grace and the centrality of Christ in such acts. To be virtuous is, therefore, to submit to the lordship of Christ.

To appreciate both the significance of "the peace" (ἡ εἰρήνη) and the means through which such "peace" can rule in one's hearts, one should refer back to the act of "making peace" (εἰρηνοποιήσας) in 1:20. As we noted there, "peace" was a powerful

32. Harris, *Colossians and Philemon*, 164 – 65.

33. Thus also Lightfoot, *St. Paul's Epistles to the Colossians and to Philemon*, 222; Moule, *Epistles to the Colossians and to Philemon*, 123 – 24; Moo, *Letters to the Colossians and to Philemon*, 281; and Sumney, *Colossians*, 218.

34. Lohse, *Colossians and Philemon*, 149; O'Brien, *Colossians, Philemon*, 203 – 4; MacDonald, *Colossians and Ephesians*, 141.

35. In Eph 4:15 – 16, this unity is also described in reference to "love" that produces the bond between the believers and Christ.

36. Cf. Andrew T. Lincoln, "The Letter to the Colossians," in *The New Interpreter's Bible*, vol. 11 (ed. Leander E. Keck; Nashville: Abingdon, 2000), 648.

37. Yates, "A Reappraisal of Colossians," 112.

word in both Jewish and Greco-Roman contexts. For Jews, this "peace" is the fulfillment of the eschatological hope of Israel, one that transcends interpersonal relationships as it acquires cosmic significance. For the Gentile readers in first-century Asia Minor, this peace that only Christ can provide ("of Christ")[38] challenges the imperial claims proclaimed through military pacification.

The means through which the rule of Christ's peace can be realized is "the blood of his cross" (1:20). An act that appears to reveal the utter impotence of the subject becomes the most powerful creative act through which creation is reconciled with its Creator (cf. 1:20). For Paul, therefore, the evocation of this "peace" again reminds the readers of both the means through which God's salvation is accomplished and the cosmic effect of such an accomplishment.[39] To incorporate this "peace" in one's life is to behave with the realization of the reality of this divine accomplishment.

The verb translated here as "rule" (βραβευέτω) carries the sense of to "judge, decide, control, rule."[40] It appears only here in the NT, but a related compound verb is used in 2:18 (καταβραβευέτω) in reference to acts of judgment and condemnation carried out by the false teachers. The reappearance of this word group may be an attempt to respond again to the false teachers: instead of being judged by others, believers should only be judged by "the peace of Christ." This not only maintains the christocentric emphasis of the argument, but it also emphasizes "peace" that has already been accomplished by God through Christ as the ultimate rule of measure. The prepositional phrase "in your hearts," then, draws a contrast with the false

teachers, who were insisting on external rituals (2:20 – 23) and cultic practices (2:18).

Nevertheless, Paul's exhortation here should not simply be understood as a polemic against the false teachers in Colossae. Elsewhere, he has emphasized the connection between peace and sanctified living (see, e.g., 1 Thess 5:23a). Moreover, the numerous references to "hearts" in this letter (Col 2:2; 3:15, 16, 22; 4:8) suggest that Paul is here primarily focusing on the full and sincere reception of the rule of the peace of Christ. Therefore, this call is consistent with Paul's understanding of the behavior of a Christian community that confesses the lordship of Christ.

3:15b To which indeed you were called in one body (εἰς ἣν καὶ ἐκλήθητε ἐν ἑνὶ σώματι). Paul further describes this peace. "To which" (εἰς ἣν) points to "peace" as the purpose of the calling of the believers. "You were called" (ἐκλήθητε) points again to God's prior act. In light of Eph 4:3 – 4 and the reference to the Spirit there, some consider the Spirit as the implied subject of this passive verb.[41] Since Paul identifies the believers as "elect of God" in v. 12, however, it seems best to consider God the Father as the implied subject of this verb.

In light of the biblical understanding of "peace," believers are not simply called to peaceful living. Instead, they are called to participate in the cosmic reconciliation brought about by God's salvific act through his Son. The interpersonal relationship is emphasized in the phrase "in one body," a phrase that recalls the earlier references to the body of Christ (1:18, 24; 2:19). Paul calls believers to be unified as they live as the reconciled people of

---

38. This interpretation take the genitive "of Christ" (τοῦ Χριστοῦ) as a subjective genitive, as made explicit in some versions: "the peace that Christ gives" (GNB; cf. NLT).

39. The relationship between the "peace" that is accomplished by God through Christ and the "peace" that is to be demonstrated in one's community can also be found in Ro-

mans, where "peace with God" that is achieved through God's justifying act (Rom 5:1) becomes the basis on which believers can "live in peace with all people" (12:18).

40. BDAG, 183.

41. Fee, *God's Empowering Presence*, 647.

God (cf. 1:22). The emphasis on "one" body argues against the "false humility" of those who claim to have achieved a higher spiritual status through ascetic and cultic practices (2:18, 21 – 23) or ethnic and social locations (3:11), and against those who disrupt that unity through their behavior (3:8 – 9). Because of the universal significance of Christ's death, insistence on the "one body" of Christ lies at the center of Paul's theology (cf. Rom 12:5; 1 Cor 10:17; 12:12 – 26; Eph 4:4).

3:15c And be thankful (καὶ εὐχάριστοι γίνεσθε). The adjective "thankful" (εὐχάριστοι) appears only here in the NT to characterize God's people as a "thankful" people. This absolute call to be thankful without any direct reference to a gift moves beyond the modern conception of reciprocity. This is consistent with Paul's call to "give thanks in all circumstances" (1 Thess 5:18), where the act of thanksgiving acknowledges one's dependence on God's grace through Christ.[42] As noted above (cf. 1:12; 2:7), the call to thanksgiving often accompanies the confession of the lordship of Christ. Thus, this call to thanksgiving is again a call to submit to the lordship of Christ (v. 17). This becomes the fitting climax in a section that discusses the behavior of those who claim Jesus to be the Lord (vv. 5 – 14) and introduces the theme of worship both in public formal settings (v. 16) and in everyday living (v. 17).

In defining this "new humanity" (v. 10) in such a manner, the readers, who live in a patron-client cultural framework, might also consider this call as one that points to Christ as their new patron, especially when gratitude is considered a proper response of clients to their patrons.[43] As acts of praise served to define the covenantal relationship between God and his people in the OT, for Paul,

thanksgiving defines the believers as people who belong to Christ.

3:16a Let the word of Christ dwell in you richly (ὁ λόγος τοῦ Χριστοῦ ἐνοικείτω ἐν ὑμῖν πλουσίως). Paul continues his focus on Christ here. "The word of Christ" (ὁ λόγος τοῦ Χριστοῦ) appears only here in Paul's letters. Some have taken this phrase as a subjective genitive, referring to particular sayings of the earthly Jesus.[44] If so, one would expect the plural form (e.g., 1 Cor 2:4; 1 Tim 6:3; cf. 1 Cor 14:19) or, more likely, the use of a different word (cf. τοῦ ῥήματος τοῦ κυρίου, Acts 11:16). A second interpretation takes the genitive "of Christ" as an objective genitive and the phrase "the word of Christ" as referring specifically to the christological hymn in 1:15 – 20.[45] "Word" (λόγος) can indeed refer to an encomium in honor of a deity (cf. Plato, *Symp.* 193D, 194D), and the reference to songs later in this verse may support this reading. Nevertheless, other uses of λόγος in Colossians (and elsewhere in Paul) fail to confirm this reading.

It is true that the genitive "of Christ" should probably be understood as an objective genitive, but it seems best to take the phrase as referring more generally to the gospel about and centered on Christ: thus, "the message about Christ" (CEV; cf. HCSB). This objective genitive reading is built on the "word" that comes from Christ himself, but this "word" is not simply his uttered words, but "the 'Word' uttered by Christ in his life and ministry and through his person and repeated by each Christian as [he or she proclaims] the Gospel by life and witness."[46] The understanding of "word" as the gospel is supported by the earlier reference in 1:5, where "the gospel" is identified as "the word of

---

42. Pao, *Thanksgiving*, 15 – 38.

43. MacDonald, *Colossians and Ephesians*, 108. The adjective "thankful" is "often found in [inscriptions] to denote the 'gratitude' of the people to their benefactors" (MM, 268).

44. David Wenham, *Paul: Follower of Jesus or Founder of Christianity?* (Grand Rapids: Eerdmans, 1995), 287 – 88.

45. Gordley, *Colossian Hymn in Context*, 207.

46. Moule, *Epistles to the Colossians and to Philemon*, 125.

truth." Equally important is that in both contexts, this "word" is portrayed as an active agent of God. In 1:6 this "word ... has come to you ... bearing fruit and growing." Here, believers are called to have the word "dwell" (ἐνοικείτω) in them.[47]

Elsewhere in Paul, one finds the indwelling of "the Spirit" (Rom 8:11) or "of God" (2 Cor 6:16). The related verb "to dwell" (οἰκέω) is also used in reference to the Spirit (cf. Rom 8:9, 11; 1 Cor 3:16). While the second half of this verse finds its parallel in Eph 5:19, the call that precedes that verse may also be relevant in this discussion: "be filled with the Spirit" (Eph 5:18). Moreover, the adverbial modifier "richly" (πλουσίως) has also been applied to the outpouring of the Spirit (Titus 3:5 – 6). The role of the Spirit is reflected in the "spiritual songs" noted below, but Paul emphasizes "the word of Christ" here probably to insist on the singular importance of the work of Christ for the believers.[48]

3:16b-f In all wisdom teaching and admonishing one another with psalms, hymns, and spiritual songs (ἐν πάσῃ σοφίᾳ διδάσκοντες καὶ νουθετοῦντες ἑαυτοὺς ψαλμοῖς, ὕμνοις, ᾠδαῖς πνευματικαῖς). Paul now identifies "teaching and admonishing" as the means through which believers can have "the word of Christ dwell" in them. The translation adopted here reflects two exegetical decisions. First, as in most versions,[49] the prepositional phrase "in all

wisdom" (ἐν πάσῃ σοφίᾳ) is understood as modifying the two participles that follow, "teaching and admonishing." This reading is supported by 1:28, where the same phrase modifies the acts of "admonishing" and "teaching."

More difficult is whether "psalms, hymns, and spiritual songs" should be taken with "teaching and admonishing," which precede (KJV, ASV, NASB, NKJV, TNIV, NIV), or "singing," which follows (NRSV, REB, CEV, NLT, NET, ESV, HCSB). Noting that "psalms, hymns, and spiritual songs" seem to be "more suitable with 'singing' than with 'teaching,'" some argue for the second option.[50] Despite the natural affinity between songs and the act of singing, the former reading is preferable.[51] First, the parallel in Eph 5:19 clearly points to the relationship between teaching and hymns, while singing belongs to a different clause: "speaking to one another with psalms, hymns, and songs from the Spirit. Sing and make music from your heart to the Lord."

Second, elsewhere in Paul, psalms and teaching have also appeared in the same context (1 Cor 14:26). As has often been stated, more theology is engrained into our hearts through singing than through the printed page or even through preaching.

Third, the datives in "psalms, hymns, and spiritual songs" go naturally with "teaching and ad-

---

47. It is difficult to decide whether the prepositional phrase ἐν ὑμῖν should be taken in an individual ("in/within you," KJV, ASV, NASB, NIV, NKJV, NRSV, NLT, NET, ESV) or a collective sense ("among you," REB, HCSB, NIV). References to "in your hearts" in vv. 15 and 16 point to the emphasis on the individual, while "in one body" (v. 15) and "one another" (v. 16) point to the significance of the collective body of Christ. Perhaps both are in Paul's mind.

48. Others have also suggested that the emphasis on "the word" here serves to distinguish Christian worship from Hellenistic cultic practices, where christological confession instead of ecstatic experience is the focus of worship; cf. Francois P. Viljoen, "Song and Music in the Early Christian Communities: Paul's Utilisation of Jewish, Roman and Greek Musical Tradi-

tions to Encourage the Early Christian Communities to Praise God and to Explain his Arguments," in *Zwischen den Reichen: Neues Testament und Römische Herrschaft* (ed. Michael Labahn and Jürgen Zangenberg; Tübingen: Francke, 2002), 210.

49. See, however, NKJV: "Let the word of Christ dwell in you richly in all wisdom" (cf. KJV, NLT).

50. Harris, *Colossians and Philemon*, 167; cf. Lohse, *Colossians and Philemon*, 151; Schweizer, *Letter to the Colossians*, 210; Sumney, *Colossians*, 224 – 25.

51. Lightfoot, *St. Paul's Epistles to the Colossians and to Philemon*, 224; O'Brien, *Colossians, Philemon*, 207 – 208; Barth and Blanke, *Colossians*, 427; MacDonald, *Colossians and Ephesians*, 143; Callow, *Semantic and Structural Analysis*, 133; Moo, *Letters to the Colossians and to Philemon*, 287 – 88.

monishing" as they express means through which instructions can be carried out. If these nouns are to be attached with "singing," they should be in the accusative case as objects of the act of singing.

Finally, this reading also highlights the parallelism between the two parts that are both introduced by a prepositional phrase beginning with ἐν,[52] followed by a participial clause:

> in all wisdom,
> teaching and admonishing one another with
>   psalms, hymns, and spiritual songs
>
> with gratitude
> singing in your hearts to God

Therefore, in terms of structure it seems best that "psalms, hymns, and spiritual songs" modify their preceding participles. Nevertheless, in parallel phrases in Greek, items that appear in the first one are often also relevant for the second one. In this case, "psalms, hymns, and spiritual songs" will thus also be relevant for the second clause.[53] To their fellow members of the body of Christ, believers are called to teach and admonish one another with psalms, hymns, and spiritual songs. To God, they are to sing these songs.

Both "teaching and admonishing" and "singing" should be considered as means though which one can allow the word of Christ to dwell in our hearts and in our midst. As in 1:28, Christ is again the focus of "teaching and admonishing," as highlighted by instrumental datives, "with psalms, hymns, and spiritual songs." In the OT, songs were means through which God's people remembered his mighty deeds, and through such deeds God

made himself known.[54] For Paul, believers also need to be educated through such confessions of God's mighty acts through his Son.

It is uncertain if clear distinctions should be made among "psalms, hymns, and spiritual songs," although they should not be considered as synonyms.[55] "Psalms" (ψαλμοῖς) often refer to OT psalms (Luke 20:42, 44; Acts 1:20), but Paul also uses it for hymns sung in a Christian worship setting (1 Cor 14:26).[56] "Hymns" (ὕμνοις), a word that appears only here and in Eph 5:19 in the NT, often refers to praises offered to deities or heroes. In the early church, it could refer specifically to hymns sung to Christ as God (Pliny, *Ep. Tra.* 10.96), a category for which the christological hymn of 1:15 – 20 comfortably qualifies. "Spiritual songs" (ᾠδαῖς πνευματικαῖς) can refer to "Spirit-inspired, and therefore often spontaneous, songs" sung in Christian worship settings (cf. 1 Cor 14:15 – 16),[57] although the word "spiritual" can be taken as modifying "psalms" and "hymns" as well.[58] Regardless of how the terms are to be understood, they all aim at confessing God's acts that climax in the life and ministry of Christ.

3:16g-j With gratitude singing in your hearts to God (ἐν [τῇ] χάριτι ᾄδοντες ἐν ταῖς καρδίαις ὑμῶν τῷ θεῷ). To a certain extent, this last phrase repeats and thus emphasizes the concerns expressed earlier in the verse: in thanksgiving believers are to remember the gracious acts of God and thus to respond with praise and submission. This represents the related means through which the word

---

52. For such parallel structures introduced by ἐν, cf. BDF §491.

53. If Paul were to write this out, one would have expected the second appearance of this phrase in accusative case.

54. Cf. G. W. Anderson, "Israel's Creed: Sung, not Signed," *SJT* 16 (1963): 277 – 85.

55. See esp. Richard C. Trench, *Synonyms of the New Testa-*

ment (repr.; Grand Rapids: Eerdmans, 1980), 295 – 301.

56. Even here, Paul may also be referring to the Old Testament Psalms; cf. Anthony Thiselton, *First Epistle to the Corinthians* (NIGTC: Grand Rapids: Eerdmans, 2000), 1134.

57. Fee, *God's Empowering Presence*, 653.

58. This interpretive possibility is left open in TNIV and NIV: "psalms, hymns, and songs from the Spirit."

of Christ can be implanted richly in the lives of the believers.

The word translated "gratitude" ([τῇ] χάριτι) can also be taken as referring to "divine grace" (cf. KJV, ASV, NKJV, NET), especially when the authenticity of the article is assumed.[59] Nevertheless, the focus on thanksgiving here (explicitly noted in vv. 15, 17) and the use of this word elsewhere in Paul for thanksgiving (Rom 6:17; 7:25; 1 Cor 10:30; 15:57; 2 Cor 2:14; 8:16; 9:15; 2 Tim 1:3) support the translation adopted here. Paul may intend this term to draw attention to the proper response required of those who experience God's grace. This connection between divine grace and thanksgiving as directed to God is noted in 2 Cor 4:15: "All this is for your benefit, so that the grace [ἡ χάρις] that is reaching more and more people may cause thanksgiving [τὴν εὐχαριστίαν] to overflow to the glory of God." There Paul points to the increase of the manifestation of God's grace as the basis of the believers' increase in thanksgiving offered to God. Here in Colossians, Paul is making the same argument for those who have participated in Christ's death and resurrection.

3:17a-b And whatever you do in word or in deed, do everything in the name of the Lord Jesus (καὶ πᾶν ὅ τι ἐὰν ποιῆτε ἐν λόγῳ ἢ ἐν ἔργῳ, πάντα ἐν ὀνόματι κυρίου Ἰησοῦ). In this final verse, Paul provides a general but forceful exhortation that relates the behavior of the believers to the confession of their hearts. Not only does this verse conclude the paraenetic section that begins in 3:1, but it also echoes the beginning of the central section, where one likewise finds a general call to submit to the lordship of Christ with an emphasis on teaching and thanksgiving (2:6 – 7). As a transition verse, v. 17 also introduces the discussion of household

relationships that follows as it highlights the role of Jesus as "Lord" (cf. 3:18, 20, 22, 23, 24; 4:1); the significance of this verse for the following section is confirmed by the appearance of a similar statement in v. 23: "Whatever you do, do it wholeheartedly, as to the Lord and not to people."

"Whatever you do" points to the comprehensive nature of this exhortation, and this is underlined by the all-encompassing pair, "in word or in deed" (ἐν λόγῳ ἢ ἐν ἔργῳ),[60] which uses the speech/act polarity to cover all areas of life (cf. Luke 24:19; Acts 7:22; Rom 15:18; 2 Thess 2:17; cf. 1 John 3:18). The power of this phrase here is not limited to its function within its formulaic use elsewhere, however, since in this letter Paul is particularly concerned with the consistency between the believers' confession of the lordship of Christ and their corresponding action. "Word," then, refers not simply to verbal acts, but includes the knowledge of the mind.

The connection between knowledge and deed is reflected in the opening thanksgiving and prayer report of 1:3 – 14, where Paul urges that the "word of truth" (1:5) that has come to the Colossian believers must be allowed to have its effect in their lives; this effect is described in an emphatic call comparable to the one we have in 3:17: "in order that you may walk in a manner worthy of the Lord, and please him in every way, bearing fruit in every good work, growing in the knowledge of God" (1:10). In the context of 3:17, the "word" represents the knowledge that can be expressed in acts of praises noted in v. 16, while "deed" points back to the behavior noted in vv. 5 – 14.

Following v. 15, this focus on both "word" and "deed" is particularly significant as it redefines true worship. In insisting that one's confession should be manifested in daily living, Paul indicates that wor-

---

59. Lightfoot, *St. Paul's Epistles to the Colossians and to Philemon*, 225 – 26. The inclusion of the article has strong external support: 𝔓⁴⁶ ℵ² B D* F G Ψ 6 1505 1739.

60. The preposition ἐν probably indicates the sphere and realm of reference (cf. Wallace, *Greek Grammar*, 372): thus "in the realm of speech/knowledge and in the realm of action."

ship is no longer limited to the verbal act within the congregational gathering; it includes all areas of life. Those who insist that this passage focuses on a "Christian's everyday life" and "thus the primary reference [of this verse] is obviously not to worship"[61] misread Paul's words here. If worship is to be defined as the submission to the lordship of Christ, worship is to be considered as a lifestyle rather than as a cultic act confined to a sacred act performed during the sacred time within the sacred space.

"Do everything in the name of the Lord Jesus" reinforces this redefinition of worship in terms of one's whole being. In the OT, the phrase "the name of the Lᴏʀᴅ" always refers to God; Paul's use of "Lord" in reference to Christ again affirms his divine status.[62] The phrase "in the name of the Lord" is often found in cultic contexts in both the OT (e.g., 2 Sam 6:18; 1 Kgs 8:44; 18:32; 1 Chr 16:2; 21:19; Pss 118:26 [LXX 117:26]; 124:8 [LXX 123:8]; 129:8 [LXX 128:8]) and the NT (1 Cor 5:4; Jas 5:10, 14).[63] The use of this phrase as the link between worship and everyday living is best illustrated in Mic 4:5:

All the nations may walk
  in the name of their gods;
but we will walk in the name of the Lᴏʀᴅ
  [ἐν ὀνόματι κυρίου]
  our God for ever and ever.

In the present context, Paul is likewise calling the believers to abandon their lives in "idolatry" (v. 5) in their worship of the one Lord of all.[64] This worship is to encompass all areas of life since only such worship can point to the universal sovereignty of the Lord Jesus.

3:17c Giving thanks to God the Father through him (εὐχαριστοῦντες τῷ θεῷ πατρὶ δι᾽ αὐτοῦ). Modifying the implied imperative "do" in the preceding clause, "giving thanks" provides the means through which believers can do everything in the name of the Lord Jesus. In this verse, "giving thanks" is not simply a verbal act; it is one that involves both "word" and "deed." This point becomes even more apparent in view of the parallel in Eph 5:20: "always giving thanks to God the Father for everything, in the name of our Lord Jesus Christ." In Col 3:17, the phrase "in the name of the Lord" modifies all acts "in word or deed." In the Ephesian parallel, however, "in the name of our Lord Jesus Christ" modifies the act of giving thanks. Taken together, it is clear that the act of giving thanks involves everything that believers do; when believers give thanks to God, they are doing everything "in the name of the Lord Jesus." As such, this verse provides the positive command that corresponds to the prohibition in Phil 2:14: "Do everything without grumbling."[65]

As noted in 1:3, 12, the act of thanksgiving is always directed to "God the Father." "Through him" (δι᾽ αὐτοῦ) parallels "in the name of the Lord Jesus," and both prepositional phrases can be considered synonymous since they refer back to the role of Christ when God reconciled all things to himself "through him" (δι᾽ αὐτοῦ, 1:20). This prepositional phrase should also be understood in light of Rom 7:25: "Thanks be to God, who delivers me through Jesus Christ our Lord!" In both Romans and here, this prepositional phrase does not point simply to the means through which believers can offer

---

61. Lohse, *Colossians and Philemon*, 153.

62. Cf. Bauckham, *Jesus and the God of Israel*, 188.

63. Most other NT references are found in the use of Ps 118:26 (LXX 117:26; e.g., Matt 21:9; 23:39; Mark 11:9; Luke 13:35; 19:38; John 12:13) and in invocation formulae, where the power or witness of the Lord is invoked (e.g., Acts 9:27 – 28; 1 Cor 1:10; 2 Thess 3:6).

64. The understanding of "in the name of the Lord Jesus" in terms of living a life that honors God is further reflected in the close parallel between this clause and 1 Cor 10:31: "whatever you do, do it all for the glory of God."

65. For a discussion of "grumbling" as an act of ingratitude, see Pao, *Thanksgiving*, 153 – 59.

thanksgiving to God; it also points to the basis on which such offering is possible (cf. 1 Cor 15:57).[66] In Colossians, the intense christocentric focus continues to dominate Paul's discussion, and this will continue in the discussion of household relationships in the next section.

Theology in Application

Grace and Forgiveness

Hidden in a subordinating participial phrase (v. 13), the note on forgiveness provides a significant link between the foundational arguments of Paul in the first half of this letter and the list of virtues in v. 12. Separated from its context, the list of virtues appears simply to point to isolated acts of kindness that might characterize any civilized society. With this note on forgiveness, however, one finds the ultimate grounds for practicing divine grace, and hence all the virtues listed above: "just as the Lord forgave you, so also forgive one another" (v. 13).

In the presentation of the sufficiency and finality of Christ's death on the cross, Paul has repeatedly emphasized the believers' freedom from sin and guilt that results from the climax of God's salvific act (cf. 1:13 – 14, 20 – 22; 2:13 – 15).[67] Here Paul urges the believers to respond to this divine act of grace with similar acts of forgiveness. Such acts do not simply belong to the realm of human ethics; more significantly, they point to the willingness to be convinced that the prior act of God indeed is able to free us to practice such grace.[68]

For the contemporary audience, the significance of Paul's point here is perhaps better appreciated if it is presented in a negative way: those who are not willing to forgive those who have sinned against them reject the principle of grace as manifested by Christ's death on the cross. This point is best illustrated by Jesus' parable of the unmerciful servant in Matt 18:21 – 35, where one finds the forgiven servant's refusal to forgive someone indebted to him. More striking, however, is the fact that although Jesus encouraged his disciples to forgive seventy-seven times (18: 22), the king immediately punishes this servant after this one offense. Behind this apparent inconsistency lies the central lesson of the parable, that those who refuse the principle of grace will not be forgiven: "This is how my heavenly Father will treat each of you unless you forgive your brother or sister from your heart" (18:35). In other

---

66. Though grammatically problematic because δία + genitive signifies means, the following translation is justifiable theologically: "as you give thanks to God the Father *because of him*" (CEV, italics added).

67. See also our discussion on "Sin and Guilt" in the Theology in Application section on 2:6 – 15.

68. The connection between the divine act of grace and one's freedom to practice such a grace is well illustrated by Henri Nouwen's words as he reflects on the difficulties of human forgiveness: "Maybe the reason it seems hard for me to forgive others is that I do not fully believe that I am a forgiven person. If I could fully accept the truth that I am forgiven and do not have to live in guilt or shame, I would really be free" (Robert Durback, ed., *Seeds of Hope: A Henri Nouwen Reader* [Doubleday: Image, 1997], 78).

words, the refusal to practice the grace of God becomes an exceptional offense because it denies one's ultimate dependence on God's prior act of grace.

In this section, therefore, Paul moves from reception of God's grace to the practice of such grace. Through the practice of this grace, one finds the manifestation of the virtues of "compassion, kindness, humility, meekness, and patience" (v. 12). Moreover, the practice of this grace culminates in "love" (v. 14), a virtue that is likewise critical in the appreciation of "all the wealth of full assurance of understanding, and the knowledge of the mystery of God, Christ" (2:2). In this community of love, forgiveness is a critical element because this community must be characterized by grace, which alone can create a community of "one body" of Christ (v. 15), one that eliminates all barriers that separate the old humanity (cf. v. 11). As Christ's death on the cross brought about the new creation (1:18 – 20), human forgiveness becomes a critical element in the upbuilding of this new creation. In forgiving those around us, we continue this act of re-creation as we "disengage that person from his hurtful act" and in doing so we "re-create him" through this grace of God.[69] Are we willing to acknowledge our own need of God's grace by extending it to those around us? Are we willing to live out the power of the cross by forgiving those who have hurt us?

Since the reception of forgiveness requires the admission of one's inadequacies and dependence on God's grace, the human act of forgiveness is likewise an act of "humility" (v. 12), as an "aspect of forgiveness is to abandon one's egocentric position of only seeing others in terms of one's own needs."[70] This redirection is again built on the christological principle that lies at the heart of Paul's arguments in this letter: "Christ is all and in all" (v. 11). It is this christological principle that brings us back to the theme of thanksgiving.

A Life of Thanksgiving

After several notes on thanksgiving (1:3, 12; 2:6 – 7), the present section provides Paul's fullest exposition of that theme in this letter. To be God's faithful people, believers are to heed Paul's call to "be thankful" (v. 15). Unlike the modern contexts where thanksgiving is often considered simply to be a matter of manners and etiquette, thanksgiving in Paul touches on the center of his theological convictions. Consistent with his emphases elsewhere, this section reveals certain distinct elements in his call to thanksgiving.

First, believers are called to give thanks to God, and to him alone. As such, it belongs to the realm of worship rather than simply the maintenance of interpersonal relationships. Second, because thanksgiving is to be directed to God alone, for

---

69. Lewis B. Smedes, "Forgiveness: The Power to Change the Past," *Christianity Today* 46 (2002): 24.

70. Jeffrey M. Brandsma, "Forgiveness: A Dynamic, Theological and Therapeutic Analysis," *Pastoral Psychology* 31 (1982): 43.

Paul it is primarily a response to the act of grace accomplished by God through his Son (v. 13). This also explains why one often finds the general call to thanksgiving without immediate references to the gifts. Finally, in a section that seeks to delineate the identity markers of believers as "the new humanity" (v. 10), the appearance of this call also forces one to reconsider its role within one's life as a faithful follower of Christ.

In regard to thanksgiving as the identity marker of this new humanity, one should begin with Paul's characterization of the old humanity. In Rom 1:21, unbelieving Gentiles experienced God's wrath because they "neither glorified him … nor gave thanks to him." Not only does this provide the definition of unbelievers as being ungrateful to God, but ingratitude is defined by their failure to glorify him. Here in Colossians, the call to "be thankful" likewise points to the willingness to "let the peace of Christ rule in your hearts" (v. 15). This life, as focused on Christ, becomes the climax of the abandonment of one's egocentric life through acts of forgiveness and love (vv. 13 – 14).

In biblical terms, to insist on one's self-sufficiency is an idolatrous act; to give thanks, by contrast, is to acknowledge one's dependence on the Creator and thus to transfer the center of one's concern to God. This understanding of thanksgiving as a humble act of admitting one's inadequacy is also recognized by psychologists who consider ingratitude as a sign of narcissism even in interpersonal relationships:

> To thank someone acknowledges our need to have been helped or enriched in the first place…. Although those of us with predominantly narcissistic concerns may go through the motions of thanking, we frequently resist expressing whole-hearted appreciation, since that would acknowledge a previous insufficiency of some sort, an insult to the grandiose self.[71]

For Paul, this thanksgiving is to be directed to Christ, to whom we owe our existence as the new humanity.

With this understanding of thanksgiving as a conviction and orientation of one's entire being, we can appreciate why Paul calls believers to give thanks in "everything" they do (v. 17). The relationship between a sanctified life that submits to the lordship of Christ and a life of thanksgiving is best noted in two verses in 1 Thessalonians:

> "It is God's will that you should be sanctified [become holy]." (1 Thess 4:3)
> "Give thanks in all circumstances; for this is God's will for you in Christ Jesus." (1 Thess 5:18)

The relationship between these two verses is clear as it is only here that Paul

---

71. Nancy McWilliams and Stanley Lependorf, "Narcissistic Pathology of Everyday Life," *Contemporary Psychoanalysis* 26 (1990): 434 – 49.

provides a definition of God's will with the formula "it/this is God's will."[72] Taken together, Paul makes it clear that to give thanks means to lead a holy life. This explains why, in a section that defines the "elect of God, [as] holy and beloved" (3:12), Paul dwells on this theme of thanksgiving. For contemporary readers, therefore, the practice of thanksgiving is not limited to the realm of interpersonal relationships, nor to the holiday season of Thanksgiving. Instead, we as believers are to acknowledge the sovereignty of God in everything that we do, because he alone is the source of all goodness, and we are his creatures who are to fulfill his will on earth.

Finally, the call to "do everything in the name of the Lord Jesus, giving thanks to God the Father through him" also argues against understanding that thanksgiving is only an emotional response to events that bring immediate gratification to one's life. In Phil 4:6, Paul calls believers to pray with thanksgiving in times of anxiety: "Do not be anxious about anything, but in every situation, by prayer and petition, with thanksgiving, present your requests to God." In times of difficulties, acts of thanksgiving not only remind us of God's past gifts, but also of the fact that he is our Creator and he is in control. In times of success and blessings, the same acts of thanksgiving remind us that security can only be found in God. Through the ups and downs of life, therefore, a life in thanksgiving is one that is anchored in the loving God.

A Worshiping Community

Any discussion of thanksgiving should naturally lead to the issue of worship, and this section provides the reader with an illuminating glimpse into Paul's understanding of worship. Without basing our entire theology on a few verses, a few comments will still be helpful. First, the mentioning of "teaching and admonishing" (v. 16) in the context of worship is important. Earlier such acts depicted the activities of the apostles (1:28); here, these acts are to be performed by the entire community.[73] Worship is no longer the privilege of the few but the responsibility of all, who are to respond to the divine acts of grace.

The fact that "psalms, hymns, and spiritual songs" (v. 16) are considered means of "teaching and admonishing" is also important since it points to doxology as means of edification. While songs of praise are addressed "to God," they are also instruments for instructing "one another." Through communal acts of worship, therefore, members can remind one another of the prior acts of God as they direct their worship toward God. In merging the vertical with the horizontal, the content of worship thereby acquires added significance. Rather than subjective expressions in the state of elation, in worship the community remembers the acts of God on their behalf and

---

72. Malherbe (*Letters to the Thessalonians*, 330) further notes that these two references form "an *inclusio* that encompasses all the paraenesis contained in chaps. 4 and 5."

73. Lohse, *Colossians and Philemon*, 151, highlights the democratization of the gifts of the Spirit (1 Cor 12:28; 14:26) that makes this shift possible.

therefore their covenantal relationship with their sovereign God. One therefore fails to find the strict demarcation between praise and teaching in Paul's understanding of worship.

As Christ, the climax of God's acts on behalf of his people, is undoubtedly the center of the content of worship, he is also its purpose. As "psalms, hymns, and spiritual songs" are means of "teaching and admonishing," "teaching and admonishing" are in turn means through which "the word of Christ [can] dwell in you richly" (v. 16). Students of Colossians should no longer be surprised by this christocentric focus. Many contemporary readers may, however, need to be reminded that worship is a "ritual" whereby one transfers the center of one's attention from self to Christ, who is to "rule in [our] hearts" (v. 15).

Finally, the striking parallel between vv. 16 and 17 should not be missed. In both verses, one finds Christ as the center of concern ("word of Christ," v. 16; "in the name of the Lord Jesus," v. 17), and in both one finds acts of praise and adoration ("teaching and admonishing ... with psalms, hymns, and spiritual songs," v. 16; "giving thanks to God," v. 17). Despite this parallelism, v. 17 extends the thought of v. 16 by the all-encompassing nature of the call: "whatever you do in word or in deed, do everything...." This critical verse redefines the act of worship in terms of one's entire existence. The power of liturgical practices in corporate worship has been well-documented and is perhaps best captured in the following statement: "With liturgy we deal with the *kinesthetics* of faith. Through the teaching power of sacrament and worship, faith gets into our bodies and bone marrow."[74]

For Paul, everyday living in worship through thanksgiving is a series of liturgical acts through which every part of our being is to be convinced thoroughly by our acts of submission that Christ is indeed the Lord of our existence. If we are to be asked the object of our worship, most will reflect on their acts Sunday morning and provide a confident response that we are worshiping the one Lord of all. If our response is to be based on our lives from Monday to Saturday, however, such confidence may no longer be justified. Paul here forces us to examine every detail of our lives to identify the true object of worship. Through acts of thanksgiving, we are called to repent and return to the one who alone deserves our worship and adoration.

---

74. James Fowler, *Weaving the New Creation: Stages of Faith and the Public Church* (New York: HarperCollins, 1991), 181, italics his.

Colossians 3:18 – 4:1

Literary Context

A discussion about the literary context of this section is particularly important because it has often been considered "a self contained unity after which the author returns to the subject he left behind at the outset of the digression."[1] Others even consider this an insertion by a later "interpolator."[2] Such a reading fails, however, to establish the focus of Paul's discussion of household relationships here and how it fits into Paul's argument in Colossians.

We must first note the focus of this section. If we can assume that Paul is drawing from the Hellenistic context in his use of this household code,[3] his striking departure from these literary conventions indicates his point here. In Hellenistic codes, the male head of the household is its sovereign ruler. Paul also focuses here on the issue of power in his repeated use of the title "Lord" (κύριος, 3:18, 20, 22, 23, 24; 4:1), but he insists that it is actually Christ who is the Lord to whom all should submit (3:24). Instead of conforming to the Hellenistic social ethic, therefore, Paul redirects our attention to the one who is truly the Lord of all.

Because of this affirmation of the lordship of Christ, Paul can further address women (3:18), children (3:20), and slaves (3:22 – 25), who are members of the household often considered by Hellenistic philosophers not to be worthy of moral exhortation.[4] Also in light of Christ's lordship, Paul can focus on the duties of the male head of the household (3:19, 21; 4:1), an element often missing in Hellenistic household discussions.

Since the lordship of Christ is the focus of this section, its connection with the surrounding sections becomes clear. That lordship is firmly established in the christological hymn of 1:15 – 20, and it becomes the foundation for Paul's critique of the Colossian false teachers in 2:8 – 23. As Paul turns his attention to the behavior of

---

1. Witherington and Wessels, "Do Everything in the Name of the Lord," 315.

2. Winsome Munro, "Col. III.18 – IV.1 and Eph. V.21 – VI.9: Evidence of a Late Literary Stratum," *NTS* 18 (1972): 440.

3. See "In Depth: Household Codes" at 3:18a.

4. See, e.g., Aristotle, *Politics* 1.1254b, who considers the male head of the household as the sole possessor of "the rational" soul who, by the law of nature, is to exercise his rule over all other animate and inanimate things.

Christians, the exalted status of the risen Christ also becomes his starting point (3:1 – 4). It is because of the acknowledgment of the power of the risen Christ that believers must take off the old humanity (vv. 5 – 11) and put on the new (vv. 12 – 17) as they participate in the community of God's new creation. Immediately preceding our present section, Paul reaffirms the significance of the lordship of Christ by urging believers to lead a life of worship through acts of thanksgiving (vv. 15 – 17).

This emphasis on submission to the Lord Jesus is best captured in v. 17, which serves as a transition: "And whatever you do in word or in deed, do everything in the name of the Lord Jesus, giving thanks to God the Father through him." And Col 3:18 – 4:1 is followed immediately by the note on thanksgiving in 4:2: "Devote yourselves to prayer, being alert in it with thanksgiving." As thanksgiving points to the acknowledgment of the Creator, the content that is bracketed by these notes on thanksgiving points to concrete ways in which believers can offer thanks to God: through a life that affirms the lordship of Christ.[5]

Moving beyond the call to refocus one's life in light of the confession of the lordship of Christ (3:1 – 4:1), Paul then proceeds to discuss the eschatological mission (4:2 – 6). This move is also anticipated by the discussion of household relationships, for the next step after affirming the lordship of Christ in one's household is the proclamation of such news to those outside of the circle of believers. Since Christ is the Lord of all, this confession must be acknowledged by all, even those who have yet to make such a confession.

V. Faithfulness of the Believers (2:6 – 4:1)

   A. Call to Faithfulness (2:6 – 7)

   B. Sufficiency in Christ (2:8 – 23)

   C. Reorientation of Christian Living (3:1 – 4:1)

      1. Focus on the Risen Christ (3:1 – 4)

      2. Take off the Old Humanity (3:5 – 11)

      3. Put on the New Humanity (3:12 – 17)

➡   **4. Lord of the Household (3:18 – 4:1)**

   VI. Eschatological Mission to the World (4:2 – 6)

5. Some have also considered this section as a response to the challenges posed by the false teachers, as Paul emphasizes the significance of a sanctified life in this earthly existence over against a preoccupation with one's visionary experiences and spiritual accomplishments; cf. Schrage, *Ethics of the New Testament*, 248 – 49; Andrew T. Lincoln, "The Household Code and Wisdom Mode of Colossians," *JSNT* 74 (1999): 108.

Main Idea

Believers' confession that Jesus is Lord of all must be manifested in their daily lives, especially in the household setting. Husbands, fathers, and masters — considered the heads of the household in Greco-Roman culture — must submit to Jesus as the Lord of all. Wives, children, and slaves — considered subordinate members — must recognize that they are serving the Lord Jesus.

Translation

Colossians 3:18 – 4:1

18a	Exhortation	**Wives, submit to your husbands,**
b	manner	as is fitting in the Lord.
19a	Exhortation	**Husbands, love your wives** and
b	expansion	**do not be harsh with them.**
20a	Exhortation	**Children, obey your parents in everything,**
b	basis	for **this is pleasing in the Lord.**
21a	Exhortation	**Fathers, do not provoke your children,**
b	purpose	so that they do not lose heart.
22a	Exhortation	**Slaves, obey your earthly masters in everything,**
b	expansion	not merely for eye service
c	manner	as people-pleasers, but
d	contrast	with single-mindedness,
e	basis	fearing the Lord.
23a	condition	Whatever you do,
b	Exhortation	**do it**
c	manner	wholeheartedly,
d	manner	as to the Lord and not to people,
24a	basis	since you know that from the Lord you will receive the reward of inheritance.
b	Exhortation	**Serve the Lord Christ.**
25a	basis	For **the wrongdoer will be repaid for his wrong,**
b	expansion	and **there is no partiality.**
4:1a	Exhortation	**Masters, provide for your slaves justice and equity,**
b	basis	since you know that you also have a Master in heaven.

Structure

Without a connecting conjunction in 3:18, the discussion of household relationships flows directly from the previous call to "do everything in the name of the Lord Jesus" (v. 17). Using imperative clauses, Paul addresses the behavior between three pairs of relationships: wives and husbands, children and fathers, and slaves and masters. All three pairs begin with a call to submit with similar compound verbs ("submit," ὑποτάσσεσθε, v. 18; "obey," ὑπακούετε, vv. 20, 22), but in all three, the attention immediately shifts to "the Lord," explicitly identified as Christ in v. 24. For the corresponding members of the pair, the focus is on their duties to those who are submitting to them (vv. 19, 21; 4:1).

In the first pair, wives are called to "submit" to their husbands (v. 18), and husbands are in turn to "love" their wives (v. 19). The second pair follows the same pattern: children are called to "obey [their] parent's (v. 20), and "fathers"[6] are to be considerate in dealing with them (v. 21).

The third pair also contains these two basic elements: slaves are called to "obey" their masters (v. 22), and the masters are to provide them "justice and equity" (4:1). What deviates from the pattern in the wider Hellenistic world is that the first part moves beyond the mere evocation of "the Lord" in the call for them to be obedient (v. 22e); it also contains a substantial subsection that explains this call to obedience with a clear note that they should do so "to the Lord and not to people" (v. 23). This focus on the Lord culminates in a direct call to "serve the Lord Christ" (v. 24b), an imperative that breaks the strict parallel of the series of the imperatives.

The move of "the Lord Christ" to center stage also transforms the second element of this pair. Unlike the earlier two pairs, where "the Lord" is evoked only in the call directed to the members who are to be obedient, 4:1 directs masters to recognize their own "Master in heaven" (4:1), a title literally rendered as "Lord in heaven" (κύριον ἐν οὐρανῷ). This completes the string of references to κύριος, where these references climax in the contrast between the two "lords": the master in an earthly household and the true Lord in heaven. With the final appearance of the title "Lord" in this household code, readers realize that this "Lord" is the focus of this entire code, the one who serves as the ultimate authority figure in human relationships.

The substantially lengthier treatment of the third pair demands an explanation. While proposals have been presented,[7] our focus should center on this household code and the context in which it is situated. If one finds the redefinition of the Lord in this code as Paul shifts the readers' attention from the earthly master of the household to the true Lord of all in heaven, it is possible that the definition of "slaves"

---

6. The word "fathers" (οἱ πατέρες) can be translated as "parents," but in this household code it most likely refers to the male heads of the households, thus the "fathers."

7. See v. 22 for a further discussion.

also undergoes similar transformation under the pen of Paul. This possibility is strengthened by v. 23 ("whatever you do, do it wholeheartedly, as to the Lord and not to people"), an encompassing call that appears to repeat Paul's earlier call to the believers: "And whatever you do in word or in deed, do everything in the name of the Lord Jesus" (v. 17). Paul here calls the believers to submit to their masters as slaves, except now their master is actually the Lord Jesus himself.[8] This explains in part the presence of this relatively lengthy treatment on the slaves, and this reading is not unexpected in light of the constant affirmation of the lordship of Christ in this letter.

Having highlighted the significance of the lordship of Christ and the servanthood of all believers, one must not deny the intent of this code to address the concrete household relationships in the first century, relationships that involved real conflicts and struggles. After all, the historical slaves addressed could also assume this dual role as slaves and believers, as Onesimus in the letter to Philemon testifies. Through the emphasis on the significance of the gospel for everyday existence, Paul provides a striking illustration that demonstrates the need for all relationships to be reconsidered in light of this gospel.

Exegetical Outline

➡ **I. Lord of the Household (3:18 – 4:1)**

A. Between wives and husbands (3:18 – 19)

1. Submission of the wives in the Lord (3:18)

2. Love of the husbands (3:19)

B. Between children and fathers (3:20 – 21)

1. Obedience of the children in the Lord (3:20)

2. Consideration of the fathers (3:21)

C. Between slaves and masters (3:22 – 4:1)

1. Obedience of the slaves in the Lord (3:22 – 25)

   a. In sincerity (3:22)

   b. Do it to the Lord (3:23 – 24a)

   c. Serve the Lord Christ (3:24b – 25)

2. Fairness of the masters (4:1)

---

8. The later reference to Epaphras as "a slave of Christ" (4:12) may further support this reading. In another prison letter likely written during the same time, Paul also identified himself and Timothy as "servants [slaves] of Christ Jesus" (Phil 1:1), and this appellation is grounded in the prior act of Christ, who had "emptied himself by taking on the form of the servant [slave]" (2:7, both pers. trans.).

Explanation of the Text

3:18a Wives, submit to your husbands (Αἱ γυναῖκες, ὑποτάσσεσθε τοῖς ἀνδράσιν). Paul begins this household code by addressing the marital relationship. In Greek, "wives" (αἱ γυναῖκες) translates a nominative plural noun with an article, a construction often used as a vocative.[9] The word "wives" can be translated as "women," but here it clearly refers to "wives"; the same applies to "husbands."

"Submit" (ὑποτάσσεσθε) is a middle present imperative, signifying that the wives should voluntarily subject themselves to their husbands.[10] The exact significance of this call must be delineated carefully. We begin with the meaning of the word "submit"; then we will discuss the historical and literary contexts within which this call is to be understood.

In the NT, as in Greek literature in general, the verb "submit" is consistently used for subordination to an authority figure. It can be used to denote subordination to older people (1 Pet 5:5), one's parents (Luke 2:51), governing authorities (Rom 13:1, 5; Titus 3:1; 1 Pet 2:13), leaders of the local church (1 Pet 5:5), the law (Rom 8:7), Christ (Eph 5:24; cf. Phil 3:21), and even God (Heb 12:9; Jas 4:7).[11] This

does not diminish the dignity and ontological status of wives, however, since Christ himself was subordinated to God, which for Paul became the basis of the submission of wives to their husbands: "the head of every man is Christ, and the head of the woman is man, and the head of Christ is God" (1 Cor 11:3).[12] In Ephesians, Paul further appeals to the submission of the church to Christ as the basis of the wives' submission to their husbands (Eph 5:23).

Some have pointed to historical and contextual factors in an attempt to understand the function of this call for wives' submission in the first-century setting: "differences in spouses' ages (the female was often significantly younger), differences in amount of formal education, differences in opportunities to acquire and hold resources, lack of informational sources within the home, women's lack of social exposure."[13] Others have suggested that Paul's note here is in response to the "inordinate freedom and enthusiasm" prompted by his gospel of grace and equality,[14] or because "an insubordinate wife was a bad witness for the gospel in a situation where non-Christian husbands expected subordination."[15] These historical factors cannot,

---

9. Wallace (*Greek Grammar*, 57) suggests that the articular nominative is often used in addressing an inferior, except in cases where a Semitic source is clearly behind the text. Here, however, since the same articular nominative is also used in addressing the husband (v. 19), this can be considered as an exceptional use, unless a sense of equality is to be read into this construction.

10. It can also be a passive, understood as a reflexive passive, which can carry this sense; cf. BDAG, 1042. Schweizer (*Letter to the Colossians*, 221), who sees this as a divine passive, argues that this is "the subjugation (brought about by God) of the powers to Christ."

11. Wayne Grudem (*Countering the Claims of Evangelical Feminism* [Colorado Springs: Multnomah, 2006], 117) argues that "no one has yet produced any examples in ancient Greek literature ... where *hupotassō* is applied to a relationship between persons, and where it does not carry this sense of being *subject to an authority*" (italics his). Even the call to "submit

to one another" (Eph 5:21) is meaningful only if this common usage is assumed.

12. Cf. George W. Knight III, "Husbands and Wives as Analogues of Christ and the Church: Ephesians 5:21 – 33 and Colossians 3:18 – 19," in *Recovering Biblical Manhood and Womanhood: A Response to Evangelical Feminism* (ed. John Piper and Wayne Grudem; Wheaton, IL: Crossway, 1991), 165 – 78, 492 – 95.

13. William J. Webb, "A Redemptive-Movement Hermeneutic: The Slavery Analogy," in *Discovering Biblical Equality: Complementarity without Hierarchy* (ed. Ronald W. Pierce, Rebecca Merrill Groothuis, and Gordon Fee; Downers Grove, IL: InterVarsity Press, 2004), 398.

14. Cannon, *Use of Traditional Materials in Colossians*, 131.

15. I. Howard Marshall, "Mutual Love and Submission in Marriage: Colossians 3:18 – 19 and Ephesians 5:21 – 33," in *Discovering Biblical Equality*, 192.

however, fully explain Paul's reference to the submission of Christ to God or the church to Christ as models for the wives' submission.

More relevant are the theological and literary contexts within which this statement should be understood. Theologically, Gal 3:28, which points to the new people of God as constituting "neither … male [nor] female" — a statement that reappears in a similar form in Col 3:11, though without reference to this particular gender contrastive pair — makes it clear that Paul's point is not the superiority of one group over another within God's people. Instead, if we take vv. 18 – 19 together, these statements point to the unity and mutual accountability as members of the one body of Christ. Clauses and phrases such as "bearing with one another and forgiving one another" (v. 13), "forgive one another" (v. 13), "put on love … the perfect bond" (v. 14), "in one body" (v. 15), "teaching and admonishing one another" (v. 16) in the preceding paragraph confirm the significance of this point. Yet it is perhaps because of his concern for the unity of the body of Christ that Paul discusses the different roles and functions of its members.

Also worth noting is that this call appears within a significant modification of the social convention reflected in Hellenistic household codes. In those codes, the fundamental principle is on the obedience of the subordinate members to the male head of the household.[16] In Paul's code, however, the focus on the lordship of Christ as emphasized in the note that immediately follows (v. 18b), as well as the attention given to the duty of the husband in v. 19, shifts the focus of this code. The power of the husband is critically and substantially relativized. With this code being a reaction to the secular convention, therefore, these qualifications deserve serious considerations. This reading is consistent with the thought of this letter that consistently emphasizes the lordship of Christ.

In our contemporary appropriation of this passage, the central point must be a christocentric one. Consequently, a translation such as CEV's can be misleading, despite its intention to soften the idea of subjection: "A wife must put her husband first." Paul's point for this code is rather: "A wife/child/slave must put the Lord first."

IN DEPTH: Household Code

Colossians 3:18 – 4:1 contains one of the best examples of the "household code" (German, *Haustafel*) in the NT, a code that addresses three pairs of relationships in the household: husband and wife, father and children, and master and slaves. The interpretation of this code in its context is affected by one's understanding of the existence and function of similar codes in Hellenistic literature.

New Testament Codes

Two primary factors have prompted many to consider the household code in Col 3:18 – 4:1 not only as an independent literary unit, but one that points to the use of a preexisting code, although it may still play a critical role in Paul's argument in this letter. First, the clear change in style and a certain disruption

---

16. Although the verb "submit" is not a term often found in such codes, the idea of subjection is; cf. Lincoln, *Ephesians*, 367.

between 3:17 and 3:18 support this conclusion. The smooth continuation of thought between 3:17 and 4:2 and the fact that this "paragraph is introduced without any connecting particle" suggest that this is a "self-contained paraenetic unit."[17] Moreover, that the exhortations within this section "are briefer and more abrupt than the preceding ones" also supports this conclusion.[18]

The existence of similar "codes" in the NT (Eph 5:22 – 6:9; 1 Tim 5:1 – 6:2; Titus 2:2 – 10; 1 Pet 2:18 – 3:7) also points to the same direction. Paul's discussion of church order is often understood as the basis for such household rules (e.g., 1 Tim 2:8 – 3:13), while others have further identified the presence of these rules behind the structure of other NT passages.[19] These codes can also be found in post-NT, early Christian literature (*Did.* 4.9 – 11; *1 Clem.* 21.6 – 9). Their existence in such diverse bodies of literature within early Christian writings suggests that these writers were using a preexisting form, even though significant modification of such a form cannot be denied.

Origin

Various attempts have been made to identify the background of these household codes,[20] and some have recently declared a consensus on this issue:

> The lengthy debate on the origin of these household rules has been recently resolved. In the past twenty years or so several scholars in quick succession have recognized that the model for the Christian household rules, insofar as there was one, was that of *oikonomia,* "household management." The point is that the household was widely recognized to be the basic unit of the state.[21]

To these scholars, the basis of these discussions rests in Aristotle's discussion of the household as the basis of the political structure of the *polis:*

> The parts of household management will correspond to the parts of which the household itself is constituted. A complete household consists of slaves and freemen. But every subject of inquiry should first be examined in its simplest elements; and the primary and simplest elements of the household are the connexion of master and slave, that of the husband and wife, and that of parents of children. We must accordingly consider each of these connexions, examining the nature of each and the qualities it ought to possess. (*Politics* 1.1253b)[22]

---

17. O'Brien, *Colossians, Philemon*, 214.

18. Leppä, *Making of Colossians*, 110.

19. Examples include Matt 19 – 20 (Warren Carter, *Households and Discipleship: A Study of Matthew 19 – 20* [JSNTSup 103; Sheffield: Sheffield Academic, 1994]) and 1 John 2:12 – 13 (K. H. Rengstorf, "Die neutestamentlichen Mahnungen an die Frau, sich dem Manne unterzuordnen," in *Verbum Dei Manet in Aeternum* [ed. W. Foerster; Wittenberg: Luther-Verlag, 1953], 133 – 34).

20. See the helpful surveys in James E. Crouch, *The Origin and Intention of the Colossian Haustafel* (Göttingen: Vandenhoeck and Ruprecht, 1972), 18 – 31; and David L. Balch, "Household Codes," in *Greco-Roman Literature and the New Testament* (ed. David E. Aune; Atlanta: Scholars, 1988), 25 – 50. See also my brief treatment in *Thanksgiving*, 109 – 10.

21. Dunn, *Theology of Paul*, 666 – 67.

22. All translations of *Politics* are taken from Ernest Barker, *The Politics of Aristotle* (New York: Oxford Univ.

Similar discussions survive in later Hellenistic literature (Dio Chrysostom 5.348 – 51; Seneca, *Ep.* 94.1; Dionysius of Halicarnassus, *Ant. rom.* 2.25.4 – 26.4). Although one may not point to one universal type in Paul's time, such understanding of the basic structure of power within the household seems widespread. Despite cautionary notes concerning the need to distinguish between social convention and literary forms,[23] it seems justifiable to see such conventions as reflected in various pieces of writings as the common tradition from which early Christian writers drew.

Without limiting this convention to one particular school of thought, this general Hellenistic background provides a helpful context within which NT household codes can be examined.[24] This is not to deny the mediation of this tradition through Hellenistic Jewish traditions (e.g., Philo, *Decalogue* 165 – 67),[25] and one should not rule out the influence of the OT traditions in the NT use of such a convention.[26] Nevertheless, the affinities of the NT codes in general, and the Colossian code in particular, come closest to the Hellenistic examples that survive as they focus on the treatment of these same three sets of relationships. Finally, those who argue from the distinctly Christian elements in these codes that these are Christian inventions[27] have only proven that these codes have been Christianized. Moreover, in genre analysis one should be careful in positing the sudden appearances of literary conventions;[28] the appearance of these codes in diverse NT writings points rather to the preexistence of this form with distinct modifications by these various writers.

Pauline Use of the Hellenistic Codes

Instead of assuming that Paul is blindly borrowing from the literary conventions of his day, to acknowledge the Hellenistic context of the household code is to allow contemporary readers to detect ways in which Paul affirms, interacts with, and qualifies the thought patterns of his contemporaries. Behind the various Hellenistic codes, one finds the basic principle of power and submission:

Press, 1958), 8. See also Plato, *Resp.* 4.433 – 34.

23. Hartman, "Code and Context," 130.

24. Many have, e.g., rejected the attempt of Martin Dibelius (*An die Kolosser, Epheser an Philemon* [HNT 12; Tübingen: Mohr, 1953], 46 – 50) to identify the Stoic background behind the NT use of this convention.

25. Crouch, *Origin and Intention of the Colossian Haustafel*, 78 – 79. See also David Daube, *The New Testament and Rabbinic Judaism* (London: Athlone, 1956), 90 – 105.

26. The influence of the Ten Commandments in particular has often been noted; cf. Grant, "The Decalogue in Early Christianity," 1 – 17.

27. Thus David Schöder, "Die Haustafeln des Neuen Testaments: Ihre Herkunft und ihr theologischer Sinn" (DTh diss.; University of Hamburg, 1959).

28. In discussing the various NT literary forms, William G. Doty ("The Concept of Genre in Literary Analysis," *SBL Proceedings* [1972]: 414) rightly notes: "the primitive Christian literary genres can best be comprehended by the approach which locates them not in terms of absolute generic identity but as positioned upon particular generic trajectories prevailing in Greco-Roman Hellenism." See also the general discussion in Alastair Fowler, *Kinds of Literature: An Introduction to the Theory of Genres and Modes* (New York: Oxford Univ. Press, 1982), 170 – 90.

subordinate members are to submit to the sovereign ruler of the household, who is at the same time the husband, the father, and the master.[29]

Many consider the household codes in the later writings of Paul as a betrayal of the theology of freedom and equality as reflected in his earlier writings. They often assume that this "Paul" of Colossians, Ephesians, and the Pastoral Letters domesticates the gospel of the authentic Paul, who only penned the earlier "authentic" letters. For them, this "Paul," who is considered a second-class disciple of the historical Paul, uses the household code to exert social control on those who assume that the gospel of freedom proclaimed by Paul "would expect release from that condition in the community of the redeemed."[30] Some even argue that this author of such household codes "reinforces male control of paternity, male control of women's sexual experience … and male control of slaves' bodies."[31]

The above conclusion not only assumes that this "Paul" simply reaffirms the ideology behind such Hellenistic codes; it also ignores the wider context within which these codes appear. A more faithful reading of the text pays attention to Paul's arguments surrounding the code, where he repeatedly affirms the lordship of Christ. This affirmation is also evident both within the Colossian code and in the context in which it is situated. In citing the code, therefore, Paul provides significant modification while situating it in a new context, thereby challenging the basic principle of the code: instead of affirming the sovereignty of the male head of the household, Paul affirms the lordship of Christ even in the household setting.

In other words, "the conventional authority structures of the ancient household are thereby subverted even while they are left in place."[32] In this reading, submission to authority is not denied, but the focus is on Christ, who himself brought about this "spiritual revolution" through his own submission and humiliation.[33] Rather than advocating a social revolt,[34] therefore, Paul is promoting something far more earth-shattering: the Christ who died on the cross is now the Lord of all whose power and glory will be fully revealed when all his people will be "revealed with him in glory" (Col 3:4).

29. See Aristotle, *Pol.* 1.1254a; David L. Balch, *Let Wives Be Submissive: The Domestic Code in 1 Peter* (SBLMS 26; Chico, CA: Scholars, 1981), 23 – 80.

30. Leppä, *Making of Colossians*, 126 – 27.

31. Margaret Y. MacDonald, "Slavery, Sexuality and House Churches: A Reassessment of Colossians 3.18 – 4.1 in Light of New Research on the Roman Family," *NTS* 53 (2007): 105 – 6.

32. Richard Hays, *Moral Vision of the New Testament: A Contemporary Introduction to New Testament Ethics* (Edinburgh: T&T Clark, 2004), 64.

33. John W. Kleinig, "Ordered Community: Order and Subordination in the New Testament," *Lutheran Theological Journal* 39 (2005): 196 – 209. See also Suzanne Watts Henderson, "Taking Liberties with the Text: The Colossians Household Code as Hermeneutical Paradigm," *Int* 60 (2006): 430.

34. For the problems of the understanding of Paul as promoting social revolt, see, in particular, John H. Elliott, "Jesus Was Not an Egalitarian: A Critique of an Anachronistic and Idealist Theory," *BTB* 32 (2002): 75 – 91.

3:18b As is fitting in the Lord (ὡς ἀνῆκεν ἐν κυρίῳ). Even within the discussion of this first pair of relationships within the household, Paul reminds the believers of the centrality of the lordship of Christ. While it is clear that "the Lord" refers to "the Lord Christ" (v. 24), the way this clause is related to the previous clause is not immediately clear. This clause is often considered to provide the basis for the previous call to submission: "that is what you should do since you are united to the Lord Jesus."[35] But if we note the common function of the comparative particle "as," it seems best to take the entire phrase as indicating manner,[36] with "is fitting" (ἀνῆκεν)[37] denoting a sense of propriety.[38] The resulting sense is therefore: submit in a manner that is appropriate for those who are in the Lord.[39] Understood in this way, this clause points to Christ as the pattern of humility and submission.[40]

It is also possible to take this clause as limiting the sphere in which the wife is to submit to her husband. She is to submit only insofar as the will of the husband aligns with that of "the Lord." Again, "the Lord" is the center of one's attention, as he alone is the criterion through which to determine what is appropriate and acceptable. Therefore, instead of understanding this verse as a call "to conduct their lives in accord with the prevalent social order,"[41] it actually suggests that "those structures stand in tension with their existence in Christ."[42]

3:19a Husbands, love your wives (Οἱ ἄνδρες, ἀγαπᾶτε τὰς γυναῖκας). Unlike Hellenistic codes, which are preoccupied with the rights of the male head of the household, Paul also addresses the duties of the husbands. The order of address itself may be important. Considered to be the heads of the households, the fact that they are addressed after their wives may be an attempt to challenge the assured position of the husbands in the household.[43]

In Hellenistic discussions of marital relationships, the focus is almost always on the rights of the husbands. According to Aristotle, husbands have the innate right to exercise "marital authority," since the "male is naturally fitter to command than the female, except where there is some departure from nature" (Aristotle, *Pol.* 1.1259a-b). Without noting such rights, Paul focuses instead on the duty of the husbands. "Love" is largely absent from Hellenistic and even Jewish discussions of marital relationships. This note on the distinctly Christian virtue of love "highlights the newness of Paul's vision of marriage."[44] In Colossians, this new vision is based on the creation of a "new humanity" (v. 10). Because this "new humanity" is first loved by God (cf. "beloved," v. 12), believers can practice the various virtues that culminate in "love, which is the perfect bond" (v. 14). In Ephesians, the call to love is directly linked with Christ's love for us (Eph 5:2; cf. Col 2:2). This imitation of Christ's love finds its concrete manifestation in the marital

---

35. Callow, *Semantic and Structural Analysis*, 141. Cf. GNB: "for that is what you should do as Christians."

36. Harris, *Colossians and Philemon*, 179.

37. Among the various ways to explain the imperfect tense, Lightfoot's (*St. Paul's Epistles to the Colossians and to Philemon*, 227) reading seems most helpful; this tense "implies an essential *a priori* obligation," i.e., an obligation stipulated prior to this discussion.

38. With the use of this verb, most see a parallel in the Stoic emphasis of duty.

39. Thus Schweizer, *Letter to the Colossians*, 221 – 22; Dunn, *Epistles to the Colossians and to Philemon*, 248.

40. Cf. Ben Witherington III, *Women and the Genesis of Christianity* (Cambridge: Cambridge Univ. Press, 1990), 152.

41. Lohse, *Colossians and Philemon*, 157, who considers the wives as "not given a specifically Christian directive."

42. Sumney, *Colossians*, 242.

43. Thus James P. Hering, *The Colossian and Ephesian Haustafeln in Theological Context: An Analysis of Their Origins, Relationship, and Message* (American University Studies 7.260; New York: Peter Lang, 2007), 83.

44. Philip B. Payne, *Man and Woman, One in Christ: An Exegetical and Theological Study of Paul's Letters* (Grand Rapids: Zondervan, 2009), 276.

relationship: "Husbands, love your wives, just as Christ loved the church and gave himself up for her" (Eph 5:25).

In light of this christological model, such love is not to be defined simply in emotional or sexual terms; it is to be defined by the will and action of one who is willing to consider the other as the object of one's concern.[45] This move away from a self-centered life is also consistent with Paul's earlier call in this letter to flee an idolatrous life that revolves around one's own needs and desires (v. 5). The move is from idolatry, and true worship therefore is to be lived out in everyday existence as symbolized by the relationships within the household.

3:19b And do not be harsh with them (καὶ μὴ πικραίνεσθε πρὸς αὐτάς). With this negative prohibition, Paul provides a further command for the husbands. The conjunction "and" (καί) has been taken as an epexegetical conjunction, explaining what it means for the husbands to "love" their wives.[46] This view, however, may unjustifiably limit the general command to "love" their wives, since loving does not simply denote the lack of harshness. Thus, some consider the conjunction as providing a specific example to illustrate the general command of love: "in particular, do not be harsh with them."[47]

On the other hand, if "do not be harsh" reflects a more general inclination and attitude, this general call may indeed serve as a corresponding call to the command to love. In the NT, the verb "be harsh" (πικραίνω)[48] is only used in reference to the taste of bitter (Rev 8:11) and sour (Rev 10:9, 10).[49] The related noun "bitterness" (πικρία) is, however, used in a variety of contexts where bitterness reflects a general evil and sinful inclination. In Acts 8:23, the "gall of bitterness" is linked with "the bondage of iniquity" (NASB) and points to a general sense of being evil rather than simply a particular violent act. This phrase points further to the anti-idol polemic since it alludes to Deut 28:18, which contains a warning for those who practice idolatry. In Rom 3, those who have "no fear of God" (3:18) are said to be filled with "cursing and bitterness" (3:14). In Eph 4:31, "bitterness" tops the vice lists that symbolizes "every form of malice." Finally, in Heb 12:15, lack of grace is understood in terms of bitterness.

These four references to bitterness reflect the general sense of wickedness and refusal to worship God.[50] Thus, if the love of one's wife reflects the general, glorious love that Christ has for his people, the bitterness that some may show to their wives will reflect the rejection of that love. Even with the understanding of the verb πικραίνω in the sense of being "angry,"[51] this call reminds the readers of the "anger" that tops the vice list in v. 8.

3:20a Children, obey your parents in everything (Τὰ τέκνα, ὑπακούετε τοῖς γονεῦσιν κατὰ πάντα). Paul now addresses the relationship between children and their parents. "Children" (τέκνα) often points to the relational status of a person instead of his or her age. Some have therefore taken this term here to mean "grown children."[52] Nevertheless, in Hellenistic codes, age is a factor. In Aristotle's paradigmatic discussion of household relationships, for example, "children" are to be subjected

---

45. This is made explicit in Eph 5:28, where the husbands are to love their wives with the love that they have for their own selves.

46. Lohse, *Colossians and Philemon*, 158.

47. Callow, *Semantic and Structural Analysis*, 141 – 42.

48. This intransitive passive verb carries the sense of to "become bitter or embittered" (BDAG, 812).

49. These references may also symbolize the wrath of God at the end of times.

50. See also the adjective "bitter" (πικρός) in reference to envy and in connection with "selfish ambition" in Jas 3:14.

51. Cf. Wilhelm Michaelis, "πικρός, κτλ.," *TDNT*, 6:125.

52. Barth and Blanke, *Colossians*, 439.

to their fathers because of their age and maturity (*Pol.* 1.1259b), and they are to be well-trained because one day they will "grow up to be partners in the government of the state" (*Pol.* 1.1260b). Moreover, in the Ephesian household code, the fathers are called to "bring them up in the training and instruction of the Lord" (Eph 6:4). This points to these children as being relatively young.

In two ways, this call demands more from these children as compared to the wives. First, the verb "obey" (ὑπακούετε) points to a stronger sense of obedience than the call for the wives to "submit" (ὑποτάσσεσθε).[53] Second, this imperative is followed by the all-encompassing phrase "in everything," which emphasizes the comprehensive scope of their obedience to their fathers. Both of these elements reappear in the following call to slaves to "obey your earthly masters in everything" (v. 22).

In the Ephesians household code, the fifth of the Ten Commandments is explicitly evoked as the basis for this call to obedience: "Honor your father and mother" (Eph 6:2). This may explain the reference to "the parents" (τοῖς γονεῦσιν) here instead of only the "fathers" (οἱ πατέρες), who are addressed in the next verse. This OT background may also help in explaining the phrase "in everything." In the OT, the call to honor one's "father and . . . mother" (Deut 5:16) is related to their duties to "teach them [i.e., the laws] to your children and to their children after them" (Deut 4:9; cf. 6:7).[54] In light of the OT teachings and the reference to "the Lord" in the second half of this verse, "in everything" undoubtedly refers to the teachings of parents that are con-

sistent with the law of God. A similar qualification can also be found in Greco-Roman philosophers such as Epictetus, who issues the call to "be obedient in everything" (*Diatr.* 2.10.7) in reference to the absolute submission to one's father even though he also affirms that the higher priority is to be given to the "good" (*Diatr.* 3.3.6).[55]

3:20b For this is pleasing in the Lord (τοῦτο γὰρ εὐάρεστόν ἐστιν ἐν κυρίῳ). As in the call for the wives to submit, Paul refers to "the Lord" in his discussion of the obedience of the children. "Pleasing" means that which is pleasant and acceptable. In both the LXX and the NT, this word is most often used (1) with a simple dative object and (2) in reference to God (e.g., Wis 4:10; Rom 12:1; 14:18; Phil 4:18). In this case, however, the word is followed by a prepositional phrase that appears to point to Christ: "in the Lord" (ἐν κυρίῳ). Several attempts have been made to make sense of this phrase in this context.

(1) In light of the presumably absent dative reference, some have supplied an additional phrase that points to Christ as the object of the pleasing act, with an additional reference to those who are united with him: "for such behavior pleases the Lord and befits those who belong to him."[56]

(2) Agreeing with (1) that an additional phrase needs to be inserted, some have insisted that God should be the object of the act of pleasing instead: "well-pleasing (to God) in the Lord (Jesus Christ)."[57]

(3) Another option considers this a conditional construction, limiting the call to be obedient "in everything": "provided that the children's

---

53. Cf. Lohse, *Colossians and Philemon*, 159, who defines this obedience as "absolute subordination."

54. That the teaching of the law is in view is made clear by Deut 4:1, which provides the same reward as those who honor their parents: "Now, Israel, hear the decrees and laws I am about to teach you. Follow them so that you may live and may go in and take possession of the land the LORD, the God of your ancestors, is giving you."

55. Peter Balla, *The Child-Parent Relationship in the New Testament and Its Environment* (WUNT 155; Tübingen: Mohr Siebeck, 2003), 134 – 35, 174.

56. Harris, *Colossians and Philemon*, 189.

57. Dunn, *Epistles to the Colossians and to Philemon*, 251, who considers this as a way to affirm both the Jewish heritage of the believers and their christocentric faith. Cf. REB: "for that is pleasing to God and is the Christian way."

obedience is ἐν κυρίῳ, on a truly Christian level of motive."[58]

(4) Finally, the phrase can simply be read in the sense of a dative construction: "for this is well pleasing to the Lord" (NKJV; cf. NAB, NASB), or "for this pleases the Lord" (TNIV, ESV, NIV; cf. NLT, NJB).[59]

In this context, (4) provides the most likely reading. In light of the direct references to "the Lord" in Paul's addresses to the wives (v. 18) and to the slaves (v. 22), it seems best to retain "in the Lord" as a reference to the Lord Jesus. That a prepositional phrase is used instead of a simple dative can be explained either by its parallels with v. 18 ("as is fitting in the Lord") or simply the formulaic nature of this phrase in Paul's writings.[60] Moreover, in some cases, one does find the use of the word "pleasing" with comparable prepositional phrases with essentially the same meaning: "pleasing to [πρός] you [i.e., God]" (Wis 9:10), and "pleasing to [ἐνώπιον] him [i.e., God]" (Heb. 13:21). In this call to the children, this phrase not only justifies Paul's call for the children to obey their parents, but this use of the christological title also redirects the attention to Jesus, who is the true Lord of all.[61]

3:21a Fathers, do not provoke your children (Οἱ πατέρες, μὴ ἐρεθίζετε τὰ τέκνα ὑμῶν). Paul now addresses the responsibilities of the "fathers." Although "fathers" can refer to both fathers and mothers (cf. Heb 11:23),[62] here the use of this term instead of the more general "parents" (see v. 20) may reflect Paul's intention to address only the "fathers." This is consistent with the Hellenistic household discussion, where the male head of the household is often addressed ("husbands," "fathers," and "masters"). Moreover, the rule of fathers over their children is often emphasized. Aristotle compares fathers to kings who have "royal authority": "A king ought to be naturally superior to his subjects, and yet of the same stock as they are; and this is the case with the relation of age to youth, and of father to child" (*Pol.* 1.1259b).

"Provoke" (ἐρεθίζετε) means to "to make resentful, to make someone bitter."[63] As a verb that refers to an act that may create an adverse reaction, it may be related to the teaching in Deut 21:20 concerning the treatment of the "rebellious" (ἐρεθίζει) son.[64] In this case, however, the focus is on the duty of the father not to turn his son into such a person. This verse may also be a reaction to the contemporary Jewish tradition that focused on the responsibilities of the children not to "provoke" their parents (Sir 3:16).[65] If so, the transposition of this concern to the command on the fathers is striking. Unlike both Hellenistic and Jewish discussions that focus on the power of the fathers, therefore, Paul focuses on the responsibility of fathers in assuring the character of their children.[66]

---

58. Moule, *Epistles to the Colossians and to Philemon*, 130.

59. Some, however, see "God" as the reference behind "Lord": "for that is what pleases God" (GNB).

60. Schweizer, *Letter to the Colossians*, 223. Cf. Rom 14:14; 16:11, 12, 13, 22; 1 Cor 1:31; 4:17; 7:39; 9:1; 2 Cor 2:12; Gal 5:10; Eph 4:17; Phil 1:14; 4:1, 2, 4; Col 4:7, 17; 1 Thess 3:8.

61. See also Lightfoot, *St. Paul's Epistles to the Colossians and to Philemon*, 227, who takes "pleasing" in an absolute sense, and "in the Lord" as a qualifying phrase: "is well-pleasing ... as judged by a Christian standard."

62. Thus "parents" (NJB, CEV, GNB); cf. O'Brien, *Colossians, Philemon*, 225; Barth and Blanke, *Colossians*, 443.

63. Louw and Nida, §86.168.

64. Moo, *Letters to the Colossians and to Philemon*, 307.

65. Sir 3:16 uses the verb παροργίζω ("to provoke") in the call to the children, the same verb used in Eph 6:4: "Fathers, do not provoke [μὴ παροργίζετε] your children" (Eph 6:4 NASB). Cf. Balla, *Child-Parent Relationship*, 98.

66. Rabbinic sources do, however, testify to a tradition that seeks to qualify Deut 21:20 by noting the duties of the fathers; cf. *b. Moʿed Qaṭ.* 17a; Crouch, *Origin and Intention of the Colossian Haustafel*, 115 – 16, who also notes that in Judaism, discussions of parental duties are always focused on the fathers as explicitly noted in *m. Qidd.* 1.7: "All the obligations of a father toward his son enjoined in the Law are incumbent on men but not on women." This may also explain the focus on the "fathers" in this Colossian code.

3:21b So that they do not lose heart (ἵνα μὴ ἀθυμῶσιν). Grammatically, this is a purpose clause that modifies the previous call to the fathers, but in this context it also provides the basis for the previous call: "do not aggravate your children, or they will become discouraged" (NLT; cf. CEV). This reading is possible especially since the negative purpose clause introduced by "so that … not" (ἵνα μή) often points to a scenario that is to be avoided (cf. Matt 7:1; 17:27; 26:5; Mark 14:38; Luke 16:28; Rom 11:25; 15:20; 1 Cor 4:6; 8:13; 11:32; Eph 2:9).

"Lose heart" refers to the state of becoming "disheartened to the extent of loss of motivation."[67] This verb is often translated as "discouraged" (KJV, ASV, NKJV, HCSB, TNIV, ESV, NIV), but that translation can be misunderstood as pointing simply to one's emotional state without implications on the actions to be carried out. NLT provides a helpful phrase noted above ("discouraged and quit trying"), although the more archaic "lose heart" (NASB, NRSV, REB, NJB) may function just as well. Paul's choice of this verb, which appears only here in the NT, may be motivated by the appearance of the related word "rage" (θυμόν)[68] in the vice list (v. 8). In warning against provoking the spirit of their children in anger, Paul points to the likely result that their provocation will lead to their state of being dispirited.

3:22a Slaves, obey your earthly masters in everything (Οἱ δοῦλοι, ὑπακούετε κατὰ πάντα τοῖς κατὰ σάρκα κυρίοις). In the third section within this household code, Paul addresses the relationship between slaves and masters. This discussion is expected in Hellenistic discussions of household relationships since a "complete household consists of slaves and freemen" (Aristotle, *Pol.* 1253b). Un-

like "wives" and "children," "slaves" are considered "an animate article of property" (*Pol.* 1253b). As such, a "slave is not only the slave of his master; he also belongs entirely to him" (*Pol.* 1254a). As "an animate article of property," they are considered unable to take part in rational discourse: "The slave is entirely without the faculty of deliberation; the female indeed possesses it, but in a form which remains inconclusive; and if children also possess it, it is only in an immature form" (*Pol.* 1260a). Although Aristotle's detailed treatment of slavery in the fourth century BC may not represent the common perception in Paul's day, these statements do reflect the sentiments among many in the first century AD.[69]

In light of these statements, we must ask whether Paul's call for the slaves to "obey your earthly masters in everything" affirms this social institution. We will limit our discussion of Paul's view of slavery to this section within Colossians. First, the mere fact that Paul is addressing slaves indicates that he considers them to be rational and moral beings who are capable of developing a relationship not only with their masters but also with the Lord Jesus.

Second, the call to obedience is qualified by numerous references to "the Lord" (vv. 22, 23, 24), who is explicitly identified with "Christ" in v. 24. This directly challenges Hellenistic household discussions that consider the male head of the household as the sole authority figure.

Third, not only is the emphasis shifted to "the Lord," but one also finds here the surprising call to "serve the Lord Christ" (v. 24). This imperative, which breaks the three sets of relationships as found in secular discussions, shifts the focus from the master to the slave.

---

67. BDAG, 25.

68. The feminine nominal form "discouragement" (ἀθυμία) does not occur in the NT although its positive masculine form "rage" (θυμός) often appears in vice lists in Paul's letters (Rom

2:8; 1 Cor 12:20; Gal 5:20; Eph 4:31).

69. For a discussion of slavery in the first century, see the Introduction to Philemon.

Fourth, Paul here qualifies the masters as "earthly masters" (τοῖς κατὰ σάρκα κυρίοις; lit., "masters according to the flesh," cf. KJV, ASV, NKJV), a phrase that limits the realm of authority of these masters. They are masters only "according to human reckoning" (NJB). "Earthly masters" serves as a good translation since it contrasts with "Christ," who is "seated at the right hand of God" (v. 1). This Christ is explicitly identified as the "Master in heaven" in 4:1, where Paul directly qualifies the authority of these masters.

Finally, the lengthier discussion on the slaves also serves to qualify the call for the slaves to be obedient to their earthly masters. Not only is the lordship of Christ repeatedly noted, but one also finds the surprising portrayal of those slaves who are faithful to the Lord Jesus as heirs who "will receive the reward of inheritance" (v. 24). As ones who by definition are the property of their masters, this striking note redefines the slaves whose primary identities are not to be defined by their earthly masters but by their relationship with Christ.

The comparative length of this section also points to its other functions. Noting the historical context of this letter and its relationship with Philemon, some suggest that this focus on slaves can be explained by the presence of Philemon and Onesimus in the church of Colossae.[70] Others suggest that Paul's audience may have included many slaves, which thus prompts him to address their roles within the household.[71]

While these historical factors cannot be denied, this extended discussion can also be explained by the development of Paul's argument in this letter. After focusing on "humility" (v. 12) and "love" (v. 14), Paul issues an all-encompassing call to submit to the Lord Jesus in "whatever you do in word or in deed" (v. 17). As noted in the Structure section, the reappearance of this call in this section addressed to slaves (v. 23) provides a critical clue to its function. Because Paul's call to slaves is identical to that of believers in general, he essentially identifies believers as those who should act like slaves when they serve "the Lord Christ" (v. 24).[72] This discussion, therefore, becomes relevant for all believers, who belong to the household of God. Instead of simply shifting the focus from the earthly masters to the Lord in heaven, Paul also forces believers to obey their Lord as slaves are to obey their earthly masters.

3:22b-e   Not merely for eye service as people-pleasers, but with single-mindedness, fearing the Lord (μὴ ἐν ὀφθαλμοδουλίᾳ ὡς ἀνθρωπάρεσκοι, ἀλλ' ἐν ἁπλότητι καρδίας, φοβούμενοι τὸν κύριον). Paul expands and qualifies this call by emphasizing true obedience together with a reference to "the Lord." "Eye service" is a compound word consisting of "eye" (ὀφθαλμός) and "servitude/slavery" (δουλεία), referring to "service that is performed only to make an impression in the owner's presence."[73] This compound word is most appropriate when addressed to "slaves" (οἱ δοῦλοι) in regards to their "servitude" (δουλεία).[74]

"People-pleasers," another compound word consisting of "people" and "pleasing," further explains the meaning of "eye service" as it refers to

---

70. Fee, *Pauline Christology*, 330. Some have further considered Paul inserting this section so that the case of Onesimus will not lead to the revolt of other slaves; cf. Winsome Munro, "Col. III.18 – IV.1 and Eph. V.21 – VI.9," 441.

71. Maier, "A Sly Civility," 346; cf. Balch, *Let Wives Be Submissive*, 96 – 97; Lincoln, "Household Code and Wisdom Mode," 108.

72. See Hering, *The Colossian and Ephesian Haustafeln*, 76 – 77, who considers this master-slave section where the issue of power is at stake as the best context for the explication of the lordship of Christ motif.

73. BDAG, 744.

74. MacDonald, "Slavery, Sexuality and House Churches," 103, further argues that "the visibility of familial relations in house churches" lies behind this note on "eye service."

the acts merely "to curry their favor" (TNIV, NIV). This compound word is also appropriate here as it alludes back to the call for the children to act in a way that is "pleasing in the Lord" (v. 20).[75] As children are called to please the Lord, the slaves are called to do the same by not having their actions based on their desire to please other people.

Instead, the slaves are called to serve with "single-mindedness." As in its cognate adjective "singleness of purpose" (ἁπλοῦς),[76] the noun ἁπλότης, often rendered "sincerity" (NASB, NKJV, TNIV, NIV; cf. GNB, NET) carries this sense of commitment, thus "singleness of heart" (KJV, ASV) and "single-mindedness" (REB).[77] Here Paul is calling the slaves to serve with a single purpose, but the object of service is to be the Lord Christ himself, as is made clear in vv. 23 – 25.

"Fearing the Lord" provides the transition to the next verses that focus on the Lord Christ. In connection with what precedes, the participle "fearing" (φοβούμενοι) can be a circumstantial participle pointing to the basis ("because of your reverent fear of the Lord," NLT; cf. REB, NJB, GNB). But in light of the following verses, Paul appears not to be primarily supporting his call to serve their earthly masters by the evocation of "the Lord"; rather, he is setting up the contrast between the earthly master and the Lord in heaven. It is best, therefore, to take this participle as expressing manner: "but with sincerity of heart and reverence for the Lord" (TNIV, NIV; cf. CEV).

While the appearance of the title "the Lord" shifts the focus to the true Lord of all, the phrase "fearing the Lord" also evokes the "fear of the Lord" formula in the OT, a formula that applies specifically to God himself (cf. Deut 6:2, 13, 24; 10:12, 20; Josh 24:14; Pss 33:8; 34:9; Prov 24:21; Jer 5:24). The call to fear the Lord and serve him wholeheartedly recalls a similar call in 1 Sam 12:24: "fear the LORD and serve him faithfully with all your heart." But here in Colossians, this formula is applied to Jesus the Lord.[78] This again reaffirms the exalted status of Christ in this letter. In light of the frequent encouragement for the slave owner to instill a sense of fear in the slaves,[79] this note on shifting fear to the true Lord acquires added significance.

3:23 Whatever you do, do it wholeheartedly, as to the Lord and not to people (ὃ ἐὰν ποιῆτε, ἐκ ψυχῆς ἐργάζεσθε, ὡς τῷ κυρίῳ καὶ οὐκ ἀνθρώποις). This sentence, which continues into v. 24, redefines (1) the masters of the slaves, (2) the believers who are to heed the call here addressed to the slaves, and (3) the slaves themselves.

(1) "Do it wholeheartedly" recalls the previous verse, "obey ... with singleness-mindedness." "Wholeheartedly" (ἐκ ψυχῆς) translates (lit.) "from the soul." It can be taken to refer to the "motivation for the effort,"[80] but in biblical idiom it often indicates the totality of one's devotion as illustrated by Mark 12:30, a passage that places "heart" and "soul" in parallel: "Love the Lord your God with all your heart [ἐξ ὅλης τῆς καρδίας] and with all your soul [ἐξ ὅλης τῆς ψυχῆς] and with all your mind

---

75. For the contrast between pleasing people and pleasing God, see also Paul's reference to his own conviction in Gal 1:10.

76. BDAG, 104. See the use in Luke 11:34 and the discussion in Susan R. Garrett, " 'Lest the Light in You Be Darkness': Luke 11:33 – 36 and the Question of Commitment," *JBL* 110 (1991): 93 – 105.

77. Thus also Lightfoot, *St. Paul's Epistles to the Colossians and to Philemon*, 228; Lohse, *Colossians and Philemon*, 160; Moo, *Letters to the Colossians and to Philemon*, 310.

78. See Bauckham, *Jesus and the God of Israel*, 188, who considers this another example of "YHWH texts" that is now applied to Jesus.

79. Cf. Cicero, *Parad.* 5.41; K. R. Bradley, *Slaves and Masters in the Roman Empire: A Study in Social Control* (New York: Oxford Univ. Press, 1987), 113.

80. Moo, *Letters to the Colossians and to Philemon*, 311, who nevertheless acknowledges the significance of Mark 12:30. Van Kooten (*Paul's Anthropology in Context*, 300) argues for "from the heart."

and with all your strength" (cf. Deut 6:5; also Matt 22:37; Luke 10:27). Therefore, this clause is best understood in terms of putting "your whole heart into it" (REB) or even putting "yourselves into it" (NRSV).

Note that Paul is now shifting his attention to the true object of one's service: "the Lord." This shift is reinforced by the contrastive pair at the end of v. 23: "as to the Lord and not to people."[81] Through this shift Paul provides yet another striking qualification to the secular ethos, where only the male head of the household is the authoritative figure.

(2) This call not only shifts the focus from the earthly masters to "the Lord," but through its parallel with v. 17 ("whatever you do in word or in deed"), Paul further identifies believers as those who are to serve this Lord wholeheartedly. As slaves should submit to their masters in all that they do, believers are also to serve their Lord. This identification has already been anticipated by 1:7, where Epaphras, presumably the founder of the Colossian church, is identified as "our beloved fellow slave" and "a faithful servant of Christ." This identification is repeated in 4:12, where Epaphras is also called "a slave of Christ Jesus." This present section in the household code provides the rationale for such an identification.

(3) Beyond the redefinition of the master as "the Lord" and the believers as "the slaves," this sentence also redefines the "slaves." As the property of their masters, they are but instruments in their hands. For Paul, however, they are heirs who will inherit an inheritance, a point established in v. 24a.

3:24a Since you know that from the Lord you will receive the reward of inheritance (εἰδότες ὅτι ἀπὸ κυρίου ἀπολήμψεσθε τὴν ἀνταπόδοσιν τῆς κληρονομίας). Paul now provides the basis for the actions required of the slaves. "Since you know" (εἰδότες) takes the participle to be a causal adverbial participle, providing the basis for Paul's call to the slaves to serve "as to the Lord" wholeheartedly (v. 23). This verb points to the reality about which these Christian slaves have to be reminded.[82] In 4:1, Paul uses the same word to remind their masters that they are not the slaves' real masters.

These slaves are promised to receive "the reward of inheritance," a phrase where the genitive "of inheritance" is best taken as an epexegetical genitive[83] that defines "the reward," thus: "the inheritance as your reward" (NRSV, ESV; cf. NLT, NET, TNIV, NIV). "The reward" can point to "the just recompense" for the earthly service or even injustice that the slaves endure[84] and the positive reward for their faithfulness as they serve the Lord.[85]

The promise of an inheritance is striking when applied to slaves. Despite possible payments made to the slaves that can be considered as constituting their inheritance,[86] legally such funds belonged to the masters. In any case, "inheritance" is technically reserved for those who are the legitimate heirs

---

81. The comparative particle "as" (ὡς) has been understood as pointing to the contrast between those who are serving the Lord: "Work wholeheartedly like those who are working for the Lord Jesus, not like those who are working merely for men" (Callow, *Semantic and Structural Analysis*, 147). In this context where one finds the contrast between the "earthly masters" (v. 22) and the "Master in heaven" (4:1), however, it is best taken as pointing to the comparison between the perceived ("earthly masters" as the object of one's service) and the ultimate reality ("heavenly Master" as the object): "as though you were working for the Lord rather than for people" (NLT).

82. The phrase "since you know that" is one Paul often uses

to introduce the basis for his arguments or exhortations (e.g., Rom 5:3; 6:8 – 9; 2 Cor 4:13 – 14; 5:6); Harris, *Colossians and Philemon*, 185.

83. Also called the genitive of apposition; cf. Wallace, *Greek Grammar*, 95 – 100.

84. Lightfoot, *St. Paul's Epistles to the Colossians and to Philemon*, 229; Sumney, *Colossians*, 250.

85. O'Brien, *Colossians, Philemon*, 229; MacDonald, *Colossians and Ephesians*, 158.

86. See, e.g., Tacitus, *Annals* 14.42, who testifies to the slaves owning private funds for the possibility of purchasing their own freedom.

within the household. Note Rom 8:15 – 17, where Paul draws a contrast between children, who are able to be "heirs," and slaves, who are not — a point also noted in Gal 4:7: "So you are no longer a slave, but God's child; and since you are his child, God has made you also an heir." In this case, therefore, the promise of an inheritance for slaves transforms their status to those who are legitimate heirs in the household of God. This transformation again challenges the cultural assumptions of the time and thus relativizes their status as the property of their masters.

As the previous verses draw parallels between the call of the believers (v. 17) and that of the slaves, this note on "inheritance" also identifies the slaves as part of the believers, who have been qualified "to share in the inheritance of the saints in the light" (1:12).[87] Just as believers who serve their Lord will be heirs, so too these slaves will participate as full members in the household of God. Though missing the striking contradiction of the portrayal of slaves as heirs, the following translation notes the significance of 1:12 for the reading of this verse: "Remember that the Lord will give you as a reward what he has kept for his people" (GNB).

3:24b Serve the Lord Christ (τῷ κυρίῳ Χριστῷ δουλεύετε). Paul now identifies the true object of one's service. Most translations take the word "serve" (δουλεύετε) as an indicative verb ("you serve the Lord Christ," e.g., NRSV), and several arguments are suggested for this reading.[88] (1) All the imperatives in this code thus far are used within the reciprocal relationships where the relationship between the male head of the household and the subordinate members is addressed. To introduce an imperative with "the Lord" seems to break this structure. (2) The identification of "the Lord" as "Christ" appears to explain the preceding clause, "from the Lord," and therefore should be taken as an indicative explanatory clause: "it is the Lord Christ whom you serve." (3) In Paul, the phrase "the Lord Christ" appears elsewhere only in Rom 16:18, where the identification of "the Lord" appears in the midst of competing claims of lordship. Therefore, this phrase has been taken primarily as one that identifies Christ as the Lord.

However, this verb should be taken as an imperative: "Serve the Lord Christ" (NET; cf. NAB), as supported by a majority of recent commentators.[89] (1) The lack of a conjunction in this clause is consistent with other imperatival clauses in this code (vv. 18, 19, 20, 21, 22; 4:1).[90] (2) Taken as an imperative, this clause parallels the imperative in v. 23, "do it wholeheartedly," but it also provides development of thought as it now explicitly identifies Christ as the Lord. (3) The "for" (γάρ) clause in v. 25, which provides the basis for this call, supports this imperative reading. (4) This imperative also provides the transition to the direct address to the masters since what is noted here is applicable to both slaves and masters.

The arguments for the indicative reading noted

---

87. See, in particular, Robert Scott Nash, "Heuristic Haustafeln: Domestic Codes as Entrance to the Social World of Early Christianity: The Case of Colossians," in *Religious Writings and Religious Systems: Systemic Analysis of Holy Books in Christianity, Islam, Buddhism, Greco-Roman Religions, Ancient Israel, and Judaism*, vol. 2: *Christianity* (ed. Jacob Neusner, Ernest S. Frerichs, and A. J. Levine; Atlanta: Scholars, 1989), 43 – 45.

88. See Lightfoot, *St. Paul's Epistles to the Colossians and to Philemon*, 229; Aletti, *Saint Paul Épître aux Colossiens*, 246; Callow, *Semantic and Structural Analysis*, 148; Wilson, *Colossians and Philemon*, 285.

89. Moule, *Epistles to the Colossians and to Philemon*, 131; Lohse, *Colossians and Philemon*, 161; Schweizer, *Letter to the Colossians*, 226; O'Brien, *Colossians, Philemon*, 229; Wright, *Colossians and Philemon*, 150; Harris, *Colossians and Philemon*, 185 – 86; Moo, *Letters to the Colossians and to Philemon*, 313 – 14; Sumney, *Colossians*, 250 – 51.

90. This also explains the insertion of the conjunction "for" (γάρ) in some manuscripts (D¹ Ψ 075 𝔐). Its omission, however, is supported by the earliest and most widely distributed manuscripts (𝔓⁴⁶ ℵ A B C D* F G 0278 33 81 365 1175 1241ˢ 1739 1881 2464).

earlier actually highlight the striking aspects of this imperative. (1) As this imperative breaks the pattern of the other reciprocal imperatives of this code, Paul draws attention to this striking redefinition of the lordship of Christ. The mere presence of yet another master in a discussion of household relationships is already noteworthy; in this call, this direct imperative establishes the Lord Christ as the ultimate and final authority of the household. (2) The identification of this "Lord" as "Christ" is also an embedded function of this imperative. The christological implications of the preceding arguments in this letter are now brought to bear in this household. (3) Consistent with the context of Rom 16:18, the identification of this Lord is indeed at stake. Nevertheless, in light of the earlier call to serve their earthly masters, this imperative makes this critical shift clear when Paul now identifies Christ as the true object of their servitude.

3:25   For the wrongdoer will be repaid for his wrong, and there is no partiality (ὁ γὰρ ἀδικῶν κομίσεται ὃ ἠδίκησεν, καὶ οὐκ ἔστιν προσωπολημψία). Paul now grounds his previous call with this statement that refers to God's justice. The connection with the previous call to "serve the Lord Christ" (v. 24) is made by the conjunction "for," which indicates the basis of the call. It is more difficult to pinpoint exactly how this general statement provides that basis. (1) It could point to the reason for serving the Lord because he is a fair and righteous judge, unlike earthly masters, who may not be. (2) Or it can serve as the basis by noting that those who do not serve the Lord are the wrongdoers, and they will face the punishment they deserve. This would motivate slaves or even believers in general to be vigilant in their daily walk. While the former reading fits the immediate context within this code, the latter is consistent with Paul's call to faithful living in vv. 5–17 and the call to be alert in 4:2.

In any case, either reading is to be preferred over the one that connects this verse with v. 22 or v. 23, seeing this as the basis for serving one's earthly masters.[91] The transitional nature of this section must be recognized as Paul is shifting the focus from the slaves to the masters and providing a section relevant for the believers in general.

This reading also affects our understanding of the identity of "the wrongdoer." Since this phrase is located within the section that deals with slaves, many argue that behind it are the slaves who may have wronged their masters.[92] The use of this verb (ἀδικέω) in reference to the possible wrongdoing of Onesimus in Phlm 18 has also been used in support of this reading.[93] Nevertheless, such a reading may assume the perspective of the masters who adopt a stereotypical portrayal of slaves as evil and irresponsible.[94] Moreover, Phlm 18 only provides a hypothetical statement and does not refer to specific wrongdoings of Onesimus.[95]

In light of the note on the harsh treatment of the slaves in texts such as 1 Pet 2:18, some take this verse as "intended to encourage slaves,"[96] in that masters must also be responsible for their own wrongdoings.[97] But closer to this Colossian house-

---

91. Thus Wright, *Colossians and Philemon*, 150.

92. See, e.g., Lohse, *Colossians and Philemon*, 161, who suggests that this verse is to warn the "miserable slaves" that they will still "be held responsible for their actions."

93. Cf. Lightfoot, *St. Paul's Epistles to the Colossians and to Philemon*, 229.

94. Allen D. Callahan, *Embassy of Onesimus: The Letter of Paul to Philemon* (Valley Forge, PA: Trinity International, 1997), 12–16.

95. See comments on Phlm 18.

96. Barth and Blanke, *Colossians*, 449.

97. The eschatological emphases in this section with notes on future "reward" (v. 24) and judgment (v. 25) may also have been particularly relevant in light of the injustice often committed by the slave-masters; cf. Hay, *Colossians*, 147.

hold code is Eph 6:8, where this general principle is applied to everyone, whether "slave or free." It is possible, therefore, that this principle is referring here to both slaves and masters; it then serves to introduce the discussion of the masters in Col 4:1.

In light of our discussion above concerning how believers are to serve their Lord just as slaves serve their masters, it is perhaps best to see this general principle as applicable to believers in general, and the wrongdoers are those who have committed the sins as noted in the vice lists above (3:5, 8 – 9).[98] Unlike Hellenistic household discussions, where the focus is on the power structure of the present realm, Paul provides an eschatological perspective within which everyone must be responsible for their action under the authority of the Lord, who will be "revealed … in glory" at the end of times (v. 4).

The term "partiality" (προσωπολημψία) here consists of two words literally rendered "to receive the face." This phrase is often used in the LXX meaning "to show partiality" (Lev 19:15; Deut 16:19; Ps 82:2 [LXX 81:2]; Lam 4:16; Mal 2:9; cf. Luke 20:21; Gal 2:6). The compound verb and its cognates are considered among "the earliest definitely Christian words."[99] This word group was used by Paul (Rom 2:11) and by others (Acts 10:34) to refer to the salvation of both Jews and Gentiles, and this usage here may allude back to Col 3:11, where the new humanity is portrayed as one "where there is neither Greek nor Jew." In Jas 2:9 the term is used in a more general sense for believers not to show favoritism.

4:1a Masters, provide for your slaves justice and equity (Οἱ κύριοι, τὸ δίκαιον καὶ τὴν ἰσότητα τοῖς δούλοις παρέχεσθε). In this final exhortation within the household code, Paul addresses earthly masters and reminds them of their duties. "Masters" (οἱ κύριοι), the same word for "Lord" (in the singular) that appears in this code for Christ, no longer evokes an unqualified sense of awe and respect. It is precisely in this climactic verse that Paul makes it clear that these "masters" also have a "Master" in heaven.

Before the final statement that relativizes the power and authority of the male heads of the households, Paul focuses on the historical reality of the master-slave relationship in the first century. After noting the principle of impartiality, Paul draws the implications of such a principle for the behavior of these earthly masters. The phrase "justice and equity" again emphasizes the duties of these authoritative figures rather than their rights. "Justice" in Paul can refer to one's standing before God; in such contexts, Paul clearly declares that "no one is righteous [just], not even one" (Rom 3:10 [Ps 14:1 LXX 13:1]). When applied to God as an authoritative judge, however, this word denotes "justice" (2 Thess 1:5, 6; 2 Tim 4:8). In a context where the power of the human authoritative figure is concerned, the same applies: masters are called to be just judges who provide justice for those over whom they rule.[100]

The term "equity" (τὴν ἰσότητα) is more difficult. It can mean either "fairness" when applied to identical treatment as each in their role deserves, or "equality" when applied to the general sense of identical status. In this context, "fairness" is probably the primary meaning intended by Paul.[101] (1) In a discussion of how to treat subordinate members,

---

98. Cf. Hering, *The Colossian and Ephesian Haustafeln*, 99. See also 2 Pet 2, where the same principle ("they will be paid back with harm for the harm they have done," v. 13) appears after the general discussion of the sins of the false prophets (vv. 1 – 12).

99. MM, 553.

100. The translation "provide your slaves with what is right" (TNIV, NIV) is appropriate when "what is right" is understood as that which they rightly deserve.

101. Most contemporary translations adopt this reading, though some older versions use "equal" (KJV, ASV).

"fairness" seems implied. This sense is consistent with the usage of this term in Greco-Roman discussions on the treatment of slaves.[102] (2) Since this is something that the masters are to grant, "fairness" fits this context more. (3) Finally, if 3:25 is to serve as the basis for this call, the urge to avoid wrongdoings fits this call to provide fair treatment to the slaves rather than to provide "equality" that is not expected of even virtuous masters.

Nevertheless, in light of the striking qualifications to the accepted societal norm in this household discussion and in anticipation of the ultimate reference to the "Master in heaven" that follows, it seems that the divine principle of "there is no partiality" that immediately precedes this call should be taken seriously. Moreover, the fact that there is neither "slave nor free" in the new humanity (3:11) encourages the reader to consider the sense of "equality" when confronted with this call. Moreover, the word "just" (τὸ δίκαιον) may evoke the Roman sense of justice where it is said to guarantee "equality" (ἰσότης) between the powerful and the powerless.[103] If so, "equality" could well be in the mind of the audience. Yet it should be noted that the implications of this implicit sense are left unsaid, and this term may not be able to bear the weight of the modern conceptions of liberation and egalitarianism.

4:1b Since you know that you also have a Master in heaven (εἰδότες ὅτι καὶ ὑμεῖς ἔχετε κύριον ἐν οὐρανῷ). Syntactically, this clause provides the grounds for the call to "provide for your slaves justice and equity." In terms of the wider flow of Paul's

argument, however, it represents one of the significant points in Paul's presentation of Jesus as "the Lord/Master."[104] The qualification of the power of the male head of the household also climaxes here where the term "Lord/Master" (κύριον) is finally used explicitly to qualify those who are considered by many to be "masters" (οἱ κύριοι).

The clause "you also have a Master in heaven" transforms these masters into slaves who are in turn to serve their own master. This new reading of reality allows Paul to call them to fulfill their duties as faithful and considerate husbands, fathers, and masters. The prepositional phrase "in heaven" should not be considered to limit the realm of power of Christ the Lord; it is not meant to divide the realm of reality into the earthly and the heavenly since Christ himself is the instrument through whom all things in heaven and in earth are reconciled to God (1:16, 20).

Instead, this phrase points to two significant aspects. First, it points to the enthronement of Christ noted in 3:1 – 4.[105] As the "Lord/Master in heaven," Christ is the Lord of all. The submission of the earthly masters is therefore required. Second, as 3:1 – 4 points also to the final revelation of Christ, who is now "seated at the right hand of God" (3:1), the eschatological aspects reemerge with this phrase (cf. 3:24 – 25). Since Christ is the final and ultimate judge of all, all who live on this earth must be mindful of this final judgment. This eschatological aspect continues to be the focus of 4:2, where Paul urges his audience to be alert in anticipation of the final consummation of God's act in history.

---

102. Seneca, *Ep.* 47; BDAG, 481.

103. Aristides, *Regarding Rome* 26.39; Angela Standhartinger, "The Origin and Intention of the Household Code in the Letter to the Colossians," *JSNT* 79 (2000): 128.

104. The title "Lord" has been applied to Christ eight times in this section, and it appears only twice in the remaining verses (4:7, 17). When applied to the earthly masters, English

translations consistently use "masters," and when applied to Jesus, "the Lord." In this case, however, the translation "Master in heaven" is necessary to highlight the contrast between the earthly masters and the true Master in heaven.

105. MacDonald, "Slavery, Sexuality and House Churches," 102.

Theology in Application

Lord of the Household

To identify this section as a household code may give the false impression that Paul is providing a comprehensive treatment of family relationships. If this were such a treatment, one would expect a discussion of significant topics such as the foundation of marriage (e.g., Eph 5:22 – 33), faithfulness within marriage (e.g., 1 Cor 6:12 – 20), divorce and remarriage (e.g., 1 Cor 7:8 – 11), status and behavior of the widows (e.g., 1 Tim 5:3 – 16), relationship between believers and unbelievers within the same household (e.g., 1 Cor 7:12 – 16), training of children in faith (e.g., 1 Tim 5:10; Titus 1:6), conflicts between masters and slaves (e.g., Phlm 16, 18), rules concerning manumission (e.g., Phlm 16), and so on. In this section, however, Paul focuses on the issue of authority within the household, especially the way the authority of Christ the Lord affects the relationships among different members of the household.

This focus on authority may explain the selective treatment of issues within members of the household. Before dealing with the particulars, however, the emphasis on Jesus as the Lord of the household must be noted. In light of the consistent affirmation of the authority of the male head of the household in Hellenistic household discussions, the repeated uses of the title "Lord" (3:18, 20, 22, 23, 24; 4:1) in reference to Christ not only qualifies the secular social conventions, but it challenges the very basis of such structures of authority by noting that this husband/father/master is but a slave to the "Master in heaven" (4:1). In other words, if one were to summarize the central message of this code, it is the confession that affirms "Christ Jesus [as] the Lord" (2:6). This reading not only takes seriously Paul's modification of common patterns behind Hellenistic household discussions, but it also explains how this section fits into the wider argument in a letter that focuses on the final and ultimate authority and status of Christ.

In light of this reading, the commands to the various members of the household can be understood. The call to submission reminds wives of their role within their families, but their obedience is to be directed to "the Lord" (3:18), and the call for the husbands to love their wives turns their "rights" into their "duties" to care for them (3:19). Children are called to obey their parents (3:20), but the authority of the fathers is qualified not simply because their children are ultimately to submit to their Lord, but also because they have their responsibility under this higher authority (3:21). Finally, since the slave-master relationship centers distinctly on the issue of authority, one finds the call to serve the masters only in anticipation of the call to serve "the Lord Christ" (3:24). This climactic call is coupled with the redefinition of the earthly masters as the slaves of the "Master in heaven" (4:1). Therefore, the often-repeated claim that "Paul had no intention of turning that world upside down"[106] is true only when such "turning" is understood primarily as blatantly disruptive acts. Such a statement undermines, however, the powerful challenge this section poses to the social, cultural, and political norms of the day. After all, this section aims at illustrating the preceding call to "do everything in the name of the Lord Jesus" (3:17).

Wives and Husbands

Within the understanding of the focus of this section, we can think of the practical implications for relationships between husband and wives and between children and fathers. Concerning marital relationships, the obvious question is the way the call for wives to submit to their husbands is to be appropriated in the contemporary setting. Several comments are in order, and they should be taken together as one considers Paul's teachings here. First, the call for submission cannot be denied despite the relativizing of this call in Paul's qualification of the Hellenistic household discussions. This call is not limited to one context, as is clarified by Paul's references elsewhere when he affirms the headship of men (1 Cor 11:3; Eph 5:23) in the context where the creation mandate is affirmed (Eph 5:33).

More difficult is the nature of this submission. What is clear is that submission is not to be equated with blind obedience, for wives are called to submit, whereas children and slaves are called to "obey" their fathers and masters "in everything" (vv. 20, 22). That Paul often calls believers to mutual submission (Gal 5:13; Phil 2:3 – 4), even in contexts where household relationships are discussed (Eph 5:21), further shows this submission of wives as one that is not based on their relative status or ability. In the context of Colossians, the calls to "put on ... humility" (3:12), to bear "with one another" (v. 13), to "love," (v. 14), to be "in one body" (v. 15), and to teach and admonish "one another" all emphasize the importance of this mutuality. The call for the husbands to "love" their wives should, therefore, be considered as contributing to this definition of submission: "true love for one's wife is not compatible with a husband completely controlling her life."[107] Within the context of love, this submission allows wives to follow their husbands in their attempt to "do everything in the name of the Lord Jesus" (v. 17).

In practical terms, what would such "submission" look like in the modern family? It is not enough to say that wives should yield to their husbands only when the wishes of their husbands conform to the general Christian value system. It is also not to be applied in numerous practical matters when a simple evaluation of technical expertise reveals the relative superiority of the wife's skill. This can but does not necessarily have to include tasks often associated with women (e.g., cooking, counseling, childrearing), for modern wives have also excelled in other areas not traditionally lim-

---

106. Garland, *Colossians and Philemon*, 255.
107. Payne, *Man and Woman*, 275. This is not to deny the significance of this call as addressed to wives, however, since husbands were never called to submit to their wives.

ited to the female gender (e.g., scientific/technical analysis, theoretical simulation, financial planning). "Submission" instead should be applied to certain life decisions in which morality and technical skills are not in question. These may include cases when the husband is "called" to serve in a particular mission field, or the way he is led to lead the family in daily/weekly devotions. In such cases, the husband has to pray that the Spirit will likewise lead his wife to share in this vision, and they should then prayerfully commit to this common vision.

As to the duty of the husbands, since in the Greco-Roman context "love" is not an expected "duty" for husbands, the distinct understanding of this virtue within Colossians must be noted. Rather than a general expression of benevolence, this love lives out the love of God the Father for his Son (1:13) and is to function as the critical ingredient in God's act in the creation of a new humanity (2:2; 3:14). As "beloved" (3:12) of God, the faithful participation of believers in the body of Christ testifies to the power of this new creation; "the removal of a husband's oppressive rule over his wife … is the removal, through love, of the effects of sin on the role relationship."[108] In light of this grand vision, few men can claim to be faithful witnesses to such creative acts of God, as Christian thinkers through the ages readily admit:

> It is painful, being a man, to have to assert the privilege, or the burden, which Christianity lays upon my own sex. I am crushingly aware how inadequate most of us are, in our actual and historical individualities, to fill the place prepared for us.[109]

This awareness of such critical inadequacies only increases our thirst for the fulfillment of God's redemptive act when his Son returns in glory (cf. 3:4). In the meanwhile, we are all called to humble living while fully recognizing the power of God's grace.

Finally, in defining the relationship between men and women, isolated statements from a code are often pulled out of their context in discussions of gender roles. Without providing a detailed discussion on this complex issue, it is sufficient to note that Paul's position must be evaluated within a wider trajectory in redemptive history.[110] In the case of the status of women, Paul is clearly rejecting his dominant culture that denies any sense of equality between the two sexes. Paul's significant qualification of the power and status of the male head of the household and his statement elsewhere that there is neither "male [nor] female" (Gal 3:28) points clearly to a vision where the term "subordination" becomes misleading in characterizing the effect of the gospel of the cross.

---

108. George W. Knight III, *Role Relationships of Men and Women: New Testament Teaching* (rev. ed.; Phillipsburg, NJ: Presbyterian & Reformed, 1989), 32.

109. C. S. Lewis, *God in the Dock: Essays on Theology and Ethics* (Grand Rapids: Eerdmans, 1970), 238 – 39.

110. See, e.g., Webb, "A Redemptive-Movement Hermeneutic," 382 – 400; Marshall, "Mutual Love and Submission in Marriage," 194. Often considered to be a strategy adopted by those who are labeled egalitarians, this is actually one that transcends this gender debate; cf. Moo, *Letters to the Colossians and to Philemon*, 297.

Children and Parents

To the modern audience, Paul's discussion of the relationship between children and their parents[111] is more palatable than his discussions of either slaves or women. Here, in distinction from Hellenistic household discussions one finds a similar trajectory that emphasizes the father's duties, although Paul's teaching is clearly consistent with the OT teaching that affirms both the obedience of the children to their parents (Exod 20:12; Deut 5:16) and the responsibility of their fathers to teach them the ways of the Lord (e.g., Exod 10:2; Deut 4:9). This background paves the way for Paul's emphasis here because in the OT, the ultimate focus of the call for the children to obey their parents and for the fathers to be responsible for their children's upbringing is on the significance of the passing on of the divine teachings and commandments. Young children are those who "do not yet know good from bad" (Deut 1:39), and fathers are to teach them "to obey carefully all the words of this law" (32:46). In this household code, the calls to the children and the fathers likewise ultimately point to "the Lord" as the ultimate object of concern.

The family should also be the context where daily struggles are to be instruments in the cultivation of lives that lead to the obedience to the ultimate Lord of all. Parents are the ones who can transform daily household activities into liturgical practices that allow members of the household to follow Paul's call: "whatever you do in word and in deed, do everything in the name of the Lord Jesus."[112] This is the overarching theme of a significant study that examines factors that lead adults back to their childhood faith:

> Effective religious socialization comes about through embedded practices; that is, through specific, deliberate religious activities that are firmly intertwined with the daily habits of family routines, of eating and sleeping, of having conversations, of adorning the spaces in which people live, of celebrating the holidays, and of being part of a community. Compared with these practices, the formal teachings of religious leaders often pale in significance.[113]

As parents who confess Christ as our Lord, the call for our children to be obedient to us highlights the responsibility we have for the wider household of God.

Equally important in the OT tradition is the use of the father-son relationship in depicting God's love for his people: "As a father has compassion on his children, so the LORD has compassion on those who fear him" (Ps 103:13). As God has compassion even on those among his children who rebelled against him (Isa 1:2), Paul urges the fathers to imitate their Lord in not being harsh to their children. The fathers are

---

111. Teachings on the "fathers" can be applied to both parents in today's setting.

112. For a discussion of faithful daily living as liturgical practices, see discussion in Theology in Application on 3:12 – 17.

113. Robert Wuthnow, *Growing Up Religious: Christians and Jews and their Journeys of Faith* (Boston: Beacon, 1999), xxxi – xxxii.

called to reenact God's gracious love for his people in a way that is consistent with their identity as members of the new humanity.

It is in this discussion of the call to reenact God's gracious love that the issue of child abuse can be addressed. While the children are to "obey" their parents, fathers (and mothers) are called not to "provoke" their children. This clearly qualifies the "power" of the fathers in their dealings with their children. Moreover, as Paul repeatedly notes, Jesus is the true "Lord" of the household. Fathers are therefore also responsible to this final authority. More importantly, as we discuss the imitation of the fatherly love of God, we are also reminded of the positive motivations for fathers to model the gracious love of God the Father. It is ultimately the identification of these fathers with the death and resurrection of Christ that allows us to serve as instruments of God's grace for those placed under our responsibility.

Slaves and Masters

With the relationship between slaves and masters, the issue of Paul's view of slavery as reflected in this household code must be dealt with first, especially because the church is often accused of silence on this issue, an accusation often repeated in reasons to reject the gospel: "The churches, as everyone knows, opposed the abolition of slavery as long as they dared."[114] Whether churches throughout history have been faithful to the NT teachings is beyond the scope of this discussion, but it is misleading to assert that Paul is silent on this issue.

As noted above, this household code challenges the underlying principle of the institution of slavery by relativizing the power and authority of earthly masters. They are but slaves of the "Master in heaven" (4:1), and "the Lord" is explicitly identified as "Christ" (3:24). Moreover, to consider slaves as heirs of an "inheritance" (3:24) affirms their spiritual status as children in "the kingdom of [God's] beloved Son" (1:13). On the basis of this status, the note on God as an impartial God (3:25) and the call for the earthly masters to provide "justice and equity" for their slaves (4:1) become understandable. Though without an explicit note on the equality between slaves and masters, this code clearly points toward this direction. This code should be read in light of the preceding description of the "new humanity" as one where the distinction between "slave" and "free" is to be eradicated (3:11).

Beyond the immediate context of this code, the relevance of Philemon is also worth noting. Written to the same area by Paul during the same Roman imprisonment, the Colossian household code should be read in light of Paul's call in his letter to Philemon for him to receive Onesimus back "no longer as a slave, but more than a slave, a beloved brother" (Phlm 16). Moreover, Paul demonstrates the primary

---

114. Bertrand Russell, "Has Religion Made Useful Contributions to Civilization?" in *Why I Am Not a Christian* (New York: Simon and Schuster, 1957), 26.

significance to reconsider the status of Onesimus within the household of God by first calling him his "child" (Phlm 10). This redefinition of the status of this slave is consistent with the trajectory one finds throughout Colossians.

Before moving beyond this question of Paul's view of slavery, contemporary readers need to be reminded of the differences between slavery in Greco-Roman society and the more recent American experience of this institution. Historians have repeatedly emphasized that "the history of ancient slavery can only be a history of Graeco-Roman society," and the same can be said concerning its modern counterpart.[115] Without providing even a brief survey of slavery in Graeco-Roman times,[116] a cautionary note should at least be sounded when we consider the isolated statements on slavery found in Paul's writings.

The message embedded in Paul's discussion of the role of the slaves here is easily overshadowed by the perceived need to defend his position on the ancient institution of slavery. For ministers of the gospel, however, it is incumbent on us to unleash the power of this message. As noted above, one of the main functions of Paul's relatively lengthy discussion of the slaves here is to draw a parallel between the behavior of slaves and that of all believers. This is best seen in 3:23, where Paul's call for the slaves ("whatever you do, do it wholeheartedly, as to the Lord and not to people") repeats the earlier call in 3:17 to believers in general ("whatever you do in word or in deed, do everything in the name of the Lord Jesus"). Shifting from the status of the slaves to the behavior of believers, Paul urges the latter to take on this self-understanding by submitting to the Lord in absolute obedience.

This reading is confirmed by Paul's reference to the founder of the Colossian church, Epaphras, as "the slave of Christ Jesus" (4:12). This appellation is rooted in the fundamental redemptive act of God through Christ, who delivers his people from the bondage of sin (Rom 6:20; 7:14; 8:21) and of the elemental spirits (Gal 4:3; Eph 2:2). In response, believers are called to be slaves of Christ and righteousness:

> Don't you know that when you offer yourselves to someone as obedient slaves, you are slaves of the one you obey — whether you are slaves to sin, which leads to death, or to obedience, which leads to righteousness? (Rom 6:16; cf. Rom 6:18; 14:18)

This call to be "slaves ... to obedience" is based on the prior act of Christ, who "emptied himself, by taking on the form of a slave" (Phil 2:7, pers. trans.). This humbling act culminates in his "becoming obedient to death" (2:8). It is in light of this imagery that the life and death of Christ become the model of obedient servitude for believers (cf. Rom 14:8 – 12; 2 Cor 5:14 – 21).[117] The references to participation in the

---

115. Moses I. Finley, *Ancient Slavery and Modern Ideology* (New York: Penguin, 1983), 66.

116. For such a survey, see the Introduction to Philemon.

117. See, e.g., I. A. H. Combes, *The Metaphor of Slavery in the Writings of the Early Church: From the New Testament to the*

Beginning of the Fifth Century (JSNTSup 156; Sheffield: Sheffield Academic, 1998), 92, who rightly claims that "it is only in relation to this theology of the cross that Paul's metaphor of slavery makes sense."

death and resurrection of Christ in Colossians (Col 2:11 – 13, 20 – 23; 3:1 – 4) form the basis for this further call to be his slaves.

To appreciate what it means to be a slave to Christ, Aristotle's definition of slaves in reference to their function and status may be helpful:

> First, that "anybody who by his nature is not his own man, but another's, is by his nature a slave"; secondly, that "anybody who, being a man, is an article of property, is another's man"; and thirdly, that "an article of property is an instrument intended for the purpose of action and separable from its possessor." (*Pol.*1.1254a)

Since believers are called "do everything in the name of the Lord Jesus" (3:17), we are likewise called to be his slaves; those who belong to him and are instruments for his glory and honor. Pastors who wish to develop this point further may consider using musical instruments as an illustration of our role as the slaves of Christ. As an instrument is useless without being played, we are useless unless we become Christ's instrument; as the instrument brings glory to its master, our only goal is to bring glory to our Master. Moreover, as instruments we do not have our own "will" since we are called to be an extension of the "will" of our Master.

10

Colossians 4:2 – 6

Literary Context

After a clearly defined unit about household relationships, Paul moves to a seemingly random collection of "somewhat general exhortations."[1] Many have simply labeled this section as "Concluding Exhortations"[2] or even "Various Admonitions."[3] If we read these verses in light of the wider development of the arguments of Paul, however, both the connection of this passage with its preceding context as well as its focus will become evident.

This section begins with a call to persevere in prayer and to be alert (v. 2). These words evoke the eschatological overtones that can also be identified behind the preceding household code (3:18 – 4:1). The references to the future "reward of inheritance" (3:24), the Lord as the impartial judge who will repay each according to their own behavior (3:25), and Jesus as the "Master in heaven" (4:1) all point back to the note on the final revelation of Christ with his followers in glory at the end of times (3:4). In this passage, the call to persevere and be alert becomes the general call for believers to act in light of the reality of the eschaton that began with the death and resurrection of Jesus.

The prepositional phrase "with thanksgiving" (v. 2) also recalls the repeated emphasis on thanksgiving in the section that precedes the household code (3:15 – 17). In a sense, then, these references to thanksgiving provide the framework for reading the household code. As believers are called to acknowledge the Creator as their Lord through a life of thanksgiving, the household code provides a concrete illustration as to how the lordship of Christ can find its manifestation within the basic unit of social relationship.

"Prayer" (v. 2) dominates the first half of this section (vv. 2 – 4). It also links this section with the opening of this letter, where Paul describes his prayer for the Colossian believers that they can grow in the knowledge of God (1:9 – 14). Paul now

---

1. Sumney, *Colossians*, 255.

2. Dunn, *Epistles to the Colossians and to Philemon*, 261; cf. Aletti, *Saint Paul Épître aux Colossiens*, 257; Barth and Blanke, *Colossians*, 451.

3. Moule, *Epistles to the Colossians and to Philemon*, 132.

returns to the theme of prayer and requests the Colossian believers to pray for him so that their fulfillment in the gospel can be experienced by others.

While vv. 2 – 4 focus on prayer, vv. 5 – 6 focus on Christian behavior that glorifies God. Some have considered these two sections as dealing with two separate topics.[4] In both sections, however, Paul is clearly concerned with reaching those outside the community of believers. In vv. 2 – 4, he requests prayer for open doors to "declare the mystery of Christ" (v. 3), and in vv. 5 – 6 he encourages the believers to "walk in wisdom toward outsiders" (v. 5) and to speak with wisdom to them (v. 6). Instead of a random collection of general exhortations, Paul deliberately moves to the climax of his presentation. This move is made clear when the mediatorial roles of both Paul and the believers are recognized as they preach the gospel of God's redemptive act through his own Son:

- continuous work of the Father (1:3 – 14)
- climactic work of the Son (1:15 – 23)
- apostolic mission of Paul (1:24 – 2:5)
- faithfulness of the believers (2:6 – 4:1)
- eschatological mission to the world (4:2 – 6)

After this focus on the mission to the world, Paul concludes with the introduction of the messengers he sent (vv. 7 – 9), words of greeting from his coworkers (vv. 10 – 14) and those directed to others near Colossae (vv. 15 – 17), and finally a signature by his own hand (v. 18).

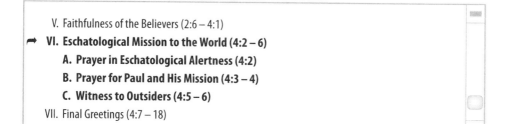

V. Faithfulness of the Believers (2:6 – 4:1)

➡ **VI. Eschatological Mission to the World (4:2 – 6)**

    A. Prayer in Eschatological Alertness (4:2)

    B. Prayer for Paul and His Mission (4:3 – 4)

    C. Witness to Outsiders (4:5 – 6)

VII. Final Greetings (4:7 – 18)

Main Idea

Being alert in prayer, believers are called to participate in the proclamation of God's redemptive acts. They must pray faithfully for the expansion of the gospel, and their lives must also be a proclamation of the gospel.

---

4. See Callow, *Semantic and Structural Analysis*, 150, who considers the common ground between the two sections as simply that they both "deal with Christian behavior."

Translation

Colossians 4:2 – 6

2a	Exhortation	**Devote yourselves to prayer,**
b	circumstance	being alert in it with thanksgiving,
3a	simultaneous	at the same time
		praying for us as well,
b	content	that God may open for us a door for the word
c	purpose	so that we may declare the mystery of Christ,
d	explanation	on account of which I am bound,
		and
		that I may proclaim it clearly,
		as it is necessary for me to speak.
4a	content	
b	manner	
5a	Exhortation	**Walk in wisdom toward outsiders,**
b	expansion	making the most of every opportunity.
6a	Exhortation	**Let your speech always be full of grace,**
b	illustration	seasoned with salt,
c	purpose	so that you may know
		in what way it is necessary for you to answer each one.

Structure

Paul has demonstrated the need to translate one's confession into one's pattern of life. The discussion of appropriate and inappropriate Christian behavior (3:5 – 17) culminates in the call to "do everything in the name of the Lord Jesus" (3:17), which expands the discussion about affirming the lordship of Christ in all areas of life. The discussion of household relationships that follows (3:18 – 4:1) provides a concrete setting where the lordship of Christ must take precedence. In the present section, Paul extends this concern in his address to the behavior of the believers outside of their Christian communities.

Paul begins by reminding the believers to persevere in prayer (v. 2a). This call is accompanied by a note on alertness, one that points to the eschatological urgency of Paul's message (v. 2b). Grounding this section on this eschatological note, Paul points to ways the believers can participate in the unfolding of God's redemptive plan. First, Paul requests that they pray for God to open doors for him and his coworkers as they proclaim the mystery of Christ (v. 3a-c). Second, Paul requests that they pray specifically for him as he fulfills the task given to him (v. 4a). Both requests are grounded in Christ's call to Paul as one who is to suffer for him (v. 3d) and who participates in the foreordained plan of God, which carries a sense of necessity (v. 4b).[5]

Paul then turns to the responsibilities of the believers in their own witness to those outside of their Christian communities (vv. 5 – 6). This two-part section begins with the call to act wisely towards the "outsiders" (v. 5a), which is followed by a participial clause that again highlights the eschatological urgency of this call: "making the most of every opportunity" (v. 5b). The second call focuses on the need to speak graciously (v. 6a-b), and the theme of necessity reappears when Paul grounds this call in the need to know the essentials in the faith in responding to the questions and challenges of the outsiders (v. 6c). As Paul is faithful in his mission to proclaim the gospel, believers are called to imitate him and continue his mission.

---

5. The themes of suffering and necessity can be found together in the context of Paul's call to proclaim the gospel of Christ: "This man is my chosen instrument to proclaim my name to the Gentiles and their kings and to the people of Israel. I will show him how much he must [δεῖ] suffer for my name" (Acts 9:15 – 16).

Exegetical Outline

➜ **I. Eschatological Mission to the World (4:2 – 6)**

　A. Prayer in eschatological alertness (4:2)

　B. Prayer for Paul and his mission (4:3 – 4)

　　1. So that God may open a door (4:3a-b)

　　2. So that Paul may reveal the mystery of Christ (4:3c – 4)

　C. Witness to outsiders (4:5 – 6)

　　1. Walk in wisdom (4:5)

　　2. Speak in grace (4:6)

Explanation of the Text

4:2 Devote yourselves to prayer, being alert in it with thanksgiving (τῇ προσευχῇ προσκαρτερεῖτε, γρηγοροῦντες ἐν αὐτῇ ἐν εὐχαριστίᾳ). The reference to prayer after the discussion of the household code may be a bit surprising to modern readers, but this theme of worship continues the focus of 3:15 – 17. In light of the preceding (re)definition of worship in terms of leading a God/Christ-centered life "in word" and "in deed" (3:17), the call to act in a prayerful way in this section becomes understandable since Paul is not focusing narrowly on one's prayer but is defining one's entire existence as having prayerful alertness.

The call to "devote yourselves in prayer" points to the need to be consistent and faithful in one's worshipful existence. The imperative "devote yourselves" can carry the sense of "perseverance," especially in contexts where endurance in the midst of persecution is noted (cf. Rom 12:12). In this context, however, it points to the total devotion of oneself in the life of prayer, and the translation "devote yourselves in prayer," as adopted by many contemporary versions, reflects this sense (e.g., NASB, NRSV, HCSB, NLT, TNIV, NIV). Elsewhere, the community of believers is depicted as those who

"joined together constantly in prayer" (Acts 1:14). Here in Colossians, the note on prayer may also remind the audience of Paul's earlier note on his diligence in praying for them: "we ... have not ceased praying for you and asking God that you may be filled with the knowledge of his will in all spiritual wisdom" (1:9). As Paul prays persistently for the Colossian believers for their faithfulness in Christ, Paul now calls on them to participate in this same act for the continued spread of the gospel.

Reading this verse with 1:9, we can appreciate the significance of prayer in Paul's writings and in the NT in general. To Paul, prayer is not simply an act of presenting one's personal wishes and desires to God; rather, it is a way for believers to participate in the unfolding of God's redemptive plan in history.[6] Elsewhere, one also finds the paradigmatic prayer of the early Christians in Acts 4:24 – 30, where, in the midst of persecution, they pray not to be delivered from such sufferings, but to continue to preach the word boldly. Here Paul encourages believers to continue to participate in this mission of the gospel through prayers.

The participle "being alert" (γρηγοροῦντες) has been taken as an imperative and thus "an inde-

---

6. This is consistent with the observation that Paul's mission is often centered on the gospel (Rom 15:30 – 33; Eph 1:15 – 23;

3:14 – 21; Phil 1:9 – 11; Col 1:9 – 14; 1 Thess 3:11 – 13); Carson, "Paul's Mission and Prayer," 175 – 84.

pendent command."[7] But, as elsewhere, this participle should be taken as a circumstantial participle modifying the previous call to "devote yourself to prayer."[8] The verb γρηγορέω appears elsewhere with the call to pray in a critical situations ("watch [be alert] and pray [γρηγορεῖτε καὶ προσεύχεσθε] so that you will not fall into temptation" [Mark 14:38; cf. Matt 26:41]), and it is often used in eschatological contexts where the end of the ages is in view (e.g., 1 Thess 5:6; Rev 3:3; 16:15; cf. 1 Cor 16:13).[9] In light of numerous terms and phrases in this section that carry eschatological overtones,[10] "being alert" here should also be read within this eschatological framework.

This focus is highlighted as well in the Ephesian parallel, where the call to be "alert" (Eph 6:18)[11] follows the call to put on the armor of God in fighting "against the rulers, against the authorities, against the powers of this dark world and against the spiritual forces of evil in the heavenly realms" (Eph 6:12). In Colossians, the dawn of the eschatological era has already been noted in 1:12–14. Paul is now emphasizing the need for believers to be alert in anticipation of the return of Jesus Christ in glory (cf. 3:4). By participating in the critical victory already accomplished by Christ on the cross (2:15), believers are called to live in light of the final consummation of this victory.

In light of the numerous references to gratitude and thanksgiving in 3:15–17, the reappearance of this theme in the phrase "with thanksgiving" (ἐν εὐχαριστίᾳ) is noteworthy. This phrase not only provides the proper conclusion to the previous section, where the lordship of Christ is so strongly affirmed, but it also points to the need to continue living a life of thanksgiving as believers affirm the lordship of Christ. The appearance of this note on thanksgiving in an eschatological context may surprise modern readers, but unlike our notion of gratitude as an expression of thanks for a prior act of kindness, for Paul thanksgiving can be forward-looking as it represents a call to respond to God's future act as if it is already an accomplished reality.

In 1 Cor 15:57, for example, Paul calls believers to be thankful for the final consummation of his redemptive act: "But thanks be to God! He gives us the victory through our Lord Jesus Christ."[12] Moreover, the call to thanksgiving is appropriate where believers are called to live in light of the future, full revelation of Christ's glory. Here, then, the thanksgiving motif serves to affirm both the certainty of the future manifestation of Christ's glory and the need for the believers to submit to the lordship of Christ as they live in view of this future reality.

4:3a-b At the same time praying for us as well, that God may open for us a door for the word (προσευχόμενοι ἅμα καὶ περὶ ἡμῶν, ἵνα ὁ θεὸς ἀνοίξῃ ἡμῖν θύραν τοῦ λόγου). Paul now shifts his attention from the Colossian believers to those outside their community. Paralleled with "being alert," the participle "praying" also modifies the call

---

7. Lohse, *Colossians and Philemon*, 164.

8. To determine the exact function of this circumstantial participle is more difficult. It has been taken as a participle of means, thus: "by keeping alert in it with thanksgiving" (James P. Sweeney, "The Priority of Prayer in Colossians 4:2–4," *BSac* 159 [2002]: 318). But this reading has difficulty explaining the function of the next participle, "praying" (v. 3) because "at the same time praying for us as well" (v. 3) seems not to point to the means of the imperative in v. 2. It seems best to take these two as dependent verbs that can take on imperative force but only as subordinating acts.

9. For the eschatological significance of this term, see Evald Lövestam, *Spiritual Wakefulness in the New Testament* (Lund: Gleerup, 1963), 76–77.

10. Dunn (*Epistles to the Colossians and to Philemon*, 262) points to the following terms/phrases in Col 4:2–6: "the mystery of Christ," "proclaim," "it is necessary" (2x), and "making the most of every opportunity."

11. The verb used here for the call to alertness is ἀγρυπνοῦντες.

12. Outside of Paul, a clear note of thanksgiving in light of the future act of God occurs in the eschatological, thanksgiving prayer in Rev 11:17–18.

to "devote yourselves to prayer" (v. 2). While this note clearly specifies the content of the "prayer" to which believers are to be devoted, the parallel between this clause and the previous one is important:[13] to pray for the further proclamation of the mystery of Christ is the manifestation of one's alertness in prayer in this eschatological era.

The pronoun "us" that appears twice in this clause (ἡμῶν, ἡμῖν) points likely to Paul and his coworkers, including Timothy (1:1) and Epaphras (1:7; 4:12),[14] although he later focuses on his own mission with the use of the singular pronoun ("me," v. 4) and first person singular verbs ("I am bound," v. 3; "I may proclaim," v. 4). Instead of seeing the plural pronoun here as an epistolary plural, therefore, it seems best to consider Paul making a general statement concerning the eschatological mission before focusing on his own mission.

In the context of prayer, "that" (ἵνα) indicates the content of the prayer (cf. 1:9) rather than its purpose. Paul's focus is on the continuous growth of the word. Elsewhere, Paul has used the metaphor of an open "door" for opportunities of gospel proclamation (cf. 1 Cor 16:9; 2 Cor 2:12).[15] The opening of a door "for the word" (τοῦ λόγου)[16] reminds the audience of the powerful "word of truth, the gospel" in 1:5, the "word" that can "come" to the audience while "bearing fruit and growing" (1:6).[17] The focus of this active and powerful word points to the inherent power of the gospel message. It is

therefore problematic to supply the pronoun "our" here, as in "our message" (NIV).

The parallel between this and the previous participial clause demands further attention as it points to the connection between alertness and missions. Instead of passively being alert in anticipation of Christ's return, Paul is pleading with believers to recognize the urgency of this eschatological moment as he calls them to participate with him and his coworkers in the mission that is to take place before Christ's return.

This focus on the alertness of the believers and their active responsibility can also be found in Jesus' teachings. This is best illustrated in the two eschatological parables in Matt 25. In the first, the parable of the ten virgins, believers are called to be alert in anticipation of the return of their Master. Significantly, eschatological terms that appear in the Colossians context also appear in Matthew: "door" (25:10), "open" (25:11), and "keep watch" (25:13). In the second, the parable of the bags of gold (Matt 25:14 – 30; cf. Luke 19:11 – 27), the focus shifts to the responsibility of the believers as they are called to use their time wisely before the return of Christ.[18] This focus on faithfulness (cf. Matt 25:21, 23) highlights the active mission of believers as they live in the eschatological moment. In line with the teachings of Jesus, Paul also emphasizes both alertness and missions in this context, especially where "being alert" (v. 2) is coupled with the call to make "the most of every opportunity" (v. 5).

---

13. Most contemporary versions take this participle as an imperative (e.g., NRSV, NLT, NET, CEV, TNIV, ESV, HCSB, NIV) and thus downplay the significance of this parallelism. Note Barth and Blanke (*Colossians*, 452), who highlight the parallelism between the two participial clauses. Note also the parallelism between "praying" and "being alert" in Matt 26:41 and Mark 14:38.

14. This plural may also anticipate the list of names presented in vv. 10 – 14 below.

15. Pokorný, *Colossians*, 186, points to the particular relevance of "door" as a soteriological metaphor as it depicts (1) a narrow opening, (2) the possibility of closing the door, thus the theme of judgment, and (3) the entrance into a new existence.

16. This translation takes the genitive as an objective genitive.

17. See comments on 1:5. Also note the depiction of the active and powerful word of God in Acts 6:7; 12:24; 19:20. In Jewish wisdom traditions, the powerful word becomes an instrument through which God's purposes can be accomplished (cf. Wis 18:14 – 16).

18. For a response to those who see this parable as addressing the time before the judgment on Jerusalem rather than the return of Christ, see Klyne R. Snodgrass, *Stories with Intent: A Comprehensive Guide to the Parables of Jesus* (Grand Rapids: Eerdmans, 2008), 533 – 35.

4:3c-d So that we may declare the mystery of Christ, on account of which I am bound (λαλῆσαι τὸ μυστήριον τοῦ Χριστοῦ, δι᾽ ὃ καὶ δέδεμαι). Paul now specifies the purpose for his request for believers to pray to God for an open "door for the word." Paul focuses here on his and his coworkers' mission to "declare the mystery of Christ." The eschatological significance of this "mystery" is clear in light of its previous appearances in this letter. The parallel between Paul's discussion here and 1:25 – 26 is particularly clear as "the mystery" stands in apposition to "the word of God." This "mystery" is that which has been "hidden for ages and generations, but now revealed to his [i.e., God's] saints" (1:26).[19] When Paul further identifies this "mystery" as "Christ in you," he also continues to emphasize the eschatological significance of this mystery as Christ, who is also "the hope of glory" (1:27). In 2:2, Paul identifies his mission as that which aims at proclaiming "the mystery of God, Christ."

These references help explain this phrase in 4:3. First, "the mystery of Christ" should again be understood in eschatological terms. After dealing with the situation in Colossae, Paul is looking forward to the continuation of this eschatological mission. Moreover, in light of 2:2, "of Christ" should be understood as an epexegetical genitive ("the mystery, that is, Christ"),[20] instead of a possessive genitive ("his secret plan," NLT) or a genitive of reference ("mystery about Christ," CEV).[21] Even in the earlier discussion on eschatology, Paul insists on a christocentric perspective in which the fulfillment of God's promises is contained in the final revelation of Christ's glory (cf. 3:1 – 4).

"On account of which I am bound" points directly to Paul's imprisonment for the sake of the gospel. In light of the reference to "mystery" that evokes 1:24 – 2:5, this reference to Paul's imprisonment becomes a concrete example of Paul's suffering noted in 1:24. As 1:24 is to be understood within the wider context of eschatological suffering, Paul here is also situating his imprisonment within the context of such suffering. In both the Pauline (Rom 15:22 – 33) and the Lukan (Acts 20 – 26) accounts, Paul's imprisonment is directly a result of his preaching of the gospel, which includes both Jews and Gentiles.

Paul's note on the relationship between his imprisonment and the revelation of the mystery of Christ, a mystery that points specifically to the inclusion of both Jews and Gentiles in God's redemptive plan (cf. Eph 3:1 – 7), takes on added rhetorical force here. Since Paul the Jew is imprisoned when he takes on the mission to proclaim the gospel among Gentiles, these Gentiles all the more are to carry on this mission among "the outsiders" around them (v. 5).

4:4 And that I may proclaim it clearly, as it is necessary for me to speak (ἵνα φανερώσω αὐτὸ ὡς δεῖ με λαλῆσαι). Paul now mentions the second item in his request for prayer as he seeks to be a faithful minister of the gospel. The relationship between this clause and that which precedes has been debated. Two major options are available:

(1) The first option is to be read as a purpose clause indicating the purpose of the request for God to open "the door" (v. 3), thus:

> Pray that God may open a door
> so that we may declare the mystery
> of Christ … [and]
> so that I may proclaim it clearly.…[22]

---

19. For the OT background of the term "mystery," see comments on 1:26a.

20. Harris, *Colossians and Philemon*, 194; MacDonald, *Colossians and Ephesians*, 171.

21. Callow, *Semantic and Structural Analysis*, 152.

22. Lightfoot, *St. Paul's Epistles to the Colossians and to Philemon*, 229; O'Brien, *Colossians, Philemon*, 240; Moo, *Letters to the Colossians and to Philemon*, 325. See also NRSV: "so that I may reveal it clearly" (cf. HCSB).

(2) The second option is to be read as the second item in the content of the prayer, thus:

Pray for us

that God may open a door ... [and]

that I may proclaim it clearly....[23]

Of the two options, the latter is to be preferred. First, the word "that" (ἵνα) is clearly paralleled to "that" (ἵνα) in v. 3b above ("that [ἵνα] God may open for us a door"). Paul is therefore describing the second item in the believers' petition. Second, one finds a natural progression of thought between the two petitions. The first focuses on God, who will be opening the door, while the second focuses on Paul, who is to proclaim this gospel. This reading does not, however, deny the close connection between the last clause of v. 3 and the present verse, especially when one finds the two verbs "declare/speak" (λαλέω) and "bound/[it is] necessary" (δέω) appearing in both clauses.[24]

The verb "I may proclaim ... clearly" (φανερώσω) often carries the sense of "revelation": "that I may reveal it clearly" (NRSV; cf. HCSB). This verb is used in this sense in 1:26 in reference to God's revelation of his mystery and in 3:4 to the final revelation of Christ in glory. Elsewhere in Paul, this word most often occurs in reference to divine acts in redemption (e.g., Rom 1:19; 3:21; 16:26; 1 Tim 3:16; 2 Tim 1:10) and in the final judgment (1 Cor 4:5; 2 Cor 5:10; 7:12; Eph 5:13 – 14). Some have therefore considered this verse as yet another piece of evidence that challenges the authenticity of this letter.[25]

In this context, however, God's act of opening a door is already mentioned together with the emphasis on the active work of the word (4:3). Moreover, the phrase "it is necessary" that follows also points to the redemptive plan of God. Paul is, therefore, but an instrument within this plan as he proclaims the gospel in obedience to his divine call. The description of the prior act of God in the revelation of his mystery together with Paul's role in such revelation has already been noted in 1:25 – 26:

... I became a servant according to the commission from God given to me for you, to fulfill the word of God, the mystery hidden for ages and generations, but now revealed (ἐφανερώθη) to his saints.

Our present text must be read in light of this previous note, as Paul understands himself to be merely an instrument of God's own act of revealing his mystery. The same understanding of his role appears in Titus 1:3: "at his appointed season he has brought to light [ἐφανέρωσεν] [his word] through the preaching entrusted to me by the command of God our Savior." Here Paul is simply situating himself as one who clarifies what has already been revealed.[26]

"As it is necessary for me to speak" can also be considered as a rephrasing of 1:25: "according to the commission from God given to me." This equation hinges on the Greek verb rendered "it is necessary" (δεῖ). Elsewhere in the NT, this verb can point to the series of events as necessitated by the

---

23. Harris, *Colossians and Philemon*, 195; MacDonald, *Colossians and Ephesians*, 172; Sumney, *Colossians*, 259. See also TNIV, NIV: "Pray that I may proclaim it clearly" (cf. KJV, ASV, NAB, NASB, REB, NJB, CEV, GNB, NKJV, NLT, NET, ESV).

24. A chiastic structure that involves the verbs, λαλέω, δέω, δέω, λαλέω, has been noted by Bockmuehl (*Revelation and Mystery*, 192) in support of the connection between the final clauses of v. 3 and v. 4.

25. Cf. Aletti, *Saint Paul Épître aux Colossiens*, 260.

26. On the semantic range of the term "to reveal/to pro-

claim clearly" (φανερόω), see also Bockmuehl, *Revelation and Mystery*, 192: "the word φανερόω is not in the first instance synonymous with ἀποκαλύπτω; it means rather 'to demonstrate' or 'to manifest' (in the empirical or logical sense). This is surely what is meant here: Paul desires to make the gospel manifest, as indeed he is bound to."

27. This is particularly evident in Luke-Acts; cf. Charles H. Cosgrove, "The Divine ΔΕΙ in Luke-Acts: Investigations into the Lukan Understanding of God's Providence," *NovT* 26 (1984): 168 – 90.

foreordained plan of God.[27] Some suggest that the significance of δεῖ finds its roots in the eschatological discourse.[28] The use of this verb here for Paul's apostolic mission in proclaiming the gospel is comparable to Luke's description of Paul's Damascus call to be God's "chosen instrument ... [and] must [δεῖ] suffer" for the name of Christ (Acts 9:15 – 16). In this Colossian context, this verb should likewise be understood as referring to the divine necessity as Paul seeks to be obedient to his role in God's redemptive plan.

Paul does not specify the intended audience of his obligation "to speak," but if the idea of necessity is connected with Paul's call to be an apostle among the Gentiles, the object would be the Gentiles, to whom Paul is expecting to preach if he were to be released from the prison. The reference to his imprisonment in the previous verse, however, may point also to the more immediate context of his Roman imprisonment, when he speaks boldly in the presence of those who accuse him. The use of the verb "to declare fearlessly" (παρρησιάσωμαι) in the Ephesian parallel (Eph 6:20) may also support this reading since courage (παρρησία) is more appropriate when the apostles continue to preach the gospel even as they are being persecuted (Phil 1:20; cf. Acts 4:13; 28:31).

4:5a Walk in wisdom toward outsiders (Ἐν σοφίᾳ περιπατεῖτε πρὸς τοὺς ἔξω). After focusing on his and his coworkers' mission to proclaim the gospel, Paul turns to the responsibility of the Colossian believers to act appropriately in the eschatological era. "Walk" (περιπατεῖτε) is the Jewish way of speaking about leading a way of life. Paul's concern for the way believers lead their lives is reflected in the repeated appearances of this verb in this letter (1:10; 2:6; 3:7). The fact that this verb appears

in the different parts of this section argues against the conclusion that this is simply a concern with outward behavior. Refusing to dichotomize between mind/understanding and body/behavior, Paul emphasizes how one's knowledge of the true gospel will lead to right thinking and an acceptable response to such a gospel.

This connection between knowledge and behavior is well illustrated by the phrase "in wisdom." The translation "wisely" (NAB, NRSV, NJB, NLT, cf. REB, GNB, TNIV, NIV), although it accurately reflects the adverbial function of this prepositional phrase, fails to reflect the significance of "wisdom" in this letter. While "wisely" could imply that believers simply have to act according to their own considered judgment,[29] "wisdom" in Colossians points to the unique wisdom that comes from and focuses on God. In 1:9 – 10, for example, the basis of "walk[ing] in a manner worthy of the Lord" is "the knowledge of his will in all spiritual wisdom and understanding." There, the "spiritual wisdom" is contrasted with human wisdom or the wisdom of the world (cf. 1 Cor 2:1 – 13). In Col 2:6, the christocentric emphasis emerges as believers are now called to "walk in him [i.e., Christ]." Closer to our passage, believers are called to reject the idolatrous practices in which they "once walked, when [they] were living in them" (3:7); instead, they are called to "put on the new humanity, being renewed in knowledge according to the image of their Creator" (3:10).

In light of all these references, it is clear that to "walk in wisdom" is to walk in the spiritual wisdom that centers on Christ, "in whom all the treasures of wisdom and knowledge are hidden" (2:3; cf. 3:16). Behind this call one may also detect a subtle response to the false teachers who possess only "an

---

28. Walter Grundman, "δεῖ, κτλ.," *TDNT*, 2:23.

29. Cf. Moule, *Epistles to the Colossians and to Philemon*, 133: "Behave with tact towards non-Christians." Others (e.g.,

Lightfoot, *St. Paul's Epistles to the Colossians and to Philemon*, 232) further compare this call to Jesus' exhortation for his disciples to be "shrewd as snakes" (Matt 10:16).

appearance of wisdom" (2:23).[30] Beyond this polemical intent, however, Paul's focus is on the positive call for believers to submit to the lordship of Christ as they walk in conformity to the knowledge of God's will.

"Outsiders" clearly refers to nonbelievers (cf. 1 Cor 5:12–13; 1 Thess 4:12), "those who are not Christians" (NLT). The insistence on the lordship of Christ does not create a community that values its own supreme status as the redeemed;[31] on the contrary, because Christ is the Lord of all, his lordship must be proclaimed among all (cf. 1:15–20).

4:5b Making the most of every opportunity

(τὸν καιρὸν ἐξαγοραζόμενοι). The eschatological urgency of the call to witness to nonbelievers becomes explicit here. In Greek, "making the most" translates a compound verb that can be literally rendered as "buying out," which is used elsewhere in the sense of redemption (Gal 3:13; 4:5).[32] The phrase has thus been rendered as "redeeming the time" (KJV, ASV, NKJV). Although a theological sense of redemption does not seem to be present here, the idea of buying out is supported by the additional clause in the Ephesian parallel ("because the days are evil," Eph 5:16) — that is, since "the prevailing evil of the times makes the opportunities for good more precious."[33]

More significant is the presence of a parallel in Daniel, where a similar phase is used: "I am certain that you are trying to gain time" (Dan 2:8). In that context, the Babylonian king has accused his astrologers of attempting to buy time in their delay to provide the proper interpretation for his

dreams. Beyond the apparent similar use of this phrase in Paul, this Danielic context may provide a further clue for this Colossian text if Paul is indeed alluding to this text. The Babylonian astrologers failed to comprehend the "mystery" presented to them and therefore needed to "buy time." But the believers, who now possess the knowledge of this revealed "mystery," should now seize every opportunity to proclaim this "mystery."[34]

In this context, the participle "making the most of" should best be taken as an attendant circumstantial participle modifying the preceding imperative, "walk." "Opportunity" (τὸν καιρόν) is often used to refer to the critical eschatological moment (Rom 5:6; 9:9; 13:11; 1 Cor 4:5; Gal 6:9; Eph 1:10), and such eschatological flavor can be detected here.[35] In this verse, however, this word does not refer to one particular point of time, but the opportunity that remains in this eschatological moment.[36] In light of the urgency presented by the revelation of God's mystery, believers are to proclaim this mystery to those outside their community. In this way, the Colossian believers will continue the work of Paul, who has struggled so that they can obtain "the knowledge of the mystery of God, Christ" (2:2).

4:6a-b Let your speech always be full of grace, seasoned with salt (ὁ λόγος ὑμῶν πάντοτε ἐν χάριτι, ἅλατι ἠρτυμένος). Paul now turns to the proper witness of the believers through their "speech." The word translated "speech" (ὁ λόγος) can also be translated as "word." While the "word" in v. 3 refers to the gospel message, the second per-

---

30. Cf. MacDonald, *Colossians and Ephesians*, 172.

31. Again, one may be able to detect a challenge to the false teachers who insist on a certain set of external boundary markers that separate them from those who are excluded from their community (cf. 2:16–23).

32. BDAG, 343.

33. Lightfoot, *St. Paul's Epistles to the Colossians and to Philemon*, 232.

34. Beale, "Colossians," 868–89.

35. Thus Barth and Blanke, *Colossians*, 456; Sumney, *Colossians*, 262.

36. While Paul focuses here on reaching out to the "outsiders," similar phraseology is used elsewhere in the call to care especially for those who are inside the church (see Gal 6:10).

sonal plural pronoun "your" (ὑμῶν) suggests that this is referring to human speech.

It is possible, however, that this human speech is to be understood as the vehicle for proclaiming God's word — thus, "the message" (CEV). This reading is supported by the connection between this verse and v. 5. In v. 5, Paul focuses on the deeds of the believers to bear witness for the gospel to the outsiders; here, Paul focuses on their words as vehicles of this gospel. These twin emphases point back to Paul's call earlier for believers to submit to the lordship of Christ: "whatever you do in word or in deed, do everything in the name of the Lord Jesus, giving thanks to God the Father through him" (3:17). Here, Paul is affirming that this christological confession through "word" and "deed" is to be extended in one's interaction with the "outsiders."

Does this "grace" (χάριτι) refer to divine grace[37] or human graciousness?[38] Without denying that the combination of "grace" and "word" often appears in ancient literature in reference to gracious or winsome speech,[39] in this context it seems best to consider this "grace" as containing a further reference to divine grace and the human response of gratitude. First, in both 1:2 and 1:6, χάρις is used for the grace of God. The relationship between "word" and "grace" is particularly clear in 1:5 – 6, where the "word of truth" is depicted as coming to the Colossian community of believers and enables this community to understand "the grace of God in truth." Now Paul is urging believers to extend the work of this "word" through the power of the same "grace" as they witness to "outsiders."[40]

Second, as we noted on 1:6, this "grace" represents the powerful act of God among his people. This reading may explain the purpose clause that follows here: "so that you may know in what way it is necessary for you to answer each one." It is not human graciousness but divine grace and power that will allow one to defend the gospel message. This use of "grace" reminds one of Luke's portrayal of Stephen in Acts 6:8 – 10, who, empowered by God's grace, becomes mighty in words and deeds in response to those who challenge the gospel.

Finally, the connection between this passage and 3:17 (as noted above) may also illuminate the use of the term "grace" (χάριτι) here. Prior to the call to submit to the lordship of Christ "in word and in deed" (v. 17), Paul uses essentially the same phrase in his call to thanksgiving (v. 16), a call that reappears in v. 17 with the participle, "giving thanks." For Paul, thanksgiving is a response to God's grace (cf. 2 Cor 4:15), and the term "grace" may carry both meanings when used in a theological context. In this section, which begins with a note on "being alert in [prayer] with thanksgiving" (v. 2), one should not be surprised to find both terms in reference to God's grace and the response that is required (as we have already seen in 3:15 – 17). The striking contrast between inappropriate speech and thanksgiving is explicitly made in a related passage in Ephesians: "Nor should there be obscenity, foolish talk or coarse joking, which are out of place, but rather thanksgiving" (Eph 5:4).[41] Therefore, if both senses of "grace" and "thanksgiving" are implied here as the believers are to extend their

---

37. Thus, "full of grace" (TNIV, NIV); Barth and Blanke, *Colossians*, 457.

38. Thus, "gracious" (NRSV, NLT, NET, ESV, HCSB); cf. Wilson, *Colossians and Philemon*, 292; Moo, *Letters to the Colossians and to Philemon*, 330.

39. See esp. Hultin, *The Ethics of Obscene Speech*, 168.

40. See also the Ephesian parallel, where "grace" clearly refers to the grace of God: "You must let no unwholesome word

come out of your mouth, but only what is beneficial for the building up of the one in need, that it may give grace [χάριν] to those who hear" (Eph 4:29 NET).

41. As repeatedly noted above, this Ephesian passage is understandable only if we assume that thanksgiving in Paul points essentially to the grateful submission to the lordship of Christ. Note Eph 5:5, where one who refuses to submit in thanksgiving is labeled as "an idolater."

christological confession in their witness, a paraphrase that may convey this call is: "Let your words be full of the power of God as you speak in submission to and with the objective of proclaiming the lordship of Christ."

The metaphor of "salt" in the phrase "seasoned with salt" clearly refers to the care in "choosing the right word."[42] Those who compare this use with Jesus' call for his followers to be "the salt of the earth" (Matt 5:13; cf. Mark 9:50; Luke 14:34) suggest that "salt" points to the "religious and moral quality which must characterise the speech of the Christian."[43] Nevertheless, here believers are not called to be "salt," but their speech is to be like salt. More relevant is the use of salt in the sense of winsome and witty speech.[44] This winsome speech is not an end in itself, for Quintilian notes that "salty" speech can arouse a "thirst for listening" (*Inst.* 6.3.19).[45] At the end of this section on reaching the world, believers are to present the gospel in a winsome way so that outsiders can be attracted to this message of salvation.

4:6c So that you may know in what way it is necessary for you to answer each one (εἰδέναι πῶς δεῖ ὑμᾶς ἑνὶ ἑκάστῳ ἀποκρίνεσθαι). As the "word" that has come to the Colossian community is now to move to outsiders through "speech" that is "full of grace," this final purpose clause further indicates the continuity of the movement of this word by means of the witness of believers. This continuity is highlighted by the impersonal verb "it is necessary" (δεῖ), a verb used in v. 4 for Paul's own gospel ministry. As it is necessary for Paul to speak, it is also necessary for the believers to continue this ministry of the word.

"To answer each one" points to the significance of addressing each unbeliever according to his or her own context and situation.[46] Although Jesus is Lord of all, each person must receive this grace as a divine gift. The preceding focus on "grace" and the present focus on "each one" reminds one of Eph 4:5 – 7, where the affirmation of the "one Lord" is followed by the emphasis on the individual distribution of the divine grace: "But to each one of us grace has been given as Christ apportioned it" (Eph 4:7). Here, Paul concludes the body of his letter by emphasizing the need for every individual to provide the proper response to this cosmic Christ.

Theology in Application

Prayer and Missions

At the beginning of this letter, Paul has provided us with a model of prayer that centers on God's redemptive act and his redeemed people.[47] Here, Paul picks up this discussion by pointing to the significance of prayer as believers reach beyond those within their own communities. Moving beyond his own prayer report in 1:9 – 14, Paul here provides the critical link between missions and prayer.

First, Paul points to the need to be watchful in one's prayer life. "Being alert" (v. 2)

---

42. Lohse, *Colossians and Philemon*, 169.
43. Friedrich Hauck, "ἅλας," *TDNT*, 1:229.
44. Cf. Plutarch *Mor.* 514E-F; Sumney, *Colossians*, 262.
45. Hultin, *The Ethics of Obscene Speech*, 172.

46. Cf. Harris' (*Colossians and Philemon*, 198) paraphrase: "so that you may know how you should give an answer suitable for each occasion and each need to each separate individual."
47. See discussion in the Theology in Application section on 1:9 – 14.

points not simply to a general sense of wakefulness; it points to the eschatological context that requires a proper ability to comprehend the present reality on the part of the believers. A parallel can be found in the Gethsemane scene, where Jesus urges his followers to "watch and pray so that you will not fall into temptation" (Mark 14:38; cf. Matt 26:41). In that context, the eschatological significance is apparent, as Jesus is about to be delivered to the authorities and be sentenced to death. Here, Paul's call to the believers to be devoted "to prayer [while] being alert" (v. 2) likewise points to the eschatological moment that demands one's watchfulness (cf. also Luke 21:36). In prayer, one is able to move away from and beyond one's self-centeredness in the discernment of the urgency of the eschatological moment.

Within this focus on the eschatological moment, the urgency of Paul's call to pray becomes understandable. In this specific context, the prayer is to be directed to God's opening of doors for the apostles to preach the word, and for Paul in particular in his fulfillment of his call as an apostle to the Gentiles. Although syntactically a different sentence, the call to witness to others in speech (v. 6) and deeds (v. 5) should likewise be considered as a practical outcome of one's prayerful alertness. As believers recognize the urgency of the eschatological moment, a natural response is to participate in the proclamation of the gospel of the cross.

Beyond this call to duty, not to be missed is the importance of prayer in confirming one's status within redemptive history. Instead of believers simply being passive recipients of God's drama of salvation, Paul emphasizes the active role of each believer. Through prayer, one recognizes one's dignity in the ability to play a part in redemption history. In a passage that emphasizes the necessity in the unfolding of God's foreordained plan (cf. vv. 4, 6), Paul also emphasizes the significance of prayer as a means through which believers can participate in this plan. Through prayers, God will continue his work through his messengers in claiming his lordship among all creation.

In this note on participation in God's redemptive plan, one can perhaps detect Paul's attempt to provide a reorientation of prayer from the "worship of angels" (2:18) to the ministry among unbelievers in this world (4:2 – 6). Throughout church history, many have emphasized the need to transcend the world in one's prayer life. From the pen of the fourth-century Egyptian monk Evagrios Pontikos, for example, one finds a similar understanding of prayer:

> Do you have a longing for prayer? Then leave the things of this world and live your life in heaven, not just theoretically but in angelic action and godlike knowledge.[48]

This understanding of prayer assumes a dualism between the spiritual and the material world, and prayer is possible only when the observance of commandments

---

48. G. E. H. Palmer, Philip Sherrard, and Kallistos Ware, eds. and trans., *The Philokalia: The Complete Text* (London: Faber and Faber, 1983), 1:70.

is able to control the bodily desires, which will allow the soul to guide the mind in one's communion with God:

> When the soul has been purified through the keeping of all the commandments, it makes the intellect steadfast and able to receive the state needed for prayer.[49]

Without denying the significance of communion with God, Paul focuses here on the kind of prayer that allows believers to be engaged with the world through the discernment of God's will through the intercession of the Spirit (Rom 8:26–27). This engagement is clearly stated here when Paul points to the mission to the "outsiders" as one's goal of prayer, instead of one's own ascent to the heavenly realm. In this context, therefore, missions and evangelism take on added significance.

Evangelism

Paul provides significant guidance here for believers as they are to be involved in evangelism. Before focusing on the human act of spreading the gospel, Paul begins with the prior act of God in such an endeavor. First, the believers are to pray that "God may open ... a door for the word" (v. 3). Fully realizing that it is God who will create for his followers the opportunity to preach the word, Paul reminds the audience that evangelistic efforts depend on God. This is consistent with Paul's own missionary activities when he, for example, describes God's opening of a door for him: "I went to Troas to preach the gospel of Christ and found that the Lord had opened a door for me" (2 Cor 2:12). In the Colossian context, the emphasis on "the word" also reminds one of the activity of the powerful word of God that "has come" to the Colossian believers, "bearing fruit and growing" among them (1:6). The word becomes the subject of evangelism rather than its object.

The prior act of God is also implied in the use of the term "grace" in describing believers, who are to be vehicles of the "word" (v. 6). To consider this "grace" simply as a reference to human graciousness is to deny the power of this term throughout Colossians (1:2, 6; 3:16; 4:18), as also elsewhere in Paul.[50] In Eph 3:7, Paul also describes the prior act of God in the provision of his grace that has enabled him to be an effective evangelist: "I became a servant of this gospel by the gift of God's grace given me through the working of his power." It is this emphasis on the prior act of God that the idea of necessity (Col 4:4, 6) should be understood: God provides both the design and the fuel for the proclamation of the word, and human beings who are obedient to his call are but instruments of this powerful word. It is this understanding of God's act in the human proclamation of the gospel that explains the connection between eschatology and missions in this context:

---

49. Ibid., 1:57.

50. See Wright, *Colossians and Philemon*, 153, who sees here a reference to both divine grace and human graciousness.

Eschatology is a vision of the coming of the kingdom of God that was initiated in Jesus of Nazareth, was experienced and cherished by the community that developed after his death and resurrection, and is now within the grasp of those who repent and receive the gift of the Holy Spirit; yet the kingdom remains to come in all its glory and fullness. If this vision is correct, there is good news for the world; there is indeed a gospel worth sharing. Moreover, evangelism is an activity of the followers of Jesus that should be rooted and grounded in this dynamic, mysterious, numinous reality of the rule of God in history.[51]

Shifting the attention from the prior acts of God to the role of human beings, Paul emphasizes the need for believers to be actively involved in evangelism. The call for believers to pray for his apostolic mission (vv. 3 – 4) is already a call for them to be involved in the partnership of the gospel mission. This understanding takes seriously the power of prayer. For Paul, prayer is not just a ritual to be performed. It is rather a critical means through which the gospel mission can be accomplished. As Paul has prayed that the Colossian believers "may be filled with the knowledge of his will in all spiritual wisdom and understanding" (1:9) and that Epaphras has also always been "striving on behalf of [them] in prayers" (4:12), the believers are now to join these acts of prayer in the anticipation of God's further acts among the nonbelievers. In the consideration of Paul's emphasis on missions and evangelism, therefore, such calls to prayer should not be ignored.[52]

Beyond being prayer partners in Paul's mission, believers are also called to be active and independent witnesses. In 3:17, believers are already called to "do everything in the name of the Lord Jesus," whether "in word or in deed," a call that is essentially repeated in 3:23. Here, the calls to "walk in wisdom" (v. 5) and "let your speech always be full of grace" (v. 6) echo the previous call to submit to the lordship of Christ "in word or in deed." Evangelism in word and evangelism in deed are not separate acts; they are part of living out the confession that Christ is Lord of all.

Evangelism in word and in deed means that every aspect of one's existence will have to be devoted to the proclamation of the gospel. Empowered by the sovereign God,[53] believers can claim everything for him (1:15 – 20).[54] Two points need to be made here. First, in examining the explosion of the early Christian movement after Paul when one can no longer identify a single group of outstanding missionaries that follow his model of missions, many sociologists have now recognized that "most conversions are not produced by professional missionaries conveying a new

---

51. William J. Abraham, *The Logic of Evangelism* (Grand Rapids: Eerdmans, 1989), 38 – 39.

52. The emphasis on the participation of believers as partners in Paul's apostolic mission is even clearer in Philippians (1:5, 27, 30; 4:14 – 15); cf. Andreas J. Köstenberger and Peter T. O'Brien, *Salvation to the Ends of the Earth: A Biblical Theology of Mission* (Downers Grove, IL: InterVarsity Press, 2001), 194.

53. See, e.g., 2 Thess 2:16 – 17: "May our Lord Jesus Christ himself and God our Father, who loved us and by his grace gave us eternal encouragement and good hope, encourage your hearts and strengthen you in every good deed and word."

54. The connection between the universal authority of Christ and evangelism/missions is clearly stated in Matt 28:18 – 20.

message, but by rank-and-file members who share their faith with their friends and relatives."[55]

Second, conversions produced by these "friends and relatives" are often produced by a lifestyle that demonstrates the vitality and power of one's faith. In "making the most of every opportunity" (v. 5), believers are called to demonstrate the power of the gospel in various contexts and situations. According to 1:4, when Paul discusses how the "faith" of the Colossian believers is demonstrated through "the love" they have for those around them, here this love is also likely in Paul's mind when he discusses the relationship between the believers and the outsiders. The power of this love, emphasized throughout Colossians (1:8, 13; 2:2; 3:14), can therefore become the basis for one's interaction with outsiders "in wisdom" (v. 5).

A study of the spread of Christianity in the modern era has also demonstrated that "individuals, families, clans, groups and societies from anywhere and everywhere have been drawn to God by cords of divine love."[56] It is precisely because of this divine love that one finds in Christianity "a religion of nearly infinite flexibility"[57] as it reaches every individual where he or she is.

Finally, in a letter that focuses on correcting wrong practices grounded in a wrong understanding of the status and work of Jesus Christ, this call to witness is also a call for believers to be assured of the faith they have in the all-sufficient Christ. The final purpose clause, "so that you may know in what way it is necessary for you to answer each one" (v. 6), can also point to the need for believers to stand firm in what they believe. This is explicitly noted in the closely related letter written to Philemon: I pray "that your partnership in the faith may become effective in gaining the knowledge of every good thing that is in us for Christ" (Phlm 6). Being a witness to outsiders, therefore, can in turn strengthen one's faith in Jesus Christ. Moreover, to witness how others come to Christ becomes the most powerful testimony of the grace of God, to both believers and to "outsiders."

---

55. Rodney Stark, *Cities of God: The Real Story of How Christianity Became an Urban Movement and Conquered Rome* (New York: HarperCollins, 2006), 13, who further argues that "only monotheism can generate the level of commitment to a particular faith sufficient to mobilize the rank and file to engage in missionizing activities."

56. Mark A. Noll, *The New Shape of World Christianity: How American Experience Reflects Global Faith* (Downers Grove, IL: InterVarsity Press, 2009), 192.

57. Ibid.

Colossians 4:7 – 18

Literary Context

This final section of Colossians not only provides closure to the letter, but it also provides the historical link between this letter and its historical audience. If the previous section (4:2 – 6) can be considered as the "body closing" of Paul's main arguments, this section serves as the "letter closing" that provides critical envelope material.[1] These two closings do, however, function in similar ways as they both aim at ensuring the proper reception of the letter. As the previous "body closing" provides the eschatological urgency of Paul's message, this "letter closing" secures the social relationships and network among Paul, his coworkers, and the recipients, upon which rests the personal and theological appeal of this letter.[2]

This letter closing is also connected with the opening greetings (1:1 – 2) and the thanksgiving and prayer reports that follow (1:3 – 14). The mentioning of Paul's co-workers, especially Epaphras in 1:7, occupies a significant part of the final section (vv. 12 – 13). These references are important especially because Epaphras is considered as the founder of the church at Colossae. Without bypassing this significant leader of the church, Paul emphasizes that this letter does not simply contain a discussion of a private matter; it is rather a correspondence between the apostolic authorities and a young and growing church.

Another connection with the opening sections of this letter is the importance of the theme of prayer. The reference to prayer as the context of thanksgiving in 1:3 together with the report in 1:9 – 14 highlights the theological dimension of Paul's discourse. In this final section that follows the call to prayer (4:2 – 4), Paul likewise points to Epaphras as a model of prayer (v. 12). In addition, the call for the believers to "remember" his "chains" (v. 18b), together with the final benediction ("Grace be with you," v. 18c), concludes this letter with a word of prayer. Taken as a whole, this

---

1. See Klauck, *Ancient Letters and the New Testament*, 321 – 22.

2. See John L. White, *The Form and Function of the Body of the Greek Letter: A Study of the Letter-Body in the Non-Literary Papyri and in Paul the Apostle* (SBLDS 2; Missoula, MT: Society of Biblical Literature, 1972), 39, who points to the significance of the relationship established by the frame of a typical papyrus letter that ensures a proper reception of the information transferred through the letter body.

letter, as other Pauline letters, are liturgical acts that are not simply concerned with the social-historical reality of the community, but they are also concerned with allowing the recipients to act and respond in light of the spiritual reality as impressed on them throughout the letter.[3]

In light of other Hellenistic letters, it has long been recognized that while the letter body is "fluid, flexible, and adaptable to a wide variety of situations and subjects," the letter opening and closing are much more predictable.[4] Nevertheless, individual emphases emerge. In this closing, several elements reflect Paul's emphases as well as the context of this epistolary situation. First, the identification of Tychicus as a "fellow slave" (4:7) and of Epaphras as a "slave of Christ Jesus" (v. 12) highlights the significance of this label in Colossians. This is consistent with Paul's emphasis on the responsibility of the slaves in 3:22 – 25, and on the believers, who are to act as slaves who serve the Lord (3:15 – 17).[5]

Second, the request for the exchange of letters with the church of Laodicea is striking (v. 16). This verse points to the relevance of Colossians for a wider area beyond one local church.[6] While Colossians as a document must be read in its literary and historical contexts, its relevance is not limited to the believers in first-century Colossae. Moreover, the circulation of letters may point to the impetus for the later collection of Paul's letters.

Finally, the absence of the discussion of Paul's itinerary in this letter closing also demands an explanation.[7] The concern about his own absence is not left untreated. Instead of his own presence, Paul begins by drawing attention to the presence of God's word among the Colossian believers (1:5 – 6). This focus on the word helps explain the relative absence of a discussion on his own presence/absence. In 2:5, however, Paul does deal with this topic in a different way. The claim "though I am absent in body, I am with you in spirit" points to this very letter as representing Paul's own presence and authority.

This concern can also be detected in the present section where Paul closes his letter with a reference to his emissaries (vv. 7 – 9), the people sent by Paul. While they serve as Paul's letter carriers, Paul's note here also secures their position as those who will be the faithful interpreters of the apostolic message. With this guarantee of the continuation of the faithful interpretation of the gospel message, Paul concludes his letter to the Colossians.

---

3. For the possible influence of synagogue liturgy on Christian prayer traditions, and therefore also on the Pauline letters that are framed by such prayers, see Wiles, *Paul's Intercessory Prayers*, 161.

4. Loveday Alexander, "Hellenistic Letter-Forms and the Structure of Philippians," *JSNT* 37 (1989): 90.

5. Paul's note that is he in "chains" (v. 18) may also be read in light of his emphasis on believers being slaves of Christ.

6. The references to Laodicea in vv. 13 – 14 and Hierapolis in v. 13 confirm this point.

7. See Funk, "The Apostolic *Parousia*: Form and Significance," 249 – 68; see comments on 1:6.

VI. Eschatological Mission to the World (4:2 – 6)

➡ **VII. Final Greetings (4:7 – 18)**

    A. Messengers of the Letters (4:7 – 9)

    B. Greetings from Paul's Coworkers (4:10 – 14)

    C. Greetings to and Instructions for Others (4:15 – 17)

    D. Paul's Signature (4:18)

Main Idea

Paul concludes this letter by naming his emissaries, conveying greetings from himself and his coworkers, providing final instructions, and sealing the letter with his own signature. In doing so, he provides his audience with models of faithfulness and calls others to follow such examples of faith.

Translation

Colossians 4:7 – 18

7a	Assertion	**Tychicus will tell you all the news about me;**
b	apposition	he is a beloved brother,
c	apposition	faithful servant, and
d	apposition	fellow slave in the Lord,
8a	identification	whom I am sending to you for this very purpose,
b	purpose	so that you may know the things concerning us and
c	purpose	that he may comfort your hearts.
9a	association	I am sending him
		with Onesimus,
b	apposition	the faithful and beloved brother,
c	description	who is one of you.
d	Summary	**They will tell you everything that has happened here.**
10a	Assertion	**Aristarchus ... greets you,**
b	apposition	my fellow prisoner,
c	List	**as does Mark,**
d	apposition	the cousin of Barnabas,
e	description	(concerning whom you received instructions,
f	condition	if he comes to you,
g	exhortation	receive him), and

Continued on next page.

Continued from previous page.

11a	List	**Jesus,**
b	identification	who is called Justus.
c	description	These Jews are the only ones among my coworkers for the kingdom of God;
d	description	they have been a comfort to me.
12a	Assertion	**Epaphras … greets you,**
b	identification	who is from you;
c	apposition	he is a slave of Christ Jesus,
d	description	always striving on behalf of you in prayers,
e	content	that you may stand mature and
f	expansion	fully assured in all the will of God.
13a	Assertion	For **I bear witness to him**
b	content	that he has labored much for you and
c	list	for those in Laodicea and
d	list	in Hierapolis.
14a	Assertion	**Luke … greets you,**
b	apposition	the beloved physician,
c	list	as does **Demas.**
15a	Assertion	**Send my greetings to the brothers in Laodicea,** and
b	list	to Nympha and
c	list	the church in her house.
16a	time	After this letter has been read to you,
b	Exhortation	**have it also read in the church of the Laodiceans;**
c	Parallel	and **read in turn the letter from Laodicea.**
17a	Exhortation	And **say to Archippus,**
b	content	"See to it that you complete the ministry
c	identification	you have received in the Lord."
18a	Assertion	**I, Paul, write this greeting with my own hand.**
b	Exhortation	**Remember my chains.**
c	Desire	**Grace be with you.**

Structure

As Paul provides a list of greetings and instructions, he begins by introducing Tychicus and Onesimus and their mission (vv. 7 – 9). Tychicus is apparently the primary emissary who will carry the letter and explain Paul's current condition to the Colossian believers. Paul's description of him (v. 7) not only allows the Colossians to trust him and accept his authority; it also points to him as a model whom the believers are to imitate. This may explain the lengthier descriptions attached to some of the persons noted in this section (e.g., vv. 9, 11c-d, 12b – 13). The description of Onesimus (vv. 9a-c) is particularly relevant, especially because the letter to Philemon is also addressed to the same community.

After providing a third person description of his emissaries, Paul shifts to greetings from his coworkers (4:10 – 14). The first three (Aristarchus, Mark, Jesus, vv. 10 – 11b) are identified as being "of the circumcision" (lit.; cf. 4:11c), while the final three (Epaphras, Luke, Demas, vv. 12 – 14) are apparently Gentiles. Paul uses this arrangement to convey how Jews and Gentiles are now participating as a unified body in Paul's gospel mission. This list of greetings thus provides a concrete illustration of what it means to put on the new humanity, "where there is neither Greek nor Jew, circumcised nor uncircumcised" (3:11). Embedded in these greetings is the call to receive Mark, Barnabas's cousin (4:10e-g). Also noteworthy is the detailed description of Epaphras (vv. 12 – 13), who was probably the founder of the Colossian church (cf. 1:7).

Moving beyond his coworkers, Paul turns his attention to the believers in Colossae and Laodicea (vv. 15 – 17). After greeting them (v. 15), he calls for the exchange of letters among them (v. 16). Paul then singles out Archippus by calling him to complete the ministry he has received in the Lord (v. 17).

In his own hand, Paul concludes this letter with his own greetings (v. 18a), a call to remember him in his imprisonment (v. 18b), and a benediction that focuses again on the grace of God (v. 18c). After all, this "grace" has formed the basis of Paul's argument in this letter (1:2c; cf. 1:6d; 4:6a).

Exegetical Outline

➡ **I. Final Greetings (4:7 – 18)**
    A. Messengers of the letters (4:7 – 9)
        1. Identity of Tychicus (4:7)
        2. Mission of Tychicus (4:8)
        3. Identity of Onesimus (4:9a-c)
        4. Restatement of the mission of these messengers (4:9d)
    B. Greetings from Paul's coworkers (4:10 – 14)
        1. From Aristarchus (4:10a-b)
        2. From Mark (4:10c-g)
            a. Identity of Mark (4:10c-d)
            b. Call to receive Mark (4:10e-g)
        3. From Jesus (4:11a-b)
        4. Identities of these men (4:11c-d)
            a. Ethnic and spiritual identity (4:11c)
            b. Relationship with Paul (4:11d)
        5. From Epaphras (4:12 – 13)
            a. Greetings (4:12a)
            b. Identity of Epaphras (4:12b-c)
            c. Example of Epaphras (4:12d – 13)
        6. From Luke (4:14a-b)

7. From Demas (4:14c)

C. Greetings to and instructions for others (4:15–17)

    1. Greetings to the believers in the surrounding areas (4:15)

    2. Call for the exchange of letters (4:16)

    3. Call for Archippus to complete his ministry (4:17)

D. Paul's signature (4:18)

    1. Paul's own greetings (4:18a)

    2. Call to remember his imprisonment (4:18b)

    3. Final benediction (4:18c)

Explanation of the Text

4:7a Tychicus will tell you all the news about me (Τὰ κατ᾿ ἐμὲ πάντα γνωρίσει ὑμῖν Τυχικός). Paul introduces Tychicus, the letter carrier and the one who will provide news concerning Paul. In Acts 20:4, Tychicus appears as one who accompanied Paul on his third missionary journey when he returned from Corinth to Macedonia. He is mentioned there with Trophimus, one who apparently traveled with Paul from Asia Minor back to Jerusalem (Acts 21:29). Some have suggested that Tychicus is also among Paul's travel companions in his journey to bring the collection to Jerusalem.[8]

Tychicus's appearance here in Colossians as well as in the similarly worded description in Eph 6:21 points to his contact with Paul during his Roman imprisonment.[9] Apparently, he will serve as the letter carrier to believers in Colossae and Ephesus.[10] His mission to this area may reflect his background as one who is from "the province of Asia" (Acts 20:4). The fact that the phrase "who is one of you" is only applied to Onesimus probably means that Tychicus is not from the city of Colossae.

In the final period of Paul's ministry, Tychicus also appears as Paul's trusted coworker. In Titus 3:12, Paul sends him to Crete, where Titus is. In plausibly his final letter, Paul sends Tychicus to Ephesus (2 Tim 4:12). The fact that Tychicus appears a number of times in relation to Ephesus suggests that he is from Ephesus and he is a convert of Paul's ministry there.[11]

"[He] will tell you all the news about me" points to the role of Tychicus not only as a letter carrier, but also as one who will provide a report concerning Paul. "All the news about me" literally reads "all the things concerning me." This most likely refers to Paul's condition in his imprisonment (v. 18) — thus, "how I am getting along" (NLT).[12] Nevertheless, this translation may limit the wider sense

---

8. Lightfoot, *St. Paul's Epistles to the Colossians and to Philemon*, 233.

9. This similarly worded statement has been used to argue that Ephesians is dependent on Colossians (C. Leslie Mitton, *The Epistle to the Ephesians: Its Authorship, Origin and Purpose* [Oxford: Clarendon, 1951], 58–99) or that both were products of the same "Pauline school" (Ernest Best, *Ephesians* [ICC; Edinburgh: T&T Clark], 613). Even to those who argue for a Pauline authorship for both letters, these verses suggest that "the author still had the first letter while he was penning the other" (Hoehner, *Ephesians*, 828).

10. We can also assume that he is also the one who delivers Paul's letter to the Laodiceans (cf. v. 16).

11. Cf. Eckhard Schnabel, *Early Christian Mission* (Downers Grove, IL: InterVarsity Press, 2004), 2:1228.

12. In a different context, a similar phrase ("the things concerning me," Phil 1:12, lit. trans.) is indeed used with specific reference to Paul's condition in chains. In the Ephesian parallel, this phrase is used together with an additional phrase, "how I am doing" (Eph 6:21 NET), in specifying the content of Tychicus's report.

of this phrase, as Tychicus apparently will provide additional instructions and probably interpretation for the words Paul has written (cf. v. 8).[13]

Beyond informing the Colossian believers of Paul's situation, Tychicus is to carry out a number of other tasks, including bringing Onesimus back to the house of Philemon (v. 9). In addition, a letter carrier of ancient times often brought gifts or supplies from the author and his circle of friends (cf. Phil 4:18). This carrier will likely be responsible for publicly reading the letter (cf. 1 Thess 5:27), and as such may be expected to provide the authoritative oral commentary on the letter.[14] In this context, Paul's authorizes Tychicus to do this.

4:7b-d He is a beloved brother, faithful servant, and fellow slave in the Lord (ὁ ἀγαπητὸς ἀδελφὸς καὶ πιστὸς διάκονος καὶ σύνδουλος ἐν κυρίῳ). Since Tychicus is to function as the official representative of Paul and the authorized interpreter of this letter, the descriptions provided here are not unexpected. These appellations do not draw attention to the personal relationship between Tychicus and Paul; they point rather to his respected status in the ministry of the gospel.

"Beloved brother"[15] should best be considered as a title depicting Tychicus's status as Paul's coworker. "Beloved" is here used together with the sibling metaphor, but it can stand on its own with the same intended reference to a metaphorical sibling relationship (cf. Rom 12:19; 1 Cor 10:14; 2 Cor 7:1; 12:19; Phil 2:12).[16] In the letter to Philemon, the significance of the title "beloved" is noted by

its parallel "coworker" when Philemon is addressed with both terms (Phlm 2). Significantly, he is later addressed as "brother" (Phlm 20), a title often also applied to Paul's coworkers, especially in the openings and closings of his letters (1:1; 4:9; cf. Rom 16:23; 1 Cor 1:1; 2 Cor 1:1; Eph 6:21; Phlm 1).[17] Here, therefore, "beloved brother" should also be considered as a title; "beloved" likely has God as the implied subject (cf. Rom 1:7), although Paul may also have in mind his own love for Tychicus (cf. Phil 4:1).[18]

"Faithful servant" (πιστὸς διάκονος) further highlights Tychicus's role in his service for God. The term "servant" denotes servitude[19] — in Colossians for service rendered to Christ (1:7; cf. 2 Cor 11:23; 1 Tim 4:6), the church (1:25), and the gospel (1:23; cf. Eph 3:7). In such contexts where the object of such service is an authoritative figure or institution, the authority of this "servant" is emphasized: "In relation to those they assist, διάκονοι are subordinate, but in relation to others they share in the authority of the one whose assistants they are, whether God, the gospel, the church, the apostle, or in due course the bishop."[20] The term "faithful" (πιστός) likewise highlights Tychicus's dedication to the gospel ministry. As in the case of the founder of the Colossian church (cf. 1:7), this description highlights his honorable status and thus ensures a proper reception by the Colossian believers.

The adjective "faithful" applies not only to "servant" but also to "fellow slave" (σύνδουλος); the final prepositional phrase, "in the Lord" (ἐν κυρίῳ),

---

13. Cf. Moule, *Epistles to the Colossians and to Philemon*, 136.

14. Randolph Richards, *Paul and First-Century Letter Writing: Secretaries, Composition, and Collection* (Downers Grove, IL: InterVarsity Press, 2004), 200–201.

15. The definite article (ὁ) used here can carry the function of a personal pronoun, thus "our beloved brother" (NASB; cf. GNB; see also 1:2).

16. In these references, the term "brother(s)" is implied.

17. Significantly, in Paul the appellation "brother" is also

the most frequently used ecclesiastical title for early Christian leaders. This points to Paul's understanding of the ecclesiastical structure of the early Christian communities.

18. See Aasgaard, *"My Beloved Brothers and Sisters,"* 244.

19. Only rarely is this term used in reference to an official ecclesiastic office (i.e., "deacon;" cf. Rom 16:1; Phil 1:1; 1 Tim 3:8, 12).

20. R. Alastair Campbell, *The Elders: Seniority within Earliest Christianity* (New York: T&T Clark, 2004), 134. See also Collins, *Diakonia*, 195–234.

should also be understood as modifying both appellations. Thus: Tychicus "is a faithful helper who serves the Lord with me" (NLT). The term "fellow slave" is particularly important in this context because of Paul's emphasis on believers who are to serve the Lord like slaves serving their masters (3:15 – 17, 22 – 25).[21] This is also an important title here since Tychicus is to escort Onesimus, the slave of Philemon, back to Colossae. Significantly, the only other appearance of this title in Paul is in 1:7 – 8 regarding Epaphras, a verse that resembles the present description: "as you learned it from Epaphras, our beloved fellow slave, a faithful servant of Christ on our behalf, who has also told us of your love in the Spirit."

The fact that Paul describes Tychicus in a similar way to Epaphras is important since this connection reinforces the status of Tychicus in the church that Epaphras founded. Such parallelism also points to their similar roles in this epistolary situation: Epaphras reported to Paul concerning the situation in Colossae, and Tychicus is now to report to the Colossian believers the situation concerning Paul.

4:8 Whom I am sending to you for this very purpose, so that you may know the things concerning us and that he may comfort your hearts (ὃν ἔπεμψα πρὸς ὑμᾶς εἰς αὐτὸ τοῦτο, ἵνα γνῶτε τὰ περὶ ἡμῶν καὶ παρακαλέσῃ τὰς καρδίας ὑμῶν). Paul explains further the purpose of sending Tychicus to Colossae. "I am sending" (ἔπεμψα) has rightly been recognized to be an epistolary aorist, that is, "the use of the aorist indicative in the letters in which the author self-consciously describes

his letter from the time frame of the audience."[22] In English, it is therefore appropriate to translate the phrase in the present tense.[23] The use of this aorist also implies that Tychicus is officially the letter carrier designated by Paul.

This verse is reproduced verbatim in Eph 6:22, thus referring to the same epistolary context.[24] Numerous coworkers of Paul are described to have been sent by Paul (e.g., 1 Cor 4:17; Phil 2:19, 23, 25, 28; 1 Thess 3:2; Titus 3:12). Not only does this point to his own apostolic authority in sending out messengers to the different churches, but it also testifies to the beginning of a social network that connects local churches through letters and emissaries.

The two listed purposes here make explicit what is implied in the clause in v. 7, "Tychicus will tell you all the news about me." Though v. 8 appears to repeat the stated purpose of v. 7, it extends that clause in two ways. First, "the things concerning us" expands the previous reference to Paul to include his coworkers. This "us" would include Timothy (1:1) and possibly also Epaphras (1:7; 4:12; cf. Phlm 23). Paul is making it clear that Tychicus is not simply a personal friend; he also represents the ministry team of which Paul is a part.

Second, "he may comfort your hearts" (παρακαλέσῃ τὰς καρδίας ὑμῶν) points to the role of Tychicus as one who is more than merely a news reporter. Earlier, Paul used the same verb to describe his own mission: "so that their hearts may be comforted [παρακληθῶσιν] as they are united in love, to obtain all the wealth of full assurance of un-

---

21. See comments on 3:22 – 25.

22. Wallace, *Greek Grammar*, 562. This explanation assumes, however, that tenses of Greek verbs are temporally based. For a different explanation that considers the aorist tense as representing the entire writing of the letter and is equally appropriate in expressing the present temporal sphere of reference, see Porter, *Verbal Aspect*, 228 – 30.

23. Thus NAB, REB, CEV, NJB, NKJV, TNIV, NIV; *contra* KJV, ASV, NASB, NRSV, NLT, NET, HCSB, ESV.

24. Beyond the issues of the relationship between Ephesians and Colossians (see n. 9, above), Richards (*Paul and First-Century Letter Writing*, 215) further suggests that this points to Paul's use of secretaries (cf. v. 18) since "this was the type of material secretaries often merely recopied from one letter to another."

derstanding, and the knowledge of the mystery of God, Christ" (2:2). Here Tychicus is sent to "comfort" the hearts of the Colossians. As noted above,[25] this verb can carry significant theological weight as it points to the comfort brought about by God's eschatological act of salvation (cf. Isa 40:1 – 2; 2 Cor 1:6). Tychicus is to provide such comfort for the Colossian believers. Although Paul is absent from this community, Tychicus will represent Paul as he continues to minister as his representative.

4:9a-c I am sending him with Onesimus, the faithful and beloved brother, who is one of you (σὺν Ὀνησίμῳ τῷ πιστῷ καὶ ἀγαπητῷ ἀδελφῷ, ὅς ἐστιν ἐξ ὑμῶν). Paul now mentions Onesimus, who will accompany Tychicus as they travel to Colossae. In Greek, this verse begins with a prepositional phrase connected to the relative clause in v. 8, thus: "whom I am sending to you … with Onesimus…." Apart from the letter to Philemon, the name "Onesimus" only appears here in Paul's writings. The name means "useful," and it was a common name of a slave (cf. Phlm 11).[26] From the letter to Philemon, we know that he is Philemon's slave who has left his master and met Paul in prison, where he became a believer (Phlm 10). The exact reason for his separation from Philemon (cf. Phlm 15) is unclear,[27] although it seems there is tension between him and Philemon (cf. Phlm 11, 18). Among the purposes of the writing to Philemon, Paul urges him to receive Onesimus back "no longer as a slave, but more than a slave, a beloved brother" (Phlm 16).

"The faithful and beloved brother" recalls a similar description of Tychicus, except Onesimus is not labeled as "servant" or "fellow slave" (v. 7). This omission may be due to Paul's attempt not to draw attention to the (former) status of Onesimus as literally a slave, though it may also point to the fact that Onesimus is not (yet) considered to be one of Paul's coworkers.[28] Yet another reason for the omission of such titles is to highlight the sibling metaphor as applied now to a slave. As noted above, in his letter to Philemon Paul urges him to receive Onesimus back as a "beloved brother" (Phlm 16). Paul also reminds him that Onesimus is now a "son" to him (Phlm 10). This reframing of reality through the use of family terms points to a new existence in Christ where there is neither slave nor free (cf. 3:11). In this case, therefore, to call Onesimus a "faithful and beloved brother" may reflect the wider argument Paul will make in his letter to Philemon.[29]

"Who is one of you" has been read to denote Onesimus's new status as a believer and thus a member of the wider Christian community.[30] For this to be Paul's focus, one would expect a first personal plural pronoun ("us"), however. Those who deny Pauline authorship further suggest that this is a subtle reference to the Onesimus who later was recognized as a church leader in western Asia Minor.[31] Nevertheless, there is no hint in the text that Paul is highlighting Onesimus's leadership role, at least in comparison to the status of

---

25. See comments on 2:2, esp. on translating this verb as "to comfort."

26. BDAG, 711. An analysis of the name Onesimus in more recently published inscriptions and papyri shows, however, that this name "could be borne by free persons of no insignificant status and that it is far from being a sure indication of servile status" (A. L. Connolly, "Onesimos," *NewDocs* 4:180).

27. See the Introduction to the commentary on Philemon.

28. Schweizer, *Letter to the Colossians*, 238; Moo, *Letters to the Colossians and to Philemon*, 336. Some consider the term "faithful and beloved brother" as already implying that he is a

"servant and fellow slave"; cf. Pokorný, *Colossians*, 191.

29. Cf. S. Scott Bartchy, "Undermining Ancient Patriarchy: The Apostle Paul's Vision of a Society of Siblings," *BTB* 29 (1999): 68 – 78.

30. See Wright, *Colossians and Philemon*, 156, who sees a double reference behind this phrase: "The church already knows that he *is one of you*, and needs to be assured that he is now this in a deeper sense, not merely a Colossian but also a Christian" (italics his).

31. Cf. *Apostolic Constitutions* 7.46; Ignatius, *Eph.* 1.3 – 2.1; Sumney, *Colossians*, 270.

Tychicus. It seems best to read this phrase to refer to Onesimus as a native of Colossae.

To evoke a person's connection with the community may appeal to the audience and thus provide the basis for a proper reception of the letter. In this case, however, evoking the name of a slave who apparently is not (yet) an honorable member of the community may accomplish a different purpose. Instead of ensuring a proper reception of the letter, Paul is here ensuring a proper reception of this slave. This is, after all, the purpose of the letter to Philemon.

4:9d They will tell you everything that has happened here (πάντα ὑμῖν γνωρίσουσιν τὰ ὧδε). The final statement of this subsection essentially repeats the earlier statement concerning the task of Tychicus (vv. 7 – 8). This statement could simply be summarizing this subsection, but since it is a restatement after the reference to Onesimus, it includes Onesimus as one of Paul's emissaries. If so, the honorable status of Onesimus is implicitly asserted, a move that may have been intended to influence the audience in their perception and eventual reception of Onesimus.

4:10a-b Aristarchus, my fellow prisoner, greets you (Ἀσπάζεται ὑμᾶς Ἀρίσταρχος ὁ συναιχμάλωτός μου). In this new subsection, Paul provides greetings from his coworkers. Three types of greetings can be found in Hellenistic papyri; only the first type, which is relatively rare in papyri letters,[32] is missing in this closing section:

1. Direct greetings from the author to the audience

2. Forwarded greetings from a third party to the audience (vv. 10 – 14)
3. Greetings from the author to a third party (v. 15)

Paul begins with forwarded greetings from his coworkers. As with the name Onesimus in the previous verse, all the names listed here except for Jesus/Justus reappear in Philemon (vv. 23 – 24), which thus reaffirms the common contexts between the two letters.

In Acts, "Aristarchus" is called "a Macedonian from Thessalonica" (Acts 27:2), who is one of Paul's travel companions on his third missionary journey (19:29; 20:4). Since he appears in two of the so-called "we-passages" (20:3 – 15; 27:1 – 28:16), which likely contain Luke's own eyewitness accounts of Paul's journeys,[33] it is not surprising to find Luke also in this greetings section (cf. v. 14).

Aristarchus was with Paul during the riot in Ephesus (Acts 19:21 – 41); if we can assume an Ephesian imprisonment, then "my fellow prisoner" may literally refer to their sharing time in prison there and possibly also in Rome: "who is in prison with me" (NLT).[34] But this title can also carry a metaphorical sense referring to their submission to Christ's lordship, as in the title "fellow slave" in v. 7. If so, this title points primarily to the idea that he is "Christ's captive like myself" (REB).[35] A similar metaphoric sense can be identified in Phlm 1, where Archippus is called our "fellow soldier" (cf. Phil 2:25).

4:10c-d As does Mark, the cousin of Barnabas (καὶ Μᾶρκος ὁ ἀνεψιὸς Βαρναβᾶ). This "Mark" is

---

32. Klauck, *Ancient Letters and the New Testament*, 24 – 25.
33. See esp. the defense of this reading in William S. Kurz, *Reading Luke-Acts: Dynamics of Biblical Narrative* (Louisville: Westminster John Knox, 1993), 123 – 24.
34. Since Paul is now writing from Rome, it seems likely that Aristarchus is imprisoned with him in Rome. Lightfoot (*St. Paul's Epistles to the Colossians and to Philemon*, 236) further suggests the possibility that Aristarchus "voluntarily

shared the Apostle's captivity by living with him." The purpose of doing so was to serve him in prison (cf. Phil 2:25).
35. The fact that Epaphras and not Aristarchus is called "my fellow prisoner in Christ Jesus" in Phlm 23 may further support this metaphoric reading, although some (Lohse, *Colossians and Philemon*, 172 n. 20) point out that the omission of the phrase "in Christ Jesus" may suggest a literal reading instead.

possibly the one who first appears as John Mark when Luke identifies a believers' meeting in the house of his mother (Acts 12:12). After their Jerusalem relief visit, Paul and Barnabas brought Mark from Jerusalem to Antioch (12:25). He joined Paul and Barnabas on their first missionary journey, but he left them in Pamphylia (15:38). Paul refused to bring him along in his second journey; this led to a "sharp disagreement" between him and Barnabas, with the result that they parted company, with Barnabas and Mark sailing to Cyprus (15:39). In Colossians and Philemon (Phlm 24), Mark reappears in Paul's own writings. Together with the later description of Mark as being "helpful" in his ministry (2 Tim 4:11),[36] it seems evident that they were eventually reconciled.

Mark is identified here as "the cousin [ἀνεψιός] of Barnabas."[37] Since "Mark" is a common name, the phrase may help identify the person to whom Paul is referring. The reference to Barnabas also reinforces the apostolic authority that stands behind this letter. Beyond his relationship with Barnabas, Mark is also identified as a Jewish Christian who is a coworker with Paul "for the kingdom of God" (v. 11).

4:10e-g (Concerning whom you received instructions, if he comes to you, receive him) (περὶ οὗ ἐλάβετε ἐντολάς, ἐὰν ἔλθῃ πρὸς ὑμᾶς δέξασθε αὐτόν). Breaking the sequence of the list of greetings, Paul reminds the audience of the instructions they have received about the reception of Mark.[38]

It is unclear when this previous instruction was given, and it is not even clear who gave the instruction. Since Paul has never been to Colossae, and since there is no evidence that he had prior contact with that church, most likely someone else gave the instruction.[39] Possible candidates include Peter (cf. 1 Pet 5:13) and Barnabas.

This parenthetical note may reflect "a hint of lingering tension" in whether Mark will make the journey or whether the Colossian believers will receive him because of Mark's past.[40] It is possible, however, to read this third-class conditional sentence not as reflecting doubt, but as a general command to ensure that Mark is being received.[41] This is important especially because Mark is to represent Paul and his coworkers. The fact that Mark is one of Paul's "coworkers for the kingdom of God" (v. 11) further supports this reading. If so, this is yet another way for Paul to deal with his own absence among the Colossians. Together with this letter, Mark's presence will represent Paul's person and authority. This reading is consistent with the rhetorical thrust of this closing section insofar as the mere possibility of the impending visit of an apostolic representative would strengthen the bond between Paul and the Colossian community.[42]

4:11a-b And Jesus, who is called Justus (καὶ Ἰησοῦς ὁ λεγόμενος Ἰοῦστος). The final name in this list of Jewish coworkers of Paul is "Jesus" (Ἰησοῦς), the Greek form of a common Jewish name, Joshua (cf. Luke 3:29; Acts 7:45; Heb 4:8). "Who is called

---

36. The fact that Mark turns out to be a reliable and faithful proclaimer of the gospel is evident in the writing of his gospel, likely prior to Paul's writing of Colossians and Philemon.

37. The term ἀνεψιός has been misunderstood to mean nephew ("sister's son," KJV), but ancient sources consistently use it in the sense of "cousin"; Num 36:11; Tob 7:2; Philo, *Embassy* 67; Josephus, *War* 1.662; *Ant.* 1.290; BDAG, 78.

38. Most commentators and versions rightly consider the reference behind this relative pronoun ("whom," οὗ) to be "Mark."

39. Of course, one cannot rule out the existence of a prior

letter (Moule, *Epistles to the Colossians and to Philemon*, 137) or other means of contact (Lightfoot, *St. Paul's Epistles to the Colossians and to Philemon*, 237 – 38) between Paul and the Colossian believers.

40. MacDonald, *Colossians and Ephesians*, 180.

41. Moreover, the use of the aorist subjunctive ("if he comes," ἔλθῃ) in the protasis generally indicates a relatively high degree of probability; Harris, *Colossians and Philemon*, 207.

42. Cf. C. Clifton Black, *Mark* (ANTC; Nashville: Abington, 2011), 53 – 54.

Justus" helps to distinguish this "Jesus" from others of the same name. The Roman name "Justus," which means just or law-abiding, was also a common name applied to both Jews and Gentiles[43] (see Acts 1:23; 18:7). We know nothing more about this Jesus.

4:11c These Jews are the only ones among my coworkers for the kingdom of God (οἱ ὄντες ἐκ περιτομῆς οὗτοι μόνοι συνεργοὶ εἰς τὴν βασιλείαν τοῦ θεοῦ). This clause provides critical information for the three persons named above, but its meaning is not clear.[44] As far as the syntactical relationship between these two parts is concerned, two major options emerge:

(1) "These are the only ones of the circumcision among my coworkers for the kingdom of God" (cf. NRSV, NKJV, NLT, ESV, TNIV, NIV).

(2) "Among those of the circumcision these alone are my coworkers for the kingdom of God" (cf. NJB, CEV, NEB, NET, HCSB).

The first option provides the contrast between the three names just given and the three below, as only those above are "of the circumcision." The second option highlights that only the three above "of the circumcision" are Paul's coworkers. In light of the three names below that apparently are not "of the circumcision," option (1) provides a better reading.

Two further readings can be identified behind option (1), and these depend on the exact meaning of the phrase "of the circumcision" (ἐκ περιτομῆς).

(1a) "These are the only ones of the circumcision among my coworkers for the kingdom of God" (cf. NKJV, NRSV, ESV).

(1b) "These are the only Jews among my coworkers for the kingdom of God" (cf. NLT, TNIV, NIV).

Option (1a) leaves open the possibility of the reading the phrase "of the circumcision" to refer to conservative Jewish Christians who insist on the observance of the Jewish law. Option (1b) understands this phrase as referring specifically to the "Jews" or "Jewish Christians" in general. While the phrase "of the circumcision" may remind one of the "circumcision party" (τοὺς ἐκ περιτομῆς) in Gal 2:12,[45] the phrase can also be used simply in reference to the Jews in general (cf. Rom 4:12).[46] In this case, it seems that Paul is simply pointing to the Jews above and the Gentiles below as participating in the gospel mission.[47] This would testify to the fact that both Jews and Gentiles are part of this new humanity (cf. 3:11). Moreover, in the greetings in Romans, one also finds the identification of several of Paul's coworkers explicitly as his "kinspeople" (Rom 16:7; cf. 16:11; NIV, "fellow Jews"), probably making the same point about the gospel that includes both Jews and Gentiles.[48]

"Coworkers" (συνεργοί) points to the participation of these Jews in God's mission. Unlike other civil associations where the honor of the office holders is reflected in the exalted title, this one does not draw attention to a unique and exalted

---

43. Cf. James the brother of the Lord is later called "James the Just"; see Eusebius, *Hist. eccl.* 2.23.4).

44. The ambiguity lies partly in the fact that the "plain reading" ("these Jews are my only coworkers for the kingdom of God") does not make sense with three other coworkers named below.

45. See E. Earle Ellis, "'Those of the Circumcision' and the Early Christian Mission," *SE* 4 (1964): 390–99.

46. For the use of "circumcision" as an ethnic marker in the NT, see Lieu, *Christian Identity in the Jewish and Graeco-Roman World*, 128.

47. Lohse, *Colossians and Philemon*, 173 n. 28; O'Brien, *Colossians, Philemon*, 251–52; Wilson, *Colossians and Philemon*, 301.

48. Cf. Andrew D. Clarke, "Jew and Greek, Slave and Free, Male and Female: Paul's Theology of Ethnic, Social and Gender Inclusiveness in Romans 16," in *Rome in the Bible and the Early Church* (ed. Peter Oakes; Carlisle, UK: Paternoster, 2002), 103–25.

status (cf. Rom 16:3, 9, 21; 1 Cor 3:9; 2 Cor 1:24; 8:23; Phil 2:25; 4:3; 1 Thess 3:2; Phlm 1, 24).[49] Although the term may point to Paul's inner circle, the emphasis lies in the common work they have in the common mission. In this sense, then, they are not primarily Paul's coworkers, but God's: "for we are co-workers in God's service" (1 Cor 3:9; cf. 1 Thess 3:2).[50]

The prepositional phrase "for the kingdom of God" appropriately draws attention to this theocentric emphasis. Here, "the kingdom of God" should be identified with "the kingdom of his beloved Son" (1:13). The close relationship between the two is well illustrated by the description in Eph 5:5: "the kingdom of Christ and of God."[51]

4:11d They have been a comfort to me (οἵτινες ἐγενήθησάν μοι παρηγορία). The word "comfort" (παρηγορία) appears only here in the NT, and it can refer to assistance, encouragement, and consolation. Paul's comment may have several functions. For those who consider the phrase "of the circumcision" as a reference to the "circumcision party," their cooperation with Paul may symbolize an act of reconciliation after the Antioch incident (Gal 2:11 – 12) and thus provide some comfort to Paul in his later years.[52] If "of the circumcision" refers to "Jews," however, this note more likely points to the cooperation between Jews and Gentiles in the gospel mission, which brings satisfaction to Paul, who is concerned about the relationship between them (cf. Rom 9 – 11; Eph 1 – 2). Not to be ruled out is the specific help these coworkers might have provided Paul during his imprisonment.

4:12a-b Epaphras, who is from you, greets you (ἀσπάζεται ὑμᾶς Ἐπαφρᾶς ὁ ἐξ ὑμῶν). Paul shifts now to the greetings offered by his Gentile coworkers. Epaphras has already been introduced in 1:7 – 8. His appearance in both the opening and the closing of this letter confirms his significance in both Paul's ministry and among the Colossian believers. "Who is from you" (ὁ ἐξ ὑμῶν) repeats Paul's description of Onesimus and confirms Epaphras as a native of Colossae. In 1:7 – 8, we learned that Epaphras is both the founder of the church and the one who informs Paul of the situation there.[53] Paul and Epaphras have been speaking with one voice in the letter in their attempt to challenge the false teachers. This connection reaffirms both Epaphras's standing and Paul's apostolic authority within that community.

4:12c-f He is a slave of Christ Jesus, always striving on behalf of you in prayers, that you may stand mature and fully assured in all the will of God (δοῦλος Χριστοῦ [Ἰησοῦ], πάντοτε ἀγωνιζόμενος ὑπὲρ ὑμῶν ἐν ταῖς προσευχαῖς, ἵνα σταθῆτε τέλειοι καὶ πεπληροφορημένοι ἐν παντὶ θελήματι τοῦ θεοῦ). Epaphras was earlier described as "our beloved fellow slave, a faithful servant of Christ on our behalf," 1:7); here he is identified as a "slave of Christ Jesus."[54] Paul applies to Epaphras the title he applies primarily to himself (Rom 1:1; Gal 1:10; Titus 1:1; cf. 1 Cor 7:22; 2 Cor 4:5; Eph

---

49. Clarke, *A Pauline Theology of Church Leadership*, 46 – 47.

50. Cf. Kathy Ehrensperger, *Paul and the Dynamics of Power: Communication and Interaction in the Early Christ-Movement* (London: T&T Clark, 2007), 47 – 48.

51. George Eldon Ladd, "Paul's Friends in Colossians, 4:7 – 16," *RevExp* 70 (1973): 510, points to 1 Cor 15:25 ("For he [i.e., Christ] must reign until he has put all his enemies under his feet"), which suggests that the Son will turn over his kingdom to his Father when the ultimate victory is achieved.

52. John Gillman, "Justus," *ABD*, 3:1134.

53. Epaphras's ability to travel to Rome to seek Paul's advice suggests he is a person of means. Some even argue that he is a businessman; cf. Murphy-O'Connor, *Paul*, 235.

54. "Jesus" (Ἰησοῦ) is included in some of the best uncial (א A B C I L 0278) and minuscule (33 81 365 629 1175 2464) manuscripts, but is omitted by the generally reliable papyrus (𝔓[46]) together with other manuscripts of various textual families (D F G Ψ 075 1739 1881 𝔐). The shorter reading is probably to be preferred.

6:6; Phil 1:1). Moreover, after the detailed description of "slaves" who are to submit to their masters (3:22 – 25) and the connection between such submission and the believers' submission to their heavenly Lord (cf. 3:15 – 17), Epaphras becomes the prime example of such a "slave of Christ Jesus."

Epaphras is someone who is "always striving" in prayers on behalf of the Colossian believers.[55] Paul uses the same verb here as he used to describe his own "striving" (ἀγωνιζόμενος, 1:29) on behalf of the Colossian believers (cf. "for you," ὑπὲρ ὑμῶν, 2:1).[56] As the believers are called to continue Paul's mission in proclaiming the gospel in their own contexts (4:2 – 6), Paul again symbolizes such continuation by portraying Epaphras as the one who extends Paul's own labor of love.[57]

The content[58] of Epaphras's prayer is that the Colossian believers "may stand mature and fully assured in all the will of God." This short report consists of four major components: (1) "stand"; (2) "mature"; (3) "fully assured"; and (4) "the will of God." The second and fourth items point again to the connection between Epaphras's ministry and Paul's. In 1:28, the maturity (τέλειοι) of the Colossian believers was highlighted as the focus of Paul's gospel ministry: "Him [i.e., Christ] we proclaim, admonishing everyone and teaching everyone with all wisdom so that we may present everyone mature [τέλειον] in Christ." Here, Epaphras likewise prays for their maturity. The reference to "the will of God" (θελήματι τοῦ θεοῦ) also points back to Paul's prayer in 1:9 on behalf of the Colossian believers.

The first and third items, however, find no direct linguistic parallels to earlier parts of this letter. They focus rather on the need for the Colossians to resist the false teachers. The verb "stand" (σταθῆτε)[59] means to "stand firm" (cf. 1 Cor 10:12; 2 Cor 1:24; Eph 6:14; 2 Tim 2:19) in the foundation of faith,[60] that is, to "continue in your faith, established and steadfast, not shifting from the hope of the gospel" (1:23).[61] The participle "fully assured" (πεπληροφορημένοι) in turns points to "all the wealth of full assurance [πληροφορίας] of understanding" that can only be found in Christ (2:2). With both terms, therefore, Paul points to Epaphras's continued prayer and mission to ensure that the Colossian believers remain faithful to Christ and his gospel.

4:13 For I bear witness to him that he has labored much for you and for those in Laodicea and in Hierapolis (μαρτυρῶ γὰρ αὐτῷ ὅτι ἔχει πολὺν πόνον ὑπὲρ ὑμῶν καὶ τῶν ἐν Λαοδικείᾳ καὶ τῶν ἐν Ἱεραπόλει). Paul now testifies that Epaphras "has labored much" for the believers in the Lycus Valley. The conjunction "for" (γάρ) is left untranslated in some versions (e.g., NAB, REB, CEV, GNB, NLT, NIV) since it does not provide grounds for

---

55. The connection between "striving" and "prayer" recalls Jesus' own agonizing prayer in Gethsemane (cf. 4:2); Moule, *Epistles to the Colossians and to Philemon*, 138.

56. Ostmeyer, *Kommunikation mit Gott und Christus*, 124. For the wider parallels between 1:25 – 2:1 and 4:12 – 13, see also Martin Brändl, *Der Agon bei Paulus: Herkunft und Profil paulinischer Agonmetaphorik* (WUNT 2.222; Tübingen: Mohr Siebeck, 2006), 367.

57. The emphasis on Epaphras's labor in his prayer on behalf of the Colossian believers is well captured in REB: "He prays hard for you all the time."

58. As in the prayer report/requests above, the word "that"

(ἵνα) points to the content rather than the purpose of the prayer (1:9; 4:3 – 4).

59. This aorist passive subjunctive takes on an intransitive active meaning; cf. BDAG, 482.

60. Scholars debate whether "in the will of God" is connected directly with "stand" or "fully assured." Our translation here allows for both readings, though it may be best to consider the phrase as directly modifying the verb "stand": "that you may stand firm in all the will of God, mature and fully assured" (TNIV, NIV; cf. GNB, CEV).

61. Cf. Paul's double use of this verb in Eph 6:11, 13 in his call for believers to be "stand" (στῆναι) firm in their spiritual warfare against the evil one.

v. 12; rather, it provides additional information relevant in this context.[62] "I bear witness" (μαρτυρῶ) evokes an oath formula in emphasizing the truth of this statement (cf. Rom 10:2; 2 Cor 8:3; Gal 4:15). The verb "labored" translates the noun "hard labor" (πόνον).[63] Together with "striving," this underlines Epaphras's dedication to building up the believers.[64] NLT captures this sense well: "he has agonized for you...."

This statement should not be separated from the previous note on prayer. In Paul's mind, prayer must not be separated from labor since one's intense work is but an instrument of God's own power. The working of God through a human being has already appeared in Paul's description of his own toil for the believers in the Lycus Valley: "For this I toil, striving with his energy that powerfully works in me" (1:29).

"For you and for those in Laodicea and in Hierapolis" recalls the earlier statement concerning the scope of Paul's toil: "how great a struggle I have for you and those in Laodicea and those who have not seen my face in the flesh" (2:1). "Hierapolis," which appears only here, is probably included in the previous note. The prominence of Laodicea is reflected not only in its several appearances in this letter (cf. 2:1; 4:15–16), but also in the presence of yet another letter from the hand of Paul to the be-

lievers of this city (4:16). Hierapolis here suggests that with Colossae and Laodicea, these three represent the most prominent cities in the Lycus Valley. Paul is thus emphasizing Epaphras's ministry in that general area.

Hierapolis was about fifteen miles northwest of Colossae; as with Colossae, a Jewish settlement there probably formed the basis of the earliest converts to Christianity in that region.[65] Epaphras's involvement in these cities shows that he is not simply a leader of a local church, but a missionary involved in areas beyond his local house church.[66] These geographical references may also explain what Paul meant by "outsiders" (v. 5), who included not simply those outside one's believing community, but also those outside their own *polis*.

4:14 Luke, the beloved physician, greets you, as does Demas (ἀσπάζεται ὑμᾶς Λουκᾶς ὁ ἰατρὸς ὁ ἀγαπητὸς καὶ Δημᾶς). Paul concludes this subsection with the greetings from Luke and Demas. Elsewhere in the NT, the name "Luke" appears only in Paul's later letters (cf. 2 Tim 4:11; Phlm 24), neither of which adds to the information we have about him except for his presence with Paul in his second Roman imprisonment (2 Tim 4:11). Though he rarely appears in the NT, Luke is significant because overwhelming external evidence points to this companion of Paul as the author of

---

62. Cf. Wallace, *Greek Grammar*, 673. See, however, Callow (*Semantic and Structural Analysis*, 165), who connects this conjunction with the description of Epaphras's struggles for the believers in the Lycus Valley. This conjunction would then provide the basis for Paul's statement concerning Epaphras's prayer for them.

63. BDAG, 852.

64. The connection between the "striving" (ἀγών) word group and "hard labor" (πόνος) is one that can also be found in ancient Greek literature (e.g. Plato, *Phaedr.* 247 B); Lightfoot, *St. Paul's Epistles to the Colossians and to Philemon*, 240.

65. It is difficult to reconstruct the history of the earliest missionary movements among the various communities in the Lycus Valley. It is possible that different groups were re-

sponsible for the founding of the local churches in Colossae, Laodicea, and Hierapolis. Cf. Alastair Kirkland, "The Beginnings of Christianity in the Lycus Valley: An Exercise in Historical Reconstruction," *Neot* 29 (1995): 109–24.

66. Some have taken this reference to the three cities as indicative that Epaphras's activity is "regional rather than urban." Undoubtedly Epaphras believed in Christ as the cosmic Lord, who transcends all social and political spheres (cf. Trainor, *Epaphras*, 90–91). For the possibility of Epaphras reaching to other cities in the area such as Aphrodisias, which had a significant Jewish population as testified to by the second-century synagogue inscription, see Schnabel, *Early Christian Mission*, 2:1246–47.

Luke-Acts,[67] two works that surpass the length of Paul's own writings. That Luke is with Paul in Rome is consistent with the understanding that he himself was Paul's travel companion on his second and third journeys, as implied by the "we-passages" in Acts (16:10 – 17; 20:5 – 15; 21:1 – 18; 27:1 – 28:16),[68] which brings Luke all the way to Rome with Paul.

The significance of this reference of Luke is twofold. First, if our reading of v. 11 is correct, Luke is among the Gentile coworkers of Paul. This in part may explain Luke's polished Greek style as well as his broad knowledge of the institutions and geography of the wider Roman world. His knowledge of the LXX can also be explained by the possibility that he is a God-fearer who worshiped in the synagogue.[69]

Second, the phrase "the beloved physician" (ὁ ἰατρὸς ὁ ἀγαπητός) provides further information about Luke. Although attempts to show that Luke is a medical doctor through the identification of the medical language used in Luke-Acts have not produced conclusive results,[70] his prologue (Luke 1:1 – 4) is consistent with those found in the scientific writings of the time, including writings in the field of medicine.[71] Moreover, his interest in travel-ling is also consistent with the itinerant doctors of ancient times.[72] The reason why Luke's profession is noted here is perhaps due to Paul's need for medical attention during his imprisonment,[73] although this reference may simply aim at distinguishing him from other persons of the same name.

In the NT "Demas" appears only in two other passages, where one also finds Luke mentioned (Phlm 24; 2 Tim 4:10 – 11). In 2 Tim 4:10, Paul notes that this Demas has "deserted" him and that he "loved this world." If that verse can shed light on our present verse, "deserted" may point to Demas's fear of being associated with someone in chains,[74] while "loved the world" may point to his refusal to continue to support Paul in his imprisonment or even in his future missions.[75] In this first Roman imprisonment, which is perhaps several years prior to the writing of 1 Timothy, Demas is still counted among Paul's trusted coworkers.

4:15 Send my greetings to the brothers in Laodicea, and to Nympha and the church in her house (Ἀσπάσασθε τοὺς ἐν Λαοδικείᾳ ἀδελφοὺς καὶ Νύμφαν καὶ τὴν κατ᾽ οἶκον αὐτῆς ἐκκλησίαν). Paul now begins with words of greeting to those be-

---

67. The most important external support can be found in (1) 𝔓[75], the oldest manuscript of the gospel of Luke, which identifies him as the author in the attached title; (2) the roughly contemporary Muratorian canon points to the same direction (for a survey of the debate about its date, see P. Henne, "La datation du canon de Muratori," *RB* 100 [1993]: 54 – 75); (3) at the end of the second century Irenaeus provides the same conclusion (*Haer.* 3.1.1, 3.3.3).

68. Cf. John Wenham, "The Identification of Luke," *EvQ* 63 (1991): 3 – 44.

69. This would also explain his interest in the "God-fearers" in his own work (Acts 10:2, 22, 35; 13:16, 26, 50; 16:14; 17:4, 17; 18:7).

70. The classic attempt is that of W. K. Hobart, *The Medical Language of St. Luke* (Dublin: Hodges, Figgis, 1882). Henry J. Cadbury, however, demonstrated that the medical vocabularies Luke uses do not belong to the technical lingua of the medical profession, though they do point to him being an educated writer (*Studies in the Style and Literary Method of Luke* [HTS 6;

Cambridge, MA: Harvard Univ. Press, 1920]).

71. Loveday C. A. Alexander, *The Preface to Luke's Gospel: Literary Convention and Social Context in Luke 1.1 – 4 and Acts 1.1* (SNTSMS 78; Cambridge: Cambridge Univ. Press, 1993).

72. G. H. R. Horsley, *NewDocs* 2:19 – 21; and Martin Hengel and Anna Maria Schwemer, *Paulus zwischen Damaskus und Antiochien: Die unbekannten Jahre des Apostels* (WUNT 108; Tübingen: Mohr Siebeck, 1998), 18 – 22.

73. See, e.g., Ben Witherington III, *Conflict and Community in Corinth* (Grand Rapids: Eerdmans, 1995), 495 – 64, who argues from the reference to the "thorn in [the] flesh" in 2 Cor 12:7 that Luke's service may have been required in light of Paul's chronic medical condition.

74. Towner, *Letters to Timothy and Titus*, 622.

75. Jerome D. Quinn and William C. Walker, *The First and Second Letters to Timothy* (ECC; Grand Rapids: Eerdmans, 2000), 800 – 801. This understanding is consistent with the later memory of Demas as a hypocrite who had ulterior motives in following of Paul (cf. *Acts Paul* 3.1).

yond the Colossian community. "The brothers in Laodicea" likely refers to all believers in Laodicea and can thus justifiably be translated as "the brothers and sisters in Laodicea" (NRSV; cf. REB, CEV, GNB, NLT, NET, TNIV, NIV). That the Laodiceans would also receive a letter from Paul (cf. v. 16) has made this word of greeting a bit puzzling for some commentators. Several explanations can be offered. First, since the Colossians are to bring their own letter to the Laodiceans (v. 16), this greeting is most appropriate.[76] Second, this greeting may be meant for one particular person, Nympha. Third, since greetings acquire a significant social function, it points to the connection and unity among the various local communities. To have the Colossians greet the Laodiceans on behalf of Paul may also serve this function.[77]

The function of "and" (καί) after the reference to Laodicea has been variably understood. (1) If it is taken as a coordinating conjunction, Nympha and her church are not part of the Laodicean community of believers: "Greet the brethren who are in Laodicea and also Nympha and the church that is in her house" (NASB).[78] (2) If it is understood to intensify a particular member within the class, Nympha and her church becomes the particular focus of Paul's greetings among the several churches in Laodicea: "Give my greetings to the followers at Laodicea, especially to Nympha and

the church that meets in her home" (CEV).[79] (3) If it is taken in an epexegetical sense, the church in Nympha's house represents all the brothers and sisters in Laodicea: "Send my greetings to the brothers in Laodicea, that is, to Nympha and the church in her house." Because of the reference to an entire community with a geographic marker followed by the note of an individual, option (2) seems to provide the best interpretation.

The greetings to "Nympha and the church in her house" conclude the list of greetings in Colossians. Debates concerning the gender of "Nympha" (Νύμφαν) depend on the exact form of her name as well as the authenticity of the feminine form of "her" (αὐτῆς). The accusative Νύμφαν could be derived from either a masculine (Νυμφᾶς) or a feminine (Νύμφα) name. The gender identification therefore depends on the pronoun. The masculine pronoun ("his," αὐτοῦ) receives the support of the later majority text (𝔐),[80] and thus led to the KJV reading: "Nymphas, and the church which is in his house" (cf. NKJV). Earlier manuscripts from the relatively more reliable Alexandrian family[81] support the feminine reading, however, and this reading is adopted by most contemporary versions. The feminine original can also explain the change to the masculine when many after the second century considered male leadership as the norm.[82]

Even with this gender identification, the role

---

76. Schweizer, *Letter to the Colossians*, 241.

77. This verse literally reads "greet the brothers in Laodicea," although most versions assume that Paul is requesting that they send such greetings on his behalf. It can, however, be read as a command by Paul for the Colossians themselves to greet the Laodiceans on their own behalf (cf. Wilson, *Colossians and Philemon*, 304). Some versions leave such an option open: "Give greetings to the brothers in Laodicea" (NAB).

78. Because of the lack of reference to the believers in Hierapolis here (cf. v. 13), some suggest that Nympha is a resident of Hierapolis; cf. Marlis Gielen, "Zur Interpretation der paulinischen Formel ἡ κατ᾽ οἶκον ἐκκλησία," *ZNW* 77 (1986): 123 – 24.

79. See Barth and Blanke, *Colossians*, 486.

80. Also D [F G] Ψ.

81. B 0278 6 1739[*] 1881. Because of the affinity of the minuscule manuscript 1739 with one of the most reliable manuscripts of the Pauline corpus (𝔓⁴⁶), one can conceivably argue that this reading also receives the support of this important papyrus.

82. For a parallel development in the case of Junia in Rom 16:7, see Bernadette Brooten, "Junia . . . Outstanding among the Apostles (Romans 16:7)," in *Women Priests: A Catholic Commentary on the Vatican Declaration* (ed. Leonard and Arlene Swidler; New York: Paulist, 1977), 141 – 44.

of Nympha in this church is unclear. She could be a widow who had inherited a sizeable property that could accommodate the church meeting in her house (cf. 1 Tim 5:9 – 16). She could also be a woman of means who had been converted to Christianity (cf. Luke 8:1 – 3; Acts 13:50; 17:4) and would thus be a patron of the church (cf. Rom 16:2). One can also imagine Nympha being a coworker in the gospel mission (cf. Rom 16:1, 3, 6 – 7, 12; Phil 4:3), but whether she can be considered the "leader" of this church is not clear. In any case, this verse clearly points to the "church" meeting in a house (cf. Acts 2:46; 5:42; 8:3; Rom 16:5; 1 Cor 16:19).

4:16 After this letter has been read to you, have it also read in the church of the Laodiceans; and read in turn the letter from Laodicea (καὶ ὅταν ἀναγνωσθῇ παρ' ὑμῖν ἡ ἐπιστολή, ποιήσατε ἵνα καὶ ἐν τῇ Λαοδικέων ἐκκλησίᾳ ἀναγνωσθῇ, καὶ τὴν ἐκ Λαοδικείας ἵνα καὶ ὑμεῖς ἀναγνῶτε). This instruction provides significant information concerning reading practices of the NT churches as well as the early circulation of Paul's letters. Since this letter originated from the apostle and his coworker(s) and is addressed to an entire community, it is apparently a public letter. This is confirmed perhaps by the passive verb "has been read," which suggests the letter was read by one person for the entire community.[83] This reading is implicit in the phrase "to you" (παρ' ὑμῖν), which can be translated as "among you." Either translation reflects the likelihood of the presence of only one copy of the letter, so that a public lector would be used for such a reading.[84] Translating the clause as "after you have read this letter" (NLT; cf. GNB) is misleading as it may lead us to understand this phrase in light of the modern private act of reading.

Elsewhere, Paul also explicitly called for his letter to be read to the appropriate audience: "I charge you before the Lord to have this letter read to all the brothers and sisters" (1 Thess 5:27). This not only confirms our reading about the significance of this passive verb, but the evocation of "the Lord" in that context points to the authority attached to the public reading of the letter. As Jews were used to having the law read aloud in synagogue worship,[85] the call to have his own letter read in the presence of a community may itself be an authority claim as Paul (and his coworkers) underlines his own apostolic authority.[86]

"Have it also read in the church of the Laodiceans" points out the relevance of this letter for the surrounding churches, while "read in turn the letter from Laodicea" provides a piece of information concerning yet another letter by Paul, one written to the believers in Laodicea.[87] It is unclear when the letter to the Laodiceans was written. It could have been sent to that community before Colossians, but it is equally possible that this letter is also carried by Tychicus as he is about to travel to the Lycus Valley (cf. vv. 7 – 8).

The letter to the Laodiceans has been identified

---

83. Thus "*read aloud* for public hearing" (BDAG, 60, italics original). In antiquity, most people read aloud, even in private reading; and public reading was common because of the scarcity of manuscripts and the high illiteracy rate of the general public. For a further discussion, see Harry Y. Gamble, *Books and Readers in the Early Church: A History of Early Christian Texts* (New Haven, CT: Yale Univ. Press, 1995), 203 – 4.

84. Cf. "before you" (NAB).

85. Cf. 2 Cor 3:15: "Even to this day when Moses is read, a veil covers their hearts" (cf. Acts 15:21).

86. As Gamble (*Books and Readers in the Early Church*, 205,

326) notes, the public reading of Christian texts takes place primarily in a worship setting. Not surprisingly, from the earliest post-NT period, the Pauline letters have been read alongside the Jewish Scriptures in such a setting (cf. 2 Pet 3:16; Polycarp, *Phil.* 3.2).

87. Grammatically it is possible to understand this as a letter written by the Laodiceans to Paul. It is difficult, however, as to why Paul would like the Colossians to read such a letter. In light of the preceding request to have the letter to the Colossians read among the Laodiceans, it is more natural to understand this clause as a reference to yet another letter authored by Paul.

as the letter to the Ephesians,[88] Philemon,[89] or even the present letter to the Colossians (one that contained both the letter to the Colossians and one to the Laodiceans).[90] Most are convinced, however, that this letter remains lost. This note provides room for the later forger to pen the apocryphal "Epistle to the Laodiceans," containing phrases taken mainly from Philippians and Galatians.[91]

These two clauses also point the earliest evidence of the exchange of Paul's letters. This itself is important for a number of reasons. First, the wider relevance for Paul's letters is evident, and the problems the Colossians believers encounter are apparently not limited to their local community. Second, the call for Paul's letters to be circulated points again to his apostolic authority. Finally, this may point to the earliest stages of the collection of Paul's letters, a process that eventually led to their canonization.[92]

4:17 And say to Archippus, "See to it that you complete the ministry you have received in the Lord" (καὶ εἴπατε Ἀρχίππῳ, Βλέπε τὴν διακονίαν ἣν παρέλαβες ἐν κυρίῳ, ἵνα αὐτὴν πληροῖς). The final note before Paul's signature and greetings is an instruction to "Archippus." In the NT this name appears as one of the recipients of Paul's letter to Philemon, where Paul labels him as "our fellow soldier" (Phlm 2). From this label and from his appearance in Paul's address there, he apparently belongs to the household of Philemon and is involved in Paul's ministry in some way.

Paul does not specify the nature of the "ministry" that Archippus is to complete. The word translated "ministry" (τὴν διακονίαν) can refer to any "work" (NLT, TNIV), "task" (NRSV, GNB), or "service" (NJB). In light of the phrase "in the Lord" (ἐν κυρίῳ), however, this service is likely related to the gospel ministry.[93] Moreover, in light of previous uses of the related term "servant/minister" (διάκονος; 1:7, 23, 25; 4:7), this service is perhaps connected to Paul's own mission. The translation "ministry" (KJV, ASV, NAB, NASB, NKJV, HCSB, NET, ESV, NIV) seems most appropriate here.

Speculations abound concerning the exact nature of this "ministry." For those who take this in a general sense of godly service, this call would carry a sense of warning if not rebuke as Archippus is called to remain faithful in his service to God.[94] The verb "complete" could denote one particular type of ministry without assuming that Archippus has been or would be unfaithful.[95] For those who consider Archippus as the primary intended recipient of the letter to Philemon, this "ministry" is understood to refer to the proper reception of Onesimus.[96]

88. Lightfoot, *St. Paul's Epistles to the Colossians and to Philemon*, 244.

89. John Knox, *Philemon among the Letters of Paul* (London: Collins, 1960), 38 – 47.

90. M.-É Boismard, *La lettre de saint Paul aux Laodicéens* (CahRB 42; Paris: Gabalda, 1999).

91. This work only survives in Latin, but a Greek original can be dated no earlier than the second century; cf. J. K. Elliott, *The Apocryphal New Testament* (Oxford: Clarendon, 1993), 544.

92. For a recent evaluation of the various theories concerning the origin of the collection of Paul's letters, see Stanley E. Porter, "When and How Was the Pauline Canon Compiled? An Assessment of Theories," in *The Pauline Canon* (ed. Stanley E. Porter; Pauline Studies; Leiden: Brill, 2004), 95 – 127, who argues for the personal involvement of

Luke for the earliest collection of Paul's letters.

93. The phrase "in the Lord" has been taken as indicating realm of service ("the task you were given in the Lord's service," GNB), agency ("the work the Lord gave you," NLT; cf. NJB, CEV), or grounds ("since you are united to the Lord Jesus," Callow, *Semantic and Structural Analysis*, 168).

94. Lightfoot, *St. Paul's Epistles to the Colossians and to Philemon*, 244.

95. The exhortation for Archippus may aim at affirming the authority of Archippus so that his ministry may receive a warm reception; cf. Sumney, *Colossians*, 281.

96. Knox, *Philemon among the Letters of Paul*, 49 – 51; Lamar Cope, "On Re-thinking the Philemon-Colossians Connection," *BR* 30 (1985): 35 – 50. This depends, however, on a problematic reading of Phlm 2 (see comments there).

It is more plausible to understand this ministry as centering on the proclamation of the gospel as well as the edification of the community.[97] First, as noted above, the word "ministry" most naturally refers to works related to the gospel mission. Second, in Eph 4:12 Paul explicitly defines "works of service" (ἔργον διακονίας) in terms of the gospel ministry: "so that the body of Christ may be built up." Third, in light of Paul's concern in this section that his ministries continue in the communities of believers in the Lycus Valley (cf. vv. 8, 11 – 12), this verse should also be understood as extending Paul's gospel ministry. The words "complete" and "ministry" may evoke Paul's earlier description of his own ministry: "I became a servant [διάκονος] according to the commission from God given to me for you, to fulfill [πληρῶσαι] the word of God" (1:25). Finally, the clause "you received in the Lord" also reflects the language used in 2:6: "just as you received Christ Jesus the Lord, continue to walk in him."[98] Here, Paul may be asking Archippus to proclaim this christocentric gospel so that the believers can continue to grow in the Lord.

4:18a I, Paul, write this greeting with my own hand

(Ὁ ἀσπασμὸς τῇ ἐμῇ χειρὶ Παύλου). Paul concludes this letter with his own signature, a brief call for the audience to remember his situation, and a short benediction. The signature in Paul's own handwriting appears in some of his letters (1 Cor 16:21; Gal 6:11; 2 Thess 3:17; Phlm 19). This likely points to Paul's use of a secretary in the composition of his letter. In another letter where such an autograph is missing,[99] one finds the explicit note of the secretary "Tertius" (Rom 16:22). The absence of the name of a secretary here can be explained by the fact that "using a secretary was standard procedure in antiquity and does not require explicit evidence in each letter."[100]

The intended purpose of this autograph is not, however, simply to suggest that a secretary is being used. It can testify to the authenticity of the message written (2 Thess 2:2; 3:17), and it can also serve as a seal that transforms the letter into a legally binding document.[101] In terms of the rhetorical function of this practice, a study on illiteracy and ancient writing practices further points to the significance of such signature in emphasizing the literate ability of the author.[102] Again, an implicit authority claim seems clear here.

4:18b-c Remember my chains. Grace be with you

(μνημονεύετέ μου τῶν δεσμῶν. ἡ χάρις μεθ᾽ ὑμῶν). Paul's call for the readers to remember his "chains" is apparently a call to remember him in their prayers.[103] It may also suggest an implied request

---

97. See O'Brien, *Colossians, Philemon*, 259; Wright, *Colossians and Philemon*, 125; Pokorný, *Colossians*, 195.

98. See comments on 2:6 concerning the technical use of "to receive" (παραλαμβάνω).

99. Even without the explicit presence of an autograph, the closing section is likely written by the author's own hand, thus essentially functioning as an autograph. This can be assumed in the remaining Pauline letters, as well as in other Greco-Roman letters; see Jeffrey A. D. Weima, *Neglected Endings: The Significance of the Pauline Letter Closings* (JSNTSup 101; Sheffield: JSOT, 1994), 119 – 21.

100. Richards, *Paul and First-Century Letter Writing*, 81. For a further discussion of Paul's use of secretaries, see also idem, *The Secretary in the Letters of Paul*. Paul J. Achtemeier, "*Omne verbum sonat*: The New Testament and the Oral Environment of Late Western Antiquity," *JBL* 109 (1990): 12, also

points to dictation as a "normal mode" of letter writing.

101. G. J. Bahr, "The Subscriptions in the Pauline Letters," *JBL* 87 (1968): 31. Although Colossians is not a formal business contract, the evocation of the coworkers of Paul in both its opening (1:1) and closing (4:10 – 14) may aim precisely at stressing the binding nature of this document.

102. Chris Keith, " 'In My Own Hand': Grapho-Literacy and the Apostle Paul," *Bib* 89 (2008): 56: "When Paul signs his own name and writes the formulaic statement 'the greetings in my hand' ... he demonstrates both his identity as an educated individual who 'knows letters' (and Greek ones at that) and that he is a person of true prestige — able to write, but able to avoid it as well and have an amanuensis write the bulk of the epistle."

103. See O'Brien, *Colossians, Philemon*, 260; and Moo, *Letters to the Colossians and to Philemon*, 353, who point to Paul's frequent use of the nominal form ("remembrance," μνεία) in

for personal and financial help.[104] This must not be understood simply as a personal request, however. Consistent with the emphasis of this final section, it is a call for the believers to participate with Paul for the sake of the gospel: "both in my imprisonment [τοῖς δεσμοῖς μου] and in the defense and confirmation of the gospel all of you became partners in God's grace together with me" (Phil 1:7 NET).

This wider reference to the gospel mission is confirmed by the fact that to Paul, his "imprisonment" is not a symbol of embarrassment but a participation in the "afflictions of Christ" (1:24). Elsewhere in Paul's writings, every reference to his "chains" appears in connection with the gospel mission (Phil 1:13, 14, 17; 2 Tim 2:9; Phlm 10, 13). This is consistent with his request for prayers in Col 4:2 – 3, where he makes reference to his imprisonment but focuses on the gospel mission: "Devote yourselves to prayer … that God may open for us a door for the word so that we may declare the mystery of Christ, on account of which I am bound." In this context, therefore, Paul's request for the believers to remember his "chains" should again be read as an invitation for them to extend his own gospel ministry.

This letter concludes with a brief benediction or prayer wish: "Grace be with you." As noted in the letter opening (1:2c), implied in this formula is probably the verb "may … be" (εἴη), and the notion that the "grace" is ultimately "from God our Father" (1:2), although Christ can justifiably be considered the immediate agent. This reference to grace appears in the closing benediction of all Paul's letters, and it is often qualified by the genitival phrase, "of our/the Lord Jesus [Christ]." These references to "grace" are likely meant to replace the "farewell wish" in secular letters.[105]

Though a consistent presence in Paul's closing formula, this reference to "grace" forms an appropriate conclusion to this letter. From the beginning, Paul reminds the readers of "the grace of God in truth" (1:6) that they have received. It is precisely the sufficiency of this grace that he emphasizes throughout this letter.[106] Moreover, this "grace" is to be manifested in their grateful living in the eschatological age (cf. 3:17; 4:6). It is this "grace" of our Lord Jesus Christ that Paul points as he concludes this christocentric letter.

Theology in Application

Teachings Embodied

The closing greetings sections in Paul's letters have often been considered to "possess little intellectual content but are more emotionally oriented."[107] Though the emotional import of such sections cannot be denied, their intellectual content should not be ignored. Here Paul is not only demonstrating his skill in enhancing the rhetorical force of this letter, but we also see a passionate Paul, who transforms this formulaic section as he continues to appeal to the believers to be faithful to the gospel mission.

---

reference to prayer (Rom 1:9; Eph 1:16; Phil 1:3; 1 Thess 1:2; 2 Tim 1:3; Phlm 4).

104. Dunn, *Epistles to the Colossians and to Philemon*, 289.

105. In Hellenistic papyri letters, two verbs represent two different forms of closing: "Be strong!" (ἔρρωσο) and "Prosper!"

(εὐτυχεῖ); cf. Weima, *Neglected Endings*, 29 – 34.

106. See the use of the related verbal "to forgive" (χαρίζομαι) in 2:13 and 3:13.

107. Weima, *Neglected Endings*, 39, who challenges this assumption in his study.

Such appeals take on two aspects in this section. First, Paul focuses on individuals who serve as living examples who embody his teachings. Tychicus is not only a "beloved brother" and "faithful servant"; he is also a "fellow slave in the Lord" (v. 7). In Paul, the title "fellow slave" only appears in Colossians (cf. 1:7), and it illustrates Paul's teachings as he calls believers to serve their Lord in all they do (3:15 – 17), a teaching that evokes the paradigm of the slave-master relationship (3:22 – 25). This emphasis on being the slave of Christ reappears in the greetings to Epaphras, who is called "a slave of Christ Jesus" (v. 12). Rather than seeing such appellations as incidental, Paul is using such examples to illustrate the models that the believers are to follow.

The further description of Epaphras as one who is "always striving on behalf of you in prayers" (v. 12) and one who "has labored much for you" (v. 13) repeats Paul's self-portrayal (1:29; 2:1). The believers are also called to continue to participate in such prayer and labor in 4:2 – 6, and Epaphras, one of their own, provides a living example. The descriptions applied to others provide further models for emulations: "faithful and beloved brother" (v. 9), "fellow prisoner" (v. 10), and "coworkers for the kingdom of God" (v. 11).

Although Paul is absent from these believers, accompanying this letter is yet another "letter from Christ, the result of our ministry, written not with ink but with the Spirit of the living God, not on tablets of stone but on tablets of human hearts" (2 Cor 3:3). For the Colossians, this "letter from Christ" consists of the lives of these faithful servants of God, who serve as the living voice that continues to testify to the gospel of Christ. The pastoral intent of the closing section is captured in the final instruction to be conveyed to Archippus, as it may also aim as the reminder for those who are to convey it: "See to it that you complete the ministry you have received in the Lord" (v. 17).

Beyond the individual examples, the second aspect in this greetings section must also be noted. In a letter that emphasizes the full sufficiency and final authority of Christ the Lord of all, this lengthy greeting section points to the mutual dependence of believers as they ultimately rest on their dependence on Christ. Tychicus, for example, is to "comfort" (v. 8) the hearts of the Colossian believers, and Epaphras is always praying and striving "on behalf of" these believers (v. 12; cf. v. 13). These believers in turn are to "receive" (v. 10) Mark, and Paul is dependent on the "comfort" of the "coworkers for the kingdom of God" (v. 11).

In this closing section, therefore, acts of greetings point to the interdependence of believers. Insufficient in themselves, as the "body" of Christ (1:18) they become "holy, without blemish, and blameless before him [i.e., Christ]" because of the reconciliation in Christ's own "body" (1:22). In the mutual greetings, therefore, human insufficiency is acknowledged alongside the all-sufficiency of Christ.

It is in this sense that such greetings can also be considered acts of worship because worship is an act that challenges "the myths of self-sufficiency," while greetings are "the lack of self-sufficiency … affirmed horizontally":

> It is not only sin that makes us dependent upon others; our very finitude, as creatures, impels us to relationality because we need the gifts, talents, and resources of others. And such dependence is part of the very fiber of God's good creation. Worship is a space of welcome because we are, at root, relational creatures called into relationship with the Creator, in order to flourish as a people who bear his image to and for the world.[108]

Through individual examples as well as the emphasis on the corporate nature of the body of Christ, Paul reaffirms the christocentric gospel he has emphasized in the body of this letter.

Fellowship of Believers

The horizontal interdependence of believers noted above leads us to a related aspect in this closing section: the significance of the connections between individual believers and of the networking among local communities of believers. In terms of individual believers, this long section of greetings, recommendations, and instructions links the various individuals to an organic whole as they participate in the gospel mission in various capacities. In the major subsection in this closing, where Paul conveys the greetings from his coworkers (vv. 10 – 14), the significant commentary provided at the center identifies one half of the group as "Jews" (v. 11) and the other half as Gentiles by implication. This identification is important as Paul reemphasizes the significance of the gospel of Jesus Christ that creates a new humanity, "where there is neither Greek nor Jew, circumcised nor uncircumcised" (3:11). The fact that they are all identified as "coworkers for the kingdom of God" (4:11) points to the unity among the believers as they serve the one God and Lord of all.

Not only does Paul focus on the relationships among individuals, but the networking among the various communities of believers is also highlighted here. The connection between the apostolic authorities and the Colossian believers is noted by the identifiers "who is one of you" (v. 9) and "who is from you" (v. 12) as applied to the leaders of the Colossian church. Beyond such connections with the apostolic authorities, the relationship among the local communities in the Lycus Valley is also repeatedly noted. The ministry of Epaphras itself provides a personal link between the churches in Colossae, Laodicea, and Hierapolis (v. 13). Paul's call for the Colossian believers to convey his greetings to "the brothers in Laodicea, and to Nympha

---

108. James K. A. Smith, *Desiring the Kingdom: Worship, Worldview, and Cultural Formation* (Grand Rapids: Baker, 2009), 169.

and the church in her house" (v. 15) further emphasizes this relationship. Finally, the request for the exchange of letters between the Colossians and the Laodiceans (v. 16) binds these communities in the wider community of believers who are to submit to Paul's apostolic authority. The relationship between the apostolic authorities with these communities as well as that among these local communities is secured with this note.

When discussing this networking among communities and individual believers, the structure of power revealed in such a depiction of relationships is also worth noting. Although Paul does speak with an authoritative voice in this letter and even in this closing section, his uses of titles such as "fellow slave" (v. 7), "brother(s)" (vv. 7, 9, 15), "fellow prisoner" (v. 10), and "coworkers" (v. 11) direct one's attention to the unique lordship of Christ. It is, therefore, possible to claim that "the power-over operative between Paul and the communities is aimed at rendering itself obsolete, in that their asymmetrical relationship will be transformed and Paul should eventually become one among many siblings."[109] In a section where his unique authority can be further exerted, Paul instead chooses to emphasize the primacy of their common mission "for the kingdom of God" (v. 11).

Authority of the Word

Through the appellations he applies to his coworkers, Paul clearly refuses to be labeled as the *solus apostolus*, as some have insisted that he is so described in this letter.[110] This should not, however, be construed as a refusal to insist on the unique authority of the gospel he preaches. It is in view of this gospel that every person listed in this greetings section is to be related. It is also because of this gospel that messengers are sent, so that the faithfulness of the gospel can be maintained (vv. 7 – 9). Even his "chains" (v. 18) are for the sake of this gospel (cf. vv. 2 – 3). Perhaps most importantly, the call to have this letter read in public and to have its impact felt beyond its immediate audience (v. 16) points to the authority of this gospel message as embedded in the written words. Not to be considered simply as an occasional document whose relevance is limited by one particular historical context, this letter is to serve the church in ways that go beyond the false teachings it seeks to encounter.

The information included in this closing section also testifies to Paul's understanding of this letter as carrying particular authority. The adaptation of the form of the "official letter" is again evident as "his communications were prepared, sent, and delivered according to official logistics to the extent that Paul could command them." Moreover, "careful arrangements were made for delivery; and the letters must

---

109. Ehrensperger, *Paul and the Dynamics of Power*, 62.

110. Cf. J. Christiaan Beker, *Heirs of Paul: Paul's Legacy in the New Testament and in the Church Today* (Minneapolis:

Fortress, 1991), 68, who, believing this letter as written by a disciple of Paul, considers Paul as the *solus apostolus* who "has been given a heroic status."

have been read before the assembled congregation."[111] In adopting the form of the letter, Paul seeks to provide instructions and corrections to a community that needs to hear the gospel anew. In both form and content, Paul emphasizes the need for the embedded gospel to be heard in obedient submission.

Just as Paul began his letter by emphasizing how "the word of truth, the gospel ... has been bearing fruit and growing among [the Colossians] since the day [they] heard and understood the grace of God in truth" (1:5 – 6), so at the end of this letter he fully expects this gospel to continue to empower the believers as they continue to grow in the Lord Jesus. As Paul reminded his first readers that this letter is to be heard beyond the confines of their local community, we are also called to submit to this gospel after two thousand years as the gospel continues to bear fruit and grow among those who have heard and understood it.

111. M. Luther Stirewalt Jr., *Paul the Letter Writer* (Grand Rapids: Eerdmans, 2003), 118. While not ignoring other letter forms available to Paul, Stirewalt draws attention to Paul's indebtedness to the form of the official letter. This identification is directly related to implicit authority claims as "Paul saw himself as a representative of Christ ministering between the Lord and the people of the ecclesiae. It was an authoritative position in the religious community similar to that of numerous officials in the secular world" (25 – 26). His adaptation of the official letter form thus reflects his self-understanding as "an apostle of Christ Jesus" (1:1).

The Theology of Colossians

In this short letter, Paul presents a robust Christology that clearly and powerfully explains the status and significance of Christ in order to instruct the Colossians on proper behavior. Though intimately tied with the Christology contained in his earlier writings, this letter provides a "Pauline Christology in a New Key"[1] as Paul brings his earlier discussions of Christ to their climax in addressing the needs of a new context. Not only is the title "Christ" the focus of the first part of this letter where the theoretical foundation is laid, but this title also floods the second half, which explains the implications of Paul's christocentric message.[2]

Beyond these general observations, substantial and significant statements of the status of Christ can be found both in the earlier section, which climaxes in the christological hymn (1:15–20), and in the second half, where believers are called to total submission to Christ: "Whatever you do in word or in deed, do everything in the name of the Lord Jesus" (3:17). In our analysis of the theology of this letter, therefore, we will focus on Christ and his impact on our understanding of God his Father and on the different realms of creation.

Christ and the Fullness of Deity

Paul begins by grounding his apostolic calling in the "will of God" (1:1) and by praying to "God" (1:3). In Colossians, this God is portrayed primarily in his relationship with Jesus Christ. Even in the opening prayer, God is "the Father of our Lord Jesus Christ" (1:3). That God the Father is the one who empowers Christ is repeatedly noted. He is the one who raised Jesus from the dead (2:12), and he is the power behind the gospel that centers on Jesus Christ (1:6, 27).[3] In addition to this, one finds the close association between the Father and the Son in spatial and relational terms

---

1. Frank Matera, *New Testament Christology* (Louisville: Westminster John Knox, 1999), 145.

2. Ten out of twenty-five occurrences of the title "Christ" appear after 3:1. It should be noted, however, that the strict distinction between the "theoretical" and the "practical" sections in Colossians cannot be made since the lordship of Christ over

the cosmos is not to be distinguished from his authority over various areas of the lives of the believers.

3. See also 2:19, where believers are called to hold fast to Christ "the head, from which the entire body ... grows with a growth from God."

as Christ is said to be "seated at the right hand of God" (3:1) and believers are "hidden with Christ in God" (3:3).

More importantly, the identification of Christ with God forms the basis of the message of Colossians. Paul clearly articulates this emphasis in the christological hymn (1:15 – 20), which serves as the foundation for his argument. Preceding this hymn, one already finds the work of God as related to the "kingdom of his beloved Son" (1:14), which serves as "the theological grounding of Christology" as developed in the hymn.[4]

The hymn makes several significant claims. First, Christ is "the image of the invisible God" (1:15). He is the authoritative representation of God and the mediator through whom God is revealed. Second, Christ is identified as the agent of creation, "for in him all things were created ... all things were created through him and for him" (1:16). Because God is often identified as the one and only Creator in the OT (cf. Gen 14:19, 22; Pss 96:5; 121:2; 146:5 – 6; Isa 40:12 – 31; 51:13), to consider Christ as an agent of creation is to identify him with God the Father. Third, since Christ is an agent of creation, he becomes supreme "in all things" (1:18), as God is. Fourth, the reference to "the kingdom of his beloved Son" (1:13) should be understood as equivalent to "the kingdom of God" (4:11). Finally, the full deity of Christ is explicitly noted in the statement: "in him all the fullness was pleased to dwell" (1:19).

Throughout this letter, this relationship between Christ and God the Father is assumed and reaffirmed. In 2:2, for example, "Christ" is identified as the "mystery of God." The parallelism between "do everything in the name of the Lord Jesus" and "giving thanks to God the Father through him" (3:17) points to the inextricable relationship between the two. Christ is, therefore, the work of God in history.[5] This understanding of the relationship between the two forms the foundation of the theological affirmations embedded in this letter.

Victory of Christ through His Death and Resurrection

Embedded in the christological hymn is the affirmation of the central significance of Christ's death and resurrection. What is striking here is the parallel between the first (old) and second (new) creations. In the first creation (1:15 – 16), Christ's power is revealed through the manifestation of his creative power. In the second (1:18b – 20), his power is revealed "through the blood of his cross" (1:20), and this new creation is embodied in Christ, "the firstborn from the dead" (1:18). That the power of his blood shed on the cross is the focus of the christological hymn is

---

4. Udo Schnelle, *Theology of the New Testament* (trans. M. Eugene Boring; Grand Rapids: Baker, 2009), 540.

5. Thus Marianne Meye Thompson, *Colossians and Philemon* (THNTC; Grand Rapids: Eerdmans, 2005), 111: "christological statements do not stand on their own but serve to articulate convictions about the character, purposes, and work of God in the world."

confirmed by the section that follows, where Paul argues that those alienated from God are now reconciled to him through Christ's "body of flesh through death" (1:22).

The same description of Christ's death and resurrection occurs in 2:11 – 12, and this is followed by a focus on the power of the cross, where Christ took that which opposes those who belong to him and "nail[ed] it to the cross" (2:14). This represents one of the most significant NT statements on the atoning significance of Christ's death,[6] and the language used here may also reflect Paul's awareness of the gospel passion narratives.[7]

The resurrection is equally important in Paul's portrayal of Christ for it points to his victory over death (cf. 3:1 – 4). This understanding of "victory" provides a helpful category in understanding both the death and resurrection of Christ.[8] In Colossians, this victory is almost always portrayed in relation to Christ's powerful work on behalf of those whom he delivered. In the paragraph that precedes the christological hymn, the "power" of God's "glorious might" is manifested in the "redemption" that can be found in Christ's work (1:11 – 14). Believers are not to be taken captive by the false gospels because Christ "is the head of every ruler and authority" (2:10), and such headship is testified by Christ's resurrection (2:12). This victory is immediately restated in reference to Christ's accomplishment on the cross as he "disarmed the rulers and authorities" (2:15). Those who have died and are raised with him "will be revealed with him in glory" (3:4).

Behind this emphasis on the resurrection, which testifies to the power and sufficiency of the atoning death of Christ, is the need to counter the false teachers, who insist on additional visionary experiences and ascetic practices in order to attain a state of perfection and divine acceptance. In response to these teachers, Paul claims that Christ's death and resurrection have achieved cosmic reconciliation. For individual believers who respond positively to Christ, such reconciliation provides complete and final forgiveness of sins.

In cosmic terms, Christ's death and resurrection bring about universal reconciliation. In 1:20, Paul makes clear that through Christ's death on the cross, "all things" are reconciled to him. In personal terms, those who "were once alienated and hostile in mind" are now "reconciled . . . in his body of flesh" (1:21 – 22).[9] Those reconciled to God have already been "delivered . . . from the dominion of darkness and transferred . . . into the kingdom of his beloved Son, in whom we have redemption, the forgiveness of sins" (1:13 – 14). These believers are now presented as "holy, without blemish,

6. For the significance of this verse in the construction of a theory of atonement, see Eugene C. Best, *An Historical Study of the Exegesis of Colossians 2,14* (Rome: Pontificia Universitas Gregoriana, 1956), 11 – 133.

7. See the recent discussion in Dale C. Allison Jr., *Constructing Jesus: Memory, Imagination, and History* (Grand Rapids: Baker, 2010), 413 – 14.

8. On this point, see esp. Colin Gunton, "*Christus Victor* Revisited: A Study in Metaphor and the Transformation of Meaning," *JTS* 36 (1985): 129 – 45.

9. This personal aspect must not be understood simply in "individualistic" terms, however. For the ecclesiological significance of Christ's death, see comments on Christ's lordship over the church, below.

and blameless before him" (1:22). As Christ died on the cross, believers once were dead in their transgressions (2:13), and as Christ is raised from the dead, believers will no longer be judged or condemned by those who refuse to acknowledge the finality of his work (2:16 – 19).[10] The next act in the plan of salvation lies not in the acts of individual believers, but in Christ's final revelation in glory (3:4).

In personal terms, for Paul to participate in the victory of Christ's death and resurrection is to be "in/with Christ." Already in the opening greetings, Paul identifies the Colossian believers as "faithful brothers in Christ" (1:2). This "in Christ" formula points to Paul's emphasis on the final sufficiency of the work of Christ (cf. 1:27 – 28). For the believers, the importance of being "in Christ" lies in the fact that "in him all things were created" (1:16), "in him all things are held together" (1:17) and "in him all the fullness was pleased to dwell" (1:19). The intersection between the high Christology and the sufficiency of Christ's work for believers lies, therefore, in this "in Christ" formula, since one's faith should rest solely "in Christ" (1:4; 2:5) and true maturity can only be found "in Christ" (1:28).

Beyond such general assertions, Paul uses the "with Christ" formula in drawing attention to the believers' identification with Christ in his death (2:20) and resurrection (3:1). In the present age as believers await the final consummation, Paul also notes that "your life is hidden with Christ in God" (3:3). In this letter, therefore, the "in/with Christ" formula becomes a link that draws out the critical significance of God's work in Christ for believers.

Lordship of Christ

Building on the foundation of the full deity of Christ and of his death and resurrection, Paul provides a sustained argument for the lordship of Christ in every realm of existence. From creation to the lives of individual believers, the final authority of Christ is affirmed in both the theoretical and the paraenetic sections.

Over Creation

Christ's lordship over creation is most clearly established in the christological hymn (1:15 – 20). This lordship claim consists of several critical elements. First, as the "firstborn of all creation" (1:15)[11] and as an agent of creation through whom "all things were created" (1:16), Christ's sovereignty over "all things . . . in heaven and on

---

10. Our discussion here presents the gift of forgiveness within the paradigm of the substitutionary atonement of Christ. For a reading of this gift within the benefaction paradigm, where the lordship of Christ is the primary framework of reference, see Richard B. Hays, "The Story of God's Son: The Identity of Jesus in the Letters of Paul," in *Seeking the Identity of*

Christ: A Pilgrimage (ed. Beverly Roberts Gaventa and Richard B. Hays; Grand Rapids: Eerdmans, 2008), 193 – 95.

11. On the understanding of "firstborn" as a reference to rank and status rather than (simply) temporal priority, see comments on 1:15b.

earth, visible and invisible, whether thrones or dominions or rulers or authorities" (1:16) is emphasized in a most emphatic way. This is particularly important when understood against an OT and ancient Near Eastern background, in which creation language is used to establish the power claim of a deity.[12] Here, Christ is portrayed as the one and only agent of creation; this fact provides an even stronger claim to power within the framework of Jewish monotheism.

Second, the need for a new creation (1:18b–20) presupposes the fall and highlights the critical significance of Christ's death. This new creation dispels any suspicion of a "sacred cosmology," as Paul does not assume that creation is of any inherent value apart from the creative and redemptive act of Christ. Even the new creation awaits its final redemption in the final revelation of Christ's glory (3:4).

Third, Christ's lordship over creation does not simply denote subjugation and submission; it also provides meaning and purpose within the created order ("all things were created … for him," 1:16). Moreover, he sustains all things, for "in him all things are held together" (1:17); this act must not be understood in a mechanistic sense but in a way that points to Christ as the ground of all existence.[13] Again, perhaps the OT and ancient Near Eastern context helps in drawing attention to the fact that creation is not simply an act that brings about existence; it is also an act that provides order to a chaotic and meaningless existence.

Over the Church

The christological hymn also establishes Christ's claim over the church, for the new creation brought about by his death and resurrection centers on "the church," and Christ is "the head" of this church, his "body" (2:18; cf. 1:24). This is consistent with the OT understanding of God's creation as culminating in the creation of his own people (cf. Pss 74:12–17; 89:5–37). As Christ is "head" of the church, he has final authority over her. This "head" also provides necessary nourishment for the entire body as the body holds fast to the head and "grows with a growth from God" (2:19).

As members of one body of Christ, the church also testifies to the unity of this body. Already in the OT, one finds the creation of an eschatological community as the climax of the new creative work of God (cf. Isa 43:12; 45:9–18; 51:12–16). In Colossians, the identity of this community is revealed in a new humanity, "where there is neither Greek nor Jew, circumcised nor uncircumcised, barbarian, Scythian, slave nor free" (3:11). Rather than relying on identity markers like circumcision (2:11), Sabbath, and purity laws (2:16), which characterize ethnic Israel, this new people

---

12. Cf. Lee, "Power not Novelty: The Connotations of בָּרָא in the Hebrew Bible," 199–212.

13. Barclay, *Colossians and Philemon*, 80, rightly notes that 1:17 points to "not merely some primeval role in bringing creation about, nor some 'headship' imposed from without on an alien world, but an inner relation between Christ and creation concerning its meaning and integrity."

is to be identified solely as a people who have "received Christ Jesus the Lord" and who now "continue to walk in him" (2:6). Just as Christ is "the image of the invisible God" (1:15), so the church as his body must live as one people in unity and harmony "according to the image of their Creator" (3:10).

Over Households

The household is the social institution that occupies the space between the church and the individual. It is not unrelated to the church since believers in the first century met in private houses (cf. 4:15). It is related to the behavior of individuals, for the household is the most basic social unit within which individuals are to relate to one another. This explains the presence of a discussion on household relationships in this letter (3:18 – 4:1).

The fundamental principle of many of the secular Hellenistic household codes is the affirmation of the authority of the male head of the household since the husband/father/master is considered the only person designated by nature to lead the household (cf. Aristotle, *Pol.* 1.1259).[14] In the Colossian household code, however, one finds the repeated use of the title "Lord" (ὁ κύριος) in reference to Christ himself (3:18, 20, 22, 23, 24; 4:1). It is the "Lord Christ" who alone should be considered as the object of one's complete submission and obedient service (3:24). Even the earthly masters must recognize that they have a "Master [i.e., Lord, κύριον] in heaven" (4:1).

This discussion of household relationships is, therefore, an application of the confession that "Christ Jesus [is] Lord" (2:6).[15] The true Lord is Christ Jesus himself. This shift in focus signals the importance of living out the christological confessions expounded in the first half of this letter in one's everyday existence. Christ's lordship is not limited to the cosmological realm or the life of the church; it also extends to every set of human relationships.

Over Believers

The fact that Jesus is Lord has direct implications for believers' actions. Within the household code, one finds a discussion of the expected behavior of slaves, as they are to serve their masters "in everything" (3:22). What is striking is the considerable length of Paul's address to the slaves (3:22 – 25). His emphasis on slaves here is understandable since the slave-master relationship depicts the relationship between believers and the Lord Jesus Christ himself.

Paul's emphasis on the metaphor of slavery is reinforced by several observations.

---

14. Under Roman law, the male head of the household, the *paterfamilias*, is likewise the only person recognized by the law; cf. Barry Nicholas, *An Introduction to Roman Law* (Oxford: Clarendon, 1975), 65 – 68.

15. For a discussion on other ways Paul transforms the expectations of how the household should be managed, see the Theology in Application section on 3:18 – 4:1.

First, the call for slaves to submit to their masters "wholeheartedly, as to the Lord and not to people" 3:23), is comparable to the call for believers to submit to their Lord in 3:17, which precedes the household code ("whatever you do in word or in deed, do everything in the name of the Lord Jesus"). The expected behavior of a Greco-Roman slave provides a model for Paul as he describes the expected behavior of believers under the lordship of Christ.

Second, the fact that within the household code "slave" and "free" is the only set of relationships that has already been alluded to in the significant definition of the new humanity in 3:11 points to the function of this discussion within the wider argument in this letter.

Finally, that believers are called to be "slaves" of Christ is confirmed by the use of the slavery metaphor elsewhere in Colossians. Epaphras, the founder of the Colossian church, is identified as "our beloved fellow slave" (1:7) and "a slave of Christ Jesus" (4:12), while Tychicus, the primary emissary of this letter and apparently a respected figure in the community, is a "fellow slave in the Lord" (4:7). The significance of this metaphorical use of "slave" is highlighted by Onesimus, who is literally a slave but is identified not as a "slave," but as "the faithful and beloved brother" (4:9). In this letter, therefore, the historical and social institution of slavery is not the focus of Paul's discussion. Instead, he is using such a well-known institution in depicting the expected behavior of believers.[16] After all, if one is to claim another person as a "lord" in all realms of existence, one must submit to this person as a "slave," whose sole purpose is to align his or her will to the master's will.

To be slaves of Christ, believers must reject the old pattern of behavior (3:5 – 9) and act so as to build up the community of God's people (3:10 – 17). For Paul, such ethical admonitions are built on the confession of the believers' identity in the exalted Christ (3:1 – 4). The call to reject the old pattern of behavior begins with a catalogue of sinful desires (3:5), which provides the readers with selected manifestations of hearts that worship idols.[17] This catalogue does not provide an exhaustive list of sinful acts, but it does point to the pattern of behavior that characterizes the rebellious past of believers (cf. 3:6). The second vice list points to violent offenses in interpersonal relationships (3:8 – 9) and culminates in the exhortation "do not lie to one another" (3:9); that exhortation is not simply concerned with matters of speech, but with a life of falsehood that denies the reality of one's participation in Christ's death and resurrection.

In positive terms, Paul encourages believers to "put on" a new set of behaviors consistent with their identity as the "elect ... holy and beloved" people of God (3:12).

---

16. For a discussion of the use of the slave metaphor in the NT, see Combes, *Metaphor of Slavery*, 68 – 94, who claims that Paul's prevalent use of this metaphor draws on his own experience of enslavement, which is in turn understood within the framework of Christ's own life and acts (77).

17. The connection with idol-worshiping is made explicit in the final explanatory phrase of the verse: "which is idolatry" (v. 5).

This list of virtues focuses on what builds up the community of God's people and culminates in the call to forgive one another (3:13). This again points to the christological foundation of Paul's ethics since believers are called to live out the power of forgiveness that is demonstrated in God's act of grace through Christ's death on the cross. This is confirmed by the call to "put on love" (3:14), since being "united in love" is part of what it means to "obtain all the wealth of full assurance of understanding, and the knowledge of the mystery of God, Christ" (2:2).

Responses to the Lordship Claim of Christ

Beyond identifying one as the "slave" of the Lord Jesus Christ, this letter also points to other responsibilities of believers, two of which deserve our extended discussion: worship and thanksgiving.

Worship

In response to the lordship claim of Christ, believers are to provide a response that is "worthy of the Lord" (1:10). If worship is defined as a reorientation of one's actions and being in response to God's redemptive act through Christ, what Paul demands is nothing less than a life of worship. In negative terms, believers are to flee from idolatry. Teachings that take attention away from Christ are portrayed as an "empty and deceitful philosophy according to human tradition" (2:8), language that recalls OT anti-idol polemic, for idols are nothing but products of the human hands (cf. Isa 40:18–24; 41:4–7; 44:9–11). In 2:22, such "deceitful philosophy" is further described as being "according to human commands and teachings." By definition, these human traditions must be rejected because they are "not according to Christ" (2:8). In contrast to the traditions and practices of the false teachers, Paul reminds the believers that they were circumcised by a circumcision "not performed by human hands" (2:11). What Paul is concerned with is, therefore, not simply lifestyle choices, but the two options of worship: either the Creator or the created beings (cf. 1:15–20).

The life of idolatry is illustrated by the two vice lists in Col 3. In the first one, which culminates in "covetousness, which is idolatry" (3:5), one finds acts that manifest a refusal to submit to the lordship of Christ. In the second list, the various vices point to expressions of the "mouth[s]" of those who refuse to live out their confession, which is also uttered through their mouths as they sing praises to God in acknowledging Jesus Christ as their Lord (3:8).

In positive terms, believers are called to act out their confession of Jesus as the Lord of all. The most striking note is found in 3:16–17, where language of worship is paralleled by the call to a christocentric lifestyle. In 3:16, believers are to teach and admonish one another "with psalms, hymns, and spiritual songs, with gratitude singing in [their] hearts to God." This cultic language is immediately followed by an all-encompassing call to "do everything in the name of the Lord Jesus" (3:17). The discussion of household relationships that follows illustrates how a life of worship affects every aspect of human existence.

This positive outworking of one's life of worship is reflected in the virtue list in 3:12 – 14. As one worships the God whose Son has given his life on the cross, believers are called to respond by a life of grace and forgiveness. Individually, the acceptance of the final redemptive grace of God compels one to respond by living out the grace that justifies one's existence in this new creation. Corporately, this principle of grace points to the existence of one people of God regardless of one's ethnic, cultural, and social identities (3:11). It is only in this sense that this new humanity can be understood as a worshiping community.

Thanksgiving

A theme closely tied to worship is that of thanksgiving. For Paul, thanksgiving is not simply a matter of proper etiquette and manners; it is an acknowledgment of the Creator as the one and only source of all goodness.[18] Thus, the readers should not be surprised to find an emphasis on this theme in a letter that emphatically affirms the lordship of Christ.

As he does in many of his letters, Paul begins with a thanksgiving prayer that acknowledges God's work through his Son among the believers in Colossae (1:3 – 8). In 1:10 – 12, together with "bearing fruit," "growing," and "being strengthened," "giving thanks" is a means through which one can please Christ in every aspect of life. This is a significant piece as Paul points to "giving thanks" as a sign of maturity as believers hold firm to their dependence on the Lord Jesus Christ. The next appearance of the thanksgiving theme reinforces this reading: "abounding in thanksgiving" follows "rooted [in him]," "built up in him," and "established in the faith" as signs of one's continued faithfulness in their confession of Jesus as Lord (2:7).

The most significant discussion of thanksgiving appears in 3:15 – 17, where submission to the lordship of Christ is explicitly tied to the call to thanksgiving. The call to "be thankful" is understood in the sense of letting "the peace of Christ rule in your hearts" (3:15). Likewise, the call to worship with "psalms, hymns, and spiritual songs" is followed by the phrase "with gratitude" as Paul highlights the importance of a worshipful submission to Christ. Moreover, believers must "do everything in the name of the Lord Jesus, giving thanks to God the Father through him" (3:17). Here one finds the call to thanksgiving providing a bridge between the grateful confession of the heart and an outworking of that confession in a life of thanksgiving.

The final note on thanksgiving appears in 4:2 in a context that calls for eschato-

---

18. This is best illustrated in another prison letter of Paul, where "thanksgiving" is contrasted with acts of "idolatry" (Eph 5:3 – 4). For more on this aspect of the thanksgiving motif in Paul, see Pao, *Thanksgiving*, 15 – 38.

logical alertness. Although gratitude is often linked with past acts of kindness, for Paul such past acts provide the foundation to look forward to the consummation of God's gracious acts through his Son. In the interim, believers are called to give thanks to God as they respond to the covenantal faithfulness of God with corresponding acts of faithfulness.

Mediation of the Power of the Lordship of Christ

In a letter that focuses on the final authority of Christ and the complete sufficiency of his death and resurrection, the proper mediation of the power of such divine acts becomes a critical concern. Because of the finality of Christ's work and authority, various forms of this mediation do not contribute to the divine redemptive act, but they do provide links to those who have yet to encounter this power. Several that acquire this mediatorial role are highlighted.

Gospel

In Paul, the "gospel" embodies what God has accomplished for humanity through his Son. This gospel is rightly "the power of God that brings salvation to everyone who believes" (Rom 1:16). As the embodiment of this power, that gospel accomplishes what it was sent to accomplish. In 1:5, this "gospel" is understood as "the word of truth." As an active agent of God, it "has come to you, just as in the whole world it is bearing fruit and growing" (1:6). The significance of this gospel is illustrated by Paul's claim that he himself is its "servant" (1:23). The emphasis on the prior act of the active gospel is important as Paul argues for the need to move away from "human tradition" (2:8). Separated from the realm of human possibility, this gospel "has been proclaimed in all creation under heaven" (1:23) as it builds up those who have received this gospel.

Intimately related to the "gospel," this "word" also provides the medium through which the gospel can be received and appropriated.[19] This "word" does not cease to act with one's initial reception of the gospel, however. This "word" "dwells" among God's people and allows them to lead lives that center on Christ (3:16). As Paul exhorts believers to act in a way that is worthy of their calling, he makes clear that this "word" is able to accomplish such tasks. Finally, beyond one's own community, Paul asks God to "open … a door for the word" so that his redemptive power can be experienced among other groups (4:3). His emphasis on the power of the "word of Christ" (3:16) is consistent with the christocentric gospel he presents.

---

19. It should be noted, however, that "word" in this context denotes the entire gospel message, not just the words that are uttered. The fact that the gospel is not simply such uttered words is made clear in 1 Thess 1:5: "our gospel came to you not simply with words but also with power, with the Holy Spirit and deep conviction."

Apostles

To include a section on the "apostles" is not to downplay the significant categorical difference between the mediatorial role of the gospel and that of its human agents. In this letter, however, Paul does emphasize his own role as an apostle of the gospel, but only as its "servant" (1:23). A proper understanding of his role is important in appreciating God's redemptive plan.

At the beginning of this letter, Paul identifies himself as "an apostle of Christ Jesus," chosen and sent "by the will of God" (1:1). This designation points to the source of both his authority and power. His specific role as an apostle is highlighted in 1:24 – 2:5, a section sandwiched between his presentation on Christology (1:15 – 23) and his exhortation to the Colossian believers (2:6 – 4:1). The mere placement of such a discussion reflects his self-understanding as a bearer of the gospel of Christ to the church, if not explicitly its mediator.

Here Paul reiterates his conviction that his calling is based on "the commission from God … to fulfill the word of God" (1:25). In terms of God's redemptive plan, he specifically points to his responsibility as one who is called to proclaim the gospel in a time when God's salvation is to be made known to both Jews and Gentiles (1:26 – 28). With the dawn of the eschatological era, Paul considers himself to be one who has the privilege to witness God's new creation in the formation of the new humanity (3:11).

Although the title "prophet" is not used in his self-portrayal, Paul does seem to consider himself as taking on the role of a prophet in proclaiming God's word, especially an eschatological prophet as portrayed in Isaiah. There one finds both the "gospel" word group used for the proclamation of the eschatological good news (εὐαγγελίζομαι, Isa 40:9; 52:7; 60:6; 61:1), and the "comfort" word group in reference to the content of such good news (παρακαλέω, Isa 40:1, 2, 11; 49:10, 13; 51:12; 61:2; παράκλησις, Isa 57:18). This same combination of terms occurs in Colossians. In 1:24 – 2:5, Paul identifies himself as the servant of the "gospel" (τοῦ εὐαγγελίου, 1:23), and he makes it clear that he struggles "so that their hearts may be comforted [παρακληθῶσιν]" (2:2). The ultimate purpose of such acts of comfort is that believers can "obtain all the wealth of full assurance of understanding, and the knowledge of the mystery of God, Christ" (2:2). In proclaiming the gospel as prophesied by the prophets of old, Paul becomes a prophet himself who fulfills such prophecies.[20]

Reading through the lens of the office of OT prophets, one can better understand Paul's self-reflection in 1:24 – 2:5. Instead of seeing "fabricated self-references" that aim at exalting his role as apostle,[21] one can easily view such self-understanding

---

20. See Karl Olav Sandnes, *Paul — One of the Prophets?* (WUNT 2.43; Tübingen: Mohr Siebeck, 1991), 218. The connection of "prophets" and "apostles" is clearly noted in Eph

2:20; 3:5, a prison letter that resembles some of the thematic emphases of Colossians.

21. Cf. Nicole Frank, *Der Kolosserbrief im Kontext des pau-*

within the prophetic framework as the work of the authentic Paul. Moreover, as he did elsewhere, what Paul focuses on is not his power or charisma, but his suffering as he lives out the suffering of Christ (1:24; cf. 2 Cor 11:30; 12:9). Through participating in Christ's suffering, the subversive gospel can challenge false perceptions of reality and allow the true glory of Christ's resurrection and return to be manifested (cf. 3:4).

Believers

The inclusion of a short section (4:2 – 6) on the responsibility of the community of believers toward the world should not be ignored. As Paul (1:24 – 2:5) stands between Christ (1:15 – 23) and the church (2:6 – 4:1), the church (2:6 – 4:1) stands between Paul (1:24 – 2:5) and the world (4:2 – 6). As Paul recognizes his role in God's redemptive plan, believers also must recognize their roles in allowing others to experience the power of the gospel accomplished through the death and resurrection of his Son.

In this final section in the body of this letter, the connection between the missions of the church and that of Paul is noted in two ways. First, believers are called to participate in the ministry of prayer as Paul and his companions continue to serve the gospel (4:2 – 4). Second, believers themselves are called to be mediators of the power of the gospel. While this sudden focus on the responsibilities of believers toward outsiders may be surprising, in context it is an extension of Paul's call for believers to submit to the lordship of Christ. As believers live out this confession "in word" and "in deed" (3:17), they are now called to "walk in wisdom" (4:5) and have their "speech always … full of grace" (4:6). To witness to outsiders is not an incidental charge; rather, it lies at the heart of the demand of the gospel.

Final Consummation of the Lordship of Christ

Noting Paul's statement about the believers' experience of participating in the resurrection of Christ (cf. 2:12 – 13; 3:1), some have concluded that "given his own theological presuppositions, [Paul] cannot speak in this way, so that here a decisive difference must be seen between the eschatology of Colossians and Paul's own eschatology."[22] But since Paul is writing to a new audience among whom the finality of Christ's redemptive work is in doubt, one can understand why he focuses not only on the completion of Christ's work but also on believers' participation in such work. Moreover, in Rom 6:4, Paul also focuses on believers' being raised with Christ to "a new life." The relationship between this metaphorical resurrection and the future

---

linischen Erbes: Eine intertextuelle Studie zur Auslegung und Fortschreibung der Paulustradition (WUNT 2.271; Tübingen: Mohr Siebeck, 2009), 89 – 124.

22. See, e.g., Schnelle, *Theology of the New Testament*, 555.

literal resurrection should be readily understood by those who are exposed to similar teachings in Second Temple Judaism, as noted by N. T. Wright:

> In the Jewish thought where "resurrection" was used metaphorically for "return from exile," one central part of that hope was that Israel's sins would finally be forgiven. Throughout this sequence of thought, the *present* metaphorical "resurrection" of Christians, replacing the metaphorical usage in some Jewish texts, denotes their status "in the Messiah" who has himself been concretely raised from the dead; and it takes its meaning from the fact that it anticipates their *future* literal "resurrection," their eventual sharing of the Messiah's glory.[23]

It seems presumptuous, therefore, to suggest that Paul "cannot speak in this way" in a letter that addresses a particular problem among the Colossians. His note on the present reality of the resurrected lives of believers should best be taken as his firm conviction of the resurrection yet to come.

Equally important are references in this letter to the future consummation of God's redemptive plan. Two references in particular should be noted, both of which contribute substantially to Paul's argument. First, in 1:27 Paul identifies Christ as "the hope of glory." This identification is important in light of the common identification of the Torah as the instrument through which the "glory" of Israel will be revealed. Here, Paul argues that it is Christ himself who is both the instrument and the content of this glory. This reference is also important insofar as the context discusses Paul's role in God's redemptive plan (1:24 – 2:5). His present suffering is justifiable in light of the future glory found only in Christ.

Second, in 3:4, Paul points to the future glory when Christ returns with and for those who belong to him: "when Christ is revealed, who is your life, then you also will be revealed with him in glory." Steering away from the false teachers' emphasis on the present attainment of glory and fulfillment through visionary experiences and ascetic practices, Paul evokes the christological argument that such glory can only be found at the end of time when Christ returns in glory. The false teachers are at fault for taking away from the glory of Christ and for ignoring the consummation of God's redemptive plan.

While other notes reflecting on Paul's future eschatology can be identified in this letter,[24] these two themes are particularly important since they contribute to Paul's main argument. To deny the significance of these references is to miss a critical element in Paul's argument in Colossians as he makes his case for the centrality of the death, resurrection, and final revelation of Christ. It is this element that provides cohesion for the entire letter.

---

23. N. T. Wright, *Resurrection of the Son of God* (Minneapolis: Fortress, 2003), 238 – 39 [emphasis his].

24. See, e.g., "the wrath of God" (3:6) and the call to be "alert" (4:2). For more on future eschatology in this letter, see Still, "Eschatology in Colossians," 125 – 38.

Introduction to Philemon

Though Philemon has been described as "one of the most charming letters ever written,"[1] some have seen it as disturbing since Paul seems to deal with the issue of slavery without voicing any explicit critique of such an oppressive institution. Others have dismissed it as insignificant, not only because of its size, but also because its subject matter (dealing with a personal matter between two private individuals). Moreover, Paul seems less than clear about what he wishes to accomplish with this letter. Finally, to the contemporary audience, this letter, which deals neither with significant doctrinal matters nor with prominent Christian spiritual practices, seems at best an archaic note limited in value.

This commentary attempts to correct such misunderstandings while drawing attention to the power embedded in the letter. Philemon is not an exclusively private letter, and it promises to bring about fundamental changes in our understanding of the power of the gospel as well as in ways that such an understanding can be practiced on both a personal and corporate level. Behind the paucity of theological formulations lies a profound conviction of Paul, who insists on the paradigmatic significance of Christ's redemptive death on the cross and its effect on the community of God's people. Through the application of the gospel message to one historical audience, we can appreciate how this same gospel can be applied in our own contexts.

People, Place, and Time

This letter begins with the self-identification: "Paul, a prisoner of Christ Jesus."[2] In the early church, there is almost a universal acceptance of Paul's authorship for this letter, as testified even by Marcion's critical hands. Despite the challenges from a few nineteenth-century German scholars,[3] most modern scholars also accept the authenticity of this letter. Although closely related to Colossians, even those who

---

1. John Knox, *Philemon among the Letters of Paul* (London: Collins, 1960), 9.

2. For the role of Timothy in this letter opening, see comments on v. 1.

3. See esp. Ferdinand Christian Baur, *Paul, the Apostle of Jesus Christ: His Life and Works, His Epistles and Teachings. A Contribution to a Critical History of Primitive Christianity* (London: Williams & Norgate, 1875), 2:84, who considers this letter as one that "contains nothing of importance either in relation to doctrine or to Church history."

doubt the authenticity of Colossians find no reason to ascribe this letter to anyone other than Paul.[4] Moreover, some who doubt Paul's authorship of other letters have argued for the authenticity of Colossians in light of its close affinity with this letter to Philemon.[5]

Most scholars rightly consider Philemon the primary recipient of this letter. Not to be missed is the title attached to this name: "our beloved and coworker" (v. 1). This identification points to his status in the gospel ministry and may suggest that this is not simply a private letter written to a personal friend. The list of names with their corresponding titles confirms this reading: "Apphia, our sister" and "Archippus, our fellow soldier" (v. 2). The final note in the opening greetings ("to the church in your house," v. 2) demonstrates that Paul is writing to the entire church that meets at Philemon's house.[6]

Reading Philemon as a public letter explains Paul's emphasis on Philemon's "partnership in the faith" (v. 6) and the relevance of his work "for all the saints" (v. 5). More importantly, this reading of the letter considers the issue addressed here and its corresponding requests to affect not simply one person and his family, but also the entire household of God. For the contemporary audience, to understand this as a public letter also highlights its significance and continued relevance for the community of God's people.

In Col 4:9, Onesimus, apparently the slave of Philemon, is described as being "one of you [i.e., the Colossians]." Thus, it is likely that Philemon and his household reside at Colossae. The closing greetings of this letter (vv. 23 – 24) and that of Colossians (4:10 – 17), where one finds the names of Epaphras, Mark, Aristarchus, Demas, and Luke, also point to the two letters as addressing the same community.

The place of origin is more difficult to determine, although clearly Paul is writing from prison (vv. 1, 9, 10, 13, 23). As with Colossians, major options include Caesarea,[7] Ephesus,[8] and Rome.[9] The presence of Luke in Col 4:14 and Phlm 24 may suggest a Caesarean origin for both letters since Luke is with Paul in Caesarea as testified by the "we" in Acts 27:1 – 2. But none of Paul's captivity letters mentions Caesarea, and a Caesarean origin receives little support from early Christian sources.

If we focus on Philemon itself, Ephesus is a favorite candidate primarily because

---

4. Cf. Raymond Brown, *Introduction to the New Testament* (New York: Doubleday, 1977), 612.

5. Cf. W. Kümmel, *Introduction to the New Testament* (rev. and enlarged; Nashville: Abingdon, 1986), 345.

6. It was common for ancient letters to mention multiple recipients even if it targeted one primary recipient; cf. Peter Arzt-Grabner, *Philemon* (Papyrologische Kommentare zum Neuen Testament 1; Göttingen: Vandenhoeck & Ruprecht, 2003), 111 – 14. The mentioning of "the church" that meets in Philemon's house highlights the public nature of this letter.

7. For a defense of a Caesarean origin, see E. Earle Ellis, *The Making of the New Testament Documents* (BIS 39; Leiden: Brill, 1999), 266 – 75.

8. Eduard Lohse, *Colossians and Philemon* (trans. William R. Poehlmann and Robert J. Karris; Hermeneia; Philadelphia: Fortress, 1971), 188; Charles B. Cousar, *Philippians and Philemon: A Commentary* (NTL; Louisville: Westminster John Knox, 2009), 187.

9. See esp. Markus Barth and Helmut Blanke, *The Letter to Philemon* (ECC; Grand Rapids: Eerdmans, 2000), 122 – 26.

of its proximity to Colossae, which would explain both the possibility of Onesimus fleeing to this nearby city and Paul's own plan to return to Colossae soon after his release (cf. v. 22). But this assumes that Onesimus did "flee" from Philemon using his own limited resources[10] and that Paul's future plan was only limited to nearby areas. Moreover, there is no explicit evidence of an Ephesian imprisonment in the canonical writings. If we take Philemon and Colossians as originating from the same geographical and temporal location, Rome remains the best option.[11] This also boasts the strongest support in subscriptions attached to relatively early manuscripts and versions.[12] If a Roman provenance is accepted, Philemon can be dated to AD 60 – 62.

Circumstances behind the Text

Most would agree that Paul is less than direct in stating the purpose of writing this letter. Perhaps equally unclear are the circumstances that led to its writing. Several interpretive options have been suggested.

(1) The traditional interpretation is best represented by the concise statement of Calvin: "Sending back a runaway slave and thief, he [i.e., Paul] supplicates pardon for him."[13] An expanded version points to several statements made by Paul that appear to support this reading:

> Onesimus was a slave of Philemon in Colossae (cf. Col. 4:9) who had not only run away from his master (Phlm. 15 – 16) but had also absconded with some of Philemon's money or possessions (vv. 18 – 19). Attracted by the anonymity and excitement of a large metropolis, he traveled furtively to Rome ... where somehow he met the imprisoned Paul."[14]

Although this interpretation enjoys the support of many commentators throughout history, a growing number of interpreters have pointed to its weaknesses. First, the thesis that Onesimus was a runaway slave[15] is never explicitly stated in the text itself.[16] The conjecture that he is a "thief" comes from reading the conditional clause

---

10. See Circumstances behind the Text (the next section below).

11. For further discussion on this issue, see the introduction to Colossians.

12. Cf. Bruce M. Metzger, *Textual Commentary on the Greek New Testament* (2nd ed.; Stuttgart: United Bible Societies, 1994), 589 – 60.

13. John Calvin, *Commentaries on the Epistles to Timothy, Titus, and Philemon* (trans. William Pringle; Grand Rapids: Baker, 2003), 347 – 48.

14. Murray J. Harris, *Colossians and Philemon* (Exegetical Guide to the Greek New Testament; Grand Rapids: Eerdmans, 1991), 241.

15. Noting Paul's use of the metaphor of slavery elsewhere in his letters, some have even questioned whether Onesimus is really Philemon's slave; Allen D. Callahan, "Paul's Epistle to Philemon: Toward an Alternative Argumentum," *HTR* 86 (1993): 357 – 76; idem, *Embassy of Onesimus: The Letter of Paul to Philemon* (Valley Forge, PA: Trinity International, 1997). This reading is, however, improbable; see comments on vv. 15 – 16.

16. See Sarah B. C. Winter, "Paul's Letter to Philemon," *NTS* 33 (1987): 1 – 15.

in v. 18 ("if he has wronged you in any way, or owes you anything") as an indicative statement that affirms the reality of such an act.[17]

Moving from the text to the historical reality of the first-century Roman world:

the runaway theory on its own does not explain adequately how Onesimus came to be in prison with Paul, or how Paul had the authority to send him back. Nor does it explain the remarkable coincidence that Onesimus came into contact with — of all people — the one person in prison who knew his master and was in a position to intercede on his behalf.[18]

More specifically, a slave would not be kept in the same prison with a Roman citizen, and Paul would not be allowed to harbor a runaway slave even if he was not a prisoner. Furthermore, by receiving a runaway slave, Paul would have put his entire ministry and his coworkers at risk.[19]

Coupled with these historical observations is the lack of support from the literary parallels in the Greco-Roman letters that make explicit appeals for runaway slaves. The alleged parallels in Pliny the Younger (*Ep.* 9.21; 9.24) only highlight the lack of a description of Onesimus's repentant attitude or an explicit call for Philemon to forgive and have mercy on Onesimus.[20]

(2) While the problems with the traditional interpretation are apparent, the choice among the other alternative interpretations is less than clear. Accepting that Philemon and Onesimus were not on good terms, some suggest that Onesimus fled to Paul to seek asylum from his own master.[21] In the first century, temples could be used as places of asylum for runaway slaves, and houses with a dominant family cult could conceivably be considered as such a sanctuary.[22] With Paul in prison (or in

---

17. For the rhetorical function of this verse, see Clarice J. Martin, "The Rhetorical Function of Commercial Language in Paul's Letter to Philemon (Verse 18)," in *Persuasive Artistry: Studies in New Testament Rhetoric in Honor of George A. Kennedy* (ed. Duane F. Watson; JSNTSup 50; Sheffield: Sheffield Academic, 1991), 321 – 37.

18. I. Howard Marshall, "The Theology of Philemon," in *The Theology of the Shorter Pauline Letters* (ed. Karl P. Donfried and I. Howard Marshall; Cambridge: Cambridge Univ. Press, 1993), 178. For the various places to which a runaway slave could escape, see Peter Stuhlmacher, *Der Brief an Philemon* (4th ed.; EKKNT 18; Neukirchen-Vluyn: Neukirchener and Düsseldorf: Banziger, 2004), 22 – 23.

19. Brian M. Rapske, "The Prisoner Paul in the Eyes of Onesimus," *NTS* 37 (1991): 189 – 90.

20. Craig S. Wansink, *Chained in Christ: The Experience and Rhetoric of Paul's Imprisonments* (JSNTSup 130; Sheffield: Sheffield Academic, 1996), 176. Equally important is the difference in "tone" between these two groups of letters; see J. A.

Harrill, "Paul and Slavery," in *Paul in the Greco-Roman World: A Handbook* (ed. J. Paul Sampley; Harrisburg, PA: Trinity International, 2003), 590. Some consider, however, such lack of explicit requests in this letter as emerging from Paul's own predicament as he found himself harboring a fugitive; David M. Russell, "The Strategy of a First-Century Appeals Letter: A Discourse Reading of Paul's Epistle to Philemon," *JOTT* 11 (1998): 1 – 25. Others who likewise hold to the traditional interpretation suggest that Paul's intention is not to settle a private matter, but to promote "love and brotherhood" among those within the church; F. Forrester Church, "Rhetorical Structure and Design in Paul's Letter to Philemon," *HTR* 71 (1978): 32. These proposals do not provide sufficient defense of the traditional interpretation, although they do point to the problems of reading Philemon in light of the letters of Pliny the Younger.

21. E. R. Goodenough, "Paul and Onesimus," *HTR* 22 (1929): 181 – 82.

22. Cf. Barth and Blanke, *Letter to Philemon*, 28 – 30.

house arrest), however, it is difficult to consider such a temporary place of residence as a sanctuary, not to mention the improbability that Paul would reside in such a sanctuary for a pagan god.

(3) More plausible is the hypothesis that Onesimus purposefully approached a friend of his master in the hope that, through mediation, he might be restored.[23] In the first-century Roman world, an alienated slave could approach such a mediator and would not be considered a runaway. Paul would qualify as such a friend because "his religious power outweighs the potential drawback of his being a prisoner in the enterprise of pleading as an *amicus domini*."[24] This interpretation also accommodates the absence of any reference to Onesimus as a runaway slave. Moreover, in such a scenario, one does not have to assume the slave is the only party at fault; the absence of any reference to Onesimus's repentance can therefore be explained.[25]

Despite its explanatory power, this hypothesis is not without problems. First, there is no evidence that Onesimus himself is seeking to be restored to his master, Philemon. Instead, his return seems closely tied to Paul's own desire for Onesimus to follow the implications of the gospel (vv. 10 – 14).[26] Second, Paul does not speak primarily as the friend of the master; instead, he speaks as the friend of the slave. This reversal of role may argue against this understanding of Onesimus's meeting with Paul in the first place.[27] Third, as with the traditional interpretation, the lack of any explicit plea on behalf of Onesimus is striking.[28] Even if the slave does not bear a substantial responsibility for the strained relationship with his master, such appeals are to be expected. Finally, this hypothesis fails to explain the purpose of this letter, at least in a way consistent with the data contained in the text.

(4) The alternative hypothesis favored by this commentary does reject the traditional interpretation that Onesimus is a *runaway* slave, but rather argues that Onesimus was sent by Philemon to help Paul. Championing this reading, Winter argues that "Onesimus was with Paul in prison because the former had been sent by the

---

23. Peter Lampe, "Keine 'Sklavenflucht' des Onesimus," *ZNW* 76 (1985): 135 – 37. See also C. F. D. Moule, *The Epistles of Paul the Apostle to the Colossians and to Philemon* (Cambridge: Cambridge Univ. Press, 1957), 20; Lohse, *Colossians and Philemon*, 187; Jerome Murphy-O'Connor, *Paul: A Critical Life* (Oxford: Clarendon, 1996), 177; James D. G. Dunn, *The Epistles to the Colossians and to Philemon* (NIGTC; Grand Rapids: Eerdmans, 1996), 303 – 5; J. M. G. Barclay, *Colossians and Philemon* (Sheffield: Sheffield Academic, 1997), 101; Reidar Aasgaard, *"My Beloved Brothers and Sisters!" Christian Siblingship in Paul* (JSNTSup 265; London: T&T Clark, 2004), 242.

24. Rapske, "The Prisoner Paul in the Eyes of Onesimus," 202.

25. Max Turner, "Human Reconciliation in the New Testament with Special Reference to Philemon, Colossians and Ephesians," *EuroJTh* 16 (2006): 39.

26. See also Neil Elliott, *Liberating Paul: The Justice of God and the Politics of the Apostle* (Maryknoll, NY: Orbis, 1994), 51; Harrill, "Paul and Slavery," 590; idem, "Using the Roman Jurists to Interpret Philemon: A Response to Peter Lampe," *ZNW* 90 (1999): 135 – 38.

27. See Donald M. Steele, "Releasing the Captives — Release the Captors: The Letter to Philemon and the Relationship of North American Christians and the Peoples of the Two-Thirds World" (PhD.diss., Graduate Theological Union, 1994), 92 – 93.

28. Cf. Wansink, *Chained in Christ*, 188: "If Paul is interceding on Onesimus's behalf, his subtlety is overwhelming."

congregation in Colossae."[29] Winter's detailed analysis of the thanksgiving section with her particular emphasis on phrases and clauses like "I hear" (v. 5), "your love and faith in the Lord Jesus and for all the saints" (v. 5), "your partnership in the faith" (v. 6), and "the hearts of the saints have been refreshed through you" (v. 7) adds considerable strength to this argument since it points to the prior act of kindness on the part of Philemon as the basis of Paul's further appeal in this letter.[30]

Moreover, one has to agree with Winter when she adds that "under a loose house arrest visitors were not only allowed, they were necessary to provide food and services for the imprisonment," and "this construction of the circumstances agrees with what is known about the situation portrayed in Philippians, where Epaphroditus is sent to Paul in prison."[31] Perhaps the reference to Paul's being "refreshed" (v. 7) by Philemon was precisely through his sending of Onesimus to help him during his time of need.[32] This reading not only provides a plausible background, but it also explains its public nature as Paul is concerned with the involvement of Philemon and the church that meets at his house in the gospel ministry.[33]

Instead of the letters of Pliny that supposedly provide appropriate parallels to Paul's letter to Philemon, a closer parallel is Ignatius's letter to the Ephesians, where one finds the request for the continued service of the slave sent for the refreshment of a servant of the gospel (cf. *Eph.* 2.1 – 2).[34] Some have further suggested that the occasion of Paul's writing is his delayed return of this dispatched slave, an occasion that is also paralleled by other ancient letters (Cicero, *Fam.*, 9.3; *Att.* 11.2 – 3).[35]

Those who object to this reading often point to the unlikelihood of Philemon sending a "useless" slave to serve Paul on his behalf (cf. v. 11).[36] It should be noted, however, that the word "useless" is a wordplay on Onesimus[37] and should not be taken as an absolute statement concerning the value of Onesimus.[38] As to whether

---

29. Winter, "Paul's Letter to Philemon," 3. See also idem, "Methodological Observations on a New Interpretation of Paul's Letter to Philemon," *USQR* 39 (1984): 203 – 12. See also Wolfgang Schenk, "Der Brief des Paulus an Philemon in der neueren Forschung," *ANRW* II.25.4 (1987): 3439 – 95. John Knox offers an early version of this in *Philemon among the Letters of Paul*, 18 – 27, when he suggests this letter was actually addressed to Archippus, whom he considers the owner of Onesimus. For Knox, the purpose of this letter is to have Archippus free Onesimus so that he can serve together with Paul in his future ministries.

30. For a more detailed reading of this entire letter that supports this hypothesis, see Brook W. R. Pearson, "Assumptions in the Criticism and Translation of Philemon," in *Translating the Bible: Problems and Prospect* (ed. Stanley E. Porter and Richard S. Hess; JSNTSup 173; Sheffield: Sheffield Academic, 1999), 253 – 80.

31. Winter, "Paul's Letter to Philemon," 3. On this, see also

Brian M. Rapske, "The Importance of Helpers to the Imprisoned Paul in the Book of Acts," *TynBul* 42 (1991): 3 – 30.

32. In two letters of Ignatius (*Trall.* 12.1; *Mag.* 15.1), the same word group was used regarding those who had served him during his imprisonment (Wansink, *Chained in Christ*, 195).

33. This reading points to the significant ecclesiological as well as missiological significance of this letter, one that reflects Paul's passion and conviction.

34. Wansink, *Chained in Christ*, 196.

35. Harrill, "Paul and Slavery," 591.

36. Thus, e.g., Barclay, *Colossians and Philemon*, 100; Douglas J. Moo, *The Letters to the Colossians and to Philemon* (PNTC; Grand Rapids: Eerdmans, 2008), 166.

37. See comments on v. 11.

38. See also a similar wordplay on the words "useful" (χρηστός) and "Christ" (Χριστός) in 1 Cor 15:31 – 33; cf. Steele, "Releasing the Captives," 93 – 103.

Philemon should have sent a non-Christian slave to serve Paul, one must reconsider the reading of v. 10 in light of the social reality among first-century converts to Christianity. When the head of the household was converted to Christianity, it is likely that his entire household was also "converted" at least in name. The description of Onesimus as becoming Paul's son should therefore be understood as a rededication of his commitment to the gospel.[39] If so, it is entirely conceivable for Philemon to have sent this slave to Paul and for Onesimus to gain a more personal and profound experience of the power of the gospel during his stay with Paul.

Although the evidence may appear to favor this emissary hypothesis, the data in the text itself fail to prove that this is indeed the occasion behind Onesimus's meeting with Paul. Moreover, one can also imagine a combination of any two of these readings, such as the possibility of Onesimus being sent by Philemon only to confess later that he had stolen from his master.[40] The presence of these various possibilities only points to the tentative nature of any hypothesis concerning the situation behind the text.

Purpose

Regardless of what circumstances occasioned the writing of Philemon, the question of purpose still needs to be raised: What is Paul asking for in this letter? This general question embraces two more specific ones: Did Paul desire Onesimus to be manumitted? And is there an underlying purpose other than Philemon's acceptance of Onesimus?

Concerning Onesimus's legal status, attention has been focused on vv. 15–16: "so that you may have him back forever, no longer as a slave, but more than a slave, a beloved brother." While some have argued that Paul is clearly suggesting here that Philemon should manumit his slave,[41] it is more likely that Paul is not at all concerned with the question of Onesimus's legal status.[42] Paul's primary concern is to have Onesimus welcomed back as a Christian brother and be treated as Paul himself. "No longer as a slave" does not necessarily mean that Philemon is to receive Onesimus back as a freedman, or that he is to free him immediately. Rather, "as" (ὡς) expresses the idea that Philemon should accept Onesimus as a brother *in spite of* his physical status. In other words, "whether Onesimus remained a slave or not, he could

39. Thus N. H. Taylor, "Onesimus: A Case Study of Slave Conversion in Early Christianity," *R&T* 3 (1996): 259–81.

40. Gary Wills, *What Paul Meant* (New York: Viking, 2006), 112–13.

41. F. F. Bruce, *Epistles to the Colossians, to Philemon, and to the Ephesians* (NICNT; Grand Rapids: Eerdmans, 1984), 217; Norman R. Petersen, *Rediscovering Paul: Philemon and the So-*

ciology of Paul's Narrative World (Philadelphia: Fortress, 1985), 97; Stuhlmacher, *Der Brief an Philemon*, 54.

42. Lohse, *Colossians and Philemon*, 203; J. M. G. Barclay, "Paul, Philemon and the Dilemma of Christian Slave Ownership," *NTS* 37 (1991): 170; Dunn, *Epistles to the Colossians and to Philemon*, 334–35; Barth and Blanke, *Letter to Philemon*, 414–16.

no longer be regarded as a slave."[43] In the next section we will return to the issue of manumission in the ancient world.

In requesting that Philemon receive Onesimus back as a beloved brother, Paul is altering the social system by which characters relate to each other. Under the framework of God as "Father" and Jesus as "Lord" (v. 3), Philemon, Apphia, and Archippus are to be related as siblings and coworkers within this household of God. As a "brother," Onesimus is addressed in the same way as Philemon (vv. 7, 20); he too has been incorporated into the body of Christ, and this new framework becomes the primary reference as far as the interrelationships among the characters are concerned.[44]

Within this new framework, Paul hints at the underlying purpose of this letter. In v. 21 he writes, "I write to you, because I know that you will do even more than what I say." Paul has already expressed his wish to have Philemon receive Onesimus as he would himself (v. 17); Paul seems more concerned, therefore, with more than simply the legal release of Onesimus. Earlier (v. 13) Paul expressed his desire to keep Onesimus so he could serve Paul in the gospel ministry. Reading between the lines, it seems possible to consider this "more" in v. 21 as a desire for Onesimus to be returned to Paul for the service of the gospel.[45] If so, Paul's note of Philemon's indebtedness to him in v. 19 may pave the way for this implicit request.

Moreover, phrases like "in the Lord" and "in Christ" in v. 20 may also be understood as implying that Philemon's returning Onesimus to Paul for the service of the gospel will truly be an act that will refresh Paul "in the Lord" and "in Christ." Finally, the public nature of this letter with multiple destinations and the evocation of Paul's coworker (v. 1)[46] may further confirm that this letter is to deal with an issue that involves the wider Christian circle: Philemon and his church are to send Onesimus as a servant of the gospel ministry.

None of these observations is decisive, however. But if there is indeed an underlying purpose in this letter and no viable competing proposal, this one can function as a working hypothesis as we read the letter.

Paul and Slavery

To understand further the situation behind the text, we must dig deeper into the institution of slavery in the ancient world. Not only does this provide a window for us into the world of Onesimus, but it also sheds light on the issue of manumission of

43. Peter O'Brien, *Colossians, Philemon* (WBC 44; Waco, TX: Word, 1982), 287.

44. For a further discussion of this restructuring of human relationships, see the Theology of Philemon section.

45. This understanding of the purpose of this letter is consistent with, but not necessarily tied to, our understanding of the occasion behind Onesimus's initial meeting with Paul; cf. Marshall, "Theology of Philemon," 179; S. H. Polaski, *Paul and*

the Discourse of Power (Biblical Seminar 62; Sheffield: Sheffield Academic, 1999), 66.

46. Some have also considered Paul's naming Onesimus as a "brother" (v. 16) as pointing to his intended position as his coworker in the gospel ministry (cf. Rom 16:1, 23; 1 Cor 1:1; 16:12; 2 Cor 1:1; 2:13; Phil 2:25; 1 Thess 3:2); Aasgaard, "*My Beloved Brothers and Sisters,*" 249–50, 296–97.

slaves. In the Hellenistic world, Aristotle's understanding of the slave as "an animate article of property" (*Pol.* 1253b) probably reflects the opinion of most. In Roman times, this understanding of the slave as a "thing" (*res*) continues at least in legal texts (cf. Justinian, *Digest* 21.1.23.3).[47] Although the actual experience of slaves may vary according to individual circumstances and geographical locations, socially they were considered to be "natally alienated and generally dishonored persons."[48] Even reports of various degrees of "freedom" granted to slaves fail to contradict their clear legal status as those who fell outside of the protection of Roman law.

Slaves were generally divided into two types: (1) agricultural and industrial slaves, and (2) domestic slaves. The former often consisted of prisoners of wars and convicted criminals; their treatment was harsh and prospect of manumission low. Domestic slaves, however, performed a variety of functions throughout the household, and skilled laborers received considerably better treatment with the possibility of gaining upward social mobility.[49] The distinction between the two types is by no means clearly demarcated, however, and they may reflect the historical development of the sources of slavery from periods of war and conquest to the more peaceful times of the early Imperial period.[50] Moreover, in the early Imperial period, the fact that many sold themselves into slavery because of debt or the prospect of upward social mobility points to the diversity of such an institution and its related practice in the first century. For the contemporary (Western) readers, it is worth noting that unlike the more recent American experiences, race did not play a role in Greco-Roman slavery.

Being a domestic slave, Onesimus could be in charge of a number of household duties, from administrative to menial tasks. His absence from Philemon would have caused some problems in the operation of the household, but he was likely not the only slave in Philemon's possession.[51] If Onesimus were a runaway slave, a penalty would be imposed on anyone who might run into such a fugitive without reporting it within a period of twenty days.[52] This seems to be an accepted understanding among the Romans:

> A man who conceals a runaway is a thief. The senate has decreed that runaways should not be allowed into woodland nor protected by the bailiffs or procurators of

---

47. Other definitions include "chattel" (*mancipium*) and "mortal object" (*res mortales*); S. Scott Bartchy, *First-Century Slavery and 1 Corinthians 7:21* (SBLDS 11; Atlanta: Scholars, 1973), 38.

48. Orlando Patterson, *Slavery and Social Death: A Comparative Study* (Cambridge, MA: Harvard Univ. Press, 1982), 13.

49. This would only apply to male slaves since female slaves received less specific training and were exploited in numerous ways; cf. Lynn H. Cohick, *Women in the World of the Earliest Christians: Illuminating Ancient Ways of Life* (Grand Rapids: Baker, 2009), 257–84.

50. Cf. Keith Hopkins, *Conquerors and Slaves* (Sociological Studies in Roman History 1; Cambridge: Cambridge Univ. Press, 1978), 11.

51. In the ancient Greco-Roman world, it would be a sign of severe poverty not to own at least a few slaves (cf. Libanius, *Oratio* 31.11); Barclay, "Paul, Philemon and the Dilemma of Christian Slave Ownership," 166 n. 19.

52. Apuleius, *Metam.* 6.4; William Linn Westermann, *The Slave Systems of Greek and Roman Antiquity* (Philadelphia: American Philosophical Society, 1955), 108.

the owners, and it has fixed a fine; but if within twenty days they either return the runaways to their owners or produce them before magistrates, the senate has granted them pardon for their previous conduct. (Justinian, *Digest* 11.4.1)[53]

For slaves ancient and modern, being freed is understood as the goal of one's labor and life. This is testified by the numerous tomb inscriptions in Rome, where freedmen celebrated the event of their manumission as the most important event in their life.[54] To many, however, manumission was not always desirable, nor did it automatically translate into an independent state of existence. First, when a slave was manumitted, he was legally freed, but socially and economically his obligation to his former master continued. Owing his former master *operae* (work days) and *obsequium* (loyalty), the freedman then entered into a patron-client relationship with his former master and continued to serve. Manumission should not be understood as emancipation, and freedom and slavery were but two poles on a continuum of a complicated picture of social and political relationship.[55]

Although manumitted slaves in Rome could become Roman citizens, they never ceased to be recognized as ex-slaves. Entering society without a network of support, these freedmen were "never wholly free."[56] They often found themselves in a less secure position since protection and sustenance could no longer be expected. Unless closely bound with his former master, now his patron, he would find himself "slave to several instead of one" (Epictetus, *Disc.* 4.1.35 – 37).[57] Equally important was the recognition that manumission could easily reinforce the institution of slavery as masters imposed their will on their slaves so that the faint hope of manumission became the tool for control and manipulation.[58] Any discussion of manumission must, therefore, be construed as a support of the institution of slavery.

It is in light of this background that the omission of an explicit call for the manumission of Onesimus should be understood. In this letter, however, Paul appears to be moving beyond manumission in an attempt to reinstate Onesimus within the more significant network of the household of God. The call to consider Onesimus "no longer as a slave, but more than a slave, a beloved brother" (v. 16), is no longer simply a metaphorical way of speaking, but has significant implications as Paul considers not only his departure from his identity as a slave but also his entry into

---

53. Translation taken from Theodor Mommsen, Paul Krueger, and Alan Watson, eds., *The Digest of Justinian* (Philadelphia: Univ. of Pennsylvania Press, 1985), 1:344.

54. Orlando Patterson, *Freedom*, vol. 1: *Freedom in the Making of Western Culture* (New York: HarperCollins, 1991), 236.

55. See esp. Bartchy, *First-Century Slavery*, 40; Craig S. de Vos, "Once a Slave, Always a Slave? Slavery, Manumission and Relational Patterns in Paul's Letter to Philemon," *JSNT* 82 (2001): 99. It should be noted, however, that although urban slaves were often manumitted, this was not an automatic pro-

cess, nor was there a definite time line through which they were to be manumitted; cf. Harrill, "Paul and Slavery," 580 – 81.

56. R. Zelnick-Abramovitz, *Not Wholly Free: The Concept of Manumission and the Status of Manumitted Slaves in the Ancient Greek World* (Mnemosyne Supplementa 266; Leiden/Boston: Brill, 2005), 333.

57. K. R. Bradley, *Slaves and Masters in the Roman Empire: A Study in Social Control* (New York: Oxford Univ. Press, 1987), 82.

58. Ibid., 83 – 112.

a new network of relationships. Thus, what Paul is advocating is "far more radical than manumission," since "what he expected effectively undermined the collectivist, authoritarian and patriarchal values of Graeco-Roman society."[59]

Beyond this significant consideration, one can also imagine various other reasons for Paul's lack of an explicit call for manumission. First, within the political reality of the first-century Roman world, an explicit call to manumission would place the church in a politically dangerous position.[60]

Second, Paul's concern with the ministry of the gospel probably eclipses that of his social program. Some put it bluntly: "The emancipation of Onesimus is as nothing compared with his being furnished to spread the gospel in Phrygia and elsewhere."[61] Understood in eschatological terms, this concern for missions can again explain Paul's discussion of this issue apart from the context of the life of the household church.[62]

Third, some suggest that Paul's omission reflects the fact that "he did not know what to recommend" because of the difficulties involved in both the call to manumission and the call to remain in the status quo.[63] But this fails to take into account what Paul does advocate in his discussion of the new reality in Christ. Moreover, it fails to recognize the rhetorical force behind Paul's mode of discourse.[64]

Finally, in light of Paul's emphasis on a new social world for Onesimus that finds its basis on the power of the gospel, one can claim the call to manumission would have been an easier route, but Paul is more concerned with the deeper structure of reality.[65] Instead of focusing on what the readers may have expected, we should focus on what is advocated in this letter. Only then can the power of this short letter be fully appreciated.

Significance

The above discussion has already pointed to the significance of this short letter. Instead of dealing exclusively with the private relationship between a slave and his master, Paul points to the power of the gospel in restructuring personal and social relationships with the goal of the ministry of God's Word. If our reading of the purpose of this letter is correct, it also addresses the issue of how one house church can participate in the apostolic mission in fulfilling God's salvific plan in history. The full

---

59. De Vos, "Once a Slave, Always a Slave?" 104.

60. J. B. Lightfoot, *St. Paul's Epistles to the Colossians and to Philemon* (London: Macmillan, 1897), 322–23.

61. J. Duncan M. Derrett, "The Function of the Epistle to Philemon," *ZNW* 79 (1988): 84–85.

62. For some, Paul's failure to discuss the issue of manumission reflects his conviction of the imminent end of the present world; Marion L. Soards, "Benefitting from Philemon," *Journal of Theology* 91 (1987): 49–50; Mark D. Chapman, "The Short-

est Book in the Bible," *ExpTim* 118 (2007): 546. This fails, however, to explain passages where social and political institutions are indeed addressed (e.g., Rom 13:1–7; Col 3:18–4:1; etc.).

63. Barclay, "Paul, Philemon and the Dilemma of Christian Slave Ownership," 175.

64. Elliott, *Liberating Paul*, 44.

65. James Tunstead Burtchaell, *Philemon's Problem: A Theology of Grace* (Grand Rapids: Eerdmans, 1998), 28.

implications of a seemingly private matter are explored in a skillful and pastorally sensitive way.

It is in this sense that the rhetorical art and tact of Paul in this short letter should be appreciated.[66] The Paul of this letter has often been criticized for not making his request(s) explicit, but it is precisely in this respect that one can identify the power of this letter. Instead of issuing an explicit command, Paul provides a framework within which Philemon is compelled to be obedient to the authority of this apostle. The two pillars of this framework, faith and love, are introduced already in vv. 4 – 7, and these two pillars are grounded in Christ (v. 6), who is the basis of the partnership between Paul and Philemon (v. 17).

Beyond this theological foundation, Paul also appeals through his own relationship with Onesimus (vv. 8 – 16) and his relationship with Philemon (vv. 17 – 20). In doing so, Paul evokes a wide range of emotions to bolster the rhetorical power of his arguments: joy (v. 7), comfort (v. 7), sympathy (vv. 1, 9, 10, 13, 23), indebtedness (vv. 13, 19), respect (v. 19), and honor/shame (vv. 1 – 2, 23 – 24).[67] Finally, Paul exerts his own apostolic authority by claiming not to exert such authority (v. 8) and by expressing confidence in Philemon's obedient response (v. 21); these are further secured by the threat of his own presence (v. 22). In contrast to his letter to Colossians, where he is confronting an explicit form of a false gospel, Paul's rhetorical strategy here demonstrates his skill and sensitivity in handling an issue that appears to be personal in nature but with profound theological ramifications.

We can recognize another contribution of this letter even when Paul does not make his request explicit. It provides the lengthiest and most nuanced discussion on the relationship between a slave and his master in the NT. Not only is Paul's discussion important for the issue of liberty and equality within the Christian household, but the way he articulates the vision of the new reality introduced by the work of God through Christ also allows readers to move beyond the narrow discussion of slavery to the wider impact of the gospel in every level of human existence. This wider discussion informs readers as to how particular social issues are to be handled.

Finally, one is probably justified, inferring from the inclusion of this letter in the NT, in seeing the successful fulfillment of Paul's demand in this letter.[68] Such success should not, however, be considered the sole criterion by which this letter is to be judged.

---

66. To some, this is the major contribution of this letter; Todd D. Still, "Philemon among the Letters of Paul: Theological and Canonical Considerations," *ResQ* 47 (2005): 139 – 40.

67. Peter Lampe, "Affects and Emotions in the Rhetoric of Paul's Letter to Philemon: A Rhetorical-Psychological Interpretation," in *Philemon in Perspective: Interpreting a Pauline Letter* (ed. D. Francois Tolmie; BZNW 169; New York/Berlin: de Gruyter, 2011), 65 – 66.

68. Stanley E. Porter, "Is Critical Discourse Analysis Critical? An Evaluation Using Philemon as a Test Case," in *Discourse Analysis and the New Testament: Approaches and Results* (ed. Stanley E. Porter and Jeffrey T. Reed; JSNTSup 170; Sheffield: Sheffield Academic, 1999), 63.

Outline

As with Colossians, this letter has also been read as an example of deliberative rhetoric.[69] This classification does not, however, control the way Paul develops his arguments.[70] A detailed discussion of the development of Paul's argument will be provided at the beginning of our discussion of its various sections. Here a general outline will suffice:

I. Opening Greetings (vv. 1 – 3)
II. Faith and Love (vv. 4 – 7)
    A. Thanksgiving (vv. 4 – 5)
    B. Intercession (vv. 6 – 7)
III. Requests concerning Onesimus (vv. 8 – 20)
    A. Appeals from the Relationship between Paul and Onesimus (vv. 8 – 16)
    B. Instructions from the Relationship between Paul and Philemon (vv. 17 – 20)
IV. Final Greetings (vv. 21 – 25)
    A. Further Instructions (vv. 21 – 22)
    B. Greetings from Paul's Coworkers (vv. 23 – 24)
    C. Benediction (v. 25)

---

69. Cf. Martin, "The Rhetorical Function of Commercial Language," 321 – 37.

70. For the limitations of applying models found in ancient rhetorical handbooks to Paul's letters, see the Introduction to Colossians.

Select Bibliography on Philemon

(In addition to works listed in the Colossian bibliography)

Aasgaard, R. *"My Beloved Brothers and Sisters!"*: *Christian Siblingship in Paul.* JSNTSup 265. London: T&T Clark, 2004.

Allen, David L. "The Discourse Structure of Philemon: A Study in Textlinguistics." Pages 77–96 in *Scribes and Scripture: New Testament Essays in Honor of J. Harold Greenlee.* Ed. David Alan Black. Winona Lake, IN: Eisenbrauns, 1992.

Arzt-Grabner, Peter. *Philemon.* Papyrologische Kommentare zum Neuen Testament. Göttingen: Vandenhoeck & Ruprecht, 2003.

Barclay, J. M. G. "Paul, Philemon and the Dilemma of Christian Slave Ownership." *NTS* 37 (1991): 161–86.

Bartchy, S. Scott. *First-Century Slavery and 1 Corinthians 7:21.* SBLDS 11. Atlanta: Scholars, 1973.

Barth, Markus, and Helmut Blanke. *The Letter to Philemon.* ECC. Grand Rapids: Eerdmans, 2000.

Barton, S. C. "Paul and Philemon: A Correspondence Continued." *Theology* 90 (1987): 97–101.

Bieberstein, Sabine. "Disrupting the Normal Reality of Slavery: A Feminist Reading of the Letter to Philemon." *JSNT* 79 (2000): 105–16.

Burtchaell, James Tunstead. *Philemon's Problem: A Theology of Grace.* Grand Rapids: Eerdmans, 1998.

Callahan, A. D. *Embassy of Onesimus: The Letter of Paul to Philemon.* Valley Forge, PA: Trinity International, 1997.

Chapman, Mark D. "The Shortest Book in the Bible." *ExpTim* 118 (2007): 546–48.

Church, F. Forrester. "Rhetorical Structure and Design in Paul's Letter to Philemon." *HTR* 71 (1978): 17–33.

Clarke, Andrew D. "'Refresh the Hearts of the Saints': A Unique Pauline Context." *TynBul* 47 (1996): 277–300.

Cousar, Charles B. *Philippians and Philemon: A Commentary.* NTL. Louisville: Westminster John Knox, 2009.

Daube, David. "Onesimos." Pages 40–43 in *Christians among Jews and Gentiles: Essays in Honor of Krister Stendahl on His Sixty-fifth Birthday.* Ed. George W. E. Nickelsburg and George W. MacRae. Philadelphia: Fortress, 1986.

Derrett, J. Duncan M. "The Function of the Epistle to Philemon." *ZNW* 79 (1988): 63–91.

De Vos, Craig S. "Once a Slave, Always a Slave? Slavery, Manumission and Relational Patterns in Paul's Letter to Philemon." *JSNT* 82 (2001): 89–105.

Du Plessis, Isak J. "How Christians Can Survive in a Hostile Social-Economic Environment: Paul's Mind concerning Difficult Social Conditions in the Letter to Philemon." Pages 387–413 in *Identity, Ethics, and Ethos in the New Testament.*

Ed. Jan G. van der Watt. BZNW 141. Berlin/New York: de Gruyter, 2006.

Elliott, Neil. *Liberating Paul: The Justice of God and the Politics of the Apostle*. Maryknoll, NY: Orbis, 1994.

Fitzmyer, Joseph. *The Letter to Philemon: A New Translation with Introduction and Commentary*. AB 34C. New York: Doubleday, 2000.

Frilingos, Chris. "'For My Child, Onesimus': Paul and Domestic Power in Philemon." *JBL* 119 (2000): 91 – 104.

Getty, Mary Ann. "The Theology of Philemon." *SBLSP* 26 (1987): 503 – 8.

Glancy, Jennifer A. *Slavery in Early Christianity*. New York: Oxford University Press, 2002.

Harrill, J. A. "Paul and Slavery." Pages 575 – 607 in *Paul in the Greco-Roman World: A Handbook*. Ed. J. Paul Sampley. Harrisburg, PA: Trinity International, 2003.

———. *The Manumission of Slaves in Early Christianity*. Tübingen: Mohr Siebeck, 1998.

Harris, Murray J. *Slave of Christ: A New Testament Metaphor for Total Devotion to Christ*. NSBT 8. Downers Grove, IL: InterVarsity Press, 1999.

Haykin, Michael A. G. "Praying Together: A Note on Philemon 22." *EvQ* 66 (1994): 331 – 35.

Hays, Richard. "Crucified With Christ: A Synthesis of the Theology of 1 and 2 Thessalonians, Philemon, Philippians, and Galatians." Pages 227 – 46 in *Pauline Theology,* vol. 1: *Thessalonians, Philippians, Galatians, Philemon*. Ed. Jouette M. Bassler. Minneapolis: Fortress, 1991.

Heil, John Paul. "The Chiastic Structure and Meaning of Paul's Letter to Philemon." *Bib* 82 (2001): 178 – 206.

Hock, Ronald F. "A Support for His Old Age: Paul's Plea on Behalf of Onesimus." Pages 67 – 81 in *The Social World of the First Christians: Essays in Honor of Wayne A. Meeks*. Ed. L. Michael White and O. Larry Yarbrough. Minneapolis: Fortress, 1995.

Kea, Perry V. "Paul's Letter to Philemon: A Short Analysis of Its Values." *PRSt* 23 (1996): 223 – 32.

Kumitz, Christopher. *Der Brief als Medium der ἀγάπη: Eine Untersuchung zur rhetorischen und epistolographischen Gestalt des Philemonbriefes*. Europäische Hochschulschriften 23.787. Frankfurt: Peter Lang, 2004.

Lampe, Peter. "Keine 'Sklavenflucht' des Onesimus." *ZNW* 76 (1985): 135 – 37.

Lyons, Kirk D., Sr. "Paul's Confrontation with Class: The Letter to Philemon as Counter-Hegemonic Discourse." *Cross Currents* 56 (2006): 116 – 32.

Marshall, I. Howard. "The Theology of Philemon." Pages 177 – 91 in *The Theology of the Shorter Pauline Letters*. Ed. Karl P. Donfried and I. Howard Marshall. Cambridge: Cambridge University Press, 1993.

Martens, John W. "Ignatius and Onesimus: John Knox Reconsidered." *Second Century* 9 (1992): 73 – 86.

Martin, Dale. *Slavery as Salvation: The Metaphor of Slavery in Pauline Christianity*. New Haven, CT: Yale University Press, 1990.

Mitchell, Margaret M. "John Chrysostom on Philemon: A Second Look." *HTR* 88 (1995): 135 – 48.

Mullins, Terence Y. "The Thanksgivings of Philemon and Colossians." *NTS* 30 (1984): 288 – 93.

Nordling, J. G. "Onesimus Fugitivus: A Defense of the Runaway Slave Hypothesis in Philemon." *JSNT* 41 (1991): 97 – 119.

Olson, Stanley N. "Pauline Expressions of Confidence in His Addressees." *CBQ* 47 (1985): 282 – 95.

Osiek, Carolyn. *Philippians, Philemon*. ANTC. Nashville: Abingdon, 2000.

Pearson, Brook W. R. "Assumptions in the Criticism and Translation of Philemon." Pages 253 – 80 in *Translating the Bible: Problems and Prospect*. Ed. Stanley E. Porter and Richard S. Hess. JSNTSup 173. Sheffield: Sheffield Academic, 1999.

Petersen, Norman R. *Rediscovering Paul: Philemon and the Sociology of Paul's Narrative World.* Philadelphia: Fortress, 1985.

Polaski, S. H. *Paul and the Discourse of Power.* Biblical Seminar 62. Sheffield: Sheffield Academic, 1999.

Porter, Stanley E. "Is Critical Discourse Analysis Critical? An Evaluation Using Philemon as a Test Case." Pages 47 – 70 in *Discourse Analysis and the New Testament: Approaches and Results.* Ed. Stanley E. Porter and Jeffrey T. Reed. JSNTSup 170. Sheffield: Sheffield Academic, 1999.

Rapske, Brian M. "The Prisoner Paul in the Eyes of Onesimus." *NTS* 37 (1991): 187 – 203.

Russell, David M. "The Strategy of a First-Century Appeals Letter: A Discourse Reading of Paul's Epistle to Philemon." *JOTT* 11 (1998): 1 – 25.

Ryan, Judith M. "Philemon." Pages 167 – 261 in *Philippians and Philemon.* SP 10. Minneapolis: Liturgical, 2003.

Sanders, Laura L. "Equality and a Request for the Manumission of Onesimus." *ResQ* 46 (2004): 109 – 14.

Schenk, Wolfgang. "Der Brief des Paulus an Philemon in der neueren Forschung." *ANRW* II.25.4 (1987): 3439 – 95.

Shyman, A. H. "A Semantic Discourse Analysis of the Letter to Philemon." Pages 83 – 99 in *Text and Interpretation: New Approaches in the Criticism of the New Testament.* Ed. P. J. Hartin and J. H. Petzer. Leiden: Brill, 1991.

Soards, Marion L. "Some Neglected Theological Dimensions of Paul's Letter to Philemon." *PRSt* 17 (1990): 209 – 19.

Steele, Donald M. "Releasing the Captives — Release the Captors: The Letter to Philemon and the Relationship of North American Christians and the Peoples of the Two-Thirds World." PhD diss., Graduate Theological Union, 1994.

Still, Todd D. "Philemon among the Letters of Paul: Theological and Canonical Considerations." *ResQ* 47 (2005): 133 – 42.

Stuhlmacher, Peter. *Der Brief an Philemon.* 4th ed. EKKNT 18. Neukirchen-Vluyn: Neukirchener and Düsseldorf: Benziger, 2004.

Taylor, N. H. "Onesimus: A Case Study of Slave Conversion in Early Christianity." *R&T* 3 (1996): 259 – 81.

Tolmie, D. Francois, ed. *Philemon in Perspective: Interpreting a Pauline Letter.* BZNW 169. New York/Berlin: de Gruyter, 2011.

Urbainczyk, Theresa. *Slave Revolts in Antiquity.* Berkeley and Los Angeles: University of California Press, 2008.

Vanhoozer, Kevin J. "Imprisoned or Free? Text, Status, and Theological Interpretation in the Master/Slave Discourse of Philemon." Pages 51 – 94 in *Reading Scripture with the Church: Toward a Hermeneutic for Theological Interpretation.* Ed. A. K. M. Adam et al. Grand Rapids: Baker, 2006.

Wansink, Craig S. *Chained in Christ: The Experience and Rhetoric of Paul's Imprisonments.* JSNTSup 130. Sheffield: Sheffield Academic, 1996.

Wilson, Andrew. "The Pragmatics of Politeness and Pauline Epistolography: A Case Study of the Letter to Philemon." *JSNT* 48 (1992): 107 – 19.

Winter, Sara B. C. "Methodological Observations on a New Interpretation of Paul's Letter to Philemon." *USQR* 39 (1984): 203 – 12.

———. "Paul's Letter to Philemon." *NTS* 33 (1987): 1 – 15.

———. "Philemon." Pages 301 – 12 in *Searching the Scriptures: A Feminist Commentary, II.* Ed. Elisabeth Schüssler Fiorenza. New York: Crossroad, 1994.

Witherington, Ben, III. "Was Paul a Pro-Slavery Chauvinist? Making Sense of Paul's Seemingly Mixed Moral Messages." *BR* 20:2 (2004): 8, 44.

Wright, N. T. "Putting Paul Together Again: Toward a Synthesis of Pauline Theology (1 and 2 Thessalonians, Philippians, and Philemon)." Pages 183–211 in *Pauline Theology*, vol. 1: *Thessalonians, Philippians, Galatians, Philemon*. Ed. Jouette M. Bassler. Minneapolis: Fortress, 1991.

Zelnick-Abramovitz, R. *Not Wholly Free: The Concept of Manumission and the Status of Manumitted Slaves in the Ancient Greek World*. Mnemosyne Supplementa 266. Leiden/Boston: Brill, 2005.

Philemon 1 – 7

Literary Context

As in Colossians, Paul begins by identifying the letter's coauthor and recipients and offering a brief greeting (vv. 1 – 3). Unlike Colossians, however, Paul identifies himself here as a "prisoner" (v. 1), a title that carries significant rhetorical force in this letter. Moreover, the lengthy list of recipients with their titles (vv. 1 – 2) points to the ecclesiological significance and perhaps public nature of this letter.

The opening section consists of a thanksgiving section (vv. 4 – 5) and a prayer report (vv. 6 – 7). Both focus on the outworking of Philemon's faith in his labor of love for the community of God's people. This relationship between faith and love has already appeared in Col 1:4, where Paul speaks of the Colossians' "faith in Christ Jesus" that is expressed in their "love … for all the saints."[1] Here the relationship between "faith" and "love" appears in both the thanksgiving section and the prayer report. Through thanksgiving, Paul highlights the past acts of faith in the expression of love on Philemon's part (v. 5). In the prayer report, Paul encourages Philemon to continue his walk in faith and love as he did in the past (vv. 6 – 7). This again testifies to Paul's concern for his reader's[2] relationship with God and other believers, rather than simply his own personal relationship with him.[3]

The themes of "faith" and "love" emphasized in this introductory section point to the central concerns of this letter. In rhetorical terms, the notes on Philemon's past achievement prepare him for a favorable reception of the message that follows (cf. Quintilian, *Inst.* 4.1.5). The focus on these two virtues also allows Paul to point to the honorable path that Philemon is encouraged to follow (cf. ibid., 3.8.1). He urges Philemon to live out his "faith" for the Lord in his "love" expressed for Onesimus, and

---

1. See comments on Col 1:4 for the conjunction "and" (καί) as epexegetical.

2. Although this letter is addressed to a number of coworkers within the same house church, the primary intended recipient is Philemon (note the singular "your," σου, in vv. 2, 4, 5, 6, 7).

3. For a discussion of how this focus transforms that of the opening formula found in Hellenistic papyri letters, see comments on Col 1:1 – 8.

probably also for other saints, as Onesimus is to be allowed to serve as a "brother" in the household of God (cf. vv. 9).[4]

Other significant themes and vocabularies from this introductory paragraph occur in the rest of this letter: "participation/partner" (κοινωνία/κοινωνός, vv. 6, 17), "heart" (σπλάγχνα, vv. 7, 12, 20), and "brother" (ἀδελφός, vv. 1, 7, 16, 20). These terms not only provide the link between the introductory paragraph and the body of this letter, but they also point to the significant basis on which Paul's argument rests and underline Paul's personal and emotional involvement in this letter.

➡ **I. Opening Greetings (vv. 1 – 3)**
 II. Faith and Love (vv. 4 – 7)
  A. Thanksgiving (vv. 4 – 5)
  B. Intercession (vv. 6 – 7)
 III. Requests concerning Onesimus (vv. 8 – 20)

Main Idea

After opening greetings that underline the ecclesiological setting of this letter, Paul thanks God for the outworking of Philemon's faith in his labor of love. His faith and love become the focus of Paul's prayer as he encourages Philemon to continue this good work in Christ.

Translation

(See next page.)

Structure

Paul begins this letter with the self-identification as a "prisoner of Christ" (v. 1b), a title that contributes to the rhetorical force of Paul's plea and arguments that follow. With Timothy (v. 1c-d), Paul addresses this letter to Philemon, Apphia, Archippus, and the church that meets in Philemon's house (vv. 1e – 2). This list of names points to the ecclesiological significance of this letter; this is confirmed by the appellations attached to each of these names. The opening greeting concludes with the familiar Pauline salutation of "grace" and "peace" (v. 3).

---

4. For Winter, "Paul's Letter to Philemon," 3, the absence of the themes of "grace" and "forgiveness" in this introductory paragraph argues against a runaway slave hypothesis, for introductory paragraphs usually introduced major themes of a letter. However, the emphasis on "love" certainly includes these themes.

Philemon 1 – 7

1a	Greeting	Paul,
b	apposition	a prisoner of Christ Jesus, and
c	parallel	Timothy,
d	apposition	our brother,
e	recipient	to Philemon,
f	apposition	our beloved and
g	apposition	coworker,
2a	list	to Apphia,
b	apposition	our sister,
c	list	to Archippus,
d	apposition	our fellow soldier, and
e	list	to the church in your house:
3	desire	Grace to you and peace from God our Father and the Lord Jesus Christ.
4a	**Assertion**	**I give thanks to my God always**
b	time	when I remember you in my prayers,
5a	basis	because I hear of your love and
b	parallel	love and
		faith [a] [b]
c	identification	in the Lord Jesus and
d	identification	for all the saints. [b'] [a']
6a	content (of 4b)	so that your partnership in the faith may become effective
b	sphere	in gaining the knowledge of every good thing
c	identification	that is in us for Christ.
7a	expansion (of 5a)	I have received much joy and comfort from your love,
b	cause	because the hearts of the saints have been refreshed through you, brother.

The paragraph that follows consists of a prayer report that proceeds from thanksgiving (vv. 4 – 5) to intercession (vv. 6 – 7), both of which center on faith and love. Paul begins by thanking God because of Philemon's faith in the Lord Jesus that is expressed in "love … for all the saints." In the Greek, this inextricable relationship between faith and love is expressed through a chiastic structure in v. 5, where faith toward the Lord Jesus is enveloped by the love for all the saints.[5] This chiastic structure also highlights the fundamental basis of faith that prompts particular expressions of love.

Grammatically, v. 6 ("so that your partnership in the faith may become effective") can be taken as the purpose clause of v. 4 ("I remember you in my prayers"), although it can also be the content of an implied verb "I pray." The thanksgiving in v. 5 serves as the basis for the center of Paul's prayer that follows.[6] Paul's intercession builds on this thanksgiving as he expands on the themes of faith (v. 6) and love (v. 7). The purpose of that intercession is that the partnership built on faith might allow Philemon to experience the full knowledge of every good thing that can be found in Christ. The confidence of this intercession rests on Paul's experience of the effects of Philemon's love, which has refreshed the hearts of many. This rather cumbersome construction allows Paul to focus again on the relationship between faith and love while pointing to the implicit request that Philemon's refreshment of the hearts of others can continue to refresh Paul's own heart (cf. v. 20).

Exegetical Outline

→ **I. Opening Greetings (vv. 1 – 3)**

    A. Identification of the sender and the cosender (v. 1a-d)

    B. Identification of the recipients (vv. 1e – 2)

    C. Salutation (v. 3)

II. Faith and Love (vv. 4 – 7)

    A. Thanksgiving (vv. 4 – 5)

       1. Occasion for the prayer (v. 4)

       2. Faith in Christ and love for all (v. 5)

    B. Intercession (vv. 6 – 7)

       1. So that Philemon's faith may be deepened (v. 6)

       2. Based on his love , which has refreshed the hearts of many (v. 7)

---

5. See comments on v. 5.

6. See the structure proposed by David L. Allen, "The Discourse Structure of Philemon: A Study in Textlinguistics," in *Scribes and Scripture: New Testament Essays in Honor of J. Har-* *old Greenlee* (ed. David Alan Black; Winona Lake, IN: Eisenbrauns, 1992), 85: introduction (vv. 4 – 5), text (v. 6), reason (v. 7).

Explanation of the Text

1a-d Paul, a prisoner of Christ Jesus, and Timothy, our brother (Παῦλος δέσμιος Χριστοῦ Ἰησοῦ καὶ Τιμόθεος ὁ ἀδελφός). Paul begins by identifying the author (and coauthor) and recipients of this letter. In Colossians, a letter likely written in the same time period to Christians in the same locale, Paul identifies himself as "an apostle of Christ Jesus" (Col 1:1); here, however, he chooses the self-identification "a prisoner of Christ Jesus."

Some have suggested that this shift points to the personal nature of this letter,[7] but the title "apostle" also appears in the opening greetings of Paul's personal letters to Timothy (1 Tim 1:1; 2 Tim 1:1) and Titus (Titus 1:1). Moreover, "a prisoner of Christ" also appears in Paul's letter to the Ephesians (Eph 3:1). Others have suggested, therefore, that Paul's self-identification as "a prisoner of Christ Jesus" simply reflects the reality of his own incarceration (cf. 2 Tim 1:8).[8] But this does not sufficiently explain the absence of this self-identification in other prison letters, where his imprisonment is repeatedly noted without the use of this title (cf. Phil 1:7, 13, 14, 17; Col 4:3, 18).

The reappearance of this appellation in v. 9, together with numerous references to his imprisonment (cf. vv. 10, 13, 23), suggests that it possesses a significant rhetorical force in this letter. Perhaps Paul considers this title as "a designation which would touch his friend's heart,"[9] but in light of v. 13, where Paul apparently considers his imprisonment

for the sake of the gospel ministry an honor, evoking sympathy does not exhaust its force. It is more likely that Paul is demanding Philemon to follow his example in obeying the call of the gospel ministry. As Paul submits to God's will in fulfilling his call, Philemon is also called to obey what the gospel demands (as implied by Paul's appeal in the body of this letter).[10]

The genitive qualifier "of Christ Jesus" is equally important. It can carry the sense of "because of the preaching of the gospel of Christ Jesus,"[11] "for the sake of Christ Jesus" (GNB),[12] "belonging to Christ Jesus,"[13] and "being totally dedicated to the authority of Christ."[14] In this case, a multidimensional force of this qualifier should be assumed.

As in Col 1:1, Paul mentions "Timothy our brother" as a cosender of this letter. As his name also appears in another prison letter (Phil 1:1), his presence with Paul during his imprisonment may explain his presence in these letters. He may have also been a secretary who assisted Paul in writing this letter. His presence also encourages readers to recognize that this is not simply a private, personal letter but one written by an apostle together with his coworker, who together address a matter that concerns the church and the wider gospel ministry.

As to the rhetorical force of the presence of Timothy's name, this may again represent "a linguistic move of power on Paul's part"[15] as he evokes the endorsement of another Christian leader in

---

7. See, e.g., Moo, *Letters to the Colossians and to Philemon*, 379.

8. Murray J. Harris, *Slave of Christ: A New Testament Metaphor for Total Devotion to Christ* (NSBT 8; Downers Grove, IL: InterVarsity Press, 1999), 117 – 18.

9. Lightfoot, *St. Paul's Epistles to the Colossians and to Philemon*, 333.

10. It is also possible that "the prisoner" can carry a sense of authority, as it does elsewhere in Paul's writings (cf. Eph 3:1; 4:1; 2 Tim 1:8).

11. NTL: "Paul, a prisoner for preaching the Good News about Christ Jesus."

12. Wansink, *Chained in Christ*, 171.

13. Cf. Harris, *Slave of Christ*, 118.

14. Cf. John Paul Heil, "The Chiastic Structure and Meaning of Paul's Letter to Philemon," *Bib* 82 (2001): 189.

15. Stanley E. Porter, "Is Critical Discourse Analysis Critical?" 58.

pressuring Philemon to provide a favorable response to his request(s). Moreover, the title "our brother" may also pave the way for Paul to remind Philemon of the reality within the household of God in which believers are to be related to one another as siblings under the lordship of Christ (cf. v. 16).

1e-g To Philemon, our beloved and coworker (Φιλήμονι τῷ ἀγαπητῷ καὶ συνεργῷ ἡμῶν). The appearance of "Philemon"[16] as first among the listed recipients makes it obvious that he is the primary intended recipient.[17] If this letter is addressed to the entire household church, Philemon naturally is the head of the household. Philemon is probably a person of means: he is one that hosts a church in his house (v. 2), who is a patron to others (vv. 5 – 7), and who is able to entertain his guests (v. 22).[18]

The adjective "beloved" (τῷ ἀγαπητῷ) has often been translated as "dear friend" (NRSV, NET, TNIV, HCSB, NIV; cf. GNB), but in this context it is not simply a term of endearment that highlights the ties between the circle around Paul and Philemon. The subject of this act of love could be God (Rom 1:7; 11:28; Eph 5:1) or Paul himself (Rom 16:9; 1 Cor 4:14; Col 4:7, 9, 14); it is probably both.[19] More importantly, this title also paves the way for the emphasis on love that follows (vv. 5, 7, 9). As Philemon is the object of love, he must also continue to act as an agent of such love.

The title "coworker" (συνεργῷ) is also significant in Paul's rhetorical strategy. This title points to Philemon's participation in their common ministry.[20] As they serve God together, Paul urges Philemon to recognize this identity and to continue to participate as his "partner" (v. 17) in fulfilling his request concerning the reception and treatment of Onesimus.

2 To Apphia, our sister, to Archippus, our fellow soldier, and to the church in your house (καὶ Ἀπφίᾳ τῇ ἀδελφῇ καὶ Ἀρχίππῳ τῷ συστρατιώτῃ ἡμῶν καὶ τῇ κατ᾽ οἶκόν σου ἐκκλησίᾳ). Paul here expands the circle of this letter's recipients. The presence of this list of names demands an explanation. The well-known but rightly rejected theory of John Knox considers "Archippus" as the primary recipient of this letter and the master of Onesimus.[21] But most commentators rightly consider Philemon as the proper antecedent for "your" (σου) and, as the first of the list, the primary recipient of this letter. Some translations make this explicit by moving the phrase "the church in your house" earlier in the verse.[22]

As to the identity of these individuals, many follow early Christian interpretation in identifying "Apphia" as Philemon's wife and "Archippus" as their son.[23] While the household setting may point to the possibility of a family relationship among these three persons, the way they are introduced

---

16. This was a common name in the first century; cf. G. H. R. Horsley, "Philemon," *NewDocs* 3:91.

17. Note the shift to the singular second person pronoun (σου) in vv. 2, 4, 5, 6, 7.

18. Thus Wayne A. Meeks, *The First Urban Christians: The Social World of the Apostle Paul* (2nd ed.; New Haven, CT: Yale Univ. Press, 2003), 59 – 60, who concludes that "Philemon himself ranks high at least on the dimension of wealth and on evaluation within the sect."

19. It can also point to Philemon as someone loved by many other Christians; cf. Aasgaard, *"My Beloved Brothers and Sisters,"* 244.

20. Andrew D. Clarke, *A Pauline Theology of Church Lead-*

ership (LNTS 362; New York/London: T&T Clark, 2008), 208, has rightly noted that this title points primarily to a unity of purpose rather than equality (see comments on Col 4:11).

21. This reading is based on the close proximity between the singular "your" (σου) and the name Archippus (Knox, *Philemon among the Letters of Paul*, 49 – 61).

22. See CEV, GNB; note how the NIV uses dashes to bracket the words, "also to Apphia our sister, to Archippus our fellow soldier."

23. Cf. Lightfoot, *St. Paul's Epistles to the Colossians and to Philemon*, 333; Lohse, *Colossians and Philemon*, 190; O'Brien, *Colossians, Philemon*, 273; R. McL. Wilson, *Colossians and Philemon* (ICC; Edinburgh: T&T Clark, 2005), 334.

focuses on their own standing within the church. "Our sister" (τῇ ἀδελφῇ … ἡμῶν) should be considered a title comparable to "our brother" as applied to Timothy in v. 1 and thus highlights her independent standing as a Christian and possibly as a leader of the church.[24] The fact that she is specifically mentioned may even point to her status as a patron of this Christian community (cf. Rom 16:1).

A different title is applied to "Archippus": "our fellow soldier" (τῷ συστρατιώτῃ ἡμῶν). In Phil 2:25, this title is used with the title "coworker" in describing Epaphroditus.[25] In this context, therefore, "fellow soldier" highlights Archippus's involvement in the work of the ministry. If this Archippus is the same as the Archippus of Col 4:17 ("And say to Archippus, 'See to it that you complete the ministry you have received in the Lord' "), he would be a leader of the church. Moreover, the presence of the singular pronoun ("your house," οἶκόν σου) may argue against seeing Philemon, Apphia, and Archippus as family members, since one would have expected a plural pronoun as is found in a similar opening greeting in a papyrus letter: "Apollonios to Hippalos and Sarapion and Berenike and Pyrrhos and to all in *their* house, greetings" (P.Lond. I 33b [161 BC]).[26]

The significance of these names in a letter addressed primarily to Philemon should be noted. First, together with their titles they point to the public nature of this letter. Although this is no doubt a "personal" letter, it cannot be considered strictly a "private" letter since the relationship between Philemon and his slave Onesimus is one

that would affect the entire church.[27] This does not deny, however, the pivotal role of Philemon since he would be the one who has the power to decide whether to make the content of this letter known to others.[28]

As to the precise function of these other names, some have suggested that it is a matter of "courtesy,"[29] while others see them as enhancing the power of the requests embedded in this letter.[30] It is also probable that their presence points to the relevance of Paul's request and Philemon's response for the entire Christian community. This understanding may also at least partly explain the inclusion of this letter in the NT canon.

The phrase "to the church in your house" reconfirms the ecclesiological significance of this letter. The fact that congregations often met in a household context is noted in Col 4:15 (cf. Rom 16:3 – 5a). In the Greco-Roman context, household matters can be a concern addressed in a public "assembly" (ἐκκλησία).[31] While Paul may be following this practice, elsewhere he has noted the significance of household relationships for the entire Christian community.[32] Here, the relationship between Philemon and Onesimus is a concern for the entire church because it is built on the foundation of a gospel for which there is no distinction between "slave [or] free" (Col 3:11). Moreover, Paul explicitly expresses his wish to keep Onesimus in order to serve him in his imprisonment "for the gospel" (v. 13). These discussions are most appropriately discussed in an ecclesiological context.

24. Cf. Meeks, *First Urban Christians*, 60.

25. The use of this military imagery in these prison letters may be explained by the presence of soldiers in the prison environment; Wansink, *Chained in Christ*, 170.

26. Hans-Josef Klauck, *Ancient Letters and the New Testament: A Guide to Context and Exegesis* (trans. Daniel P. Bailey; Waco, TX: Baylor Univ. Press, 2006), 329.

27. See esp. U. Wickert, "Der Philemonbrief — Privatbrief oder apostolisches Schreiben?" *ZNW* 52 (1961): 230 – 38.

28. Artzt-Graber, *Philemon*, 111 – 15.

29. O'Brien, *Colossians, Philemon*, 273.

30. Petersen, *Rediscovering Paul*, 99.

31. Ronald F. Hock, "A Support for His Old Age: Paul's Plea on Behalf of Onesimus," in *The Social World of the First Christians: Essays in Honor of Wayne A. Meeks* (ed. L. Michael White and O. Larry Yarbrough; Minneapolis: Fortress, 1995), 77.

32. See discussion of Col 3:18 – 4:1.

**3 Grace to you and peace from God our Father
and the Lord Jesus Christ** (χάρις ὑμῖν καὶ εἰρήνη
ἀπὸ θεοῦ πατρὸς ἡμῶν καὶ κυρίου Ἰησοῦ Χριστοῦ).
As in other opening greetings in Paul's letters, this
section culminates in the salutation that evokes
the significant theological themes of "grace" and
"peace." This exact salutation can be found in
many of Paul's letters (Rom 1:7; 1 Cor 1:3; 2 Cor
1:2; Gal 1:3; Eph 1:2; Phil 1:2; 2 Thess 1:2). In Col
1:2, which shares the same historical and geographical context with Philemon, Paul omits the
final clause, "and the Lord Jesus Christ," probably
because he reserves the attention to the lordship
of Christ for the second main section of that letter
(Col 1:15 – 2:4).

"Grace" (χάρις) replaces the typical Greek
"greeting" (χαίρειν) while pointing to the salvific
act of God through Christ (e.g., Rom 3:24; 5:17),
and "peace" (εἰρήνη) points to the reconciliation
brought about by this climactic act of God (cf.
Rom 5:1; Eph 2:14 – 18; Col 3:15).[33] Though part
of Paul's typical opening formula, the concepts of
"grace" and "peace" form the foundation of his argument in this letter where human forgiveness and
reconciliation form the proper responses to divine
acts of grace. Moreover, the reappearance of "grace"
in the final benediction (v. 25) "places the totality
of the letter in the frame of the congregation's worship."[34] This may also explain the presence of the
plural pronoun here ("you," ὑμῖν) as it points to the
entire church that meets in Philemon's house.[35]

The mentioning of "God our Father" together
with "the Lord Jesus Christ" underscores the exalted status and identity of Christ. The label "our
Father" is particularly significant in this letter, as
Paul is insisting on a new frame of reference within
the household of God. While God is the "Father"
and Jesus is "the Lord," believers are to relate to
one another as "brothers" (v. 1) and "sisters" (cf.
v. 2). Philemon, being a "brother" (v. 7, 20), should
therefore treat even his own slave "no longer as a
slave, but more than a slave, as a beloved brother"
(v. 16).[36]

**4 I give thanks to my God always when I remem-
ber you in my prayers** (Εὐχαριστῶ τῷ θεῷ μου
πάντοτε μνείαν σου ποιούμενος ἐπὶ τῶν προσευχῶν
μου). Paul begins his typical thanksgiving section
here. According to Schubert, the thanksgiving section in Philemon is a perfect example of the first
type of Paul's thanksgiving formula, one that contains one or more participial constructions that follow and modify the principal verb "to give thanks"
(εὐχαριστῶ).[37] Subsequent studies have challenged
such a classification system because of the lack of
a broad sample pool.[38] Beyond formal characteristics, what is clear is that Paul situates his discourse
within a theological context that focuses on the
relationship between the readers and God. Significant themes are introduced in these thanksgiving
sections as Paul paves the way for his main argument in the letter body.

The singular verb, "I give thanks," makes it clear
that Paul is the one primarily responsible for writing this letter. He often uses this singular verb even
when his coworkers are mentioned in the opening greetings (cf. 1 Cor 1:1, 4; Phil 1:1, 3).[39] "My

---

33. For a typical Hellenistic salutation, see comments on
Col 1:2.

34. Barth and Blanke, *Letter to Philemon*, 265.

35. This second person plural pronoun appears only here
and in vv. 22, 25.

36. Within this frame of reference, it is striking for Paul
to call Onesimus his "child" (v. 10). Not only does this label
highlight the intimate relationship between Paul and Onesi-

mus, it also elevates Paul's own status as a "father," one who has
authority over Philemon.

37. Paul Schubert, *The Form and Function of the Pauline
Thanksgivings* (Berlin: Töpelmann, 1939), 13.

38. See comments on Col 1:3.

39. The clear exception can be found in Col 1:3, which emphasizes the universal impact of the gospel (cf. 1:6).

God" in the context of prayer uses the language of the psalms (cf. Pss 3:7; 5:2; 7:1, 3; 13:3; 18:2, 6, 21; 22:1, 2; 42:5, 11; 43:4 – 5; 71:22; 86:2; etc.) as Paul gives thanks to God. The adverb "always" is almost a constant feature in Paul's note on thanksgiving (Rom 1:8 – 10; 1 Cor 1:4; Phil 1:4; Col 1:3; 1 Thess 1:2 – 3; 2:13; 2 Thess 1:3; 2:13). Although some have considered this simply as a "part and parcel of the style of ancient letters,"[40] it is a theologically meaningful term for Paul.

The OT emphasis on the undivided act of worship provides a relevant background for Paul's emphasis here ("Love the LORD your God with all your heart and with all your soul and with all your strength," Deut 6:5.).[41] In Col 3:17, Paul also notes the need to worship God with one's entire being while acknowledging the lordship of Christ through acts of thanksgiving ("whatever you do in word or in deed, do everything in the name of the Lord Jesus, giving thanks to God the Father through him"). This reading is possible because for Paul, thanksgiving is not simply a matter of etiquette; it is a matter of worship.

The connection between acts of thanksgiving and remembrance in prayer points to a significant aspect of Paul's understanding of the proper acts of worship for God's people (cf. Eph 1:16; Phil 1:3; 1 Thess 1:2; 2 Tim 1:3). In secular Greek, the "remembering" word group was often used for acts of

thanksgiving.[42] In the OT, to give thanks to God is to remember his acts on behalf of his people: "I will perpetuate your memory through all generations; therefore the nations will praise you for ever and ever" (Ps 45:17). For God's people, the act of remembrance is also a covenantal act that reminds them of the need of a proper response to what God has done (cf. Deut 4:23 – 24; 2 Kgs 17:38 – 39; Isa 46:9).[43] By contrast, to ask God to "remember" his people in the act of prayer is to appeal to his continued faithfulness to his covenantal people (cf. Exod 2:24; 6:5; Lev 26:42 – 45; Deut 4:31; Pss 105:42; 106:45).

In the present context, "when I remember you" can be literally translated as "when I make remembrance of you."[44] If this is not simply a periphrastic way to express Paul's own remembrance of Philemon in his prayer, this can also mean either "when I ask God to remember you,"[45] or "when I ask him [i.e., Philemon] to remember you."[46] Perhaps both are intended here: Paul appeals to God to remember the faithfulness of his readers, and in turn these readers are to remember God with their own faithful acts.

5 Because I hear of your love for all the saints and your faith in the Lord Jesus (ἀκούων σου τὴν ἀγάπην καὶ τὴν πίστιν ἣν ἔχεις πρὸς τὸν κύριον Ἰησοῦν καὶ εἰς πάντας τοὺς ἁγίους).[47] The previous verse linked giving thanks and praying; this verse

---

40. Peter T. O'Brien, *Introductory Thanksgivings in the Letters of Paul* (NovTSup 49; Leiden: Brill, 1977), 21.

41. Cf. Roger D. Aus, "The Liturgical Background of the Necessity and Propriety of Giving Thanks According to 2 Thess 1:3," *JBL* 46 (1973): 436.

42. See Hendrik S. Versnel, "Religious Mentality in Ancient Prayer," in *Faith, Hope and Worship: Aspects of Religious Mentality in the Ancient World* (ed. H. S. Versnel; Leiden: Brill, 1981), 59.

43. See Brevard S. Childs, *Memory and Tradition in Israel* (London: SCM, 1962).

44. "When I remember you in my prayers" (μνείαν σου ποιούμενος ἐπὶ τῶν προσευχῶν μου) has also been translated

more literally as "making mention of you in my prayers" (NASB; cf. BDAG, 654; Moule, *Epistles to the Colossians and to Philemon*, 140 – 41). In light of the wider connection between "thanksgiving" and "remembering" in the OT tradition, however, the act of remembering should be reflected in the translation.

45. Moo, *Letters to the Colossians and to Philemon*, 386.

46. Barth and Blanke, *Letter to Philemon*, 269.

47. This translation deviates from that presented in the diagrammed sentence flow. In the sentence flow, the chiastic structure is indicated while the word order in Greek is followed. Here, the translation expresses the meaning intended through such chiastic structure (see comments below).

provides the basis of Paul's thanksgiving, while the next points to the purpose of his prayer. Thus, the participle that introduces this verse should be taken as a causal participle ("because I hear," ἀκούων).[48] The use of this verb of hearing and the comments that follow point to the reception of a report concerning the love and faith of Philemon.

Paul does not specify through whom he has received such information. For those who consider Onesimus as an estranged runaway slave with nothing positive to report to Paul, this report must have been given by another person from the church of Colossae — possibly Epaphras (see v. 23).[49] It is puzzling, however, to find "Epaphras" missing in this context, since he appears in the comparable context in Col 1:8. For those who consider the separation between Onesimus and Philemon taking place in a more amiable context, Onesimus could be the bearer of this positive report.[50] To imply that Onesimus is the one who has provided such reports may further prepare Paul's argument that Philemon should be consistent with what his slave has already observed. The absence of Onesimus's name can be explained by a literary strategy that allows for an increase in narrative tension that prepares for the introduction of his name in v. 10, the only verse that explicitly names Onesimus.

Following the word order in Greek, the verse literally reads: "because I hear of your love and of the faith which you have toward the Lord Jesus and toward all the saints" (NASB; cf. NAB; NJB; NKJV; REB; HCSB; ESV). Some consider this grouping of two nouns followed by two prepositional phrases an "ugly duplication."[51] For those who consider the two nouns as a group with two prepositional phrases modifying both nouns, the word "faith" would mean "faithfulness."[52] Proponents of this reading see "no reason why Paul should not have thought of both love and faith as the sum of the Christian lifestyle and therefore of both as related to both 'the Lord Jesus' and 'all the saints.' "[53]

Several scholars have, however, detected a chiastic structure here:[54]

> a Love
>   b faith
>   b´ in the Lord Jesus
> a´ for all the saints

With this construction, "in the Lord Jesus" (πρὸς τὸν κύριον Ἰησοῦν) modifies "faith" (τὴν πίστιν), while "for all the saints" (εἰς πάντας τοὺς ἁγίους)[55] modifies "love" (τὴν ἀγάπην): "because I hear about your love for all his holy people and your faith in the Lord Jesus" (NIV; cf. NRSV, GNB, TNIV).[56] This reading is preferable for a number of reasons. First, this chiastic structure explains the existence of the two prepositional phrases in successive order and maintains the usual Pauline use of the term πίστις in the sense of "trust" or "faith." Moreover,

---

48. The present tense can be taken as indicating a continuous act: "because I keep hearing" (NLT).

49. Lightfoot, *St. Paul's Epistles to the Colossians and to Philemon*, 334; Barth and Blanke, *Letter to Philemon*, 271.

50. Winter, "Paul's Letter to Philemon," 3.

51. Barth and Blanke, *Letter to Philemon*, 271.

52. Cf. F. F. Bruce, "St Paul in Rome. 2. The Epistle to Philemon," *BJRL* 48 (1965): 81.

53. Dunn, *Epistles to the Colossians and to Philemon*, 317. See also 1 Thess 1:3, where both "faith" and "love" are directed to and rooted in "Christ Jesus."

54. Lohse, *Colossians and Philemon*, 193; Stuhlmacher, *Der Brief an Philemon*, 31 – 32; O'Brien, *Colossians, Philemon*, 278;

Judith M. Ryan, "Philemon," in *Philippians and Philemon* (SP 10; Minneapolis: Liturgical, 2003), 223.

55. For the meaning of this phrase, see comments on Col 1:4. But the emphatic "all" acquires a different function in this context. While the universal impact of the gospel is the focus of Colossians as Paul combats the elitist practices imposed by the false teachers, in this context, "all" allows Paul to insist that Philemon should be consistent in expressing this Christian love toward all, including his own household slave.

56. Other versions that adopt a chiastic reading list faith first: "because I heard about your faith in the Lord Jesus and your love for all God's holy people" (cf. CEV; NLT; NET).

the Ephesian parallel with a simpler structure in Greek confirms this reading: "For this reason, ever since I heard about your faith in the Lord Jesus and your love for all God's people" (Eph 1:15).

The Colossian parallel not only provides the same two-part structure ("because we have heard of your faith in Christ Jesus and the love that you have for all the saints," Col 1:4), but the relationship between "love" and "faith" there helps illuminate the relationship between the two here. In Colossians, the conjunction "and" (καί) is probably epexegetical: "because we have heard of your faith in Christ Jesus, a faith that is expressed in the love that you have for all the saints." This is supported by the reappearance of only "love" at the end of that thanksgiving section (Col 1:8).

In Philemon, "love" is likewise the focus of Paul's discussion, as this paves the way for his appeal for Philemon to continue to express this "love" for the saints (v. 7). This appeal is explicitly linked with the fate of Onesimus in v. 9 as Paul urges Philemon to be consistent in his Christian behavior. As in Colossians, among the pair of "faith" and "love," it is "love" that reappears beyond this thanksgiving section. For both letters, however, "faith" that centers on Christ is the critical basis for an appeal to "love." This relationship is best expressed in Gal 5:6: "faith expressing itself through love" (cf. Eph 3:17).

If the letter to the Colossians can serve as a framework for reading this verse, the absence of "hope" here — it appears in Col 1:5 and elsewhere in the familiar triad of faith, love, and hope (cf. Rom 5:1–5; 1 Cor 13:13; 1 Thess 1:3; 5:8) — demands an explanation. Again, the emphasis on "love" may provide a partial explanation of its absence.[57] Moreover, it is the present reality of the impact of the gospel of Jesus Christ that lies at the center of Paul's concern here (vv. 16, 20).

6a So that your partnership in the faith may become effective (ὅπως ἡ κοινωνία τῆς πίστεώς σου ἐνεργὴς γένηται). Anticipating his requests, Paul appeals to Philemon's partnership with him and his other coworkers in the gospel ministry. Often considered to be "the most obscure verse in this letter,"[58] this part of Paul's thanksgiving section provides various possible readings. These readings are the result of various possible syntactical connections between elements within this verse as well as the semantic possibilities for a number of its key terms. Before examining the content of this verse, its relationship with the previous verses must be discussed.

Some take the conjunction "so that" (ὅπως) as indicating the result of the immediately preceding semantic unit, thus: "you have love … and faith … so that your partnership…." But this construction fails to make sense here. Most commentators, therefore, consider this clause as expressing the content of the prayer noted in v. 4 ("I remember you in my prayers … so that your partnership …"). To make this connection explicit, some have chosen to insert additional words before this clause, thus: "I pray that …" (NRSV, CEV, GNB, NJB, HCSB, NET, TNIV, NIV; cf. NASB, REB, NLT, ESV).

One locus of difficulty lies in the precise understanding of the phrase "your partnership in the faith" (ἡ κοινωνία τῆς πίστεώς σου). The various possibilities can be traced to the exact meaning of the term rendered here as "partnership," and thus also the meaning of "faith" as well as the placement of the personal pronoun "your." For the meaning of "partnership" (ἡ κοινωνία), four major options emerge.

(1) *The passive sense of "fellowship."* This reading rests on the common usage of κοινωνία in the sense of close association (1 Cor 1:9; 2 Cor 13:13;

57. Cf. Church, "Rhetorical Structure and Design," 22.

58. Moule, *Epistles to the Colossians and to Philemon*, 142.

Phil 1:5), but it takes this close association in relation to those sharing this faith, and not faith itself. Commentators who support this reading point to the contemporary use of this word in reference to close human relationship,[59] thus: "My prayer is that our fellowship with you as believers will bring about ..." (GNB). Faith then refers to the common Christian faith, although this category would also include those who see "your faith" as a reference to Philemon's faith: "I am praying that the mutual participation that arises from your faith in Christ might become effective...."[60]

(2) *The passive sense of "sharing in."* This draws from the use of κοινωνία in the sense of "participation" as is related to (1) above, except that the term is referring to direct participation in the faith rather than those who also share this faith (e.g., Phil 3:10; 2 Cor 8:4). Thus: "May your sharing in the faith become effective...."[61] A few contemporary versions adopt this reading: "I pray that your participation in the faith may become effective" (HCSB; cf. NJB, REB, NET). With this reading, "your" goes with "participation," and "faith" is the Christian faith.

(3) *The active intransitive sense of "partnership."* Instead of simply the passive "fellowship" and "sharing in" the faith, this reading assumes an active "partnership" in the ministry of the faith.[62] Though supported by many recent commentators,[63] only the TNIV and NIV explicitly adopt

this reading: "I pray that your partnership with us in the faith may be effective...." With this reading, "faith" is understood as the gospel ministry, although one can conceivably argue that the personal pronoun applies to both terms: "I pray that your partnership in the faith that you have already manifested may be effective...."

(4) *The active transitive sense of "sharing."* This sense takes "the faith" as the object, which points to the evangelistic activities of sharing one's faith with others. This is based on the relatively rare usage of the term κοινωνία in reference to the act of goodwill (2 Cor 13:13). This reading is accepted by some versions: "I pray that the sharing of your faith may become effective" (NRSV; cf. CEV, NKJV).[64] "Faith" is then the gospel message itself. Other commentators have taken this understanding of goodwill in the sense of generosity, thus: "I pray that the generosity which your faith prompts may effectively increase...."[65] This "faith" is then the personal faith of Philemon.

Although certainty is not possible, option (3) provides the best reading. With a nonpersonal genitive qualifier following the word κοινωνία, option (1) is ruled out.[66] The rare use of this noun in the active transitive sense argues against option (4). Between (2) and (3), several factors argue for (3). First, in the previous verse, where Paul gives thanks for Philemon's "love" and "faith," "faith" there is apparently understood in an active sense.

59. Cf. Arzt-Grabner, *Philemon*, 182–85.

60. Moo, *Letters to the Colossians and to Philemon*, 394. Cf. Joseph Fitzmyer, *The Letter to Philemon: A New Translation with Introduction and Commentary* (AB 34C; New York: Doubleday, 2000), 97.

61. Lohse, *Colossians and Philemon*, 192. Cf. Dunn, *Epistles to the Colossians and to Philemon*, 318.

62. While not a uniquely Pauline usage, this use of κοινωνία is widespread in secular Greek; cf. Friedrich Hauck, "κοινός, κτλ.," *TDNT*, 3:798; Nigel Turner, *Christian Words* (Edinburg: T&T Clark, 1980), 163.

63. Cf. Stuhlmacher, *Der Brief an Philemon*, 33; Ryan, "Philemon," 223. See also the discussion in Marshall, "Theology of Philemon," 183.

64. This active transitive reading takes the words "become effective" (ἐνεργὴς γένηται) in the active sense of making one's faith realized in the lives of others.

65. Harris, *Colossians and Philemon*, 254; cf. O'Brien, *Colossians, Philemon*, 279–80.

66. Cf. Harold Riesenfeld, "Faith and Love Promoting Hope: An Interpretation of Philemon v. 6," in *Paul and Paulinism: Essays in Honour of C. K. Barrett* (ed. M. D. Hooker and S. G. Wilson; London: SPCK, 1982), 254.

Second, a parallel use occurs in Phil 1:5, where the word is clearly used in the sense of "partnership": "because of your partnership in the gospel from the first day until now."[67] Most important is the reappearance of this word group in Phlm 17, which calls for Philemon to be Paul's "partner" (κοινωνόν) in the gospel ministry by receiving Onesimus back as a "brother … in the Lord" (v. 16). The emphasis on Paul's prayer that Philemon will continue to participate in this partnership of faith paves the way for Paul's further appeal to act in a similar way in response to the return of Onesimus.[68]

Finally, this reading is also consistent with the understanding that the placement of the pronoun "your" (σου) next to the word "effective" (ἐνεργής)[69] might be a wordplay on the earlier title applied to Philemon, "coworker" (συνεργῷ, v. 1), thus underlining how "κοινωνία here refers to the partnership between Paul and Philemon as coworkers in the advancement of the gospel."[70] This reading is consistent with option (4) without having to take the term κοινωνία in an active transitive sense.

6b-c In gaining the knowledge of every good thing that is in us for Christ (ἐν ἐπιγνώσει παντὸς ἀγαθοῦ τοῦ ἐν ἡμῖν εἰς Χριστόν). The second half of the verse is equally obscure, although the decision about the first half of the verse limits the interpretive possibilities. The preposition "in" (ἐν) has been taken in an "instrumental"[71] or "temporal"[72] sense, but if κοινωνία is understood in the sense of "partnership," this preposition probably refers to the "sphere" where their partnership would be effective.

The combination of "effective" and "knowledge" presupposes a verbal act, thus the insertion of "gaining" in this translation. As in a number of his prison letters, Paul again points to the "knowledge" of the reader(s) in the content of his opening prayer report (cf. Eph 1:17; Phil 1:9; Col 1:9). Particularly relevant is the passage from Colossians, written during the same time to the same community:

> For this reason we also, since the day we heard, have not ceased praying for you and asking God that you may be filled with the knowledge [τὴν ἐπίγνωσιν] of his will in all spiritual wisdom and understanding, in order that you may walk in a manner worthy of the Lord, and please him in every way, bearing fruit in every good work [παντὶ ἔργῳ ἀγαθῷ], growing in the knowledge [τῇ ἐπιγνώσει] of God. (Col 1:9 – 10)

This Colossian passage unlocks the meaning of a number of words in this passage in Philemon. First, the "knowledge" noted in Col 1:9 refers to the "knowledge" of the readers. Likewise, the "knowledge" in Philemon is also Philemon's, not that of the believers in general (as would be the case if κοινωνία means the sharing of faith). Paul is encouraging Philemon to be his partner in the gospel ministry so that he can also experience the power of this gospel.

As in Colossians, this "knowledge" is not an abstract knowledge, but "the knowledge of his will" as one seeks to lead a life faithful to the gospel that one has received (cf. Col 1:5 – 6). This also sheds light on the phrase "every good thing" (παντὸς ἀγαθοῦ), as it naturally refers to the "will" of God.[73]

---

67. Wilson, *Colossians and Philemon*, 340.

68. Winter, "Paul's Letter to Philemon," 3, who takes κοινωνία in the sense of "partnership," further argues that this verse points to Philemon's sending Onesimus to Paul to aid him during his imprisonment, thus indirectly becoming a partner in Paul's gospel ministry.

69. This adjective carries the sense of "effective," "active," and "powerful"; BDAG, 335.

70. Heil, "The Chiastic Structure and Meaning of Paul's Letter to Philemon," 192 n. 25.

71. "Through the knowledge" (NASB; cf. KJV, NKJV, HCSB).

72. "When you perceive" (NRSV).

73. Moule, *Epistles to the Colossians and to Philemon*, 143, arrives at the same conclusion, not through the Colossian parallel, but through the parallel with the Jewish concept of the

This phrase also provides a transition to the works of love noted in v. 7. In Colossians, a similar phrase ("every good work," παντὶ ἔργῳ ἀγαθῷ) refers to the practical behavior that corresponds to the "knowledge of God." Here, Paul prays that Philemon's knowledge of "every good thing" will likewise produce the works of love that are the fruits of one's knowledge of the will of God.[74]

Finally, the last prepositional phrase, "for Christ" (εἰς Χριστόν), must also be explained. This phrase has been variously translated as "unto Christ" (ASV),[75] "in Christ" (NET; cf. GNB),[76] "for the sake of Christ" (TNIV, ESV, NIV; cf. NASB, NJB, NRSV, NLT),[77] and "for the glory of Christ" (HCSB).[78] While the precise sense cannot be determined since Paul uses this phrase in various contexts, clearly he is highlighting the christocentric focus of "the knowledge of every good thing." In light of our understanding of the rest of this verse that emphasizes the partnership in carrying out the knowledge of God's will, perhaps the best reading is "for Christ." This sentiment is expressed through a different phrase when Paul appeals to Philemon to refresh his heart "in Christ" (ἐν Χριστῷ, v. 20).

7a I have received much joy and comfort from your love (χαρὰν γὰρ πολλὴν ἔσχον καὶ παράκλησιν ἐπὶ τῇ ἀγάπῃ σου). Paul concludes this section by highlighting the love that Philemon had already shown to the believers around him. In Greek, the previous verse concludes the lengthy sentence that constitutes the main part of this introductory paragraph. Some have considered this verse as extending this introductory section "beyond its formal necessity."[79] This verse is, however, important in a number of ways. First, the focus on "love" picks up the note on "love" in v. 5. As v. 6 expands on the theme of "faith," this verse expands on "love." Once again, the reader encounters a chiastic structure:

> a Love (v. 5a)
>   b Faith (v. 5b)
>   b′ Faith (v. 6)
> a′ Love (v. 7)[80]

Second, we should also note the postpositive particle here ("for," γάρ). It is left untranslated because the English word "for" cannot convey its various possible functions. It can provide the basis for the previous note. If so, it can provide the basis for Paul's thanksgiving in v. 4: "I give thanks to my God … because I hear of your love … and faith … and because I have received much joy and comfort from your love."[81] But it can also provide the basis for the immediately preceding verse: "[I pray] that your partnership in the faith may become effective … for I have received much joy and comfort from your love."[82] This particle can also be taken as a "confirmatory adverb,"[83] reinforcing the point that is made in v. 6: "I have indeed received much joy and encouragement from your love" (NRSV).

---

will of God. For the Jews, "every good thing" can be found in the law that reveals God's will. For Paul, however, it can only be found through "the faith" in Christ Jesus.

74. Note that in v. 14, Paul uses "the good" (τὸ ἀγαθόν) for that which Philemon needs to accomplish in the reception of Onesimus.

75. E.g., N. T. Wright, *The Epistles of Paul to the Colossians and to Philemon* [TNTC; Grand Rapids: Eerdmans, 1986], 177.

76. E.g., Fitzmyer, *Letter to Philemon*, 98.

77. E.g., Moo, *Letters to the Colossians and to Philemon*, 394.

78. Cf. "in expectation of Christ"; Barth and Blanke, *Letter to Philemon*, 291.

79. Ryan, "Philemon," 225.

80. Heil, "The Chiastic Structure and Meaning of Paul's Letter to Philemon," 182, further points to the use of the preposition "in/from" (ἐπί) in vv. 4 and 7 that provides an inclusio: "It is *in* his prayers that Paul thanks God for the love (v. 5) of Philemon, for it is *in* his love that Paul has had much joy and encouragement (v. 7)" (italics his).

81. Cf. Lightfoot, *St. Paul's Epistles to the Colossians and to Philemon*, 334.

82. Cf. Arthur A. Rupprecht, "Philemon," Expositor's Bible Commentary (ed. Tremper Longman III and David E. Garland; 2nd ed.; Grand Rapids: Zondervan, 2006), 12:637.

83. Herbert W. Smyth, *Greek Grammar* (rev. Gordon M. Messing; Cambridge, MA: Harvard Univ. Press, 1984), §2803.

Third, this verse also serves as a transition to the main body of the letter. This note on "love" (τῇ ἀγάπῃ) provides the basis for Paul's appeal to "love" in v. 9, and the note on the refreshment of the "hearts" (τὰ σπλάγχνα) of the believers in v. 7b also points forward to Paul's further appeal for Philemon to refresh his own "heart" in vv. 7 and 20.

In Paul, both "joy" (cf. Rom 14:17; 15:13; Gal 5:22; Phil 1:25; Col 1:11) and "comfort" (2 Cor 1:3 – 7; Phil 2:1) can refer to the positive experience of God's salvific act. They are also used for Paul's own reaction to the faithful acts of believers ("joy," 2 Cor 2:3; 7:4; Phil 4:1; "comfort," 2 Cor 7:4). The word translated "comfort" (παράκλησιν) here (cf. NASB, NLT, ESV) can also be translated as "encouragement" (cf. NRSV, GNB, HCSB, TNIV, NET, NIV); perhaps the translation "comfort" better reflects the OT idioms where the verbal form points to the arrival of God's eschatological salvation (cf. Isa 40:1). Although Paul is focusing on Philemon's acts of love, he is trying to ground such love in the prior divine act. Based on the divine acts and Philemon's past responses, Paul continues to "appeal" (παρακαλῶ, vv. 9, 10) to Philemon to act similarly. A similar combination of terms is found in 2 Cor 7:13:

> Therefore we are comforted [παρακεκλήμεθα]. And besides our own comfort [τῇ παρακλήσει], we rejoiced [ἐχάρημεν] still more at the joy [τῇ χαρᾷ] of Titus, because his spirit has been refreshed [ἀναπέπαυται] by you all. (ESV)

Here, the source of Paul's "comfort" and "joy" lies in Philemon's acts of "love" (τῇ ἀγάπῃ) for all the believers. It is this "love" that will be the focus of the rest of this letter.

7b Because the hearts of the saints have been refreshed through you, brother (ὅτι τὰ σπλάγχνα τῶν ἁγίων ἀναπέπαυται διὰ σοῦ, ἀδελφέ). Paul rejoices and is comforted because through Philemon's labor of love the "hearts" of the believers are "refreshed." The transitional nature of this verse is made clear by several significant terms. The word translated "hearts" (τὰ σπλάγχνα) originally refers to the "inner parts"[84] of a person (or an animal); in Paul, it "expresses the total personality at the deepest level."[85] This word appears three times in three different subsections of this letter: "Taken together they constitute a syllogism that is itself the touchstone of Paul's argument: if Philemon refreshes the very hearts of the saints (v. 7); and, if Onesimus is Saint Paul's very heart (v. 12); then, to refresh Paul's very heart, Philemon must refresh Onesimus (v. 20)."[86]

The verb "have been refreshed" (ἀναπέπαυται) by itself can denote the act of rest,[87] and it has been taken as such in this context.[88] Elsewhere in Paul, however, the verb is used several times for the refreshment of the human spirit and heart (1 Cor 16:18; 2 Cor 7:13; Phlm 20). In each of these passages, the "refreshment is brought on by the actions of others, not by his own actions, or indeed his own lack of action (physical rest)."[89]

Moreover, since the application of the verb "refresh" in reference to the human spirit and heart appears unique to Paul among first-century (and ancient) Greek authors, the significance of this phrase should be explored. All of Paul's references imply a positive commendation. The closest parallel to Paul's usage here is 1 Cor 16:18, where in both contexts one finds the crossing of "traditional

---

84. Cf. "bowels," (KJV).
85. Helmut Köster, "σπλάγχνον, κτλ.," *TDNT*, 7:555.
86. Church, "Rhetorical Structure and Design," 24.
87. BDAG, 69.
88. Cf. Wright, *Colossians and Philemon*, 178: "The Colossian Christians, weary in their daily battles for the Lord, find in Philemon the refreshment and rest needed to regain strength for renewed warfare."
89. Andrew D. Clarke, " 'Refresh the Hearts of the Saints': A Unique Pauline Context," *TynBul* 47 (1996): 298 – 99.

social barriers."[90] In Philemon, this verb that reappears in v. 20 clearly moves the rhetoric forward from the indicative to the imperative as Paul urges Philemon to refresh his own heart by receiving Onesimus as a "brother" (v. 16).

This understanding may explain the appearances of the vocative "brother" (ἀδελφέ) in vv. 7, 20 as Paul reminds Philemon of his own status in the household of God. As in 1 Cor 16:18 and 2 Cor 7:13, this act of refreshment is not just any benevolent act; it is one that demonstrates the power of the gospel that challenges the present conception of reality.

Theology in Application

Household of God

In this introductory section, Paul follows his customary procedure in drawing attention to the relationship between God and the recipient(s) as the basis of his further argument. Here he highlights the need to recognize the reality created through the gospel of Jesus Christ. In two ways, this reality is superimposed on the perceived reality of everyday existence.

First, a seemingly personal and private matter is transformed into an ecclesiological one because the impact of the gospel ministry will be felt in the most fundamental of all social units. This is evident in the opening salutation, where Paul not only addresses several members (and presumably leaders) of the church (Philemon, Apphia, Archippus, vv. 1 – 2) while mentioning his own coauthor, Timothy, but he also attaches various relevant titles to his coauthor ("our brother") and the recipients ("our beloved and coworker," "our sister," "our fellow soldier"). This culminates in the note on Philemon's church: "the church in your house" (v. 2). Rather than simply trying to put pressure on Philemon, this ecclesiological focus points to the significance of the issue addressed and the impact of a Christian household on the wider church. Moreover, the line between private and public blurs as Jesus the Lord is the Lord of all.

Related to this ecclesiological focus is the portrayal of the central characters of this letter as members of the wider household of God. In Colossians, we saw how Paul used a discussion of household relationships in affirming the lordship of Christ and in defining believers as those who are to serve this Lord.[91] Here it is the interrelationship among members of the Christian household under the lordship of Christ that is the focus of Paul's concern. Being one of the most focused uses of kinship language among his letters,[92] this letter demonstrates the importance of kinship labels in defining the relationships among the various members as they are called to deal with the issue at hand.[93]

---

90. Clarke, " 'Refresh the Hearts of the Saints'," 296.

91. See Theology in Application on Col 3:18 – 4:1.

92. Cf. Raymond E. Collins, *The Power of Images in Paul* (Collegeville, MN: Liturgical, 2008), 76: "Were it not for the Letter to the Galatians, one might say that in no other texts of the New Testament does kinship language have such importance as it does in the Letter to Philemon and the church in his house."

93. Though used throughout Paul's writings, this fictive kinship language can be traced back to Jesus himself, who

Reminding Philemon of his own role within this household of God, Paul begins to portray this household by naming his own coworker as a "brother" (v. 1) and a member of Philemon's own church as a "sister" (v. 2). Within this sibling relationship, Paul locates Philemon as a member of this household. In the conclusion of this introductory section, Paul uses the vocative "brother" (v. 7) in a direct address to Philemon. This vocative reappears in the final verse of the body of this letter (v. 20) as Paul reminds Philemon to act according to his own status within this household of God. Thus, the central appeal in v. 16 becomes all the more powerful when Paul appeals to Philemon to receive Onesimus back "no longer as a slave, but more than a slave, a beloved brother."[94] This appeal is possible only if the reality of the new frame of reference is acknowledged.

Within this household of God, "God" is naturally "our Father" (v. 3), and "Jesus Christ" is the "Lord" (vv. 3, 5, 25). It is under that lordship that appeals to Philemon can be made; this is attested by appearances of "in the Lord" precisely where such appeals appear in this letter (vv. 16, 20). The coexistence of the perceived reality and the reality brought about by the gospel is demonstrated by the coexistence of the two phrases in v. 16: "in the flesh" and "in the Lord." Through kinship language, Paul points to the significance of the household of God as the primary frame of reference within which decisions must be made.

Finally, in the body of the letter, one also finds Paul identifying himself as an "old man" (v. 9) while Onesimus is his "child" (v. 10). The reference to "old man" allows Paul to speak with authority even under the final authority of the Lord Jesus Christ, and to call Onesimus his "child" transforms his reality as a slave into one that belongs in the household of God. Since Paul views the status of Onesimus as already changed, Philemon is asked simply to acknowledge this reality. The relative status of Paul is further affirmed when his "child" is to be the "brother" of Philemon. Philemon is therefore but a "child" to Paul, a claim implicit in v. 19 when Philemon is said to "owe" Paul his "own self."

This discussion is not simply an abstract academic exercise; rather, it points to a critical frame of reference wherein concrete actions are to be carried out. Unlike many of Paul's letters, where one finds a clear separation between the "theoretical/ dogmatic" and the "practical/ethical" sections, Philemon does not reflect such a two-part structure. The insistence on a new frame of reference is, however, the "indicative" from which the imperative flows. No application of this letter can ignore this significant theological move.

How can this reality be appropriated in our contemporary setting? In light of the

---

referred to his disciples as "brothers" (e.g., Matt 12:50; 28:10; Mark 3:35; John 20:17). Equally important is the fact that it is because of Jesus himself that believers can relate to one another as brothers and sisters. Cf. Stanley E. Porter, "Family in the Epistles," in *Family in the Bible: Exploring Customs, Culture,* *and Context* (ed. Richard S. Hess and M. Daniel Carroll R.; Grand Rapids: Baker, 2003), 148 – 66.

94. Recall that in the ancient context, "slave" is also a household term.

prevalent individualism in the West, household language is seldom evoked outside of one's "nuclear" family. In ethnic churches, however, such language often becomes meaningful in creating a bond among various members; moreover, it also provides a vehicle through which intergenerational conflicts are resolved so that a new sense of identity can grow when filial piety is transformed through the biblical lens that focuses on the lordship of Christ.[95] Within such communities, an individual has multiple adopted parents and aunts/uncles who nurture them as they grow in that affirming community. Mutual respect, submission, and accountability testify to the transformative power of the cross. Such practices are also possible, albeit in different forms, in other Christian communities as we live out the reality of the household of God.

Perhaps churches in the modern Western world can learn from these smaller ethnic Christian communities, who model in a better way the kind of interdependent household of God that Philemon describes. We should acknowledge that size can affect the degree to which a church functions like a familial unit with accountability and other more intimate practices, but larger churches would do well to implement smaller communal units within the greater church to model such behaviors. One of the main hindrances to this intervenient household of faith is the Western ideal of individualism and self-sufficiency, both of which are challenged by this letter.

Faith and Love

The discussion of the relationship between the "indicative" and the "imperative" naturally leads to the discussion of "faith" and "love" in Philemon. That connection has appeared already in Colossians.[96] Colossians focuses on the significance of right belief as the basis of one's behavior; Philemon focuses on the right action that should come from the right belief that Philemon possesses. Though the body of this letter clearly focuses on the appeal to Philemon out of "love" (v. 9), this introductory paragraph points to the inextricable relationship between "faith" and "love."

This relationship is illustrated in two ways. First, the chiasm that explains the difficult structure in v. 5 points to the fundamental significance of "faith." The "love" that begins this verse is resumed in the final phrase, "for all the saints," and these two elements bracket the center of the verse: "faith in [πρός] the Lord Jesus." "Love for all the saints" is grounded in one's "faith toward the Lord Jesus." Second, a second chiastic structure provides organization for vv. 5 – 7 as Paul begins and ends with comments on "love" (vv. 5a, 7), with discussion of "faith" at the center (vv. 5b, 6). Here faith is likewise defined in reference to "Christ" (v. 6).

Before focusing on his appeal, therefore, Paul points to the foundational signifi-

---

95. See, e.g., the helpful discussion in Peter T. Cha, "Constructing New Intergenerational Ties, Cultures and Identities among Korean American Christians: A Congregational Case Study," in *This Side of Heaven: Race, Ethnicity, and Christian*

Faith (ed. Robert J. Priest and Alvaro L. Nieves; Oxford: Oxford Univ. Press, 2007), 259 – 73.

96. See Theology in Application on Col 1:1 – 8.

cance of confessing Jesus as Lord — a confession he shares with Philemon. The love that Paul appeals to is, therefore, not simply a general sentiment of kindness; it is a love based on the prior act of Christ, an act that believers appropriate through faith. This understanding of love explains the reference to Philemon as "beloved" (v. 1), with the implied subjects not limited to Paul and Timothy, but ultimately including God. As one who has experienced God's love through the redemptive work of Christ, Philemon is to respond to this prior act of grace.

This understanding of the relationship between "faith" and "love" is rooted in the OT confession in which love for others flows from the worship of the one God:

> The command to love is part of a comprehensive theological conception of love that is modeled on God's covenantal love and the response to it presented in Israel's fundamental confession: "Hear, O Israel: The Lord is our God, the Lord alone. You shall love the Lord your God with all your heart, and with all your soul, and with all your might" (Deut 6:4 – 5).[97]

The connection between the love of God and the love of others was already noted by the earthly Jesus when he responded to the question about the most important commandment. After quoting from Deut 6:4 – 5, Jesus added Lev 19:18: "The second is this: 'Love your neighbor as yourself.' There is no commandment greater than these" (Mark 12:31; cf. Matt 22:39 – 40; Luke 10:27).

In this short letter, although one may be unable to identify many direct theological statements, the connection between "faith" and "love" forms a critical basis for the rest of the letter. Contemporary Christians should not simply affirm a theoretical statement of faith; we are also called to live out the necessary reality that this faith affirms. Similarly, we should not simply perpetuate acts of kindness; we are called to live out a gospel that transforms our self-centered lives into ones that worship God; thus, we are able to love others as fellow members of the household of God.

Partnership in Ministry

Finally, we must provide a brief note concerning the *koinōnia* in v. 6. Although merely a subordinating clause, it is the purpose clause in a section that contains a long prayer consisting of both thanksgiving and intercession. Because it expresses the purpose of this prayer, this clause can be considered the climax of this introductory section. Despite the difficulties in discerning the exact meaning of this verse, Paul is apparently calling Philemon to participate in the work of the gospel ministry.[98] Beyond the grammatical and syntactical ambiguities lies a clear vision of ministry.

---

97. Carter Lindberg, *Love: A Brief History through Western Christianity* (Oxford: Blackwell, 2008), 28.

98. This general way of rephrasing the central point of this verse seeks to avoid building this application point only on one possible reading of this verse.

First, Paul holds that believers are to be joined together as partners in the gospel ministry. While his apostolic authority cannot be questioned, he does not consider such authority as the basis for understanding himself as the only and unique instrument that is able to accomplish the gospel mission. Paul already reflects this when he mentions Timothy as the cosender of this letter (v. 1). More importantly, Paul appeals to Philemon as a "coworker" (v. 1) and thus a "partner" in the gospel ministry. Therefore, although he can evoke his apostolic authority (v. 8), he appeals to Philemon upon the basis of the faith they share. *Koinōnia*, a word that denotes participation, association, and the sharing of common grounds, best expresses this Pauline sense of common faith and thus the common vocation within the gospel ministry.

Second, Paul's understanding of partnership in the gospel ministry should also be noted. This partnership does not point to the physical cooperation among equals within the same temporal and spatial location. It refers, however, to their participation in the same gospel ministry with the same goal "for [the sake of] Christ" (v. 6). This unity of purpose also explains texts where Paul identifies himself and others as the "coworkers" of God (1 Cor 3:9; 1 Thess 3:2).[99] In other words, to emphasize that Paul and Philemon are "coworkers" is not to emphasize their cooperative effort in a gospel project; instead, it emphasizes their individual dependence on and obedience to the gospel ministry as they share the same vocation for Christ and his kingdom. In other words, Paul is not calling Philemon to be his personal associate; he is calling him to share in their common vocation as faithful servants of God.[100]

Finally, for Paul, being partners in the gospel ministry also provides opportunities for personal growth and sanctification. Paul notes this explicitly when he prays that Philemon's "partnership in the faith may become effective in gaining the knowledge of every good thing that is in us for Christ" (v. 6). This defines Philemon not primarily as an active contributor to the gospel ministry but as an obedient witness to God's work in history. Rather than begging Philemon to accomplish an assigned task, Paul challenges him to acknowledge his dignity and honor by playing a part in God's own acts in history. In doing so, he will gain a better knowledge of the profound work of God among his people.

We are likewise called to be united in the witness of God's acts in history. This is grounded in the redemptive work of Christ, who is himself the goal of all gospel ministries. Only within such a perspective can human partners recognize their roles as obedient and dependent beings who are privileged to experience God's grace through such participation in his work. For many of us, forms of partnership can include prayer and financial support, personal evangelism and counseling, mutual forgiveness and reconciliation, and even obedience and submission to the particular call of God.

---

99. Clarke, *A Pauline Theology of Church Leadership*, 93.
100. For the relationship between Paul and the local leaders whom he considers to be his "coworkers," see also Robert Banks, *Paul's Idea of Community* (rev. ed.; Peabody, MA: Hendrickson, 1994), 163 – 65.

CHAPTER 13

Philemon 8 – 16

Literary Context

In the previous section, which contains the opening greetings (vv. 1 – 3), thanksgiving (vv. 4 – 5), and prayer report (vv. 6 – 7), Paul paves the way for this central section, which contains his requests regarding Onesimus (vv. 8 – 10). The introductory section has provided the framework for Paul's requests by identifying the various characters involved through their positions within the family of God. While God is "our Father" (v. 3) and Jesus Christ is the "Lord" (v. 3), Philemon is a "brother" (v. 7). This points ahead to Paul's urging Philemon to receive Onesimus also as a "brother" (v. 16) in view of his new position as a believer, a "son" born to Paul during his imprisonment (v. 10).

The thanksgiving and prayer report also provide the foundation for Paul's argument here. Paul's thanksgiving is based on Philemon's "love for all the saints" and "faith in the Lord Jesus" (v. 5). The prayer report likewise focuses on "faith" (v. 6) and "love" (v. 7) for one who claims to be a member of the household of God. In the letter body, "love" becomes the basis for Paul's appeal to Philemon (v. 9).

Most scholars agree that the main body begins with v. 8. But there is no consensus as to where it ends and whether a discernible division can be found within this body. This lack of consensus is due to the close connection between vv. 8 – 16 and vv. 17 – 20 on the one hand, and the presence of further instructions in vv. 21 – 22 on the other.

We should begin with the ending of the main body. Because it obviously focuses on Paul's appeal to and instructions for Philemon, some see a distinct break at the end of v. 22 (cf. GNB, CEV, NEB, HCSB, NET, NLT, ESV).[1] This is supported by the presence of a final instruction (to provide a guest room for Paul) in v. 22, while v. 23 shifts to the greetings. Those who consider the main body as focusing on the issue surrounding Onesimus see v. 21 as providing a natural break, for there Paul concludes with a final admonition to Philemon to be obedient to what is asked of him (cf. NRSV, NJB, TNIV, NIV).[2] Finally, for those who consider v. 21 as a concluding

---

1. Wright, *Colossians and Philemon*, 178 – 79; Rupprecht, "Philemon," 635; Arzt-Grabner, *Philemon*, 192.

2. Herbert Carson, *The Epistles of Paul to the Colossians and Philemon* (TNTC; Grand Rapids: Eerdmans, 1960), 112.

note that underlines the urgency for the main body of the letter, v. 20 becomes the natural conclusion to the main body (cf. NAB).[3]

The consideration of vv. 8 – 20 as containing the main body of the letter provides the best reading. First, the phrase "at the same time" (ἅμα δέ) at the beginning of v. 22 links this verse with v. 21. Since v. 22 deals with Paul's travel plan, it fits well within the closing section of Paul's letters (cf. Rom 15:22 – 32). Thus, it is best to see v. 21 as the beginning of the closing section. Second, the words "brother" (ἀδελφέ), "refresh" (ἀνάπαυσον), and "heart(s)" (τὰ σπλάγχνα), which conclude the introductory paragraph (v. 7), reappear in v. 20; they provide a corresponding conclusion to this second section of the letter.

The line between the two subsections within the main body of the letter is even less clear.[4] Our division points to the first subsection as providing Paul's appeal on the basis of his relationship with Onesimus (vv. 8 – 16), while the second one provides the instructions on the basis of his relationship with Philemon (vv. 17 – 20). This division is suggested by the absence of imperatives in vv. 8 – 16 but the presence of the verb "appeal" (παρακαλῶ) in vv. 9, 10; by contrast, vv. 17 – 20 contain three imperatives (vv. 17, 18, 20). The presence of "therefore" (διό) in v. 8 and a comparable marker (οὖν) in v. 17 further confirms these two subsections.[5]

In vv. 8 – 16, Paul evokes his authority (v. 8), though basing his appeals on love (v. 9). He also alludes to his relationship with Onesimus (v. 10), Onesimus's usefulness for him (v. 11 – 14), and his new relationship in Christ and thus his place in Paul's heart (v. 15 – 16). With such appeals, Paul provides specific instructions in vv. 17 – 20 for Philemon to receive Onesimus and thus refresh Paul's heart.

I. Opening Greetings (vv. 1 – 3)

II. Faith and Love (vv. 4 – 7)

➡ **III. Requests concerning Onesimus (vv. 8 – 20)**

    A. Appeals from the Relationship between Paul and Onesimus (vv. 8 – 16)

    B. Instructions from the Relationship between Paul and Philemon (vv. 17 – 20)

IV. Final Greetings (vv. 21 – 25)

---

3. Lohse, *Colossians and Philemon*, 198; O'Brien, *Colossians, Philemon*, 286; Stuhlmacher, *Der Brief an Philemon*, 36; Dunn, *Epistles to the Colossians and to Philemon*, 324; Barth and Blanke, *Letter to Philemon*, 487; Ryan, "Philemon," 253; Wilson, *Colossians and Philemon*, 362; Moo, *Letters to the Colossians and to Philemon*, 397 – 98.

4. Others have argued for a different two-part (vv. 8 – 14, 15 – 20; e.g., Dunn, *Epistles to the Colossians and to Philemon*, 322) or three-part structure (vv. 8 – 14, 15 – 16, 17 – 20; e.g., Moo, *Letters to the Colossians and to Philemon*, 399).

5. See also Allen, "The Discourse Structure of Philemon," 87, who further argues for the presence of an inclusio formed by the phrase "in Christ" in v. 8 and "in the Lord" in v. 16.

Main Idea

Identifying Onesimus as his child and as one useful for him and the gospel ministry, Paul urges Philemon to consider him no longer as a slave but as a beloved brother. This new sense of reality provides the basis for Paul's explicit instructions in the section that follows.

Translation

(See next page.)

Structure

Paul appeals to Philemon on the basis of Paul's relationship with Onesimus. He begins by noting his authority over Philemon, but then expresses his decision to appeal to Philemon on the basis of love instead (v. 9a). Therefore, he does not identify himself as an apostle, but as a prisoner and an old man (v. 9b-d). Although this is an appeal of love, such a self-identification does carry sufficient rhetorical force to fuel the particular appeal that follows.

In v. 10 Paul begins his appeal by identifying Onesimus as his "child," one born to him in his imprisonment. This father-son relationship transforms the requests that follow into ones that cannot be rejected. Playing on the meaning of his name, Paul describes Onesimus as someone who is "useful" to him, although he might not have been so to Philemon (v. 11). In describing his decision to send Onesimus back to Philemon, Paul further identifies Onesimus as his "heart" (v. 12). He then expresses his desire to keep Onesimus for himself so that he can serve Paul and thus also further the cause of the gospel on account of which Paul is imprisoned (v. 13). Echoing his earlier sentiment concerning love as the basis of his appeal (cf. v. 10), Paul reiterates his desire not to force Philemon into submission, but to encourage him to respond according to his own will (v. 14).

In the third sentence of this section, through the use of a divine passive ("he was separated," ἐχωρίσθη, v. 15), Paul notes a possible explanation of the divine will behind the separation between Philemon and Onesimus, with an implicit appeal that Philemon should receive Onesimus back "no longer as a slave, but more than a slave, a beloved brother" (v. 16a-c).[6] Even here, Paul calls Onesimus his "beloved brother" and urges Philemon to share this view (v. 16d-e). This paragraph shifts the attention away from the personal relationship between Paul and Onesimus to the relationship

---

6. Although neither the verb "to appeal" (παρακαλῶ) nor an imperative is found here, most scholars recognize an implicit appeal embedded in this statement concerning the divine will. The lack of an explicit appeal in this critical sentence can be partially explained by Paul's decision to appeal to Philemon on the basis of "love" (v. 9).

page 382 Philemon 8 – 16

Philemon 8 – 16

8a	concession (9a)	Therefore, though I have much boldness in Christ
b	description	to command you to do what is proper,
9a	Contra-expectation	**yet I appeal to you on the basis of love** —
b	apposition	I, Paul,
c	apposition	an old man,
d	Expansion (of 9c)	and now also a prisoner of Christ Jesus —
10a	Expansion (of 9a)	**I appeal to you concerning my child,**
b	apposition	Onesimus,
c	description	who became my son during my imprisonment;
11a	description	formerly he was useless to you,
b	contrast	but now he is indeed useful to you and to me.
12a	sequence (of 10b)	I am sending him … back to you.
b	description (of 10a)	who is my own heart,
13a	desire	I would have liked to keep him for myself,
b	purpose	so that he might serve me on your behalf
c	time	during my imprisonment for the gospel,
14a	contrast (with 13a)	but I preferred to do nothing without your consent,
b	purpose	so that your good deed would not be forced,
c	contrast	but voluntary.
15a	Assertion	**Perhaps it was for this reason that he was separated from you for a while,**
b	purpose	so that you may have him back forever,
16a	manner	no longer as a slave,
b	contrast	but more than a slave,
c	expansion	a beloved brother,
d	specification	especially to me,
e	comparison	but how much more to you,
f	sphere	both in the flesh and in the Lord.

between God and Philemon.[7] These references to God frame this appeal to consider Onesimus as a "beloved brother," one that can be considered the climax of Paul's appeal in this letter.

Exegetical Outline

→ **I. Appeals from the Relationship between Paul and Onesimus (vv. 8 – 16)**

    A. Based on love rather than on authority (vv. 8 – 9)

    B. Onesimus as Paul's child (v. 10)

    C. Onesimus as useful to Paul (v. 11)

    D. Onesimus as Paul's heart (v. 12)

    E. Paul's desire to keep Onesimus (vv. 13 – 14)

    F. Reference to divine purpose (vv. 15 – 16)

        1. Onesimus to be received as Philemon's brother (vv. 15 – 16c)

        2. Onesimus as Paul's beloved brother (v. 16d-f)

Explanation of the Text

8 Therefore, though I have much boldness in Christ to command you to do what is proper (Διό, πολλὴν ἐν Χριστῷ παρρησίαν ἔχων ἐπιτάσσειν σοι τὸ ἀνῆκον). Paul implicitly establishes his authority by claiming he will not evoke such authority. "Therefore" (διό)[8] signals the beginning of a new section. The comma after this conjunction and the one at the end of this verse reflect an exegetical decision to connect this adverb with the verb that appears in the next verse, thus: "therefore … I appeal to you."[9] In this context, the conjunction points back to v. 7 as the grounds of Paul's appeal: "because the hearts of the saints have been refreshed through you in the past, I am appealing to you…." But v. 7 is part of the wider discussion of faith and love in vv. 4 – 7. Since those verses introduce Paul's central appeal in this letter body, it is best to see

this conjunction as pointing back to the entire thanksgiving and prayer report.

The participle "though I have" (ἔχων) is a concessive circumstantial participle. The word "boldness" (παρρησίαν) can carry overlapping layers of meanings. It can refer to the "public" (Mark 8:32; John 7:4, 13, 26; 11:54) and "plain" (John 11:14; 16:25, 29) nature of one's expressions. It can also refer to "confidence" (Acts 2:29; 2 Cor 7:4; Heb 10:35) and "boldness" (Acts 4:29, 31; 28:31; Phil 1:20; 2 Cor 3:12; Eph 3:12) that is built on one's relative position of power and authority. In this context, most readings affirm the unique authority derived from Paul's relationship with and position "in Christ." For those who translate this term as "freedom," it points to "the capability to speak up freely" because the Lord "enables them to open

---

7. This not only allows God to be at the center of Paul's appeal, but it also paves the way for Paul to consider another interpersonal relationship, one between himself and Philemon, in his further instructions for Philemon (vv. 17 – 20).

8. This is a strong inferential conjunction. In the NT, its

function is comparable to the more frequently used particle οὖν; διό is mostly limited to Acts and the letters. Cf. BDF §451.

9. Among the contemporary versions, only GNB explicitly links this conjunction with the participle ("though I have," ἔχων): "For this reason I could be bold enough."

their mouths freely and courageously."[10] For those who adopt the translation "confidence"[11] or "boldness,"[12] it is a confidence derived from the authority of Christ rather than one that is based on one's inherent rights.

This "boldness" grounded "in Christ" can refer to the "boldness" that believers experience in the victory of Christ (Phil 1:20; 1 Tim 3:13; cf. Col 2:15). Here, however, when it is used with the verb "command" (ἐπιτάσσειν), Paul is clearly pointing to his unique authority over Philemon.[13] This "boldness" can then be understood as "apostolic παρρησία,"[14] one derived from his position as an "apostle of Christ Jesus by the will of God," a self-identification often found at the beginning of his letters (1 Cor 1:1; 2 Cor 1:1; Eph 1:1; Col 1:1; 2 Tim 1:1).

Significantly, elsewhere in his letters Paul never refers to his own exercise of his authority "to command."[15] Using the nominal form ("command," ἐπιταγή), more than once he expresses his hesitancy to command believers (cf. 1 Cor 7:6; 2 Cor 8:8), probably because of his conviction that only God can command (Rom 16:26; 1 Cor 7:25; 1 Tim 1:1).[16] It is striking, therefore, to find Paul affirming that authority here. Even though he claims not to use such power, the mere mentioning of such authority is in itself a striking power claim. It has been rightly noted, therefore, that in this verse "Paul parades a theoretical apostolic authority unmatched elsewhere in his letters."[17] Moreover, the expectation that Philemon will respond "in obedience" (v. 21) assumes that Paul is engaging in the exercise of his apostolic authority.[18]

Regarding "what is proper" (τὸ ἀνῆκον), the context implies a sense of duty, which is made explicit in some versions: "what is required" (ESV) and "your duty" (NRSV). Paul does not specify the basis for determining what is proper. It is possible that he is referring to the appeals that follow, thus: "what you ought to do according to the content of this letter." Nevertheless, in light of the reference to Paul's authority "in Christ," it seems best to consider the reference to be in the wider sense of proper behavior in Christ, thus: "that which is proper for one who lives under the authority of Christ." The phrase "as is fitting in the Lord" in Col 3:18 provides additional support for this reading.

9a Yet I appeal to you on the basis of love (διὰ τὴν ἀγάπην μᾶλλον παρακαλῶ). Instead of "command," Paul appeals to Philemon in love. "I appeal" (παρακαλῶ) implies making a request,[19] but it is a request made with strong emotional investment.[20] In contrast to "command," "appeal" points to a different framework of relationships within which the interaction between Paul and Philemon is to be defined. "Command" reflects a relationship between two official parties with different social and political locations; "appeal" is a request made within the sphere of personal friendship. Paul, therefore, is arguing against the use of authority based on hierar-

10. Barth and Blanke, *Letter to Philemon*, 307–8. Cf. Moule, *Epistles to the Colossians and to Philemon*, 144; Fitzmyer, *Letter to Philemon*, 104.

11. NASB, NET; Wilson, *Colossians and Philemon*, 346.

12. ASV, HCSB; cf. KJV, NKJV, NRSV, GNB, NLT, TNIV, ESV, NIV; Harris, *Colossians and Philemon*, 268.

13. Cf. Lohse, *Colossians and Philemon*, 196: "although I have full authority in Christ to command you."

14. Heinrich Schlier, "παρρησία, κτλ.," *TDNT*, 5:882.

15. Even when Paul does exercise such authority to command, he does not use this verb (cf. 1 Cor 5:1–5); Polaski, *Paul and the Discourse of Power*, 63 n. 48.

16. Paul does, however, encourage Titus to exercise such authority (cf. Titus 2:15).

17. John Howard Schütz, *Paul and the Anatomy of Apostolic Authority* (SNTSMS 26; Cambridge: Cambridge Univ. Press, 1975), 221.

18. Cf. Petersen, *Rediscovering Paul*, 132.

19. Cf. TEV: "I make a request."

20. Cf. BDAG, 764: "to urge strongly," or "to make a strong request for something."

chical structure and turning to a frame of reference derived ultimately from their individual relationships with Christ. Moreover, this "appeal" becomes an example for Philemon's own interaction with his slave: "Paul used conventions of brotherhood to appeal to Philemon to treat a runaway slave as a brother rather than a criminal."[21]

Despite the contrast between "command" and "appeal," Paul has clearly established his authority to call Philemon to obedient submission. But the focus on "appeal" points to a different use of power as Paul seeks to challenge the rhetoric of "domination and control" while seeking to emphasize the transformative power embedded in the gospel message of Jesus as Lord (cf. vv. 3, 5, 16, 20, 25).[22] It is the authority of this message that undergirds Paul's rhetoric.

As "the basis" (διά + accusative) of Paul's appeal, this "love" does not refer to his mode of appealing, but to the grounds of this appeal in Philemon's own prior acts of love.[23] If Paul were focusing on his own mode of appealing, he would have used διά + genitive, as he did elsewhere: "I appeal to you, brothers and sisters, by our Lord Jesus Christ and by the love of the Spirit" (Rom 15:30 NRSV). Here the emphasis on "love" as the basis of Paul's appeal continues the theme already mentioned in the introductory section (vv. 5, 7). That basis lies, therefore, within Philemon's own expression that grows out of his faith in the Lord Jesus Christ rather than in the external authority imposed by the apostle Paul.

9b-d I, Paul, an old man, and now also a prisoner of Christ Jesus (τοιοῦτος ὢν ὡς Παῦλος πρεσβύτης, νυνὶ δὲ καὶ δέσμιος Χριστοῦ Ἰησοῦ). Shifting from Philemon's prior acts of love, Paul now reflects on his own circumstances. The participle left untranslated here (ὤν) has been variously understood as causal ("since") or concessive ("even though"). The decision rests on whether the word πρεσβύτης is to be taken in a positive ("ambassador") or negative ("old man") sense, thus: "since I am … the aged" (NASB), or "even though I am … the ambassador of Christ Jesus" (GNB). Our translation aligns with those who consider this clause as a parenthetical clause syntactically separated from the previous clause (NRSV, NLT, NET, ESV); the repetition of "I appeal" (παρακαλῶ) in v. 10a resumes the thought begun in v. 9a.

Because of the difficulties in understanding why Paul here, and nowhere else, identifies himself as an "old man,"[24] some have suggested it means "an ambassador" (cf. 2 Cor 5:20; Eph 6:20). Those who argue for this reading point to a number of factors:[25] (1) elsewhere Paul identifies himself as "an ambassador in chains" (πρεσβεύω ἐν ἁλύσει, Eph 6:20); (2) the word "ambassador" (πρεσβυετής) is only one letter different from "old man" (πρεσβύτης), and the reading in our present Greek text may reflect an early corruption of the text; (3) even if not, one can point to several documents where πρεσβύτης is used instead of πρεσβευτής for an ambassador (e.g., 1 Macc 13:21; 14:22), probably because of a confusion between these words.

21. David Hartman, "Epistolary Conventions and Social Change in Paul's Letters," in *Ancient History in a Modern University* (ed. T. W. Hillard et al.; Grand Rapids: Eerdmans, 1998), 2:203.

22. Cf. Kathy Ehrensperger, *Paul and the Dynamics of Power: Communication and Interaction in the Early Christ-Movement* (London: T&T Clark, 2007), 174 – 75.

23. For a further discussion of Paul's rhetoric of love, see Christopher Kumitz, *Der Brief als Medium der ἀγάπη: Eine Untersuchung zur rhetorischen und epistolographischen Gestalt*

des Philemonbriefes (Europäische Hochschulschriften 23.787; Frankfurt: Peter Lang, 2004), 211 – 14.

24. In the NT, only Zechariah identifies himself as an "old man" (Luke 1:18), but not in a context where the term would enhance the rhetorical force of one's authority or appeal.

25. See Lightfoot, *St. Paul's Epistles to the Colossians and to Philemon*, 338 – 39; O'Brien, *Colossians, Philemon*, 290; Petersen, *Rediscovering Paul*, 126 – 28; Harris, *Colossians and Philemon*, 259 – 60; Barth and Blanke, *Letter to Philemon*, 321.

The majority of the contemporary versions[26] and a number of commentators continue to consider "old man" the correct reading.[27] First, the lexical support for "ambassador" is weak, and the few references likely point to scribal errors.[28] Second, there is no manuscript support for "ambassador" (πρεσβευτής) here. Third, since Paul has just given up a rhetoric of power (v. 8), it would be surprising to find him reverting to a label such as "ambassador."[29]

In Paul's argument, "old man" fits the context well since both "old man" and "prisoner" point to experiences of dependence and weakness.[30] Here, "Paul begins his argument to Philemon by evoking considerable pathos for himself — as an old man and prisoner in need of support — and at the same time by establishing Onesimus' ethos — as his child who is now responsible for his support."[31] Shifting from a rhetoric of power to one of weakness, Paul urges Philemon to consider his relationship with Onesimus within this new frame of reference.

Paul's self-identification as a "prisoner of Christ Jesus" builds on this sense of dependence and weakness and pushes his point one step forward. While being an "old man" is the natural stage in one's life journey, being a "prisoner of Christ Jesus" reflects an obedient will that has responded to the divine call.[32] Here, Paul is likewise calling Philemon to submit to the divine will in giving up his own sense of autonomy and superiority. Elsewhere, Paul also calls others to join him "in suffering for the gospel" while identifying himself as "his [the Lord's] prisoner" (2 Tim 1:8).

10 I appeal to you concerning my child, Onesimus, who became my son during my imprisonment (παρακαλῶ σε περὶ τοῦ ἐμοῦ τέκνου, ὃν ἐγέννησα ἐν τοῖς δεσμοῖς Ὀνήσιμον). Paul now gives the content of his appeal by mentioning of the name of the person who is its center. In the previous verse, "I appeal" (παρακαλῶ) is left without an object.[33] An object does appear, however, in this verse: "I appeal to you [σε]." This points to Paul's resumption of thought started at the beginning of v. 9, and the intervening material must be considered as parenthetical.

The preposition "concerning" (περί) used with the verb "I appeal" is unusual, and it lies at the center of a debate about the background and purpose of this letter. Although many versions read "I appeal to you *for* my son/child" (KJV, ASV, NASB, NKJV, NRSV, HCSB, ESV, TNIV, NIV), the meaning of "for" in these translations appears to have the sense of "on behalf of" (NAB, GNB), a reading adopted by most commentators.[34] A few have, however, suggested that this preposition points to Onesimus as the object of the appeal: "I ask for [him]."[35] Those who support this reading note that "to request on behalf of" would be represented by

---

26. With the major exceptions being GNB and REB.

27. Lohse, *Colossians and Philemon*, 199; Stuhlmacher, *Der Brief an Philemon*, 37 – 38; Fitzmyer, *Letter to Philemon*, 105; Wilson, *Colossians and Philemon*, 348; Ben Witherington III, *Letters to Philemon, the Colossians, and the Ephesians* (Grand Rapids: Eerdmans, 2007), 67; Moo, *Letters to the Colossians and to Philemon*, 405; Cousar, *Philippians and Philemon*, 102.

28. See J. N. Birdsall, "ΠΡΕΣΒΥΤΗΣ in Philemon 9: A Study in Conjectural Emendation," *NTS* 39 (1993): 625 – 30.

29. Wansink, *Chained in Christ*, 161.

30. Some suggest that "old man" was considered a title of honor in the ancient world; cf. Carolyn Osiek, *Philippians, Philemon* (ANTC; Nashville: Abingdon, 2000), 135, but this does not seem to be the focus of the text.

31. Ronald F. Hock, "A Support for His Old Age: Paul's Plea on Behalf of Onesimus," 79. Hock also points to the common sentiment as reflected in a classical description of one who is miserable: "an old man with no means of support" (Diogenes Laertius 6.51).

32. For discussion of this title, see comments on v. 1.

33. In our translation of v. 9, "to you" is supplied for the sake of clarity.

34. See O'Brien, *Colossians, Philemon*, 290; Barth and Blanke, *Letter to Philemon*, 325; Moo, *Letters to the Colossians and to Philemon*, 406 – 7.

35. Knox, *Philemon among the Letters of Paul*, 20.

a different Greek phrase: παρακαλῶ ὑπέρ (cf. 2 Cor 5:20; 2 Cor 12:8; 1 Thess 3:2).[36] But those defending the traditional reading point to papyri evidence that supports the reading of this preposition in the sense of "on behalf of."[37] Moreover, as with 1 Thess 3:2, there is a significant semantic overlap between the two prepositions.[38]

It should be noted, however, that these defenses merely point to the possibility of reading this phrase in the sense of "I appeal on behalf of"; they do not prove this is the more prevalent or even the only possible reading. The use of περί with this verb appears often in summons formulae in the papyri material,[39] and one simply cannot rule out the possibility that Paul is using that same formula in the sense of "I ask for." In short, while Paul is clearly appealing "concerning" Onesimus, it is unclear whether he is appealing "on behalf of" him (seeing this letter primarily as one that asks for forgiveness) or "for" him (seeing this letter as a request to have Onesimus returned to himself, cf. v. 13). The preposition, by itself, is not determinative enough to exclude or confirm either reading.

Paul identifies Onesimus as "my child" (τοῦ ἐμοῦ τέκνου) — an identification that also applies to Timothy (1 Cor 4:17; Phil 2:22). In both cases, "Paul is commending to the addressees a person coming to them from him."[40] In such contexts, this appellation takes on considerable rhetorical force

because their relationships with Paul impose a certain demand on the recipients as they consider ways to receive them. This relationship is made explicit in the words that follow, where the relationship between Paul and Onesimus is depicted as a father-son relationship.

In this verse, we finally encounter the name of the person at the center of Paul's discussion, Onesimus (Ὀνήσιμον).[41] A common name applied to slaves,[42] this "Onesimus" is likely the Onesimus whom Paul depicts as "the faithful and beloved brother" in Col 4:9. After identifying him as his "child," Paul further describes him as the one "who became my son during my imprisonment." This relative clause literally reads, "whom I have begotten in my imprisonment" (NASB). This is often taken to refer to Onesimus's conversion,[43] which reflects the OT tradition that considers a slave as a proper member of the household (cf. Gen 17:9 – 14).[44] In the Jewish tradition, a convert is compared to a "child just born" (*b. Yebam.* 22a) since the son is to learn the Torah from his own father.[45]

Because of this relationship, one can conceivably understand this metaphor as extending beyond the time of conversion. In Phil 2:22, for example, Timothy is identified as Paul's son because of his involvement in Paul's ministry: "you know that Timothy has proved himself, because as a son with his father he has served with me in the

---

36. Winter, "Paul's Letter to Philemon," 6.

37. P.Oxy. 7.1070.8; 10.1298.4; 12.1494.6; Fitzmyer, *Letter to Philemon*, 107; Peter Arzt-Grabner, " 'Bitten für' oder 'Bitten um'? Zur Problematik des Textvergleichs am Beispiel von Phlm 10," *PzB* 13 (2004): 49 – 55. In the NT itself, one can also point to the use of the preposition to introduce a topic ("concerning"): 1 Cor 7:25; 8:1; 12:1; 16:1, 12; 1 Thess 4:9, 13; 5:1; cf. Petersen, *Rediscovering Paul*, 179 n. 50.

38. J. G. Nordling, "Onesimus Fugitivus: A Defense of the Runaway Slave Hypothesis in Philemon," *JSNT* 41 (1991): 110.

39. P.Oxy. 1.1070.7 – 10; P.Tebt. 1.58.52.55; P.Sarap. 92; P.Sarap. 95; cf. Brook W. R. Pearson, "Assumptions in the Criticism and Translation of Philemon," 262 – 63, who also argues that the semantic overlaps between the περί and ὑπέρ go both

directions, as ὑπέρ also appears in contexts where one would have expected περί (John 1:30; 2 Cor 7:4).

40. Meeks, *First Urban Christians*, 87.

41. In Greek, this name appears at the end of the verse, thus further suspending the tension of this text (cf. ASV, REB, NJB, HCSB, NET). In English, however, this name must be placed at the center (cf. NAB, NASB, NKJV, NRSV, TNIV, ESV, NIV).

42. Though not necessarily so; cf. A. L. Connolly, "Onesimos," *NewDocs* 4:179 – 81.

43. See, e.g., "He is like a son to me because I led him to Christ here in jail" (CEV).

44. Derrett, "The Function of the Epistle to Philemon," 76.

45. Cf. Collins, *The Power of Images in Paul*, 73.

work of the gospel." It is therefore possible to see this metaphor as referring to "some other kind of changed relationship."[46] Others have hypothesized that Onesimus would have been "converted" in a more general sense when Philemon's household became part of the wider Christian community, and the present reference to his birth points to "the reincorporation of Onesimus into Christian fellowship."[47] In any case, the relationship between Paul and Onesimus is underlined with this reference, and its rhetorical force cannot be missed.

11 Formerly he was useless to you, but now he is indeed useful to you and to me (τόν ποτέ σοι ἄχρηστον νυνὶ δὲ [καὶ] σοὶ καὶ ἐμοὶ εὔχρηστον). Playing on the meaning of Onesimus's name, Paul points to his new status and function within the ministry of the gospel. In Greek, this verse is not a separate sentence but a further description of Onesimus: "who formerly was useless to you, but now is useful both to you and to me" (NASB). This text immediately follows the name "Onesimus," a name that means "useful."[48] This wordplay provides a contrast between Onesimus's past and his present status as a true believer. The pair, "useless" (ἄχρηστον) and "useful" (εὔχρηστον) has also been translated as "unprofitable" and "profitable" (cf. KJV, ASV, NKJV). Paul does not specify in what ways Onesimus has been "useless" to Philemon. Some suggest it refers to Onesimus's escape from his master,[49] while others point to the wrong he had done to Philemon (as perhaps implied in

v. 18),[50] or simply the general unreliability of his work.[51]

It should be noted, however, that this contrastive pair built on the meaning of the name Onesimus does not necessarily have to point to a reality behind both elements in the pair. If Paul is focusing on the usefulness of Onesimus, "ἄχρηστον need not function literally outside the word play."[52] Moreover, it has been noted that Phrygian slaves were notorious for their "vulgar type of slavish offenses."[53] Paul may be simply alluding to such a reputation while emphasizing the present usefulness of Onesimus. Others have suggested this uselessness may well refer to Onesimus's past as an unbeliever. As in the case of all human beings, only through God's grace can one find oneself useful in the plan of God.[54]

In any case, it is at least possible that this contrast between "useless" and "useful" aims primarily at highlighting the usefulness of Onesimus in the gospel ministry now that he is a Christian disciple.[55] The reference in v. 13 that Paul would like to keep him for his service may further support this reading. This focus on Onesimus's present usefulness rather than his past uselessness is specifically noted with the use of the word "indeed" (καί) here.[56]

With this understanding of this wordplay, one may also be able to explain the phrase "to you and to me" (σοὶ καὶ ἐμοί). These two pronouns may point again to Paul and Philemon's partnership in

46. Osiek, *Philippians, Philemon*, 127.

47. Taylor, "Onesimus," 259 – 81.

48. BDAG, 711.

49. E.g., Robert G. Bratcher and Eugene A. Nida, *A Translator's Handbook on Paul's Letters to the Colossians and to Philemon* (Stuttgart: United Bible Societies, 1977), 125.

50. E.g., Fitzmyer, *Letter to Philemon*, 108.

51. E.g., O'Brien, *Colossians, Philemon*, 292.

52. Winter, "Paul's Letter to Philemon," 4.

53. Lightfoot, *St. Paul's Epistles to the Colossians and Phi-*

lemon, 312. See also Allen D. Callahan, "Paul's Epistle to Philemon: Toward an Alternative Argumentum," *HTR* 86 (1993): 361.

54. See the discussion in Barth and Blanke, *Letter to Philemon*, 340 – 41. This is the way this contrast is used in Hermas, *Vision* 3.6; Marianne Meye Thompson, *Colossians and Philemon* (THNTC; Grand Rapids: Eerdmans, 2005), 217.

55. Ryan, "Philemon," 235.

56. This word is missing in many manuscripts from diverse textual traditions (ℵ² A C D 0278 1739 1881 𝔐).

faith (cf. vv. 6, 17).[57] In Col 4:9, Paul has already identified Onesimus as a "faithful" brother. Here, with the common ground in the gospel message, Paul may be implying that Philemon should continue to have Onesimus serve in some ways for the advancement of the gospel. Less likely is the possibility that Paul is referring to Onesimus's present usefulness to him in the gospel ministry, but his usefulness to Philemon as a slave after his return.

Beyond the wordplay on Onesimus, many also see a play on the word "Christ" (Χριστός) and a related word for "useful" (χρηστός), since both words were pronounced the same in Hellenistic Greek.[58] This wordplay fits the context well, but if this secondary wordplay is present, one would have expected Paul to use the word χρηστόν instead of εὔχρηστον for "useful" here. This wordplay seems to be less than obvious.

12 I am sending him, who is my own heart, back to you (ὃν ἀνέπεμψά σοι, αὐτόν, τοῦτ᾽ ἔστιν τὰ ἐμὰ σπλάγχνα). As Paul comments on Onesimus's return to Philemon, he again emphasizes Onesimus's importance to him. As with vv. 10b–11, this verse is actually a relative clause in Greek, providing further description of Onesimus: "whom I am sending back to you, him, who is my own heart."

This verse has a complicated textual history, prompted by the appearance of the relative pronoun ("whom," ὅν) with the seemingly redundant third person pronoun ("him," αὐτόν), thus, literally: "whom I am sending back to you, him, who is

my own heart." The reading chosen here has been considered to be one that "best explains the origin of the other readings."[59] The awkward presence of αὐτόν may emphasize Onesimus as the proper subject of the discussion without explicitly naming him,[60] and the absence of any imperative here may aim at suspending the expectation of the readers until v. 17, where the proper appeal is made when Paul again identifies Onesimus with his own self: "receive him, as you would receive me."

Almost all contemporary versions take the verb ἀνέπεμψα to mean: "I am sending … back."[61] Noting the frequent use of this verb in the NT in the sense of "referring or remitting a case," however, some have suggested the translation "I am sending up."[62] The verse then takes on a legal sense: "It is this new Onesimus — Onesimus really himself — whose case I am referring to you [ἀνέπεμψα], and now that I send him, I seem to be sending my heart."[63] While this reading may again challenge the traditional reading, some who affirm the traditional hypothesis — which sees Onesimus as a runaway slave and the letter as a letter appealing for forgiveness — consider "I am sending up" as an appropriate translation.[64] It is true that this legal meaning was a common one in ancient documents, but "sending back" is "the alternative meaning" in the Hellenistic papyri documents,[65] and it fits the context better.

The word "heart" reappears here (cf. v. 7) as Paul identifies Onesimus as "my own heart" (τὰ

---

57. See Andrew Wilson, "The Pragmatics of Politeness and Pauline Epistolography: A Case Study of the Letter to Philemon," *JSNT* 48 (1992): 113, who considers this construction as emphasizing their common needs.

58. Lohse, *Colossians and Philemon*, 200. See esp. the well-known confusion of the two terms in Suetonius, *Claud.* 25.4. One also finds the wordplay between "useful" and "Christians" in the literature of the early Christian centuries; see G. H. R. Horsley, "Christian Inscriptions from Phrygia," *NewDocs* 3:129.

59. Metzger, *Textual Commentary*, 589. This reading is supported by א* A 33. Some manuscripts supply the imperative

"receive" (προσλαβοῦ, see v. 17) as a verb to go with the accusative αὐτόν.

60. Cf. NLT: "I am sending him back to you, and with him comes my own heart."

61. As an epistolary aorist, this verb is to be translated as a present tense in English.

62. Cf. Luke 23:7; 23:15; Acts 25:21; Winter, "Paul's Letter to Philemon," 21.

63. Knox, *Philemon among the Letters of Paul*, 21.

64. Moule, *Epistles to the Colossians and to Philemon*, 145.

65. MM, 37.

ἐμὰ σπλάγχνα). This phrase can justifiably be taken as "a part of myself" (HCSB). Paul is sending his own self to Philemon, and he expects Onesimus to be treated as such (v. 17).[66] Moreover, to describe a slave as "my own heart" identifies him within the new frame of reference in Christ. This identification serves to force Philemon to accept Onesimus's new status. After all, to accept this "heart" would demonstrate Philemon's continued commitment in his labor of love for all the saints (v. 7), as well as his partnership with Paul (vv. 17, 20).

13 I would have liked to keep him for myself, so that he might serve me on your behalf during my imprisonment for the gospel (ὃν ἐγὼ ἐβουλόμην πρὸς ἐμαυτὸν κατέχειν, ἵνα ὑπὲρ σοῦ μοι διακονῇ ἐν τοῖς δεσμοῖς τοῦ εὐαγγελίου). As Paul provides further description of Onesimus, he alludes to his possible future service for Paul himself and for the gospel. In Greek, this relative clause focuses on Onesimus, who is at the center of Paul's desire in his service for the gospel: "whom I wished to keep with me, so that …" (NASB).

The emphatic first person pronoun "I" (ἐγώ) draws attention to Paul's own desire and sets up a contrast between that desire and his decision to do what is appropriate under the circumstances: thus, "I really wanted to …" (NLT). The imperfect verb "I would have liked to" (ἐβουλόμην) is to be read with the aorist verb "I preferred" (ἠθέλησα) in the next verse. The change in the vocabulary and tense is important. In this context, "the imperfect implies a tentative, inchoate process; while the aorist describes a definite and complete act."[67] The imperfect can therefore be translated as an unfulfilled

wish: "I would have liked to …" (NIV; cf. ESV),[68] while the aorist as a definitive act: "I preferred …" (NRSV). In terms of meaning, there is significant overlapping in the semantic domains of the two verbs, both being used to express "desire, want, wish."[69] If a distinction is to be made, "I would have liked to" denotes Paul's own "desire," while "I preferred" denotes his "will" or "resolution."[70] Taken together, Paul is suppressing his own desire in his own resolution to do what is appropriate.

In the previous verse, Paul has already noted he is sending Onesimus back to Philemon. Here he expresses his own desire to do the opposite, and in the next, he explains why he made the decision that he did. The discrepancy between Paul's own desires and his final decision has led some to read the infinitive "to keep" (κατέχειν) as "implying … that it was Onesimus who was anxious to return to make amends and peace with his master."[71] Others point to the possibility that "the congregation living in the city of Paul's captivity may have exerted some pressure on Paul, advising that he separate himself from the fugitive, who had been harbored long enough."[72] These readings not only assume a particular background behind the separation of Philemon and Onesimus, but they also attribute Paul's decision to external factors. What Paul himself emphasizes, however, is his own will to send Onesimus back, perhaps in order to maintain "partnership" with Philemon (vv. 6, 17). It is precisely this "partnership" that forms the basis of his argument.

The reason for Paul's desire to keep Onesimus is that "he might serve" (διακονῇ) him in his im-

---

66. While Onesimus's departure would sadden Paul, this is not the main point of this expression (cf. CEV: "Sending Onesimus back to you makes me very sad"). To reduce this term to an emotional expression misses the rhetorical force of this identification.

67. Lightfoot, *St. Paul's Epistles to the Colossians and to Philemon*, 341.

68. For this use of this verb, see Acts 25:22: "I would like (ἐβουλόμην) to hear this man myself." Cf. BDF §359(2).

69. Louw and Nida, §25.

70. Cf. BDAG, 182, 448.

71. Dunn, *Epistles to the Colossians and to Philemon*, 330; cf. Fitzmyer, *Letter to Philemon*, 110.

72. Barth and Blanke, *Letter to Philemon*, 363.

prisonment. In Paul's letters, the verb διακονέω is always used in a religious/theological context. Therefore, it seems probable that Paul is expressing his desire to have Onesimus serve as a minister of the gospel.[73] The fact that serving Paul is serving the gospel is made clear by the reference to his "imprisonment for the gospel"; his predicament is part of his calling as one who serves the gospel mission. Some even consider this verse as the heart of Paul's appeal as he expresses his desire to have Onesimus serve as a gospel missionary.[74] The presence of this implicit appeal with the absence of any note on Onesimus's repentance forces one to reevaluate the background and thus the purpose of this letter. Instead of an appeal for forgiveness, the focus on Onesimus's usefulness (v. 11) and the expression of Paul's desire to have Onesimus "serve" in the gospel ministry point to this wider ministerial and evangelistic concern as lying at the center of this letter.

The phrase "on your behalf" (ὑπὲρ σοῦ) may be important in more than one way. First, if Onesimus had been sent by Philemon to serve Paul in prison, this presupposition would assume this fact and suggest that Philemon should permanently release Onesimus so that this brother can continue to serve Paul on his behalf. Moreover, the need for Philemon to serve Paul in some ways may assume a certain indebtedness on Philemon's part. This assumption reemerges in v. 19, where Paul reminds Philemon that he owes Paul his very self. If so, the appearance of "on your behalf" also adds rhetorical force to Paul's argument in this letter.

"During my imprisonment for the gospel" takes this prepositional phrase as a description of Paul's own imprisonment. Less likely is that this refers to Onesimus's future imprisonment as he serves in the gospel mission: "In the chains of the gospel he could serve me."[75] That this refers to Paul's own imprisonment is supported by the fact that every appearance of the word "chain/imprisonment" (δεσμός) in Paul's letters refers to his own imprisonment (Phil 1:7, 13, 14, 17; Col 4:18; 2 Tim 2:9; cf. Phlm 10). The genitival phrase "for the gospel" (τοῦ εὐαγγελίου) should be taken as a genitive of reference, expressing both the cause and the purpose of his imprisonment: "for the sake of the gospel" (NET; cf. GNB).[76] What is not clear is whether "gospel" refers to the content of the gospel[77] or the act of preaching the gospel. Verse 9 ("a prisoner of Christ Jesus") points to the former reading, although both may be implied here.

14a But I preferred to do nothing without your consent (χωρὶς δὲ τῆς σῆς γνώμης οὐδὲν ἠθέλησα ποιῆσαι). As the final part of this long sentence, this verse serves as a transition from Onesimus as the center of concern to Philemon.[78] Paul wants Philemon to respond voluntarily to his appeal.

This verse also serves as a contrast to the previous clause. This contrast is highlighted not only by the adversative conjunction "but" (δέ), but also by the presence of the emphatic "your" (σῆς), a stronger possessive pronoun instead of the simple genitival form of the second person singular pronoun

---

73. Thus Winter, "Paul's Letter to Philemon," 9; Pearson, "Assumptions in the Criticism and Translation of Philemon," 276 – 77; Ryan, "Philemon," 236; Wilson, *Colossians and Philemon*, 352 – 53.

74. Cf. Wolf-Henning Ollrog, *Paulus und seine Mitarbeiter: Untersuchungen zu Theorie und Praxis der paulinischen Mission* (WMANT 50; Neukirchen-Vluyn: Neukirchener, 1979), 101 – 6.

75. Barth and Blanke, *Letter to Philemon*, 371, who further argue, "applied to Onesimus's eventual future service to Paul,

this would mean that, even when suffering cannot be avoided, the slave will occupy a place of honor and will be richly rewarded by God himself" (375).

76. Cf. Harris, *Colossians and Philemon*, 264.

77. Cf. "I am in prison for the sake of Christ" (Phil 1:13, NET).

78. Heil, "The Chiastic Structure and Meaning of Paul's Letter to Philemon," 184, maintains that this verse is the center of the chiastic structure of Paul's argument in this letter.

(σου, v. 13).[79] This pronoun corresponds to the emphatic first person pronoun "I" (ἐγώ) in the previous verse. The point is clear: despite Paul's own desire, he is willing to give up his rights in honor of Philemon's own judgment. Paul is thereby hoping that Philemon will give up his own rights to act in line with the new reality that exists in Christ.

The significance of "I preferred to" (ἠθέλησα), has already been noted in our discussion of v. 13. The translation adopted here ("I preferred to do nothing"), rather than the more idiomatic paraphrase, "I did not want to do anything" (NASB, NAB, REB, TNIV, NET, NIV; cf. HCSB, NLT), highlights the contrast with v. 13 and thus with Paul's own act according to the strength of his will and conviction.

The meaning "consent" for γνώμη is common in Hellenistic writings.[80] Behind Paul's request for Philemon's consent may lie the recognition that he is the rightful "master" of Onesimus;[81] others point to Paul's personal relationship with Philemon as the primary motivation behind this request.[82] But in light of Paul's attempt to convince Philemon to act within the new framework of the reality in Christ, it is best to see again Paul's partnership (cf. v. 6, 17) with his coworker in faith (v. 1) as the primary force that will restrain him from simply exercising his rights according to his own personal desire.

14b-c So that your good deed would not be forced, but voluntary (ἵνα μὴ ὡς κατὰ ἀνάγκην τὸ ἀγαθόν σου ᾖ ἀλλὰ κατὰ ἑκούσιον). Paul now appeals to Philemon's commitment to be consistent in his Christian walk. For the sake of contemporary readers, it is tempting to translate this "good deed" (τὸ ἀγαθόν) as "favor" (TNIV, NIV) or even with the verb "to help (me)" (GNB, NLT), but this translation is inadequate. This "good thing" refers to "every good thing" (παντὸς ἀγαθοῦ) in v. 6. There the "good thing" is described as that which "is in us for Christ." The "good thing" is not limited to kind deeds performed for others; rather, it is that which is appropriate when one lives in Christ. In this context, therefore, Paul is not simply referring to a "favor" that Philemon should be doing for him, nor is he simply asking for Philemon's help; he is instead trying to have Philemon live out the reality that he is already affirming: the new life lived out in the household of God.

With this reference to the "good thing," one again confronts the question concerning the implied request embedded here. In light of v. 13, it seems best to consider this "good thing" as the release of Onesimus to serve Paul as he himself serves the Lord in his imprisonment.[83] Those who consider this a "general expression which does not restrict the letter's recipient to the fulfillment of a precise instruction"[84] fail to recognize the importance of the previous verse in interpreting this phrase.

"Forced" (ἀνάγκην) carries the sense of "necessity" (KJV, ASV) and "compulsion" (NASB, NKJV, NET, ESV). In 1 Cor 7:37, this word is used in contrast to the one who "has control over his own will" (NIV). This is also how the term "voluntary" (ἑκούσιον) is to be understood. For readers familiar

---

79. This possessive pronoun ("your," σῆς) "serves to emphasize or to contrast"; see BDAG, 934.

80. Cf. P.Grenf. II.14(a), P.Tebt. I.6, P.Tebt. 1.104, BGU IV.1051; MM, 129. See also Arzt-Grabner, *Philemon*, 220.

81. S. R. Llewelyn and R. A. Kearsley, "'Slaves, Obey Your Masters': The Legal Liability of Slaves," *NewDocs* 7:194.

82. Wilson, *Colossians and Philemon*, 352.

83. Lightfoot, *St. Paul's Epistles to the Colossians and to Philemon*, 342; Ryan, "Philemon," 237; Wilson, *Colossians and Philemon*, 354. Others, such as Witherington, *Letters to Philemon, the Colossians, and the Ephesians*, 76, suggest that "good thing" refers to a series of things that Philemon is to accomplish: friendly reception of Onesimus, granting Onesimus freedom, and sending Onesimus back to serve (with) Paul.

84. Lohse, *Colossians and Philemon*, 202.

with the translation "spontaneous,"[85] it should be noted this word is to be understood as "the opposite not of 'premeditated' but of 'unwilling.'"[86]

It is no accident that Paul discusses this contrast between "forced" and "voluntary" in a letter that deals with the proper treatment of a slave. In setting up an example for Philemon, Paul has decided to grant him the freedom to act according to his own will in light of their partnership in Christ and the new reality found in Christ (cf. v. 15). As he does so, Philemon should similarly allow Onesimus to respond to the call to service according to his own will, and not according to the compulsion imposed on him by one who insists on his status as a slave. In addition to enhancing the rhetorical force of his argument, this verse is significant in that Paul is living out a model that Philemon is to follow.

15a Perhaps it was for this reason that he was separated from you for a while (τάχα γὰρ διὰ τοῦτο ἐχωρίσθη πρὸς ὥραν). Paul finally alludes to Onesimus's separation from Philemon, and he considers this separation to be part of God's will. The postpositive γάρ, left untranslated here (cf. "For perhaps it was for this reason," NET),[87] points to the syntactical relationship between vv. 15 – 16 and the previous sentence: Paul is sending Onesimus back although he wanted to keep him because of the possibility that Philemon and Onesimus

would be able to relate to one another within the new framework in the household of God in Christ.

"For this reason" (διὰ τοῦτο) points ahead to the second half of the verse, which provides the reason for Onesimus's temporary absence from Philemon. This is made explicit in some versions: "Perhaps the reason he was separated from you for a little while was that you might have him back forever."[88] This phrase is then connected with the "so that" (ἵνα) that follows, a clause that indicates this reason. Onesimus's temporary absence from Philemon, then, becomes the reason for God to work so that the relationship between Philemon and Onesimus can be transformed permanently.

In terms of function, both "perhaps" and "he was separated" carry considerable theological weight. In this context, "perhaps" (τάχα), "a marker expressing contingency,"[89] does not express doubt or uncertainty; rather, it calls for further deliberation and the need to see beyond what is apparent. Many, therefore, see this word as introducing "a cautious added thought,"[90] while others suggest it points to "divine involvement."[91] In any case, these two verses aim at forcing Philemon to see the events that have transpired through the eyes of faith.

In the same way, "he was separated" (ἐχωρίσθη) should be taken as implying divine involvement. This passive verb is rightly considered to be a "divine passive," so that God is the ultimate subject of

---

85. This is the reading adopted by the earlier versions of NIV (1973 – 84). Note the change to "voluntary" in TNIV and the 2011 NIV.

86. Wright, *Colossians and Philemon*, 184. In Attic legal texts, the term is used in reference to "premeditated" (ἐκούσιοι) versus "unpremeditated" (ἀκούσιοι) murders; cf. P. Dimakis, "The Vocabulary of Legal Terms," in *History of Ancient Greek* (ed. A.-F. Christidis; Cambridge: Cambridge Univ. Press, 2007), 1084.

87. This conjunction is left untranslated in many contemporary versions (cf. NAB, REV, NJB, NRSV, CEV, GNB, NLT, TNIV, NIV).

88. This is how the phrase is taken by most commentators, with the notable exception of Callahan, *Embassy of Onesimus*, 43, who confuses this phrase with the postpositive conjunction "for" (γάρ), and therefore takes this phrase as a reference to "on account of Paul's wish that Onesimus minister to Philemon."

89. BDAG, 992. Elsewhere in the NT, the word appears only in Rom 5:7.

90. Fitzmyer, *Letter to Philemon*, 112. Cf. Wright, *Colossians and Philemon*, 184.

91. Bratcher and Nida, *Translator's Handbook*, 127.

what took place.[92] Some have considered this verb as a "euphemistic verb,"[93] and Paul's use of it shows that he "clearly does not want Philemon to be reminded of the damage he has suffered."[94] Others have suggested that by using this verb, Paul intends "to protect Onesimus yet also give his master a precise hint of Onesimus's crime."[95]

These inferences are, however, without basis. Consistent with other Hellenistic uses, in the NT this verb occurs in reference to the departure from a locality (Acts 1:4; 18:1,2), separation from objects/persons (Rom 8:35–39; Heb 7:26), and also the extended meaning as in discussions of divorce (Matt 19:6; Mark 10:9; 1 Cor 7:10, 11, 15). In ancient documents, it does not refer to an escape, nor is it a euphemism for a criminal act. From this verb, therefore, one cannot argue for the presence of a criminal act that prompted this separation.[96]

It is best to see God as the focus of this verb. Paul is using it to suggest that God might have used him in his meeting with Onesimus as an instrument for a higher end: to convert Onesimus into a believer and a disciple. He has been brought into a network of relationships in which all are full members and siblings within the household of God. For Philemon, to receive Onesimus back "represents the completion of God's design."[97]

15b So that you may have him back forever (ἵνα αἰώνιον αὐτὸν ἀπέχῃς). As noted above, this clause provides the content of the prepositional phrase "for this reason," for Paul considers it God's will for Philemon to accept Onesimus as a fellow believer. "You may have … back" (ἀπέχῃς) can acquire a technical sense of "receiving full payment" in business transactions (cf. Phil 4:18),[98] but here it refers to the full and willing reception of Onesimus.

The contrast with the previous clause is highlighted by word order. The previous clause ends with "for a while" (lit., "for an hour," πρὸς ὥραν), while in this clause "forever" (αἰώνιον) immediately follows the conjunction "so that" (ἵνα). The temporary separation will now be overshadowed by a renewed relationship that lasts "forever"; this renewed relationship is the focus of the next verse. Here, "forever" likely means "permanently" (HCSB).

The use of "forever" may evoke a similar use in Exod 21:6, where a voluntary slave would have his ear pierced and would "be his [master's] servant for life [εἰς τὸν αἰῶνα]."[99] But in light of the next clause, where Paul clearly states that Philemon is to receive Onesimus back "no longer as a slave, but more than a slave," it seems certain that Paul is not saying that Onesimus will now serve Philemon permanently as a slave. To "have him back forever" should, therefore, refer to the new relationship that transcends earthly relationships, and this is likely what Paul means with the phrase "a beloved brother" (v. 16).

---

92. Lohse, *Colossians and Philemon*, 202; O'Brien, *Colossians, Philemon*, 295; Harris, *Colossians and Philemon*, 265; Fitzmyer, *Letter to Philemon*, 112; Ryan, "Philemon," 245, Moo, *Letters to the Colossians and to Philemon*, 419. Some, however, take it as a deponent verb with an active meaning of "leave" or "depart"; cf. Isak J. du Plessis, "How Christians Can Survive in a Hostile Social-Economic Environment: Paul's Mind concerning Difficult Social Conditions in the Letter to Philemon," in *Identity, Ethics, and Ethos in the New Testament* (ed. Jan G. van der Watt; BZNW 141; Berlin/New York: de Gruyter, 2006), 402; Arzt-Graber, Philemon, 103–4.

93. Lightfoot, *St. Paul's Epistles to the Colossians and to Philemon*, 342.

94. Fitzmyer, *Letter to Philemon*, 112.

95. Nordling, "Onesimus Fugitivus," 109.

96. Pearson, "Assumptions in the Criticism and Translation of Philemon," 265. See also Barth and Blanke, *Letter to Philemon*, 395: "by using the passive form, Paul did not intend to 'veil' what is declared by a majority to be the slave's 'guilt' of escaping."

97. Martin, "The Rhetorical Function of Commercial Language," 328.

98. Stuhlmacher, *Der Brief an Philemon*, 41.

99. Moule, *Epistles to the Colossians and to Philemon*, 146.

16a-c No longer as a slave, but more than a slave, a beloved brother (οὐκέτι ὡς δοῦλον ἀλλὰ ὑπὲρ δοῦλον, ἀδελφὸν ἀγαπητόν). Paul now explicitly articulates the new relationship between Philemon and Onesimus. Modifying the verb "you may have … back" (ἀπέχῃς), this verse provides further definition as to how Onesimus is to be received. This phrase modifies the purpose clause with its subjunctive verb ἀπέχῃς, so one might have expected μηκέτι rather than οὐκέτι for "no longer."[100] The use of οὐκέτι here may serve to emphasize that " 'no more than a slave' is an absolute fact, whether Philemon chooses to recognize it or not."[101] If so, the significance of this statement in Paul's rhetorical strategy should not be missed.

The particle "as" (ὡς) has been taken in a number of ways. Least likely is the reading that takes this in the counterfactual sense of "as though." This reading assumes that Onesimus is not literally a slave and should not be treated as one.[102] This use of the particle is absent from the NT (except perhaps in 2 Cor 10:9). It is best, therefore, to consider this as a "marker introducing the perspective from which a per., thing, or activity is viewed or understood as to character, function, or role."[103]

Even so, it is not clear whether this particle introduces merely a subjective perspective or one that reflects an objective reality (at least in the opinion of the author). For some, ὡς points merely to Paul's subjective reading of the situation, without challenging the objective reality of Onesimus's status as a slave.[104] But it is questionable whether Paul would consider the reality in Christ, where there is neither "slave" nor "free" (Col 3:11) in the new humanity brought about his redemptive death, as merely a subjective reading. One cannot deny, however, that ὡς does point to a reality that may escape human eyes. "No longer as a slave," therefore, points to a reception of this slave within a new framework that acknowledges the relativization of the present social and political reality without necessarily denying such a reality in the present age. This is consistent with Paul's exhortation to the slaves in Col 3:23: "whatever you do, do it wholeheartedly, as [ὡς] to the Lord and not to people."

This understanding is perhaps confirmed by the next phrase, "but more than a slave" (ἀλλὰ ὑπὲρ δοῦλον). The preposition "more than" (ὑπέρ), by itself, does not necessarily deny the reality of a slave's earthly status, but it does point to his new status as "surpassing" that of his present identity.[105] When Paul further defines this phrase through the words "a beloved brother" (ἀδελφὸν ἀγαπητόν), readers are again reminded of the ambiguity and tension with the presence of these competing realities. While some see behind this juxtaposition of labels as pointing toward a call to manumission,[106] others see Paul as less concerned with the social relationships at this point.[107] Such ambiguity has also led

---

100. See a parallel in Rom 6:6, where a similar thought concerning freedom from slavery is expressed within a purpose clause: "For we know that our old self was crucified with him so that the body ruled by sin might be done away with, that we should no longer [μηκέτι] be slaves to sin."

101. Lightfoot, *St. Paul's Epistles to the Colossians and to Philemon*, 3,43.

102. See esp. Callahan, *Embassy of Onesimus*, 44 – 47, who argues that "all indications here are that if Onesimus was a *doulos*, he was, like Paul and his associates (see Phil. 1:1), a *doulos tou theou*, a slave of God."

103. BDAG, 1104.

104. Lohse, *Colossians and Philemon*, 203; O'Brien, *Colossians, Philemon*, 297.

105. Cf. BDF §230. Cf. TNIV, NIV: "better than a slave."

106. Recognizing that an explicit call is absent, some still see at least a textual opening that allows for an implicit appeal; see, e.g., Stuhlmacher, *Der Brief an Philemon*, 43; G. Francois Wessels, "The Letter to Philemon in the Context of Slavery in Early Christianity," in *Philemon in Perspective: Interpreting a Pauline Letter* (ed. D. Francois Tolmie; BZNW 169; New York/Berlin: de Gruyter, 2011), 164 – 68.

107. See, e.g., Wright, *Colossians and Philemon*, 185.

some to conclude that Paul himself "did not know what to recommend."[108]

Before surrendering to such interpretive despair, a few points need to be made. First, within the social reality of the first-century Roman world, a simple call to manumission without changes to the entire Roman social and political system would simply be considered as an idealistic move. Moreover, in such contexts, "manumission would have diminished Philemon's obligations without increasing Onesimus' well-being or security."[109]

Second, regardless of whether Paul is calling for Philemon to manumit his slave, the progression of thought in this verse clearly points to the significance of a new set of relationships among these brothers in Christ.

Third, the adjective "beloved" (ἀγαπητόν) should also be noted. As Philemon is the "beloved" in v. 1 and as he has consistently expressed his "love for all the saints" (v. 5; cf. vv. 7, 9), he is urged to fulfill this trajectory of love in his reception of Onesimus. This love transcends the old realities that include both their former statuses as well as the possible tensions between them.

Finally, the striking juxtaposition of the titles "slave" and "brother" is noteworthy. Not only is it unique in the NT,[110] but the fact that slaves are considered aliens within the household highlights the significance of this sibling language. Note too that manumission itself would not only fail to remedy this situation; it could further alienate the slave from the household, since to "free a slave meant not only to alienate family property, but also to disengage a member, though an inferior one, from the *oikos*."[111] Within the social and political reality of the first-century world, therefore, to consider a "slave" as a "beloved brother" is at least as significant as the mere call for manumission would be.

16d-f Especially to me, but how much more to you, both in the flesh and in the Lord (μάλιστα ἐμοί, πόσῳ δὲ μᾶλλον σοὶ καὶ ἐν σαρκὶ καὶ ἐν κυρίῳ). Building on his own relationship with Onesimus, Paul now urges for the transformation of the way Philemon relates to Onesimus since both Onesimus and Philemon are Paul's sons in the faith. The combination of the superlative adverb "especially" (μάλιστα) with its comparative form "more" (μᾶλλον) has been labeled as an "enthusiastic illogicality"[112] that can be rendered literally as "most of all to me … more than most of all to thee."[113] "Especially to me" draws attention to the close relationship between Paul and Onesimus, as Onesimus became Paul's son during his imprisonment (v. 10). "How much more to you" then points to Philemon's newfound relationship with Onesimus as a sibling within the household of God.

Moreover, in the context of Paul's wider argument, this superlative-comparative combination takes on added rhetorical force. If Onesimus is most important to Paul, he is to be even more important to Philemon precisely because Onesimus is not simply his "beloved brother" in Christ; he is also Paul's son. Underlying this emphatic note is the assumption that will be made explicit in v. 17: "receive him, as you would receive me."

---

108. Barclay, "Paul, Philemon and the Dilemma of Christian Slave Ownership," 175, who further notes: "If we think about the situation in practical terms we will see that there were immense difficulties in either of the two main options to Philemon — to retain Onesimus as a slave or to manumit him."

109. Taylor "Onesimus," 271. For more on manumission, see Introduction to Philemon.

110. This is, therefore, the center of Paul's rhetorical force in this sentence; cf. Witherington, *Letters to Philemon, the Colossians, and the Ephesians,* 80; Aasgaard, *"My Beloved Brothers and Sisters,"* 257 – 60.

111. Zelnick-Abramovitz, *Not Wholly Free,* 336.

112. Moule, *Epistles to the Colossians and to Philemon,* 148.

113. Lightfoot, *St. Paul's Epistles to the Colossians and to Philemon,* 343.

The contrast between "in the flesh" (ἐν σαρκί) and "in the Lord" (ἐν κυρίῳ) completes the thought of this sentence. This contrast can be found nowhere else in Paul's writings, but the discussion of household relationships in a letter addressed to the same wider community may help. In Col 3:18 – 4:1, the lordship of Christ is repeatedly affirmed through the title "Lord" (3:18, 20, 22, 23, 24; 4:1). Significantly, it is in this context that the masters of slaves are identified as "the masters/lords of the flesh" (lit., τοῖς κατὰ σάρκα κυρίοις, 3:22). In that Colossian context, the authority of the "masters" is relativized through the reference to the "flesh." In this context, however, the strategy is reversed, and the point is striking. One would have expected Paul to say that Onesimus is to be received as a slave "in the flesh," but a "beloved brother in the Lord." Instead, Paul applies both prepositional phrases to the "beloved brother."[114] That is to say, Onesimus is

a "beloved brother" not simply in a spiritual sense, but also in an earthly sociopolitical sense.

Several implications can be drawn from this claim. First, as noted above, the climax of this sentence indeed lies in the claim that Onesimus is to be treated as "a beloved brother." This application to this contrastive pair points to the comprehensive scope of this reality within the household of God. Although manumission may not be the main point of this passage, it is Onesimus's status as a "beloved brother" that is the focus of Paul's concern here. Moreover, if he was converted as a household slave when Philemon was converted, his true conversion under the mentorship of Paul would allow him to return to his household as a full member of the household of faith.[115] At the end, Paul is as concerned with convincing Philemon of the significance of this new reality as he is with Philemon's proper reception of Onesimus as a full member of this household.

Theology in Application

More than Freedom

Contemporary readers of Philemon often focus on Paul's precise position concerning the manumission of Onesimus. Most, however, are disappointed with what they find in this text. Those who see manumission behind this text highlight v. 16 in particular: "no longer as a slave, but more than a slave, a beloved brother ... both in the flesh and in the Lord." The fact that the final prepositional phrases modify "a beloved brother" points to the earthly significance of Onesimus's new status as a brother in the household of God.

Moreover, the development of Paul's rhetoric that climaxes in his labeling

---

114. Some, such as Harris, *Colossians and Philemon*, 269, suggest that "in the flesh" describes Onesimus's earthly status as a slave, while "in the Lord" describes his spiritual identity as a brother, thus: "since he is now related to you by spiritual ties as a fellow Christian, as well as by human ties as a slave in your household." This reading is also adopted in some contemporary versions: "both as a man and as a brother in the Lord" (NLT; cf. GNB). This, however, misreads the Greek where both

prepositional phrases clearly modify the phrases, "especially to me, but how much more to you," which in turn modify "a beloved brother." See the detailed discussion in Barth and Blanke, *Letter to Philemon*, 450 – 73.

115. Taylor "Onesimus," 272, sees this return as the completion of his conversion since "he would be resocialised into the household of which he was already legally a part, but as identifying fully with its cultic life."

Onesimus as "a beloved brother" also draws attention to this new label as one that at least relativizes his (former) status as a slave. Those who do not see this as a call for manumission point to the absence of any explicit call that can be interpreted as such. Furthermore, the fact that Paul writes "no longer *as* a slave" rather than "no longer a slave" points to his lack of interest in challenging this social institution. What both sides can agree on is the fact that Paul could have been clearer in making his intention known, at least as far as this issue of manumission is concerned. This has also led some to conclude that Paul himself is not exactly certain as to what he would like to recommend.[116]

Instead of focusing on the issue of manumission, readers should allow Paul to set the agenda for his own writing. In this case, he writes as an apostle and not as a philosopher whose task is to outline an ideal state or as a political operative who has the power to bring about systemic changes to the social and political reality of the first-century world. He is not, however, ignorant of such discourses or disinterested in such visions. In this letter, however, Paul is confronted with a more immediate problem with the status and identity of Onesimus. Instead of simply seeking to disengage Onesimus from the household of Philemon so that he can serve Paul in his imprisonment, he attempts to accomplish a far more difficult task, one that leads to a far more nuanced and sophisticated letter.

Identifying himself primarily as one who serves "Christ Jesus" (v. 1), Paul sees his primary task as convincing both Onesimus and Philemon to accept the reality that the gospel of Christ introduces. As one who considers himself the father of Onesimus (v. 10), Paul seeks to have him returned to his household and to become a full member of this spiritual household. Instead of spending effort in convincing Philemon that he can live without Onesimus, he does the reverse. Thus, one finds the emphasis on Onesimus being "useful" (v. 11) and his being "no longer as a slave, but more than a slave" (v. 16). Onesimus is to return to Philemon, and with a proper reception, they will be able to testify to the new humanity that is in Christ (cf. Col 3:11). Choosing a path that transcends manumission, on the one hand, and upholding the status quo, on the other, Paul considers both options as detrimental to both Philemon and Onesimus. Instead, he insists on having them relate to one another as "beloved brothers" (cf. v. 16), because they are both "beloved" in the eyes of God. Therefore, "both in the flesh and in the Lord" (v. 16), Paul expects them to live out the reality of the gospel message.

For contemporary Christians, we must also be reminded of the primacy of this gospel message and the reality it brings. Though unpopular in some circles, evangelism and missions still form the heart of our Christian calling. But this is not to ignore the present reality of struggles or to romanticize the systemic evil that can be

---

116. Barclay, "Paul, Philemon and the Dilemma of Christian Slave Ownership," 175. See also comments on v. 16. In response, Taylor, "Onesimus," 269, notes that "it is abundantly clear from verse 21 that Paul expects to be obeyed, and this presupposes that he is issuing an unambiguous if tactful directive."

identified around us. Instead, we are called to focus on the gospel message that demands so much more from us. It is a gospel that testifies to a God who is not simply a projection of our human imagination:

> It is obvious that this God's name of Father is not merely an echo of the experience of fatherhood, masculinity, strength, and power in this world.... No, this God is a different God ... a God who does not overthrow the existing legal order and the whole social system, but who tempers it for humanity's sake; and a God who consequently wants to have the barriers of categorization between good people and bad, friends and foes, neighbors and strangers, workers and unemployed, removed. How? By humility, self-denial, love, forgiveness without end, service regardless of reward, sacrifice without compensation.[117]

Through the death of his Son on the cross, this God is able to conquer the world through an utterly powerless act, but one that challenges all powers and authorities (Col. 1:15 – 20). In refusing to use his apostolic power to proclaim freedom for Onesimus, therefore, Paul is testifying to the gospel of this cross, a gospel that refuses to challenge the structure of this world simply through the powerful instruments of the world.

Rhetoric of Weakness

In shifting the focus away from the individual thirst for freedom, Paul focuses instead on the believers' freedom to serve one another and to find their identity in Christ. In articulating this vision, Paul makes it clear that he himself is also willing to give up his freedom for the sake of the gospel. As a "prisoner" (vv. 1, 9) and an "old man" (v. 9), he submits to a reality in which the exercise of his own will is no longer his primary concern. The decision to "appeal ... on the basis of love" (v. 9) is, therefore, not merely a rhetorical ploy; it reflects the refusal to exercise the rightful power he possesses, especially since Philemon owes him his "very self" (v. 19). This also explains his decision to send Onesimus back so that Philemon can exercise his right to make the right decision through his "voluntary" will (v. 14).

This rhetoric of weakness is no mere rhetoric. For Paul, this points to the reality of the cross, and this is to live out the gospel of this cross through which reconciliation is possible (cf. Col 1:21 – 23). In this letter, therefore, Paul highlights the framework within which one should love, without explicit commands that are to be followed. Paul refuses to succumb to the temptation to exercise his power so that Philemon can give up his own. If there is a "power" about which he can "boast," it is the power in his weakness, as he states elsewhere:

---

117. Hans Küng, *Why I Am Still a Christian* (trans. David Smith et. al.; ed. E. C. Hughes; Nashville: Abingdon, 1987), 51 – 52.

I will boast all the more gladly about my weaknesses, so that Christ's power may rest on me. That is why, for Christ's sake, I delight in weaknesses, in insults, in hardships, in persecutions, in difficulties. For when I am weak, then I am strong. (2 Cor 12:9 – 10)

This rhetoric of weakness is possible because Christ "was crucified in weakness, yet he lives by God's power" (2 Cor 13:4).

This demonstration of a life that submits to weaknesses in turn becomes a powerful argument for Philemon to give Onesimus his own life. As Paul is willing to give up his claim over Onesimus (v. 13), Philemon should do the same. As Paul resists exercising his will over others (v. 14), Philemon should do the same. As God is the sovereign one who stands behind the events that have transpired (v. 15), Philemon should also yield to God's sovereignty. Following the affirmation of that sovereignty and the willful submission to God's will, Paul launches the most powerful argument possible for Philemon to give up willfully his rights over Onesimus so that he too can serve God with his own will. Even without a call to manumission, one does find a powerful basis for such a call. This call seeks neither to "accommodate" nor to "colonize" the world, but it will bring new life into this present existence simply because one has been born into this new reality:[118]

> Christians do not come into their social world from outside seeking either to accommodate to their new home (like second generation immigrants would), shape it in the image of the one they left behind (like colonizers would), or establish a little haven in the strange new world reminiscent of the old (as resident aliens would). They are not outsiders who either seek to become insiders or maintain strenuously the status of outsiders. Christians are the *insiders* who have diverted from their culture by being born again. They are by definition those who are not what they used to be, those who do not live like they used to live. Christian difference is therefore not an insertion of something new into the old from outside, but a bursting out of the new *precisely within the proper space of the old*.[119]

In Paul's letter to Philemon, one finds a striking example of such a process wherein new believers are called to reevaluate their identity in their own social and cultural locations. This message is also relevant for contemporary readers who may not be struggling with issues of slavery. From self-centered and idolatrous lives that worship individual freedoms and rights, we must submit to the powerful demands of the gospel message and serve God with all our will and might. It is only in such a posture of weakness that we can experience God's power, a power that bursts forth in our present existence.

---

118. This may also explain the significance of the indirect references to both the conversions of Onesimus (v. 10) and Philemon (v. 19) in this letter.

119. Miroslav Volf, "Soft Difference: Theological Reflections on the Relation between Church and Culture in 1 Peter," *ExAud* 10 (1994): 18 – 19, italics his.

What are some modern manifestations for such quests for individual freedoms and rights? Within our churches, these may include insisting on one's own opinion in the name of divine inspiration, competing for power and attention, or trying to dominate in committees and worship teams. In our workplace, these may include an insatiable desire to get ahead by whatever means, or the urge to establish one's status within the corporate system at the expense of Christian witness. In society at large, such quests for individual freedoms and rights lurk behind our positions in numerous social issues such as abortion, euthanasia, or sexual ethics. In all these, Paul's rhetoric of weakness reminds us not to assume the posture of the autonomous self but to recognize our place within the created order and the wider plan of God.

For the Kingdom of God

By insisting on a rhetoric of weakness that looks beyond individual freedom, the focus on the kingdom of God should not be missed. Paul's self-identification as a "prisoner of Christ Jesus" (vv. 1, 9) already points to a christocentric framework of reference. The reference to Onesimus being "useful to you and to me" (v. 11) likely refers to Onesimus's new service as a believer, and Paul's wish to keep him so that he might serve him on Philemon's behalf during his "imprisonment for the gospel" (v. 13) points to the heart of Paul's request. These statements are peripheral while the fate of Onesimus lies at the center of attention, but they are central to Paul's agenda as he focuses on what will benefit the ministry of the gospel.

Far from being a theologically deprived letter, the letter to Philemon reveals a profound theocentric and christocentric vision. Paul's indirect request to have Onesimus serve him as he is imprisoned "for the gospel" (v. 13) points to a missions-driven agenda, and the concern to have Philemon relate to Onesimus as "a beloved brother" (v. 16) situates this relationship within the wider ecclesiological discussions where the sibling language plays an important role in depicting the new community that submits to the lordship of Christ. These missiological and ecclesiological emphases are grounded in Christ's redemptive death, which may have provided the model for Paul's own offer in v. 18 (see comments). Elsewhere in Paul, it is explicitly noted that believers can relate to one another because of the death of Christ: "So, my brothers and sisters, you also died to the law through the body of Christ, that you might belong to another, to him who was raised from the dead, in order that we might bear fruit for God" (Rom 7:4).

Contemporary readers should take note of the significance of this theocentric and christocentric message, which will impact the lives of individuals navigating through the implications of their own claims as members of the household of God. In drawing attention to these dimensions that may not be the immediate concerns of Philemon, Paul reminds him of the priority of this new reality. Those among us who are also struggling with their own daily struggles will do well if they are also reminded to seek first the kingdom of God (see Matt 6:33).

Philemon 17 – 20

Literary Context

These verses form part of a larger section of Paul's requests concerning Onesimus (vv. 8 – 20).[1] In vv. 8 – 16, Paul appeals to Philemon on the basis of his relationship with Onesimus. There he identifies Onesimus as his "child" (v. 10) and his own "heart" (v. 12). This identification highlights his significance in Paul's eyes and makes it clear to Philemon that his treatment of Onesimus reflects his own evaluation of his relationship with Paul. Beyond this, Paul emphasizes Onesimus's usefulness (v. 11) and his desire to keep the slave to serve him in prison (v. 13). The previous section culminates in Paul's request to Philemon to receive Onesimus "no longer as a slave, but more than a slave, a beloved brother" (v. 16).

The present subsection makes Paul's request even clearer. The development from vv. 8 – 16 to these verses is best illustrated by the presence of three imperatives ("receive," προσλαβοῦ, v. 17; "charge," ἐλλόγα, v. 18; "refresh," ἀνάπαυσον, v. 20), whereas none is present in vv. 8 – 16. As the previous section establishes Onesimus's significance to and usefulness for Paul, this one begins with a direct call to Philemon to receive Onesimus as he would receive Paul (v. 17). This has led some to consider vv. 8 – 16 as the background and v. 17 as the request proper.[2] Others have identified v. 17 as representing "a unique summary of the book."[3] In any case, its central importance cannot be denied, and its significance is foreshadowed by Paul's previous presentation of Onesimus through a new framework.

After the explicit call in v. 17, Paul proceeds with a promise to repay Philemon for any debt incurred by Onesimus (vv. 18 – 19b) while reminding Philemon of his own indebtedness to himself (v. 19c-d). The concluding appeal for Philemon to refresh his own heart (v. 20) again reminds him of Paul's earlier identification of Onesimus as his own heart (v. 12).

---

1. Concerning the debate surrounding the limit of the main body of this letter, see the discussion of Literary Context on vv. 8 – 16.

2. Cf. Chan-Hie Kim, *Form and Structure of the Familiar Greek Letter of Recommendation* (SBLDS 4; Missoula, MT: Society of Biblical Literature, 1972), 124.

3. Allen "The Discourse Structure of Philemon," 91.

In the section that follows (vv. 21 – 25), Paul concludes the letter with a note of confidence concerning Philemon's obedience to his requests (v. 21) as well as a more specific instruction to prepare a room for him for an upcoming visit (v. 22). Both notes should, however, be considered as accomplishing the same function: to ensure that Philemon will accomplish what is asked of him. As in other Pauline letters, this one ends with words of greetings (vv. 23 – 24) and a benediction (v. 25).

III. Requests concerning Onesimus (vv. 8 – 20)
    A. Appeals from the Relationship between Paul and Onesimus (vv. 8 – 16)
➡   **B. Instructions from the Relationship between Paul and Philemon (vv. 17 – 20)**
    IV. Final Greetings (vv. 21 – 25)

Main Idea

Paul names Philemon as a partner in ministry and instructs him to receive Onesimus as he would receive Paul himself while ensuring that there is no reason for Philemon not to accept him in this way.

Translation

Philemon 17 – 20

17a	condition	If, therefore, you consider me a partner,
b	Exhortation	**receive him**
c	manner	as you would receive me.
18a	condition	If he has wronged you in any way,
b	condition	or owes you anything,
c	Exhortation	**charge it to me.**
19a	verification (of 19b)	I, Paul, am writing this with my own hand:
b	Assertion	**I will repay it —**
c	explanation	not to mention that
d	content	you owe me your own self.
20a	Entreaty	**Yes, brother, let me have some benefit**
b	source	from you
c	sphere	in the Lord.
d	Exhortation	**Refresh my heart in Christ.**

Structure

The connection with the previous sections is noted in two ways. First, the conjunction "therefore" (οὖν, v. 17) connects this passage to the previous appeals as Paul makes a specific request of Philemon to receive Onesimus as he would receive Paul himself. Second, the conditional clause also links this request with an assumption made earlier. "If ... you consider me a partner (κοινωνόν)" (v. 17) points back to v. 6, where Paul comments on Philemon's "partnership" (ἡ κοινωνία) in the faith. Paul is now prepared to make his requests explicit as he calls Philemon to act in a way consistent with the faith that he has received and affirms.

Perhaps no stronger request can be made than the one in v. 17, as Paul asks Philemon to receive Onesimus as he would receive Paul himself. This request is not only based on the assumption of Paul's partnership with Philemon as stated in the protasis of this conditional sentence, but it also extends the argument presented earlier as Paul makes it clear that Onesimus is his own child (v. 10) and his very own heart (v. 12). Instead of presenting a series of theoretical arguments as to why Philemon should accept Onesimus, Paul puts himself at the center of this discussion and turns it into an intensely personal one. His own person, therefore, becomes the key in providing the power of this argument.[4]

Vv. 18 – 19 have often been considered an amplification of Paul's earlier request and arguments.[5] Here Paul removes one possible obstacle to keep Philemon from responding positively to him by promising to repay any possible debt Onesimus has incurred. Immediately following this promise, however, is Paul's emphasis on Philemon's own indebtedness to Paul. The promissory note is, therefore, transformed into another forceful argument for Philemon to act the way Paul thinks he should.

The final request for Philemon to refresh Paul's own heart again draws attention to Paul's personal stake in this case. The reference to Paul's "heart" (σπλάγχνα) here is particularly significant since earlier Onesimus is described as his own "heart" (σπλάγχνα). To have Philemon refresh Paul's own heart is therefore to have him refresh his own slave. Moreover, in v. 7 Paul has already noted that "the hearts [σπλάγχνα] of the saints have been refreshed through you [i.e., Philemon]." Here, as he concludes, Paul urges Philemon to refresh him (and Onesimus) the way he has refreshed all the believers.

---

4. See Theology in Application section for an allusion to Christ's own example behind this verse within the wider context of Paul's argument.

5. Church, "Rhetorical Structure and Design," 28.

Exegetical Outline

→ **I. Instructions from the Relationship between Paul and Philemon (vv. 17–20)**
    A. Explicit request based on partnership between Philemon and Paul (v. 17)
    B. Promise to repay any possible debt to Philemon (vv. 18–19b)
    C. Reminder of Philemon's own indebtedness to Paul (v. 19c-d)
    D. Concluding appeal for Philemon to refresh Paul's heart (v. 20)

Explanation of the Text

17a If, therefore, you consider me a partner (Εἰ οὖν με ἔχεις κοινωνόν). Paul continues his appeal by alluding again to Philemon's partnership with him in ministry, but here he also highlights the conditionality of this partnership. The conjunction "therefore" (οὖν) connects this verse with the previous section. As "the pivot of the entire letter,"[6] this sentence builds on the previous arguments and presents the consummation of such arguments. In view of the lengthy note that qualifies the manner in which Onesimus is to be received (v. 16), οὖν may link v. 17 with v. 15, resuming the discussion concerning the proper reception of Onesimus.[7] Moreover, as the beginning of a new subsection, its function is similar to that of "therefore" (διό) in v. 8, as both are markers of the progression of thought in the main body of this letter.[8]

This protasis ("if" clause) is part of a first-class condition of which the contained assertion cannot simply be taken to be true.[9] Although one may assume the likelihood that Paul considers the claim embedded in this protasis to be true because it serves as the basis for the request that follows, the fact that Philemon's participation in this partnership is the focus of Paul's earlier prayer (v. 6) shows that this claim cannot yet be taken as a certain truth. But in this context, Paul is not simply providing an abstract hypothetical scenario. Instead, with this conditional sentence, "Paul's rhetoric shifts the focus from himself onto what *Philemon* considers and values."[10] In doing so, he is challenging Philemon to realize the conditionality of his continued partnership with Paul: if Philemon wants to continue with Paul as partners in ministry, he will have to adjust his action according to the demands of the gospel that transforms every human relationship.

The term "partner" (κοινωνόν) here should be read in light of Paul's earlier usage of the same word group ("partnership," ἡ κοινωνία) in v. 6, where that word refers to partnership in ministry ("partnership in the faith"). The word "partner" was often used in first-century Hellenistic papyri in the sense of "business partner,"[11] but here it functions as a

---

6. Russell, "Strategy of a First-Century Appeals Letter, *JOTT* 11 (1998): 20.
7. Lohse, *Colossians and Philemon*, 203; O'Brien, *Colossians, Philemon*, 298.
8. Allen, "The Discourse Structure of Philemon," 87.
9. Stanley E. Porter, *Idioms of the Greek New Testament* (2nd ed.; BLG 2; Sheffield: Sheffield Academic, 1994), 256–57; Daniel B. Wallace, *Greek Grammar beyond the Basics: An Exegetical*

Syntax of the New Testament (Grand Rapids: Zondervan, 1996), 690–91.
10. Petersen, *Rediscovering Paul*, 105, italics his.
11. Cf. Arzt-Grabner, *Philemon*, 226–29. For a reading of this term in light of the Roman concept of *societas* that is rooted in the household unit, see also J. Paul Sampley, *Pauline Partnership in Christ: Christian Community and Commitment in Light of Roman Law* (Philadelphia: Fortress, 1980), 11–20.

metaphor for mutual participation in kingdom ministry.[12] This focus on ministry is reinforced by the reference to "the Lord" in the phrase that precedes this conditional sentence (v. 16f).

This reference to partnership is particularly important in Paul's argument. First, in relation to v. 6, Paul is now claiming that Philemon should at least grant Paul the same favor and love as he bestowed on others.[13] More importantly, Paul considers a slave, Onesimus, as the critical bridge that links his relationship with Philemon. Their mutual involvement in the life of Onesimus, therefore, becomes the criterion through which they can participate with one another in the ministry of the Lord.[14] This connection not only forces Philemon to take Paul's request seriously, but it also elevates the position of Onesimus as he is now considered to have the dignity to determine (indirectly) the circle of Paul's fellowship of partners.

17b-c   Receive him as you would receive me (προσλαβοῦ αὐτὸν ὡς ἐμέ). In this apodosis ("then" clause), Paul makes his request known. The precise way Philemon is to "receive" Onesimus must be carefully unpacked. In Paul, this verb (προσλαμβάνω) is used for receiving a person with the emphasis on not passing judgment on that person (cf. Rom 14:1, 3). If this is the intended nuance, this points to the reception of Onesimus without remembering his faults or even the wrong he may have inflicted on Philemon (cf. v. 18). To acquire this sense, however, one would expect further explication of the theme, such as "receive and forgive him."

A slightly different usage can be found in Rom 15:7, where Paul urges believers to "accept one another" (προσλαμβάνεσθε ἀλλήλους). In the present context, this usage would point to the reception of Onesimus into the household of faith.[15] This is supported by a reference to the conversion or rededication of Onesimus in v. 10 as well as the call to have him back as "a beloved brother" in v. 16.

If there is any development of thought from v. 16 and any specific focus embedded in the use of the imperative "receive," it is contained in the phrase "as you would receive me" (ὡς ἐμέ).[16] This phrase points to Onesimus's status as Paul's child (v. 10) and therefore as an honorable representative of the apostle. This reception is not limited to a welcoming of a new member of the household, but the reception of one who has power over Philemon himself (cf. vv. 8, 19). If so, this is a reception that is to be offered to an honorable guest.[17]

To contemporary readers, a simple act of hosting a dinner party may come to mind. For first-century readers, however, this evokes the virtue of hospitality where a stranger is considered a member of the household of the host and equal in status, since friendship can only exist among equals. This call to receive Onesimus is such a call: "when he returns, say to him '… my home is your home.'"[18] If so, there is a clear progression from the previous note on Onesimus as a "beloved brother," since here Paul "expects even more outrageously

---

12. As such, it aims at pointing to a concrete way through which the prayer of v. 6 can be fulfilled; cf. Josef Zmijewski, "Der Philemonbrief: Ein Plädoyer für die christliche Brüderlichkeit," *TTZ* 114 (2005): 222 – 42.

13. See esp. Pearson, "Assumptions in the Criticism and Translation of Philemon," 273 – 74.

14. This would also mean that this partnership is the necessary basis for Paul's identification of Philemon as his "beloved and coworker" (v. 1); cf. Polaski, *Paul and the Discourse of Power*, 66.

15. Cf. Fitzmyer, *Letter to Philemon*, 116; Wilson, *Colossians and Philemon*, 157.

16. In Greek, the phrase literally reads "as me" and is often translated simply as "as you would me" (NASB, NAB, NJB, NKJV, HCSB, NET).

17. See Barth and Blanke, *Letter to Philemon*, 475, who points to this use in Acts 18:26: "When Priscilla and Aquila heard him, they invited [προσελάβοντο] him to their home."

18. Bratcher and Nida, *Translator's Handbook*, 129.

that Philemon ought to treat him as an honored guest, thereby treating him better than he would a brother, a spouse or a child."[19]

18 If he has wronged you in any way, or owes you anything, charge it to me (εἰ δέ τι ἠδίκησέν σε ἢ ὀφείλει, τοῦτο ἐμοὶ ἐλλόγα). To cover all bases, Paul promises to bear any costs for Philemon's proper reception of Onesimus. This conditional sentence has been variously understood according to one's wider assumption concerning the cause of the separation between Onesimus and Philemon. For those who consider Onesimus to be a runaway slave, this is the clearest statement that suggests Onesimus has stolen from his master, which prompted his escape. Even though a reference to possible wrongdoings is embedded in the protasis of a conditional sentence (where certainty is not affirmed), these interpreters consider such references as "very odd … if he [Paul] knew that Philemon had no grounds for complaint."[20]

Moreover, it is often noted that Phrygian slaves had a reputation of being immoral and evil, which provides further support for understanding Onesimus as one who has wronged his master.[21] If so, this protasis does not intend to indicate any doubt in Paul's mind but is "simply a tactful way of raising a rather delicate subject."[22] Some have

also suggested that behind this conditional clause lies an accusation that is presented in no uncertain terms.[23] Insisting on such certainty, the presence of this tactful conditional statement is understood as a way for Paul to shift the focus from Onesimus's wrongdoing to his own generosity.[24]

These readings are, however, no more than conjecture. As a first-class conditional sentence, Paul provides no indication concerning the veracity of the hypothetical scenario presented in the protasis.[25] Even if one affirms that veracity, we have no idea how Onesimus "has wronged" Philemon. This verb can refer to any act that has caused a person "loss."[26] The verb "owes" can cover a variety of debt: not only "financial" but also "social" and "moral" expectations.[27] Thus, this "loss/debt," even if it had taken place, does not have to refer to theft. It can refer to the loss of service incurred when Onesimus was away from Philemon.[28] If Onesimus was himself a debt-slave, this promise to repay such loss may be a veiled attempt to have Onesimus freed or at least transferred to serve under Paul.[29]

It is equally possible for this conditional sentence to be taken as a rhetorical note as Paul seeks to cover all possible grounds in making his own plea for Onesimus. To anticipate an objection is a well-known rhetorical strategy,[30] and to consider this as a key pillar in the reconstruction of the sce-

---

19. De Vos, "Once a Slave, Always a Slave?" 103.

20. Wright, *Colossians and Philemon*, 187; cf. Stuhlmacher, *Der Brief an Philemon*, 49.

21. Cf. Derrett, "The Function of the Epistle to Philemon," 67.

22. Wilson, *Colossians and Philemon*, 358; cf. Lightfoot, *St. Paul's Epistles to the Colossians and to Philemon*, 343.

23. Fitzmyer, *Letter to Philemon*, 117: "Paul states the matter hypothetically, but he realizes it to be true absolutely: Onesimus, he knows, has wronged Philemon in some way."

24. Nordling, "Onesimus Fugitivus," 110.

25. Wallace, *Greek Grammar*, 690 – 91.

26. BDAG, 20. To translate this verb as having "defrauded" (NET) is to limit the semantic range unjustifiably.

27. BDAG, 742.

28. Ryan, "Philemon," 248. For those who uphold the "runaway slave" hypothesis, this "loss" can also refer to Paul's harboring a runaway slave, thus being responsible for such loss of service; cf. Ralph P. Martin, *Colossians and Philemon* (NCB; London: Oliphants, 1974), 167. The language used here, however, does not hint at any apology on Paul's part.

29. The promise to repay a slave's former master is often found in documents that negotiate the manumission of a slave; cf. Adolf Deissmann, *Light from the Ancient East: The New Testament Illustrated by Recently Discovered Texts of the Graeco-Roman World* (trans. Lionel R. M. Strachan; Grand Rapids: Baker, 1965), 330 – 32. See discussion below.

30. Anaximenes, *Rhet. Alex.* 36; cf. Martin, "The Rhetorical Function of Commercial Language," 330.

nario behind this letter is problematic.[31] Moreover, the call to "charge it to me" (τοῦτο ἐμοὶ ἐλλόγα) should be noted. Adopting legal commercial terminology that carries the sense of "set to one's account,"[32] Paul assumes responsibility to repay any such loss. The concrete problem as to how Paul could repay Philemon while he himself is in prison and dependent on others for his daily sustenance is a real one.[33] Paul's inability to repay loss is less of a problem if his promise is understood in its rhetorical intent. Rather than making a false promise, Paul appears to assume that the material loss would be minimal.[34] If so, the conditionality of this note should not be downplayed.

Furthermore, it is possible that this promise of reparation would at least allow Paul to make the implicit request to have Onesimus returned to him to serve him for the sake of the gospel.[35] To assume the responsibility to repay any debt would then be considered an act that paves the way for Philemon to free Onesimus from his service.[36] These assumptions, however, are not explicit in this verse.

19a-b I, Paul, am writing this with my own hand: I will repay it (ἐγὼ Παῦλος ἔγραψα τῇ ἐμῇ χειρί, ἐγὼ ἀποτίσω). Embedded within verses dominated by imperative verbs directed to Philemon (vv. 17, 18, 20), Paul inserts a statement that contains an emphatic first person pronoun, "I" (ἐγώ), his own

name, "Paul" (Παῦλος), together with the emphatic first-person possessive pronoun ("with my own hand," τῇ ἐμῇ χειρί). These self-references are coupled with a note that contains his own promise to Philemon, one that is again introduced by an emphatic first person pronoun. The emphasis placed on this statement highlights the seriousness of Paul's earlier request to have Philemon "receive" Onesimus as he would receive him (v. 17).

This self-identification with Onesimus resurfaces in the next verse where Paul notes that the reception of Onesimus would refresh Paul's own "heart," since Onesimus himself is Paul's own "heart" (see v. 12). In this context, the repetitive focus on Paul's own self does not aim simply to highlight his own willingness to repay Philemon; rather, it reinforces Paul's identification with Onesimus and thus reinforces the rhetorical force of the requests made.

The aorist verb translated "I ... am writing" (ἔγραψα) provides yet another example of an epistolary aorist (cf. Col 4:8).[37] This reference to Paul's writing with his own hand has been compared to other endings of his letters where he provides his signature (1 Cor 16:21; Gal 6:11; Col 4:18; 2 Thess 3:17). Some consider this to be the beginning of a "summary postscript" as Paul concludes this letter.[38] Others suggest, however, that the entire letter was written by Paul himself, and this note in his

---

31. Church, "Rhetorical Structure and Design," 29–30.

32. MM, 204. See also NRSV: "charge that to my account."

33. See, e.g., Fitzmyer, *Letter to Philemon*, 118–19; Moo, *Letters to the Colossians and to Philemon*, 428.

34. Of course, one can also suggest that Paul can repay through nonmaterial means; cf. Lohse, *Colossians and Philemon*, 204.

35. Thus Marshall, "Theology of Philemon," 179–80.

36. For the legal and financial role of the third party in the process of manumission, see Bartchy, *First-Century Slavery*, 121–25; Laura L. Sanders, "Equality and a Request for the Manumission of Onesimus," *ResQ* 46 (2004): 113–14.

37. Cf. Wallace, *Greek Grammar*, 563. See also Stanley E.

Porter, *Verbal Aspect in the Greek of the New Testament* (New York: Lang, 1989), 228–29.

38. Randolph Richards, *Paul and First-Century Letter Writing: Secretaries, Composition, and Collection* (Downers Grove, IL: InterVarsity Press, 2004), 173. Richards also considers the presence of this postscript as a helpful way to explain the shift in tone in this final section, where Paul becomes more forthright: "in other Pauline postscripts (Philm 19–25; 1 Cor 16:22–24; Gal 6:12–18 and Col 4:18), there is a tendency for the language to be more abrupt and stern than that found in the body of the letter. It is quite possible that 'pure Paul' tended to be more blunt and that his coauthors (and secretaries) tended to moderate his tone" (175).

own handwriting simply highlights his commitment to Onesimus.[39] Regardless of whether Paul wrote the rest of this letter, his signature here is best understood in relation to the quasilegal nature of this promissory note.[40] With his own signature, Paul promises to honor his commitment as noted here.

"I will repay it" (ἐγὼ ἀποτίσω) is the content of this certificate of debt (cf. Col 2:14). This translation may give the false impression that Paul himself owes Philemon.[41] Some suggest, therefore, that the verb be translated: "I will pay you whatever is owed."[42] The issue of the exact nature of what is owed resurfaces here. Although it can be used in the sense of making restitution (cf. Exod 21:19, 34, 36; 22:11–13), in Hellenistic papyri this verb has also been used to refer to the missed days of service with the departure of a laborer.[43] Again, this verb is not able to provide the definitive answer as to the loss Philemon suffered as well as the circumstances of Onesimus's departure from Philemon.

19c-d Not to mention that you owe me your own self (ἵνα μὴ λέγω σοι ὅτι καὶ σεαυτόν μοι προσοφείλεις). To reinforce the rhetorical force of his appeals, Paul now mentions Philemon's own indebtedness to him. The conjunction (ἵνα) that begins this clause has been taken as modifying the imperatival clause in v. 18 ("charge it to me")[44]

or an implied clause, such as "I am silent ... so as not to mention...."[45] In light of a parallel in 2 Cor 9:4, where one finds the same words (ἵνα μὴ λέγω) without a main verb that it is supposed to modify, it is also possible that this is an idiomatic use for a parenthetical thought: "not to mention...."[46] This would then be a case of *paralipsis* (i.e., passing over), where an author mentions something that he claims not to mention. Here, this rhetorical device is used "to transform Philemon's position from creditor to debtor and so to put him under a limitless moral obligation to comply with Paul's requests."[47]

The compound verb "you owe" (προσοφείλεις) may acquire the added meaning of "in addition," thus: "In addition to your owing me any amount I might repay, you owe me yourself as well."[48] With the use of the reflexive pronoun "your own self" (σεαυτόν), this debt likely points to the conversion of Philemon through the wider ministry of Paul rather than to other material or legal obligations. Even though Paul alludes to Philemon's conversion here, it is perhaps significant that he does not call him his "son," as he did with Onesimus (v. 10). Here, the note that Philemon owes Paul his very self essentially reduces him to be Paul's slave. If so, the rhetorical intent is clear: if Paul does not insist on Philemon's status as one who owes his very self

---

39. Lightfoot, *St. Paul's Epistles to the Colossians and to Philemon*, 344, draws this conclusion precisely in light of the appearance of Paul's signature here.

40. Cf. Arzt-Grabner, *Philemon*, 240–43.

41. If so, one would expect another verb for "I will pay back" (ἀποδώσω).

42. Bratcher and Nida, *Translator's Handbook*, 130.

43. P.Oxy. 2.275; Pearson, "Assumptions in the Criticism and Translation of Philemon," 277–78.

44. A different way of punctuating this sentence is assumed: "charge it to me ... so that I will not say, 'to you, because you owe me your own self.'" Cf. BDF §495(1).

45. Rupprecht, "Philemon," 641.

46. Many contemporary versions use a dash (NKJV, REB, NJB, HCSB, TNIV, ESV, NIV) or parenthesis (NASB, GNB) here.

47. Barclay, "Paul, Philemon and the Dilemma of Christian Slave Ownership," 171–72.

48. Harris, *Colossians and Philemon*, 274. See also Cousar, *Philippians and Philemon*, 104, who considers vv. 19–21 as depicting the relationship between Paul and Philemon as that of a patron-client relationship. Equally possible is Paul's intent to highlight the commonality between Philemon and his slave Onesimus, since both owe their new lives in Christ to his ministry; cf. Porter, "Is Critical Discourse Analysis Critical?" 60.

to Paul, Philemon likewise has no rights of ownership over Onesimus.

20a-c Yes, brother, let me have some benefit from you in the Lord (ναί, ἀδελφέ, ἐγώ σου ὀναίμην ἐν κυρίῳ).

Paul now returns to calling Philemon his "brother" (ἀδελφέ), a title applied to him in v. 7. This title, together with the verb "refresh" (ἀνάπαύω), frames the main body of this letter (vv. 8 – 20) as Paul urges Philemon to think and act in light of their relationship within the household of God. Moreover, structurally "in the Lord" concludes this subsection (vv. 17 – 20) as it did the previous one (vv. 8 – 16), where one likewise finds a shift from the framework of master-slave to that of the household of God: "no longer as a slave, but more than a slave, a beloved brother … both in the flesh and in the Lord" (v. 16).

"Yes" (ναί) can carry a number of related functions, the primary of which is to lay emphasis on Paul's final appeal, one that builds on the previous series of imperatives (cf. Matt 11:9; Luke 11:51; Phil 4:3; Rev 14:13).[49] Elsewhere in Paul, this particle also serves as a way to introduce an "affectionate appeal" (Phil 4:3).[50] In certain cases when an implied or explicit question is raised, this "yes" points to the anticipation of a positive response (cf. Rom 3:29). In this case, with numerous requests made, "yes" may also serve to encourage an affirmative response from Philemon.

Behind the phrase "let me have" lies the emphatic first person pronoun "I" (ἐγώ), although such emphasis is difficult to render into English.

One possible way of highlighting this emphasis can be found in the following paraphrase: "Let me have this benefit — and it is to me, rather than even to Onesimus, that it will be such."[51] What appears to be an expression of a selfish desire is actually a request on behalf of Onesimus, as Paul is identifying himself with him in making his request known to Philemon. Whatever honor and capital Paul possesses is again made available to Onesimus as Paul appeals to Philemon.

The verb rendered here as "let me have some benefit" (ὀναίμην) represents an independent use of the optative verb to express an "obtainable wish."[52] The deliberative nature of such use of an optative justifies a more circumspective rendering: "now I come to think of it, I want…."[53] This verb, which resembles the name of Onesimus (Ὀνήσιμον, cf. v. 10), may reflect an intentional wordplay by Paul.[54] If so, Paul again may be indirectly "keeping Onesimus in the forefront of the discussion,"[55] although this wordplay can also be a veiled reference of Paul's own desire to "keep him" for himself (v. 13): "let me have some benefit from you" may imply, "let me have Onesimus from you."

Note also the prepositional phrase "in the Lord" (ἐν κυρίῳ). In v. 16, Paul has already appealed to Philemon to receive Onesimus back as a "beloved brother … in the Lord." In both contexts, this phrase points to the need to operate within a new framework since they are both now members of the same household of God. The introduction of lordship language also reminds Philemon that he also has a "Master [κύριον] in heaven" (Col 4:1).[56]

---

49. BDAG, 665; Barth and Blanke, *Letter to Philemon*, 485 – 86.

50. Lightfoot, *St. Paul's Epistles to the Colossians and to Philemon*, 344.

51. Moule, *Epistles to the Colossians and to Philemon*, 149.

52. Wallace, *Greek Grammar*, 481.

53. Wright, *Colossians and Philemon*, 188.

54. The fact that this verb appears only here in the NT increases the likelihood that a wordplay is intended; cf. Dunn,

Epistles to the Colossians and to Philemon, 341; Barth and Blanke, *Letter to Philemon*, 486; Moo, *Letters to the Colossians and to Philemon*, 432.

55. Polaski, *Paul and the Discourse of Power*, 67.

56. For a discussion of the repeated uses of the title "Lord" in the Colossian household code (Col 3:18, 20, 22, 23, 24; 4:1) in shifting attention to the Lord Christ as the final authority, see comments on Col 3:18 – 4:1.

20d Refresh my heart in Christ (ἀνάπαυσόν μου τὰ σπλάγχνα ἐν Χριστῷ). Drawing on the fact that Philemon had refreshed the hearts of the saints (v. 7), Paul is now asking that his heart may also be refreshed by Philemon. This appeal is presented as one that is more than reasonable because Philemon himself owes his very self to Paul (v. 19). As the final of the three imperatives of this section, the impact of Philemon's decision and action on Paul, Onesimus, and Philemon becomes clear. The first imperative ("receive," v. 17) highlights the impact on the life of Onesimus; the second ("charge," v. 18) ensures Philemon that he will not suffer any loss; here, "refresh" points to the pleasure Paul will receive if Philemon responds positively to Paul's appeals. Not to be missed, however, is the fact that Paul's own refreshment lies in the proper treatment of Onesimus, not in the fulfillment of his own desires.[57]

"My heart" (μου τὰ σπλάγχνα) must be read in light of v. 12, where Onesimus is described as "my own heart" (τὰ ἐμὰ σπλάγχνα). To refresh Paul's own heart is, therefore, to refresh Onesimus. The identification of Paul with Onesimus is again made clear. Moreover, with this third and final appearance of the word "heart," Paul's argument has reached its climax. Since Onesimus is Paul's own heart (v. 12) and since Philemon is said to have refreshed the hearts of "all" the saints (v. 7), Philemon has no choice but to provide a proper reception of Onesimus (i.e., "my heart," v. 20).[58]

"In Christ" (ἐν Χριστῷ) here corresponds to "in the Lord" (ἐν κυρίῳ) in the previous clause, and both point to the primacy of this framework of reality. This phrase also echoes the same formula found at the beginning of the main body of this letter (v. 8) and thus forms an inclusio that frames Paul's appeal to Philemon.

Theology in Application

Pastoral Presence

In this short paragraph, readers may be surprised by Paul's intense focus on himself. Beyond the explicit mentioning of his own name, "Paul" (v. 19), there are two appearances of the emphatic first person pronoun in its nominative form, "I" (ἐγώ, vv. 19, 20).[59] The uses of this pronoun in the oblique cases also confirm Paul's apparent intense interest in himself and his role in the affairs between Onesimus and Philemon (vv. 17, 19, 20). This focus does not, however, point to Paul's self-absorption with his own interest. On the contrary, it aims at having Philemon (re)consider his relationship with Onesimus in light of Paul's mediatorial intervention. It is striking to find Paul, a person with considerable power,[60] willing to risk his own reputation and to exhaust his "political capital" for the sake of a slave.

This willingness to stand in the place of a slave is also reflected in the conditional sentence that begins this section (v. 17). In contrast to the statement in v. 6, where

---

57. Cf. NLT: "Give me this encouragement in Christ."

58. See comments on v. 7.

59. Note too that neither Philemon's nor Onesimus's name appears in this section.

60. In the rhetorical world of this text, Paul's imprisonment is not a sign of weakness but a sign of power, since Paul's power ultimately rests on his call as an apostle of the gospel, and it is precisely for the sake of this gospel that he is in prison (cf. vv. 1, 9, 13).

Paul affirms his "partnership" with Philemon, here the conditional sentence makes this partnership contingent on Philemon's proper reception of Onesimus.[61] As Paul stands in the place of Onesimus in his own appeal to Philemon, Onesimus becomes the critical link on which their partnership rests.

This rhetorical move is substantially different from strategies of similar documents concerning slavery that survive from the ancient world. When appealing for a slave or slaves in general, such documents usually adopt one of two strategies. Some provide a theoretical argument concerning moral concerns surrounding aspects of the institution of slavery. For example, Seneca considers slaves as personal beings with individual rights and duties, and thus they are able to perform virtuous acts, including beneficial acts even for their own masters (*Ben.* 3.18–20). Others appeal to the masters while emphasizing the repentant attitude of the slaves who are to be returned to their masters (Pliny, *Ep.* 9.21; 9.24).[62] In this letter, however, neither strategy is adopted. Paul launches a "personal" argument as he considers his own self as the basis for his appeal to Philemon. For an apostle who has demonstrated his skills in launching a series of theoretical arguments and who often emphasizes the significance of individual responsibility, this focus on himself can only be interpreted as an expression of his pastoral heart and the deep conviction to be immersed in the caring for his own spiritual son.

For contemporary Christian leaders who are likewise well-trained in theological matters as well as cultural and social analyses, we are reminded of the significance of one's personal ministry even when other rhetorical strategies might be tempting. Moving from being a technician in the diagnosis and resolution of the existing condition, we are called to move away from the role of an objective observer and mediator and to allow ourselves to be placed in the midst of the situation, providing space for God's love to be manifested through our personal presence:

> The minister who cares for people is called to be skillful but not a handyman, knowledgeable but not an imposter, a professional but not a manipulator. When he is able to deny himself, to be faithful and to understand the meaning of human suffering, then the man who is cared for will discover that through the hands of those who want to be of help God shows his tender love for him.[63]

Even this short letter offers a rich demonstration of Christian leadership. This message does not simply speak to pastors and full-time Christian workers; it also applies to elders, deacons, and other Christian leaders. One thinks of Sunday school teachers, who are often not considered as members of the clergy but who nonetheless serve as critical mediators of the divine Word for their students through words and

---

61. Onesimus therefore becomes the basis of their partnership. See Polaski, *Paul and the Discourse of Power*, 66.

62. See Introduction to Philemon for discussion.

63. Henri J. M. Nouwen, *Creative Ministry* (New York: Doubleday, 1971), 65.

deeds.[64] For many children, they are the embodiment of Christ. From ordination services for ministers to installation services for deacons/elders, to Sunday school or Awana club kickoffs, this passage serves as a powerful reminder for both Christian ministers and lay leaders.

This pastoral presence can become yet another act of manipulation if it does not rest on the prior act of God through Christ, and it is to this act that we must now turn.

Imitation of Christ

Despite a common assumption that Paul's letter to Philemon offers little theology,[65] an underlying theological substructure is detectable here. In emphasizing his own willingness to take the place of Onesimus so that Philemon can receive him as he would receive Paul (v. 17), and in requesting Philemon to "refresh" his "heart" (v. 20) after having identified Onesimus as his "own heart" (v. 12), Paul essentially takes on the form of a slave. His repeated emphasis on his status as a prisoner for the sake of the gospel (vv. 1, 9, 10, 13) reaffirms this identification. It may have reminded Paul's audience of his own description of the incarnated Christ:

> but emptied himself
> by taking on the form of a slave,
> by looking like other men,
> and by sharing in human nature. (Phil 2:7 NET)

By placing himself between Philemon and Onesimus, Paul serves as a mediator of their relationship. This mediatorial function is similarly described in Phil 2:8:

> He humbled himself,
> by becoming obedient to the point of death
> — even death on a cross! (NET)

Perhaps most significant is the language of redemption embedded in v. 18: "If he has wronged you in any way, or owes you anything, charge it to me." The willingness to redeem the debt of a slave reminds one again of Paul's description of Christ, who is willing to redeem those who are slaves to sin:

> Christ redeemed us from the curse of the law by becoming a curse for us, for it is written: "Cursed is everyone who is hung on a pole." He redeemed us in order that the blessing given to Abraham might come to the Gentiles through Christ Jesus, so that by faith we might receive the promise of the Spirit. (Gal 3:13 – 14)[66]

---

64. See, e.g., the helpful discussion in Martin Marty, "The Sunday School: Battered Survivor," *ChrCent* 97 (1980): 634 – 36.

65. See, e.g., Jouette M. Bassler, ed., *Pauline Theology*, vol. 1: *Thessalonians, Philippians, Galatians, Philemon* (Minneapolis: Fortress, 1991). Despite the title, chapters are devoted to 1 and 2 Thessalonians, Philippians, and Galatians, but not to Philemon. Behind this omission is apparently the assumption that "theology" cannot be found in this short letter.

66. Cf. Rom 3:24; 7:14; 8:12 – 13; Eph 4:30; Col 1:14. See also Martin, "The Rhetorical Function of Commercial Language,"

With the lack of linguistic parallels, however, one should not immediately assume that Paul is intending to portray himself as a Christ figure. Nevertheless, in light of his focus on Christ's redemptive work elsewhere, such allusions are possible. One can at least understand Paul as imitating Christ as he seeks to be faithful to the gospel he preaches.[67] It is in the practicality of everyday existence that one finds Paul living out a christocentric gospel as he takes on the role of a slave and offers to redeem this slave for the sake of further gospel service (v. 13).[68]

How should contemporary readers apply these Pauline allusions to the works of Christ? Instead of seeking an immediate application behind every verse, Paul's own model as demonstrated throughout this letter reminds us of the prior act of God through Christ that allows Paul to act the way he does. These acts also form the basis for his appeals to Philemon as Philemon himself also needs to live in light of the reality of this gospel message. For Christians, who are sinners redeemed from the slavery of sin, we also need to extend this grace to others by humbling ourselves in taking the place of powerless ones as we serve as mediators who are able to preach the gospel through our living. Our everyday existence becomes the discourse through which our theology can become evident. As Paul has reminded us: "Be imitators of me, just as I also am of Christ" (1 Cor 11:1 NET).

---

335 – 36. Though not referring specifically to v. 18, the meta-narrative that frames this letter is considered to be nothing less than the drama of redemption: "Paul is saying to Philemon: keep on playing your part in the divine comedy of redemption as well as you have been playing it up to now" (Kevin J. Vanhoozer, "Imprisoned or Free? Text, Status, and Theological Interpretation in the Master/Slave Discourse of Philemon," in *Reading Scripture with the Church: Toward a Hermeneutic for Theological Interpretation* [ed. A. K. M. Adam et al.; Grand Rapids: Baker, 2006], 85).

67. For other possible allusions to the life of Christ in this letter, see also Kirk D. Lyons Sr., "Paul's Confrontation with Class: The Letter to Philemon as Counter-Hegemonic Discourse," *Cross Currents* 56 (2006): 125 – 26, who sees Paul's reference to his own apostolic presence in v. 22 as a veiled reference to the parousia of Christ.

68. The phrase "in Christ" (ἐν Χριστῷ) in v. 20 and throughout Philemon (vv. 8, 23; cf. v. 6) serves as constant reminders of the significant christological basis of Paul's argument.

Philemon 21–25

Literary Context

As we noted in our discussion of the delineation of the main body of this letter, it is best to see v. 21 as beginning the concluding remarks of this letter.[1] The previous subsection (vv. 17–20) builds on the relationship between Paul and Philemon as Paul listed his demands. This is highlighted by the repeated use of the first person pronoun ("I" in vv. 19, 20; "me"/"my" in all verses). Paul urged Philemon to act properly in light of their partnership and also offered to repay any debt owed to Philemon while reminding him of his own indebtedness to Paul (vv. 18–19). He concluded by asking Philemon to refresh his own heart (v. 20; cf. v. 7).

In this final section, Paul begins by expressing his confidence that Philemon will be obedient to his demands and requests (v. 21). This note of confidence signals the beginning of the closing section as it refers back to the entire main body of the letter.[2] In v. 22, one finds another specific instruction as Paul requests Philemon to prepare a room for him for an upcoming visit. In light of the presence of this specific instruction, some consider the main body of the letter as extending to v. 22. (cf. GNB, CEV, NEB, HCSB, NET, NLT, ESV).[3] It is clear, however, that the instruction in v. 22 is of a different nature than those provided in vv. 17–20. First, the instructions in vv. 17–20 are all focused on Onesimus, although Paul grounds such instructions on his relationship with Philemon. In v. 22, however, the instruction focuses squarely on Paul's visit. Second, by the time of Paul's future visit (v. 22), all the requests noted in vv. 17–20 should have been performed. This again points to the disjunction between the two sections. Finally, this note of Paul's visit is consistent with distinct sections of his letters where he discusses his travel plans (cf. Rom 1:8–15; 15:14–33; 1 Cor 4:14–21; 2 Cor 12:14–13:13; Gal 4:12–20; Phil 2:19–24; 1 Thess 2:17–3:13).[4]

---

1. See the Literary Context on vv. 8–16.

2. Also worth noting is the fact that while the previous section is flooded with imperatives, this section begins with a participle ("confident," πεποιθώς), thus signaling a shift in focus and tone. See also Allen, "The Discourse Structure of Philemon," 92.

3. Wright, *Colossians and Philemon*, 178–79; Rupprecht, "Philemon," 635; Arzt-Grabner, *Philemon*, 192.

4. In form-critical terms, this has been identified as "apostolic *parousia*"; cf. Robert Funk, "The Apostolic *Parousia*: Form and Significance," in *Christian History and Interpretation: Studies Presented to John Knox* (ed. W. R. Farmer et. al.; Cambridge: Cambridge Univ. Press, 1967), 249–68.

III. Requests concerning Onesimus (vv. 8 – 20)

➡ **IV. Final Greetings (vv. 21 – 25)**

    A. Further Instructions (vv. 21 – 22)

    B. Greetings from Paul's Coworkers (vv. 23 – 24)

    C. Benediction (v. 25)

Main Idea

Paul reinforces his preceding arguments by expressing confidence in Philemon's obedience as well as noting his own impending visit. This letter concludes with a list of greetings and a closing benediction, thus framing its content with references to the wider ecclesiological and theological contexts.

Translation

Philemon 21 – 25

21a	manner	Confident of your obedience,
b	Assertion	**I write to you,**
c	cause	because I know that
d	content	you will do even more than what I say.
22a	Entreaty	**At the same time, also prepare me a guest room,**
b	explanation	for I hope that
c	means (of 22d)	through your prayers
d	content	I will be restored to you.
23a	Assertion	**Epaphras ... greets you,**
b	apposition	my fellow prisoner in Christ Jesus,
24a	list	as do Mark,
b	list	Aristarchus,
c	list	Demas, and
d	list	Luke,
e	apposition	my coworkers.
25	Desire	**The grace of the Lord Jesus Christ be with your spirit.**

Structure

After the main body of this letter (vv. 8 – 20), Paul gives further instructions that underline the need for his requests to be followed (vv. 21 – 22). Shifting from his earlier emphasis on appealing to Philemon on the basis of love (v. 9) rather than command (v. 8), Paul now uses the language of "obedience" (v. 21a) in expressing his expectations for Philemon. He goes on to mention that he expects Philemon to do even more than what is specified in this letter (v. 21c-d). Despite the difficulties in discerning exactly what is implied in this statement, it is clear that Paul's desire is not limited to what is explicit in the main body of the letter. This subtle hint aims at forcing Philemon to act beyond the requests made, so that he can be faithful to the faith he confesses as well as to the partnership he shares with Paul.

The instruction for Philemon to prepare a room for him in his next visit (v. 22) also acquires significant rhetorical force as Paul reminds Philemon that he will be held responsible for fulfilling the stated and implied requests of the letter. Obscured by contemporary English usage, the shift from the singular verb to the plural pronoun should be noted: "prepare [second person singular] me a guest room, for I hope that through your [plural] prayers I will be restored to you [plural]" (v. 22). This shift paves the way for the greetings that follow as the wider circle of believers becomes witnesses ensuring that Philemon will provide the proper response.

In the final greetings, Paul first conveys greetings from Epaphras, whom he identifies as his "fellow prisoner in Christ Jesus" (v. 23). Likely the founder of the church of Colossae (cf. Col 1:7; 4:12), Epaphras is singled out in this final greeting section, perhaps again to make it clear that this is not simply a personal and private letter. The others listed (Mark, Aristarchus, Demas, and Luke) are all identified as Paul's "coworkers" (v. 24).[5] As in his other letters, Paul closes with a final benediction (v. 25).

---

5. All four appear also in Colossians with further descriptions (4:10, 14).

Exegetical Outline

→ **I. Final Greetings (vv. 21 – 25)**

    A. Further instructions (vv. 21 – 22)

        1. Expected Obedience from Philemon (v. 21)

        2. Call to prepare for Paul's visit (v. 22)

    B. Greetings from Paul's coworkers (vv. 23 – 24)

        1. From Paul's fellow prisoner, Epaphras (v. 23)

        2. From Paul's coworkers (v. 24)

            a. Mark (v. 24a)

            b. Aristarchus (v. 24b)

            c. Demas (v. 24c)

            d. Luke (v. 24d)

            e. Summary (v. 24e)

    C. Benediction (v. 25)

Explanation of the Text

21a-b Confident of your obedience, I write to you (Πεποιθὼς τῇ ὑπακοῇ σου ἔγραψά σοι). Though refusing to evoke his apostolic authority, Paul expresses confidence that Philemon will be obedient to his requests. Some prefer to see this statement as the climax of the previous section "since there is no abrupt shift in subject matter."[6] This, however, ignores several shifts in both focus and tone. First, the use of a perfect participle ("confident," πεποιθώς) at the beginning of this sentence is significant since it is the first nonfinite verb after vv. 17 – 20. Although the imperative reappears in v. 22, this section is no longer dominated by specific instructions for Philemon.

Second, in the previous section, Paul focuses on appeals based on love (v. 9); here he uses language of "obedience." This shift in tone should not go unnoticed no matter how the concept of "obedience" is to be understood.

Finally, the reference to "more than what I say" also serves as a marker as Paul now moves beyond the previous discussion in pointing to what must yet be uttered.

The word translated "confident" (πεποιθώς) carries the nuance of "persuade, trust, obey." In the perfect tense, it can refer to the act of being "so convinced that one puts confidence in someth[ing]."[7] Most contemporary English translations rightly render this verb as "having confidence" (KJV, ASV, NASB, NKJV) or simply "confident" (NRSV, REB, TNIV, ESV, NIV).[8]

The reference to Philemon's expected "obedience" (τῇ ὑπακοῇ) is a bit surprising, especially in light of Paul's earlier decision not to evoke his (apostolic) authority (see vv. 8 – 9). In Paul, this term often refers to the believer's obedience to God (Rom 6:16; 15:18; 16:19)[9] or to Christ (2 Cor 10:5), and by logical extension also to the gospel message

---

6. Bratcher and Nida, *Translator's Handbook*, 131.

7. BDAG, 792.

8. This participle is a causal circumstantial participle, as is clear in some translations: "since I am confident" (HCSB; cf. NET).

9. It is also used for Christ's complete obedience to his Father (Rom 5:19).

(Rom 1:5; 16:26). Some suggest that "obedience" should be understood here in a weaker sense of "compliance"[10] or "acquiescence."[11] That meaning is, however, unattested in Paul's writings. Others, therefore, consider the implied object of obedience here as "Christ's command,"[12] "the will of God,"[13] or "the gospel."[14]

While the ultimate object of the believers' obedience is certainly God and his Son, the role of Paul here cannot be ignored. His reference to Philemon's obedient response to his own requests is implied in the second half of this verse: "because I know that you will do even more than what I say." This is consistent with his repeated focus on his own role in his appeal to Philemon (cf. vv. 17 – 20). Elsewhere Paul also uses similar language as he considers himself as an intermediary agent of God; thus, he rightfully deserves such "obedience" (ὑπακοήν in 2 Cor 7:15; cf. Phil 2:12).[15] Beyond the canonical corpus, one can also point to examples where such language within the "confidence-formula" can be used even among equals.[16] Moreover, in vv. 8 – 9, Paul's mere claim not to impose his authority on Philemon is itself a power claim, and Philemon's obedience is expected. Therefore, Paul's return to such language of authority is not unexpected as he provides a climactic note in his appeals to Philemon.[17]

"I write" (ἔγραψα) should again be taken as an "epistolary aorist." Because of the same verb form in v. 19, however, some argue that it does not refer to the literal act of writing and should thus be rendered as "I send this letter to you."[18] In any case, it points to the authority embedded in this letter penned and sent by Paul.

21c-d Because I know that you will do even more than what I say (εἰδὼς ὅτι καὶ ὑπὲρ ἃ λέγω ποιήσεις). With this clause that also begins with another perfect causal circumstantial participle, Paul makes another ambiguous request of which the meaning is left unspecified. Much speculation surrounds the reference behind "more than what I say." Many are confident that this "more" refers to "Philemon's bringing the legal aspect of his worldly relationship with Onesimus into conformity with the social structural ground of their new churchly relationship, presumably by legally freeing Onesimus."[19] Others consider this ambiguity as a way for Paul to allow Philemon to respond in his own way to the wider theological framework laid out in this letter.[20] An extreme version of this reading is the conclusion that Paul himself is unsure as to the best course of action to recommend.[21]

To suggest that Paul does not have a solution in mind fails to take into account the carefully crafted main body of this letter, where Paul does provide a detailed theological vision within which Philemon is to act. Manumission does not seem to be

---

10. E.g., Harris, *Colossians and Philemon*, 277 – 78 (see also NJB; NAB).

11. Fitzmyer, *Letter to Philemon*, 121 – 22.

12. Wilson, *Colossians and Philemon*, 364.

13. O'Brien, *Colossians, Philemon*, 305; Barth and Blanke, *Letter to Philemon*, 491.

14. Moo, *Letters to the Colossians and to Philemon*, 435.

15. Cf. Martin, *Colossians and Philemon*, 168.

16. Cf. Ps.-Demetrius, *Typoi* 1; Stanley N. Olson, "Pauline Expressions of Confidence in His Addressees," *CBQ* 47 (1985): 289.

17. Noting the shift of tone, Richards (*Paul and First-Century Letter Writing*, 175) considers this as another example of Paul's use of a secretary in a letter body. To him, the bold Paul reflected in the letter ending reflects the true Paul.

18. Bratcher and Nida, *Translator's Handbook*, 131.

19. Petersen, *Rediscovering Paul*, 97 – 98. Those who see manumission behind this phrase include Wright, *Colossians and Philemon*, 189; Martin, *Colossians and Philemon*, 168; Stuhlmacher, *Der Brief an Philemon*, 53 – 54. Others see a shift from the ethical to the eschatological as "Paul expects Philemon to go on living *sub specie theodramatis* — 'under the perspective of the theodrama'" (Vanhoozer, "Imprisoned or Free?" 87).

20. Lohse, *Colossians and Philemon*, 206.

21. Barclay, "Paul, Philemon and the Dilemma of Christian Slave Ownership," 161 – 86.

the embedded meaning behind this clause, however, since in v. 16 he has already moved beyond the limited concern of the legal status of Onesimus. If a solution can be found in this letter, it is located in v. 13, where Paul explicitly desires to keep Onesimus so that he can be of service to him and the gospel he preaches. If so, this "more" should be considered as a veiled request for Philemon to allow (or free) Onesimus so that he can return to Paul for the further service of the gospel mission.[22] Manumission is not quite enough for Paul since Onesimus is not simply to be disengaged from his household; he is also to be engaged in the household of God to play a role in God's mission on which a new humanity is being built (cf. Col 3:11).

22a At the same time, also prepare me a guest room (ἅμα δὲ καὶ ἑτοίμαζέ μοι ξενίαν). Paul concludes his appeal to Philemon with a note of his impending visit. The particle translated "at the same time" (ἅμα) is a "marker of simultaneous occurrence."[23] The translation of this phrase as "and one thing more" (TNIV, NIV; cf. NRSV) is acceptable if it is not understood merely as a casual thought that happens to come into Paul's mind.[24] Our translation sufficiently highlights the connection between this request and the previous one as Paul concludes this letter.

In Hellenistic Greek, the word "guest room" (ξενία) is most often used in the sense of "hospitality,"[25] but both of its occurrences in the NT refer to a place where hospitable acts are performed (cf. Acts 28:23). The two usages are not entirely

divorced from one another, however, especially in this context where Paul is likely not simply referring to an empty space for temporary lodging, but "a hospitable reception with all the amenities that good hospitality entails."[26] As his "partner" in faith (v. 17; cf. v. 6), Paul will also feel the need to receive such hospitality when he visits Philemon after his release from prison.

The significance of Paul's request for Philemon to have a guest room prepared for him has been variably understood. On one end of the spectrum, this request is read as a "thinly veiled" statement comparable to Paul's earlier statement in 1 Cor 4:21: "What do you prefer? Shall I come to you with a rod of discipline, or shall I come in love and with a gentle spirit?"[27] Others see it as a promise as Paul looks forward to being restored to his partner.[28] Based on both the rhetorical force of Paul's preceding argument and his commitment to appeal to Philemon "on the basis of love" (v. 9), it seems best to consider Paul as intending to exert gentle pressure here as he expects Philemon to act appropriately in light of the theological framework outlined above.[29]

22b-d For I hope that through your prayers I will be restored to you (ἐλπίζω γὰρ ὅτι διὰ τῶν προσευχῶν ὑμῶν χαρισθήσομαι ὑμῖν). Paul here expresses a wish to visit Philemon through God's gracious answer of the prayers of believers. While some argue that "I hope" (ἐλπίζω) completes the triad with "love" (v. 5) and "faith" (v. 5), this verb when used to describe Paul's travel plans (cf. Rom

22. Thus also O'Brien, *Colossians, Philemon*, 306; Dunn, *Epistles to the Colossians and to Philemon*, 345; Barth and Blanke, *Letter to Philemon*, 492.

23. BDAG, 49.

24. As reflected in the paraphrase of Wright, *Colossians and Philemon*, 190: "oh, and by the way…."

25. BDAG, 683.

26. Osiek, *Philippians, Philemon*, 142.

27. Petersen, *Rediscovering Paul*, 267.

28. Wright, *Colossians and Philemon*, 190.

29. Lightfoot, *St. Paul's Epistles to the Colossians and Philemon*, 344; Jeffrey A. D. Weima, *Neglected Endings: The Significance of the Pauline Letter Closings* (JSNTSup 101; Sheffield: JSOT, 1994), 256. Transcending this debate, some have simply suggested that Paul's request is "but a deliberately phrased convention, known from epistolary forms in the Graeco-Roman

15:24; 1 Cor 16:7; Phil 2:19, 23) necessarily hints at a "tentativeness" that is absent in Paul's other uses of this verb in reference to the hope that one finds in Christ.[30] Here, Paul's reference to "prayers" defers to God as the one who will ultimately determine the future plans and fate of Paul.

With this clause, one finds the return of the second person plural pronoun "your" (ὑμῶν) and "to you" (ὑμῖν). On the most fundamental level, this plural pronoun points to Paul's belief that the entire community of believers in Philemon's house church is praying for him (cf. Rom 15:30).[31] In its immediate context, it also evokes the other members and leaders of this house church to hold Philemon accountable to the demands presented to him. This plural also paves the way for Paul's final greetings to the believers there.

One can also identify "a strong recapitulating function" here as Paul points back to the beginning of this letter where other members of Philemon's house church are noted (vv. 1 – 3).[32] Thus, Paul again makes it clear that this is not a private letter. Not only will the other church leaders serve as witnesses to Paul's demand and Philemon's response, but they and their entire community will also be affected by Philemon's decision.

"I will be restored" (χαρισθήσομαι) often carries the sense of "gracious provision" (cf. Rom 8:32; 1 Cor 2:12; Gal 3:18; Phil 1:29; 2:9),[33] and its passive voice is best taken as a divine passive especially in a context where "prayers" are mentioned. Some translations, therefore, render this verb, "I will be given (back) to you" (NASB, NET), or even "I will be graciously given to you" (ESV), although such renditions may be awkward to our ears. In any

case, Paul's focus is not on restoration but on God's gracious act of leading Paul to Philemon.

Many have considered this note on Paul's desire to visit Philemon in Colossae as a strong evidence for this letter being written in Ephesus rather than in Rome, especially because Paul himself had expressed his desire to travel to Spain after his Roman imprisonment (cf. Rom 15:24, 28).[34] This verse does not, however, necessitate this conclusion. First, the rhetorical intent of this note must be emphasized. While one cannot doubt Paul's sincerity as he hopes to visit Philemon, this note reminds Philemon of the need to take the letter seriously. Moreover, a travel note such as this one serves more to express his desire to be with the recipient rather than outlining an itinerary. Finally, in light of the strong tradition in both the canonical text and in early Christian tradition that Paul did return to Asia after his Roman imprisonment, the actual distance between his place of imprisonment and Philemon's location should no longer be considered a critical factor in this discussion.

23 Epaphras, my fellow prisoner in Christ Jesus, greets you (Ἀσπάζεταί σε Ἐπαφρᾶς ὁ συναιχμάλωτός μου ἐν Χριστῷ Ἰησοῦ). As in his other letters (e.g., Rom 16:3 – 16, 21 – 23; 1 Cor 16:19 – 20; Col 4:10 – 15; 1 Thess 5:26), this letter ends with words of greeting. The closest parallel to this section is Col 4:10 – 15, where Epaphras, Mark, Aristarchus, Demas, and Luke are also mentioned. In light of such similarities, the differences between this final section and the concluding section of Colossians (4:7 – 18) should also be noted. First, Paul's signature in Col 4:18 is missing in Philemon,

---

world" (Martin, *Colossians and Philemon*, 169). Paul is not, however, bound to Greco-Roman epistolary practices.

30. Dunn, *Epistles to the Colossians and to Philemon*, 346.

31. Michael A. G. Haykin, "Praying Together: A Note on Philemon 22," *EvQ* 66 (1994): 331 – 35.

32. Weima, *Neglected Endings*, 256. Also here one finds the use of the second person plural pronoun ("to you," ὑμῖν, v. 3).

33. An extended usage can be found in reference to acts of forgiveness (cf. 2 Cor 2:7, 10; 12:13; Eph 4:32; Col 2:13; 3:13).

34. Wright, *Colossians and Philemon*, 190; Wilson, *Colossians and Philemon*, 365.

though see his handwritten note in Phlm 19, which may function in a similar way to Col 4:18; as we noted on v. 19, it is also possible that this shorter and more personal letter was entirely written by Paul.

Second, Tychicus, the letter carrier, is mentioned in Col 4:7 – 8, while Philemon has no such reference. This omission can probably be explained by the fact that the introduction of Tychicus in Colossians is meant to highlight his function as one who will explain Paul's own circumstances. If we assume that Philemon is among the Colossian believers who have already received such information, to reintroduce Tychicus is unnecessary. Moreover, since this letter is likely to be carried by Onesimus himself, there is no need for yet another letter carrier.[35]

Third, in Colossians, the list of names is divided between Jews and Gentiles, while no such division is obvious here. This can be explained by the emphasis on the unity of God's people in Colossians (cf. Col 3:11), whereas an ethnic concern is not the focus of Philemon.

Finally, the omission of "Jesus, who is called Justus" (Col 4:11) here should also be noted. Some have suggested that the final word of this verse should have a final sigma, thus referring not to Christ, but to this "Jesus": "Epaphras, my fellow prisoner in Christ, greets you, so does Jesus" (ἀσπάζεταί σε Ἐπαφρᾶς ὁ συναιχμάλωτός μου ἐν Χριστῷ, Ἰησοῦς).[36] Attractive as this emendation may be, it has no manuscript support. Therefore, it seems best to adopt the traditional reading even

though it remains unclear why this "Jesus" is omitted from this list of greetings.

"Epaphras" is mentioned first, probably because of his prominent status among the Colossian believers. Since he was the one who spread the gospel to the Colossae area (cf. Col 1:7; 4:12), his name would no doubt further exert pressure on Philemon.

The term "fellow prisoner" (ὁ συναιχμάλωτός) can be understood in either a literal or a metaphorical sense. Those who argue for a literal reading[37] must explain why the title is applied to Aristarchus rather than Epaphras in Colossians (Col 4:10; cf. Rom 16:7).[38] In this case, however, the presence of the phrase "in Christ Jesus" suggests that this title should be taken metaphorically, both here and in Col 4:10.[39] Moreover, since this term literally means "fellow prisoner of war,"[40] Paul himself would not literally fit this category. The use of a different word group for his own imprisonment in v. 1 ("prisoner," δέσμιος) also argues against taking this literally.[41] It seems best, then, to take Paul as again evoking this imagery to urge Philemon to imitate those who are willing to give up their rights for the sake of the gospel.

24 As do Mark, Aristarchus, Demas, and Luke, my coworkers (Μᾶρκος, Ἀρίσταρχος, Δημᾶς, Λουκᾶς, οἱ συνεργοί μου). "Greets you," which starts the Greek sentence in the previous verse, applies to each one of these names. Most English translations insert either "and so do" or "as do" to clarify the relationship between these two verses.

---

35. See Llewelyn and Kearsley, "Letters in the Early Church," *NewDocs* 7: 52.

36. Among the recent proponents of this reading is Lohse, *Colossians and Philemon*, 207, who argues that the phrase "in Christ Jesus" is never used by Paul elsewhere in his letters.

37. Cf. CEV: "Epaphras is also here in jail" (cf. GNB).

38. Moo, *Letters to the Colossians and to Philemon*, 438, suggests that they were with Paul in different times during his imprisonment. Those who argue for an Ephesian imprisonment

face the same difficulty; cf. Jerome Murphy-O'Connor, "The Greeters in Col 4:10 – 14 and Phlm 23 – 24," *RB* 114 (2007): 416 – 26.

39. Thus Moule, *Epistles to the Colossians and to Philemon*, 136 – 37; Harris, *Colossians and Philemon*, 280.

40. Cf. LSJ, 45.

41. See esp. Harris, *Slave of Christ*, 117, who argues that if Paul were referring to his literal fellow prisoners, he would have used συνδεσμώτης.

All four names appear in the final greetings in Colossians (Col 4:10, 14). "Mark," the one identified as "the cousin of Barnabas" in Col 4:10, is likely the John Mark who joined Paul and Barnabas in their first missionary journey, but did not complete the journey and abandoned them in Pampylia (Acts 15:38), an act that caused the rift between Paul and Barnabas (15:39). His appearance in Colossians and here points to the reconciliation between Paul and Mark, and most probably also Paul and Barnabas. In a letter that emphasizes acts of reconciliation, the appearance of this name provides added significance.

"Aristarchus" is among Paul's travel companions in Acts (19:29; 20:4). Originally from Macedonia (cf. 27:2), he was with Paul during the riot in Ephesus (19:21 – 41). In Colossians, he is identified as Paul's "fellow prisoner" (Col 4:10), probably reflecting on their commitment to Christ and his gospel.

Unlike Mark and Aristarchus (identified as "Jews" in Col 4:11), "Demas" and "Luke" are likely Gentiles. Demas (see Col 4:14) is later described as one who deserted Paul (2 Tim 4:10 – 11). "Luke," however, was a longtime companion of Paul, if we assume that he is the author of Luke-Acts and the character identified in the "we-passages" in Acts (16:10 – 17; 20:5 – 15; 21:1 – 18; 27:1 – 28:16). In Col 4:14, he is also identified as "the beloved physician." By grouping Jews with Gentiles, longtime partners with more recent partners, and those who have at times failed with those who have always been faithful, Paul further emphasizes the breakdown of social and hierarchical boundaries in the gospel ministry.

These four are labeled as Paul's "coworkers" (οἱ συνεργοί). This term is used elsewhere to identify those who serve with Paul (cf. Rom 16:3, 9, 21; 2 Cor 8:23; Phil 2:25; 4:3; Col 4:11),[42] but its presence in the final section of the letter should be read in light of the appearance of the same term in v. 1, where Paul identifies Philemon as his and Timothy's "coworker." Since the entire letter is enveloped by such references, Paul points to a "common action and accountability" within which Philemon is to play his own part.[43] Once again the public nature of this personal letter carries a significant rhetorical function. Moreover, to identify Philemon with other notable coworkers of Paul is to make the assertion that Philemon's appropriate acts of obedience will also qualify him to be among those who participate in the ministry of the gospel.[44]

25 The grace of the Lord Jesus Christ be with your spirit (Ἡ χάρις τοῦ κυρίου Ἰησοῦ Χριστοῦ μετὰ τοῦ πνεύματος ὑμῶν). As in Paul's other letters, this grace benediction is likely meant to replace the "farewell wish" often found in secular letters.[45] Various forms of this benediction can be found in Paul's letters, and the one Paul uses here is identical to that of Phil 4:23. Although formulaic in nature, such a benediction is not without significance in its own literary context as Paul concludes his presentation. Here, "grace" (ἡ χάρις) again evokes the opening "grace" and "peace" benediction (v. 3) as Paul frames his discussion with the theology of grace and reconciliation. Without the revelation of the grace "of the Lord Jesus Christ,"[46] the transformation depicted by Paul will remain an unachievable ideal. In light of the reality of

---

42. Paul has also identified himself and others as "coworkers of God" (1 Cor 3:9; 1 Thess 3:2).

43. Stanley E. Porter, "A Functional Letter Perspective: Towards a Grammar of Epistolary Form," in *Paul and the Ancient Letter Form* (ed. Stanley E. Porter and Sean A. Adams; Pauline Studies; Leiden/Boston: Brill, 2010), 29.

44. Cf. C. Clifton Black, *Mark* (ANTC; Nashville: Abington, 2011), 52.

45. See comments on Col 4:18.

46. This genitive phrase is best taken as a subjective genitive, where "the Lord Jesus Christ" is the one who grants this "grace" among his people.

such divine grace, however, this transformation becomes a necessity demanded by the gospel of the cross.

"With your spirit" (μετὰ τοῦ πνεύματος ὑμῶν; cf. also Gal 6:18) should be understood simply as "with you."[47] "Spirit" here, even with the definite article, points to the human spirit rather than the divine Spirit. The exact reason for the inclusion of this word in these closing benedictions remains unclear,[48] but the combination between the singular "spirit" and the plural "your" is noteworthy. This combination provides an emphatic note on the distribution of the divine grace among every single believer.[49] It is this divine provision that allows Paul to write what he did and Philemon to respond the way he should.

Theology in Application

Obedience and Accountability

In this closing section of Philemon, Paul draws attention to the need to provide a proper response to what he has just written. The use of the word "obedience" (v. 21) is particularly important. As noted above, this word is most often used for one's obedience to God or Christ. Such uses may suggest that behind this use of the word Paul is also pointing to the need for Philemon to be obedient to Christ and God. Nevertheless, to use this term here further bolsters the power of what is written in this letter: Philemon's obedience to Christ and God is to be measured in light of the way he is obedient to the specific instructions embedded in this letter. The written word, therefore, provides the specific and concrete expressions of God's will.

Setting himself apart from the moral philosophers of his time, Paul's teachings carry an authority that demands an obedient response. This authority is derived from "Christ Jesus," because of whom Paul is "a prisoner" (v. 1). Even though Paul's mode of discourse in this letter is an appeal "on the basis of love" (v. 9), the source and basis of this appeal is Christ Jesus himself, and it carries a substantial force that cannot be ignored. For contemporary believers who encounter Paul's letters, we are called to submit to the gospel embedded in these pages.

In this letter, the vocabulary of obedience is particularly important because obedience language often appears in the discussions of the relationship between masters and slaves (cf. Eph 6:5; Col 3:22). Elsewhere, Paul has already used this metaphor in the contrast between slavery to sin and obedience to righteousness:

Don't you know that when you offer yourselves to someone as obedient slaves, you

---

47. Some have argued for the translation "with you" since "in English, at least, 'with your spirit' carries overtones and implications not present in Paul's use of the word"; Bratcher and Nida, *Translator's Handbook*, 133.

48. Some, such as Gordon Fee, *God's Empowering Presence: The Holy Spirit in the Letters of Paul* (Peabody, MA: Hen-

drickson, 1994), 469, suggest that the use of the word in these benedictions reflects significant emotional involvement on the part of Paul. It is unclear, however, if one should consider other benedictions without this "spirit" reference as reflecting the lack of emotional investment.

49. Weima, *Neglected Endings*, 82.

are slaves of the one you obey — whether you are slaves to sin, which leads to death, or to obedience, which leads to righteousness? (Rom 6:16)

In this letter where the issue of slavery is at the forefront, the use of such language is particularly striking. In calling Philemon to be obedient to the gospel that Paul himself preaches, he reminds Philemon that he is no different from Onesimus, for they are both slaves to a higher authority. Moreover, they are no different from Paul (v. 1), who is also a slave of Christ. This relativizes Philemon's own relationship with Onesimus and puts this earthly relationship in its right perspective. Such use of the obedience language is, therefore, comparable to Paul's own exhortation to the earthly masters: "Masters, provide for your slaves justice and equity, since you know that you also have a Master in heaven" (Col 4:1).

Paul makes it clear that this obedience is not simply an individual and personal response; it should characterize an entire community of believers. Here, the interconnectedness of believers is highlighted. First, in his request for Philemon to prepare a guest room for him for his next visit (v. 22), Paul reminds Philemon of his own presence as he expects to witness Philemon's obedience to his earlier appeals. Second, the greetings from his "coworkers" (v. 24) also point to the public nature of this letter as Paul fully realizes that this personal matter is one that will involve the entire community of believers. In this closing section, therefore, Paul calls for the creation of a moral community defined by its obedience to God, Christ, and his gospel.[50] It is within this community that this gospel message can become a living reality.

In an age when the gospel is often understood in therapeutic terms, the concept of "obedience" must be reintroduced in our churches. As individuals, we must be obedient to God's will as expressed in the written Word. As God's people, we must develop into communities accountable to one another as we seek to grow the body of Christ. Christian leaders should not shy away from disciplining or rebuking their flocks all the while allowing themselves to be open to warnings and corrections. Are we willing to build and participate in accountability groups so that we can be reminded of the need to be faithful to God? Are we willing to grow so that our local communities of believers can be mature in Christ?

Primacy of the Gospel Ministry

Paul reminds his audience here again of the primacy of Christ and his gospel. Returning to the issue of freedom and slavery, he reminds them that he himself is in chains, and he asks for prayers so that he can be released from his imprisonment (v. 22). His plans after his release are, however, no different from the reason why

---

50. For a characterization of God's people as a moral community that obeys God and him alone, see Patrick D. Miller, "The Good Neighborhood: Identity and Community through the Commandments," in *Character and Scripture: Moral Formation, Community, and Biblical Interpretation* (ed. William P. Brown; Grand Rapids: Eerdmans, 2002), 63 – 65.

he was imprisoned in the first place, since his release from prison will not affect his status as "a prisoner of Christ Jesus" (v. 1). Taking the appellation attached to Epaphras, "my fellow prisoner in Christ Jesus" (v. 23), in the metaphorical sense, Paul emphasizes that it is not freedom but obedience that is the ultimate goal of the gospel message.

The passing reference to "prayers" (v. 22) points to Paul's dependence on and submission to the divine will, and the formulaic note on "the grace of the Lord Jesus Christ" (v. 25) that concludes this letter is formulaic because of Paul's conscious choice of words for the endings of all of his letters. Without such "grace," Paul would have no gospel to preach, and Philemon would not be expected to be able to act the way Paul expects him to. All of these are possible because "it is by grace you have been saved, through faith — and this is not from yourselves, it is the gift of God" (Eph 2:8). This "grace" allows one to participate in God's cosmic act of reconciliation through his Son (Col 1:6; cf. 1:15 – 23), and it is also this "grace" that allows two individuals to relate to one another in strikingly different terms (cf. vv. 15 – 16). Readers of these two letters, and of this commentary, can do no better than to rely on this divine grace as we seek to live lives consistent with the message we have received.

The Theology of Philemon

It has been noted that "few ideas in New Testament studies produce higher levels of agreement than the notion that Paul's letter to Philemon has little or no theological substance."[1] In fact, few treatments of Pauline theology devote a substantial section to this particular letter.[2] Several factors contribute to this conclusion: the relative length of Philemon, the personal tone and private nature of the letter, and the lack of explicit theological arguments. To many, these considerations provide sufficient justification for downplaying this letter as an important resource for Pauline theology, much less the theology of the NT.

This consensus further rests on the assumption that this letter must be evaluated against the categories established by the modern study of Paul's theology. The letter lacks explicit treatment of topics such as justification by grace through faith, the justice and mercy of God the Father, the atoning death of Christ, and the unity of Jews and Gentiles as the one body of Christ. Others who attempt to evaluate this letter according to categories familiar to the works of the systematic theologians would also easily conclude that this work does not focus on Theology proper, Christology, Pneumatology, Ecclesiology, or Eschatology.

Our evaluation of the theological contribution of Philemon, however, must begin with the text in order to reconstruct the framework within which Paul's letter was understood by believers in the first century. In doing so, we must focus on two interrelated aspects: the underlying presuppositions on which Paul's appeals are made,[3] and the narrative that can be identified behind the various assertions in this letter.[4] The presentation below provides a sketch of such a "theology," which points to the profound reservoir of theological thought.

---

1. Marion L. Soards, "Some Neglected Theological Dimensions of Paul's Letter to Philemon," *PRSt* 17 (1990): 209.

2. This is best illustrated by the treatment in Bassler, ed. *Pauline Theology*, vol. 1, which ignores Philemon.

3. Cf. James D. G. Dunn, "Prolegomena to a Theology of Paul," *NTS* 40 (1994): 407–32.

4. Ben Witherington III, *Paul's Narrative Thought World: The Tapestry of Tragedy and Triumph* (Louisville: Westminster John Knox, 1994), 1–5.

God the Father

Although not the subject of extensive discussion, the few references to "God" are consistent with Paul's emphasis in his other letters. In the opening section, "God" is identified as "our Father" (v. 3), an appellation found in other opening sections of Paul's letters (Rom 1:7; 1 Cor 1:3; 2 Cor 1:2; Gal 1:3; Eph 1:2; Phil 1:2; Col 1:2; 2 Thess 1:1; 2:16). This God is also the object of Paul's thanksgiving prayer (v. 4). The significance of such an affirmation should not be underestimated. Paul writes with the fundamental assumption that God is the one and only object of worship.

The act of thanksgiving is an act of worship;[5] it is an act in which Paul not only affirms the centrality of God but also situates human interaction and relationships within the wider plan of God. In focusing on the "love and faith" (v. 5) that Philemon has for all the saints, Paul foregrounds his relationship with God as the primary area of concern. This letter is, therefore, not to be read as a discourse in philosophical ethics, but rather as an appeal to Philemon to continue acting in a way consistent with his commitment to worship the one true God.

Beyond the appearances of the name "God," two passive verbs point to God as the sovereign one who controls history. In v. 15, the assertion that Onesimus "was separated from" Philemon should be interpreted as an affirmation of divine providence: despite human intentions, God has a wider purpose for the human characters. In v. 22, Paul's use of "I will be restored to you" together with the reference to prayer points to his own submission to the divine will.[6] The God presented in this letter is a God who acts in history and to whom humans are responsible.

Returning to the title "our Father," in light of the prominence of the household metaphor in this letter, this title acquires special significance. God the Father is the *paterfamilias*, who has power over his entire household. This note on divine authority introduces a proper perspective with its implied call for accountability.[7] Some have also detected an anti-imperial claim here as God, not the Roman emperor, is now to be considered the ultimate head of the cosmic household.[8]

---

5. For the relationship between the opening thanksgiving sections in Paul's letters and his theology of thanksgiving, see David W. Pao, "Gospel within the Constraints of an Epistolary Form: Pauline Introductory Thanksgivings and Paul's Theology of Thanksgiving," in *Paul and the Ancient Letter Form* (ed. Stanley E. Porter and Sean A. Adams; Pauline Studies 6; Boston/Leiden: Brill, 2010), 101–28.

6. See also Soards, "Some Neglected Theological Dimensions," 215, who considers the content of Paul's prayer, "so that your partnership in the faith may become effective" (v. 6), as reflecting the belief in the active work of God (see comments on v. 6).

7. Burtchaell, *Philemon's Problem: A Theology of Grace*, 48–49, rightly draws attention to the God embedded in this letter as the God of love, one who "loves us as he must" because "He is love." His claim, however, that this God is "a Father who has no wrath" goes beyond the biblical evidence.

8. See S. Scott Bartchy, "Undermining Ancient Patriarchy: The Apostle Paul's Vision of a Society of Siblings," *BTB* 29 (1999): 76, who draws attention to the fact that "Christians were to 'call no man father on earth' — not even the emperor — and many of them were forced to pay with their lives for this radical redefining of family values."

Christ the Lord

Though not a letter that focuses on the supreme ontological status of Christ, this letter contains numerous references to Christ, upon whom Paul grounds his appeals. He begins by identifying himself as a "prisoner of Christ Jesus" (v. 1). The significance of this identification is reinforced by its reappearances in vv. 9 and 23, as well as several references to his own imprisonment (vv. 10, 13, 22). Paul lives out the confession that Jesus is the Lord to whom all should submit.

The lordship of Christ is explicitly noted in v. 3 with the title "the Lord Jesus Christ." In a letter that urges Philemon to be obedient to Christ and his gospel,[9] this emphasis on lordship acquires special meaning as Philemon must act in a way consistent with this confession. This explains the phrase "in the Lord" at the end of both subsections of the main body of this letter (vv. 16, 20). In framing the entire discussion under the lordship of Christ, Paul reminds Philemon that he also has a "Master/ Lord in heaven" (Col 4:1).[10] This relativization of his own power and authority allows Paul to attempt to change Philemon's behavior toward his own slave. After all, Paul does have "boldness in Christ" (v. 8) to command Philemon to act in light of Christ's lordship as he continues in his expression of "love and faith in the Lord Jesus" (v. 5). Through these references to the Lord Jesus Christ, this letter can be considered a christocentric one, where Christ is both the basis and the goal of Paul's appeals (cf. v. 6). Without Christ, Paul has no grounds to appeal to Philemon, and Philemon will find no reason to receive Onesimus as his brother.[11]

Redemption and Reconciliation

Beyond explicit references to Christ, one also finds indirect references to his redemptive work through Paul's own acts as the mediator of reconciliation.[12] Instead of proposing a series of moral arguments, Paul places himself between Onesimus and Philemon in an attempt to seek reconciliation. In identifying himself with Onesimus, he urges Philemon to receive Onesimus as he would receive Paul (v. 17) since Onesimus is his "own heart" (v. 12; cf. v. 20). This is consistent with the force of the conditional clause in v. 17, where Paul considers Philemon's acceptance of Onesimus

---

9. The close identification of Christ with his gospel is illustrated by the coexistence of the title "prisoner of Christ Jesus" (vv. 1, 9; cf. v. 23) and the description "imprisonment for the gospel" (v. 13) in this letter.

10. Another marker that frames this main body is the phrase "in Christ," which is found at the beginning (v. 8) and end (v. 20) of this section.

11. Thus Still, "Philemon among the Letters of Paul," 137: "In Philemon, Christ is not only a part of the letter's warp and woof, but he is also the one who binds Paul to both Philemon and Onesimus. Paul was persuaded that Christ could bring believers together, even a slave and a master."

12. For a more detailed discussion, see Theology in Application on vv. 17 – 20.

as the condition of his own partnership with Philemon.[13] In this way, he imitates the reconciliatory work of Christ, who stands between the holy God and those who are disobedient to him. Moreover, as Christ himself takes on the role of a slave (cf. Phil 2:6 – 11), Paul gives up his freedom in serving the gospel as a "prisoner of Christ Jesus" (vv. 1, 9).[14]

Most striking is Paul's adoption of redemption language in v. 18: "If he has wronged you in any way, or owes you anything, charge it to me." This willingness to purchase the freedom of a slave resembles Christ's own redemptive work on the cross (cf. Gal 3:13 – 14). In bearing the cost of this reconciliation, Paul stands between the two parties, willing to pay for such redemption with his own person.

This is consistent with Paul's behavior elsewhere. At the end of Romans, for example, he intends to return to Jerusalem to deliver the collection to the Jews (Rom 15:25 – 29) since that money symbolizes the unity of Jews and Gentiles (cf. Gal 1:9 – 10; 1 Cor 16:1 – 4; 2 Cor 8 – 9).[15] There Paul is also willing to risk his life for the sake of the unity of the church (cf. Rom 15:30 – 33). Moreover, discussion of his plans to return to Jerusalem culminates his arguments presented earlier in Romans, chapters that contain theological arguments.[16] If Paul's words in Philemon can be compared to that of Romans, his willingness to stand between Philemon and Onesimus should also be read in light of the wider theological arguments that find their climax in Christ's redemptive work on the cross. The lack of explicit theological expressions should, therefore, not be considered a sign of the lack of theological depth.

Structure of the New Reality

Building on the prior work of God through Christ, Paul provides a radical new vision of reality in which the full transformation of human relationships testifies to the power of God's salvific acts. Unlike Colossians, where the power of Christ's death and resurrection is carefully articulated (cf. 1:15 – 23), Paul here focuses on the implications of such events. It is nonetheless correct to argue that in this letter, "Paul's premise is nothing less than Christ's resurrection: there is a new creation; all things have become new."[17]

One significant way this new reality is presented is through the use of household

---

13. See also v. 22, where Paul presents his own reception by Philemon as comparable to Philemon's own reception of Onesimus; cf. Polaski, *Paul and the Discourse of Power*, 70.

14. See Lyons, "Paul's Confrontation with Class," 125 – 26, who further considers Paul's self-portrayal as following Christ's incarnation: self-abnegation, challenge of existing hierarchical social structure, redemptive sacrifice, and an anticipated *parousia*.

15. For a discussion of the theological significance of Paul's collection, see esp. Dieter Georgi, *Remembering the Poor: The History of Paul's Collection for Jerusalem* (Nashville: Abingdon, 1992).

16. This is confirmed by the appearance of four OT quotations in Rom 15:9 – 12 that forms the climax of Paul's preceding discussion.

17. Vanhoozer, "Imprisoned or Free?" 85.

labels. First and most important, God is the "Father" and Jesus Christ is the "Lord" (v. 3). In a household setting, both titles point to the *paterfamilias*. This is yet another piece in Paul's writings that points to a high Christology, where Paul considers Christ to be of the same status as God the Father. Under the headship of God and the lordship of his Son, members of this household are to relate to one another under the presence of this higher authority.

With God and Christ being the heads of the household, the sibling metaphors become meaningful. Timothy, Paul's coworker, is identified as a "brother" (v. 1), while Apphia, apparently a member of Philemon's community, a "sister" (v. 2). Within this framework, the identification of Philemon as a "brother" (vv. 7, 20) becomes important as he is to be considered no more and no less than a member of the household of God. These labels pave the way for v. 16, where Philemon is called to receive Onesimus back "no longer as a slave, but more than a slave, a beloved brother."[18]

This structuring of reality is theologically significant. First, God's people, who have been defined by blood lineage, are now defined by their participation in the gospel of Christ. Both Jews and Gentiles are now able to participate in the Israel who has been called God's "firstborn" (Exod 4:22) and "daughter" (Lam 2:13).[19] As "brothers" and "sisters" who can now call God "Father" and Christ "Lord," they acquire the privilege to receive the inheritance reserved for the legitimate heirs (cf. Col 1:12).

Second, in this reconstruction of reality, the marginal members of the community can claim their rightful places within this household of God. It is not surprising for Paul to mention "Apphia, our sister" at the beginning of this letter, as she is to serve as the witness of this gospel of reversal, where the powerless ones can experience the powerful grace of God.[20] Rather than a narrow treatise on the treatment of slaves, this letter is concerned with the wider perception of reality, a reality constructed by the power of the gospel of Christ.

Third, Paul considers the local church as the proper setting for the implementation of this new vision of reality. In this community of faith, this vision ceased to be a theoretical model, for it testifies to the transformative power of the gospel. Without discussing the responsibilities of various office holders, this letter does provide one of the strongest views of the local church. It is in this ecclesiological setting that one

---

18. For the further discussion of the labels of "old man" (v. 9) and "child" (v. 10) in Philemon, see comments on vv. 9–10.

19. See esp. Stephen C. Barton, "The Relativisation of Family Ties in the Jewish and Graeco-Roman Traditions," in *Constructing Early Christian Families: Family as Social Reality and Metaphor* (ed. H. Moxnes; London/New York: Routledge, 1997), 81–100.

20. See, e.g., Sabine Bieberstein, "Disrupting the Normal Reality of Slavery: A Feminist Reading of the Letter to Phi-

lemon," *JSNT* 79 (2000): 115: "Precisely here, where social normality is broken open, the letter to Philemon summons a woman, Apphia, as witness. She brings before our eyes the relational structure of the early communities of believers in Christ, where a new relationship to the slave Onesimus is now being sought." Assuming that Archippus is Philemon's son, others have considered him as a symbol of the marginal member of the household; cf. Mary Ann Getty, "The Theology of Philemon," *SBLSP* 26 (1987): 506.

can experience the eschatological reality of the new age: "Therefore, if anyone is in Christ, a new creation has come: The old has gone, the new is here!" (2 Cor 5:17).[21] It is to this ecclesiology that we must now turn.

Community of the New Age

With the dawn of the new age, Paul expects the community of God's people to live out this new reality. As a natural extension of this point, the church is to represent the new humanity, one that testifies to the powerful work of a gospel that transcends social and ethnic barriers. If this letter is to be read with Colossians, also addressed to believers in the same geographical region, that letter's theoretical discussion provides the rationale for the practices advocated in Philemon. In Col 3:11, the new humanity is defined in strikingly universal terms: "there is neither Greek nor Jew, circumcised nor uncircumcised, barbarian, Scythian, slave nor free, but Christ is all and in all." Here, Paul urges Philemon to live out this reality.[22]

In light of this wider vision, the public nature of Philemon can be properly understood. The address to the various individuals with their (official) titles at the beginning of this letter (vv. 1 – 2) and the greetings from a number of Paul's coworkers at the end (vv. 23 – 24) make it clear that although Paul is dealing with a personal issue, this is also a public one that involves the entire community of believers.[23] Beyond the concern of individual virtue, therefore, Paul focuses on such community with individual members united through the "grace ... and peace from God our Father and the Lord Jesus Christ" (v. 3). This focus as well as its basis that transcends personal friendship distinguishes Paul's letters from the writings of other moral philosophers of his time.[24] It also points to the continued relevance of this letter for the contemporary audience as Paul here "appears to speak about the interests of the whole Church rather than the private affairs of a single individual."[25]

In considering a personal matter as one that involves the entire ecclesial community, Paul highlights the connection between individual acts and the life of the church. In commenting on Philemon's past acts of love, Paul has already noted how "the hearts of the saints have been refreshed" through him (v. 7), and such isolated acts of kindness are the outworking of his "faith in the Lord Jesus," with "all the saints" being the beneficiaries (v. 5). Instead of being a rhetorical device to manipu-

---

21. Only when "eschatology" is limited to the final culmination of God's work in Christ can one argue for the absence of "eschatology" in this letter; cf. Still, "Philemon among the Letters of Paul," 138.

22. Some have further suggested that this new humanity is to fulfill the role of Israel as the true Adam, God's true humanity; cf. N. T. Wright, "Putting Paul Together Again: Toward a Synthesis of Pauline Theology," in *Pauline Theology*, vol. 1: *Thessalonians, Philippians, Galatians, Philemon*, 204.

23. See also the explicit mentioning of "the church in your [Philemon's] house" (v. 2).

24. See Steele, "Releasing the Captives," 81.

25. Calvin, *Commentaries on the Epistles to Timothy, Titus, and Philemon*, 348.

late Philemon, these words highlight how acts of an individual become instruments of God through which the lives of all the saints are affected.

Because of his insistence on the connection between individual acts and the Christian community, Paul emphasizes the issue of accountability. The coworkers noted in this letter become witnesses both to the exercise of Paul's authority and the need for Philemon to respond appropriately. The final reminder of his own impending visit (v. 22) underscores this issue. This focus on accountability within the community creates a space within which the reality of the new age can be realized and experienced. One can perhaps also detect an embedded polemic here as Paul argues against the status quo of the wider society.[26] It is in this sense that one can consider this letter as presenting a countercultural vision for those who are not included in the eschatological people of God.

From Conversion to Missions

In presenting a new vision of reality for the community, Paul also emphasizes the significance of conversion. This new vision is not imposed from without by Paul or any other church leaders; it is rather developed from within as individuals are transformed by the gospel of Jesus Christ. This letter deals with the effects of conversion: the conversion of Philemon and his household and the conversion of Onesimus. With Philemon's conversion, he must live and act within a different frame of reference.[27] An underlying purpose of Paul's appeal is to have Philemon fully obtain "the knowledge of every good thing that is in us for Christ" (v. 6). In this respect, the function of this letter is comparable to that of the early Christian catechetical instructions, through which new believers learn to live out their new identity.

The conversion of Onesimus is the focus of a major subsection of this letter (vv. 8 – 16). If we can assume that the entire household of Philemon was converted when Philemon himself received the gospel message, Onesimus's "conversion" during his stay with Paul signifies a personal and independent commitment to the gospel. Paul's identification of this regenerated Onesimus as his "son" points to his incorporation into the household of God. This appellation does not function as a term of endearment; it reflects the Jewish understanding of conversion as a new birth. In light of the prevalence of kinship language in this letter, this conversion

---

26. Thus also Bieberstein, "Disrupting the Normal Reality of Slavery," 112: "This public dimension of the community functions as a counterweight not only to the private sphere between Paul and Philemon, but also vis-à-vis the public dimension of state and society, which not merely accepted slavery as the normal state of affairs, but in fact required for its own maintenance a system that divided the population into free and unfree persons."

27. I assume Philemon received the gospel from the evangelistic activities of Epaphras when he first brought the gospel to the city of Colossae (cf. Col 1:7); this also explains the mention of Epaphras at the end of this letter (v. 23). Nevertheless, according to v. 19, Paul also seems to have played a part in Philemon's conversion, and thus Philemon is indebted to him.

acquires added significance. Onesimus does not simply obtain eternal life; he is now part of a community that worships God as Father and Jesus Christ as Lord.

With the conversion of both Philemon and Onesimus, the relationship between them can no longer remain as it was. Philemon must receive Onesimus back "no longer as a slave, but more than a slave, a beloved brother" (v. 16). This statement clearly points to the reframing of the relationship between these two. For the discussion of the theology of conversion, the phrase that follows is equally significant: "both in the flesh and in the Lord" (v. 16). Instead of arguing for two separate realms of existence, Paul clearly points to the interrelatedness of one's earthly existence and spiritual identity. The fact that both Philemon and Onesimus are now part of this same community, grounded in grace, makes it necessary that their relationship be transformed according to the new rules of this kinship group.

For Paul, conversion cannot be separated from mission, because one is not simply converted to benefit from the joy of eternal life; one is also called to participate in the unfolding plan of God.[28] It is not surprising, therefore, to find Paul discussing how Onesimus is "useful" immediately after noting his conversion. He is "useful" because he is serving Paul, who is serving Christ in his imprisonment (v. 13). If we can assume that by saying that "you will do even more than what I say" (v. 21), Paul is appealing to Philemon to release Onesimus for service to the gospel, this letter is intensely focused on missions and the wider unfolding of the salvific plan of God. This in part explains the canonical status of this letter.

Identity, Missions, and the Moral Life

One does not find a separate section on Christian ethics here, although the entire letter is often considered to center on slavery, an issue of significant moral importance. While Paul does not provide a systematic discussion on the issue of slavery,[29] several general principles concerning the life and behavior of believers are worth noting.

First, to Paul, ethics is intimately connected with the identity of believers and their roles in the wider salvific plan of God (as noted above). Instead of presenting an abstract set of ethical principles, Paul focuses on one's response to the gospel of the cross. Moreover, ethics is not limited to acts of an individual; it is also concerned with the function and well-being of the entire community of believers. Ethics is, therefore, but a way to live out the reality that is introduced by the dawn of the new age.

More specifically, Paul grounds one's behavior on the gospel itself. This is well

---

28. See also Paul's description of his own conversion/call account in Gal 1:13–17.

29. For Paul's view of slavery, see introduction to Philemon.

illustrated by the chiastic structure in v. 5, where the "love ... for all the saints" is intimately related to one's "faith in the Lord Jesus." This faith worked out in one's acts of love is that which determines the right course of behavior for Philemon, as it does for all believers.[30] Within this broad framework, particular themes become meaningful: forgiveness, reconciliation, kindness, justice, respect, and responsibility.

Finally, in framing this discussion with a thanksgiving prayer report (vv. 4 – 7) and a benediction (v. 25), Paul refuses to draw a line between worship and ethics.[31] He is concerned with a certain course of action because it is consistent with the gospel message and because it participates in the unfolding of God's plan in history. As such, the "right" course of action is one that testifies to God's powerful work in history. This testimony becomes an act of praise through which the work of God through Christ can be proclaimed.

Authority and Obedience

No discussion of the theology of Philemon is complete without noting Paul's understanding of his authority and his expectation of Philemon's obedience. By reminding Philemon that he has the authority "to command [him] to do what is proper" (v. 8), Paul makes it clear that the appeals "on the basis of love" (v. 9) that follow cannot be taken lightly. This authority is based on his call to be an apostle, as implied by the reference to the consequence of such a call, his own imprisonment for the sake of Christ and his gospel (vv. 1, 9, 23). Moreover, by identifying himself as an "old man" (v. 9) with Onesimus as his "son" (v. 10)[32] and Philemon as Onesimus's "brother" (v. 16), Paul is speaking on behalf of God the "Father" and Jesus Christ the "Lord" (v. 3). His unique authority is a significant part of this new structure of reality as it reflects the will of the head of this household.

Paul expects nothing short of the absolute "obedience" (v. 21) of Philemon. Today's audience should also be reminded of the significance of this letter and the authority it carries. Rather than a series of friendly recommendations, Paul's words convey the divine will. Christian leaders are to continue the proclamation of God's Word, including this short letter of Paul, as we all submit to the lordship of Christ.

---

30. Cf. Marshall, "Theology of Philemon," 186. For a general discussion of the ethical import of this letter, see William J. Richardson, "Principle and Context in the Ethics of the Epistle to Philemon," *Int* 22 (1968): 301 – 16.

31. Such liturgical language points to community worship as the proper setting of the reading of this letter, thus transforming this discussion into one that concerns the life of worship of the entire community; cf. Getty, "Theology of Philemon," 504.

32. The identification of Onesimus as his own son is also a power claim since Philemon is to receive him as he would Paul. For a discussion of the consideration of a son as a mirror image of his father, see Cassius Dio 56.3.4; cf. Chris Frilingos, " 'For my Child, Onesimus': Paul and Domestic Power in Philemon," *JBL* 119 (2000): 100 – 101.

Scripture and Apocrypha Index

Genesis

1:1 . . . . .93, 96, 100
1:26 – 27 227
1:27 94
1:28 . . . . .55, 94
2 – 3 227
3:7 225
3:17 . . . . .169, 212
3:21 225
3:23 – 24 169
5:1 – 2 94
14:19 . . . . .111, 329
14:20 111
14:22 329
17 178
17:9 – 14 . . . . .164, 387
17:11 . . . . .169, 177
17:14 169
17:23, 24, 25 169
20:4, 6 195
40:20 100

Exodus

2:24 367
3:15 81
3:21 – 22 159
4:12, 15 137
4:22 . . . . .95, 431
4:25 – 26 166
6:5 367
6:6 76
6:8 75
6:12 164
6:25 100
6:30 164
10:2 282
10:21 – 23 76
12:34 – 35 159
14:20 76

15:11 – 13 82
19:4 – 6 241
19:15 195
20:2 – 6 218
20:12 282
20:17 220
21:6 394
21:19, 34, 36 409
22:11 – 13 409
22:30 48
26:33 108
28:43 108
29:1 108
29:4 – 9 225
29:37 108
30:29 195
31:3 69
33:19 242
34:6 – 7 242
34:15 – 16 220
34:28 185
35:31 69
40:10 108
40:15 129

Leviticus

1:3 108
2:3 108
3:17 129
5:2 195
5:3 . . . . .195, 220
6:18, 27 195
10:9 185
10:12 108
11:24 – 39 195
11:34, 36 185
14:13 108
15:3, 30 – 31 220
16:3 – 4 225
16:16 220

16:29 – 31 202
17 – 26 217
19:15 277
19:18 377
22:4 – 5 220
23:26 – 32 202
25:55 82
26:1, 30 165
26:41 – 42 164
26:41 178
26:42 – 45 367

Numbers

6:3 185
6:14 108
12:9 224
14:34 224
15:37 – 41 234
15:40 75
18:8, 9, 19, 32 108
19:13 220
32:14 224
36:11 313

Deuteronomy

1:8 75
1:39 282
4:1 269
4:9 . . . . .269, 282
4:23 – 24 . . . . .81, 367
4:31 367
5:6 – 8 218
5:16 282
5:21 220
6:2 273
6:4 – 5 377
6:5 . . . . .274, 367
6:7 269
6:13, 24 273

7:6 241
8:18 – 19 174
9:9 185
10:6 164
10:12, 20 273
11:22 70
13:17 224
14:2 75
16:19 277
18:5, 7 108
21:5 108
21:20 270
22:12 234
28:18 268
30 178
30:6 . . . . 165, 178
30:15 – 16 217
31:16 220
32:9 74
32:21 174
32:46 282

Joshua

7:26 224
19:9 74
19:49 190
24:14 273

Judges

13:7 220
19:3 54
20:26 185

1 Samuel

12:21 174
12:24 273
16:11 95
18:22 188

2 Samuel

6:18 251
7:8 – 17 . . . . 76, 77
15:26 188

1 Kings

8:8 108

8:39, 43 102
8:44 251
8:49 102
10:9 188
18:32 251

2 Kings

4:23 185
17:15 174
17:38 – 39 . . . . .81, 367

1 Chronicles

16:2 251
16:26 174
21:19 251
23:31 185
29:10 – 19 96

2 Chronicles

2:4 185
6:18, 21 102
6:30, 33, 39 102
18:18 211
28:11 224
29:5, 16 220
31:3 185

Ezra

8:21 188

Nehemiah

9:17 242
10:33 . . . . .108, 185

Job

1:6 108
2:1 108
40:19 100

Psalms

1 157
1:6 217
2:7 77

3:7 367
5:2 367
7:1, 3 367
11:4 211
13:3 367
14:1 277
18:2, 6, 21 367
22:1, 2 367
25:7 242
31:19 242
33:6 61
33:8 273
33:9 61
34:9 273
34:13 188
35:18 50
40:13 101
42:5, 11 367
43:4 – 5 367
44:17 80
45:17 367
51:16 101
52:8 157
68 102
68:10 242
68:16 . . . . .102, 161
71:22 367
74:12 – 17 . . . . 113, 332
77:12 – 20 113
82:2 277
85:1 101
86:2 367
86:11 54
86:15 242
89:5 – 37 . . . . 113, 332
89:9 – 14 96
89:10 242
89:27 95
92:12 – 14 157
96:3 – 6 114
96:5 . . . . 111, 174, 329
96:13 54
97:7 . . . . .160, 174
100:4 50
102:25 109
103:8 242
103:13 282
103:19 211
104:24 97
105:6 240
105:42 367
105:43 240

106:45. 367
109:30. 50
110:1 – 2 77
110:1 211
114:1 – 8 113
115:2 – 16 114
115:4 – 7 160
115:5 – 8 174
118:26. 251
121:2. . . . . .111, 329
124:8. 251
129:8. 251
131:1. 242
135:5 – 18 114
135:15 – 18 . . . . .160, 174
136:4 – 17 113
146:5 – 6 .111, 329
147:10. 188

Proverbs

2:1 – 8 139
2:12 – 13 217
2:17 174
3:19 97
4:5 – 6, 12 – 14 70
4:18 – 19 217
6:17 – 19 216
8 92
8:22 – 23 100
8:22 . . . . .93, 95
8:27 – 30 97
12:10 241
24:3 97
24:21 273

Isaiah

1:2. 282
2 175
2:6 – 8 175
2:18. 165
4:3 75
5:25. 224
6:1 . . . . .102, 211
6:2 – 3 189
6:9 – 10 174
10:11. 165
11:2, 9. 69
16:12. 165
19:1 165
21:9 165

29:13 . . . . 159, 196, 199
29:14. 196
31:7 165
40:1 – 2 311
40:1 . . . . .136, 338
40:2 .78, 136, 338
40:8 61
40:9 . . . . .54, 338
40:11 . . . . .136, 338
40:12 – 31 . . . . 111, 113, 329
40:13, 14. 137
40:18 – 24 . . . . 96, 114, 160, 174,
                                    186, 217, 335
41:4 – 7 . . . . 114, 160, 174, 217, 335
41:14. 76
41:27. 54
42:5 113
42:7, 16. 76
42:17 174
43:1 76
43:12. 332
43:14. 76
43:15. 114
43:20. 240
44:9 – 11 . . . . 160, 174, 217, 335
44:9. 174
44:18. 174
44:21 83
44:22 – 23 76
44:22. 78
44:24. . . . . .103, 113
45:4 240
45:9 – 18 . . . . .114, 332
45:16. 174
45:22 – 23 82
46:1 – 4 114
46:6 – 7 .160, 174
46:6. 165
46:9 . . . . .80, 367
47:10. 220
48:12 – 13 114
49:8 75
49:10, 13. 338
49:25. 159
51:3 136
51:12 – 16 . . . . .114, 332
51:12. 338
51:13. . . . . .111, 329
52:6 – 7 104
52:7. . . . . .50, 54, 338
52:11 – 53:12 .78
53:12 159

54:13 104
55:10 – 11 61
57:2 50
57:13 174
57:15 242
57:18 338
58:3, 5. 188
58:6 78
60:6 338
61:1 – 2 . . . . .78, 338
63:18. 108
65:9, 15. 240
66:1 211
66:23. 185

Jeremiah

2:4 – 8 160
2:5. 196
2:19. 101
3:9 220
3:16. 55
4:3 – 4 164
5:24. 273
6:10 164
7:9 216
9:24 – 25 164
9:26 178
10:1 – 16 217
10:16. 103
11:16 166
14:10, 12. 101
14:22. 174
17:8, 12. 157
19:13. 220
21:8 217
23:3 55
31:9. 95
32:34. 220
35:19. 108
36:6 185
51:19. 103

Lamentations

2:13. 431
4:16. 277

Ezekiel

6:9 81

7:20 220
23:8 220
36:10 – 11 55
36:25 – 26 178
36:25 220
36:29 – 30 55
42:13 108
43:5 102
43:22 108
44:4 101
44:6 – 9 164
44:7, 9 178
44:10 196
44:13 108
45:17 185
46:1 185
47 157

Daniel

2:8 296
2:18, 19 129
2:9 – 22 139
2:27, 28, 29 129
2:30, 47 129
5:4, 23 165
6:28 165
7:9 211
7:10 . . . . 108, 211
7:13 108
7:21 – 27 125
9:3 185
10:2 – 3, 12 185
12:1 – 3 170
12:1 125

Hosea

2:10 220
2:23 241
4:2 216
10:6 174
13:14 76

Joel

2:13 242

Amos

8:5 185

Jonah

4:2 242

Micah

1:7 220
4:5 251
4:10 76
5:10 – 15 175

Haggai

2:7 102

Zechariah

10:2 174

Malachi

1:10 188
2:9 277

Matthew

4:2 201
5:3 – 11 216
5:5 242
5:12 73
5:13 298
5:21 – 26 244
5:29 – 30 219
6:12, 14 – 15 244
6:16 – 18 201
6:33 401
7:1 271
7:25 109
8:3 195
9:14 – 17 . . . . 199, 202
10:16 295
11:9 410
11:14 186
11:29 242
12:29 158
12:31 224
12:50 375
15:8 – 9 199
15:9 195
15:19 224
17:5 241

17:17 243
17:27 271
18:4 242
18:21 – 35 252
18:22 252
18:23 – 35 244
18:35 252
19 – 20 246
19:6 394
21:5 242
21:9 251
22:37 274
22:39 – 40 377
23:12 242
25 292
25:10, 11, 13 292
25:14 – 30 292
25:21, 23 292
26:5 271
26:41 . . . . 291, 292, 299
26:65 224
27:9 197
28:10 375
28:19 – 20 301

Mark

2:7 244
2:18 – 22 199
2:18 – 20 202
3:27 158
3:35 375
4:22 139
7:6 – 7 199
7:7 196
7:8 . . . . 159, 199
7:9 200
7:21 – 22 216
7:22 224
8:32 . . . . 173, 383
9:7 241
9:19 243
9:50 298
10:9 394
11:9 251
11:24 68
11:25 244
12:30 273
12:31 377
13:20 126
14:38 . . . . 271, 291, 292, 299
14:64 224

Luke

1:1 – 4	318
1:6	199
1:18	385
1:52	242
2:7	95
2:36 – 38	202
2:51	262
3:29	313
4:2	201
4:18 – 19	78
5:13	195
5:21	224
5:33 – 39	199
5:33 – 35	202
6:37	244
7:41 – 42	244
8:1 – 3	320
8:15	55
8:17	139
9:22, 23	144
9:35	241
9:41	243
10:27	274, 377
11:4	244
11:21 – 22	159
11:30	243
11:34	273
11:51	410
12:11	97
13:21	213
13:35	251
14:11	242
14:34	298
16:1 – 4	127
16:28	271
17:10	244
17:26	243
18:9 – 14	201
18:14	242
19:11 – 27	292
19:20	53
19:38	251
20:20	97
20:21	277
20:42, 44	249
21:36	299
22:27	57
23:7, 15	389
24:19	250
24:46	101

John

1:1	61
1:14	107
1:30	387
3:14	243
6:51	107
7:4, 13	383
7:26	173, 383
7:35	227
8:31 – 32, 51	116
10:33	224
11:14, 54	383
12:13	251
12:50	243
15:4	243
15:18 – 21	145
16:25, 29	383
18:20	173
20:17	375

Acts

1	143
1:4	394
1:14	290
1:20	249
1:23	314
2:29	383
2:34 – 35	211
2:34	111
2:36	51, 111
2:46	59, 320
3:7	141
3:14	170
3:15	101
3:19	111
4:2	132
4:10	101
4:13	173, 295
4:24 – 30	290
4:29	173, 383
4:31	383
4:34	197
5:41	73
5:42	59, 68, 132, 155, 320
6:7	55, 61, 292
6:8 – 10	297
6:8	134
7:22	250
7:39 – 41	160
7:41	165

7:45	313
7:48 – 50	160
7:48	165
7:53	189
7:58	47, 142
8:1 – 3	142
8:1	47
8:3	59, 320
8:23	268
9	143
9:1 – 2	142
9:1	47
9:9	201
9:15 – 16	128, 289, 295
9:15	47
9:16	126
9:22	155
9:26	123
9:27 – 28	251
10:2, 22	318
10:34	277
10:35	318
10:36	61
11:16	247
11:25	47
12:12	313
12:24	55, 61, 292
12:25	313
13:2 – 3	201
13:5	132
13:16, 26	318
13:30, 34	101
13:50	318, 320
14:1	227
14:23	201
15:5, 9, 11	200
15:21	320
15:36	132
15:38	313, 423
15:39	313, 423
16:1 – 3	47
16:5	141
16:10 – 17	318, 423
16:14	318
17:3	101, 132
17:4	318, 320
17:14	47
17:17	318
17:24 – 31	160
17:24 – 25	165
17:31	101
18:1, 2	394

18:4 227
18:5 . . . . 47, 155
18:7 . . . . 314, 318
18:26 406
18:28 155
19:10 . . . . 24, 227
18:17 227
19:20 . . . . 55, 61, 292
19:21 – 41 . . . . 312, 423
19:22 47
19:29 . . . . 312, 423
20 – 26 293
20:3 – 15 312
20:4 . . . . 308, 312, 423
20:5 – 15 . . . . 318, 423
20:19 188
20:20 59
20:21 227
20:31 24
20:32 . . . . 56, 61
21:1 – 18 . . . . 318, 423
21:21 – 22, 28 135
21:29 308
21:39 142
22:3 142
22:14 – 15 47
22:21 – 22 135
25:21 389
25:22 390
26:17 – 18 47
26:18 . . . . 76, 78
26:23 . . . . 101, 135
27:1 – 28:16 . . . . 312, 318, 423
27:1 – 2 . . . . 23, 342
27:2 . . . . 24, 312, 423
28:2, 4 228
28:23 420
28:30 – 31 24
28:31 . . . . 132, 173, 295, 383

Romans

1:1 . . . . 47, 315
1:4 . . . . 47, 51
1:5 419
1:7 . . . . 48, 309, 364, 366, 428
1:8 – 15 415
1:8 – 10 367
1:9 323
1:13 135
1:14 228
1:16 . . . . 227, 337

1:17 129
1:18 – 32 221
1:18 54
1:19 294
1:20 110
1:21 . . . . 73, 254
1:24 . . . . 169, 220
1:25 – 31 216
1:25 . . . . 54, 217, 225
1:26 – 30 225
1:26 – 27 . . . . 217, 232
1:26 220
1:29 . . . . 69, 224
2:1 184
2:4 . . . . 73, 242
2:5 . . . . 221, 225
2:7 – 8 221
2:7 . . . . 73, 216
2:8 . . . . 54, 225, 271
2:10 227
2:11 277
2:25 – 29 . . . . 164, 178
2:25 – 27 . . . . 171, 228
2:25 166
2:28 – 29 214
2:29 166
3 268
3:5 98
3:9 227
3:10 – 18 223
3:10 277
3:14 268
3:18 268
3:20 . . . . 109, 171
3:21 . . . . 107, 129, 294
3:24 . . . . 50, 55, 80, 366, 413
3:29 410
3:30 228
4:9 – 12 228
4:12 314
4:15 171
4:16 55
5:1 – 5 . . . . 52, 369
5:1 – 2 51
5:1 . . . . 50, 246, 366
5:2 . . . . 52, 55
5:3 . . . . 123, 274
5:5 – 9 77
5:5 . . . . 52, 58
5:6 296
5:7 393
5:8 . . . . 103, 106, 169, 176, 244

5:9 – 13 105
5:9 . . . . 172, 221
5:10 . . . . 103, 104
5:11 103
5:15 55
5:17 . . . . 50, 55, 366
5:19 418
5:21 47
6 . . . . 21, 167, 169, 194
6:1 – 14 204
6:3 – 4 166
6:4 . . . . 70, 101, 132, 194,
                                        216, 243, 339
6:5 – 11 167
6:6 – 7 219
6:6 . . . . 226, 395
6:8 – 9 274
6:9 101
6:11 – 12 219
6:11 . . . . 167, 169
6:12 220
6:13 219
6:15 – 16 75
6:16 . . . . 108, 135, 284, 418, 425
6:17 250
6:18 284
6:19 . . . . 107, 108, 166
6:20 . . . . 229, 284
7:4 . . . . 101, 401
7:5 166
7:7, 8 220
7:12 . . . . 171, 199
7:14 . . . . 284, 413
7:18 . . . . 107, 166
7:25 . . . . 47, 74, 107,
                                        191, 250, 251
8:3 169
8:4 . . . . 69, 70, 166
8:5, 6 166
8:7 262
8:8 71
8:9 248
8:10 169
8:11 . . . . 168, 248
8:12 – 17 116
8:12 – 13 413
8:15 – 17 275
8:17, 18 144
8:19, 20 110
8:21 . . . . 110, 115, 196, 284
8:22 110
8:26 – 27 299

8:29 . . . . .94, 227
8:32 421
8:35 – 39 394
8:38 21
9 – 11 315
9:9 296
9:15 – 18 242
9:22 . . . . .221, 242
9:23 . . . . .130, 241
9:25 241
10:2 317
10:9 . . . . 101, 155, 168, 212, 223
10:12 . . . . .227, 229
11:12 69
11:13 . . . . .47, 127
11:15 103
11:22 242
11:23 109
11:25 – 32 126
11:25 . . . . 69, 129, 135, 271
11:28 364
11:30 107
11:31 241
11:33 139
12:1 – 2 212
12:1 . . . . 108, 241, 269
12:2 . . . . 117, 133, 226
12:3 212
12:4 – 5 . . . . .99, 100
12:5 247
12:12 290
12:16 212
12:17 109
12:18 246
12:19 309
13:1 – 7 351
13:1 262
13:3 71
13:5 262
13:6 68
13:8 69
13:10 . . . . .69, 244
13:11 296
13:12 – 14 223
13:13 . . . . 216, 217, 232
13:14 . . . . .220, 226
14 . . . . .184, 185
14:1 406
14:3 . . . . .185, 406
14:5 185
14:8 – 12 284
14:10 . . . . .108, 185

14:14 . . . . .185, 270
14:17 . . . . .77, 373
14:18 . . . . .269, 284
14:21 185
14:22 109
15 23
15:1 71
15:2 71
15:7 406
15:8 . . . . .54, 157
15:9 – 12 430
15:9 241
15:13 . . . . .69, 73, 373
15:14 – 33 415
15:14 . . . . .69, 132
15:18 . . . . .250, 418
15:19 . . . . .69, 128
15:20 271
15:22 – 33 293
15:22 – 32 380
15:24 . . . . .23, 421
15:25 – 29 430
15:28 421
15:29 69
15:30 – 33 . . . . .65, 290, 430
15:30 – 32 20
15:30 . . . . .58, 385, 421
15:32 73
15:33 79
16:1 . . . . 57, 98, 309,
                      320, 348, 365
16:2 320
16:3 – 16 421
16:3 – 5 365
16:3 . . . . 315, 320, 423
16:5 . . . . .59, 127, 320
16:6 – 7 320
16:6 134
16:7 . . . . 98, 314, 319, 422
16:9 . . . . 315, 364, 423
16:11 . . . . .270, 314
16:12 . . . . .270, 320
16:13 270
16:18 276
16:19 418
16:21 – 23 421
16:21 . . . . .315, 423
16:22 . . . . 21, 48, 70, 270, 322
16:23 . . . . .309, 348
16:25 129
16:26 . . . . 129, 294, 384, 419

1 Corinthians

1:1 . . . . 47, 50, 309, 348, 366, 384
1:2 . . . . .48, 240
1:3 . . . . .91, 366, 428
1:4 . . . . .50, 366, 367
1:6 . . . . .157, 311
1:8 . . . . .108, 157
1:9 . . . . .47, 51, 369
1:10 251
1:11 58
1:12 139
1:17 47
1:18 61
1:23 . . . . .132, 138
1:24 227
1:29 109
1:31 270
2:1 – 13 . . . . .69, 295
2:1 129
2:4 247
2:6 – 13 129
2:6 – 8 21
2:6 – 7 129
2:7 . . . . .91, 98
2:12 421
3:9 . . . . 315, 378, 423
3:10, 12, 14 156
3:16 . . . . .135, 248
4:4 169
4:5 . . . . .294, 296
4:6 271
4:9 . . . . .21, 126
4:12 . . . . .134, 243
4:14 – 21 415
4:14 364
4:17 . . . . 270, 310, 387
4:18, 19 191
4:20 77
4:21 420
5:1 – 5 384
5:2 . . . . .171, 191
5:3 . . . . .54, 141
5:4 251
5:6 135
5:8 54
5:9 – 10 217
5:10 – 11 . . . . 216, 217, 232
5:11 123
5:12 – 13 296
6:2, 3 135
6:9 – 11 222

6:9 – 10 217
6:9 135
6:10 220
6:12 – 20 279
6:15, 16 135
6:20 197
7:1 . . . . .194, 195
7:6 384
7:8 – 11 279
7:10 394
7:11 . . . . .103, 394
7:12 – 16 279
7:14 169
7:15 394
7:19 228
7:21 – 22 229
7:22 315
7:23 197
7:25 . . . . .384, 387
7:32, 33 71
7:37 392
7:39 270
8:1 387
8:6 . . . . .51, 91, 132
8:9 158
8:13 271
9:1 – 2 47
9:1 270
9:13 135
9:14 132
9:16 – 17 127
9:16 143
9:24 135
9:25 134
10:1 135
10:4 91
10:12 . . . . .158, 316
10:14 309
10:17 247
10:26 96
10:30 250
10:31 251
10:33 71
11:1 . . . . .56, 414
11:2 154
11:3 . . . . 100, 135, 262, 280
11:7 94
11:23 154
11:27 – 32 155
11:32 271
11:34 127
12:1 . . . . .135, 387

12:3 . . . . .51, 155, 212
12:8 139
12:12 – 30 100
12:12 – 26 . . . . 192, 219, 247
12:12 99
12:13 229
12:20 . . . . .123, 271
12:27 100
12:28 255
13:2 52
13:4 191
13:10 133
13:13 . . . . 46, 52, 244, 369
14:11 228
14:15 – 16 249
14:19 247
14:26 . . . . 89, 248, 249, 255
14:31 136
14:40 141
15 215
15:1 – 2 116
15:3 – 4 154
15:9 47
15:10 . . . . .133, 134
15:12 – 13 155
15:12 . . . . .101, 138
15:20 – 24 215
15:20 101
15:22 226
15:23 54
15:24 – 28 76
15:24 . . . . .77, 97
15:25 315
15:31 – 33 346
15:32 23
15:38 – 39 107
15:42 196
15:45 – 49 94
15:45 226
15:49 114
15:50 . . . . .77, 196
15:51 129
15:53 – 54 216
15:56 – 57 74
15:57 . . . . 250, 252, 291
15:58 110
16 23
16:1 – 4 430
16:1 387
16:7 421
16:9 292
16:12 . . . . .348, 387

16:13 291
16:17 124
16:18 . . . . .373, 374
16:19 – 20 421
16:19 . . . . .59, 127, 320
16:21 . . . . .322, 408
16:22 – 24 408

2 Corinthians

1 – 9 23
1:1 . . . . 47, 48, 309, 348, 384
1:2 . . . . .366, 428
1:3 – 7 . . . . .146, 373
1:3 241
1:5 243
1:6 . . . . .123, 136
1:8 135
1:9 – 10 52
1:21 157
1:23 132
1:24 . . . . .315, 316
2:3 373
2:7, 10 421
2:12 . . . . 270, 292, 300
2:13 348
2:14 . . . . .126, 250
3:1 98
3:3 324
3:6 – 12 157
3:6 74
3:12 . . . . .173, 383
3:15 320
4:2 . . . . .98, 109
4:3 – 6 75
4:4 94
4:5 315
4:7 139
4:10 – 12 215
4:11 126
4:13 – 14 . . . . .132, 274
4:14 108
4:15 . . . . .250, 297
4:16 226
5:2 – 4 166
5:2 169
5:3 109
5:6 274
5:10 . . . . .215, 294
5:12 98
5:14 – 21 . . . . .105, 284
5:17 . . . . .110, 432

5:18 – 19 104
5:18, 19 103
5:20 . . . . 103, 385, 387
6:4 – 6 73
6:4 98
6:5 133
6:6 – 7 216
6:6 . . . . .241, 244
6:10 123
6:12 241
6:16 248
7:1 309
7:4 . . . . 373, 383, 387
7:6 242
7:11 98
7:12 . . . . .109, 294
7:13 . . . . .373, 374
7:15 . . . . .241, 419
8 – 9 430
8:3 317
8:4 370
8:7 244
8:8 384
8:16 250
8:21 109
8:23 . . . . .47, 315, 423
9:4 409
9:12 124
9:15 250
10:1 242
10:2 54
10:5 418
10:9 395
10:10 141
10:11 54
10:12, 18 98
11:4 243
11:9 124
11:19, 20 243
11:23 . . . . .133, 309
11:30 . . . . .143, 339
12:2 98
12:7 318
12:8 387
12:9 – 10 400
12:9 . . . . .56, 143, 339
12:11 98
12:13 421
12:14 – 13:13 415
12:19 309
12:20 217
12:21 220

13:2 54
13:4 400
13:10 54
13:13 . . . . .369, 370
13:14 79

Galatians

1:1 . . . . .47, 101
1:3 .51, 366, 428
1:6 55
1:7 158
1:9 – 10 430
1:9 154
1:10 . . . . .273, 315
1:12 154
1:13 – 17 434
1:17 98
1:23 107
2:2 138
2:5 54
2:6 277
2:7 228
2:8 . . . . .47, 127
2:12 . . . . .98, 314
2:16 200
2:18 98
2:20 . . . . .176, 215
3:4 109
3:10 199
3:13 – 14 . . . . .413, 430
3:13 296
3:17 139
3:18 421
3:19 189
3:23 – 25 28
3:23 98
3:27 226
3:28 . . . . .229, 263, 281
4:1 – 3 28
4:3 .28, 160, 284
4:4 – 5 91
4:5 296
4:7 275
4:8 – 9 107
4:9 – 10 28
4:9 .28, 160, 161
4:11 133
4:12 – 20 415
4:15 317
4:18 54
4:19 126

4:20 54
4:21 – 31 229
5:5 52
5:6 . . . . .51, 228, 244, 369
5:10 270
5:12 73
5:13 . . . . .107, 166, 241, 280
5:15 158
5:16 . . . . .70, 220
5:17 – 24 218
5:19 – 23 218
5:19 – 21 217
5:19 220
5:20 271
5:21 77
5:22 – 23 . . . . .58, 216
5:22 . . . . .73, 241, 244, 373
5:24 107
6:1 – 2 244
6:8 196
6:9 296
6:10 . . . . .71, 296
6:11 . . . . .322, 408
6:12 – 18 408
6:15 . . . . .110, 228
6:16 79
6:18 424

Ephesians

1 – 2 315
1:1 .47, 48, 384
1:2 .51, 366, 428
1:4 – 7 130
1:4 98
1:7 78
1:10 . . . . .69, 296
1:13 . . . . .53, 58, 169
1:15 – 23 .65, 290
1:15 .52, 68, 369
1:16 . . . . .323, 367
1:17 . . . . .58, 69, 72, 139, 371
1:18 130
1:19 – 20 134
1:20 – 21 173
1:20 72
1:21 . . . . .97, 186
1:23 69
2:1 – 2 222
2:1 169
2:2 – 3 221
2:2 . . . . .129, 172, 284

2:4 241
2:7 242
2:8 . . . . .56, 426
2:9 271
2:11 – 13 166
2:11 – 12 315
2:11 . . . . .169, 228
2:12 . . . . .106, 169
2:13 – 16 105
2:13 169
2:14 – 18 . . . . .50, 366
2:14 – 15 171
2:16 . . . . .103, 171
2:17 169
2:18 58
2:19 – 21 156
2:20 338
2:22 58
3:1 – 11 147
3:1 – 9 129
3:1 – 7 293
3:1 363
3:2 .109, 127, 169
3:4 131
3:5 . . . . .58, 338
3:7 . . . . 56, 134, 300, 309
3:8 131
3:9 214
3:10 97
3:12 . . . . .173, 383
3:13 123
3:14 – 21 . . . . .65, 290
3:16 . . . . 58, 73, 80, 227
3:17 369
3:18 52
3:19 69
4 241
4:1 – 16 192
4:1 . . . . .70, 241, 363
4:2 – 3 216
4:2 . . . . 188, 243, 244
4:3 – 4 246
4:3 . . . . .58, 245
4:4 . . . . .58, 247
4:5 – 7 298
4:5 241
4:10 69
4:11 70
4:12 322
4:13 . . . . .69, 133
4:15 – 16 245
4:15 100

4:16 137
4:17 . . . . .169, 270
4:18 – 19 106
4:20 56
4:21 109
4:22 – 25 223
4:29 297
4:30 . . . . .58, 413
4:31 – 32 241
4:31 . . . . 224, 268, 271
4:32 . . . . 170, 243, 421
5:1 364
5:2 . . . . 108, 244, 267
5:3 – 14 218
5:3 – 5 73
5:3 – 4 . . . . .216, 336
5:3 . . . . 217, 220, 223, 232
5:4 . . . . 223, 224, 297
5:5 . . . . 77, 217, 223, 297, 315
5:6 – 14 75
5:6 221
5:8 222
5:9 75
5:11 76
5:13 – 14 294
5:15 158
5:16 296
5:18 . . . . .58, 69, 248
5:19 – 20 89
5:19 . . . . .248, 249
5:20 . . . . .50, 251
5:21 . . . . .262, 280
5:22 – 6:9 264
5:22 – 33 279
5:23 . . . . 100, 262, 280
5:24 262
5:25, 28 268
5:33 280
6:2 269
6:4 . . . . .269, 270
6:5 424
6:6 316
6:8 . . . . .229, 277
6:10 . . . . .72, 296
6:11 316
6:12 . . . . 76, 97, 172, 291
6:13, 14 316
6:17 58
6:18 . . . . .52, 58, 291
6:20 . . . . .295, 385
6:21 . . . . .308, 309
6:22 310

Philippians

1:1 . . . . .48, 50, 52, 57, 261, 309,
316, 363, 366, 395
1:2 . . . . .51, 366, 428
1:3 . . . . 50, 323, 366, 367
1:4 .73, 79, 367
1:5 . . . . 301, 370, 371
1:6 71
1:7 . . . . 323, 363, 391
1:9 – 11 . . . . .65, 290
1:9 . . . . .79, 371
1:12 308
1:13 . . . . 323, 363, 391
1:14 . . . . 270, 323, 363, 391
1:15 138
1:17 – 18 132
1:17 . . . . 323, 363, 391
1:18 – 19 123
1:20 . . . . 295, 383, 384
1:21 215
1:23 167
1:25 373
1:26 54
1:27 . . . . .70, 301
1:29 421
1:30 . . . . .134, 301
2:1 . . . . 146, 241, 244, 373
2:2 212
2:3 – 4 280
2:3 . . . . .188, 242
2:6 – 11 . . . . 89, 91, 146, 430
2:6 94
2:7 . . . . 261, 284, 413
2:8 . . . . 242, 284, 413
2:9 . . . . .85, 104, 421
2:10 21
2:11 111
2:12 .54, 309, 419
2:14 251
2:16 133
2:19 – 24 415
2:19 . . . . .310, 421
2:22 387
2:23 . . . . .310, 421
2:25 . . . . 47, 56, 310, 312,
315, 348, 365, 423
2:28 310
2:30 124
3:2 – 4 25
3:10 – 11 125
3:10 370

3:17 56
3:19, 20 – 21 .212
3:21 . . . . .134, 262
4:1 . . . . 270, 309, 373
4:2 270
4:3 . . . . 315, 320, 410, 423
4:4 270
4:6 255
4:8 . . . . .216, 241
4:9 56
4:14 – 15 301
4:18 . . . . 56, 108, 269, 309, 394
4:21, 22 52
4:23 423

Colossians

1:1 – 2:5 149
1:1 – 8 . . . . .359, 376
1:1 . . . . .20, 21, 131, 310, 322,
                327, 328, 338, 363, 384
1:2 . . . . .70, 74, 96, 130, 131,
                240, 292, 297, 300, 307,
                309, 323, 331, 366, 428
1:3 – 14 . . . . . . 84, 118, 133, 250, 287, 303
1:3 – 8 . . . . 64, 68, 78, 84, 150, 336
1:3 – 6 109
1:3 . . . . .64, 68, 73, 131, 158,
                223, 243, 251, 253,
                303, 328, 366, 367
1:4 – 8 68
1:4 . . . . .69, 71, 74, 109, 130,
                131, 168, 331, 359, 369
1:5 – 7 127
1:5 – 6 . . . . . . 64, 110, 297, 304, 327, 371
1:5 . . . . .24, 34, 75, 110, 159,
                247, 250, 292, 337, 369
1:6 . . . . .65, 68, 69, 71, 72, 80,
                119, 127, 128, 229, 243,
                292, 297, 300, 304, 307,
                323, 328, 337, 366, 426
1:7 – 8 . . . . 68, 131, 310, 315
1:7 . . . . .24, 111, 127, 131, 274, 292,
                303, 307, 309, 310, 315,
                321, 324, 334, 417, 422, 433
1:8 . . . . 24, 302, 368, 369
1:9 – 14 . . . . 44, 84, 286, 290, 298, 303
1:9 – 10 . . . . .295, 371
1:9 . . . . .58, 63, 64, 71, 93, 132,
                133, 138, 139, 156, 290,
                292, 301, 316, 371
1:10 – 20 20
1:10 – 12 . . . . .156, 336

1:10 . . . . .34, 51, 60, 63, 64, 71,
                84, 138, 155, 156, 157,
                243, 250, 295, 335
1:11 – 14 330
1:11 – 12 123
1:11 . . . . 65, 130, 216, 373
1:12 – 14 . . . . .221, 291
1:12 . . . . .25, 44, 48, 64, 130, 158,
                190, 223, 240, 247,
                251, 253, 275, 431
1:13 – 23 113
1:13 – 14 . . . . . 84, 103, 158, 243, 252, 330
1:13 . . . . .49, 65, 88, 93, 160, 219,
                239, 281, 283, 302, 315, 329
1:14 . . . . 167, 329, 413
1:15 – 2:4 366
1:15 – 23 . . . . .119, 142, 154, 202, 287,
                338, 339, 426, 430
1:15 – 20 . . . . .25, 29, 34, 51, 55, 64, 67,
                70, 74, 77, 82, 111, 118,
                122, 125, 131, 145, 149,
                156, 180, 202, 205, 211,
                214, 218, 226, 227, 230,
                247, 249, 257, 296, 301,
                328, 329, 331, 335, 399
1:15 – 16 . . . . 64, 65, 118, 192, 329
1:15 . . . . 64, 76, 227, 329, 331, 333
1:16 . . . . .76, 138, 160, 161, 163,
                167, 174, 189, 211, 213,
                214, 278, 329, 331, 332
1:17 – 18 118
1:17 . . . . 138, 167, 331, 332
1:18 – 20 . . . . .65, 118, 125, 192, 203,
                222, 229, 253, 329, 332
1:18 . . . . . . 100, 118, 126, 127, 129, 144,
                162, 163, 168, 187, 191, 192,
                207, 226, 246, 324, 329
1:19 . . . . .138, 159, 161, 162,
                167, 329, 331
1:20 – 23 221
1:20 – 22 252
1:20 . . . . .78, 103, 118, 129, 144, 162,
                168, 172, 205, 213, 219,
                230, 246, 251, 278, 329
1:21 – 23 . . . . 118, 122, 149, 399
1:21 – 22 . . . . 103, 243, 330
1:21 . . . . 169, 221, 222
1:22 . . . . .48, 52, 59, 103, 118, 124,
                125, 133, 144, 162, 166,
                187, 191, 192, 202, 240,
                246, 324, 330, 331
1:23 . . . . .21, 22, 46, 50, 51, 52,
                56, 78, 118, 127, 131,
                132, 138, 150, 229, 309,
                316, 321, 337, 338

1:24 – 4:1 106
1:24 – 2:5 . . . . .47, 60, 85, 154, 287,
                293, 338, 339, 340
1:24 – 29 149
1:24 . . . . .23, 47, 84, 99, 162, 166,
                187, 202, 207, 246,
                293, 323, 332, 339
1:25 – 2:1 316
1:25 – 26 294
1:25 . . . . .54, 61, 69, 111, 293,
                294, 309, 321, 322, 338
1:26 – 28 338
1:26 . . . . 48, 215, 293, 294
1:27 – 28 . . . . .49, 331
1:27 . . . . .25, 46, 47, 52, 53, 214,
                216, 293, 328, 340
1:28 . . . . .47, 84, 93, 108, 155,
                248, 249, 255, 316, 331
1:29 . . . . 168, 316, 317, 324
2 230
2:1 – 5 149
2:1 . . . . 24, 49, 316, 317, 324
2:2 – 5 69
2:2 – 3 196
2:2 . . . . .47, 58, 69, 70, 71, 84,
                131, 239, 246, 253, 267,
                281, 293, 296, 302, 311,
                316, 329, 335, 338
2:3 . . . . 69, 84, 93, 131, 159, 213, 295
2:4 . . . . 25, 56, 64, 158, 159, 184
2:5 . . . . .22, 47, 51, 52, 58, 109,
                119, 123, 304, 331
2:6 – 4:1 . . . . 119, 287, 338, 339
2:6 – 23 . . . . 34, 106, 142, 174
2:6 – 15 . . . . 63, 118, 130, 186, 252
2:6 – 7 . . . . 44, 51, 74, 109,
                132, 239, 250, 253
2:6 . . . . .47, 49, 51, 56, 70, 83,
                181, 203, 210, 219, 222,
                243, 279, 295, 322, 333
2:7 . . . . .22, 52, 109, 181,
                191, 247, 336
2:8 – 23 . . . . 149, 158, 257
2:8 – 15 183
2:8 – 10 . . . . .72, 180, 191
2:8 . . . . .19, 25, 26, 28, 47, 140, 180,
                186, 189, 191, 196, 198,
                200, 212, 230, 335, 337
2:9 – 10 . . . . .98, 125
2:9 . . . . .84, 102, 191
2:10 . . . . .69, 76, 84, 97,
                114, 211, 330
2:11 – 15 . . . . 184, 186, 221, 225
2:11 – 14 181

2:11 – 13 . . . . 192, 193, 203, 285
2:11 – 12 . . . . 180, 219, 222, 330
2:11 . . . . 25, 26, 31, 47, 84,
187, 200, 202, 203,
214, 228, 240, 332
2:12 – 15 53
2:12 – 13 . . . . 54, 193, 339
2:12 . . . . 21, 26, 51, 101, 109,
134, 210, 230, 328, 330
2:13 – 15 . . . . 78, 180, 230, 252
2:13 – 14 . . . . 75, 105, 222, 239
2:13 . . . . 84, 106, 107, 196, 219,
228, 243, 323, 331, 421
2:14 – 15 . . . . 125, 212, 219, 243
2:14 . . . . 22, 84, 180, 190,
194, 199, 330, 409
2:15 . . . . 27, 29, 76, 84, 97, 103,
180, 189, 191, 194, 195,
211, 229, 291, 330, 384
2:16 – 3:17 241
2:16 – 23 . . . . . . 20, 25, 28, 49, 52, 63, 78,
137, 149, 162, 228, 296
2:16 – 19 . . . . 72, 206, 331
2:16 – 17 230
2:16 . . . . 26, 31, 119, 140,
210, 214, 219, 332
2:17 . . . . 25, 47, 84, 162, 212
2:18 – 23 108
2:18 – 19 . . . . 21, 116
2:18 . . . . 25, 27, 29, 30, 31, 53,
96, 97, 96, 130, 133, 140,
160, 204, 211, 230, 242,
246, 247, 299, 332
2:19 . . . . 22, 84, 99, 100, 137,
207, 245, 246, 328, 332
2:20 – 3:4 193
2:20 – 23 . . . . 144, 166, 204, 205, 246, 285
2:20 – 21 . . . . 26, 31, 204, 214
2:20 . . . . 26, 28, 47, 108,
210, 213, 222, 331
2:21 – 23 247
2:22 . . . . 160, 335
2:23 . . . . 27, 29, 31, 93, 107, 124,
133, 139, 204, 242, 296
3:1 – 4:1 . . . . 63, 106, 150, 184, 258
3:1 – 14 192
3:1 – 7 34
3:1 – 4 . . . . . 21, 32, 63, 96, 126, 167, 181,
193, 203, 236, 239, 258,
278, 285, 293, 330, 334
3:1 . . . . 26, 47, 49, 53, 57, 108, 180,
181, 184, 193, 219, 236, 272,
278, 328, 329, 331, 339
3:2 . . . . 84, 96

3:3 – 4 130
3:3 . . . . 47, 139, 180, 329, 331
3:4 . . . . 21, 46, 47, 53, 139, 167, 180,
214, 266, 277, 281, 286, 291,
294, 330, 331, 332, 339
3:5 – 4:1 . . . . 199, 206, 214
3:5 – 17 . . . . 276, 289
3:5 – 14 . . . . 236, 247, 250
3:5 – 11 . . . . 236, 239, 258
3:5 – 9 . . . . 181, 203, 334
3:5 – 8 192
3:5 . . . . 31, 84, 105, 236, 241,
251, 268, 277, 334, 335
3:6 . . . . 21, 105, 167, 334, 340
3:7 – 8 187
3:7 . . . . 34, 169, 295
3:8 – 9 . . . . 31, 236, 247, 277, 334
3:8 . . . . 169, 236, 238, 240, 241,
242, 268, 271, 335
3:9 – 14 192
3:9 – 12 223
3:9 – 11 . . . . 100, 178
3:9 . . . . 116, 165, 166, 172, 334
3:10 – 17 334
3:10 – 14 203
3:10 – 12 225
3:10 – 11 . . . . 239, 240
3:10 . . . . 69, 84, 114, 138, 236, 240,
247, 254, 267, 295, 333
3:11 . . . . 26, 34, 47, 52, 55, 59, 105,
137, 147, 236, 245, 247, 253,
263, 277, 278, 283, 307, 311,
314, 325, 332, 334, 336, 338,
365, 395, 398, 420, 422, 432
3:12 – 4:1 229
3:12 – 17 . . . . 258, 282
3:12 – 14 . . . . 31, 181, 204, 205,
218, 224, 336
3:12 . . . . 48, 73, 188, 223, 225,
267, 272, 281, 334
3:13 . . . . 51, 105, 155, 170, 225,
263, 280, 323, 365, 421
3:14 . . . . 52, 58, 137, 217, 263,
267, 272, 281, 302
3:15 – 4:1 32
3:15 – 17 . . . . . 31, 44, 150, 204, 205, 223,
258, 286, 290, 291, 297,
304, 310, 316, 324, 336
3:15 . . . . . 47, 84, 105, 180, 187, 191, 192,
205, 207, 263, 280, 336, 366
3:16 – 17 335
3:16 . . . . 47, 54, 58, 61, 84, 89, 93,
132, 180, 263, 295,
297, 300, 335, 337

3:17 . . . . 26, 50, 51, 74, 83, 111, 151,
180, 258, 260, 261, 264, 272,
274, 275, 280, 284, 285, 289,
290, 297, 301, 323, 328, 329,
334, 336, 339, 367
3:18 – 4:1 . . . . 204, 205, 236, 237, 239,
286, 289, 333, 351,
365, 374, 397, 410
3:18 – 19 229
3:18 . . . . 51, 59, 237, 250,
333, 384, 397, 410
3:20 . . . . 51, 59, 237, 250,
333, 397, 410
3:22 – 4:1 229
3:22 – 25 . . . . 304, 310, 316, 324, 333
3:22 . . . . 51, 59, 237, 246, 250,
333, 397, 410, 424
3:23 . . . . 51, 59, 83, 237, 250, 301,
333, 334, 395, 397, 410
3:24 . . . . 21, 47, 51, 59, 83, 135,
167, 237, 240, 250,
286, 333, 397, 410
3:25 286
4:1 . . . . 51, 59, 83, 84, 135,
237, 250, 286, 333,
397, 410, 425, 429
4:2 – 6 . . . . 79, 229, 258, 303,
316, 324, 339
4:2 – 3 . . . . 323, 326
4:2 . . . . 32, 44, 78, 119, 150,
215, 239, 258, 264, 276,
278, 316, 336, 340
4:3 – 6 32
4:3 – 4 316
4:3 . . . . 23, 47, 119, 123,
135, 337, 363
4:5 – 6 192
4:5 . . . . 93, 317, 339
4:6 . . . . 307, 323, 339
4:7 – 18 421
4:7 – 9 287
4:7 – 8 422
4:7 . . . . 25, 49, 51, 57, 127,
270, 278, 334, 364
4:8 . . . . 246, 08
4:9 . . . . 23, 49, 57, 334, 342,
343, 364, 387, 389
4:10 – 17 342
4:10 – 15 421
4:10 – 14 . . . . 287, 292
4:10 . . . . 23, 24, 123,
417, 422, 423
4:11 . . . . 329, 364, 422, 423
4:12 – 13 . . . . 24, 131, 316

4:12 . . . . .22, 24, 47, 56, 79, 163,
        261, 274, 284, 292, 301,
        310, 334, 417, 422
4:13 . . . . 24, 49, 56, 136
4:14 . . . . 23, 57, 342, 364, 417, 423
4:15 – 17 .287
4:15 . . . . 49, 59, 127, 333, 365
4:16 .49, 136
4:17 . . . . 51, 270, 278, 365
4:18 . . . . . 21, 23, 48, 119, 123, 287, 300,
        363, 391, 408, 421, 422, 423

1 Thessalonians

1:1 . . . . .47, 50
1:2 – 3 367
1:2 . . . . 50, 79, 323, 367
1:3 . . . . .52, 368, 369
1:5 337
1:6 . . . . .73, 123
1:8 130
1:9 – 10 221
2:2 134
2:4 71
2:9 . . . . .133, 134
2:12 . . . . .70, 77
2:13 .68, 367
2:15 71
2:17 – 3:13 415
2:17 141
2:19 54
3:2 . . . . 48, 310, 315, 348,
        378, 387, 423
3:5 . . . . .68, 133
3:8 270
3:11 – 13 . . . . .65, 290
3:12 79
3:13 . . . . .54, 74
4:1 – 2 111
4:1 . . . . .71, 154, 155
4:3 254
4:5 220
4:9 387
4:12 296
4:13 . . . . .135, 387
4:15 54
4:16 – 17 .216
4:17 . . . . 111, 167, 220
5:1 387
5:6 291
5:8 .52, 369
5:12 134

5:18 . . . . .247, 254
5:23 .54, 246
5:26 421
5:27 . . . . .309, 320

2 Thessalonians

1:1 . . . . .47, 428
1:2 366
1:3 367
1:4 243
1:5, 6 277
1:7, 10 74
1:11 79
2:1 54
2:2 . . . . .134, 322
2:6 – 7 126
2:7 – 11 134
2:8 54
2:9 134
2:10 – 13 54
2:11 134
2:13 – 14 74
2:13 .50, 367
2:16 – 17 .301
2:16 428
2:17 250
3:6 .154, 251
3:8 134
3:17 . . . . .322, 408

1 Timothy

1:1 . . . . 47, 131, 363, 384
1:2 . . . . .47, 51, 241
1:3 50
1:5 .52, 244
1:9 – 10 . . . . .216, 218
1:9 217
1:10 . . . . .217, 232
1:15 91
2:3 109
2:6 177
2:7 .47, 127
2:8 – 3:13 264
3:1 – 7 218
3:2 216
3:5 .59, 127
3:8 – 13 .218
3:8 .57, 309
3:10 108
3:12 .57, 309

3:13 384
3:16 . . . . 55, 89, 94, 111, 128, 294
4:6 309
4:8 186
4:10 134
4:12 241
5:1 – 6:2 .264
5:3 – 16 279
5:4 109
5:9 – 16 320
5:10 279
6:3 247
6:4 – 5 . . . . .216, 218
6:4 224
6:11 . . . . .241, 244
6:12 241
6:16 72
6:19 186

2 Timothy

1:1 . . . . .47, 363, 384
1:2 51
1:3 . . . . 250, 323, 367
1:8 .363, 386
1:9 – 10 132
1:9 98
1:10 294
1:12 123
2:4 71
2:8 101
2:9 .323, 391
2:15 53
2:19 . . . . .141, 316
2:22 241
3:2 – 4 82
3:10 . . . . .72, 73, 241
3:11 123
4:1 76
4:7 134
4:8 .53, 277
4:10 – 11 . . . . .318, 423
4:11 . . . . .313, 317
4:12 308
4:18 76
4:21 98

Titus

1:1 . . . . .47, 315, 363
1:2 98
1:3 294

1:6 – 16 218
1:6 – 7 108
1:6 279
2:2 – 10 264
2:2 244
2:13 . . . . .52, 131
2:15 384
3:1 – 3 218
3:1 . . . . .71, 97, 262
3:3 . . . . .221, 224
3:4 – 7 132
3:4 242
3:5 – 6 248
3:5 . . . . 226, 227, 241
3:12 . . . . .308, 310

Philemon

1 – 3 . . . . .379, 421
1 – 2 . . . . .352, 432
1 . . . . .23, 50, 56, 309, 315, 341,
             342, 348, 352, 392, 398,
             399, 401, 406, 411, 413,
             422, 423, 424, 425, 426,
             429, 430, 431, 435
2 . . . . 59, 309, 321, 342, 431, 432
3 . . . . .348, 379, 385, 421, 423,
             429, 431, 432, 435
4 – 7 . . . . 352, 383, 435
4 – 5 379
4 . . . . .50, 323, 428
5 . . . . .52, 342, 346, 379, 385, 396,
             420, 428, 429, 432, 435
6 – 7 379
6 . . . . 302, 342, 346, 352, 379, 389,
             390, 392, 404, 405, 406, 411,
             414, 420, 428, 429, 433
7 . . . . 346, 348, 352, 379, 380, 383,
             385, 389, 390, 396, 404,
             410, 411, 415, 431, 432
8 – 20 . . . . 380, 402, 410, 417
8 – 16 . . . . 402, 410, 415, 433
8 – 9 . . . . .418, 419
8 . . . . .352, 378, 405, 406, 411,
             414, 417, 429, 435
9 . . . . .23, 342, 352, 360, 363,
             364, 373, 375, 376, 411,
             413, 417, 418, 420, 424,
             429, 430, 431, 435
10 – 14 345
10 . . . . .23, 284, 311, 323, 342, 347,
             363, 366, 368, 373, 375, 402, 404,
             406, 409, 410, 413, 429, 431, 435

11 . . . . 311, 346, 352, 402
12 . . . . .360, 373, 402, 404,
             408, 411, 413, 429
13 . . . . .23, 323, 342, 348, 352,
             363, 402, 410, 411, 413,
             414, 420, 429, 434
14 372
15 – 16 . . . . 343, 347, 426
15 . . . . 311, 405, 428
16 . . . . 279, 283, 311, 350, 360, 364,
             366, 369, 371, 374, 375,
             379, 402, 405, 406, 410,
             420, 429, 431, 434, 435
17 – 20 . . . . .352, 379, 380, 383,
             415, 418, 419, 429
17 . . . . 348, 352, 360, 364, 371, 380,
             389, 390, 392, 396, 420, 429
18 – 19 . . . . .343, 415
18 . . . . .276, 279, 311, 344,
             380, 388, 401, 430
19 – 25 408
19 – 21 409
19 . . . . .322, 352, 375, 391, 399,
             400, 415, 419, 422, 433
20 . . . . .309, 348, 360, 362, 366,
             369, 373, 374, 375, 380,
             385, 390, 415, 429, 431
21 – 25 403
21 – 22 379
21 . . . . .348, 352, 379, 380, 384,
             398, 403, 434, 435
22 . . . . .23, 343, 352, 364, 366,
             379, 380, 403, 414,
             428, 429, 430, 433
23 – 24 . . . . 312, 342, 352, 403, 432
23 . . . . .23, 24, 56, 310, 312,
             342, 352, 363, 368, 379,
             414, 429, 433, 435
24 . . . . .23, 24, 313, 315,
             317, 318, 342
25 . . . . 366, 375, 385, 403

Hebrews

1:3 . . . . .94, 98
1:6 95
1:10 109
1:13 211
2:1 – 18 116
2:2 189
4:8 313
4:11 – 16 116
5:11 – 6:20 116
6:6 226

7:26 394
8:1 211
9:23 – 28 202
9:27 53
10:1 . . . . .186, 187
10:10 108
10:12 – 13 211
10:14 108
10:22 – 24 52
10:35 383
11:3 61
11:23 270
11:28 95
12:2 211
12:9 262
12:15 268
12:23 95
13:21 270

James

1:2 – 3 73
1:19 233
1:21 223
1:26 233
2:9 277
3:1 – 12 233
3:1 – 6, 9 – 11 .223
3:9 . . . . .224, 233
3:14 . . . . .233, 268
4:6 242
4:7 262
4:10 242
4:11 – 12 233
5:9 233
5:10 251
5:12 . . . . .98, 233
5:14 251

1 Peter

1:18 – 19 108
1:21 – 22 52
2:1 . . . . .223, 224
2:13 262
2:16 229
2:18 – 3:7 264
2:18 276
3:8, 15 241
3:22 211
4:3 216
4:8 98

4:13 73
4:17 59
5:5 . . . . 188, 242, 262
5:9 141
5:13 313

2 Peter

1:5 – 7 241
1:5 – 6 241
1:7 244
1:10 241
2:1 – 12 277
2:10 97
2:13 277
3:5 . . . . .61, 98
3:16 320

1 John

2:12 – 13 .246
2:20 – 25 .116
3:2 130
3:18 250
5:1 155

3 John

6 70

Jude

8 97

Revelation

1:5 101
3:3 291
3:5 170
3:14 – 22 .135
3:15 – 16, 17 – 18 135
4:11 96
5:13 110
6:9 – 11 126
6:15 229

7:14 126
8:11 268
10:9, 10 268
11:17 – 18 291
12:13 – 17 126
13:1, 5 – 6 224
13:16 229
14:13 410
16:15 291
17:3 224
19:13 61
19:19 229

Tobit

7:2 313

Judith

14:10 177
15:10 101

Additions to Esther

15:8 242

Wisdom of Solomon

1:7 102
4:10 269
6:22 139
7:13 – 14 .139
7:15 70
7:26 94
9:10 270
13:1 – 15:19 217
14:8 165
16:1 70
18:14 – 16 292

Sirach

1:19 69
1:24 – 25 .139
1:25 – 27 .62

1:26 70
3:16 270
4:8 242
6:37 62
10:28 242
14:11 70
19:17 62
19:20 70
24:23 62
34:19 101
36:23 242
43:26 98
45:4 242
45:19 101

Baruch

3:15 139
4:1 62

1 Maccabees

1:60 – 61 .177
1:60 164
13:21 385
14:22 385

2 Maccabees

2:30 190
6:10 177
14:35 101

3 Maccabees

5:31 108

2 Esdras

7:95, 97 131

4 Maccabees

4:25 177
5:11 159

Subject Index

Adam
first, 94, 225, 226
last (*see* Christ, as last Adam)
ambassador, 385, 386
angel, 29, 31, 74, 97, 173, 189, 195, 198, 211, 299
apostle, 20, 34, 43, 46, 47, 47n7, 48, 57n62, 58, 59, 106, 118, 119, 122, 123, 125, 126, 127, 131, 135, 140, 141, 142, 143, 144, 156, 215, 255, 295, 299, 309, 312n34, 320, 327, 338n20, 338 – 39, 352, 363, 381, 384, 385, 398, 406, 411n60, 412, 435
ascetics/asceticism, 27, 29, 49, 78, 105, 112, 133, 144, 162, 166, 171, 180, 181, 183, 187, 188, 191, 193, 195, 195n77, 197, 198, 213, 214, 232, 247, 330, 340
authority, 19, 25, 31, 43, 47, 57, 58, 59, 61, 63, 72, 73, 76n53, 77, 85, 94, 95, 99, 102, 102n94, 111, 119, 123, 126, 127, 140, 156, 163, 172, 173, 180, 191, 215, 218, 260, 262, 262n11, 266, 267, 270, 271, 272, 276, 277, 279, 283, 301n54, 304, 306, 309, 310, 313, 315, 320, 321, 321n95, 322, 324, 326, 327n111, 328n2, 330, 331, 332, 333, 337, 338, 344, 352, 363n10, 363, 366n36, 375, 378, 380, 381, 383, 384n13, 384n15, 384n16, 384, 385, 385n24, 397, 410n56, 418, 419, 424, 425, 428, 429, 431, 433, 435

baptism, 21n8, 155n6, 155n7, 164n56, 164, 166, 167, 168n78, 210, 218, 219, 225, 225n76, 230, 241n13, 243
benediction, 303, 307, 322, 323, 366, 403, 416, 417, 423, 424, 424n48, 435
blessing, 50n28, 79, 179, 255, 413
blood, 49, 59n70, 77, 78, 84, 91, 101, 104, 105, 107, 107n124, 108, 112, 113, 114, 172, 219, 246, 329, 431
boast, 49, 51, 103, 128, 143, 343, 399, 400
body (*see also* flesh), 20n3, 27, 52, 84, 85, 87, 93, 98n72, 99, 99n82, 100, 106, 107, 107n124, 108, 114, 114n145, 118, 123, 124, 126, 127, 140, 144, 145, 146, 149, 161, 162, 163, 165, 165n62, 166, 166n66, 169, 172, 176, 177, 179, 187, 187n236, 188, 191, 192, 195, 196, 197, 198, 202, 206, 207, 212, 213, 215, 216, 219, 219n48, 226, 229, 231, 236, 238, 245, 246, 247, 248n47, 249, 253, 263, 280, 281, 295, 298, 304, 322, 324, 325, 328n3, 330, 332, 333, 348, 401, 425, 427
boldness, 173, 173n107, 383, 384, 429
bondage, 78, 115, 176, 268, 284

calling, 46, 70, 111, 126, 241n12, 246, 328, 337, 338, 391, 398
captives, 19, 140, 158, 159, 172, 173, 173n112, 312, 330
chiastic structure, 34n74, 71, 87, 87n11, 89, 122, 222, 241n10, 294n24, 362, 367n47, 368, 368n56, 372, 376, 391n78, 435,
Christ
as head (*see* head/headship)
as last Adam, 55, 93, 93n35, 94n42, 215, 432n22
as Lord (*see also* Christ, lordship of), 26, 31, 47, 47n11, 50, 51, 55, 58, 63, 67, 70, 75n46, 111, 112, 132n57, 144, 145, 149, 151, 154, 155, 156, 158, 170n87, 172, 174, 174n113, 194, 200, 205, 212, 215, 222, 223, 229, 236, 237, 239, 241, 243, 244, 247, 250, 251, 251n64, 255, 256, 257, 258, 259, 260, 261, 267, 269, 270, 271, 272, 273, 274n81, 275, 276, 277, 278, 278n104, 279, 280, 282, 283, 284, 285, 286, 289, 296, 297, 298, 301, 317n66, 321n93, 322, 323, 324, 327, 328, 329, 346, 348, 362, 366, 367, 368, 368n56, 369, 374, 375, 376, 377, 379, 380n5, 384, 385, 410n56, 423n46, 423, 426, 429, 431, 432, 434, 435
as Son of God, 88, 112, 176
burial of, 166, 167, 168, 173, 176, 180, 184
death of, 19, 21, 54, 56, 92, 144, 147, 149, 150, 162, 165, 166, 168, 173, 175, 176, 177, 178, 180, 181, 184, 186, 192, 193, 202, 203, 206, 207, 210, 215, 219, 225, 229, 230, 231, 240, 250, 283, 285, 286, 301, 329, 330, 331, 334, 337, 339, 340, 430
exaltation of, 85, 85n5, 104, 173, 203, 215
lordship of, 19, 31, 49, 57, 59, 63, 74, 97, 111, 114, 116, 155, 158, 205, 212, 221, 223, 224, 227, 229, 233, 234, 236, 237, 237n3, 239, 241, 242, 245, 246, 247, 250, 251, 254, 257, 258, 261, 263, 266, 267, 272, 272n72, 275, 276, 286, 289, 291, 296, 297, 297n41, 298, 299, 301, 312, 326, 328n2, 330n9, 331 – 40, 331n10, 364, 366, 367, 374, 375, 376, 397, 401, 410, 431, 435
preexistence of, 98, 265
reign of, 77, 104, 163, 315n51
resurrection of, 19, 21, 54, 56, 92, 100, 101, 103, 108, 112, 113, 129, 144, 147, 149, 150, 162, 165, 166, 168, 169, 170, 173, 175, 176, 177, 178, 180, 181, 184, 186, 192, 193, 203, 204, 206, 207, 210, 211, 212, 213, 215, 218, 219, 225, 226, 229, 230, 231, 239, 240, 250, 283, 285, 286, 301, 329, 330, 331, 334, 337, 339, 340, 430

(Christ *cont.*)

return of, 206, 211, 214, 215, 230, 231, 281, 291, 292, 292n18, 339, 340

sufficiency of, 49, 125, 145, 148, 151, 158, 161, 176, 187, 198, 213, 244, 252, 324, 330, 331, 337

supremacy of, 21, 47, 57, 67, 88, 95, 98, 99, 100, 101, 149, 151, 156, 158, 161, 162, 163, 176,

work of, 49, 52, 71, 85, 97, 103, 106, 111, 114, 125, 149, 248, 331, 377, 378, 430

Christology, 19, 20, 21, 31, 32, 58, 92n31, 104, 105n109, 111, 112, 113, 115n146, 115, 138, 211, 214, 328, 329, 331, 338, 427, 431

Adam (*see* Christ, as last Adam)

wisdom, 93, 93n35

church (*see also* house church/household church), 20, 24, 26, 27, 43, 46, 47, 48, 50, 56, 57, 58, 59, 71, 79, 84, 87, 88, 91, 93, 97, 99, 99n82, 100, 100n83, 103, 107, 113, 114, 116, 118, 119, 125, 126, 127, 135, 136, 140, 143, 145, 147, 148, 161, 162, 187, 192, 205, 217, 218, 218n42, 218n46, 226, 231, 232, 235n120, 249, 262, 263, 264, 268, 272n74, 274, 283, 284, 296n36, 303, 304, 307, 309, 310, 311n30, 313, 315, 317, 317n65, 318, 319, 320, 325, 326, 330n9, 332, 333, 334, 338, 339, 341, 342, 342n6, 344n20, 346, 348, 351, 359n2, 360, 363, 364, 365, 366, 368, 374, 374n92, 375, 376, 401, 417, 421, 425, 430, 431, 432, 432n23, 433

circumcision, 25, 26, 28, 31, 163, 164, 164n56, 165, 165n68, 166, 167, 168, 168n78, 169, 171, 177, 178, 179, 200, 203, 228, 307, 314, 314n45, 314n46, 315, 332, 335

cleansing (*see also* washing), 165, 178

commission, 127, 140, 143, 294, 322, 338

community, 19, 21, 24, 25, 26, 31, 32, 55, 59, 61, 73, 80, 99, 100, 104, 105, 114, 115, 116n149, 123, 125, 140, 141, 144, 145, 146, 147, 148, 155, 155n7, 156, 161, 177, 192, 200, 203, 205, 206, 207, 213, 217, 218, 223, 224, 225, 226, 227, 227n86, 228, 229, 233, 234, 234n116, 238, 239, 241, 243, 244, 245, 246, 246n39, 253, 255, 258, 266, 282, 287, 290, 291, 296, 296n31, 297, 298,

301, 304, 306, 311, 312, 313, 315, 317, 319, 320, 321, 322, 326, 327, 327n111, 332, 334, 335, 336, 337, 339, 341, 342, 359, 365, 371, 376, 388, 397, 401, 421, 425, 425n50, 431, 432, 433, 433n26, 434, 435n31

completeness and sufficiency of God's power, 72

confess/confession, 19, 31, 50, 51, 73, 75, 76, 78, 80, 81, 82, 85, 85n5, 91, 94, 98, 101n86, 110, 111, 112, 114, 118, 122, 128, 128n33, 132, 149, 155, 156, 158, 174, 180, 207, 212, 218, 223, 224, 229, 233, 234, 241n13, 246, 247, 248n48, 249, 250, 258, 259, 279, 282, 289, 297, 298, 301, 333, 334, 335, 336, 339, 347, 377, 417, 429

cornerstone, 156

cosmic, 21, 27, 55, 87, 91n28, 98n72, 98n74, 98, 100, 103, 104, 110, 112, 114n143, 118, 129, 151, 162, 163, 192, 205, 216, 246, 298, 317n65, 330, 426, 428

covenant (*see also* new covenant), 75, 81, 174n115, 177, 241

covenantal people, 217, 367

covenantal relationship, 247, 256

creation, 19, 30, 65, 69, 84, 85, 87, 88, 92, 93, 94, 94n44, 95, 95n48, 96, 97, 98, 99, 100, 101, 102n94, 103, 104, 105, 109, 110, 111, 112, 113, 114, 114, 142, 115, 116, 118, 125, 129, 149, 150, 172, 183, 192, 201, 202, 205, 212n16, 216, 225, 226, 227 228, 231, 233, 244, 246, 253, 258, 267, 280, 281, 299, 325, 328, 329, 331, 332, 332, 332n13, 336, 337, 338, 425, 430

Creator, 19, 78n65, 96, 99, 103, 106, 111, 113, 114, 115, 150, 160, 175, 207, 213, 225, 226, 227, 231, 233, 237, 239, 246, 254, 255, 258, 286, 295, 325, 329, 333, 335, 336

creed, 155

cross, 32, 52, 61, 78, 84, 85, 88, 91, 92, 101, 102, 103, 104, 105, 110, 112, 114, 115, 116, 144, 148, 166, 169, 171, 171n97, 172, 172n105, 173, 178, 186, 206, 212, 213, 218, 219, 226, 230, 234, 239, 240, 242, 243, 244, 246, 253, 266, 281, 284n117, 291, 299, 329, 330, 331, 335, 336, 341, 376, 399, 413, 424, 430, 434

curse/cursing, 199, 223, 224, 233, 268, 413

Damascus, 47, 295

darkness, 65, 70, 74, 75, 75n48, 76, 76n52, 77, 78, 78n66, 81, 113, 219, 222n61, 330

death, 19, 21, 52, 54, 56, 59, 76, 78, 85, 88, 92, 93, 101, 102, 103, 104, 105, 105n109, 106, 107, 108, 112, 112n140, 113, 114, 115, 116, 118, 125, 129, 133, 141n112, 144, 145, 147, 149, 150, 162, 165, 166, 166n65, 166n68, 167, 168, 169, 171, 172, 173, 175, 176, 177, 178, 180, 181, 184, 186, 192, 193, 194, 202, 203, 204, 204n2, 207, 210, 213, 214, 215, 216, 219, 222, 225, 229, 230, 231, 232, 239, 240, 242, 243, 247, 250, 252, 253, 283, 284, 285, 286, 299, 301, 329, 330, 330n9, 331, 332, 334, 335, 337, 339, 340, 341, 395, 399, 401, 413, 425, 427, 430

deception, 140, 159, 171, 174

deeds, 50, 51, 80, 105, 106, 109, 115, 215, 217n34, 219, 221, 222, 223, 237, 249, 250, 251, 252, 256, 258, 261, 272, 274, 282, 284, 290, 297, 299, 301, 301n53, 328, 334, 339, 367, 392, 413

Demas, 307, 317, 318, 318n75, 342, 416, 421, 422, 423

demonic spiritual power, 172

demonology, 189

discernment, 299, 300

doxology, 72n33, 255

elders/leaders, 43, 59, 60, 61n74, 134, 165, 196, 218n42, 262, 282, 303, 309n17, 311, 317, 320, 325, 363, 365, 374, 378n100, 412, 413, 421, 425, 433, 435

election, 157, 197n87, 240, 241, 241n9

emperor, 104, 428, 428n8

empowering/empowerment, 63, 72, 134, 142, 143, 213, 297, 301, 327, 328

Epaphras, 24, 46, 49, 53, 56, 56n59, 57, 57n62, 58, 59, 68, 79n70, 127, 261n8, 274, 284, 292, 301, 303, 304, 307, 310, 312n35, 315, 315n53, 316, 316n57, 317, 317n62, 317n66, 324, 325, 334, 342, 368, 417, 421, 422, 422n37, 426, 433n27

eschatology, 19, 20, 21, 25, 32, 32n63, 46, 50, 53, 54, 55n5, 61, 69, 74, 75, 76, 77, 78, 90, 93, 97, 101, 104, 110, 111, 116, 117, 122, 123, 126, 128,

129, 130, 131, 133, 135, 136, 142, 167n73, 178, 179, 186, 202, 205, 206, 207, 215, 221, 226, 229n104, 230, 231, 242, 246, 258, 276n97, 277, 278, 286, 287, 289, 291, 291n9, 291n12, 292, 293, 295, 296, 299, 303, 311, 323, 332, 338, 339, 340, 340n24, 351, 373, 419n19, 427, 432, 432n21,

ethics, 19, 31, 32, 62, 63, 73, 80, 108, 138, 156, 176, 183, 200, 201, 204n1, 218, 229, 232, 233, 239, 243, 252, 257, 334, 335, 375, 401, 419, 428, 434, 435

evangelism, 132, 300 – 302, 301n54, 370, 378, 391, 398, 433n27

evil one, 76, 316n61

faith, 26, 26n32, 31, 43, 44, 46, 51n32, 51, 51n33, 52, 57, 58, 60, 62, 62n76, 68, 109, 141, 141n117, 142, 151, 156, 157, 158, 163, 166, 167, 168, 168n78, 176, 200, 229, 232, 241, 244, 256, 269n57, 279, 282, 289, 302, 302n55, 305, 316, 336, 342, 346, 352, 359, 360, 362, 367, 368, 38n53, 368n56, 369, 370, 370n64, 371, 372, 376 – 77, 378, 379, 383, 385, 389, 392, 393, 396, 397, 404, 405, 406, 413, 417, 420, 426, 427, 428, 428n6, 429, 431, 432, 435,

faithful/faithfulness, 109n131, 109, 112, 116, 119, 127, 131, 132, 135, 143, 145, 149, 150, 151, 154, 156, 171, 174, 200n93, 213, 216, 218, 221, 230, 231, 233, 241n13, 253, 254, 266, 272, 273, 276, 278, 279, 281, 282n112, 283, 287, 290, 292, 293, 304, 305, 309, 310, 311, 311n28, 313n36, 315, 316, 321, 323, 324, 326, 331, 334, 336, 337, 367, 368, 371, 372n73, 373, 378, 387, 389, 412, 414, 417, 423, 425,

false teacher, 21, 25, 31, 32, 32n63, 52, 53, 54, 56, 58, 62, 64, 68, 72, 73, 75, 85, 109n134, 119, 124, 126, 133, 139, 140, 149, 158, 159, 162, 163n51, 171, 181, 183, 184, 186, 187, 188, 190, 191, 192, 193, 194, 195, 196, 197, 198, 199, 201, 204, 205, 206, 207, 211, 212, 213, 214, 218, 226, 228, 229n104, 230, 242, 244, 245, 246, 257, 258n5, 295, 296n31, 315, 316, 330, 335, 340, 368n55

false teaching, 21, 25, 26, 26n32, 27, 28,

28n43, 29, 29n52, 30, 31, 31n62, 91, 119, 122, 136, 141, 142, 149, 151, 158, 160, 161, 162, 164, 174, 176, 180, 183, 184, 186, 187, 189, 191, 192, 195, 196, 198, 200, 202, 204n1, 210, 218, 229, 326

falsehood, 56, 207, 334

family, 49, 59, 60, 175, 279, 280, 281, 282, 311, 319, 342, 344, 364, 365, 376, 379, 396, 428n8

Father/father, 24, 34, 46, 48, 48n14, 50, 51, 58, 59, 73, 74, 75, 77, 84, 94, 95, 102n95, 107, 111, 119, 123, 156, 172, 214, 215, 223, 227, 233, 237, 239, 243, 246, 251, 252, 252n66, 255, 258, 259, 260, 260n6, 263, 266, 268, 269, 270n65, 270, 270n66, 271, 278, 279, 280, 281, 282, 283n111, 287, 297, 301n53, 315n51, 323, 328, 329, 333, 336, 348, 366, 366n36, 367, 375, 379, 381, 387, 398, 399, 418n9, 427, 428, 428n7, 428n8, 431, 432, 434, 435, 435n32

fear, 161, 268, 272, 273, 282, 318

flesh (see also body), 52, 85, 106, 107, 107n124, 107n125, 111, 119, 123, 124, 125, 128, 135, 136, 140, 141n112, 164, 165, 165n62, 166, 168, 169, 169n83, 171, 172, 178, 178n122, 179, 191, 193, 195, 196, 197, 201, 212, 220n49, 272, 317, 318n71, 330, 375, 396, 397, 397n114, 398, 410, 434

foolish talk, 223, 297

forgiveness/forgiving, 78, 78n66, 81, 113, 169, 170, 170n87, 176, 177, 218, 225, 239, 242, 243, 243n22, 244, 244n25, 244n26, 252, 252n68, 253, 254, 263, 323n105, 330, 331n10, 335, 336, 340, 344, 360n4, 366, 378, 387, 389, 391, 399, 406, 421n33, 435

freedom, 24, 32, 76n53, 78n65, 115, 116, 130, 160, 177, 180, 194, 203, 213, 229, 252, 252n68, 262, 266, 274n86, 349, 350, 383, 392n84, 393, 395n100, 397, 399, 400, 401, 425, 426, 430

fullness, 68, 69, 79, 84, 101, 102, 102n95, 107, 150, 159, 159n28, 161, 161, 162, 163, 163n51, 180, 191, 193, 301, 328, 329, 331

Gentiles, 25, 47, 75, 79, 104, 105, 122, 123, 126, 127, 128, 129, 130, 131,

133, 135, 147, 169, 171, 178, 185, 200, 207, 222, 225, 228, 229, 240, 241, 246, 2554, 277, 293, 295, 299, 307, 314, 315, 318, 325, 338,

gift, 55, 56, 134, 247, 254, 255, 255n73, 298, 300, 301, 309, 325, 331n10, 426

glory, 24, 53, 72, 74, 75n48, 82, 110, 111, 112, 115, 128, 129, 130, 130n47, 131, 131n50, 139, 144, 145, 146, 173, 201, 203, 205, 206, 211, 213, 214, 215, 216, 219, 221, 230, 232, 243, 250, 251n64, 266, 277, 281, 285, 286, 291, 293, 294, 301, 330, 331, 332, 339, 340, 372

God
   fullness of (see fullness)
   glory of, 82, 214, 250, 251n64
   grace of, 55, 56, 56n54, 134, 142, 202, 253, 297, 297n40, 302, 307, 323, 327, 336, 431
   wrath of, 215, 221, 221n57, 224, 231, 268n49, 340n24

God the Father, 46, 50, 58, 73, 74, 77, 84, 119, 214, 215, 227, 237, 239, 246, 251, 252, 255, 258, 281, 283, 297, 328, 329, 336, 367, 427, 428, 431

God-fearers, 318, 318n69

goodness, 75, 116, 132, 239, 255, 336

grace, 48, 49, 50, 55, 56, 56n54, 80, 127, 134, 142, 143, 200, 202, 218, 237, 241, 243, 244, 244n25, 245, 247, 250, 252, 252n68, 253, 254, 255, 262, 268, 281, 283, 296, 297, 297n37, 297n40, 298, 300, 300n50, 301, 301n53, 302, 303, 307, 322, 323, 327, 335, 336, 339, 360, 360n4, 366, 377, 378, 388, 414, 423, 423n46, 424, 426, 427, 431, 432, 434

growth, 56, 71, 99, 133, 134n63, 138, 191, 192, 192n61, 198, 245, 292, 328n3, 332, 378

guilt, 171, 176 – 77, 252, 252n67, 252n68, 394n96

head/headship, 84, 87, 93, 99, 99n78, 99n79, 100, 100n83, 114, 126, 127, 156, 163, 177, 180, 183, 191, 192, 192n57, 245, 257, 257n4, 259, 260n6, 262, 263, 266, 267, 270, 271, 274, 275, 277, 278, 279, 280, 281, 328n3, 330, 332, 332n13, 333, 333n14, 347, 364, 428, 431, 435 holiness, 52, 75, 82, 195, 217, 218, 220, 230

honor (*see also* shame), 51, 110, 127, 173, 197, 197n87, 221, 231, 247, 285, 314, 352, 363, 378

hope, 21, 43, 44, 46, 51n32, 52, 53, 60, 62, 62n76, 90, 109, 110, 130, 131, 144, 145, 175, 214, 215, 244, 246, 293, 301n53, 316, 340, 345, 350, 369, 417, 420, 421

house church/household church, 272n74, 317, 351, 359n2, 364, 421

household code, 19, 257, 260, 260n6, 262, 263, 264, 265, 266, 269, 271, 274, 277, 279, 282, 283, 286, 290, 333, 334, 410n56

humility, 104, 188, 197, 233, 240, 241, 242, 243, 247, 253, 267, 272, 280, 399

husbands, 110n83, 192n58, 229, 259, 260, 262, 262n9, 263, 264, 266, 267, 268, 268n45, 270, 270, 279, 280, 280n107, 281, 333

hymn, 19, 29, 64, 77, 82, 84n3, 84, 85, 87, 87n6, 88, 89 – 93, 93n36, 94, 94n45, 95n48, 96, 97, 98, 99, 100, 100n84, 101, 103, 104, 105, 105n109, 106, 107, 107n122, 109, 110, 111, 112, 113, 114, 115, 116, 118, 125, 126, 128n33, 138, 146, 149, 158, 162, 163, 168, 172, 214, 247, 248, 249, 249n58, 255, 256, 257, 328, 329, 330, 331, 332, 335, 336

idolatry/idols, 29n51, 31, 73n41, 81, 114, 116, 160, 165, 165n61, 174 – 76, 174n114, 178, 179, 185, 186, 186n22, 189, 196, 200, 207, 217, 218, 219, 220, 221, 223, 224, 225, 231, 232, 233, 251, 254, 268, 295, 297n41, 334, 334n17, 335, 336n18, 400

image, 75n48, 84, 87, 91, 94, 94n37, 94n38, 94n41, 94n42, 95, 95n46, 114, 114n145, 115, 116, 125, 157, 175, 186, 207, 226, 227, 227n86, 227n87, 231, 232, 233, 295, 325, 329, 333, 400, 435n22

imitation, 56, 57, 123, 125, 146, 170, 242, 243, 244, 267, 282, 283, 289, 306, 353n70, 413, 414, 422, 430

immorality, 217, 217n41, 219, 220, 220n50, 220n51

imprisonment, 23, 24, 48, 123, 135, 135n71, 146, 283, 293, 295, 307,

308, 312, 312n34, 315, 317, 318, 323, 343, 346, 346n32, 363, 365, 371n68, 379, 381, 386, 387, 390, 391, 392, 396, 398, 401, 411n60, 421, 422, 422n38, 425, 426, 429, 429n9, 434, 435

impurity 106, 219, 220

in Christ, 26n32, 31, 32, 43, 44, 48, 49, 49n21, 51, 52, 58, 59, 60, 62, 81, 96, 98, 98n74, 102, 106, 109, 116, 117, 119, 122, 129, 131, 133, 139, 141, 141n117, 142, 144, 147, 149, 150, 15, 156, 157, 159n28, 161, 162, 166, 167n72, 168, 169, 170, 170n87, 173, 176, 178, 179, 186, 187, 191, 200, 204, 210, 213, 214, 215, 219, 222, 225, 226, 227, 229, 230, 232, 233, 235, 239, 243, 245, 254, 267, 290, 311, 312n35, 316, 317n66, 329, 331, 340, 348, 351, 352, 359, 360, 362, 369, 370, 372, 372n73, 380, 380n5, 383, 384, 384n13, 390, 392, 393, 395, 396, 398, 399, 409n48, 411, 411n57, 414n68, 417, 421, 422, 422n36, 425, 426, 429, 429n10, 431n20, 432, 432n21

inheritance, 25, 74, 75, 75n47, 76, 79, 81, 95, 130, 190, 240, 272, 274, 275, 283, 286, 431

inner self, 136, 226

Israel/Israelites, 28, 48, 61, 70, 75, 78, 82, 83, 90, 91, 93n35, 95, 114, 114n142, 128, 165, 165n61, 175, 177, 178n122, 195, 196, 218, 234n114, 240, 246, 269n54, 289n5, 332, 340, 377, 431, 432n22

Jerusalem, 20n4, 128, 156, 165, 292n18, 308, 313, 430

Jewish angelology, 189, 211
   angelic power, 160
   angelic worship, 53, 96, 161n39, 183, 187, 188, 189, 190, 193, 195, 198, 201, 204, 299,

Jews, 24, 25, 30, 75, 105, 130, 133, 135, 135n72, 147, 147n129, 164, 171, 177, 178, 185, 200, 214, 218, 226, 227, 228, 228n96, 229, 229n102, 234, 234n114, 236, 240, 246, 277, 293, 307, 314, 314n44, 315, 320, 325, 332, 338, 372n73, 422, 423, 427, 430, 431, 432

judgment, 21, 24n30, 76, 108, 184, 188, 207, 215, 221, 231, 246, 276n97, 278, 292n15, 292n18, 294, 295, 392, 406

justification, 33, 162, 427

kindness, 50, 73, 239, 240, 242, 243, 243n22, 252, 253, 291, 337, 346, 377, 432, 435

kingdom of God/Christ, 49, 65, 75, 76, 76n55, 77, 79, 113, 132, 145, 215, 219, 231, 232, 283, 301, 313, 314, 314n44, 315, 315n51, 324, 325, 326, 329, 330, 378, 401

knowledge, 21, 27, 44, 55n53, 58, 63, 64, 65, 67, 68, 69, 69n16, 70, 71, 71n29, 72, 75n48, 79, 80, 81, 84, 118, 119, 131, 132, 137, 138, 139, 146, 147, 156, 157n17, 159, 186n23, 192, 206, 213, 226, 227, 239, 241, 244, 250, 250n60, 253, 286, 290, 295, 296, 299, 301, 302, 311, 318, 335, 338, 362, 371, 371n71, 372, 378, 433

Laodicea (also Laodiceans), 24, 25n31, 49, 56, 119, 122, 134, 135, 135n72, 136, 136n75, 304, 304n6, 307, 308, 316, 317, 317n65, 318, 319, 319n77, 320, 320n87, 321, 325, 326

law, 28, 28n43, 70, 131, 157, 159, 170, 170n94, 171, 171n95, 186, 189, 199, 200, 220, 244, 244n26, 257n4, 262, 269, 269n54, 270n66, 282, 314, 320, 332, 333n14, 349, 372n73, 401, 413

leaders, 43, 59, 60, 61n74, 134, 165, 218n42, 262, 282, 303, 309n17, 311, 317, 320, 325, 363, 365, 374, 378n100, 412, 413, 421, 433, 435

leadership, 311, 319, 412

life, 31, 46, 51, 55, 61, 63, 65, 69, 63n78, 64, 68, 70, 71n27, 74, 80, 80n74, 81, 84, 106, 107, 107n125, 108, 111, 115, 123, 125, 129, 141, 143, 144, 145, 146, 148, 155, 156, 158, 162, 163, 163n51, 167n72, 168, 168n79, 170, 176, 177, 178, 179, 186, 194, 196, 201, 203, 204, 205, 206, 207, 210, 213, 214, 215, 218, 221, 222, 222n60, 222n61, 223, 224, 230, 231, 232, 237, 238, 243, 245, 246, 247, 249, 250, 251, 251n64, 253, 254, 255, 256, 258, 258n5, 259, 267, 268, 280, 281, 284, 286, 287, 289, 290, 291, 295, 298, 299, 324, 328n2, 331, 333, 334, 334n6, 335, 336, 339, 340, 350, 351, 370n64, 371, 377, 384, 386, 392, 394, 397n115, 400, 406, 409n48, 411, 414n67, 426, 428n8, 430, 432, 433, 434, 435n31 liturgical practice, 256, 282, 282n112

love, 24, 43, 44, 46, 51, 51n33, 52, 57, 58, 58n67, 59, 60, 62, 62n76, 70, 71, 74, 76, 76n55, 77, 81, 82, 101, 122, 136, 137, 145, 146, 147, 159, 165, 176, 178, 192, 217, 223, 224, 231, 232, 237, 239, 241, 241n9, 243, 244, 245, 253, 254, 255, 260, 263, 267, 268, 268n45, 272, 273, 279, 280, 281, 282, 283, 301n53, 302, 309, 310, 316, 318, 335, 344n20, 346, 352, 359, 360, 360n4, 362, 364, 364n19, 367, 368, 368n53, 368n55, 368n56, 369, 370, 372, 372n80, 373, 376, 377, 379, 380, 381, 381n6, 383, 384, 385, 385n23, 390, 396, 399, 406, 412, 417, 418, 420, 424, 428, 428n7, 429, 432, 435

love in the Spirit, 24, 51, 57, 60, 310

lust, 219, 220, 232

manumission, 279, 348 – 50, 395, 396, 396n109, 397 – 99, 400, 407n29, 408n36, 419, 420

marriage, 267, 279

masters (*see also* slaves), 57n60, 145, 167, 194, 229, 259, 260, 261, 263, 264, 266, 269, 270, 271, 272, 272n72, 273, 274, 274n81, 275, 276, 276n97, 277, 278, 278n103, 279, 280, 283 – 85, 286, 292, 310, 311, 316, 324, 333, 334, 343, 344, 345, 347, 350, 351, 352, 364, 388, 390, 392, 394, 397, 407, 407n29, 410, 412, 414n66, 424, 425, 429, 429n11

maturity, 24, 80, 122, 129, 133, 147, 268, 271, 315, 316, 331, 336, 425

mercy, 90, 107, 241, 344, 427

Messiah, 51, 125, 155, 340

mind, 63n78, 88, 105, 106, 116, 117, 128, 145, 176, 183, 190, 191, 197, 204, 212, 212n15, 217, 221, 222, 236, 241, 250, 273, 274, 295, 300, 330

mission (*see also* evangelism), 32, 57, 81, 117, 118, 122, 126, 127, 128, 130, 131n49, 132, 133, 135n71, 135, 142, 143, 145, 227n90, 258, 287, 289, 290, 290n6, 292, 293, 295, 298 – 300, 301 – 2, 306, 307, 308, 310, 312, 314 – 15, 316, 317, 317n65, 318, 320, 321, 322, 323, 325, 326, 339, 351, 378, 391, 401, 420, 423, 433 – 34

monotheism, 102n95, 103n102, 115, 302n55, 332

mystery, 25, 27, 30

mysticism, 28, 29, 30, 31

new community, 147, 177, 203, 226, 401

new covenant (*see also* covenant) 156

new creation, 19, 69, 100, 101, 103, 104, 112, 114, 115, 150, 205, 225, 226, 227, 228, 231, 253, 258, 281, 329, 332, 336, 338, 430, 432

new identity, 49, 218, 225, 241, 433

new humanity, 226

Nympha, 318, 319, 319n78, 320, 325

obedience, 63, 65, 70, 71, 218, 221, 221n58, 222n60, 231, 260, 263, 269, 269n53, 270, 271, 272, 279, 280, 282, 284, 294, 378, 384, 403, 416, 417, 418n9, 418, 419, 423, 424, 425, 426, 435

old humanity, 207, 219, 226, 395n100

Onesimus, 23, 25, 49, 261, 272, 272n70, 276, 283, 284, 306, 308 – 12, 311n26, 315, 321, 334, 342 – 52, 343n15, 345n28, 346n29, 348n45, 348n46, 359, 360, 364, 365, 366n36, 368, 369, 371, 371n68, 372n74, 374, 375, 379 – 80, 381, 383, 386 – 401, 390n66, 391n75, 392n83, 393n88, 397n114, 400n118, 402 – 13, 407n23, 409n48, 411n59, 412n61, 415, 419, 420, 422, 425, 428, 429, 429n11, 430, 430n13, 431, 431n20, 433, 434, 435, 435n32

parousia, 126, 148, 215, 414n67, 430n14

participation in/of Christ, 111, 135, 143, 166, 167, 168, 169, 170, 176, 181, 185, 189, 192, 203, 204, 210, 211, 212, 213, 221, 226, 230, 239, 281, 284, 299, 301n51, 314, 323, 334, 339, 360, 364, 370, 378, 405, 406, 431

pastor, 24, 63, 145, 285, 412

patience, 63, 72, 72n36, 73, 79, 80, 240, 242, 243, 253

peace, 48, 49, 50, 61, 84, 101, 104, 105, 239, 245, 246n38, 246, 246n39, 254, 336, 360, 366, 390, 423, 432

perseverance, 290

possession, 75, 158, 175, 190, 241, 269n54, 343, 349

power of God, 61, 111, 134, 168, 216, 298, 330, 337

practices
 ascetic, 27, 29, 198
 cultic, 25, 29, 30, 31, 185, 187, 198, 203, 204, 246, 247, 251,

praise, 32n68, 50, 50n28, 51, 51n29, 73, 82, 90, 90n19, 110, 141, 142, 223, 225, 233, 247, 248n48, 249, 250, 255, 256, 335, 367, 435

prayer, 19, 24, 44, 46, 49, 51, 64, 65, 65n6, 67, 68, 69, 69n20, 71, 73, 77, 78n68, 79, 79n68, 79n70, 79n72, 81, 82n77, 84, 132, 138, 145, 250, 255, 258, 286, 287, 289, 290, 291, 291n12, 292, 293, 294, 297, 298, 299, 300, 301, 303, 304n3, 315, 316, 316n55, 316n57, 316n58, 317, 317n62, 322, 323, 323n103, 324, 328, 336, 339, 359, 360, 362, 366, 367n44, 367, 368, 369, 370, 371, 372n80, 377, 378, 379, 383, 405, 406n12, 417, 420, 421, 425, 426, 428, 428n6, 435

pride, 191

Priscilla and Aquila, 406n17

proclamation, 51, 53, 54, 101, 110, 115, 123, 128, 129, 130, 131, 132, 132n56, 133, 135, 147, 258, 287, 292, 299, 300, 301, 322, 338, 435

prophet, 76, 156, 277n98, 338, 338n20

purity, 31, 73, 185n13, 195, 200, 241, 332

reconciliation, 50, 78, 84, 85, 88, 93, 97, 101, 102, 103, 104, 105, 106, 107, 112, 113, 115, 116, 118, 168, 205, 229, 230, 246, 315, 324, 330, 366, 378, 399, 423, 426, 429 – 30, 435

redemption, 65, 75, 76, 77, 78, 80, 81, 82, 99, 113, 114n142, 116, 133, 137, 143, 146, 162, 170, 231, 240, 294, 296, 299, 330, 332, 413, 414n66, 429 – 30

renewal/renewing, 115, 179, 226, 226n83, 227, 295, 373n88, 394

repentance/repenting, 116, 256, 301, 344, 345, 391, 412

resurrection (*see* Christ, resurrection of)

revelation, 25, 28n43, 58, 61, 62n77, 69, 92, 94, 97, 115, 123, 127, 129, 129n36, 130, 139, 139n103, 144, 146, 147, 147n129, 168, 206, 212, 213, 214, 215, 219, 221, 230, 278, 286, 291, 293, 294, 296, 331, 332, 340, 423

rhetoric, 22, 25, 26n33, 32, 32n64, 32n68, 33, 62, 75, 84n2, 103n102,

106, 10n114, 112, 140, 142, 151, 184, 197, 216, 240, 242, 293, 313, 322, 323, 344n17, 351, 352, 353, 359, 360, 363, 364, 374, 381, 385n23, 385, 385n24, 386, 387, 388, 390n66, 391, 393, 395, 396, 396n110, 397, 399, 400, 401, 405, 407, 408, 409, 411n60, 412, 417, 420, 421, 423, 432

righteousness, 70n24, 75, 79, 82, 147n129, 177, 203, 241, 284, 424, 425

sacrament, 256

sacrifice, 92n32, 108, 113, 166, 202, 244, 399, 430n14

saints, 25, 46, 48, 49, 51, 52, 64, 70, 71, 74, 74n43, 75, 76, 79, 129, 130, 132, 135, 139, 214, 240, 275, 293, 294, 342, 346, 359, 360, 362, 367, 368, 369, 373, 376, 379, 383, 390, 396, 404, 411, 428, 432, 433, 435

salvation, 19, 43, 53, 53n41, 54, 62n76, 69, 74, 75, 76, 77, 81, 100, 104, 105, 107, 113, 114, 124, 126, 129, 133, 135, 136, 139, 143, 144, 149, 150, 181, 199, 200, 202, 206, 213, 231, 246, 277, 298, 299, 311, 331, 337, 338, 373

salvific act/plan/work of God, 19, 50, 55, 61, 69, 74, 75, 79, 80, 82, 84, 105, 136, 138, 166, 170, 174, 198, 213, 214, 215, 221, 241, 242, 246, 252, 351, 366, 373, 430, 434

sanctification, 117, 133, 378

Savior, 81, 131, 212, 294

Second Temple Judaism/Jewish tradition/Jewish thought, 21, 62n77, 70, 91, 94n42, 114n145, 126n24, 164, 164n60, 211, 340

service, 57, 272, 272n74, 273, 274, 274n81, 275, 309, 315, 318n73, 321, 321n93, 322, 333, 346, 348, 388, 390, 391n75, 393, 399, 401, 407, 407n28, 408, 409, 413, 414, 420, 434

sexual immorality, 217, 217n41, 219, 220, 220n50, 220n51, 386n30, 391n75, 392

shame (*see also* honor), 173, 174, 197n87, 252n68, 352,

sin, 78, 78n66, 78n67, 81, 103, 113, 115, 146, 150, 154, 165n62, 167n72, 169, 169n82, 170, 171, 171n100, 176–77, 194, 207, 217n41, 219,

220, 222, 223, 224, 225, 226, 229, 252, 252n67, 277, 277n98, 281, 284, 325, 330, 340, 395n100, 413, 414, 424, 425

slaves/slavery (*see also* masters), 23, 23n26, 24, 28, 32, 56, 57, 57n60, 57n61, 59, 76, 127, 159, 172, 218, 219, 226, 227, 228, 228n99, 229, 234, 236, 257, 259, 260, 261, 261n8, 263, 264, 266, 269, 270, 271, 271n69, 272, 272n70, 272n72, 273, 274, 274n86, 275, 276, 276n92, 276n97, 277, 277n100, 278, 279, 280, 282, 283–85, 284n117, 304, 304n5, 309, 310, 311, 311n28, 312, 315, 316, 324, 326, 332, 333, 334, 334n16, 335, 341, 342, 343, 343n15, 344, 344n18, 345, 346, 347, 348, 349, 349n49, 349n51, 350, 350n55, 351, 352, 360n4, 365, 366, 368, 368n55, 375, 375n94, 381, 385, 387, 388, 389, 390, 391n75, 393, 394, 394n96, 395n100, 395n102, 395, 395n105, 396, 396n108, 397, 397n114, 398, 400, 402, 404, 406, 407n28, 407, 407n29, 409, 409n48, 410, 411, 412, 413, 414, 414n66, 424, 425, 429n11, 430, 431, 431n20, 432, 433n26, 434, 434n29

soteriology, 19, 32, 117

sovereign/sovereignty, 99, 105, 111, 112, 116, 130 164, 211, 212, 224, 231, 251, 255, 256, 257, 266, 301, 331, 400, 428

spirit, elemental, 28, 151, 155, 159, 160, 162, 193, 284

Spirit, Holy, 58, 80n73, 141, 227, 301, 337n19

spiritual being/force/power, 21, 28, 29, 97, 97n63, 114, 114n143, 116, 160, 161, 162,163, 171, 172, 173, 189, 193, 194, 211, 213, 291,

spiritual discipline, 201

spiritual exercise/practice, 32n63, 49, 82n77, 137, 198

spiritual experience, 72

spiritual gift (*see also* gift), 73, 255n73

spiritual growth, 133, 192

spiritual reality, 167, 304

spiritual rulers and authority, 163, 172

spiritual songs, 248, 249, 249n58, 255, 256, 335, 336

spiritual status, 49, 201, 231, 245, 247, 283

spiritual warfare, 316n61

spiritual wisdom (and understanding), 64, 68, 69, 79, 132, 156, 290, 295, 301, 371

spirituality, 62, 62n75, 69, 80–81, 80n73, 80n74, 100, 145, 160, 230–32,

strengthening, 65, 67, 71, 72, 72n35, 73, 74, 79, 80, 80n73, 136, 141, 156, 157, 301n53, 336

submission, 54, 82, 83, 105, 110, 111, 112, 115, 185, 212, 221, 237, 239, 241, 242, 249, 251, 256, 258, 262, 263, 265–66, 267, 269, 278, 279, 280–81, 297n41, 298, 312, 316, 327,328, 332, 333, 336, 376, 378, 381, 385, 400, 426, 428

suffering, 73, 112, 118, 119, 122, 123, 123n7, 124, 125, 125n18, 126, 126n25, 126n26, 127, 128, 131, 134, 135, 136, 138, 142, 143, 144, 144n124, 144n125, 145, 146, 149, 289n5, 290, 293, 339, 340, 386, 391, 412

sufficiency of the gospel, 113

syncretism, 29, 30, 31, 113, 164, 189, 189n41, 190

syncretistic nature/tendency (*see* syncretism)

temple, 102, 156, 157, 165, 344

temple tax, 135, 135n72

thanksgiving, 19, 43, 43n1, 43n3, 44, 46, 50, 50n28, 51, 51n29, 54, 57, 58, 60, 60n71, 60n72, 61, 64, 68, 71, 73, 73n41, 74, 77, 78, 80, 81, 82, 84, 150, 151, 156, 157, 158, 205, 223, 239, 244, 247, 249, 250, 251, 252, 253, 254, 255, 256, 258, 286, 290, 291n8, 291n12, 297, 297n41, 303, 335, 336, 336n18, 346, 359, 362, 366, 367, 367n44, 368, 369, 372, 377, 379, 383, 428, 428n5, 435

Timothy, 46, 47, 47n8, 48, 48n14, 50, 57, 58, 59, 68, 261n8, 292, 310, 341, 360, 363, 365, 374, 377, 378, 387, 423, 431

tolerance, 31, 243

Torah, 30, 62n77, 70, 92, 131, 142, 147n129, 157, 157n17, 160, 171, 189, 190, 200, 340, 387

tradition
    Jewish apocalyptic, 29, 30
    human, 19, 25, 27
    Middle Platonic thought 27
    mystic, 30

wisdom, 29

Trinity, 58

Tychicus, 24, 25, 49, 127, 304, 306, 308 – 12, 308n12, 324, 334, 422

uncircumcision, 168, 169, 177, 178, 178n122, 218, 226, 227, 228, 234, 236, 240, 307, 325, 332, 432

union with Christ (*see* Christ, participation in)

vices/vice lists (*see also* virtues/virtue lists), 19, 31, 204, 207, 212, 216 – 18, 216n30, 219, 220, 220n49, 221, 222, 223, 224, 225, 232, 233, 236, 239, 241, 241n13, 242, 268, 271, 277, 334, 335

victory, 26, 114, 151, 172, 173, 176, 180, 181, 193, 216, 219, 291, 315n51, 329 – 31, 384

virtues/virtue lists (*see also* vices/vice lists), 19, 31, 51, 58, 62, 62n76, 73, 188, 204, 207, 216 – 18, 216n30, 220, 224, 225, 236, 237, 238, 239, 240, 241, 241n11, 241n12, 241n13, 243, 243n22, 244, 245, 252, 253, 267, 281, 335, 336, 359, 406, 432

walk, 63, 67, 69, 70, 70n24, 71, 72, 73, 74, 79, 80, 83, 109, 144, 151, 155, 155n7, 156, 157, 175, 203, 221, 222, 222n60, 222n61, 244, 250, 251, 276, 287, 295, 296, 301, 322, 333, 339, 359, 371, 392

washing (*see also* cleansing), 225

well-being, 60, 79, 79n71, 396, 434,

wisdom, 27, 29, 62n77, 64, 68, 69, 69n16, 69n19, 70, 79, 81, 91, 92, 92n30, 92n31, 92n32, 92n33, 93, 94, 94n44, 94n45, 95, 96n55, 97, 98, 100, 102, 112, 114, 114n145, 129, 131, 132, 132n59, 133, 138, 139, 142, 147, 155, 156, 159, 193, 196, 196n80, 197, 198, 213, 214, 248, 248n49, 249, 287, 290, 292n17, 295, 296, 301, 302, 316, 339, 371

wives, 100n83, 192n58, 229, 259, 260, 262, 263, 264, 267, 267n41, 268, 268n45, 269, 270, 271, 279, 280, 280n107, 281, 364

word of God, 54, 55, 61, 61n73, 127, 128, 132, 142, 144, 292n17, 293, 294, 300, 322, 338,

worship, 27, 29, 29n46, 29n51, 31, 32, 51, 53, 54, 60, 73, 79, 80, 81, 82, 83, 96, 96n59, 111, 112, 113, 114, 150, 156, 157, 158, 160, 165, 165n61, 174, 175, 176, 178, 183, 185, 186, 187, 188, 189, 189n37, 190, 193, 195, 196, 198, 199, 200, 201, 203, 204, 205, 206, 207, 213, 218, 221, 222, 223, 225, 230, 231, 232, 235n119, 236, 237, 239, 245, 247, 248n48, 249, 250, 251, 253, 255, 256, 258, 268, 290, 299, 318, 320n86, 324, 325, 334, 335, 336, 366, 367, 377, 400, 401, 428, 434, 435, 435n31

wrath, 171, 172, 215, 217, 221, 221n57, 224, 225, 231, 242, 254, 268n49, 340n24, 428n7

Zeus, 99

Author Index

Aasgaard, Reidar, 48, 309, 345, 348, 355, 364

Abraham, William J., 301

Achtemeier, Paul J., 322

Adams, Edward, 161

Adams, Sean A., 33, 44, 423, 428

Aletti, Jean-Noël, 35, 44, 58, 106, 122, 124, 131, 181, 243, 275, 286, 294

Alexander, Loveday C. A., 304, 318

Allen, David L., 355, 362, 380, 402, 405, 415

Allen, Diogenes, 201

Allison, Dale C., Jr., 126, 244, 330

Anderson, G. W., 96, 249

Arnold, Clinton E., 10, 11, 29, 30, 31, 35, 76, 97, 99, 102, 160, 163, 172, 189, 190, 192

Arzt-Grabner, Peter, 43, 342, 355, 365, 370, 379, 387, 392, 394, 405, 409, 415

Aune, David E., 218, 264

Aus, Roger D., 367

Bahr, G. J., 322

Bailey, Daniel P., 33, 365

Bailey, James L., 216

Balch, David L., 264, 266, 272

Balchin, John F., 87, 89, 91

Balla, Peter, 269, 270

Baltzer, Klaus, 136

Banks, Robert, 378

Barclay, J. M. G., 22, 23, 27, 28, 35, 332, 345, 346, 347, 349, 351, 355, 396, 398, 409, 419

Barker, Ernest, 264

Barram, Michael, 205

Bartchy, S. Scott, 311, 349, 350, 355, 408, 428

Barth, Markus, 24, 30, 35, 48, 51, 64, 71, 124, 132, 137, 139, 155, 164, 166, 214, 219, 248, 268, 270, 276, 286, 292, 296, 297, 319, 342, 344, 347, 355, 366, 367, 368, 372, 380, 384, 385, 386, 388, 390, 391, 394, 397, 406, 410

Barton, Stephen C., 355, 431

Bassler, Jouette M., 35, 413, 427

Bauckham, Richard, 22, 35, 96, 103, 112, 115, 126, 211, 233, 251, 273

Baugh, Steven M., 89

Baur, Ferdinand Christian, 341

Beach, Waldo, 201

Beale, Gregory K. 28, 35, 55, 69, 74, 76, 94, 95, 129, 139, 169, 174, 196, 211, 226, 227, 296

Beetham, Christopher A., 28, 35, 55, 69, 74, 77, 94, 102, 166, 169, 185, 186, 190, 211

Beker, J. Christiaan, 326

Benoit, Pierre, 138

Berger, Klaus, 43

Berkley, Timothy W., 178

Best, Ernest, 22, 308

Best, Eugene C., 330

Betz, Hans Dieter, 33, 35, 125, 141

Betz, Otto, 220

Bevere, Allan R., 28, 35, 77, 95, 168, 171, 185, 189, 215, 217, 229, 242

Bieberstein, Sabine, 355, 431, 433

Birdsall, J. N., 386

Black, Clifton, 313, 423

Black, David Alan, 193, 355, 362

Blanke, Helmut, 24, 30, 35, 48, 51, 64, 71, 124, 132, 137, 139, 155, 164, 166, 214, 219, 248, 268, 270, 276, 286, 292, 296, 297, 319, 342, 344, 347, 355, 366, 367, 368, 372, 380, 384, 385, 386, 388, 390, 391, 394, 397, 406, 410, 419, 420

Blumenfeld, Bruno, 35, 72, 100

Bock, Darrell L., 35, 226

Bockmuehl, Markus, 27, 35, 129, 130, 138, 139, 147, 294

Boismard, M.-É., 321

Bornkamm, Günther, 35, 125, 128, 159

Bossman, David M., 52

Boyarin, Daniel, 36

Bradley, K. R., 273, 350

Brändl, Martin, 316

Brandsma, Jeffrey M., 253

Bratcher, Robert G., 388, 393, 406, 409, 418, 419, 424

Breytenbach, Cilliers, 103

Broek, Lyle D. Vander, 216

Broekhoven, Harold van, 26, 41, 85

Brooten, Bernadette, 319

Brown, Raymond, 128, 342

Brown, William, 38, 126, 425

Bruce, F. F., 25, 36, 139, 347, 368

Burney, C. F., 93

Burridge, Richard A., 203

Burtchaell, James Tunstead, 351, 355, 428

Cahill, Michael, 127

Callahan, Allen D., 276, 343, 355, 388, 393, 395

Callow, John, 36, 204, 239, 248, 267, 268, 274, 275, 287, 293, 317, 321

Calvin, John, 19, 115, 116, 343, 432

Campbell, Douglas A., 36, 228, 229

Campbell, R. Alastair, 309

Cannon, George E., 21, 36, 74, 169, 217, 218, 262

Carman, John B., 30

Carr, Wesley, 26, 170, 172

Carson, D. A., 28, 35, 65, 129, 290

Carson, Herbert, 379

Carter, Warren, 264, 377

Cha, Peter T., 376

Chan, Simon, 231

Chang, Eileen, 234

Chapman, Mark D., 351, 355

Charles, J. Daryl, 244

Chen, Carolyn, 235

Chester, Andrew, 36

Childs, Brevard S., 174, 367

Christensen, Richard L., 116

Christopher, Gregory T., 241

Church, F. Forrester, 344, 355, 369, 373, 408

Clarke, Andrew D., 36, 48, 57, 314, 315, 355, 364, 373, 374, 378

Classen, Carl Joachim, 33

Clifford, Richard J., 114

Cohen, Shaye J. D., 36, 234

Cohick, Lynn H., 349

Cole, H. Ross, 36, 185, 187

Cole, Robert, 157

Cole, Susan G., 232

Collins, Gary R., 63

Collins, John N., 127, 309

Collins, Raymond E., 374, 387

Combes, I. A. H., 284, 334

Connolly, A. L., 311, 387

Cope, Lamar, 36, 321

Coppens, Joseph, 36, 130

Cosgrove , Charles H., 294

Cousar, Charles B., 342, 355, 386, 409

Crouch, James E., 264, 265, 270

Cullmann, Oscar, 155

Dan, Joseph, 30, 36, 135

Daube, David, 265, 355

Davies, W. D., 244

Dawn, Marva J., 112

De Boer, Martinus C., 36, 160

De Vos, Craig S., 350, 351, 355, 407

Deissmann, Adolf, 407

Delling, Gerhard, 154, 160

DeMaris, Richard E., 27, 36, 189

Derrett, J. Duncan M., 36, 351, 355, 387, 407

Dibelius, Martin, 36, 265

Dimakis, P., 393

Dines, Jennifer, 97

Dippenaar, M. C., 65

Doty, William G., 43, 265

Douglas, Mary, 36, 217

Du Plessis, Isak J., 355, 394

Dunn, James D. G., 28, 36, 41, 77, 94, 102, 125, 139, 155, 162, 167, 188, 214, 224, 264, 267, 269, 286, 291, 323, 345, 347, 368, 370, 380, 390, 410, 420, 421, 427

Dunne, John Anthony, 93

Easton, Burton Scott, 216

Ehrensperger, Kathy, 36, 315, 326, 385

Elior, Rachel, 29, 36

Elliott, J. K., 321

Elliott, John H., 266

Elliott, Neil, 345, 351, 356

Ellis, E. Earle, 23, 36, 78, 314, 342

Engberg-Pedersen, Troels, 217

Epictetus, 224, 269, 350

Evans, Craig A., 29

Fee, Gordon, 37, 58, 69, 73, 77, 92, 96, 102, 114, 141, 156, 227, 246, 249, 262, 272, 424

Ferreira, Christina, 59

Finley, Moses I., 284

Fitzgerald, John T., 37, 103

Fitzmyer, Joseph, 356, 370, 372, 384, 386, 387, 388, 390, 393, 394, 406, 407, 408, 418, 419

Flemington, W. F., 37, 124, 125

Fletcher-Louis, Crispin H. T., 37, 92, 114, 189

Fossum, Jarl, 29, 94

Fowl, Stephen E., 89

Fowler, Alastair, 265

Fowler, James, 256

Fraade, Steven D., 37, 195

Francesco, D'Andreia, 49, 104

Francis, Fred O., 29, 37, 188, 189, 190

Frank, Nicole, 37, 338

Freedman, David Noel, 220

Frilingos, Chris, 356, 435

Funk, Robert W., 54, 304, 415

Gamble, Harry Y., 320

Garland, David E., 37, 162, 188, 280

Garrett, Susan R., 37, 159, 273

Gebauer, Roland, 37

Georgi, Dieter, 430

Getty, Mary Ann, 356, 431, 435

Gielen, Marlis, 23, 37, 319

Gillman, John, 315

Glancy, Jennifer A., 356

Goodenough, E. R., 344

Gordley, Matthew E., 37, 84, 89, 90, 94, 247

Gorospe, Athena E., 177

Goulder, M. D., 37, 136

Gourgues, Michel, 87, 105

Gräbe, Petrus J., 37

Grant, Robert M., 217, 265

Grayston, Kenneth, 167

Grudem, Wayne A., 99, 262

Grundman, Walter, 295

Gunton, Colin, 330

Hafemann, Scott J., 144

Halbertal, Moshe, 176

Harrill, J. A., 344, 345, 346, 350, 356

Harris, Murray J., 37, 53, 64, 70, 75, 77, 95, 99, 130, 132, 136, 137, 140, 157, 159, 167, 169, 185, 188, 192, 194, 197, 222, 226, 242, 245, 248, 267, 269, 274, 275, 293, 294, 298, 313, 343, 356, 363, 370, 384, 385, 391, 394, 397, 409, 419, 422

Hartman, Lars, 37, 140, 220, 265, 385

Hauck, Friedrich, 298, 370

Hay, David M., 37, 276

Haykin, Michael A. G., 356, 421

Hays, Richard, 266, 331, 356

Heil, John Paul, 34, 38, 356, 363, 371, 372, 391

Henderson, Suzanne Watts, 102, 162, 266

Hengel, Martin, 91, 172, 318

Henry, Carl H., 80

Hering, James P., 38, 267, 272, 277

Hermas, 388

Hobart, W. K., 318

Hock, Ronald F., 356, 365, 386

Hoehner, Harold W., 56, 308

Hollenbach, Bruce, 197

Hooker, Morna D., 26, 38, 70, 131, 183

Hopkins, Keith, 349

Horgan, Maurya P., 90

Horsley, G. H. R., 318, 364, 389

Hughes, Franks W., 32
Hultin, Jeremy F., 38, 224, 297, 298
Hunt, J. P., 164, 166

Jeal, Roy R., 234
Jervis, L. Ann, 38, 126
Jobes, Karen H., 92
Johnson, Lee A., 54
Jónsson, Gunnlaugur A., 94

Kasch, Wilhelm, 98
Kea, Perry V., 356
Kearsley, Rosalind, 128, 392, 422
Keener, Craig S., 231
Keesmaat, Sylvia C., 42, 97
Keith, Chris, 322
Kellerhals, Jean, 59
Kern, Otto, 99
Kiley, Mark, 20, 134
Kim, Chan-Hie, 402
Kim, Jung Hoon, 38, 225
Kirkland, Alastair, 317
Klauck, Hans-Josef, 33, 303, 312, 365
Kleinig, John W., 38, 266
Kleinknecht, H. 94
Knight, George W., III, 38, 262, 281
Knowles, Michael P., 38, 116, 194, 242
Knox, John, 321, 341, 346, 364, 386, 389
Kobelski, Paul J., 90
Koester, Craig R., 135
Koester, Helmut, 60, 373
Koskenniemi, Heilli, 141
Köstenberger, Andreas J., 301
Kraabel, A. Thomas, 189
Kreitzer, Larry J., 22, 38, 110, 141, 170
Kremer, Jacob, 38
Kumitz, Christopher, 356, 385
Kümmel, Werner Georg, 20, 342
Küng, Hans, 399
Kurz, William S., 312
Kyrtatas, D. J., 57

Lack, Rémi, 160
Ladd, George Eldon, 315
Lamarche, Paul, 38, 180
Lampe, Peter, 345, 352, 356
Le Déaut, R., 165
Lee, Stephen, 96, 332

Lemke, Werner E., 38, 164
Lependorf, Stanley, 254
Leppä, Outi, 22, 38, 91, 100, 101, 125, 264, 266
Levenson, Jon D., 82, 99
Lewis, C. S., 281
Libanius, 349
Lieu, Judith M., 38, 164, 314
Lightfoot, J. B., 23, 24, 31, 38, 98, 104, 110, 125, 131, 136, 137, 155, 156, 158, 159, 162, 165, 167, 169, 170, 172, 188, 194, 197, 215, 222, 224, 228, 242, 244, 245, 248, 250, 270, 273, 274, 275, 276, 293, 295, 296, 308, 312, 313, 317, 321, 351, 363, 364, 368, 372, 385, 388, 390, 392, 394, 395, 396, 407, 409, 410, 420
Lincoln, Andrew T., 22, 28, 39, 53, 74, 97, 206, 211, 212, 214, 245, 258, 263, 272
Lindberg, Carter, 377
Llewelyn, S. R., 392, 422
Loader, William R. G., 39, 199
Lohmeyer, Ernst, 39
Lohse, Eduard, 39, 50, 71, 72, 74, 76, 87, 90, 95, 98, 103, 105, 127, 131, 132, 138, 140, 141, 155, 161, 162, 167, 169, 185, 189, 190, 197, 217, 219, 243, 245, 248, 251, 255, 267, 268, 269, 273, 275, 276, 291, 298, 312, 314, 342, 345, 347, 364, 368, 370, 380, 384, 386, 389, 392, 394, 395, 405, 408, 419, 422
Lorenzen, Stefanie, 39, 114
Louw, J. P., 72, 135, 170, 193, 204, 228, 270, 390
Lövestam, Evald, 291
Lure, Alison, 234
Luttenberger, Joram, 39, 170
Lyall, Francis, 95
Lyonnet, Stanislas, 31, 39
Lyons, Kirk D., Sr., 356, 414, 430

MacDonald, Dennis R., 229, 247, 248
MacDonald, Margaret Y., 39, 71, 131, 134, 149, 164, 195, 197, 214, 245, 247, 248, 266, 272, 274, 278, 293, 294, 296, 313
Maier, Harry O., 39, 104, 229, 272
Main, Keith, 202
Malherbe, Abraham J., 60, 220, 255
Manns, Frédéric, 93

Margalit, Avishai, 176
Marshall, I. Howard, 262, 281, 344, 348, 356, 370, 408, 435
Martens, John W., 356
Martin, Clarice J., 344, 353, 394, 407
Martin, Dale, 356
Martin, Mike W., 146
Martin, Ralph P., 23, 39, 90, 139, 163, 407, 419, 420
Martin, Troy W., 28, 39, 185, 188, 228
Marty, Martin, 413
Matera, Frank, 328
Mayerhoff, Ernst Theodor, 22
McClure, John S., 61
McGrath, Alister, 62
McKnight, Scot, 202
McNeill, Donald P., 146
McWilliams, Nancy, 254
Meeks, Wayne A., 39, 155, 156, 210, 218, 364, 365, 387
Menninger, Karl, 176
Merkel, H., 39
Metzger, Bruce M., 24, 107, 138, 198, 215, 343, 389
Michaelis, Wilhelm, 268
Michel,Otto, 228
Migliore, Daniel, 234
Miller, Ed. L., 220
Miller, Patrick D., 136, 425
Missiou, A., 173
Mitchell, Margaret M., 47, 356
Mitton, C. Leslie, 308
Moo, Douglas J., 39, 44, 45, 50, 53, 54, 64, 69, 72, 77, 98, 103, 107, 118, 122, 129, 131, 137, 139, 155, 156, 164, 167, 169, 173, 188, 190, 223, 244, 245, 248, 270, 273, 275, 281, 293, 297, 311, 322, 346, 363, 367, 370, 372, 380, 386, 394, 408, 410, 419, 422
Morrison, Douglas A., 146
Moule, C. F. D., 39, 51, 56, 72, 73, 102, 108, 110, 123, 125, 132, 137, 139, 141, 155, 156, 160, 165, 169, 190, 195, 197, 219, 226, 227, 244, 245, 247, 270, 275, 286, 295, 309, 313, 316, 345, 367, 369, 371, 384, 389, 394, 396, 410, 422
Mounce, William D., 218
Mullins, Terrence Y., 54, 356
Munro, Winsome, 257, 272

Murphy-O'Connor, Jerome, 36, 105, 124, 315, 345, 422

Nash, Robert Scott, 275
Nebe, Gottfried, 99, 163
Neumann, Kenneth J., 20
Neyrey, Jerome, 39, 51
Nicholas, Barry, 333
Nida, Eugene A., 72, 135, 170, 228, 270, 388, 390, 393, 406, 409, 418, 419, 424
Nielsen, Charles M., 27, 40, 125
Nock, Arthur D., 190
Noll, Mark A., 302
Nordling, J. G., 356, 387, 394, 407
Nouwen, Henri, 146, 252, 412

O'Brien, Peter, 40, 50, 68, 72, 97, 103, 107, 123, 125, 129, 131, 136, 137, 156, 166, 169, 185, 186, 213, 224, 245, 248, 264, 270, 274, 275, 293, 301, 314, 322, 348, 364, 365, 367, 368, 370, 380, 385, 386, 388, 394, 395, 405, 419, 420
O'Neill, J. C., 89
Olbricht, Thomas H., 26
Ollrog, Wolf-Henning, 391
Olson, Stanley N., 356, 419
Osiek, Carolyn, 356, 386, 388, 420
Ostmeyer, Karl-Heinrich, 79, 316

Palmer, G. E. H., 299
Pao, David W., 44, 61, 73, 165, 223, 247, 251, 336, 428
Parsons, Michael, 40
Pate, C. Marvin, 40
Patterson, Orlando, 349, 350
Payne, Philip Barton, 99, 267, 280
Pearson, W. R., 346, 356, 387, 391, 394, 406, 409
Percy, Ernst, 161
Perrenoud, David, 59
Perriman, Andrew, 125
Petersen, Norman R., 347, 357, 365, 384, 385, 387, 405, 419, 420
Peterson David G., 133
Peterson, Eugene H., 79
Peterson, Robert A., 109
Pfitzner, Victor C., 125
Piper, John, 232

Pizzuto, Vincent A., 20, 40, 85, 87, 89
Pokorný, Petr, 40, 161, 189, 195, 222, 292, 311, 322
Polaski, S. H., 348, 357, 384, 406, 410, 412, 430
Porten, Bezadel, 49
Porter, Stanley E., 33, 40, 77, 92, 101, 103, 104, 106, 157, 224, 310, 321, 352, 357, 363, 375, 405, 408, 409, 423
Priest, Kersten Bayt, 235
Priest, Robert J., 235

Quinn, Jerome D., 318

Rabey, Steve, 63
Rapske, Brian M., 344, 345, 346, 357
Reardon, Bryan P., 143
Rengstorf, K. H., 47, 264
Rennie, Niel, 143
Reumann, John, 40
Richards, E. Randolph, 48, 309, 310, 322, 408, 419
Riesenfeld, Harold, 370
Robinson, James M., 50, 84
Roose, Hanna, 20, 40
Roth, Robert Paul, 40, 230
Rowland, Christopher, 29
Royalty, Robert M., Jr., 29, 40
Rupprecht, Arthur A., 372, 379, 409, 415
Rusam, Dietrich, 40, 160
Russell, Bertrand, 283
Russell, David M., 344, 357, 405
Ryan, Judith M., 357, 368, 370, 372, 380, 388, 391, 392, 394, 407

Sabourin, Leopold, 21
Sampley, J. Paul, 405
Sanders, Laura L., 357, 408
Sandnes, Karl Olav, 338
Sappington, Thomas J., 21, 29, 40, 74, 78, 85, 139, 160, 170, 189, 190
Saunders, E. W., 40
Scharlemann, Martin, 40, 93
Schenk, Wolfgang, 346, 357
Schnabel, Eckard J., 40, 92, 139, 308, 317
Schnackenburg, Rudolf, 40, 225
Schneider, Andrew, 148
Schnelle, Udo, 40, 329, 339

Schniewind, Julius, 132
Schöder, David, 265
Scholem, Gershom, 29
Schrage, Wolfgang, 40, 218, 258
Schubert, Paul, 43, 366
Schütz, John Howard, 384
Schweizer, Eduard, 21, 28, 40, 58, 64, 87, 90, 91, 94, 125, 130, 161, 171, 173, 183, 187, 188, 196, 213, 216, 223, 225, 248, 262, 267, 270, 275, 311, 319
Schwemer, Anna Maria, 318
Seesemann, Heinrich, 69
Seifrid, Mark, 49, 129
Sherrard, Philip, 299
Shogren, Gary S., 40, 75
Shyman, A. H., 357
Smedes, Lewis B., 253
Smith, Barry D., 144
Smith, Derwood C., 157
Smith, Ian K., 29, 40, 91, 97, 103, 160, 166, 170, 173, 188, 189, 214
Smith, James K. A., 325
Smith, R. R. R., 103
Smyth, Herbert W., 372
Snodgrass, Klyne R., 292
Soards, Marion L., 351, 357, 427, 428
Söding, Thomas, 52
Son, Sang-Won Aaron, 41, 187
Stairs, Jean, 231
Standhartinger, Angela, 23, 27, 41, 125, 141, 278
Stark, Rodney, 302
Steele, Donald M., 345, 346, 357, 432
Sterling, Gregory E., 41, 96
Stettler, Christian, 41, 89, 160, 189, 194
Stettler, Hanna, 41, 126
Still, Todd D., 21, 41, 77, 167, 340, 352, 357, 429, 432
Stirewalt, M. Luther, Jr., 327
Stowers, Stanley K., 32
Stuckenbruck, Loren T., 41
Stuhlmacher, Peter, 54, 344, 347, 357, 368, 370, 380, 386, 394, 395, 407, 419
Sumney, Jerry L., 30, 41, 55, 68, 95, 106, 107, 119, 124, 126, 134, 136, 137, 142, 158, 164, 181, 184, 193, 195, 211, 222, 245, 248, 267, 274, 275, 286, 294, 296, 298, 311, 321

Swart, Gerhard, 214
Sweeney, James P., 291

Talbert, Charles H., 41, 64, 215
Taylor, Jeremy, 233
Taylor, N. H., 347, 357, 388, 396, 397, 398
Thiselton, Anthony, 249
Thompson, Marianne Meye, 41, 204, 229, 329, 388
Thornton, T. C. G., 41, 185
Thurston, Bonnie, 41
Tolmie, D. Francois, 357
Tomson, Peter J., 41, 204, 229
Towner, Philip H., 128, 318
Trainor, Michael, 41, 56, 115, 317
Trench, Richard C., 249
Tripp, David, 102
Turner, Max, 345
Turner, Nigel, 77, 99, 370

Urbainczyk, Theresa, 357

Van Broekhoven, Harold, 26, 41, 85
Van der Watt, J. G., 41
Van Kooten, George H., 27, 41, 87, 98, 162, 163, 192, 227, 273
Vanhoozer, Kevin J., 357, 414, 419, 430
Versnel, H. S., 50, 367

Viljoen, Francois P., 248
Volf, Judith M. Gundry, 109
Volf, Miroslav, 400

Walker, William C., 318
Wallace, Daniel B., 47, 51, 68, 95, 97, 99, 101, 109, 137, 161, 185, 193, 243, 250, 262, 274, 310, 317, 405, 407, 408, 410
Walsh, Brian J., 42, 97, 160, 174
Wanamaker, Charles A., 32
Wansink, Craig S., 344, 345, 346, 357, 363, 365, 386
Ware, Kallistos, 198, 299
Watson, Duane F., 33
Webb, William J., 262, 281
Wedderburn, A. J. M., 28, 31, 42, 125, 162, 205
Weima, Jeffrey A. D., 322, 323, 420, 421, 424
Weitzman, Steven, 90
Wenham, David, 42, 247
Wenham, John, 318
Wesley, Charles, 177
Wessels, G. François, 42, 225, 257, 395
Westermann, William Linn, 349
White, John L., 303
Wickert, U., 365
Wiles, Gordon P., 79, 304
Wilkins, Michael J., 56

Williamson, Lamar, Jr., 173
Willis, William Beniah, 146
Wills, Gary, 347
Wilson, Andrew, 389
Wilson, R. McL., 31, 50, 75, 95, 97, 124, 156, 194, 222, 275, 297, 314, 319, 364, 371, 380, 384, 386, 391, 392, 393, 407, 419, 421
Windisch, Hans, 124
Wink, Walter, 42
Winter, Sarah B. C., 343, 345, 346, 357, 360, 368, 371, 387, 388, 389, 391
Witherington, Ben, III, 22, 32, 42, 48, 84, 125, 225, 257, 267, 318, 357, 386, 392, 396, 427
Witulski, Thomas, 42
Wright, N. T., 42, 69, 87, 89, 93, 132, 139, 158, 173, 184, 190, 194, 216, 222, 242, 275, 276, 300, 311, 322, 340, 358, 372, 373, 379, 393, 395, 407, 410, 415, 419, 420, 421, 432
Wuthnow, Robert, 282
Wyatt, Peter, 116

Yates John W., 21, 42
Yates, Roy, 29, 42, 91, 125, 164, 171, 172, 173, 225, 239, 245
Yinger, Kent L., 42, 188

Zelnick-Abramovitz, R., 350, 358, 396
Zmijewski, Josef, 406